1,000,000 Books

are available to read at

---

www.ForgottenBooks.com

Read online
Download PDF
Purchase in print

ISBN 978-1-333-68418-1
PIBN 10535423

This book is a reproduction of an important historical work. Forgotten Books uses state-of-the-art technology to digitally reconstruct the work, preserving the original format whilst repairing imperfections present in the aged copy. In rare cases, an imperfection in the original, such as a blemish or missing page, may be replicated in our edition. We do, however, repair the vast majority of imperfections successfully; any imperfections that remain are intentionally left to preserve the state of such historical works.

1 MONTH OF
FREE
READING

at
www.ForgottenBooks.com

By purchasing this book you are eligible for one month membership to ForgottenBooks.com, giving you unlimited access to our entire collection of over 1,000,000 titles via our web site and mobile apps.

To claim your free month visit: www.forgottenbooks.com/free535423

English
Français
Deutsche
Italiano
Español
Português

www.forgottenbooks.com

Mythology Photography **Fiction**
Fishing Christianity **Art** Cooking
Essays Buddhism Freemasonry
Medicine **Biology** Music **Ancient
Egypt** Evolution Carpentry Physics
Dance Geology **Mathematics** Fitness
Shakespeare **Folklore** Yoga Marketing
Confidence Immortality Biographies
Poetry **Psychology** Witchcraft
Electronics Chemistry History **Law**
Accounting **Philosophy** Anthropology
Alchemy Drama Quantum Mechanics
Atheism Sexual Health **Ancient History**
Entrepreneurship Languages Sport
Paleontology Needlework Islam
Metaphysics Investment Archaeology
Parenting Statistics Criminology
Motivational

E

A twentieth century history
of Delaware County, Indiana

A TWENTIETH CENTURY

HISTORY

OF

DELAWARE COUNTY, INDIANA

ILLUSTRATED

G. W. H. KEMPER, M. D.
EDITOR

VOLUME I

CHICAGO
THE LEWIS PUBLISHING COMPANY
1908

PREFACE

The time seems opportune for a new History of Delaware County. It is twenty-six years (1881) since the "History of Delaware County" was issued by Kingman Brothers, of Chicago. In 1894, "A Portrait and Biographical Record of Delaware County, Indiana," was issued by A. W. Bowen & Co., of Chicago. The publishers did not claim it was a *history*. In 1898, Mr. John S. Ellis published a work of 194 pages, entitled, "Our County, Its History and Early Settlement by Townships." This work, while valuable, was not comprehensive as to historical matter.

In the present work the chapter on Military History of Delaware County is contributed by Hon. Asbury L. Kerwood, himself a veteran who entered the service during the Civil war from this county. The article is historical, exhaustive, and intensely interesting. Mr. Kerwood is to be complimented for the pains he has bestowed upon his work.

Miss Artena M. Chapin, librarian of our City Library, furnishes a valuable resume of the rise and development of our present magnificent library.

Mr. C. H. Church, cashier of the Delaware County National bank has contributed the article on Banks. His well known standing as a banker and contributor to financial literature, is a sufficient guarantee of its value.

The Editor has spared no pains, and has bestowed a great deal of time in collecting facts for the Medical Chapter.

Mr. Charles A. Van Matre, County Superintendent of Schools, has generously furnished the material for the Educational Chapter.

Mrs. Edward A. Olcott, daughter of the late Frederick E. Putnam, has kindly permitted the use for publication of her father's diary,—rich in facts relating to the early history of Muncietown as far back as 1842.

The articles on the History of the several Churches, Lodges, Societies, Clubs, Labor Unions, etc., have been supplied by members of these respective orders and, doubtless, in the main are correct. Generally the illustrations of the churches have been loaned for the work by the respective societies, for which thanks are hereby tendered.

A number of interesting features have been added that will attract the attention of the reader. Official records have been searched; elderly persons consulted and their statements verified; correspondence has been carried on with persons remotely situated; family Bibles have been consulted, and cemeteries have been visited and inscriptions on tombstones transcribed. In short, every available source of information has been sought; and while much that is valuable has necessarily been omitted, on the other hand it will be found that much that is valuable has been recorded.

In the preparation of this work a vast amount of information has been

iii

discovered that properly belongs to a County Historical Society. Delaware County should not long delay the formation of such a society.

The Editor wishes especially to thank those who have aided this work by the contribution of articles. Also to thank all persons who have so kindly assisted in furnishing information that has contributed to the value of the work. Every name can not be mentioned here, but a few have rendered such valuable assistance that it seems proper to make special mention: Judge Joseph G. Leffler, Samuel B. Murphy, Michael Dunkin, James R. Turner, Robert M. Snodgrass, Mrs. Julia A. Williamson, Mrs. Mary Carpenter, William A. Blair, Samuel A. Dickover, William H. Peacock, David M. Bell, Mrs. Mary M. J. Mock, Miss Ida Ludlow, Thomas H. Kirby, William H. Murray, James S. Rigdon, Calvin Crooks, Nathan N. Spence, Joel R. McKimmey, Abraham McConnell, Prof. George L. Roberts, Hon. George W. Cromer, Mrs. W. W. Shirk, Hon. J. Harvey Koontz, Dr. Lewis Payton, Mrs. Cynthia Randall, Jesse H. Williamson, George Louthain, Thomas Applegate, Mrs. Madaline Knox, Mrs. Julia Allegre, Cornelius Vanarsdol, Mr. and Mrs. Jacob Erther, Isaac Wright, James H. Childs, George W. Hoover, Mrs. Massy Green, Rev. F. A. Robinson, Eli M. Thornburg, C. M. Wingate, Mrs. C. B. Templer, H. P. Holmes, N. F. Etnell, Belty Dragoo, Edmund Aldredge, Mrs. R. H. Long, John Cunkle, P. M. Carmichael, Mary Berry, J. L. Hutchins, and David Craw, all of Delaware County. Dr. Jonas Stewart, Anderson, Ind., J. Wesley Whicker, Attica, Ind., and John Sanders, Matthews, Ind.

The Lewis Publishing Company of Chicago are to be congratulated for the excellent manner in which they have executed the mechanical part of the two handsome volumes.

The Editor asks indulgence for all mistakes and errors, hoping they will be overruled, forgotten, and he trusts—forgiven.   G. W. H. K.

Muncie, Indiana, December, 1907.

CONTENTS

CHAPTER I.
Delaware County a Part of the French Empire.................................. 1

CHAPTER II.
Indian Inhabitants—American Conquest... 5

CHAPTER III.
Advance of Civilization—Delaware County Opened to Settlement............... 10

CHAPTER IV.
Public Survey of Delaware County—First Occupants of Land.................. 15

CHAPTER V.
The Record of the Original Possessors of Delaware County's Soil.............. 21

CHAPTER VI.
A Study of Origins and Sources—Prominent Pioneer Types.................... 44

CHAPTER VII.
The County as a Civil Organization... 57

CHAPTER VIII.
The Courts—Bench and Bar... 64

CHAPTER IX.
Early Transportation and Communication...................................... 77

CHAPTER X.
Turnpikes and Railroads... 84

CHAPTER XI.
Beginning of Centers of Population... 95

CHAPTER XII.
Muncie 103

CHAPTER XIII.
The Putnam Diary.. 116

CHAPTER XIV.
Muncie and Vicinity at the Beginning of the Last Quarter Century............. 126

CHAPTER XV.
Natural Gas 138

CHAPTER XVI.
Natural Gas Makes a City of Muncie.. 143

CHAPTER XVII.
Progress and Change in the Smaller Centers................................... 161

CHAPTER XVIII.
Chronology of the Last Quarter Century.................................. 167

CHAPTER XIX.
City and Country in the Twentieth Century—The Results of Three-quarters of a
    Century of Progress.. 207

CHAPTER XX.
Education in Delaware County.. 237

CHAPTER XXI.
The Delaware   y Press.. 278

CHAPTER XXII.
Medical History of Delaware County.................................... 288

CHAPTER XXIII.
Banking and Finance.. 302

CHAPTER XXIV.
Military History of Delaware County................................... 307

CHAPTER XXV.
Church Organizations of Delaware County.............................. 426

CHAPTER XXVI.
The Spread of Culture Through Organization........................... 481

CHAPTER XXVII.
Fraternal and Social Organizations................................... 501

CHAPTER XXVIII.
Politics and Civil Records of County, Township and Town.............. 527

INDEX

Abbott, James, 314.
Albany, 98; luring last 25 years, 102.
Albany State Bank, 163; 306.
Aldredge, Edmund, 315.
Allison, Hiram, 420.
A ruse rents, 233.
Ancient Order of Hibernians, 524; Ladies'
   Auxiliary, 524.
Anderson, Alexander H., 959.
Anderson, Nathan, 655.
Anderson, Rhoda C., 960.
Anderson, William F., 1054.
Andrews, Daniel H., 293.
Andrews, G. R., 661.
Andrews, George R., 666.
Andrews, W. J., 290.
Anthony, Elwin C., 51.
Anthony, Joseph, 69.
Anthony, Samuel P., 50; 90; 292.
Anthony, Thomas C., 69.
Apollo Club, 495.
Applegate, John, 316.
Arnold, James W., 915.
Art, Literature and Music, 481; 493.
Art Students' League, 496.
Associate Judges, 534.
Associated Charities of Muncie and Dela-
   ware County, 234.
Athenaeum Club, 486.
Atkinson, James M., 802.
Attorneys, First A l rittel, 66.
Auditors, 533.
Austin, Charles R., 965.
Automobiles, 218.
Avondale, 160.

Bach, William, 979.
Bailey, William, 1005.
Baird, John V., 929.
Baird, J. Walter, 622.
Baird, M. B., 650.
Baker, Stephen H., 316.
Ball Brothers, 550.
Ball, Edmund B., 550.
Ball, Frank C., 550.
Ball, George A., 550.
Ball, L. L., 667.
Ball, Walter L., 1084.

Banks of Delaware County, 302.
Baptist Churches—Regular Baptist, Mun-
   cie, 443; 17th Street, 447.
Bar, Personnel of, 67.
Bartlett, Josiah P., 1004.
Barlow, John, 316.
Battle List of Civil War, 411.
Baughn, James H., 1001.
Baur, Emil, 838.
Beech Grove Cemetery, 229.
"Bee Line," The, 92.
Bell, David, 317.
Bell, John N., 1015.
Bellefontaine and Indianapolis R. R., 51;
   Completion of, 92.
Benadum, Ellen, 888.
Benadum, Francis H., 888.
Benadum, Spencer H., 884.
Bench and Bar, 64, fol.
Benevolent and Protective Order of Elks—
   Muncie Lodge, 521.
Bennett, Beecher W., 664.
Berry, Noah D., 659.
Berry, Stephen D., Sr., 318.
Bethel, 102.
Benoy, Benoni, 714.
Benoy, Charles T., 716.
Benoy, Randolph, 793.
Bicycles, 218.
"Big Four," The, 92.
Birkenstock, John, 608.
Bishop, E. W., 639.
Bloss, John M., 265; 899.
Bloss, Mary W., 904.
Blount, William, 307.
Bobo, Martin, 317.
Bond, Lewis, 738.
Booher, Levi, 953.
Bowles, T. J., 650.
Boxell, Oscar O., 839.
Boyce block, 131.
Boyce, James, 137; 145; 150; 561.
Boyce, Mrs. Minnie T., 498.
Boyceton, 160.
Braly, Arthur W., 73; 1084.
Braly, John, 48; 163.
Braly, Thomas J., 201; 348.
Braly, William, 49.
Brandt, David, 161; 910.

vii

Brandt, Robert L., 815.
Brandon, Winfield S., 1060.
Branson, Isaac, 51; 318.
Braun, August, 606.
Brissey, James W., 690.
Brooks, George W., 665.
Brotherton, William, 71.
Brotherton, William R., 73.
Brown, Henry, 319.
Brown, William H., 895.
Broyles, Joseph A., 792.
Broyles, Oliver A., 767.
Brunton, Gilbert A., 862.
Bryan, James A., 763.
Bryan, Milo, 986.
Bryan, Sarah C., 763.
Buckles, Abraham, 51.
Buckles, Joseph S., 51; 71; 187.
Bucklin, G. W., 642.
Bunch, R. A., 635.
Burlen, William J., 956.
Burdick, Claude A., 939.
Burgess, John, 739.
Burgess, Lydia A., 740.
Burris, Samuel O., 910.
Burson Banking Company, 303.
Burt, Dickinson, 288.
Burt, Ludlow K., 927.

California Forty-niners from Delaware
    County, 113.
Camack, David, 199.
Campbell, Samuel G., 1008.
Campbell, William, 925.
Carmichael, Oliver, 644.
Carmichael, Patrick, 319.
Casman, Samuel, 19.
Carpenter, Morton F., 875.
Carroll, John, 319.
Carter, Charles, 99; George, 99.
Carter, George W., 140.
Carter, Levi L., 719.
Catholic Benevolent Legion, 523.
Catholic Churches — St. Lawrence, 465;
    467; Albany, 472.
C., C. & L. E. R. R., 217.
Cemeteries, Muncie, 106.
Center Township, 26.
Chalfant, Joel, 1058.
Chalfant, Nancy, 1058.
Chapin, Artena M., 268.
Charman, James, 605.
Christian Churches—Jackson St. Christian,
    459; First Christian of Muncie, 455;
    White Chapel, 456; Albany, 457; York-
    town, 457; Philadelphia, 458; Daleville,
    458; Hoffherr Chapel, 459; Pleasant
    Run, 459.
Christian Scientists, Society of, 479.
Chronology, 1882-1906, 167, fol.
Church, Charles H., 302; 558.
Church Organizations of Delaware County,
    426, fol.

C., I. & E. R. R., 217.
Circuit Judges, 530.
Ciscus, Francis, 319.
Citizens' Enterprise Company, 152.
Citizens' National Bank, 154; 177; 303.
Citizens' Street Railway Co., 175.
City Council of Muncie, 537.
Civil Organization of Delaware County, 57.
Civil Records of County, Townships, and
    Towns, 527, fol.
Civil War, 347, fol.
Civil War, in Putnam Diary, 119-121.
Civil War, Special Companies, 410.
Clark, Albert W., 998.
Clark, Charles, 981.
Clark, George Rogers, 6.
Clark, John, 779.
Clark, John Allen, 292.
Claypool Bank, 303.
Claypool, Marcus S., 623.
Clerks, of County, 533.
Clerks of Muncie, 536.
Clevenger, Henry, 883.
Clouse, Henry, 320.
Coffeen, Eleazer, 46; 173.
Coffeentown, 46.
Commercial and Manufacturing Interests
    in 1880, 131.
Common Pleas Judges, 534.
Communication, 1.
Congerville, 160.
Conner, John M., 871.
Connor, William, 18.
Consolidated Schools, 248; History of, 251.
Conversation Club, 484.
Coroners, 533.
Cory, Michael, 718.
Cory, William L., 944.
County Buildings, 59.
County Commissioners, 531.
County Government, Beginning of, 59.
County Medical Society, 290.
County Officials, First, 59.
County Seat Land Donations, 58.
County's Financial Status, 209.
Court House, 56; 61; First, 59.
Court House Square, 60.
Court Practice, Early, 64.
Cowan, 101.
Cowing, Hugh A., 699.
Crabbs, Oscar W., 669.
Craig, William, 294.
Crampton, Mahlon, 847.
Cromer, George W., 73; 555.
Cross, John A., 972.
Crow, William, 836.
Culture Club, 486.
Cunningham, Joseph B., 1028.
Cunningham, Lewis S., 1029.

Dale Family, 98.
Daleville, 98.
Daleville Commercial Bank, 306.

Daniel Boone Rifle Club, 526.
Darter, Samuel, 321.
Daugherty, William, Sr., 308.
Daugherty, William H., 320.
Daughters of American Revolution, 492.
Davis, Matthew, 976.
Davis, Walter L., 634.
Dearth, Clarence W., 662.
Delaware County Agricultural and Mechanical Society, 493.
Delaware County Children's Home Association, 500.
Delaware County Democrat, 280.
Delaware County Free Press, 281.
Delaware County in 1880, 126; Increase of Wealth, 208; Lands in 1819, 17; Settlement of, 10.
Delaware County National Bank, 304.
Delaware County Seminary, 242.
Delaware Guards, 348.
Delaware Indians, 5.
"Delaware Towns," 18.
Delaware Township, 39.
Depoy, Martin, 321.
De Soto, 164.
De Soto School, 259.
De Witt, John W., 731.
Dick, Peter B., 1062.
Dickover, Jacob, 321.
District Attorneys, 534.
Dorton, John, 733.
Dorton, Monroe, 795.
Dowell, John A., 934.
Downing, J. Frank, 1071.
Downing, William T., 846.
Dragoo, John W., 581.
Driscoll, John L., 1046.
Driscoll, W. E., 1049.
Drumm, Samuel, 1053.
Duke, Scott S., 984.
Duling, B. Frank, 734.
Dunkin, William, Sr., 323.
Dunn, Alexander, 814.
Dunn, Francis S., 815.
Dunn, J., 724.
Dunn, Thomas L., 724.
Dynes, Jeremiah, 293.

Early Dramatics, 497.
Early Muncie Merchants, 47.
Early Officials, 61.
Early Physicians, 291.
Eastern Indiana Normal University, 267.
Eastes, William T., 747.
Eaton, 99; 161.
Eaton Advertiser, 287.
Eaton Bank Company, 162.
Eaton Gas Light, 287.
Eaton State Bank, 306.
Eber, James E., 683.
Edgington, Calvin C., 977.

Education, in Delaware County, 237, fol.; (see sketch John M. Bloss, 903-904;) History of, in Indiana, 239.
Edmunds, Mary J., 45.
Eighth Cavalry, 374.
Eighth Regiment Infantry, 349.
Eighty-fourth Regiment, 386.
Electric Communication and Transportation, 210.
Electric Lights, in Muncie, 136.
Electric Street Railway System, 176.
Elizabethtown, 100.
Elliott, John L., 324.
Ellis, Frank, 601.
Ellis', John S., History, 21.
Ellis, John S., 493; 586.
Emigration, Course of, 8.
English Conquest of Indiana, 3.
Entries, Original Land, 21.
Episcopal Churches—Grace Church, Muncie, 459.
Erie Canal, 81.
Ethell, John, 324.
Ethell, N. F., 132.
Evangelical Churches—First, Muncie, 478; German Evangelical, 478; Cross Roads, 478.
Evans, Albert W., 828.
Evans, Charles A., 968.
Evening News, 284.

Farmers' State Bank of Eaton, 162; 306.
Federate Club of Clubs, 490.
Feely, Frank, 641.
Ferguson, Josiah, 852.
Fifty-seventh Regiment, 379.
Finch, Cyrus, 68.
Fires, Thomas, 325.
Fire Department, Muncie, 127; in '90s, 160.
First Brick House, 46.
First County Election, 57.
First Heavy Artillery, 365.
First Inhabitants, 18.
First Railroad, 89.
First Schoolhouse, 237.
First School in Muncietown, 245.
First Settlement, 1.
First Telephone, 129.
Fitch, J. Monroe, 685.
Fleming, Silas, 325.
Fort Wayne, 3.
Forty-first Regiment, 376.
Forty-seventh Regiment, 379.
Foster, John W., 752.
Fourth of July, 1848, 110.
Frank, William, 970.
Fraternal Orders, 501, fol.
Fraternal Order of Eagles, 525.
Freeman, John, 928.
Freeman, William, 822.
Free Roads, 87.

Free Schools, 241; in Muncie, 109.
French Explorers, 2.
Frielle, Columbus L., 950.
Friends' Society, Muncie, 472; 473.
Fulge, C. B., 573.
Fuson, Thomas, 1057.

Galliher, Martin, 170.
Gallivan, H. R., 226; 696.
Garland, William, 964.
Garner, Enoch, 326.
Garner, Job, 102.
Garrard, Jeremiah, 638.
Garst, George W., 292.
Gas and Electric Lighting, Introduction of, 128.
Gas Territory, Development of, 140.
Gas, History of, 138; Waste of, 141.
Cass, Frank L., 703.
Gaston, 165.
Gaston Banking Company, 166; 306.
Gaston Gazette, 287.
Gates, Albert L., 1025.
Charky, David, 278.
Gibson, Garret B., 1037.
Gibson, Jonas, 1044.
Gibson, Taylor G., 796.
Gileonites, 479.
Gilbert, Goldsmith C., 20; 45; 104.
Gilbert, Suel, 309.
Gilbert, William, 326.
Gilman, 166.
Gilmer, John W., 769.
Ginn, Liberty, 834.
Gollard, Joseph A., 146; 593.
Golwin, George W., 294.
Goff, Elijah, 1002.
Goldsmith C. Gilbert's, House as Court House, 58.
Gool, A. H., 659.
Goolpasture, Clinton, 1067.
Goontz, William W., 962.
"Government Road," 82.
Gough, Albert H., 1001.
Cough, Eli M., 995.
Grand Jury, First, 65.
Granville, 99.
Gravel Roads, 85; in 1880, 86.
Gray, Myron H., 631.
Green, G. R., 629.
Green, William H., 327.
Green, William W., 961.
Greenville, Treaty of, 5; 8.
Gregory, Ralph S., 73; 673.
Griffith, Roscoe C., 633.
Grindle, Alfred, 692.
Guthrie, Leonidas A., 574.
Guthrie, Thomas S., 616.
Gwinnup, Charles, 689.

Hackley, Rebecca, 103.
Hackley Reserve, 20; 103.

Haimbaugh, Frank D., 670.
Haines, David T., 93; 191.
Haines, David T., Jr., 643.
Haines, James L., 656.
Hall, John, 327.
Hall, John A., 735.
Hamilton, Milton, 923.
Hamilton, Stephen, 52.
Hamilton Township, 33.
Hancock, John M., 1069.
Harris, John M., 755.
Harrison Township, 36.
Harter, George M., 328.
Hartley, John J., 626.
Hathaway, Stephen, 293.
Haymond, George L., 686.
Haymond, H. C., 568.
Heath Family, 51.
Heath, Frederick W., 635.
Heath, Jacob W., 198; 568.
Heath, John T., 1051.
Heaton, William, 654.
Hefel, Anton C., 676.
Heffner, Lawrence, 328.
Helm, George T. S., 1021.
Helm, John C., 293.
Helm, Peter A., 1019.
Hemingray Brothers, 149.
Henry, Thomas C., 1056.
Hensley, J. W., 1075.
Hiatt, Alexander, 891.
Hiatt, Jonathan A., 863.
Hiatt, William, 782.
Hibbets, Wallace, 45.
Highlands, S. M., 135.
Hines, John R., 657.
Hitchcock, Francis, 1007.
Hitchcock, W. E., 557.
Hittle, Benjamin F., 294.
Hoffman, William C., 787.
Holbert, John, 346.
Holmes, John, 328.
Holsclaw, Wickliff B., 751.
Hook, John J., 974.
Horne, John, 295.
Hotel, An Early, 47.
Hoover, Miles L., 840.
Howell, Colwell, 1027.
Huber, George W., 721.
Huffman, Josiah, 695.
Huffman, Thompson M., 973.
Huffman, Wilmuth A., 696.
Hurtt, Clement, 328.
Hutchins, Sewell, 329.
"Hydraulic, The," Canal, 98.
Hyer, Henry, 816.

Improved Order of Heptasophs, 523.
Indiana Bridge Company, 149.
Indiana Business College, 267.
Indiana Signal, 281.
Indiana Territory, 9.

Inlians in 1685, 2.
Inlian Inhabitants, 5.
Iulian Lands, Cession of, 7.
"Inlian Mounls," 11.
Inlian Trails, 78.
Inlian Village in 1813, 13.
Interurban Lines, 213.
Iron Brigale, 359.

Jack, John, 47.
Jackson, John A., 625.
Jackson, John F., 860.
Jackson, Thomas, 329.
Jackson, William, 11.
Jails, 63.
James, Milton, 173.
Janney, Aaros F., 737.
Jauney, Willia T., 682.
Jefferson School, 236.
Jewett, Frel E., 708.
Jewett, Silney A., 707.
Johnson, Abbott L., 134; 545.
Johnson, John C., 202; 543.
Johnson, Lewis, 420.
Johnson, Lucian A., 869.
Jones, Davil H., 1059.
Jones, Davil L., 100.
Jones, Gilbert, 330.
Jones, John W., 1045.
Jones, William F., 172.
Jorlan, Willia A., 1016.
Juip, Charles A., 997.
Juip, Samuel V., 101; 293; 1011.
Juip, S. G., 997.

Keesling, George W., 1015.
Keesling, Lewis, 1026.
Keller, Henry J., 601.
Kemper, Arthur T., 542.
Keiper, G. W. H., 290; 540.
Kemper, Willia W., 542.
Kennely, Anlrew, 69; 70.
Kennely, Evender C., 70.
Kennely, P. A. B., 70.
Kerwool, Asbury L., 307; 423.
Keys, Craven P., 1082.
Kilgore, Davil, 69; 90; 245.
Kilgore, Franklin T., 1069.
Kimbrough, Charles M., 710.
Kirby House, 48.
Kirby, Thomas, 47; 52.
Kirk, Charles B., 640.
Kirklin, John W., 790.
Kirselman Wire Works, 165.
Klela, A. M., 52; 171.
Klopfer, Frel, 611.
Knights and Lalies of Honor, 522.
Knights and Lalies of the Maccabees, bolies—Muncie Tent, 520; Gollen Hive, 520; Muncie Hive, 520; Albany Tent, 521; Eaton Tent, 521.
Knights of Colu bus, Muncie Council, 522.

Knights of Khorassan, Dra atic Orler of, 524.
Knights of Pythias bolics—Welcoie Lolge, 511; Silver Shiell Lolge, 512; Valentine Lolge, 512; Daleville Lolge, 512; Valentine Teiple, Pythian Sisters, 513; Muncie Teiple, Pythian Sisters, 513.
Koons, George H., 73; 552.
Koons, Mrs. George H., 498.
Koons, Willia P., 653.
Koontz, Harv M., 590.
Koontz, J. Harv., 590.
Kyle, Saiuel, 330.

Laboyteaux, Jaies M., 615.
Lalies' Matinee Musicale, 495.
Lalies of the Gollen Eagle, 525.
Lake Erie and Western Railroal Lines, 92.
Laibert, Charles E., 672.
Laibert, Davil A., 703.
Lanl Sales, 17.
La Salle, 2.
Lawyers, in 1881, 72; in 1891, 73; in 1907, 74.
Leairl, Thoias, 808.
Lee, John D., 852.
Lee, Willia H., 851.
Leffler, J. G., 549.
Leffler, J. H., 637.
Lenon, Alonzo R., 993.
Letter Writing in 1848, 109.
Lewellen, Arthur L., 908.
Lewellen, John O., 244; 676.
Lewis, Evan L., 938.
Liberty Township, 25.
Linlsey, Willia, 1021.
Linlsey, Willia L., Jr., 1025.
Linville, Boyl, 106.
Literacy in Delaware County, 240.
Loar, L. T., 704.
Long, John W., 161; 800.
Loss of the Sultana, 418.
Lotz, Orlanlo J., 72; 196; 579.
Lotz, Walter J., 625.
Love, Nannie, 494.

McCarty, Jaies W., 796.
McClanahan, Isaac, 331.
McClellan, Frelerick F., 645.
McConnell, John, 310.
McCorick, Walter P., 936.
McCorick, Willia, 100.
McCowan, Charles, 101.
McCreery, John W., 844.
McCreery, John Wesley, 780.
McCreery, Nathan A., 890.
McCreery, Saiuel, 785.
McCreery, Saiuel J., 785.
McCulloch, Carrie J., 483.
McCulloch, George F., 213; 708.
McCulloch, James, 295.

McCulloch Park, 229.
McCullough, Tho1 as B., 621.
McIntosh, Charles W., 749.
McKinley, Benja1 in II., 770.
McLaughlin, George N., 645.
McMahan, Minerva, 811.
McNett, Sa1 uel F., 854.
McPhee, John, 668.
McRae Club, 485.
McRae, Hamilton S., 263.
Macelonia, 101.
Magazine Club, 487.
Magic City Gun Club, 525.
Maitlen, Isaac, Sr., 330.
Mann, Isaac, 954.
Manring, A1 brose A., 881.
Mansfiell, Ja1 es, 331.
Mansfiell, Tho1 as J., 924.
Manufacturing, 232.
Manufacturing before and after Gas
  Boo1, 148.
Manufactories in 1895, 155.
Manufacturing at Eaton, 162.
March, Walter, 71; 168.
Maring, George W., 556.
Maring, Hart & Co1 pany, 150.
Market Prices in 1848, 110.
Markle, Sa1 uel E., 749.
Marsh, John, 169.
Marsh, John R., 594.
Marsh, John W., 943.
Marsh, W. M., 146.
Marshall, Tho1 as, 1022.
Martha Washington Club, 484.
Martin, Isaac, 330.
Mary Martha Club, 489.
Masonic Bodies — Delaware Lodge, 501;
  Muncie Lodge, 502; Muncie Chapter,
  502; Muncie Co1 1anlery, 503; Muncie
  Council, 503; Anthony Lodge, 504;
  Whitney Lodge, 504; Eaton Lodge,
  505; Muncie Chapter, O. E. S., 506;
  Albany Chapter, O. E. S., 506.
Matthews, Elias, 331.
Maynard, David S., 716.
Maynard, Washington, 713.
Medford, 101.
Medical History, 288, fol.
Meeks, Jacob A., 652.
Meeks, Ja1 es W., 579.
Meeks, Robert, 596.
Merchants' National Bank, 304.
Methodist Churches — High Street, 426;
  Si1 pson Chapel, 429; Ma1 ison St., 433;
  Whitely, 433; Avondale, 433; Nor1 al
  City, 434; Yorktown, 434; Mt. Zion,
  439; Daleville, 440; Wheeling, 440;
  Pleasant Valley, 441; Delaware Chapel,
  441; Bethel (Albany Circuit), 441;
  Muncie African, 441; Trinity, 442;
  First Methodist Protestant, 442.
Mexican War, 343, fol.

Michael, David, 941.
Millan1 Railroa1, 217.
Milhollin, Sa1 uel, 772.
Military History of Delaware County, 307,
  fol.
Military Recor1 of Civil War, Recapitula-
  tion, 414.
Mill at Muncie, 45.
Miller, Alfre1, 833.
Miller, Charles E., 651.
Mills, Jonathan, 52.
Mills, Joseph A., 1023.
Mills, Orliff W., 1024.
Miltenberger, J. D., 636.
Minshall, Levi, 52; 291.
Miscellaneous Co1 panies, in Civil War,
  409.
Mitchell, Harvey, 291; 294; 580.
Mitchell, Sa1 uel E., 294.
Mitchell, Walter P., 723.
Mon1 ay Afternoon Club, 487.
Monroe, John M., 958.
Monroe, Robert W., 687.
Monroe Township, 32.
Mooly, Ma1 ison M., 1003.
Moore, Ja1 es, 346.
Morgan's Rail Regi1 ents, 394.
Mt. Pleasant Township, 22; 101.
Mullin, E1 1itt, 886.
Muncie, 5; Architecture, 231; after Dis-
  covery of Gas, 143; beco1 es County
  Seat, 58; Business Directory, 1848, 111;
  Business Houses in 1880, 131; Business
  Men in 1887, 146; Early Buildings, 69;
  Early Business, 106, 107; Early History
  of, 103, fol.: in 1837, 105; in 1848, 109;
  in 1880, 126; History, 1842-1881, in
  Putna1 Diary, 116; the County Seat,
  105; Financial Status, 224; Fire De-
  partment, 226; First Officials, 113; Gen-
  eral Progress, 233; Incorporation of,
  112; Municipal Status, 127; Municipal
  I1 prove1 ents after Gas Discovery, 157;
  as a Municipality, 223; Post1 asters,
  223; Postoffice, 156; 220; Sewers, 158;
  Streets, 157; Streets and Paving, 230;
  Water Works, 132; 224; Streets and
  Sewers in '80s, 136.
Muncie Art Association, 496.
Muncie Bar Association, 75.
Muncie Business and Manufacturing As-
  sociation, 169.
Muncie Co1 1 ercial Club, 180.
Muncie De1 ocrat, 283.
Muncie Electric Light Co., 224.
Muncie Electric Street Railway Co., 212.
Muncie Heral1, 284.
Muncie Journal, 281.
Muncie News, 284.
Muncie Observer, 283.
Muncie Public Library, 268.
Muncie Savings and Loan Co1 pany, 306.

Muncie Schools, 259.
Muncie Star, 286.
Muncie Street Railroad, 211.
Muncie Suburbs, 158.
Muncie Times, 282.
Muncie Trust Company, 303; 305.
Muncietonian, The, 278.
Muncietown Yeoman, 280.
Muncietown becomes Muncie, 108.
Muncietown, Indian Village, 11.
Muncietown Telegraph, 280.
Munsee Indians, 5.
Murray, Albert P., 931.
Murray, Alfred L., 824.
Murray, Viretta, 825.
Murray, William H., 1000.
Mutual Home and Savings Association, 306.

National Road, The, 78.
Natural Gas, 188.
Nash, Darius A., 1080.
Neely, Thomas S., 89; 195.
Neiswanger, Charles W., 678.
Nelson, Joseph A., 693.
New Burlington, 101.
New Corner, 100; 165.
Newspapers, History of, 278, fol.
Nihart, Charles L., 682.
Nihart, David H., 990.
Niles township, 38.
Nineteenth Regiment, 357.
Ninetieth Regiment, 394.
Nixon, George W., 842.
Northwest Territory, Conquest of, 6.
Nolin, Peter, 59.

Oakville, 102.
Oarl, James, 1055.
Observer, The, 286.
Odd Fellows, Independent Order of, bodies
  —Muncie Lodge, 507; Energy Lodge,
  507; Muncie Encampment, 508; Canton
  Muncie, 508; Eaton Lodge, 508; York-
  town Lodge, 509; New Corner Lodge,
  509; Cowan Lodge, 509; Bethel Lodge,
  509; Charity Lodge, 510; Heart and
  Hand Lodge, 510; Daleville Lodge, 510;
  Wheeling Lodge, 510; Naomi Rebekah
  Lodge, 511; Omega Rebekah Lodge, 511.
Official Lists, 529, fol.
Oil Production in Delaware County, 219.
"Oil Fort," The, 19.
Old Letters, Historic, 52.
Oliver, Hortense L., 684.
One Hundred and Eighteenth Regiment,
  397.
One Hundred and Eleventh Regiment, 395.
One Hundred and First Regiment, 394.
One Hundred and Fortieth Regiment, 405.
One Hundred and Forty-seventh Regiment,
  407.

One Hundred and Nineteenth Regiment,
  398.
One Hundred and Seventeenth Regiment,
  396.
One Hundred and Twenty-first Regiment,
  399.
One Hundred and Thirtieth Regiment, 403.
One Hundred and Thirty-first Regiment,
  403.
One Hundred and Thirty-fourth Regiment,
  404.
One Hundred and Twenty-fourth Regi-
  ment, 401.
Ordinance of 1787, 7.
Over Glass Works, 150.
Owens, O. W., 640.

Pace, William B., 331.
Panic of 1893, 154.
Parker, Archibald, 332.
Parkison, Isaac N., 726.
Patterson, Arthur F., 195; 550.
Patterson, Harriet L., 271.
Patterson, Robert I., 498; 583.
Patterson, William M., 550.
Paving in Muncie, 180.
Payton, Lewis, 671.
Peacock, James R., 1052.
Peacock, William H., 419; 1043.
Ferline, Lewis L., 662.
Perdieu, Stafford B., 563.
People's Home and Savings Assn., 306.
People's National Bank, 305.
Perry Township, 23.
Perry Township Schools, 251.
Peyton, Jacob, 332.
Peyton, William, 333.
Physicians, List of, 297.
Phillips, William H., 999.
Pierce, Calaway, 1061.
Pierce, Walter F., 678.
Pioneers, The, 44; Association of Dela-
  ware County, 185; Mentioned in Putnam
  Diary, 116; Incidents and Customs, 53;
  (see Chronology, 167 fol.;) (see Sol-
  diers of Early Wars.)
Plank Roads, 85.
Poland, Albert M., 931.
Poland, Samuel, 927.
Poland, Ulysses G., 649.
Political History of Delaware County, 527.
Pontiac's War, 4.
Post Coaches, 108.
Potter, J. O., 623.
Powers, Mark, 166; 711.
Powers, James H., 294.
Powers, Ulysses G., 933.
Presbyterian Churches — First Presbyte-
  rian, Muncie, 447; First United Pres-
  byterian, Muncie, 449.
Price, Alexander, 333.
Probate Court, 67.

Probate Judges, 534.
Prophet, The, 10.
Prophet's Town, 11.
Props, J. Cooper, 822.
Props, William R., 819.
Prosecuting Attorneys, 530.
Public Roads, 218.
Pugh, Elwin R., 937.
Putman, Frederick E., 116; 194.

Quaker Settlers, 9; 50.
Quinn, John, 310.

Railroads, 84; 89; in 1907, 1; in North-
  Delaware County, 165; Recent
  Growth, 214.
Randal, Cynthia A., 310.
"Rat Row," 131.
Rea, Clarence G., 634.
Real Estate Boom, 145.
Reasoner, Archiball, 332.
Recorders, 532.
Rector, Arthur, 894.
Rector, Charles W., 845.
Rector, James A., 892.
Red Men, Improved Order of, bodies—
  De Erber Tribe, 513; Munsy Tribe,
  514; Twa Twa Tribe, 514; Torahawk
  Tribe, 514; Keechewa Tribe, 515; Ionia
  Council, D. of P., 515; Washatella Coun-
  cil D. of P., 515; Musco Council, D.
  of P., 515; Seneca Council, D. of P.,
  516; Kickapoo Tribe, 516; Iola Coun-
  cil, D. of P., 516; Ouray Tribe, 517;
  Sioux Tribe, 517; Delaware Tribe, 517;
  Pueblo Tribe, 518; Pueblo Council, D.
  of P., 518; Mocassin Tribe, 518; White
  Feather Tribe, 519; Nodawa Tribe, 519;
  Koka Tribe, 519.
Rees, Carl, 1030.
Renner, W. G., 69.
Revolutionary Soldiers in Delaware Coun-
  ty, 307.
Reynolds, James A., 1051.
Richarls, Daniel, 758.
Richardson, George H., 262.
Richey, Webster S., 674.
Richey, William H., 980.
Richwood, 102.
Riverside, 159.
Rivers and Settlement, 41.
Roads, 77; to Delaware County, 82.
Rose, T. F., 135; 146.
Ross, Garret, 1034.
Ross, John C., 688.
Ross, William W., 1030.
Ross, Wycliffe W., 946.
Round Table Club, 487.
Rowlett, George W., 618.
Royerton, 94; 102.
Royerton, schools, 251; 255; 257.
Rural Free Delivery, 96; 188; 219.
Ryan, John W., 71.

St. Clair, James W., 945.
Salem township, 28.
Salvation Army, 490.
Sample, Thomas J., 72.
Sanders, Asa B., 757.
Sanders, Robert, 320; 334.
Saunders, George, 335.
Schmilt, William G., 469; 471.
School Supervision in County, 244.
Schools, 237; fol.
Schools, Mt. Pleasant township, 245;
  Delaware township, 246; Salem town-
  ship, 246; Liberty township, 247; Mon-
  roe township, 247; Hamilton township,
  247; Union township, 247; Niles town-
  ship, 248; Harrison township, 248;
  Washington township, 248.
Scott, William, 335.
Seerist, Jacob, 335.
Selma, 96; 166; 219; 203; schools, 249;
  250.
Selvy, Clarrenda, 967.
Selvy, Samuel G., 966.
Settlement, General Course of, 41.
Settlers, Early, Classification of, 44; from
  North Atlantic States, 45; from South
  Atlantic States, 50.
Seventy-first Regiment, 386.
Shafer, John W., 653.
Shaffer, Peter R., 839.
Shannon, Joseph, 336.
Sharp, Florence A., 790.
Sharp, Jacob E., 789.
Sharp, Thompson, 773.
Shaw, Francis A., 694.
Shellenberger, Isaac, 336.
Sheller, George S., 942.
Sheriffs, 532.
Shideler, 94; 102.
Shideler, Isaac H., 915.
Shiner's Point, 234.
Shipley, Carlton E., 72; 204.
Shroyer, George W., 101.
Shroyer, John A., 993.
Shroyer, Sherman J., 991.
Shults, Henry, 336.
Simmons, Daniel, 337.
Sites, John A., 872.
Sixteenth Regiment, 356.
Sixty-ninth Regiment, 383.
Skiff, Clark, 295.
Slack, George W., 294.
Slickville, Muncie, 108.
Smallpox Epidemic, 178.
Smith, Caleb B., 68.
Smith, George M., 337.
Smith, Henry, 831.
Smith, John, 48.
Smith, John E., 827.
Smith, J. H., 602.
Smith, M. C., 192.
Smith, Oliver H., 19; 68.

Smith, Septi*us, 68.
Smithfield, 96; 219.
Snider, Alexander, 925.
Snider, John, Sr., 907.
Snyder, W. R., 265.
Social Conditions in Muncie During Gas Boom, 151.
Soldiers in Various Regiments of Civil War (see under different regiment numbers).
Soldiers of War of 1812, settlers in Delaware County, 314, fol.
Soldiers Draft in Civil War, 417.
Soldiers Relief in Civil War, 415.
Southeastern Indiana, Settlement of, 9.
Spaker, George W., 190; 274.
Spiritualists, Society of, 479.
Spurgeon, William A., 584.
Stafford, Cyrus J., 947.
Stafford, Samuel W., 911.
Stanley, Amos O., 663.
Star of Hope Mission, 479.
State Bank of Indiana, 302.
State Representatives, 530.
State Senators, 529.
Stephenson, G. W., 74.
Stevenson, Robert E., 666.
Stewart, Edwin R., 1065.
Stewart, James, 337.
Stewart, Louis R., 1073.
Stewart, Samuel, 1078.
Stoner, Lewis H., 949.
Stout, 102.
Street Railroad, 171.
Strong, George R., 957.
Strong, Harrison, 813.
Sultana, The, 418.
Surber, Alva C., 630.
Surveyors of County, 533.
Survey of Lands in County, 15.
Swain, Job, 52.
Sweeny, Henry, 754.

Taylor P. O., 102.
Taylor, Samuel K., 687.
Taylor, Valentine, 686.
Telegraph, 210.
Templer, Clayton B., 74; 669.
Tenth Regiment, 356.
Tecumseh, 10.
Thirteenth Regiment, 356.
Thirty-sixth Regiment, 368.
Thomas, William C., 859.
Thompson, David, 337.
Thompson, Ephraim, 339.
Thompson, E. S. L., 498.
Thompson, W. A., 575.
Thornburg, Asahel, 341.
Thornburg, George H., 1012.
Thornburg, Joseph H., 1028.
Tidrick, R. O., 667.
Tippecanoe, Battle of, 12.

Toll, O. M., 244.
Toll Roads, 85.
Tourist Club, 485.
Town Building and Railroads, 94.
Towns and Country after Discovery of Gas, 161.
Towns, Formation of, 95.
Township Trustees, 534.
Townships, Survey of, 16.
Townships, Property Valuations, Comparison, 207.
Transportation and Communication, 77.
Trask, Ezra S., 201.
Treasurers, 533; of Muncie, 536.
Treaty of St. Mary's, 14.
Truitt, James, 90.
Tuhey, Edward, 700.
Tulley, John L., 935.
Turner, Minus, 40; 66; 169.
Turnpikes, 84.
Tuttle, Darlin M., 1038.
Tuttle, John R., 759.
Twelfth Regiment, 356.
Twelve Mile Purchase, 9; 10; 57.
Twentieth Century Club of Albany, 490.

Union National Bank, 185; 305.
Union Passenger Station, Muncie, 215.
Union township, 35.
Union Traction Company of Indiana, 213.
United Brethren Churches—Normal City, 475; First Brethren, 475; Riverside, 476; Congerville, 476; Selma, 476; Beech Grove, 477; Maple Grove, 477.
Universalist Churches — First Universalist, Muncie, 465.

Vannarsdoll, Cornelius, 341.
Vanlerburg, James M., 933.
Van Matre, Charles A., 244; 672.
Van Matre, William, 50.
Venard, William, 98.
Vincennes, Sieur le, 3.
Vinton, Arthur E., 632.
Voting Tax for First Railroad, 91.

Wachtell, Calvin S., 576.
Wachtell, F. L., 681.
Wall, Harold C. R., 697.
Wallace, Benjamin, 311.
Walling, Mark, 188.
Walling, Quince, 660.
Walling, Thompson, 114.
Walling, William, 190.
Walterhouse, T. S., 167.
Walters, William A., 1064.
Warner, Rollin, 74; 611.
Warner, Thomas W., 616.
War of 1812, Delaware County in, 12; 314.
Washington township, 30.

Water Works, Muncie, 132; 224.
Wayne County, 9.
Wayne's Victory, 8.
Webster, Oliver E., 764.
West Muncie, 163.
West Side, 159.
Wheeling, 100.
Whicker, Matthew, 342.
Whicker, William, 311.
Whig Banner, 281.
White, Robe C., 564.
Whitely, 175.
Wilcoxon, Lloyd '87; 343.
Willard block, 68.
Willard ... F., 49.
Wil... William C., 292.
Williams, Duncan, 174; 698.
Williams, Henry H., 760.
Williams, John C., 983.
Williams, Sarah J., 699.
Williams, William, 313.
Williams, William H., 993.
Williamson, Alan, 922.
Williamson, Alexander, 347.
Williamson, James, 921.
Wills, James H., 725.
Wills, John W., 762.
Willson, Volney, 49; 61.

Wilson, Joseph, 100.
Wilson, S. A., 134; 146.
Wilson, Samuel P., 342.
Winans, Henry C., 295.
Wingate, Norval T., 987.
Wingate, Phillip, 343.
Wingate, William P., 988.
Winton, Robert, 289; 293.
Witamyer, Henry, 825.
Woman's Club of Muncie, 481.
Woman's Club of Selma, 490.
Women's Clubs, 481.
Women's Temperance Crusade of '70s, 123.
Woollen of the World, 523.
Wysor, Harry R., 546.
Wysor, Jacob H., 52; 203; 546.
Wysor Opera House, 131.
Wysor's Grand Opera House, 175.

Yorktown, Indian Village at, 11; 19; 97; schools, 249.
Yorktown Woman's Club, 488.
Young, Abraham C., 818.
Young, Ira J., 664.
Younts, family, 99.

Zehner, Benjamin J., 940.

HISTORY OF DELAWARE COUNTY

CHAPTER I.

DELAWARE COUNTY A PART OF THE FRENCH EMPIRE.

Though Indiana was organized as a territory in 1800 and admitted to statehood in 1816, the region that we now know as Delaware county did not receive a permanent settler until about 1820. Old Vincennes·had been a name in history and a center of stirring events for nearly a century. The first legislature of the new state had assembled at Corydon, near the southern end of the state, while Indians were the only inhabitants of the wilderness which is now the rich and prosperous agricultural county of Delaware. Not alone in the southern end of the state were there numerous villages and organized counties, but before the first permanent settlement had been made in Delaware county many people had homes to the north along the Wabash, and there was a well defined settlement and trading post at Fort Wayne, a site that had been designated on the maps through the greater part of the previous century.

On a map showing Indiana in 1907, the most conspicuous feature is the network of railroads that run in all directions over the state, and make practically every county and large town accessible by that means of communication. Radiating from Muncie alone are more than a dozen steam and electric lines leading toward all sections of Indiana and insuring uninterrupted communication with all the states and large cities of the Union. If, supposing these means of communication to remain, the lands of Indiana were uninhabited and once more thrown open to settlement, it is probable that the entire state could be occupied in a single day and Delaware county and its neighbors would be taken up as quickly as any of the counties in southern or northern Indiana.

It is not meant to imply that the absence of transportation lines was the sole reason why the first white men discriminated against Delaware county when they settled the state. But it was the prime cause in directing migration until sixty years ago. Up to that time the great trunk lines of communication in the middle west were the rivers and here and there a canal. In a map of the region about the great lakes, including northern Indiana, drawn about 1755, the rivers Miamis, Wabache and Theakaki (Kankakee) are the most conspicuous features of topography. A century ago the Naumee river, the portage at Fort Wayne across to the Wabash, the latter river as the principal water route through the central part of the state, the Ohio river along the southern border, and such tributaries as the Whitewater and the two branches of the White river, were the routes of travel first to be considered and most valuable in the settlement and economic development of the state. So far as seriously affecting the transportation facilities of the neighboring country, the Wabash river could now be dispensed with, for railway trains have long carried the burdens that once were borne on this stream. For the first seventy-five years in the history of this country, however, the Wabash was the principal connecting link between the great lakes on the north and the Ohio and Mississippi valleys. The first settlements in the valley of the Wabash were planted in order to protect this line of communication between the northern and southern divisions of New France.

French Explorers.

During the latter half of the seventeenth century, by the discoveries and explorations of Marquette, Hennepin, Joliet and LaSalle, all the country drained by the Mississippi and Ohio rivers and their tributaries was added to the vast claims of the French empire in the new world. For nearly a century the statecraft and military power of France were tested and tried to the utmost in strengthening and maintaining the authority of the empire in the territory between New Orleans and Montreal. During LaSalle's explorations about the lower end of Lake Michigan and in his journeyings from there to the Mississippi, he penetrated northwestern Indiana, going as far east as the site of South Bend. Another result of his activities was the organization of the various Indian tribes outside of the Iroquois confederacy and the concentration of them all about a central seat in Illinois, so that in 1685 it is probable that Indiana was no longer the home of a single Indian tribe.

To secure all the country between the Mississippi and the Alleghanies against English aggression, the French projected and founded many posts that would command the rivers and the outlets of trade. Several forts were established at the lower end of the Mississippi, and a vigorous policy of commercial development and expansion begun. Other posts were established higher up the river, Kaskaskia above the mouth of the Ohio becoming a strategic point of much importance. The French captain, Cadillac, by anticipating the English in the settlement of Detroit, secured a post of wonderful advantage in dealing with the Indian inhabitants west of Lake

Erie and south of Lake Michigan. The Indian tribes that had been drawn into LaSalle's Illinois confederacy were now drifting east to the Wabash, the Maumee and about Detroit. To control these tribes and prevent their being approached by the English, the French authorities in Canada, who claimed jurisdiction on the upper courses of the Wabash,* planned the relocation of the tribes and the founding of posts among them. The principal settlement of the Miamis was then at the head of the Maumee, at a place called Kekionga (the site of Fort Wayne). The Ouiatanons lived lower down on the Wabash, and about 1720 post Ouiatanon was established among them (near the site of Lafayette), this being the first military post on the Wabash. At this point, controlling the Miamis and the Ouiatanons, was stationed Sieur de Vincennes. The authorities of Louisiana, very much exercised by the reported encroachments of English traders within the Ohio valley, about 1726 won over Vincennes from his service with Canada, and a year or so later that intrepid pioneer of France founded on the lower course of the Wabash the post which soon became known as Vincennes. In a few years some French families from Canada settled around the post, and thus was established the first European village in Indiana. Until the close of the French occupation in 1763, Vincennes was included in the District of Illinois, which, in turn, was part of the Province of Louisiana. The dividing point between the jurisdiction of Canada and that of Louisiana was Terre Haute, "the Highlands of the Wabash."

By such means the authority of France was extended throughout all this country including the present state of Indiana. Vincennes became a village of French soldiers and traders and their families, where Lafayette now stands was another French post, and another at the site of Fort Wayne. The inevitable conflict between France and England, closing with the victory of Wolfe on the plains of Abraham and with the treaty of Paris in 1763, by which England became the dominant and principal territorial power in the new world, has only a remote interest in this discussion. The French and English met at the site of Pittsburg in 1754, where Fort DuQuesne was built by the former, and this meeting brought on the war which began with the disastrous defeat of Braddock by the French and their Indian allies.

After Wolfe's victory the English took possession of Detroit and the posts on the upper Wabash, but Vincennes continued a part of French Louisiana until the treaty in 1763. The numerous Indian tribes northwest of the Ohio, though at first treated with much respect by the English, were

* The lower Ohio and Wabash and Mississippi were governed as part of the Louisiana province of New France. Boisbriant, who had been appointed governor of Illinois, founded Fort Chartres (sixteen miles above Kaskaskia) for the protection of the upper colony. in 1720.

later wrought upon by the brusque behavior of the English and the secret persuasion of the French who still remained in the country. A powerful confederacy of the western tribes was formed under the brilliant leadership of Pontiac, and during the spring of 1763 a general outbreak against the English posts occurred, which has since been known in history as Pontiac's war. Few of the inland posts escaped capture, the small English garrisons at Ouiatanon and Miamis (Fort Wayne) surrendering with the rest. It was not until the following year that such energetic measures were taken by the English forces as to break the Indians' strength and force the Delawares, Shawnees, Miamis and other bands to sue for peace. Henceforth until the American revolution, the Indian inhabitants north of the Ohio gave little trouble to the English, who maintained an easy and almost nominal jurisdiction over the posts and settlements along the Wabash and down the Mississippi.

CHAPTER II.

INDIAN INHABITANTS — A N ERICAN CONQUEST.

During the first half of the eighteenth century, while St. Ange was second governor of Post Vincennes, the only Indians in Indiana lived along the Wabash and to the north of it. There were no villages and no resident tribes to the south of the Wabash valley.* Within historical times, the Indians most closely identified with the central and eastern Indiana counties were the Delawares. The Delawares were originally eastern Indians, of the Algonquian stock, calling themselves Lenape or Leni-lenape, and figured more than once in the history of the early colonies in New York, New Jersey, Delaware and Pennsylvania. After being forced out of their eastern abodes on the Delaware river, partly by the hostility of the Iroquois and partly by the extension of the white settlements, they moved into western Pennsylvania, then through the gateway of the Alleghanies, and finally settled in eastern Ohio, where, being within reach of the French, and backed by the western tribes, they asserted their independence of the Iroquois, and in the subsequent wars, up to the treaty of Greenville in 1795, showed themselves the most determined opponents of the advancing whites.†

About the year 1770, having received permission from the Miami and Piankishaw to occupy the country between the Ohio and White rivers in Indiana, the Delawares became seated in central and eastern Indiana, their presence here being commemorated in the county that contains but a small portion of the territory over which these Indians wandered. At one time they had six villages. In 1789, by permission of the Spanish government, a part of them removed to Missouri, and afterwards to Arkansas, together with a band of Shawnee. By 1820 the two bands had found their way to Texas. The Delawares, including the Munsee, now number about 1,900, most of them in Oklahoma, Indian Territory and Kansas.

The Munsee.

The Munsee were one of the three principal divisions of the Delawares, called, because of their totem, the "Wolf tribe" of the Delawares. From this tribe the county seat and metropolis of Delaware county takes its name. The original significance of the word " Munsee" is defined as "at the place where stones are gathered together," a meaning that has, of course, no relation to the city in Delaware county. Besides the Muncie in Indiana, two

* Dunn's Indiana.
† Handbook of American Indians, Bureau of Ethnology reports, 1906.

other towns in the United States bear that name, one in Illinois and the other
in Kansas; while in Pennsylvania three localities have the name form of
"Muncy." The Munsee, as a tribe of the Delawares, dwelt originally in
New York, New Jersey and Pennsylvania, about the Delaware river. About
the middle of the eighteenth century they moved to the Allegheny river.
The Moravian missionaries had already begun their work among them, and
a considerable number under their teaching drew off from the tribe and
became a separate organization. The others moved west with the Delawares
into Indiana, where most of them were incorporated with that tribe, while
others joined the Chippewa, Shawnee and other tribes, so that the Munsee
practically ceased to exist as an organized body. Many removed to Canada,
and settled near their relatives, the Moravian Indians. In 1885 the only
Munsee officially recognized in the United States were living with a body
of Chippewa in Franklin county, Kansas, both together numbering only 72.

In 1774 all the country northwest of the Ohio was put into the boundaries of the Province of Quebec, and several years later the lieutenant governor of Detroit assumed the title of "superintendent of St. Vincennes," and
took personal command there in 1777. Throughout all the years since the
first exploration of her territory Indiana was but a part of a province. "For ninety years her provincial seat of government vacillated
between Quebec, New Orleans and Montreal, with intermediate authority at
Fort Chartres and Detroit, and the ultimate power at Paris. Then her capital was whisked away to London, without the slightest regard to the wishes
of her scattered inhabitants, by the treaty of Paris. Sixteen years later it
came over the Atlantic to Richmond, on the James, by conquest; and after
a tarry of five years at that point it shifted to New York city, then the
national seat of government, by cession. In 1788 it reached Marietta, Ohio,
on its progress to its final location. In 1800 it came within the limits of the
state."*

Clark's Conquest of Northwest Territory.

During the Revolutionary war, the danger most dreaded by the colonists
was that which came from across the western frontier, produced by the
Indians and their English leaders. At this time a considerable population
had crossed the mountains from the Atlantic colonies into the country along
the Ohio, and the county of Kentucky had already been organized as a part
of Virginia by George Rogers Clark. This young Virginian, when it became
apparent that a frontier force must be maintained to subdue the Indians and
check their invasions under English leadership into the colonies, was selected
by the government of Virginia to organize and command such a force on
the frontier. Owing to lack of money, of supplies, the small number of set-

* Dunn's Indiana.

t!ers from whom his force was to be recruited, and the vast extent of country to be covered by his force, the success of Clark's campaign has long been a glorious addition to American annals, and his fame fitly symbolized with the designation "The Hannibal of the West." Setting out with a small force of men, recruited largely in Kentucky, and relying on the support or at least the neutral attitude of the French settlers, he surprised the post at Kaskaskia, July 4, 1778, and in the course of the same month Vincennes became an American post, an American flag was floated for the first time in Indiana, and the French residents welcomed the American invaders as friends of their nation. Vincennes was later captured by the British and again retaken by Clark, but the details of his campaign are not here pertinent. Suffice it to say that he held the vast region of his conquest against all expeditions of the English until the close of the war, and when the treaty of Paris was signed in 1783 the conquered region became a part of the new American republic. By the Ordinance of 1787 all this country northwest of the Ohio was organized as the Northwest Territory, and provided with a temporary government directed by officials appointed by Congress.

By Clark's conquest, by the Ordinance of 1787 for the government of the Territory, and by ordinances, dated in 1785 and 1788, providing for the survey and disposal of the public lands of the Territory, the region now embraced in the states of Ohio, Indiana, Illinois, Michigan and parts of others became a part of the United States and opened to the settlement of the pioneer homemakers who formed the first wave of western expansion. However, the Indian inhabitants were a factor that proved an obstacle to the settlement of this region for many years, and it was only when they gradually yielded, by war and treaty, their rights to the land that the white men were permitted, to come in and possess the fertile regions north of the Ohio.

When the war of the revolution came to a close in the colonies, the Indian hostilities in the west were continued with renewed bitterness. When the territory north of the Ohio was surrendered to the colonies and it became understood that in a short time the Americans would push out and possess and settle this country, the Indians were aroused to make one long and determined effort to resist this invasion. For more than ten years hostilities were continued, during which time the settlement of the Ohio country was retarded and only a meager number of pioneers came as far west as the present state of Indiana. Campaign after campaign was made against the Indian tribes, conference followed conference, and at each treaty the Indians ceded some portion of their aboriginal heritage.

The eastern half of Ohio was ceded to the United Colonies in 1785. The Shawnees, who resisted every advance of the whites, were induced, by the Fort Finney treaty in 1786, to remove to a tract of country between the upper courses of the Great Miami and the Wabash—probably including the part of Indiana that is now Delaware county. After the passage of the Ordinance of 1787 and the institution of government in the Northwest Territory, the period of actual settlement began. But for some years all the region between what is now eastern Ohio and the valley of the Wabash was a wilderness. In a short while the line of settlement extended across the entire north and south length of Ohio at its eastern border. But the emigration did not advance in even line to the west; rather the earliest settlers pioneered down the water course of the Ohio, turning aside only at the larger tributaries, so that during the last decade of the eighteenth century the fringes of population had extended all along the course of the Ohio and had penetrated inland for some distance along the Miami in Ohio and the White-water and the Wabash and its tributaries in Indiana.

Settlement would have proceeded more rapidly had not the Indians continued hostile. It will be remembered the English did not withdraw their garrisons from all the posts in the western country until 1796, and the presence of the British had served as an inspiration to the Indians. About the time the British garrisons were withdrawn, Anthony Wayne won his notable victory over the allied tribes at the rapids of the Maumee, in 1794, and soon after established at the old post of Kekionga a fort that has since borne his name. Previously, under Wayne's instructions, posts had been established called Fort Greenville and Fort Recovery (both only a short distance east of the Indiana line). At Fort Greenville, in August, 1795, was negotiated the Greenville treaty between General Wayne and the delegates of the various tribes inhabiting the portions of country under dispute. The boundary line setting off the Indian country from that ceded to the whites, fixed by this treaty, has more significance in the history of Delaware county than would be supposed in the case of an event so remote from the date of first settlement in the county. By this treaty nearly all of the present state of Ohio with the exception of the northwest corner was surrendered by the Indians. The western line ran from Fort Recovery (not far from the present Celina, Ohio) in a slightly southwesterly direction to the mouth of the Kentucky river on the Ohio. In the territory to the west of this line numerous other cessions were made by the Indians, among them a military reservation at Fort Wayne, lands about the various Wabash settlements, and the Clark grant at the falls of the Ohio. Excepting the minor cessions along the Wabash, the principal territory thrown open to settlement by this treaty in what is now Indiana was the triangular piece, shaped like a church spire with the base resting on the Ohio river, lying east of the Greenville Treaty Line to the present Ohio state line. When, in 1800, Congress divided the Northwest Territory, this Greenville line became part of the dividing line between Ohio and Indiana territories, but on the admission of Ohio to the Union in 1802 the western boundary became what it is to-day.

It will be seen that this three-cornered strip in what is now southeastern Indiana contained territory that has since been made to comprise several entire counties at the southern end, and the narrower northern point contributed portions to the present Wayne, Randolph and Jay counties. Population at once began moving into the lands ceded by the Greenville treaty. In 1795 a few families made a beginning of the town of Lawrenceburg, in the extreme southeast corner of Indiana, and from that date settlements increased over that portion of the cession. Of course, during the first two years of the territorial government of Indiana, this region belonged to Ohio and its population was counted with that of the latter territory. In 1800 the total population of what is now Indiana was estimated at 2500, the majority of whom were French, in the settlements along the Wabash. When Ohio became a state in 1802 the section above described was added to Indiana, and from this Dearborn county was organized in 1803. Dearborn county and the valley of the Whitewater attracted a large number of Quaker immigrants. Their influence on the early politics of Indiana is a matter that can not be considered here; but these Quaker settlers, who later formed the bulk of the early population of Wayne county, comprised the stock from which many of Delaware county's pioneers came, and their influence can be easily traced in this county's history.

In February, 1809, Indiana territory was reduced to practically the present limits. But at that time the Indians still retained more than two thirds of the territory, so that the white settlements were restricted to the region along the Ohio, along the Wabash from Vincennes south, to the southeastern corner (Dearborn county) and several smaller grants. In September, 1809, a large area was opened to settlement, by treaty. By the larger cession the north boundary of settlement was fixed at a line running from the Wabash above Terre Haute to the east fork of White River near Brownstown. At the same time another tract was ceded, twelve miles in width and lying west of and parallel to the Greenville Treaty Line, being commonly known as the "twelve mile purchase." By this purchase the boundary of civilization was extended so as to include what is now a small portion of Jay county, the larger part of Randolph county, almost the entire Wayne county, and the other counties lying to the south. In 1815 this strip, then divided among the counties of Wayne, Franklin, Dearborn and Switzerland and parts of others, contained more than twenty thousand inhabitants, which was one third of the population of the entire territory which was just about to be made into a state. While Wayne county (then comprising the northern end of the strip and considerably greater area than it now has) had nearly seven thousand inhabitants in 1816, the area of Delaware county, almost adjoining, was still without a permanent inhabitant and belonged to the wilderness and the red men.

CHAPTER III.

ADVANCE OF CIVILIZATION; DELAWARE COUNTY OPENED TO SETTLEMENT.

A number of interesting matters are brought up for consideration when we inquire into the reasons why civilization did not sooner advance its bounds over the region now called Delaware county. From a population of 2500 in 1800, Indiana had about 25,000 in 1810, and over 60,000 in 1815. But during the next five years population increased to nearly 150,000, and to nearly 350,000 in 1830. The rush of settlement began about 1815, and in fifteen years settlements had been made in every portion of the state. It is remarkable how such a county as Delaware became "settled up" in ten years' time, how a wilderness was so quickly transformed into civilization, and homes and institutions established on every section where shortly before the Indian and the hunter had been the only human visitors. The power of American civilization to transform the wild prairies and the rapidity with which the transformation was effected doubtless inspired the poet who spoke thus of the uninhabited plains:—

> "I listen long
>   . . . and think I hear
> The sound of that advancing multitude
> Which soon shall fill these deserts. From the ground
> Comes up the laugh of children, the soft voice
> Of maidens, and the sweet and solemn hymn
> Of Sabbath worshippers. The low of herds
> Blends with the rustling of the heavy grain
> Over the dark brown furrows."

The treaty of 1809, above mentioned, by which the "twelve mile purchase" was gained, had one result that contributed very materially to the slow development of Indiana during the next five years. The Indians had not failed to regard with jealousy the gradual encroachment of the whites upon their hunting grounds. But after Wayne's victory and the treaty of Greenville, no concerted movement in opposition had been carried out. But a worthy leader, brave warrior and shrewd chieftain arose among them in the person of the Shawnee, Tecumseh, who was ably assisted in his endeavors to rouse the Indians to resist by his brother, Law-le-was-i-kaw, but best known as the "Prophet." These two dwelt in one of the Delaware villages in the present Delaware county in the year 1805, and here it was that the Prophet began his exhortations, reinforced by his claims to divine power, by which he acquired a powerful hold on the superstitious minds of his followers and gradually inflamed them to open hatred of the whites.*

Tecumseh and Harrison.

Leaving the Delaware villages on White river about 1806, Tecumseh and his followers removed first to Greenville, Ohio, where their conduct soon aroused the suspicions of the American officers, and in the spring of 1808 they moved their settlement to the banks of the Wabash, near the mouth of the Tippecanoe, their village being known as Prophet's Town. Tecumseh's efforts were now directed toward the formation of a great Indian confederacy, and he lacked little of complete success. When, in 1809, as above mentioned, several of the tribes ceded a large tract of territory to the American government, Tecumseh opposed it, declaring that one or several of the tribes could not barter away the lands that belonged to all the Indian nations in the confederacy. Despite the efforts of Governor Harrison toward breaking up the confederacy which had its center about Prophet's Town, the Indians became more hostile every day. Small parties appeared in different parts of the territory, stealing and occasionally taking the lives of settlers. Tecumseh and his brother became more insolent in the conferences with the governor, and, on the eve of the second war with Great Britain, a secret British influence increased the disaffection of the tribes.

* Until recently it was supposed that the following incidents, as described by Dillon, took place in the Indian village which stool at the site of Yorktown: "An oll Delaware chief, whose name was Tate-c-bock-o-she, through whose influence a treaty had been made with the Delawares in 1804, was accused of witchcraft, tried, condemned and tomahawked. His boly was then consumed by fire. The wife of the oll chief, his nephew, who was known by the name of Billy Patterson, and an aged Indian whose name was Joshua, were then accused of witchcraft, and condemned to death. The two men were burnt at the stake; but the life of the wife of Tate-c-bock-o-sho was saved by her brother, who suddenly approached her, took her by the hand, and, without meeting with any opposition from the Indians who were present, led her out of the council-house. He then immediately returned, and checked the growing influence of the Prophet by exclaiming, in a strong, earnest voice: 'The evil spirit has come among us, and we are killing each other.'"

A comparison of the different authorities has led Judge Dunn (in an article in the Indianapolis News, March 17, 1906) to the conclusion that "Joshua was killed at the principal Delaware town, which was what the whites called Muncietown and the Indians Woopicamikink or Wapecomckoke. This is commonly spoken of as being on the site of Muncie, but it was on the north side of the river, directly opposite where Muncie now stands. The traditional site of the mission [the old Moravian mission] where Tatapachkse [Tate-c-bock-o-she] was executed is the southeast quarter of section 17, range 8 east, township 19 north, the location of Little Munsee town," in Malison county at the resort now known as "Indian Mounds."

Concerning the oll Indian village on the north bank of the river at Muncie there is the following testimony by a pioneer, William Jackson: "The old Indian village and graveyard stool on the north bank of White river, a short distance to the westward of the bridge, on the Muncie and Granville pike. When I came here many distinct features of the graveyard were still visible. The graves in many instances were surrounded with pens, or poles piled around them. Many skeletons were exhumed and a number of skulls have been preserved."

Finally in the fall of 1811 General Harrison, with a force of about a thousand regular troops, Indiana militiamen and Kentucky volunteers, marched up the Wabash into the heart of the Indian country. While encamped about seven miles northeast from the site of Lafayette, on the early morning of November 7, a furious attack was made by the Indians, "so suddenly," wrote Governor Harrison, "that the Indians were in the camp before many of the men could get out of the tents." Tecumseh was not present in the battle of Tippecanoe, but the Prophet, standing near the scene of action, lent encouragement to his followers by singing a war song that could be heard above the rattle of musketry and the din of battle. The loss in killed and wounded was almost equal on both sides, but substantial victory remained with the whites, the power of the Prophet was broken and the confederacy dissolved soon after the battle. Some six or seven tribes were represented at the battle of Tippecanoe, but it is of interest to note that only a few of the Miamis and none of the Delawares were present, the tribe whose homes were in what is now Delaware county and vicinity having withheld full allegiance to Tecumseh and his league.

Though the settlers were relieved of the worst dangers by the victory at Tippecanoe, the war with Great Britain which was declared in June, 1812, placed new obstacles in the path of peaceful progress, and created a state of almost constant apprehension throughout the settlements. It was uncertain how far the Indians would be influenced by the state of hostilities, and to guard against any outbreaks from the tribes residing near the settlements it was deemed best to inaugurate a state of defense along the frontiers. Block houses were built from Wayne county to Vincennes. The Delawares on White river professed friendship for the Americans, and in order that they should not be involved in any collisions between the whites and other tribes they were directed to remove from their villages to the Auglaize river in Ohio. The Miamis, on the lower courses of the Mississinewa, as well as other tribes in northern Indiana, became troublesome after the Fort Dearborn massacre and Hull's surrender of Detroit to the British. An expedition, for the destruction of the Miami villages on the Mississinewa, was organized late in the year 1812, under the command of Lieut. Col. Campbell. Leaving Dayton on December 14th, and marching eighty miles in three days, early on the morning of the 17th the force reached an Indian town on the Mississinewa inhabited by a number of Delawares and Miamis. After killing eight warriors and capturing forty-two of the inhabitants, the Americans burnt the village, and in the course of the day destroyed several other Indian villages in that vicinity. At night camp was pitched at the village first destroyed, and here, on the following morning, the Indians made a furious attack, engaging the troops for an hour, and killing and wounding about fifty of the whites. The Indians were repulsed, but Colonel Campbell at once began his return to Greenville, where the force arrived after much suffering and almost unfit for further duty. The location of the villages which were destroyed has been placed, by Dillon and successive writers, at points fifteen or twenty miles distant from the junction of the Mississinewa with the Wabash. If Campbell's official report of the campaign can be relied upon at all in its figures as to days' march, it is difficult to understand how, if he left Dayton on the 14th and after marching a distance he estimates at eighty miles reached the first Indian village on the morning of the 17th, he could have traversed the wilderness at least as far as the present site of Marion, which is distant by an air line nearly a hundred miles from Dayton. Accepting the figures of the official report, it seems more reasonable to conclude that the villages which were burnt and where the bloody fight occurred in December, 1812, were located somewhere along the Mississinewa in its course through northern Delaware county.

One other Indian campaign during the war of 1812 deserves mention because it was directed against the Delaware villages in what are now Madison and Delaware counties. Depredations upon the white settlements continued during 1813, and in June of that year an expedition was formed to punish some hostile Indians supposed to be sheltered in the Delaware villages. The troops, under the command of Colonel Joseph Bartholomew, left Valonia, in Jackson county, and proceeded north and northeast, "about one hundred miles, to the upper Delaware town on White river.* We arrived there on the 15th, and found the principal part of the town had been burnt three or four weeks previous to our getting there. We found, however, a considerable quantity of corn in the four remaining houses. We went from thence down White river, a west course, and passed another village three or four miles below, which had been also burnt. At the distance of twelve miles below the upper town, we came to another small village, not burnt." A skirmish was had with the Indians in this neighborhood, but nothing of consequence was effected by the expedition further than the burning of the Indians' corn. Soon after another expedition visited the Delaware towns and the Indians on the Mississinewa, but because of the comparative neutrality of the Delawares throughout the war this county did not become the scene of important campaigns. In 1814 the tide of victory set in strongly toward American arms, and with the battle of the Thames in October the British and Indian power ceased to cause serious alarm in the west. The tribes in Indiana soon sought terms with the American leaders, and to the close of the war they professed to live on terms of peace with the Americans.

* Bartholomew's report, in Dillon's History.

Treaty of St. Mary's.

The return of peace in 1815 marked the beginning of such an era of expansion as no other century and no other land than America has ever witnessed. The supremacy of our national arms, the ability to assert and protect our rights as a nation, were impressed upon the world at large, and among Americans themselves the success of the war produced an independence, an expansiveness of thought and action, and a degree of self-confidence that became the dominating qualities in the American character during the nineteenth century. The original colonies at once seemed too small and confined for the restless energy of the people, and the movement to the west became a great overflow that soon peopled all the lands east of the Mississippi.

It was from the emigration that set in after the war of 1812 that Delaware county was settled. On the east and southeast, a large part of the territory of Randolph and Wayne counties, as we have already seen, had been opened to settlement and by this time contained a large and flourishing population. One barrier must be removed in order that the tide of settlement might reach Delaware county: the Indian title to all this region had to be extinguished before anyone could legally make a home there.

This was accomplished in the treaty of St. Mary's, in Ohio, concluded October 3, 1818, when the Delaware Indians ceded to the United States all their claims to lands lying within the boundaries of the state of Indiana. However, the Delawares reserved the right to occupy these lands for a period of three years from the date of the treaty, and as the experience of the pioneer settlers of Delaware county testifies, these Indians were familiar visitors and neighbors of the whites for some years after settlement had begun.

CHAPTER IV.

PUBLIC SURVEY OF DELAWARE COUNTY—FIRST OCCU-PANTS OF LAND.

However, even after the land was ceded by the Indians, it was not quite ready to be occupied by homeseekers. A very important preliminary work had to be done. A few settlers probably entered the ceded region before it was finished, but they were what are properly known in American usage as "squatters," who could have no legal and recorded rights in the land on which they settled.

Before people could begin to live upon the land and form such associations with one another as constitute a county, it was necessary that a survey of the public lands should be made. Too often the employes of the government who performed this arduous and essentially pioneer work are overlooked or passed by with scant honor. They were the avant couriers of actual settlement, and the substance of their work has continued as a benefit to all who have come after them. Only on condition of their work having been properly done, could definite individual ownership exist, and those mutual rights and duties of men with one another be established which make an organic body such as a county possible. The legislature of the state of Indiana were able to declare where and what the area of this county should be, because the United States measurers of land had already laid their measuring chain upon the land out of which the county was to be made.

Survey of Lands.

In 1796 Congress enacted the law in accordance with which all the public lands were to be surveyed. The system embodied in this act is known as the "Rectangular System." The entire territory of the present state of Indiana has been surveyed and divided into townships in accordance with this system and with reference to a certain "meridian" and "base line." The first principal meridian is the north and south line that forms the boundary between Ohio and Indiana, but the meridian spoken of so frequently in determining the location of townships in Delaware county is the Second Meridian, which is just forty-seven miles west of the west boundary of this county. The "base line," or the east and west line from which reckoning was made in the survey, is a line one hundred and ten miles south of the south line of Delaware county. With this principal meridian and this base line established, the surveyors of the general government began to go over the public land of Indiana with compass and chain, and to mark trees and set posts for the boundaries of townships and sections and quarter sections. These surveyors knew, of course, no names of counties and townships as we know them, neither did they give names at all to townships or groups of townships as they surveyed them. They recorded and dated carefully day by day their measurements and topographical notes in their note-books, thus creating the original "Field Notes," which in every county today are of such primary and incalculable importance for titles, deeds, mortgages and all transactions involved in buying, selling or owning of land. As they tramped over the surface of the country, measuring and marking it off into portions each exactly six miles square, making a township, they gave no names to the townships, but merely numbered them in relation to meridian and base line.

These divisions of land six miles square, laid off by the surveyors, do not correspond in meaning nor generally in fact with the civil townships such as Perry, Center, etc. Taking the civil township of Delaware, for example, it lacks six sections of comprising the area of a congressional or surveyed township. The surveyors' description of this area stated that it was Town 21 North, Range 11 East; meaning, in the first place, that it was the 21st block of land six miles square surveyed in going north from the base line; and in the second place, that it was the 11th block of similar size surveyed in going east from the second meridian. The congressional or surveyed township comprising the civil township of Delaware also contains the north row of sections in Liberty township. Not one of the twelve civil townships of Delaware county corresponds in both limits and area to a congressional township. All the townships in the two east tiers have the regulation width of six miles, and the range lines form their east and west boundaries. But the town lines, i. e., the east and west lines, laid off at regular intervals of six miles from the base line, in only one case form the boundaries of the civil townships. The southern boundary of Niles, Union and Washington is the same as Town Line 21 North; but the townships named lack one mile of extending to next town line on the north, and hence are only fractional congressional townships. South of these townships, Hamilton and Delaware both lack a row of sections on the bottom to make them surveyed townships, while Harrison township, though six miles from north to south, extends one mile into Range 8 and therefore contains six sections more than the congressional township. Harrison township is the largest civil township in area in the county. Center and Liberty are the only civil townships in the county that are six miles square; but they are made of two fractional parts of congressional townships. It seems that the legislature of Indiana, in forming county boundaries, and the county government in dividing the county into civil townships, did not endeavor to make range and town lines correspond with county and township limits. In other states, notably Michigan, the counties usually are made to contain a certain number of complete surveyed townships, and the civil townships are generally the same in area and limits as the congressional townships.

Land Sales.

The survey having been completed, the next step was to provide for the disposal of the land to settlers. The land of some of the older cessions had been entered in land offices at Vincennes, Dayton and one or two other places. But for the sale of lands granted by the treaty of St. Mary's, the Fort Wayne land office and district was created, by act of Congress May 8, 1822. Up to this time the lands in the St. Mary's cession east of the principal meridian had been sold at the Brookville and Jeffersonville land offices, but it appears that all the land in Delaware county was sold at the Fort Wayne office except one or two entries to be mentioned later.

E. Dana was a speculator in western lands and had been very active in directing eastern investors and settlers to various points in the west. In 1819 he published a book, called "Geography of the West," in which he had this to say concerning the tract of land from which Delaware county was carved. "Among the lands purchased of the Indians in 1818 are 8,500,000 in Indiana. . . . The purchase is now being surveyed. . . . At the northeast [i. e., of the purchase], although the lands will make valuable plantations, the surface over a considerable part approaches too near, perhaps, a perfect champaign to embrace all the conveniences of the best agricultural situations. The soil is, however, strong and durable. The prevailing growth here is beech, although there be considerable sugar maple and other forest trees that indicate a rich soil. The infrequency of running streams, and level surface in the northeast cause a scarcity of good mill seats. The lands bordering on the waters of the White river and its tributary streams are considered among those of the best quality. . . . Much of this tract is delightfully situated, and the surface consisting of gentle undulations, supplied with good water, and variegated with numerous, small, rich, dry prairies."

This description, which would fit Delaware county (though whether the writer ever visited this section is uncertain), no doubt was read by many who afterwards came to Indiana and perhaps by some who became permanent settlers of Delaware county. Such a book as Dana's was not the least of the influences which directed settlers to the western country. We can imagine how eagerly those contemplating the journey west would seize upon every piece of information that would be of value to them in selecting a home. That was not the day of railroad emigration bureaus, supplying handsomely illustrated and glowingly written descriptions of every available section of the country. Yet there were various land companies with eastern agencies that supplied prospectuses and other printed' matter concerning western lands. The newspapers published letters from easterners who had gone west and become well situated and satisfied with their surroundings. These and other avenues of information were open to the prospective settler, and the above quotation may serve to indicate what the pioneer looked forward to when he journeyed toward that part of Indiana now included in Delaware county.

Some of the First Inhabitants.

Here and there in the wilderness of Indiana, and among the Indians, some few white men had chosen a place to live before the transfer of the land from the Indians. Usually such men adopted Indian ways, married Indian wives, and merged their identity so completely with the wildness and the life of their neighbors that the record of very few is left. These men were often misanthropes, fleeing from their natural society because of crime, or sorrow, or morbid desire of loneliness. In some cases their eccentricities marked them as "characters" among the pioneers, and their queer doings and speech were remembered long afterward. Seldom were they substantial settlers, the kind that clear the forests, raise crops of corn and wheat and contribute the proceeds of their work to the institutions of civil society. Rather, they were hunters or fishermen, having a cabin remote in the woods, surrounded, perhaps, by a small garden plot, and their days were passed in ranging the woods or fishing in the running streams.

When we approach the subject of the early settlement of Delaware county, we find mention of one or two such characters, although the items are too meager to compose anything resembling a portraiture. In the records of Congress for the year 1820 is contained, under date of March 13th, a favorable report to the senate upon a petition from William Connor, who, so the petition averred, had resided for years at a place called Delaware Towns among the Delaware Indians. After the St. Mary's treaty he petitioned Congress for a pre-emption for 640 acres, on which he claimed to have made a number of improvements, and on which he should be permitted to remain and rear his family of half breeds. The lands had not yet been surveyed, hence no method was provided for this sale, and it was for this reason that Connor desired the right to "pre-empt." The location of the land he desired has not been ascertained except that it was at "Delaware Towns," which allows the supposition that they were in Delaware

county. Nothing more is known of Connor, except that it is likely he as_
sisted the government forces as scout during some of the Indian campaigns.

In the treaty of St. Mary's (1818) one of the articles directs that "one
half-section of land shall be granted to each of the following persons,
namely: Isaac Wobby, Samuel Casman, Elizabeth Pet-cha-ka and Jacob
Dick; and one quarter of a section of land shall be granted to each of the
following persons, namely: Solomon Tindell and Benoni Tindell; all of
whom are Delawares; which tracts of land shall be located, after the coun_
try is surveyed, at the first creek above the old fort on White river, and
running up the river; and shall be held by the persons herein named, re_
spectively, and their heirs; but shall never be conveyed or transferred with_
out the approbation of the president of the United States."

The words of the treaty state that all those named were Delawares;
but several of them surely only by adoption into the tribe. Most of those
named in the treaty are again mentioned in the records showing the original
land entries, and from the two we get some of the earliest history concern_
ing Delaware county.

"The old fort" referred to in the above treaty probably meant the
Indian town or fortifications along White river toward Anderson. "The
first creek," however, is without doubt Buck creek, that joins White river
in the village of Yorktown. So it happened that, after the land was sur_
veyed, those granted land under the treaty became residents of what is now
Mt. Pleasant township and their land was situated near the site of the
present village. Samuel Casman, who was to receive a half section of
land, was a half-breed. The date of his land entry is the earliest in Dela_
ware county, bearing date of September 16, 1820. His land was the north
half of section 22 in what is now Mt. Pleasant township. Such facts as are
known of him do not honor him in his distinction as the first recorded land
owner in this county. He had the Indian thirst for whisky, and had neither
the thrift nor industry to develop his land and become a factor of civiliza_
tion. His first wife was a negro, and after her death he married again
and shortly afterward sold his land to Oliver H. Smith, a transaction that
involved obtaining the consent of the president of the United States. Cas_
man joined his Indian associates on one of the reserves in Indiana. His
existence was unprofitable, and some years later his dead body was dis_
covered in the hollow of a tree in Madison county.

Of the other grantees according to the St. Mary's treaty, grants were
made on February 25, 1824, to Solomon Tindell of the southeast quarter of
section 15 (lying just north of Casman's grant) and to Benoni Tindell,
consisting of the northwest quarter of section 23, just east of Casman's.
Isaac Wobby, first mentioned in the treaty clause, died before his grant

could be confirmed to him, and the south half of section 14 was reserved for his heirs. Further up the river, in what is now section 18 of Center township, the southeast quarter, was another reservation under the St. Mary's treaty. At a very early date this came into the possession of Goldsmith C. Gilbert, who also, about 1825 or later, purchased what was known as the Hackley reserve (the widow Hackley being an Indian who inherited this land). The Hackley reserve is now covered by the city of Muncie.*

* See History of Muncie.

CHAPTER V.

THE RECORD OF THE ORIGINAL POSSESSORS OF DELAWARE COUNTY'S SOIL.

The tract book in the auditor's office establishes a sort of pioneer land-owning aristocracy for Delaware county. There are written the names of those who entered the lands of the county from the government, thus in a legal sense becoming the first actual possessors. Those who thus entered land and became permanent settlers upon it are entitled above all others to the honor of being pioneers. It is true that many came to the county, bought land that had already been entered but had not been improved, and by the toil and hardship encountered in reclaiming the land from the wilderness became as truly entitled to the praise bestowed upon pioneers as those who entered land. Moreover, there was another class of men who made a practice of speculating in public lands, buying up great quantities, and holding them till the general increase in values afforded opportunities for large profits. These men—and there were such among those who entered the lands of this county—deserve none of the worthy merit of the pioneer. To discriminate among these classes and point out the actual pioneers is obviously impossible, even if the tract book were supplemented by extended individual comment. But in the course of the narrative, it will appear that many of the names mentioned among the land entrymen are honored settlers in those localities, and beyond this it is impossible to designate the career of the many names found in this old record.

The tract book is a very matter-of-fact record about facts and persons that are now generally forgotten, and therefore is seldom called for or consulted. Mr. John S. Ellis, in his little book on the history of Delaware county, has used the land entries as the basis of his work, in which he has given some historical statement about every section of the county's area. The material of the tract book is worthy of preservation, and perhaps no better way of arranging it could be found than that adopted by Mr. Ellis. For the purpose of this history, however, it has been deemed best to abbreviate the record as far as possible and arrange it with the view of supplementing the general narrative that precedes and follows it. In line with this purpose the townships have been considered in the chronological order of the entries. Mt. Pleasant having the earliest entry comes first. Then, instead of giving the record concerning the separate sections in the order of their position, they are taken up according to the date of their first entries. The advantage of this is that the parts of each township that were first selected and settled are first named in the record. After each section the record first gives the date of the first entry of land therein and then the date of the last entry; these dates are followed by the names of those who entered the land, usually in the order in which the entries were made.

MT. PLEASANT TOWNSHIP.

Sec. 22—Sept. 1820, 1835: Samuel Casman, William Hardwick (1827), Abner McCartney, Theodore R. Lewis, Charles Jones.

Sec. 20—Oct. 1822, 1834: Uriah Bulla, Joseph and William Van Matre, Stafford and Madison Hunt, William Miller, Joseph Landry, Thomas Hardwick, William Daugherty Sr., Peter Smelser.

Sec. 29—Oct. 1822, 1835: David Hillis, Line Newland, Joseph Van Matre, David Kilgore, Jefferson Reed.

Sec. 23—1824, 1835: Benoni Tindal, Thomas Brumfield, David Yount, Oliver H. Smith.

Sec. 30—1824, 1835: James M. Van Matre, Isaac Jones, John Neely, Amos D. Kennard, Morgan Van Matre, Oliver H. Smith, Jacob Redding.

Sec. 15—1824, 1835: Solomon Tindal. Robert Gordon (1829), John Gordon, William Daugherty Sr., Jonas Cummings.

Sec. 21—1825, 1832: Joseph Bell, Joseph Van Matre, William Hardwick, Absalom Daugherty, Timothy and William Jones, Samuel Parkison.

Sec. 27—1827, 1835: Samuel Bell, Timothy Stewart, Thomas and Robert Hasket, Henry Enilseizer, Oliver H. Smith.

Sec. 13—1830, 1834: Joseph Emerson, Isaac Norris, James Williamson, John Fuller, John Howell.

Sec. 25—1830, 1833: John B. Brown, James Tomlinson, Purnell Tomlinson, Edward Aldredge, Kezia Keasby.

Sec. 26—1830, 1835: John B. Brown, Kezia Keasby, Isaac Norris, Thomas Brumfield, Oliver H. Smith.

Sec. 24 (R 8)—1830, 1836: Zimri Moon, Joseph and Jonathan Dillon, Oliver H. Smith, Fleming Reed, Daniel R. Moon.

Sec. 24—1831, 1834: John Beeth, William Templeton, Jeremiah Wilson, John B. Finley, Thomas Brumfield, James Stewart, Oliver H. Smith.

Sec. 1 (R 8)—1832: John Gronendyke.

Sec. 6—1832, 1836: John D. Jones, Thomas Draper, Peter Shepherd, James Wiley, Nathan Williams, Solomon McLaughlin, John McLaughlin, Mark Martin.

Sec. 9—1832, 1836: Robert Gordon, Andrew Cummings, Samuel Danner, Thomas M. Gordon, William McKinley.

Sec. 12—1832, 1836: James Williamson, Martin J. Williamson, John Howell, Henry Merritt, Samuel W. Harland, Jonathan T. Merauda.

Sec. 14—1832, 1836: Isaac Wobby, Lemuel G. Jackson, William Daugherty, Sophia Prince, William T. Scott, Oliver H. Smith, Christopher Wilson.

Sec. 16—Sold 1832: James Reed, William Antrim, Willis Hardwick.

Sec. 10—1833, 1836: Washington Reed, John Antrim, Jefferson Reed, Samuel McKinley, William McKinley, Robert Antrim, Christopher Terrell, Christopher Wilson.

Sec. 11—1833, 1836: James Williamson, Samuel McKinley, Benjamin Owen.

Sec. 19—1833, 1837: Amos D. Kennard, James T. Watson, William Van Matre, Peter Smelser, Oliver H. Smith, Fleming Reed, Adam Antrim, Timothy Stewart.

Sec. 28—1833, 1835: Timothy Stewart, Thomas Hardwick, Theodore R. Lewis, Willis Hardwick, Joseph Stewart.

Sec. 5—1834, 1837: Thomas Palmer, Thomas Draper, James Cummings, Robert Antrim, James Justice, Israel H. Shepherd, James Wiley, Beltshazer Dragoo, Samuel Proud.

Sec. 17—1834, 1837: Peter Smelser, Beltshazer Dragoo, Stephen Brewer, Oliver H. Smith, Benjamin F. Laing, William Antrim, James Clark, Zadoc Stewart, John Reed, Robert Watkins.

Sec. 18—1834, 1837: Peter Smelser, Edward Redington, Oliver H. Smith, Phylonzo Redington, Joseph Danner, James H. Jones, William Stewart.

Sec. 1—1834, 1836: Sarah Swisher, Thomas C. Anthony, John Hayhurst.

Sec. 12 (R 8)—1835, 1836: Robert Griffis, James Gronendyke, Aaron Adamson, William Jones, Purnell F. Peters, Harlan Stone, Robert S. Jones, Bethene Norris.

Sec. 13 (R 8)—1835, 1836: Robert Griffis, Thomas H. Sharpe, Thomas Fife, Abner Ratcliff.

Sec. 25 (R 8)—1835, 1836: Absalom Van Matre, Oliver H. Smith, John Walters, Daniel R. Noon.

Sec. 4—1835, 1836: John Danner, William Reed, James Cummings, Samuel Danner, William Palmer, William N. Stewart.

Sec. 7—1835, 1837: Thomas Draper, William C. Parks, John Greer, John H. Moore, William Palmer, Joel Clem, Isaac Darter.

Sec. 2—1835, 1836: Martin Williamson, John Van Buskirk, Oliver H. Smith, John T. Drummond.

Sec. 3—1835, 1836: Andrew Danner, Oliver H. Smith, Stacia Haines, Jesse Coil.

Sec. 8—1836, 1837: Thomas Danner, Phineas B. Kennedy, Samuel Parker, William C. Parks, Stephen Reed, Samuel Proud, Wesley Oliver.

PERRY TOWNSHIP.

Sec. 31—Nov. 1822, Oct. 1830: Cornelius Van Arsdoll, George Ribble. Lewis Reese, Thomas Hackett, Garret Gibson.

Sec. 32—Dec. 1822, Sept. 1833: Wilder Potter, Daniel Ribble, Daniel Thompson, Aaron Cecil, John W. Cecil, George Ribble.

Sec. 33—Dec. 1822, Mar. 1836: William Poff, Isaac Jackson, Martin Keesling, Wilder Potter, Jacob Marshall.

Sec. 1—Oct. 1822, Mar. 1837: William King, John Fetters, Bowater Bates, John Connor, William Locke, Thomas Clevenger, William Baird, Norris Fleming, Joseph Whitaker.

Sec. 4—Dec. 1822, ———: James Bryson, Joseph Walling, David Hoover, William N. Rowe, John Will, Louisa Thayer, William J. Cecil.

Sec. 13—June 1822, Feb. 1837: Benjamin Carr, Edward Thornburg Sr., Isaac Thornburg, Joseph McClurkin, Isaac Beeson, Alexander Thornburg, John A. Locke.

Sec. 17—1823, 1836: Solomon Sanford, William Underhill, William Bennel, Harvey Bates, Jesse Jackson.

Sec. 5—Oct. 1826, Oct. 1834: Aaron Cecil, Benjamin Walker, George Ribble, William J. Cecil.

Sec. 8—1829, 1836: Aaron Richardson, Benjamin J. Blythe, Solomon Johnson, Calvin Cecil, James Cary, William Cecil, Almeron Spencer, William Drum, Ephraim Cary.

Sec. 9—1829, 1835: William Powers, William R. Roe, Eli Hoover, William Baltimore, William J. Cecil, Stephen Bunnel.

Sec. 21—Sept. 1829, 1836: Leonard Stump, James Lindley, Thomas Keener, Hosea Sisk, Joseph Cowgill, Hervey Bates, William Lindley, Rachel D. Ummit, Daniel Kessler, Charles Lindley.

Sec. 23—1829, 1836: Tarah Templin, John Lenington, Eli Fox, Robert Templeton, John Elliott, Michael Wolfe, Isaac Blount, Calvin Ball, Robert Worrell.

Sec. 6—1830, 1836: Samuel Cecil, Joseph Keesling, James Cecil, John Van Arsdoll, Daniel Keesling, Henry Mulkins.

Sec. 16—Sold Aug. 14, 1830: Samuel Harvey, John Armentrout, Israel Shoemaker, Leonard Stump, John Reese, Jesse Delaney, Stephen Bunnell, William H. Underhill.

Sec. 19—1830, 1836: Mahalon Branson, John Lewis, Samuel Poff, Peter Dragoo, Isaac Branson, Robert Franklin.

Sec. 3—1830, 1836: William M. Clark, Lyman Halstead, Peter Halstead, Joseph Walling, Samuel Halstead, David Hoover.

Sec. 12—1830, ———: John Thornburg, Thomas Clevenger, Norris Flemming, Jacob Branson, Joseph Whitaker, Solomon H. May, Samuel Rooks, Evan Jay, John Helms, Henry Hill, Ephraim Emmons.

Sec. 10—1831, 1837: John Buck, Samuel Halstead, William Locke, William Ball, Joseph Fifer, Thomas Edwards, Martin Hoover, Henry Hart, Stephen Bunnell.

Sec. 2—1832, 1837: Robert R. Barr, Henry Way, Andrew McAlister, William Dilts, James Barr, John Brooks, Nelson Thayer.

Sec. 11—1832, 1836: Moses Hudson, Benjamin J. Blythe, George Holloway, Charles Miller, Hall Way, John Buck, Henry Way.

Sec. 24—1832, 1837: Hugh McCune, Lemuel Hamilton, James Lindley Jr., William C. Swan, Abraham Lennington, John Beckelshymer, Isaac Wrightsman, Samuel Bedwell.

Sec. 20—1833, 1837: John Armentrout, Isaac N. Delaney, William Honnell, David Fetrick, Elias Burkett, Henry Riggs, William Heaton, Abraham Slover, William P. Mathews.

Sec. 7—1834, 1836: James Cecil, David Robinson, John Kirkpatrick Sr., William Drum, Isaiah Gandy, Samuel Hutchings, Joseph R. Pratt, Keder Homan.

Sec. 18—1834, 1836: Martin Galliher, Thomas C. Anthony, Jesse Jackson, Isaac Branson, Elijah Harrold, Morgan Thornburg, Joseph Cheeseman, Jonathan Thornburg.

Sec. 14—1835, 1836: James Warren, David Stephens, James Livingston, Robert Hindman, William Locke, Michael Wolfe, Jackson Brewer, Isaiah Templin.

Sec. 15—1835, 1837: Michael Wolfe, William C. Ball, Henry Way, James Hart, Jesse Pugh, Jonathan Warren, William Locke, Leonard Stump.

Sec. 22—1836: John Elliott, Ebenezer Elliott, Leonard Stump, William Locke.

LIBERTY TOWNSHIP.

Sec. 21—Nov. 1822, 1835: James Jackson, David Stout, Parker Truitt, Andrew Collins, John Stout, James Truitt.

Sec. 28—Dec. 1822, 1837: William Blunt Sr., Wilder Potter, William Barnes, William Pallen, Samuel Cecil, James H. Cecil, Henry Bates, William I. Poff.

Sec. 29—Dec. 1822, 1832: Wilder Potter, William Stansbury, John Smith, Asahel Thornburg, John Richey, Thomas Wilcoxon, Isaac DeWitt, John Smith, John W. Cecil.

Sec. 22—1823, 1836: David Branson, Morgan Thornburg, Thomas Cox, William Wire, James Jackson, John Richardson, Abraham Bush.

Sec. 24—1823, 1837: George Blalock, John Connor, Michael Mayer, James Barr, Thomas Wallace, Joseph Lewis, Samuel Cray, Lewis Shroyer.

Sec. 30—1823, 1834: Alson Ashley, Henry Bolton, Samuel Simmons, Thomas Crawford, Jacob Payton, Samuel Hutchings, Samuel Cecil.

Sec. 23—1824, 1837: John G. Decas, Asa M. Thornburg, John and Solomon Stout, Levi Bawlsby, John Rush Deeds, Eleazer Coffeen, Christian Life, John Richardson, Loring A. Waldo, Landrine Rash, Thomas Rash.

Sec. 25—1825, 1836: John Fowler, Michael Pepper, John B. Bailes, John Connor, John Gardner, Henry Clyne, Isaac Cline, John Pennington.

Sec. 18—1829, 1835: Elijah Casteel, Washington Downing, David Hamer, Joseph Mulkins, James Tilden, John Guthrie.

Sec. 27—1830, 1836: Peter Halstead, Loring A. Waldo, David Stout, Norse Main, William Williams Sr., George Turner Jr., Jonas Hammer, Francis Collins, Joseph Shields.

Sec. 8—1831, 1836: Eli Babb, John Robinson, John Barton, John Richey, Ranzel Barton, Thomas Sweetman, Peter Clark.

Sec. 19—1831, 1833: John Moore, Reuben Preston, William Payton, Jacob Payton Jr., Joseph Dungan.

Sec. 20—1831, 1839: James Truitt, Reuben Preston, Thomas Whitney, Lewis Smith, Thomas Hamilton, Asahel Thornburg, William N. Smith, Parker Truitt, John Smith, David Rench.

Sec. 31—1832, 1836: Lewis Smith, Jefferson Cox, John Guthrie, Stewart Cecil, Monroe Goff, John Dragoo, John Moody, Jesse Holland.

Sec. 16—Sold May 12, 1832: Jacob Earhart, William Barnes, Samuel G. Campbell, William Stansbury, William Poland, Frederick Goings, James F. Davis, A. R. East.

Sec. 1—1833, 1836: Benjamin E. Blythe; rest of sec. 1 and all sec. 2 reserved for school purposes in 1836.

Sec. 7—1833, 1836: Charles Points, Joseph Rash, Willis Hance, Henry Phillips, John Richey, Washington Heck.

Sec. 17—1833, 1837: Joseph Humphreys, William Payton Jr., Jacob Payton, Frederick Goings, George Dickey, John Morgan, Lewis Kendall, Alexander Addis, John Norris.

Sec. 4—1834, 1837: John Morrison, James H. Neal, James Huffman, George Barton, Jonas Huffman, Samuel N. Kinsley, John Givan.

Sec. 5—1834, 1836: William Bromfield, Joseph Howrey, George W. Miller, William Broadick, William L. Gough, Willis Ball.

Sec. 6—1834, 1836: Reuben Preston, John Kinsley, Washington Heck, Dr. Samuel P. Anthony.

Sec. 9—1834, 1838: William Barnes, Aaron Stout, John Neal, Gilbert Winsett, Ranzel Barton, Charles Melone, William N. Clark.

Sec. 33—1835, 1836: John Sparr, Thomas Zarner, Joseph Newman, Thomas Bloom.

Sec. 34—1835, 1837: James Orr, Adam Boots, William H. Williams, Ila Lake, Robert Lake, ——— Pendroy.

Sec. 35—1835, 1836: John Dinsmore, Daniel Fox, William Woods, Samuel Lewellen.

Sec. 10—1835, 1837: East half reserved for schools; west half to Isaac Barnes, John Neal, Daniel Lutz, John McConnell.

Sec. 32—1836: Thomas Points, Joseph Newman, John Newcom, George Moody, Thomas H. Weirman, John Moody, Jesse Holland, Samuel Moody.

Sec. 36—1836, 1837: Samuel S. Swain, David Fox, Samuel Malcolm, Solomon Rohrbaugh, John W. Vaughn, Elijah Reeves, Samuel Lewellen, John Hines, James Sparr, Thomas Gough.

Sec. 3—1836, 1837: James H. Neal, Moses E. McConnell, Mecker Shroyer, John Givan.

Sec. 11—1836: Isaac Dunn, John A. Gilbert, Thomas Wallace, John Van Buskirk.

Sec. 12—1836: Joseph Brandon, Jacob M. Johnson, Peter Clyne.

Sec. 13—1836: Levi Bowersby, George Dickey, John Van Buskirk, Lewis Kendall.

Sec. 14—1836, 1837: Eleazer Coffeen, Benjamin Plantz, Daniel Ellenberger, Lewis Shroyer, John McConnell.

Sec. 15—1836, 1837: Henry Ellenberger, Daniel Ellenberger, David Mays, Aaron Marshall, George Dickey, Chester Searles, William Weir, Gilbert Winsett, William McConnell.

CENTER TOWNSHIP.

Sec. 25—Dec. 24, 1822, 1835: James Bryson, Henry Massburg, Samuel Simmons, Samuel Cecil Jr., Samuel Cecil, Johnson King, Littleton Dowty.

Sec. 10—Oct: 1826, 1833:   William Blynk Sr., William Brown, James Howell.

Sec. 13—1826, 1839:   George Truitt, John Moore, Lewis Moore, James Blackford, Michael Sills.

Sec. 9—1827, 1831:   Elemuel Jackson, Conrad Mutter, Philip Mose, Jacob Calvert, John Nottingham, Samuel Merrill.

Sec. 11—1827, 1835:   John Trimble, Elijah Casteel, Elijah Walden, Moses Wilson, Thomas Kirby, Charles F. Willard, George Howell, Jesse Bracken.

Sec. 14—1827, 1834:   John Brown, Solomon Hobaugh, George Truitt, Elijah Reeves, Littleton Dowty, James Franklin, James B. Eastburn, Joseph Walling.

Sec. 15—1827, 1833:   William Brown, James Murphy, James Thompson, Jonathan Reeder, Samuel P. Anthony, James Franklin, Daniel Thompson, William Clary.

Sec. 24—1827, 1833:   Charles Stout, James Jackson, Johnson King, John Moore, Lloyd Wilcoxon, Joseph Dungan, Littleton Dowty.

Sec. 34—1829, 1835:   Joseph Bennett, Jacob Holland, Mayor Powers, David Adams, George Lieber, Ezekiel Bazzill.

Sec. 35—1829, 1836:   Thomas Reeves, Joseph Bennett, Stephen Hamilton, Owen Russell, Jacob Holland, Daniel Lieber.

Sec. 3—1829, 1835:   Joseph Bennett, Owen Russell, James Howell, David B. Buckles, William H. Brumfield.

Sec. 17—1829, 1832:   Isaac Fielder, Levi Bishop, David Gharkey, John Collins, James McKee, John McKee, George Calvert.

Sec. 18—1829, 1835:   Thomas Collins, John McKee, Levi Bishop, Morgan Johns.

Sec. 36—1830, 1837:   Thomas Gibson, John Guthrie, Archibald Dowden, Truman Conklin, Thomas Albin.

Sec. 8—1830, 1835:   Jacob Calvert; John, William, James and Mayor Nottingham, Joseph Williamson, Isaac E. Beck, George Shafer, Joseph Emmerson, Elijah Reeves.

Sec. 16—Sold April, 1830:   David Gharkey, Samuel G. Jackson, Thomas Galyon, James Jackson, Peter Nolin, M. Buck, James Hodge, James Murphy, Ezekiel Jewell, William Fitzpatrick, Joseph A. Vestal, John Marshall, Abner Smith, I. Edwards, Joel Russell, Thomas C. Anthony, Samuel W. Harmon, William Van Matre, D. Thompson, D. W. Lyons.

Sec. 22—1830, 1835:   Isaac Tilden, Pierpoint Blowers, Daniel Thompson, Anderson Redman, Oliver H. Smith, George Thompson.

Sec. 27—1830, 1836:   Pierpoint Blowers, Thomas Goble, Charles Mansfield, James Mansfield, Anda Gibson, William Kiger, Thomas C. Anthony.

Sec. 2—1831, 1836:   Joseph Bennett, William Helbie, James Sears.

Sec. 7—1831, 1835:   Isaiah E. Beck, George Shafer, Nathan Stansberry, William Nottingham, Isaac White, Thomas Collins, John H. Collins, Jeremiah Howell.

Sec. 19—1831, 1835:   Jeremiah A. Wilson, William Briggs, John Tomlinson, Asher Storer, Abner Perdieu, Thomas Bishop, Absalom Perdieu, Joseph Yount.

Sec. 20—1831, 1836: William McConnell, John McConnell Jr., William
    Y. Williams, Samuel and Asher Storer, Daniel Wilson, John Mc-
    Connell, Charles Storer.
Sec. 21—1831, 1833: Job Garner, Benjamin I. Blythe, James Garner, Dan-
    iel Cline, Asher Storer, William Clary, Samuel Storer, David
    Storer.
Sec. 28—1831, 1835: John Brown, Charles Mansfield, James Mansfield,
    William H. Brumfield, William Chipman, Oliver H. Smith, Eliza-
    beth Brumfield.
Sec. 30—1831, 1836: William Finley, Jeremiah A. Wilson, Jesse McKin-
    ney, Abner Perdieu, Asher Storer, Patrick Justice, Daniel Wil-
    son, Warren Stewart, Joseph Thomas.
Sec. 4—1832, 1835: Aaron Taff, Abraham Buckles, John Buckles, John
    Blackford, William Diltz, Thomas Gustin.
Sec. 5—1833, 1836: Peter Nolin, Thomas Kirby, Charles F. Willard,
    James Nottingham, John Collins, John Buckles, Peter Shanks,
    John Sutherland.
Sec. 6—1833, 1836: Thomas Kirby, Charles F. Willard, William Beatty,
    Peter Shanks, Thomas J. Collins, Nathan Stansberry, Thomas C.
    Anthony.
Sec. 32—1834, 1836: C. M. Preston, William P. Williams, Charles F.
    Willard, John A. Gilbert, Daniel Jarrett, John Whiteside, George
    Lieber.
Sec. 26—1834, 1836: William Heaton, Littleton Dowty, Henry Mass-
    burg, Samuel Moore, William Fowler, James Homan, Arthur Mor-
    rison, Henry Keys, Thomas C. Anthony, Samuel Heaton, Robert
    Gibson, Daniel Heaton.
Sec. 31—1835, 1836: John H. Collins, Bowen Rees, John Miller, Daniel
    Jarrett.
Sec. 33—1835, 1836: William and David S. Collins, George Lieber, Jo-
    seph Dean, Mayor Powers.
Sec. 1—1835, 1836: Benjamin Goodin, Penelope Anthony, Dr. G. W.
    Garst.
Sec. 12—1835, 1836: Jesse Brackin, Michael Sills, Daniel Sills, George
    Howell, Esop Gilbert, Archibald Dowden.
Sec. 23—1835, 1836: Thomas Kirby, Joseph Jackson, Oliver H. Smith,
    Stewart Boltin, George Thompson, Joseph Johnson, Henry Henkle.
Sec. 29—1835, 1836: Oliver H. Smith; Arnold, Naudine, Edward, Tat-
    nall and Merritt Canby; William Y. Williams, Thomas Brumfield,
    John Brooks, David Storer.

SALEM TOWNSHIP.

Sec. 31—May, 1823, 1835: Joshua Baxter, John Suman (1827), George
    Michael, Francis Pugsley, Joseph Van Matre, William Nelson,
    Jonathan Sheff.
Sec. 20—Nov., 1826, 1836: John Van Matre, James Marsh, William Sum-
    mers, Joseph Chapman, Van Matre Stewart, William Roberts,
    John Rinker.
Sec. 21—Nov., 1826, 1831: John and David Van Matre, Samuel Johnson,
    Naomi Van Matre, Alexander McAllister, Mathias Pitser.

Sec. 22—1826, 1832: Robert Williams, John Perdue, Francis Colburn, Edward Sharp, Rufus Perdue, Mathias Pitser, William Summers.

Sec. 23—1826, 1834: Robert Williams, John Myers, William Sharp, Enoch Nation, Abraham Davis, Samuel Davis.

Sec. 12 (R. 8)—1827, 1835: Campbell Dale, Isaac Carpenter, Thomas Fostnaugh, Allen Makepeace, Joel Copher.

Sec. 1 (R. 8)—1827, 1835: Campbell Dale, Chamberlain Hutton, Jason Hudson, William C. Van Matre, John Bronenburg, Frederick Bronenburg.

Sec. 6—1827, 1836: John Suman, Ransom Makepeace, Justin Steele, Samuel Rogers, Thomas Fosnot, James Griffith, Oliver H. Smith.

Sec. 32—1828, 1836—Powell Scott, John Knoop, David Kilgore, James W. Brown, Benjamin F. Hancock, Oliver H. Smith.

Sec. 36—1829, 1836: Ralph Heath, Samuel Stewart, Jesse McKinney, James Moffett, James Knott, James Goff.

Sec. 1—1829, 1836: John Lane, James McKinney, Asa Bishop, James Knott, Thomas Perdue, William Simpson, John Jones.

Sec. 14—1829, 1833: John Tomlinson, John Fitser, Aquilla Davis, Asa B. Watkins, Christian Pence, Lambert Moffett, David McNutt.

Sec. 15—1829, 1835: Daniel Shawhan, G. Young, John Tomlinson, Christian Wall, Isaac Pitser, William Parent.

Sec. 24 (R. 8)—1829, 1836: B. F. Nichols, Joseph Nichols, John Fleming, Peter Miller, Jonas Gallahan, Joshua Hurley, William Fleming, Benjamin Bartlett, William O'Briant, Abraham Dipboye.

Sec. 2—1830, 1836: Robert Heath, John Adams, Jr., Adam Campbell, Samuel G. Sunderland, Eben Pitser, Francis McNairy, William McAllister.

Sec. 9—1830, 1836: Thomas Pierce, Thomas Windsor, Lawrence Wilson, William C. Windsor, David Van Matre, William Price, David Strickler.

Sec. 12—1830, 1836: Bailes E. Jones, John B. Finley, Abner Perdieu, William Scruggs, Lambert Moffett, Abraham Hall, Edward Sharp, Daniel Miller.

Sec. 13—1830, 1834: John H. Taylor, Thomas Kidd, Samuel Clevenger, Reece Carter, William Miller.

Sec. 36 (R. 8)—1831, 1836: O. H. Smith, William C. Van Matre, Aaron Brewer, Samuel Brown, James M. Chambers, William Nelson, Jesse Dearth, Frederick Bronenburg, Jr., John McClanahan.

Sec. 33—1831, 1836: John Stewart, Willis Hardwick, William Antrim, Jacob Saunders, Theodore Lewis, Oliver H. Smith.

Sec. 4—1831, 1836: John Marsh, John Kennedy, James Leviston, Oliver H. Smith.

Sec. 11—1831, 1836: Eben Pitser, Adam Campbell, William Summers, Lambert Moffett, Samuel G. Sunderland, David Strickler, John T. Vardaman.

Sec. 17—1831, 1835: Homer Brooks, John Simpson, David Crist, Ephraim Cole, William Schofield, Samuel Stephens, David Strickler, John Fessler.

Sec. 19—1831, 1836: John Groves, Zachariah Clevenger, James Marsh,

Lemuel Fleming, Abraham Dipboye, William Fleming, William Roberts, Arbena Doubt.

Sec. 24—1831, 1837: Edward Davis, Timothy Ives, Enoch Witt, Eliakim Wilson, Christian Sourwine.

Sec. 35—1832, 1836: Daniel Prilaman, Thomas Brumfield, Sr., Oliver H. Smith, Thomas Pierce, Joseph Prilaman.

Sec. 8—1832, 1835: Morgan Van Natre, James Fenwick, Mathias Furrow, David Strickler, John Fessler, Henry Richman, Jesse Windsor.

Sec. 10—1832, 1836: Obadiah Meeker, Adam Campbell, John Davis, David Strickler, Asa French, William Tomlinson, William McAllister, Samuel Dusang.

Sec. 13 (R. 8)—1833, 1836: Robert L. Bartlett, Joshua Hurley, Joseph Dipboye, Lewis Rogers, Arbena Doubt.

Sec. 7—1833, 1835: James Fenwick, Michael Gronendyke, John Simpson, Stephen Rogers, Henry Rogers, Abraham Pugsley.

Sec. 18—1833, 1836: Lemuel Fleming, Eben Stephens, Francis Lonsdale, John Graham.

Sec. 5—1834, 1836: Haden Makepeace, John Knoop, William Stewart, John Stewart, Jacob Saunders, Tandy Reynolds, Jonas Shoemaker, William Fenwick.

Sec. 34—1835: Oliver H. Smith.

Sec. 3—1835, 1836: Abner McCarty, Griffith Thompson, William McAllister, Theodore Lewis, John Stewart.

Sec. 16—Sold 1836: Samuel McCulloch, David Strickler, James Windsor, John Fessler, William Windsor.

WASHINGTON TOWNSHIP.

Sec. 15—Dec. 1823, 1837: David Conner, William McCormick (1831), David Beouy, John Dunn, Thomas Beouy.

Sec. 11—Sept. 1829, 1834: William Heal, Thomas Littler, Eli Lansing, Thomas Wharton, William McCormick.

Sec. 12—1829, 1830: John Dillie, Robert Wharton, Joseph Wilson, James Watson, John Ginn.

Sec. 13—1830, 1837: Joseph Wilson, Thomas Reynolds, John Ginn, William Richeson, John Sanders, Margaret Watson, Jacob H. Bowers, Jesse W. Thompson.

Sec. 14—1830, 1836: Robert Sanders, William McCormick, John Wharton, John Crow.

Sec. 10—1831, 1837: William McCormick, Samuel Moore, Thomas Beouy, John Dunn, William Wharton, Thomas Dunn, John W. McCormick.

Sec. 30—1831, 1839: Michael Messenger, Samuel Richardson, Felix E. Oliphant, John Rains, John Farley Jr., Thomas Morely.

Sec. 22—1832, 1853: Samuel Carmin, John Knight, Peter Thorn, Robert Winton.

Sec. 25—1833, 1837: James Ashcraft, Mowery H. Thompson, Absalom Williams, John Kain, David Williams, James Hamilton.

Sec. 36—1833, 1841: James Ashcraft, Mathew Xorner, William Daily, Hanna Corner.

Sec. 23—1834, 1836: John Kain, Samuel Knotts, John Johnson, Mowery H. Thompson, John S. Thompson.

Sec. 7—1834, 1838: John Beouy, James Hinton, William Knight, David Hinton, Elles Jones, David McCormick, John Hanway, George Kramer.

Sec. 8—1834, 1850: Sampson Brewer, Thomas Beouy, Samuel Beouy, Gabriel Ginn, John Beouy, Richard Dickerson, William Beouy, Joshua Dickerson.

Sec. 24 (R. 8)—1835, 1838: William and Henry Walker, Jediah Adams, Anderson H. Broyles, Thomas Broyles, John Farley.

Sec. 21—1835, 1839: Jonathan McCarty, John Dunn, John Johnson, Joseph Grimes, Samuel P. Anthony, William Vannater.

Sec. 24—1835, 1837: William Carman, Mowery H. Thompson, Stephen Swain, Moses Hinton.

Sec. 26—1836, 1838: John S. Thompson, James Ashcraft, Jonathan Barton, William Conner, Henry Smith, Amos Grubb, George Tippin, Margaret Taylor.

Sec. 27—1836, 1839: John Johnson, Philip Woodring, Isaac Coe, James Burgess, John Burgess, Christopher Grimes, Jacob Miller.

Sec. 12 (R. 8)—1836, 1837: Frederick Ice. Robert Burke, Christopher Hudson, Robert Hudson, Joseph Farley, Christopher Scott, John Ellison.

Sec. 13 (R. 8)—1836, 1850: George Lewis, Ephraim Lewis, Isaac Foster, Patrick O'Brien, Hiram Lee, Madison Broyles, James Paine, Francis Ice, Lewis Hull.

Sec. 25 (R. 8)—1836, 1838: Amos Ratcliff, Eli Hockett, Solomon Fussell, Jesse Munden, Nathan Macy, Thomas Broyles, Wilson Burass.

Sec. 36 (R. 8)—1836, 1838: Samuel Brown, Isaac Marshall, Jesse Munden, William Burass, Phineas Hall, John Hall, William Laurk, Asa Davis.

Sec. 9—1836, 1837: John W. McCormick, John Hawkins, Gabriel Ginn, Amos Janney, Samuel Knight, Ira Swain.

Sec. 17—1836, 1837: Amos Janney, Isaac Whiteley, Wright Anderson, William Miller.

Sec. 18—1836, 1839: Isaac Farmer, Joseph Jones, Jacob Miller, Robert Dunlap.

Sec. 20—1836, 1853: Amos Janney, John Johnson, Hugh Hazelbaker, William Carmin, Simeon Dickenson, Nathan Maynard, Dr. Robert Winton.

Sec. 28—1836, 1839: John Johnson, Thomas Beouy, Elizabeth Umphreys, Ann Umphreys, Michael Messenger, John Black.

Sec. 29—1836, 1853: John Johnson, James Porter, David Hatfield, Orin Chapin, John Summers, Levi Miller, Hiram Hendricks, Hugh Sharpe, Thomas Morley, Jeremiah Wilson, John McCulloch.

Sec. 34—1836, 1838: Thomas Veach, Sarah Wharton, Jefferson N. Horine, John G. Collins, Thomas Cobalt, John Burgess, Thomas Dillon, James Hamilton.

Sec. 35—1836, 1838: Lewis and William H. Veach, Joseph Tippin, John Tippin, Samuel Nickson.

Sec. 19—1837, 1839: Samuel Sweaney, Robert Dickey, Nathan Henderson, Griffin Tira, William Drennen, John C. Gustin, Michael Messenger.

Sec. 33—1837, 1839: Thomas Bartlett, Benjamin Bartlett, William Vannata.

Sec. 32—1838, 1839: Woodson Cummins, Levi Miller, Purnell F. Peters, John R. Williams, Samuel Clevenger, Levi Miller, John Hanway, George Kramer.

Sec. 16—Sold 1855: Levi Adison, John Dickeson, Thompson Gherton, William McCormick, David Beouy, Streeter and Ginn, Robert Winton.

MONROE TOWNSHIP.

Sec. 10—Jan. 1827, 1836: Amaziah Beeson, Peter Simmons, John Mansfield, Samuel Merrill, Andrew Carmichael, Miles Harrold, Samuel Underhill, John Branson, Allen Beeson.

Sec. 15—July 1827, 1834: John Crum, Rebecca Gable, Homer Brooks, William Mansfield, Andrew Carmichael, David Williams.

Sec. 12—1828, 1837: William Gibson, Robert Gibson, Alexander Cheesman, John H. Payton, William Townsend, Robert Maples.

Sec. 23—1828, 1836: Zenas Beeson, Lauvel Brown, James Mansfield, John Howell, Aaron Stout, John Mansfield, Abel Williams, James Orr, William Underhill, Sarah Davis.

Sec. 31—1830, 1836: Ralph Heath, Edmond Aldredge, Enoch Tomlinson, Jesse McKinney, William Hutton; Arnold, Nadine, Edward, Tatnall, and Merritt Canby.

Sec. 36—1830, 1836: Lewis Rees, Thomas Hackett, Stewart Boltin, Samuel Cecil.

Sec. 1—1830, 1836: Bowater Gibson, Rebecca Keasling, Daniel Keasling, John W. Rhoades, Valentine Gibson, Jacob Keasling.

Sec. 13—1830, 1836: Daniel Ribble, Daniel Yandes, John Johnson, William Cheesman, Jonathan Beeson, Joseph Cheesman, Isaiah Lee, Elisha Ogle, Alexander Cheesman.

Sec. 14—1830, 1836: Jonathan Beeson, Jonathan Harrold, Homer Brooks, John Mansfield, Abel Williams, Henry Bower, Joseph Brown, William Hickman.

Sec. 22—1830, 1834: Michael Bonner, John Howell, John Rutledge, Abel Williams, Temple Smith, Daniel Williams.

Sec. 2—1831, 1837: Valentine Gibson, Elisha Gibson, William Clark, John Gibson, David Beard, Otho Williams, Boyd Linville.

Sec. 3—1831, 1837: Isaac Branson, Abel Williams, Jacob Whitinger Jr., French Triplett, John Crum, Homer Brooks; Arnold, Nadine, Edward, Tatnall and Merritt Canby; Absalom Gibson, Benjamin Antrim.

Sec. 6—1831, 1836: Aaron Ross, James McKinney, the Canbys, Abner McCarty, Harvey Heath.

Sec. 11—1831, 1836: Garrett Gibson, John Lenox, Daniel Dewitt, Henry Taylor, Ezekiel T. Hickman, Otto Wilson, William Culberson, Samuel M. West.

Sec. 21—1831, 1835: David Williams, Abel Williams, James Orr, John Dusthimer.

Sec. 18—1832, 1836: John Swope, Jacob Bowers, Henry Richman, William Andes, John Tuttle, Adam Banks.

Sec. 19—1832, 1835: William Clevenger, Michael Thompson, John Fessler, Eleakim Wilson.

Sec. 24—1832, 1837: David Ogle, James Ogle, Samuel Shockley, Valentine Gibson, Jonas Turner, John Brown, Jonathan Turner, Elisha Ogle, David C. Martin, William Morris, Gilbert C. Millspaugh, Robert Morris.

Sec. 34—1832, 1836: Charles Mansfield, William Clark, John Mansfield, Samuel Andrews, Jacob Whitinger, Anda Gibson, Amos Harrold, Samuel Heaton, Henry Whitinger, James Mansfield.

Sec. 35—1833, 1836: James Allison, Christian Acker, John Acker, Garrett Gibson, Samuel Heaton, William Heaton, William Abrams.

Sec. 5—1834, 1836: George W. Finley, William Owen, Robert Heath Jr., Mary St. Clair, Abner McCarty.

Sec. 8—1834, 1836: Mary St. Clair, Mary Moore, John Resler.

Sec. 33—1835, 1836: Isaac Branson, Oliver H. Smith, Patrick Carmichael, William H. Brumfield, Mary St. Clair.

Sec. 4—1835, 1836: John R. Palmer, the Canbys, Mary St. Clair.

Sec. 9—1835, 1836: John Gibson, Enos Strawn, Mary St. Clair, John Beard, Thomas Strawn Jr.

Sec. 17—1835, 1838: Jacob Bowers, Samuel Fessler, Peter Shively, Philip Shively, John S. Resler, Edward Jones, William M. Clark.

Sec. 20—1835, 1837: James Jones, John Dusthimer, Jesse Raider, John J. Bulingall, George Hinecker, A. Rhoton, John Howell.

Sec. 32—1836: Abner McCarty, William Hutton, the Canbys, Mary St. Clair, John Rupe, Jeptha Johnson.

Sec. 7—1836, 1837: Harvey Heath, William Drumm, John Losh Sr., William Tamsett, Ephraim Bundy, Richard S. Taylor, Thomas Fleming, Buford Jones.

Sec. 16—Sold July, Aug. 1847: Allen C. Perdieu, Walter Gibson, Joseph Clevenger, Enoch Nation, Isaac McLain, William J. Hightower.

HAMILTON TOWNSHIP.

Sec. 25—Oct. 1829, 1835: Peter Williamson, Adam Shafer, Alexander Crawford, Stephen R. Martin, Joel Russell, Archibald Hamilton.

Sec. 26—Oct. 1829, ——: Owen Russell, Morgan Conner, William Conner, Joseph Williamson, George Lieber, James D. Collier, Henry Slover, James Nottingham.

Sec. 22—1830, ——: Adam Shafer, Archibald Smith, Stephen Kennedy, James H. Fitzpatrick, Thomas Pritchard, Thomas Brumfield.

Sec. 23—1831, 1836: Adam Shafer, Samuel Martin Jr., Elijah Reeves, George Lieber, Peter Williamson, Owen Russell.

Sec. 24—1831, 1835: Owen Russell, Mordecai Massey, Stephen R. Martin, Thomas Reeves, Isaac Massey, James Massey, Joel Russell.

Sec. 18—1832, 1836: Elijah Casteel, Jeremiah Gard, Jacob Holiday, Solomon Ismael, Joseph Turner, Samuel Snyder, William Harlan, Robert Ismael.

Sec. 12—1834, 1836: Catherine and Margaret Chancy, Archibald Smith, Robert Kirkpatrick, Henry Shafer, Henry Huddleston, Barbara Huddleston, James McCormick.

Sec. 15—1834, 1836: Henry Shafer, Stephen Davis, Daniel Smith, Archibald Smith.

Sec. 29—1834, 1837: Samuel Snyder, John Nottingham, Stanley L. Robertson, Isaac Branson, Joshua Turner, Robert Ismael, Josiah Williams.

Sec. 10—1835, 1836: Cyrus Pence, Henry Shafer, Stephen Davis, William Commons.

Sec. 11—1835, 1836: James McCormick Sr., William McCormick, Robbins R. Wilson, Henry Shafer. Jonathan Johns, James McCormick Jr.

Sec. 17—1835, 1836: William Daily, Samuel Snyder.

Sec. 27—1835, 1836: Samuel R. Collier, Abraham Slover, Jeremiah Miller, William H. Brumfield, James P. Mathews, John Snyder, Peter D. Green, James Bowman.

Sec. 30—1835, 1836: Solomon Burris, Lewis Moore, William Moore, Samuel Moore, Isaac Freeman. Peter D. Green.

Sec. 1—1836: Jesse C. Dowden, John Gamble, John M. Thomas, William Free, Elizabeth Martin, William Silvers, William Phagan, George Laird, George Baldridge.

Sec. 2—1836, 1837: Joseph Hamer, Jackson Green, Isaac Shideler, John Richeson, William Martin, Rebecca Comer, William McCormick, William Silvers.

Sec. 3—1836, 1837: Thomas Erell, John Richeson, Samuel P. Anthony, Howard Mitchell, Samuel W. Mitchell, Samuel Cromer.

Sec. 4—1836, 1837: Thomas Erell, Alvin Sleeth, Joseph Hance, Howard Mitchell.

Sec. 5—1836: James Kennedy, Thomas Kennedy, Joseph Garrard, Thomas Stafford.

Sec. 6—1836, 1837: Joseph Garrard, William Singler, William Arnold.

Sec. 7—1836, 1837: George Stafford, Barnard F. Hook, John Roop, Richard Chandler.

Sec. 8—1836, 1837: Charles F. Willard, Jonathan Mason, Ralph Stafford, Cyrus Pence, Noah Tracy.

Sec. 9—1836, 1837: James Stafford, Cyrus Pence, Jacob Fortney, Noah Tracy, Howard Mitchell.

Sec. 13—1836: John D. Alvin, Waitsell W. Cary.

Sec. 14—1836: Alexander Gilfillan, Henry Shafer.

Sec. 19—1836, 1848: John Meeks, Thomas Pritchard. Benjamin Campbell, John Weedman, Thomas Adams, Samuel P. Anthony.

Sec. 20—1836: John Weidner, Garrett Williamson, Jacob Weidner, Jeremiah Miller.

Sec. 21—1836: Samuel Weidner, John Snider.

Sec. 28—1836, 1837: Naomi Powers, William Harlan. George Lieber, Stephen Norris, Mary Butcher, Thomas Brumfield.

Sec. 16—Sold Jan. 1838: A. C. Custar, Robert Ismael, Jacob Hardesty, Samuel R. Collier, Jacob Holland, William Parker, Alexander Hewitt.

Sec. 22—May, 1829, 1836: Nimrod Jester, Tristram Starbuck, John Essley, Abraham Zemar, Samuel Elliot, James Harter, James Galbreath.

Sec. 7—1830, 1835: John Ginn, Josiah McVickar, William Jobes, Isaac Swisher, John Hamilton.

Sec. 18—1830, 1836: John Ginn, David Ashby, Havilla Green, John W. Harter, Liberty Ginn, Joseph Ginn.

Sec. 25—1830, 1836: William Essley, Francis Harris, Reason Iams, Jacob Shideler, Roland Hughes, Mary James, James B. Harter.

Sec. 24—1831, 1835: William McCallister, Junius McMillan, George Shearon, William Shearon, Aaron Note, James McMillan.

Sec. 20—1832, 1836: William Flummer, Elijah Collins, Richard Craw, John Flummer, Charles Royster, Daniel Cochran, George Comstock.

Sec. 21—1832, 1836: William Cox, Isaac Cox, Samuel Wilson, Jacob Shideler, Jesse Lincomb, Peter Grimes.

Sec. 8—1833, ——: Leonard Cline, John Seecors, John Reasoner, Nathaniel Skinner, Henry Skinner, James Chenowith, Isaac Swisher.

Sec. 17—1833, 1837: Samuel Skinner, William Craw, Elizabeth Flummer, Maria S. Flummer, Richard Craw, Samuel L. Black, Elijah Collins.

Sec. 19—1833, 1837: Havilla Green, Sarah Ginn, John W. Harter, Moses Hinton, Reason Tiffin, Thomas Carter, George Carter Jr.

Sec. 23—1833, 1836: Abraham Shideler, Washington Heldren, John Irvin, Absalom Edwards, Reuben Hampton, Isaac Edwards, Samuel Kite, Ochmig Bird, Benjamin Harris, James Harter.

Sec. 26—1833, 1836: Joseph Battereal, Jacob Gump, Joseph Snider, Hannah Studebaker, James Bowman, John Neck, William Mendenhall.

Sec. 36—1833, 1836: William Gregory, Ephraim Laird, Peter R. Bradshaw, Samuel Payton, George Laird, Nancy Egnew, William Guthrey.

Sec. 29—1834, 1836: James Love, Matthew Smith, John Fipper, Charles Royster, Jonathan Jones.

Sec. 9—1835, 1837: John W. Pyke, Isaac Miller, Ashford Roberts, John Flummer, William Adsit, John Reasoner Sr., Letice Shideler.

Sec. 12—1835, 1837: Ephraim Link, William Shearon, Aaron Note, Patrick Carmichael, John Lambert.

Sec. 14—1835, 1836: Hiram Cochran, Peter Shideler, John Van Buskirk, Abraham Shideler, David Shideler.

Sec. 30—1835, 1836: Matthew Smith, Matthew R. Smith, John J. Adsit, William Martin, Jonathan Jones.

Sec. 31—1835, 1838: Stephen Dunlap, Eliza W. Wilson, William Adsit, William Daily, John W. Stafford, Thomas Williams, Joseph Wilson Jr.

Sec. 32—1835, 1836: Stephen Dunlap, Robert Huston, Willis Hance, Isaac Mendenhall, John W. Stafford.

Sec. 33—1835, 1836: William Mendenhall, John Houston, Vincent Martin, Samuel Martin, Abraham C. Culbertson, Nicholas Sherry, Simeon Maxson.

Sec. 13—1835, 1836: John McLain, Aaron Note, William Ray, Samuel Mote.

Sec. 15—1835, 1836: Joshua Shideler, Abraham Shideler, David Shideler, Peter Shideler, Benjamin Harris, Sarah Rardon, Nancy Rardon.

Sec. 27—1835, 1837: David Studebaker, James Galbreath, Mary Ann Mc-Cormick, James Frazer, Philip Hedrick, Jesse Lincome, Emelie Galbreath, William Lewis.

Sec. 10—1836: Jacob Shideler, Jacob Gayman, William Adsit.

Sec. 11—1836: John Lambert, John Gayman, Abraham Gray, Abraham Shideler, Archibald Ray, Daniel Haynes.

Sec. 16—Sold 1836: Caleb Sharon, William Adsit, John Craw.

Sec. 28—1836: James Frazer, Virginia Royster, Nancy Royster.

Sec. 34—1836, 1837: David Sherry, Eli H. Ross, Daniel Sherry, Thomas Ewell, James Egnew, Israel Martin, Elizabeth Martin, Vincent Martin.

Sec. 35—1836, 1837: John Gregory, Maitsell M. Cary, Harvey Millspaugh, George Pyke, David Sherry, Thomas McCormick, Joseph S. Austin, Sarah Simonton, Joseph Hance, Michael Thomas, Solomon McKee, William Sleeth.

HARRISON TOWNSHIP.

Sec. 36 (R. 8)—Oct. 1832, 1837: Isaac Adamson, Archibald Parker, John Parker, John Fenny, John Crawson, Stephen Crawson, Samuel Langley, Miles Marshall, Nathan Hodgson.

Sec. 31—Oct. 1833, 1836: Oliver P. Jones, William Miller, James Fortner, Jacob Crouson, Samuel Adamson.

Sec. 27—1833, 1835: Isaac Tildon, George Shafer, James Garner, Christopher Wilson, William Patten.

Sec. 20—1834, 1837: Job Garner, Isaac Ridout, William Ridout, Tobias Renner, James Stout, Isaac Stout, Joel Biggs, Levi Lynn.

Sec. 21—1834, 1837: William B. Wilson, William Newhouse, James Newhouse.

Sec. 26—1834, 1836: James Smith, George Shafer, Nicholas Maceltree, John Applegate, Thomas Applegate, Daniel Jarrett, Thomas Nottingham, Peter Simmons, John Nottingham.

Sec. 28—1834, 1836: Jacob M. Holloway, William Patten, John Coon, John Woods, Elias Wilson, Caviner Conner, Job Garner, Thomas Haworth, Jacob Cline.

Sec. 29—1834, 1836: Job Garner, Joel Biggs, Charles Stout, John Woods, Jacob Cline, Jonathan Eddy, Jesse Stout.

Sec. 25 (R. 8)—1834, 1839: Robert Swift, Jonathan Langley, Joseph Cox, Samuel Langley, John Starr, Francis Davis, Curtis Langley.

Sec. 30—1835, 1836: Hugh Finley, Abraham Smith, Nicholas Reel, Luke Wright, Jonathan Langley, James Wright, John Langley.

Sec. 25—1836: William Cantwell, John Applegate, William Moore, Josiah Williams, James Freeman.

Sec. 35—1836: John McBride, Daniel Jarrett, James Williamson, John Van Buskirk, William H. Brumfield.

Sec. 18—1836, 1852: John Starr, Benajah French, David W. Cook, William Brady, James H. Swoor.

Sec. 19—1836, 1838: John Starr, Henry W. Smith, John Smith, William Campbell, Job Garner.

Sec. 33—1836, 1838: James McLaughlin, Thomas Patton, Dickson Thomas, Jacob Cline, Daniel Van Buskirk, William Reed, Elias Humbert, Amos Jenna.

Sec. 36—1836: Daniel Jarrett, John Hayhurst, Thomas Williamson, Thomas Brumfield.

Sec. 3—1836, 1838: Gideon McKibben, John Tomlinson, John Collins, Samuel McCreery.

Sec. 15—1836: James Newhouse, Thomas Haworth, Joseph Lafavour, George Griffin.

Sec. 24—1836: John Applegate, William Cavitt, Charles Thatcher, Jacob Haynes.

Sec. 1—1836, 1841: Jonathan Johns, Bernard F. Hook, John Sutton, John Conner, James Ashcraft, David Enry, William Gard, Samuel P. Anthony.

Sec. 12—1836, 1837: Oliver H. Cogshill, Owen Morris, Asher Storer, Watson W. Fitzpatrick, Jonas Sutton, James Stafford, Abraham McConnell.

Sec. 2—1836, 1839: Jonathan Johns, Jonathan Stewart, Job Garner, John D. Jones, Samuel P. Anthony, David Hays.

Sec. 13—1836, 1839: Samuel Moore, Samuel Snider, Daniel Jarrett, Hiram Adams, William Beaty, Jacob Miller.

Sec. 11—1836, 1837: Lewis M. Wilson, Anderson Merritt, John Tomlinson, Thomas Brumfield, Thomas Collins, James Cload, John Collins.

Sec. 17—1836, 1838: Thomas I. Collins, Jonathan West, George Rouse, Stephen C. Collins, Michael Null.

Sec. 1 (R. 8)—1836, 1852: Otis Preble, John Robb, Milton Lawrence, John Perdue, Almon B. Brand, Allen Makepeace.

Sec. 5—1836, 1839: Samuel Brady, Joseph McGilliland, George W. and Jefferson N. Horine, Reason Davis, Jacob C. Palsley, Elisha Galemon, Harrison Dean.

Sec. 9—1836, 1838: Anderson Miller, Aaron Adamson, William Gard, Job Garner, Michael Null.

Sec. 16—Sold Nov. 1836: Bigger and Kennedy, John Coon, Eleazer Coffeen, William Martendale, A. Adamson.

Sec. 8—1836, 1837: Thomas Dean, Josiah Robe, Robert Robe.

Sec. 12 (R. 8)—1836, 1839: Otis Preble, W. H. Carter, James F. Robb, John Perdue, John Hodson, Richard Justice, Harrison Dean, Michael Null.

Sec. 24 (R. 8)—1836, 1839: Tobias Benner, Jonathan Langley, Joseph Cox, Jesse H. Healey, James Marshall, Thomas Worley, Curtis Langley.

Sec. 4—1836, 1839: Joseph Gobie, Joseph Gilliland, Samuel Richerson,

. Henry W. Smith, Samuel McCreery, Andrew Welch, William Bentley.

Sec. 7—1836, 1851: Amos Ratcliff, Vincent Garner, John Perdue, Robert Robe, Henry Garner, Gideon McKibben, Jacob French, James H. Swoor.

Sec. 10—1836, 1837: Samuel McCune, Prior Rigdon, Matthew Burroughs, John Woods.

Sec. 14—1836, 1839: George Griffin, Thomas Anthony, Thomas B. Jenett, Isaac Barnes, Benjamin Wallingsford, Jacob Miller.

Sec. 22—1836, 1838: Isaac Ridout, John McCarty, James Newhouse, Thomas Brumfield, Solomon Williams, Elijah Newhouse, John H. Garner, Mary Jones, Vincent Garner.

Sec. 23—1836, 1839: Joseph Lefavour, Jacob Calvert, Oliver H. Smith, James Marshall.

Sec. 32—1836, 1837: Jacob Miller, Moses Shepherd, William Palmer, Solomon McLaughlin, James McLaughlin, James Williams.

Sec. 34—1836, 1837: Samuel C. Bradford, Oliver H. Smith, Christopher Wilson, Jane Williamson, Philander Cassman, Samuel P. Anthony.

Sec. 13 (R. 8)—1837: Enoch Garner, George Turner, Joseph Cook, Adam C. Lewis, Miles Marshall.

Sec. 6—1837, 1839: Reason Summers, Jacob Beals, Zachariah Cook, Jesse Mellett, John Perdue, Harrison Dean.

NILES TOWNSHIP.

Sec. 34—May, 1831, 1837: Samuel Gregory, Robert Kimball, George Huffman, Jacob Peterson, Michael Hedkin, Joseph Stafford.

Sec. 31—1831, 1836: Peter Thomas, John Gregory, William O'Neal, John Engard, Jonathan Ruggles, Jacob Battereal, Andrew Battereal, Jacob Battereal.

Sec. 32—1831, 1836: Alexander Price, John Sutton, Samuel Kite, John Battereal, Isaac Martin, William Battereal, William Downing.

Sec. 33—1831, 1836: James Gregory, William Lee, Alexander Price, Andrew Battereal, Jesse Clark, William Downing, Samuel Gregory.

Sec. 19—1832, 1836: Philip Stoner, Philip Essley, James Black, Elisha Essley, Jesse Essley, Junius McMillan, Stephen Butler.

Sec. 28—1832, 1839: George Shearon, Samuel Martin, David Smith, John Lewis, Robert M. Boyd, Israel Martin, William Custer, Robert Huston, Noble Gregory, Glass Ross, Henry Shearon, Stephen Berry.

Sec. 30—1832, 1836: Thomas Hillman, Ralph Shaw, Willis Hance, William Gregory, John Gregory, Reason Iams, Norris Venard.

Sec. 20—1833, 1836: James Black, Francis A. Essley, William Constant, Elisha Essley, Cyrus McMillan, Jeremiah Priest, James L. Veach.

Sec. 25—1833, ——: John Wilson, Samuel Kyle, John Dinsmore, Daniel Dean Jr., William H. Houston.

Sec. 29—1833, 1836: John Blakeary, John Thomas, Samuel Clark, James Robinson, James Hetton, Charles Redding.

Sec. 36—1833, 1836: Isaac Pavy, John Boots, Eli H. Anderson, Jacob Noggle, Warren Mann, Ezra Bantz.

Sec. 17—1834, 1839: John Black, Rachel Chandler, Ralph Stafford, John Barley, John D. Highway.

Sec. 35—1834, ——: Eli Anderson, Thomas Vincent, John Shrack, Adam Keaver, John Dinsmore, John Mann, Eli Pendroy.

Sec. 15—1835, 1836: George W. Stafford, Samuel Sprinkle, Richard Higman, John Constant.

Sec. 21—1835, 1837: Alfred Barnett, William Lee, David Mason, Frederick Thornburg, Andrew Wilson, Albert Boyd, David Moore.

Sec. 27—1835, 1836: Jeremiah Veach, William McCoy, Jacob Moore, Robert Kimball, William Foster.

Sec. 7—1836, ——: Stephen Hayward, Thomas N. Sinks, Ephraim Sinks, George Leedon, Jonathan Ballinger.

Sec. 8—1836: William J. Knight, William J. Essley, John C. Corbley, John Black.

Sec. 9—1836, 1837: James Wooster, John Black, George Huffman, John Thomas.

Sec. 10—1836, 1837: William D. Field, George Huffman, Dennis Wilson, Jacob Huffman, John Constant, John Mellit.

Sec. 11—1836, 1837: John Buckles, Joel B. Low, Eldridge Addison, William Bell, Valentine Bone.

Sec. 12—1836, 1838: Joseph Heaton, Adam Reader, Samuel P. Anthony, John Buckles, Hugh Campbell, Noah Shearly, James Peterson.

Sec. 13—1836, 1837: Banlin Smith, John Buckles, Nathaniel Poor, James Peterson, Hugh Campbell, William Shrack.

Sec. 14—1836, 1837: James Peterson, Elisha Bartlett, Richard Higman, Nathaniel Polk, William Lee, Daniel Fisher, Hugh Campbell.

Sec. 18—1836: Ezra Wasson and Thomas Moore.

Sec. 22—1836: Jacob Moore, James Bolton, Augustus A. Root, Loxley A. Rickand, Samuel T. Kyle.

Sec. 23—1836, 1838: Isaac Spence, Thomas Berry, Ezra Porter, Daniel Bosman, William Scott, Ira Ingraham.

Sec. 24—1836: Amos Wooster, Nathaniel Dickson, Adam Michael, Isaac Mailten.

Sec. 26—1836: John Blakely, Sarah Kimball, Robert Kimball, John W. Vincent, John Shrack.

Sec. 16—Sold Nov. 1838: Morton C. East, William Richardson, Andrew Black, James Black, Mary Gorton, James McMillan.

DELAWARE TOWNSHIP.

Sec. 19—Oct. 1830, 1837: Henry Harmon, Daniel Pittenger, Elijah Reeves, James Russell, Stephen R. Martin, Thomas Albin, John Pepper, William Stansbury.

Sec. 2—1831, 1836: David Jones, John Dinsmore, William Venard, Reuben Strong, John Quinn, Stephen Venard, Morrison Quinn, Emson H. Venard, Henry S. Eron, Joseph Eron, Absalom Boots.

Sec. 5—1831, 1836: Archibald Dowden, Isaac Martin, Thomas Wilson, John T. Wilson, William Thomas, David Sutton, Adam Wilson.

Sec. 6—1831, 1836: Israel Martin, Thomas Williams, William H. Green, Benoni Wilson, Adam Wilson, William Thomas, Ezekiel Thomas, John Baldridge.

Sec. 11—1831, 1836: Solomon Boots, John Quinn, Joseph O'Neal, Alfred Lee, Adam Keaver, William Custer, Jonathan Bergdoll, Joseph H. Hulse.

Sec. 18—1831, 1836: Elizabeth Friend, William Custer, Henry Huddleston, Isaac Martin, A. Custer, William Pence, Philip Cochran.

Sec. 1—1832, 1835: Abraham Custer, Reuben Strong, Lewis Stoner, John W. Strong, Jacob Pendroy, Ezra Bantz.

Sec. 7—1832, ——: John Boyles, Lloyd Wilcoxon, John Batreall Jr., Archibald Dowden, William Boyles, Squire Boyles, Charles F. Willard, Jefferson Walburn.

Sec. 8—1832, 1836: William Moody, Wilson Lennon, William Thomas, Andrew Wilson, Robbins Wilson, George Richeson, John Funderburg.

Sec. 10—1832, 1836: Joshua Bantz, John Quinn, David Bright, John Bantz, Henry Bright, John Sparr, John H. Taylor.

Sec. 12—1832, 1833: John W. Strong, James Dean, Reuben Strong, Lewis Stoner, Frederick Stoner.

Sec. 13—1832, 1837: Nehemiah Burden, Abner Woolverton, Adam Keever, James Campbell, Levi Boots, James Dean.

Sec. 14—1832, 1836: Adam Keever, Joseph Templer, Eli Thornburg, Stephen Kennedy.

Sec. 20—1832, 1836: Benjamin Drummond, John Godlove, Ebenezer Halstead, Aquilla Hensley, George McCullough, Robbins R. Williams, John Pepper.

Sec. 28—1832, 1836: William E. Pendroy, Thomas Humphreys, Jesse McCray, Nicholas Pittenger, Daniel Richardson, Ila Lake, Uriah Lennon, John Moody.

Sec. 30—1832, 1837: Thomas Crawford, Thomas F. Wilson, Daniel Pittenger, James Sparr, William Dragoo, John B. Gough, Benjamin Dragoo.

Sec. 17—1833, 1836: Edward Marshall, Joseph Berry, Abraham Godlove, Daniel Cochran, Philip Cochran, Thomas Martin, Ebenezer Halstead.

Sec. 29—1833, 1837: Jacob C. Harmon, Thomas Harmon, Josiah Wade, Henry Pittenger, Wilson Lennon, Uriah Lennon, Jacob Furrow, Thomas H. Weirman.

Sec. 3—1833, 1837: Francis Venard, Ralph Stafford, Susannah Thomas, Joshua Bantz, Robert Malcolm, George Mills, Martin Depoy, David Bright, Henry Judy.

Sec. 4—1833, 1836: William Black, McCoy Malcolm, Morrison Quinn, Joseph Godlove, William Martin, Samuel P. Anthony.

Sec. 9—1833, 1836: Stephen Berry Jr., Moses C. White, David Sutton, Reuben Eppert, Silas Sparr.

Sec. 16—Sold 1833, 1834: Joseph Godlove, George F. Hastings, Robert Malcolm, David Jones, Samuel Calaway.

Sec. 15—1834, ——: Joseph Puckett, Joseph H. Hulse, John Bantz, Solomon Rohrbaugh, Samuel P. Anthony, John H. Taylor, Martin

Forbes, John Kennedy, Andrew S. Kennedy, Granville F. Hastings.

Sec. 21—1834, 1836: Jonathan Rardon, Jacob Sellers, Glass Ross, Samuel Thomas, Christopher Humphreys, John Pittenger.

Sec. 26—1834, 1836: Solomon Rohrbaugh, Warren Mann, Joseph Humphreys, William Jameson, Thomas Jones, James Johnson.

Sec. 22—1835, 1836: Daniel Perrine, Stephen Kennedy, Michael Beeghley.

Sec. 25—1835, 1837: William Bartlett, Solomon Rohrbaugh, Samuel Johnson, Edwin Johnson.

Sec. 23—1835, 1837: Solomon Rohrbaugh, John Boots, Benjamin Manor, Martin Boots, Elias Beeghley, Thomas Berry.

Sec. 24—1835, 1837: James Campbell, James Dean, Joseph Orr, George Iman, Solomon Rohrbaugh, James Pendroy, William Woods.

Sec. 27—1835, 1836: James Jones, Jabesh Jones, David Lewellen, James Orr, Justice Kitterman, Ila Lake, Adam Boots.

General Conclusions.

It requires but a brief study of the original land entries to prove the claim advanced earlier in this narrative that the rivers, being the principal transportation routes of the early days, drew the first settlers to their banks and caused a grouping of population along the streams at the expense of the higher lands that had no running streams. In this county, water transportation played a very meager part, but the two principal streams none the less directed the settlers in their location. This was natural, since along the running streams were to be found the mill sites, and also water for stock purposes. It is an interesting proof of the part taken by the rivers in settlement that the larger towns of Delaware county were all founded on the banks of either the White or Mississinewa river. Muncie, Yorktown and Smithfield on the White river, and Eaton, Albany and Wheeling on the Mississinewa, were eligible town sites in the eyes of their founders because of the rivers. It might be offered in proof that Hamilton and Harrison townships, which are the only townships in the county entirely away from the winding courses of one of these rivers, were among the last townships to be settled.

Using the table of land entries as a basis for conclusions, it will be interesting to notice what parts of the county had been settled before the beginning of the year 1830. Starting with Liberty township, we find that nine sections had been partly entered. The first entry in the township was in section 21, on the White river near Smithfield. The next sections where entries were made were 28 and 29, both crossed by this river. Then came sections 22 and 24, both on the course of the river; then section 30, with the river around two sides, and sections 23 and 25, also touched by the river. Of the nine sections, section 18 is the only one settled before 1830 that was not watered by the river.

From Liberty township, White river flows through the northwestern corner of Perry. Right in this same corner the first entries were made, in sections 31, 32, and 33, and in that order. In this township entries had been made in twelve townships before 1830, namely: 31, 32, 33, 1, 4, 13, 17, 5, 8, 9, 21 and 23. Beyond the first two sections it is not possible to affirm the positive influence of the river in directing the choice of locations. Perry township was the first point of attack, as it were, from the incoming pioneers. The movement of immigration was from the southeast, with Wayne county as the principal focus, and at an early period a road was laid out from Richmond toward Muncie and Marion, this becoming a thoroughfare that of itself exerted a great influence on settlement. So the early settlers of Perry seem to have been less restricted in their selection of land and to have quickly found homes in every part of the township. But section 31, with the White river flowing through the north half, was the only one of the twelve townships all of whose land had been entered by 1830; this of itself being proof that the settlers rather favored land that bordered the river.

Monroe township was among those later settled and White river played little or no part in its settlement. The four sections which had entries before 1830 were sections 10, 15, 12, 23.

Passing to Center township, it is found that entries had been made in thirteen townships before 1830. Section 25, in which was the first entry, lies in the southeast corner of the township, right on the course of the river. The other twelve sections, in order of the date of first entry, are 10, 13, 9, 11, 14, 15, 24, 34, 35, 3, 17, 18. All but two of these are traversed by the river or lie less than half a mile from it.

Following the course of the river into Mt. Pleasant township, it appears that before 1830 entries had been made on eight sections and that every one was adjacent to the river or Buck creek. We have already spoken of the Indian land grants, all of which lay along the river.

Turning south, White river before leaving the county passes through a considerable portion of Salem township. Land entries on fourteen sections of this township were made before 1830. The settlement of this township was an extension from Henry county on the south, and it is probable that the first settlers had some feeling of neighborly relation with the nearest settlers of that county, and, other things being equal, preferred to remain as close to them as possible. But here as elsewhere the first settler had chosen a location near the river, in section 31. Sections 20, 21, 22, 23, on the south line of the township, were next settled, and then followed the block of townships in the northwest corner, near the river, consisting of sections 12, 1, 6, and 32. The other sections to receive entries before 1830 were: 36, 1, 14, 15 and 24 (R. 8).

Of the townships away from White river few had entrymen before 1830. Washington had three sections, 15, 11, and 12, which showed entries previous to that time—all of them in the northeast corner near the Missis-sinewa. In Union township only section 22, along the river, was entered, in 1829. and in Hamilton township sections 25 and 26 had entries late in 1829. No entries were made in other townships within the time now being considered.

At the close of the decade of the twenties, entries had been recorded for land in 66 different sections in the county. Considerably more than half of the land taken up lay adjacent to the larger water courses, so that stronger proof could not be desired of the influence of the rivers in the early settlement.

CHAPTER VI.

A STUDY OF ORIGINS AND SOURCES—PROMINENT PIONEER TYPES.

Having learned the general location of the first settlements in the county, there remains a task with more personal interest. Unfortunately, it will be impossible to give more information about many of the pioneers than is contained in the list of original entrymen. Record is made there of those who purchased land of the government, whether with the intention of permanently settling or for the purpose of speculation. Several thousand different persons are named as entrymen of land from the government in this county, and yet the majority of them are unknown to the present generation. A considerable number of those purchasing land of the government never resided in the county, their purchases being simply for investment or speculation. Of these there could be nothing to say in a history of the county, since almost without exception they contributed nothing to the permanent development of the county. Then, of course, many entered land, lived on it a short while and moved out of the county, disappearing from sight and knowledge of all their neighbors. While only a comparatively small percent of the entrymen deserve historical recognition for their worth as settlers, it is unfortunate that the record is so meager of some who were strong men in their sphere and gained the high esteem of their fellows while establishing homes in their county.

Where had the early settlers lived before coming to this county? By what routes did they come? What caused them to locate here? And how did their origin influence the development of this county?

One of the most interesting themes connected with early Delaware county history is concerned with the answer to the above questions. In this modern age, when men are becoming more cosmopolitan in their conditions, when provincialism and the influences of state and section are less plainly impressed on individuals, it is less pertinent to inquire regarding birthplace and original home. Yet it is almost equally common as a question between strangers as they take the first steps to acquaintance. It is not intended to answer each of these questions categorically. A study of the early settlement of any locality suggests such questions as the above in a series, and historical curiosity impels us to endeavor to answer these queries while considering the early settlers of Delaware county.

It cannot be said of Delaware county, as of certain counties in northern Indiana and southern Michigan, that its early settlers were of New England stock. Many New Englanders can be found among the pioneers, but they were not the predominant class in numbers. All the Atlantic states from Vermont to South Carolina furnished settlers. Many of the county's best known and most influential families were from Virginia and the Carolinas. In the individual history of the settlers, going no further back than their birthplace, it would seem that a very large percent came from Ohio and Kentucky and western New York. But it will be understood that these localities were intermediate points in the westward migration, to which the family made the first stage of its journey, or stopped a few years until civilization caught up with them, and then pushed on deeper into the wilderness.

From North Atlantic States.

Of typical New England origin was the Muncie pioneer, Goldsmith C. Gilbert. He came of a family of pioneers, one of his grandfathers having been the first settler at Cavendish, Vermont. Just across the line in Washington county, New York, Goldsmith C. Gilbert was born in the last decade of the eighteenth century. Ten years later he accompanied his uncle up the valley of the Mohawk to Jefferson county on Lake Ontario, then the western frontier. In 1814 came another pioneer migration, through the sparsely settled country to Lebanon, Ohio. Mr. Gilbert in 1823 completed the final stage of his western emigration when he settled in Delaware county. The rest of his history is closely identified with this county. He bought the Hackley reserve, later donated part of it for the site of Muncie, dug the mill race on the peninsula of north Muncie and erected a mill that later became the property of Jack and Russey and finally came into the possession of the Wysor estate, and at present owned by Mr. Wallace Hibbets. He operated various mills and factories, and was no less prominent in public affairs. He took a foremost part in the railroad agitation that during the early forties seemed likely to result in a railroad from Muncie to Fort Wayne. He was a member of the legislature at that time, and his efforts to get a charter granted to the proposed railroad were his last important labors. While returning home from Indianapolis in January, 1844, he was taken ill and died at Pendleton. None of the pioneers surpassed him in enterprise, public spirit, or the energy which accomplishes the essential work of the pioneer. He had the New England conscience and adhered to the highest standards of integrity. He was a Universalist. His daughter Mary J., who was born in Muncie in 1826, was the first white child born on the site that was soon afterward selected as the county seat. She married Dr. Daniel H. Andrews, one of the early physicians, who died in 1856, and she later became the wife of Joseph W. Edmonds.

Vermont was the birthplace of another prominent pioneer of Muncie, Eleazer Coffeen, a relative of the above Goldsmith Coffeen Gilbert. Born in 1799, his parents crossed the state of New York to Jefferson county in 1801. We are not informed what route he took to reach Lebanon, in southwestern Ohio, in 1822, but it is probable the Ohio river furnished the route for the greater part of the way. Arriving in this county in 1833, Mr. Coffeen became an early merchant of Muncie, was proprietor of two saw mills, and at one time had a woolen mill on Buck creek. He lived in Muncie until 1869, and also spent his final years here. He was concerned in many affairs by which his name is permanently fixed. In 1851 he laid out a suburb of Muncie called Coffeentown. He was an associate judge, a member of the legislature, and as long as he lived in Muncie was closely connected with its progress.

In the early history of southwestern Ohio and southeastern Indiana it is interesting to note the large contribution of settlers made by the little state of Delaware. In the country north of Cincinnati it would seem that almost a majority of the pioneers were from that state. In the neighborhood of Dover, Delaware, was born Minus Turner, in 1807. His father was also a native of that state, but about 1810 joined the tide of migration down the Ohio valley, settling first at Lexington and then at Covington, Kentucky. In 1823 he moved up into that part of the "twelve mile purchase" that became Randolph county; he spent the last years of his life in Delaware county. One of the unfortunate results of the removal of a family from one of the eastern states to the new west was that the children were usually deprived of the advantages of thorough schooling. Kentucky at the time Minus Turner was a boy there had the most indifferent school facilities, and when we consider that so many of the residents of Delaware county and elsewhere in the state during the thirties and forties had been deprived of schooling while growing up in a new country, it is not surprising the census indicated so much illiteracy in this state. Minus Turner in later years made up somewhat for the lack of early advantages, and by superior business ability and native intelligence became one of Muncie's most respected citizens. He learned the trade of mason and bricklayer from his father, and after his permanent location in Muncie in 1829, he went into the business of making brick and burning lime, his brickyard being located on West Main street. His house is said to have been the first brick house in Delaware county, and about 1831 he erected the Willard block, of brick, since replaced by another Willard block, but which in its time was a very important building in the village. On the southeast corner of Main and Walnut street, where now stands the Patterson block, he completed, in 1839, a brick building which was also one of the landmarks of the city until it burned down. He burned and laid the brick, doing the latter work partly by moonlight.

He opened it as a tavern, and as such it passed through many hands—a Colonel Sayer, Hoon, Hunter, Jo Davis (and it was long known as the Jo Davis House). In December, 1844, a Muncie paper calls it the Eagle House, "formerly kept by Col. Sayer, lately by William Russey, and at this date leased by S. Giffin."

From Delaware also came one of Muncie's early merchants, John Jack, who was born at Wilmington in 1804. It will be profitable to notice, during this study, the great number of Delaware county settlers who made Wayne county, Indiana, an intermediate place of residence between the far east and this county, or entered this county through the Wayne county gateway. Mr. Jack came to Wayne county in 1825, where he followed his trade of tanner and currier several years, and in 1836 moved to Muncie. Perhaps a very few of the oldest Delaware county citizens can remember the store and trading establishment kept by the successive firms of Bloomfield and Jack, Bloomfield, Jack and Russey, and Jack and Russey. For a time he and associates conducted the woolen mill established by Mr. Gilbert. His enterprises were among the largest in Muncie during that period of its history. At one time he was engaged in pork packing, an industry then in its infancy, and he is said to have lost heavily by these transactions.

John Jack died in 1859, leaving a widow who continued to reside in the house at the northwest corner of Washington and Mulberry streets for a third of a century. Mrs. W. L. Little, Mrs. J. M. Kirby, Mrs. J. E. Howe were daughters of Mr. Jack.

Thomas Kirby had the thrift, the trading instincts, the energy, and withal the sympathy and thorough helpfulness of a typical son of Massachusetts. Born at Stockbridge in 1804, attending school between his duties in a woolen mill, in 1827 he came west to Wayne county, and at Richmond began trading in furs, skins and ginseng. Only comparatively few people of this generation know what ginseng is; though within the last few years the demands of the export trade to the orient for this article have increased its culture in many localities. In the period when the lands of eastern Indiana were first being turned over by the plow, ginseng grew wild throughout this region. In the market reports of that time ginseng was quoted alongside of butter and flour and other staples. Mr. Kirby is said to have bought about six thousand pounds of the root every year, so that it was no small item in the commerce of the country. When Minus Turner located in Muncie in 1829 Thomas Kirby was peddling goods over the country about Muncie, representing a firm in Dayton, Ohio. His increasing prosperity was indicated by his selling goods at first from a pack on his back, then going about on horseback, and finally using a horse and wagon. He also had a general store on Washington street, west of High. His energy and keen business ability made him money. He bought large amounts of land, some of it being now covered by the city, and was soon estimated as one of the wealthy men of the county. He was a trustee of his township, gave large sums for the building of turnpikes, railroads and other enterprises of public or semi-public nature, and was an influential figure in Delaware county history up to the time of his death, on August 14, 1879. He was the oldest, in years of residence, of the pioneers still living, fourteen of whom bore his remains to their last resting place; most of these a few years later had found rest in Beech Grove. Of the concrete memorials of his career, such as people see daily but which convey only superficial estimates of life, the best known is the Kirby House, which was erected by Mr. Kirby in 1871 and which more than a generation of citizens and travelers have known as one of the central points of Muncie.

In the valleys of the Miami rivers in southwestern Ohio, about the beginning of the last century, William Brady had found a home. William Brady participated in the expedition against the Indian villages along the Mississinewa during the war of 1812, as previously described, and as a result of the hardships endured lived only a short time after that event. His pioneer home in Warren county, Ohio, was the birthplace, in 1803, of John Brady, whose career and that of his family has been prominently and closely identified with Delaware county and eastern Indiana for three quarters of a century. When a boy John Brady learned how to make saddles and harness, and at the age of twenty-one advanced nearer to the frontier, and lived for some years at Richmond, Wayne county, Indiana. He came to Muncie in 1836 and until his death nearly fifty years later was a citizen whose support was considered necessary in all public enterprises and whose influence was never refused in promoting the city's progress. He died January 14, 1884, and his memory was honored by the closing of all business houses and a temporary cessation of the ordinary vocations. For years he had been honored with public office, having served as associate judge, postmaster, mayor, member of the council and township trustee, and was always a Democrat, a leader of the local party. His wife, who died August 30, 1884, was Mary Wright, who had moved to Wayne county from Maryland.

A native of Vermont, where his grandfather had settled after coming from England during the colonial period, John Smith began moving westward soon after reaching his majority, and after tarrying awhile in the mountainous region of western Virginia and on a farm in the Muskingum valley of Ohio, he came to Delaware county in 1829. Throughout the active part of his lifetime he lived in Liberty township, an industrious and prosperous farmer, rearing a large family, some of whom are still identified with this county.

To the notable group of men from the northeastern states, who did much of the essential pioneer work in developing Delaware county, was added, in 1831, a young man of nineteen years, born and reared in New Hampshire, and destined, by his remarkable energy, business ability, and thorough integrity, to become a permanent influence in this county's his. tory. Charles F. Willard was born at Charlestown, New Hampshire, in 1812. He received a good home training from his guardian (his father having died when the son was two years old) and had more than ordinary education, although he left the academy at Meriden in order to take up the active duties for which he early showed preference. At the age of fifteen he became a clerk in a store at Rochester, New York. In 1830 he moved to Dayton, Ohio, and entered the employ of the same house with which Thomas Kirby was then connected, and in February, 1831, was sent to Muncie to assist Mr. Kirby in buying furs, ginseng and other products for the Dayton house. His aggressive business ability was shown when a few months later he bought the business of the Dayton merchant, and at the age of twenty years became junior partner in the firm of Kirby and Willard. During the greater part of thirty-five years Mr. Willard continued in busi. ness in Muncie, and the family and estate established by him have remained in Muncie to the present time. He spent his last years with his son at Painesville, Ohio, where he died in 1871. His brother, Dr. William C. Wil. lard, was one of the early physicians of Muncie, and his activities in the city are mentioned in another chapter.

In the long march from pioneer times to the present the old settlers have been dropping off one by one, and of those who actually took part in the battle against the powers of the wilderness hardly any remain. And yet only a few years ago there were many who had seen the county when farming, trade and industry were in their crude beginnings. Although his death occurred in Muncie at a ripe age, on August 20, 1890, there are hun. dreds of persons who remember Volney Willson, who spent more than half a century of his lifetime in this county. His career and character were such as to make an impress on the community in which he lived. The family in the previous generation was from Vermont, but Volney was born in Wash. ington county, New York, in 1816. He had a good education, measured by the standards of the time, and taught several terms of school while a young man. During the first two years of his residence in Muncie, where he located in 1837, he taught school in the village, and for some years he gave part of his time to this work. Seven years after settling in the county he was elected county treasurer, and held the office three terms. Farming was his principal business, however, and he not only conducted a large estate but conducted it in a progressive and systematic manner that made him suc. cessful above the average. He had interests in several turnpikes of the county and also in several of the railroad lines traversing the county, and his assistance was lent to many enterprises of local importance or value at the time, but which are now forgotten. He was likewise one of the influential Republicans of the county. His wife was Elizabeth, daughter of John A. Gilbert.

From the South Atlantic States.

As elsewhere stated, the men who developed Delaware county did not own any particular section as their previous home. The settlers were per-haps as cosmopolitan as those of any county in the middle west. Here were united in society and often in family ties those whose lives had been molded by Puritan New England and those who had known no influences and cus-toms outside of Cavalier Virginia. Yankee thrift and southern liberality became valuable elements in the new social order growing up in the middle west. So far as the several recognized sections of the United States have produced each a somewhat different type of people, Delaware county has received samples from each of those types, and has developed a thoroughly American civilization, equally removed from the dominating characteristics of the north or the south, and from the peculiarities popularly ascribed to the eastern and to the western people.

From the states south of Mason and Dixon's line came not a few of the families whose activities have been recognized as important in the county for two generations. Old Virginia was the mother of colonies as well as the mother of statesmen, and even before the Revolution her sons had advanced into and across the Alleghany and parallel mountain chains, found-ing homes, clearing the forests, and forming settlements that owed allegi-ance to the mother colony until they became strong enough to be erected into separate states. Naturally, the bulk of this migration was south of the Ohio river or in its valley, but during the early decades of the nineteenth century a great many homeseekers pushed their way into the country lying midway between the great lakes and the Ohio. In addition to the usual incentives that led pioneers into new countries, some of the Virginians and settlers from other southern states were influenced to locate in the states formed from the Northwest Territory by the absence of slavery from that region. A number of examples could be found, of men who had become convinced of the moral and perhaps the economic wrong inherent in negro slavery, and had removed to northern states to practice their new ideals under favorable conditions. This was especially true of the Quakers from the Carolinas who settled in such large numbers in Wayne county and also overspread into Delaware county.

A conspicuous example of the early settlers who came from the south was Dr. Samuel P. Anthony, one of the most successful business men and one of the best citizens that the county ever had. Why he left Virginia and came into the Ohio valley is an interesting point in the history of emigration. He was born in 1792, at Lynchburg, then as now in the heart of the great

Virginia tobacco industry, and doubtless the tobacco crop had largely sup. plemented the family's yearly income ever since it located in the state. In 1813, when he was twenty years old, he and his father moved to Ohio, and after a period of the service in the army, they located in Cincinnati, in 1814, and there established the first tobacco manufacture west of the Alleghany mountains. The availability of the Ohio valley for tobacco culture drew not a few tobacco planters from Virginia, the original home of the industry, and so it was that the Anthonys first became located on the western side of the Alleghanies. While at Cincinnati, Samuel P. Anthony applied himself to the study of medicine, and following several years' practice in various parts of Ohio he located in Muncie in 1831, where he was to spend the remainder of his life, which was brought to a close in 1876, when he was almost eighty-four years old. Besides practicing medicine he sold merchandise, and, as an examination of the land entries will show, purchased great quantities of land in the county. He amassed a fortune, and, the estate which he founded is still one of the largest in the county. He was among the most liberal contributors and active promoters in the building of the first railroads through the county. He was at one time president of the Bellefontaine and Indianapolis (now the Big Four) Railroad and was a director for many years; he was also president of the Fort Wayne and Southern Railroad. His only child was Edwin C. Anthony, who was born at Cincinnati in 1818 and died in Muncie, June 7, 1884.

The Buckles family had left England in the eighteenth century and located in Virginia before the Revolution. In the years of dissent from the established church and while the seeds of discord with the mother country were bearing their first fruit, the Buckles family were active in the faith of the Baptists. Before the close of the century the family had removed to Ohio, where in 1799 was born Abraham Buckles. Thirty years later he was ordained a minister of the Baptist church, and shortly after coming to Muncie, in the fall of 1833, organized the first Baptist church. He achieved the remarkable record of serving over forty-five years as its pastor, without receiving any salary for his services. He died in 1878, when nearly eighty years of age. His son, Joseph S. Buckles, was a prominent lawyer and man of affairs in this county, whose career is outlined on other pages.

Isaac Branson was born in Virginia in 1794, and, following a common direction of migration, crossed the mountains into Kentucky, moved to High-land county, Ohio, in 1818, and the following year to Randolph county, Indiana. He came to Delaware county in 1828, where he died in 1856.

The records of the Heath family also go back to the southern states. The earliest American ancestor came from London to Maryland, but at the time Delaware county was in process of formation the family lived in North Carolina. Ralph Heath, the grandfather of the present generation in this county, came from North Carolina to Wayne county, Indiana, in 1828, and the following year settled in Salem township, this county, so that for more than three quarters of a century members of the family have been identified with the county. (See sketch elsewhere.)

The second physician in Muncie was a Virginian by birth. Dr. Levi Minshall, born in Berkeley county, Virginia, in 1804, and educated for his profession in Ohio, came to Muncie in 1829, married the daughter of one of the merchants at that time, and engaged in a successful practice until his death in 1836.

It would be easy to name many families that lived in the southern states before permanently settling in this county. Stephen Hamilton, son of the Stephen Hamilton after whom Hamilton township was named, was born in Monongalia county in what is now West Virginia, in 1825, and four years later was brought to this county. Job Swain, for many years well known in Muncie and at one time mayor of the city, was identified with the settlement south of the Ohio, having been born in Tennessee in 1806. The family were Quakers, and in 1815 moved to the chief settlement of that sect, in Wayne county, Indiana, and from there Mr. Swain came to Muncie in 1828, where he lived nearly half a century until his death in 1877. Another Tennesseean, Jonathan Mills, was the first settler of Monroe township, coming there in 1821 from Wayne county, where he had located in 1819. John Barley, one of the early settlers of Niles township, who died there March 12, 1884, was a native of Frederick county, Virginia, born in 1812. Another Virginian, one of the most prominent and successful business men that Muncie ever had, was the late Jacob H. Wysor, who was born in Pulaski county, Virginia, in 1819, and came to this county in 1834 (see sketch elsewhere). October 2, 1888, occurred the death of A. N. Klein, Muncie's pioneer jeweler, who was born in Loudon county, Virginia, in 1817. He had moved to Ohio in 1837, and the following year to Muncie, where, in order to make a living by his trade, he became an itinerant jobber, and continued this until the county was better settled and a permanent establishment became profitable.

Old Letters.

Letters are often suggestive commentaries of the time in which they are written. A number of the letters written to Thomas Kirby while he was a merchant in Muncie during the thirties have been preserved. They prove unconscious witnesses of some features of pioneer Indiana life that can no longer be readily understood.

In 1835 Thomas Kirby imported a stove to Muncie, paying fifty dollars for it. It is likely that the stove was an object of curious interest here. Some pioneer accounts make no mention of stoves of any kind, the old fireplace, with open hearth, crane, pots and bake-ovens, being the characteristic features of the pioneer house. But stoves were by no means unknown, and were used in Muncie as this letter shows. The stove was sent from Cincinnati, and the manufacturer writes: "I have sent you at the request of your brother one of the improved Franklin Alterable Cooking stoves, same as he has in use. He did not know whether or not you would want the convenience of altering it into an open stove, for which purpose the Franklin head and wings are sent, on condition that if not wanted they may be returned. . . . You will find it a great convenience if you should set the stove where you could make a dining room of it in the winter." The stove as pictured on the letter head was not an ungraceful utensil. The oven was opened when the stove was transformed into a heater, and by affixing the "head and wings" above mentioned was converted into an article of comfort and ornament.

The following letter and its request from Mr. Thomas Kirby's brother in Cincinnati piques our curiosity at the present time as much as it must have caused the former to wonder when he received the letter: "You will laugh at the purpose of my now writing. Can you procure say at $1 or $1.50 and send me say one quart of pure bear's oil when you send down your four hundred deer skins etc? I want it for a particular purpose if pure. If it will be the least inconvenience, don't do it. Should you send it through any other person don't let it appear outside what it is and direct it left at my home." This was written in February, 1831.

In Dayton Mr. Kirby had been connected with the business house of William Stone, and shortly after his arrival in Muncie he receives a letter of encouragement from his former employer, who then goes on to say: "We had a letter from Mr. Noble on Sunday. He wrote us that he started goods from New York on the 17th of this month (Sept., 1830), by the way of the Lakes, and it is probable that they will be here by the 10th of next month. I suppose you will be here by the 20th for new goods." It was a long way to transport goods up the Hudson, the Erie Canal, and from some point on Lake Erie by river and overland to Dayton.

Writing from Detroit, Zebulon Kirby, another brother, states, under date Sept. 18, 1831, that "Red Deer skins Indian handled are worth 25 cents per pound here, quick at that—they might probably fetch something more." Then asks, "Are your skins taken off and handled by the Indians? Skins which are handled by whites or Yankees do not sell as high." During the early years of this county's history deer skins were an important article of commerce. Here is a copy of a handbill printed more than seventy years ago and doubtless displayed in many public places in this county: "Cash paid for Ginseng and Red Deer skins. The subscriber will pay the highest market price in cash or goods for ginseng well washed and dried and for

Red Deer skins, delivered at his store in Muncietown, Ind., until the first day of November next [1835].—Charles F. Willard."

A letter from Zebulon written in 1844 advises Mr. Thomas Kirby to market his pork in Detroit instead of at Cincinnati. "We were struck by the prices you name as being paid there and the prices that the article commands here. A Common article sells in our streets at three and a half cents and all that will weigh 300 or thereabout brings 4 cents and some has been sold higher. A barrel of good mess pork (heavy) cannot be had here now short of 12 dollars. These prices are paid by packers, and there is considerable putting up, but they all complain they cannot obtain enough at the prices paid. Now it does strike me that if you will pack as much mess pork as you can and cure hams and shoulders as you had last summer, cart it to the canal with your lard, and come up here with it at the first opening of navigation in the spring, you cannot fail to do well at least and it strikes me you will get about twice as much as you can at home, or have it net you by sending to Cincinnati."

Court House, Muncie.

CHAPTER VII.

THE COUNTY AS A CIVIL ORGANIZATION.

The organization of counties and the fixing of their boundaries are matters of state legislation. Wayne county was organized in 1810, Randolph county about 1818, and in February, 1821, Henry county was formed. It will be remembered that previous to 1818 the region subject to settlement was limited to the "twelve mile purchase" lying west of the Greenville treaty line and lacking several townships of covering the area of the present Randolph county. But shortly after the treaty of St. Mary's, by which so much new land was acquired, all of this territory lying east of the second meridian was designated by the name of Delaware county. Delaware county, originally, therefore, was an immense country, comprising the area of half a dozen of the counties as we now know them. It is not to be understood that this original Delaware county was a civil organization; it was merely a name applied, for convenience, to a large and rather indefinitely bounded country which had not yet been settled sufficiently to be given county government. This territory, though without government of its own, nevertheless was under the jurisdiction of laws and courts. To this end it was provided that the organized counties lying adjacent should extend the operation of their civil government into the unorganized area. Accordingly the pioneers who came to the county before 1827 looked to Winchester in Randolph county or to Newcastle in Henry county as the seat of local government. When the first election was held within the limits of the present Delaware county, in 1824, the twenty odd ballots cast for the respective presidential candidates were carried to Winchester to be counted.

When Henry county was organized in 1821, the act of legislature spoke of the area to be included in the new county as "the south part of Delaware." By successive acts of the legislature, the area of the original Delaware county was rapidly reduced. A county was organized as soon as the extension of population justified it, and by 1827 the settlers on the block of country north of Henry and west of Randolph counties were given a county government. In forming a new county it was the duty of the legislature to define the boundaries, to fix the time when independent county government should begin, to appoint commissioners to locate the seat of justice, to designate the place of meeting and the first duties of the board of justices, and provide such a schedule as was necessary to transfer government from adjacent counties to the new one. The act of the legislature providing these things was signed by the governor January 26, 1827, and the new county of Delaware was to begin its official existence on the following April 1st.

Muncie Becomes County Seat.

The commissioners named in the act who should locate the county seat were: Elias Poston, of Rush county; Jonathan Platts, of Wayne county; Martin Adkins, of Decatur county; Joseph Craft, of Henry county, and William Smith, of Randolph county. The sheriff of Randolph county was instructed to inform the men of their appointment, and if he followed the usual custom in such proceedings he rode on horseback to the appointee's home in each county. The home of Goldsmith C. Gilbert was designated as the meeting place of the commissioners. On June 11, 1827, the commissioners, or a majority of them, assembled at the Gilbert home on White river, where a few settlers had already located on the site now covered by Muncie. There can be no doubt that the meeting of the commissioners was a notable occasion in the history of the county and particularly of the little settlement which was urging its claims as the seat of county government. As strangers from other counties, and clothed in official dignity, the commissioners must have been entertained with every mark of respect, and the Gilbert home, during their stay, was the center around which all thought and activities of the settlers revolved.

The commissioners examined sites and deliberated with the citizens about a week. It was finally decided to locate the county seat on the south side of White river, almost exactly in the center of the county from east to west. The commissioners were led to this decision by the donations of three men, who offered a site for the county government. They were Goldsmith C. Gilbert, Lemuel G. Jackson and William Brown. In donating land, it was their desire, as stated in the proposal, to aid "in improving the town of Muncietown, the county seat for the county aforesaid, and for the benefit and use of the said county of Delaware in the erection of public buildings and for other public purposes." Accordingly, the donated lands were transferred to the ownership of the county and were to be sold by the county officials and the proceeds applied to the buildings and other improvements essential to a county seat. The donations, which centered where the court house now stands on the public square, were as follows: Gilbert's, containing 20.09 acres, was bounded on the south by a line through the center of the court house and extending east along the alley between Washington and Main streets to the west side of Jefferson street; thence north to North street; from North street west to the river; and along the course of the river southwest until it meets a line drawn west from the center of the court house. Jackson's donation, 9.72 acres, was bounded on the east by Walnut street, on the south by Jackson street as far west as Gharkey street, and on the west by Gharkey street to Water street where it joined the Gilbert tract. Brown's donation, containing 20 acres, and lying east of Jackson's, was bounded on the south by Adams street, extending east almost to Elm street, and by a line from that point north to a point east of the court house.

These donations comprised the original area of the town of Muncie. The public square was set aside for the site of county buildings and grounds, and the rest of the land was laid off in streets and platted into lots. A certain proportion of these lots were given to the original donors, but the rest were sold by the county. The deed for the Jackson donation was executed in December, 1828, but the other two not until 1831.

Beginning of County Government.

The organizing act had provided that county government should begin April 1, 1827. It happened that this day was Sunday, so the election was postponed until Monday, when the citizens assembled and chose their first county officers. William Van Matre was elected to perform all the duties of clerk, recorder and auditor. John Rees and Lewis Rees were elected associate judges; Peter Nolin sheriff; and Valentine Gibson, Aaron Stout and Enoch Nation, justices of the peace. At that time and until the law was changed in 1831, the business of the county was performed by the justices of the peace constituting a board for that purpose.

The first meeting of the board of justices was held, in accordance with the organic act, at the house of Goldsmith C. Gilbert. This house is said to have stood on the site of the present jail. The meeting was held on the first Monday of August, 1827, and such business was transacted as was essential to set the county government in action.

County Buildings.

Naturally one of the first matters to which the county officials turned their attention was the building of a home for the county government. Courts and the meetings of the board of justices were held in private residences for a year after organization. In 1828 the board contracted for the building of a court house, and it was completed probably by the spring of 1829. It was considered a large and rather splendid building at the time. It was a two-story frame building, 20 by 40 feet, with a gable fronting the street; had a door to each of the court rooms into which the lower floor was divided, while the upper floor, lighted by half a dozen windows, was for the use of the county officials who kept offices of record. The square-hewn timbers of this building were mortised and fitted together by

means of wooden pins. A few years' use and this court house became
dilapidated. It caught fire once, and after the citizens had taken much
trouble in extinguishing the blaze they felt regretful that they had not
allowed the old structure to suffer the destruction it deserved.

Early in 1837 the board of commissioners adopted plans and awarded
a contract for a new court house. Delaware county had progressed far
since the organization of the county, and now it was proposed to erect
a building that would be an ornament to the county for years to come.
Until its removal to make place for the present court house, about twenty
years ago, the brick structure built in the thirties did service as court house.
The building was modeled after that of the court house of Wayne county
at Centerville. After the contract had been awarded and the work begun by
the contractor, Morgan John, it was decided to alter the plans and make
a better building, which would also cost more. The contractor, however,
agreed to do the work at the original terms, but failed before it was
completed. The court house was built forty-five feet square and twenty-
eight feet high, with nothing to relieve the rectangular plainness of the
whole except the cupola. There was a rather flat kind of hip roof, and from
the center rose this cupola, with no special character to distinguish it as
a thing of beauty or of architectural elevation. A bell, mounted in the
cupola, summoned the court sessions. In 1848 the old bell was removed and
placed in the seminary building, and a new bell, weighing a thousand pounds,
was hung in the tower on June 30.

The court house square in those days was a rather unattractive place,
if it may be judged from contemporaneous descriptions. One picturesque
feature, however, was a large elm tree standing at the southwest corner.
It was one of the few survivors of the wilderness, and had been permitted
to stand probably on account of its beauty and size. Here the farmers
used to hitch their teams and gather in little groups in the shade to gossip
and discuss such affairs as then concerned home and state. Along in the
forties the Muncie paper has much to say about the bareness and unkempt
conditions surrounding the square. The square should be fenced, shade
trees should be planted both in the square and along the streets. Some
response to this advice is found in the news item of April, 1847, that the
citizens on the south and east sides of the square had planted shade trees.

The old court house was not ample for the accommodation of the county
officers. In 1848 the county board advertised for bids on a brick building,
46 by 26 feet and 20 feet high, to contain offices for treasurer, recorder,
clerk and auditor. James L. Russey, John Jack and Jacob H. Wysor were
given the contract to erect this building, their bid being $2,696.46. It was
built on the ground just north of the court house, and continued in use
as originally designed until the present court house was built. The builders

had been granted the privilege of constructing a basement story to the county offices, and for a nominal sum had the use of it for fifty years. The interesting feature of their contract was this: "No liquors to be sold on the premises, except beer or cider, either for purposes of sickness or medicine."

Long before the decision was reached to build a new court house, in keeping with the county's growth and prosperity, the necessity for such a building had become plain, and both the press and the public were urging the replacing of, the old with a modern court house.* But the old brick building stood nearly half a century. Finally the county board, reinforcing their own judgment with what they deemed the best public opinion, awarded a contract, on November 6, 1884, to Charles Pearce and Company, for the building of a stone court house to cost $195,618.46. At their meeting on January 15 previous, the commissioners had decided to build the court house, and had advertised for bids. The old county offices were sold to D. C. Mitchell for ten dollars, but there were no bidders for the court house and it had to be removed at the expense of the county. During the building of the new court house Walling Hall was used for court room and clerk's office.

May 6, 1885, the first issue of court house bonds, consisting of ninety-eight $1,000 bonds, bearing five per cent interest, was sold to a Chicago firm. The bonds were dated May 15, 1885, and the first one was due in 1895. There was much discussion at this time concerning the wisdom of building such an expensive court house, many claiming that the county was already burdened. However, the financial condition of the county in July, 1885, showed the following: $2,000 outstanding bonds for free

---

*Volney Willson, opposing the purpose of the commissioners to build a new court house, argued from the economic and civil burdens on the citizens, and incidentally gave some descriptions of the first court house in 1837:

"Taking into consideration the financial condition of this county, its $89,000 of present indebtedness, the twenty odd thousand dollars' indebtedness of Muncie, in all this talk about a new court house that, as is advocated, we must build at no distant day, there is only one thing that this day entitles it to a moment's thought, viz., the safety of the county records.

"The first court house, the first court room, that I was in, was, I think, of hewn logs, weatherboarded, standing on the lot where Walling Hall now stands. I saw then inside of what, I suppose, was the bar, a part of the room enclosed with fencing boards, and an improvised kind of rostrum with a board for a shelf elevated on the front to place books, behind which was a bench, on which sat Samuel Bigger, judge, and Eleazer Coffeen and William McCormick, associates. Samuel W. Harlan, clerk, was sitting at a low table writing. William Gilbert, sheriff, or nipresent. Inside the pen sat Oliver H. Smith, afterwards known as the intellectual giant of the West; Cabel B. Smith, David Kilgore, Andrew Kennedy, John Elliott, Charles Test, —— Minchell, with Samuel W. Parker, prosecuting attorney, all sitting on benches and Jonathan Smith's best split-lolte chairs. I did not hear them say a word about ventilation or the sanitary condition of the court room, but they did look like a body of men that knew how 'Eli got there'! and they were going, and did as the history of Indiana and their biographies show; so much for the Delaware court room of 1837."—Muncie Daily News, March 28, 1884.

gravel roads; $5,000 bonds for new jail, $2,000 coming due June 1, 1886. Aside from the court house bond issue it was claimed that the county could have paid all its indebtedness and left a surplus. The court house bonds not coming to maturity until 1895, when ten thousand dollars would be payable in each of the following five years, and thereafter twelve thousand dollars each year for four years, it was argued that the county could never be in a better situation financially to expend money on public improvements.

July 23, 1885, was a day long to be remembered in Delaware county. The laying of the cornerstone of the new court house was celebrated as an event that concerned every citizen and an occasion that should bring thousands of people together. The Most Worshipful Grand Master Mason of Indiana officiated at the ceremony. The procession down the streets to the public square was headed by the U. D. Camps of the I. O. O. F. of Muncie and adjoining towns; then followed the Knight Templar commanderies; the G. A. R. posts of Muncie, New Corner, Eaton, Selma, Yorktown, Reeds and Hartford; Delaware Lodge A. F. & A. M., and speakers, officials and citizens. A rain marred the ceremony somewhat, and during its progress the news came of General Grant's long expected death.

It required two years to complete the present court house. It was accepted and the contractors released on August 13, 1887. The total cost was $227,250.06. After twenty years it is not possible to regard the court house with the same unqualified admiration that was expressed concerning it when first built. And yet the Delaware county court house for some years was claimed to be one of the finest court houses in the state, and it was a building certain to be praised by visitors. Built in the style of the French Renaissance, on ground dimensions 155 by 110 feet, on the plan of a Greek cross, the structure conformed to the most approved ideas of that time in county architecture and among court houses that were erected two decades ago it has few superiors. One of the features in the construction of both the high school building and the court house (the former built several years before the latter) is the high basement, equivalent almost to a full story, and requiring a tower of steps as direct approaches to the main floor. Much was said in praise of this feature at the time. In conformity with the predominating architectural style, the exterior presents great detail in supporting buttresses, projecting corners, heavy window casements, and other variety of ornamental construction. The office and court rooms are spacious and conveniently arranged, although the stairways are narrow and the general interior aspect unattractive. Notwithstanding some obvious defects, the court house has admirably served its purpose, and for twenty years has been a credit to Delaware county.

Jails.

It is related that the first sheriffs of Delaware county confined their prisoners by chaining them and fastening the chain by staple to one of the big puncheons in their house. But soon after the county was organized a lock-up was constructed, though so inadequate for its purposes that it soon became a subject for the grand jury's report. Another jail was constructed, which stood, according to a pioneer's account, just west of the court house and on the public square. The jail occupied the south end and the sheriff's residence the north end of the brick two-story house. The jail was of logs, surrounded with brick, and on the second floor was evidence of the extension of an obsolete custom into Delaware county—a room for the confinement of debtors.

This jail was insecure and jail deliveries caused general agitation for a better one. In December, 1858, following an examination of the jail at Winchester, Randolph county, by members of the board, the commissioners decided upon an issue of bonds to the amount of $3,000 to supplement the regular revenues in paying for the jail. In February, 1859, contracts were let for the building of the iron at $4,780, and for the construction of the building at $4,467. The jail was completed during the latter part of 1859. Two lots, lying north of the public square, were purchased for the site of the jail in March, 1859.

This jail was used a little more than twenty years. January 21, 1882, the commissioners let a contract at $20,000 for building a new jail to Myers and Company, of Fort Wayne. The work was completed in the fall of 1883.

CHAPTER VIII.

THE COURTS: BENCH AND BAR.

The day following the approval of the act organizing Delaware county another law received the signature of the governor, by which "the county of Delaware shall be, and the same is, hereby attached to the county of Randolph, for judicial purposes, any law to the contrary notwithstanding." It is highly creditable to American civilization, even in face of the apparent lawlessness of the western mining camps and cattle ranges, that means to secure the operation of regular justice have been instituted almost at the same time with the establishment of the community itself. It seems that the instinct for law and order began to operate as soon as a few settlers came together and found themselves outside the jurisdiction of organized counties.

Delaware county had settlers for seven years before organization of civil government. The legislature had seen to it that the jurisdiction of the courts should be extended over the territory acquired by the Indian treaty, and to that end had provided that the unorganized country should be attached for all judicial purposes to the organized county next adjacent. It is likely that causes arose among the first settlers that called for judicial determination. The litigants must have gone to Winchester or some neighboring county seat to obtain a court hearing, or in case of criminal action it is probable that the sheriff of Randolph county rode over with a warrant and, arresting the offender, took him back to Winchester to await trial.

A clause of the organic act provided that all suits and cases, originating within the limits of the county, and which had been begun before the organization of the county, should be continued to final settlement as though the formation of civil government had not taken place. What cases there were in this county before its organization, and any account of them cannot be presented at this time.

But with the organization of the county a complete judicial machinery was provided. The first judicial district to which Delaware county was attached covered a goodly share of the state's area, extending to the north line. In 1833 Delaware county was a part of the sixth circuit, the other counties being Randolph, Wayne, Union, Fayette, Rush, Henry, Grant. By an act approved January 28, 1839, the eleventh judicial circuit was formed, consisting of Delaware, Grant, Blackford, Wells, Adams, Jay and Randolph. Two associate judges were elected in April, 1827, John Rees and Lewis Rees, and with the president judge of the district, Miles C. Eggleston, the circuit court of Delaware county was complete. Its first session was held May 19, 1828. Gilbert's house was the court room, and it is probable that on that bright spring day the spectators, jurymen and others interested were unable to crowd into the court room and stood around by the door or leaned over the log window-sill, intent to hear all the proceedings of this first court in the new county. For many years court sessions were among the big events of the year. The arrival of the judge created much excitement, and among the children he must have been regarded with the awe due a mighty potentate. Accompanying the judge on his rounds of the circuit were the lawyers. The practice in one locality was very small, and had the lawyer depended on that alone he would have faced starvation even sooner than the traditions of the profession guarantee. Therefore, the attorneys followed the peregrinations of the court, and in the larger circuits this meant traveling over a number of counties. They rode to the county seat on horseback, with their briefs and copy of statutes in their saddlebags, and putting up at the town tavern they increased the social activity of the county seat and along with their serious business added a gayety that no other occasions of the year could produce.

After Judge Eggleston had called court to order on that day in May, 1828, the sheriff produced the panel of grand jurors, who he had summoned for that term. Familiar names are in that list. They were as follows:

Lemuel G. Jackson (foreman),	Henry Mosburgh,
joseph Thornburg,	Robert Gibson,
Jonathan Beason,	Lewis Van Sickle,
John Wardwick,	Thomas Thornburg,
William Stewart,	Joel J. Spencer,
Richard Thornburg.	Samuel McCulloch.

The grand jury returned one indictment, against John Downing for assault and battery. The latter pleaded guilty, and was fined one dollar. The regular prosecutor was Cyrus Finch, from Randolph county, but in his absence Septimus Smith was appointed and received five dollars for his services. The two associate judges each received two dollars, and the bailiff, Joab Vestal, got one dollar. The business of the court was all completed in one day and then adjourned until "court in course."

One of the lawyers, in fact, the first one to be admitted to practice at this term of court, was Charles H. Test. Three years later he was elected president judge of the judicial circuit, comprising a considerable part of the state, reaching almost from the Ohio to the northern boundary line, and his subsequent career placed him among the leaders of the Indiana bar. The only other applicant to be admitted to practice was James Rariden.

The dockets of the circuit courts in those days were not crowded with cases that must be hastened to settlement. Indeed, the course of justice might have proceeded very leisurely and no great wrong would have been done to anyone. When the second term of court came around, in November, 1828, only one associate judge was found to be present on the opening day; court adjourned. Next day none of the judges were present, and Sheriff Nolin declared court adjourned till the following day. That day came, and still no judges. In pursuance of the law, the sheriff then adjourned court till the next term. We can imagine the sheriff, assuming all the dignity of his position, spoke in loud tones the legal formula prescribed for the occasion, and thus impressed the few who had assembled about the court room with the full solemnity of the occasion.

When court convened in May, 1829, four applicants were present desiring admission to the bar, which was granted. They were: Martin M. Ray, Calvin Fletcher, Hiram Brown and Oliver H. Smith. The first named was prosecuting attorney for the third judicial circuit, which then comprised this county, and it fell to him to prosecute the case of assault and battery against James Liston. This was the first jury trial in the county, and the verdict was "not guilty."

Another incident of this session was told by Minus Turner, being reported in the History of 1881, as follows: "The grand jury held its session in the blacksmith shop on Walnut street, owned by David Baggs, the present (1881) site of the Episcopal church. The petit jury met under a buckeye tree which stood on the northwest corner of the public square. This tree was a very fine one. It had a large grapevine on it, which, with the tree's foliage, afforded a very good shade. I remember quite well, when the grand jury convened in the old blacksmith shop, that I climbed up in the loft and saw one of the jurymen creep out between the logs and go over into the hazel brush and purchase some whiskey of a fellow who was selling it there. He then crept back again, and soon became very noisy and unmanageable. His case was reported to the judge and he was fined ten dollars. Then he pulled out a long leathern sack, made, perhaps, of buckskin, which had all kinds of silver money it. It broke, and the money spilled out on the floor. He told them to take what they wanted and hand the rest back. He was a very peculiar man, and when under the influence of liquor he did not care what he said or did. His name was James Jackson, and he was familiarly known as 'Devil Jim.' He went into the Gilbert bar room, after being fined, purchased a glass of whiskey, and chewed the glass up between his teeth. I remember seeing him—chewing and damning, with his mouth bleeding."

Probate Court.

The associate judges of the circuit court by virtue of their office transacted all the probate business of the county without the formal organization of a probate court until 1830. In March of that year these associate judges constituted and held the first session of the probate court. At the first session of the circuit court, above described, the pioneer William Blount had been appointed guardian for his daughter's child, William Blount Jones. At the first regular session of the probate court the only business was the appointment of Joseph Bennett as guardian of the infant heirs of Catherine Bennett, deceased. In 1834 the associate judges ceased to act, ex-officio, as probate judges, and on the 10th of November John Tomlinson became first regular probate judge. He held the office ten years, being succeeded by Enoch Nation. Samuel W. Harlan became judge of probate in 1852, and in the same year the court was abolished and its jurisdiction transferred to the court of common pleas. Only the older generation in Delaware county know anything of any of these courts. The court of common pleas, which also had some civil jurisdiction, was abolished in 1873, and since that year probate business has been a branch of the circuit court. During the existence of the court of common pleas it had but three incumbents—Judges Walter March, J. H. Haynes and J. J. Cheeney, the last being in office when the court was abolished.

The Personnel of the Bar.

Of the attorneys who, at the various early sessions of the circuit court, were admitted to practice in Delaware county, but few maintained a regular office at Muncie or in the county, the reasons for this having already been referred to. The list of lawyers who in the course of eighty years have been admitted to practice in the county presents a notable array —representing every phase of legal ability and some of the finest types of lawyers known in the history of the Indiana bar. The claim has often been advanced. with much reason to support it, that outside of Indianapolis no county in the state has better reason to be proud of its bar, past and present, than Delaware.

The two attorneys who were granted permission to practice at the first session of the court, in May, 1828, had already achieved considerable success and later rose to prominence. Charles H. Test, son of an Indiana circuit judge during 1817-19, had begun the practice of law at Lawrenceburg in 1821 and during subsequent years practiced in many counties of the state. For a number of years subsequent to 1838 he resided in Wayne county, and finally removed to Indianapolis. He was secretary of state from 1849 to 1853. He lived to an advanced age. James Rariden, the second member of the Delaware county bar, was a native of Kentucky, and studied law in Wayne county during the second decade of the century. He resided in Wayne county until his death in 1856, though practicing in the courts of the surrounding counties. He was a man of sturdy character, self-molded, genuine but with little polish, and though his education was limited his opinion was sought as frequently as that of a more brilliant man. He was a strong Whig, and was an able member of the constitu- tional convention of 1850.

The prosecuting attorney of the circuit at the time Delaware county was organized was Cyrus Finch, and it will be remembered that he was absent from the first session of court and Septimus Smith was appointed prosecutor. Death detained him from his duties at this time, for his health had begun to fail in 1826, and he died in January, 1828.

Septimus Smith was a brother of Oliver H. Smith, so prominent in the history of Delaware county. He and Cyrus Finch, both talented lawyers, had founded the *Western Times* at Centerville, Wayne county, about 1827, and their editorials obtained more than local recognition. Smith died of consumption during the twenties.

Following Cyrus Finch as prosecutor for the circuit came Martin M. Ray, who was admitted to practice in this county in May, 1829. He had located for practice in Wayne county that year, and continued practice there until 1845, when he moved to Indianapolis and lived till his death in 1869. A native of Kentucky, he had come to Indiana shortly after its admission to the Union, and before taking up the practice of law followed the vocations of cabinet-maker, merchant and banker. He was a brother of J. B. Ray, who was governor of Indiana at the time Delaware county was organized.

The career of Oliver H. Smith, who was admitted to practice at the November session in 1829, has touched Delaware county more intimately in other ways than in the law. It is only necessary to state here that he had practiced law in Indiana since 1820. His "Reminiscences of Early Indiana Trials and Sketches" (1858) is valuable for its numerous descrip- tions of the early courts and the anecdotes and characterizations of the prominent lawyers of the state during the first half of the century.

John S. Newman was another Wayne county lawyer who followed the circuit judge in his rounds and occasionally took a case in Muncie. He had lived in Wayne county from 1807, was admitted to the bar there in 1828, continued in active practice until 1860, and from then until his death in 1882 lived in Indianapolis, where he was president of the Merchants National Bank.

At the time he presented his application to practice in Delaware county, Caleb B. Smith was a resident of Connersville. He was among the fore- most of Indiana's early lawyers, and having the gift of eloquence he rose to high positions in public life, serving as speaker of the Indiana legislature and representing his district in Congress for six years.

In the copy of the Muncietonian, for July 15, 1837, several lawyers are among the advertisers. None of those who have been mentioned ever located in Muncie, but at the time of the above publication there were several offices near the public square where the public could consult with one learned in the law. Those advertising as lawyers under that date were: Thomas C. Anthony, with "office on Main street near the tan yard"; Joseph Anthony, residing "between Miller's tan yard and Exchange Hotel"; W. G. Renner, office "on Main street, nearly opposite clerk's office"; and Andrew Kennedy, in "Willard's brick building," corner Main and Walnut. These probably were the only lawyers residing in Muncie, but one of the best known and brightest attorneys practicing in this and neighboring courts at that time was David Kilgore, whose home was in Yorktown. Born in Harrison county, Kentucky, April 3, 1804, David Kilgore accompanied the family to Franklin county, Indiana, in 1819, and soon turned his attention to the study of the law. In April, 1830, he arrived in Delaware county, after a weary tramp across the country, carrying four law books. He taught one of the first schools in Mt. Pleasant township, bought a tract of wild land, and at the same time began practicing law. To supplement his share of the meager practice then offered in this county, he was admitted to the Henry county bar in 1832 and also probably practiced in other counties of the circuit. He was pre-eminent as a trial lawyer. His rise to prominence was rapid. In 1832 he entered the legislature as a Whig, and in 1856, just after the organization of the Republican party, he was elected speaker of the house. He was the first circuit judge to come from Delaware county. His circuit, when he was elected in 1839, comprised the counties of Randolph, Delaware, Grant, Jay, Blackford, Madison, Wells and Adams. After representing this county in the constitutional convention of 1851, he went to the legislature in 1855, and from there to Congress, where he was a member of the house during the years just preceding the outbreak of the war. Always successful in his profession, and acquiring a large estate, he is honored especially for his prominence in public affairs. He was best known as "Judge Kilgore," and his record on the bench during the flourishing days of the big circuit was in keeping with his achievements at a more mature period. He died suddenly, January 23, 1879, leaving a number of descendants in Delaware county.

Joseph Anthony served as circuit judge during 1853-58. Though a lawyer by profession, he was best known to the people of Muncie for many years as proprietor of the tavern that once stood where the Kirby House is now, and was called, part of the time at least, the Eastern Hotel. It was a two-story frame structure, and was not removed until the present

Kirby House was built. Mr. Anthony was a cripple, and for many years was a familiar character in the county.

T. C. Anthony is remembered as a brilliant man, an orator with natural eloquence, refined by classic learning. He practiced a few years in Muncie, but never acquired great prominence.

Only a few of the early lawyers were college-trained men. Most of them educated themselves, reading law in the office of an attorney who had already advanced to some success in practice. Probably no lawyer in Delaware county during the first two decades of its history was more influential than Andrew Kennedy, and yet he had little training for his profession and only took it up after he had tried the two occupations of farming and blacksmithing. Born at Dayton, Ohio, in 1810, he spent most of his youth on a farm, receiving a meager education, and without showing any decided bent in life. Finally, at Connersville, where he was living with a Quaker aunt, he began the reading of law under the instruction of Caleb B. Smith and Samuel Parker, and was admitted to practice in 1830 and soon after came to Muncie. Besides a successful practice, according to the standards of the time and place, he became prominent in politics. He became state representative in 1835, state senator in 1838; in 1841 was the only Democrat elected from Indiana to Congress, and in 1847 was the nominee of his party (which was then dominant in the state) for United States senator. But in the smallpox scourge which caused an almost precipitate adjournment of the legislature Mr. Kennedy fell a victim, and died December 31, 1847, before the assembly had taken up his election. He had two sons, both born in Muncie. Evender C. was a brilliant soldier, later became a physician, and was noted for his literary productions. Philip A. B. Kennedy also served in the Civil war, and then followed his father's profession, finding success in practice and becoming well known in public life. Andrew Kennedy's daughter married Dr. Milton James, late of Muncie.

Among other lawyers admitted to practice in the county but who did not have residence, was Jehu T. Elliott, one of Henry county's ablest lawyers. He was admitted to the bar in 1834 and from that time until his death in 1876 held numerous positions of honor and trust, serving as circuit judge from 1854 to 1864, and in the latter year was elevated to the supreme bench of the state. Altogether, he served eighteen years as circuit judge and six years on the supreme bench.

In September, 1839, Jacob B. Julian was admitted to practice in this county. He had been born in Wayne county in 1815, being left an orphan at an early age, had gained a good education by persistent effort, and at the age of twenty-four was admitted to the bar. He lived in Muncie but eight months, and after his return to Wayne county soon took rank as a leading lawyer. He was president of a bank at Centerville, and after moving to Indianapolis became judge of the circuit court. His younger brother, George W. Julian, was one of the most distinguished lawyers and political leaders that Indiana produced.

John Marshall was another attorney practicing in 1846, but nothing definite is now known of his career.

Walter March for a number of years before his death ranked as the oldest member of the Delaware county bar. He honored his position as dean by brilliant ability, a career notable by its achievements in practice and in public affairs, and a most wholesome and distinguished personal character. His fellow members of the bar, at the time of his death, voiced their appreciation of his life in resolutions from which the following sentences indicate his standing in his profession: "His was a positive character. . . . His opinions were his own. . . . As an advocate one of his chief characteristics was force and strength in argument and illustration. . . . As counselor he was careful, discreet and thoroughly trustworthy. Industrious, pertinacious, energetic and thorough, he well earned the distinction he achieved as a lawyer." He had been admitted to the bar at the March term of the Delaware district court in 1841, and continued in active practice until his death, March 31, 1883. In the constitutional convention of 1851 he was senatorial delegate, and soon afterward became first judge of the newly established court of common pleas. He served in the legislature, and had a large practice in all the courts. In the constitutional convention he took a chief part in simplifying the civil code, and as one of the ablest lawyers of Indiana he impressed his learning enduringly on the fundamental laws of the state.

Joseph S. Buckles, who was one of the leaders of the Democratic party in this county and who edited the Delaware County Democrat for a time in 1844, came to Muncie during the thirties, while Andrew Kennedy was one of the few lawyers then located here. He studied law in the latter's office, and was admitted to practice in 1841. Soon after resigning the editorship of the Democrat he was elected prosecuting attorney, and from 1849 to 1853 represented his district in the state senate. In 1859 he became judge of the eleventh judicial circuit, and continued on the bench two terms. He resumed practice in 1870, in partnership with John W. Ryan, who had just been admitted. He was strong as an advocate and was a natural lawyer, effective in presentation of arguments. Possessed of a tenacious memory, he absorbed knowledge without the industrious application to books demanded of others.

William Brotherton, whose death occurred in Muncie July 11, 1888, was a Virginian by birth, and was admitted to the bar in Xenia, Ohio, in 1851, at the age of twenty-five. He came to Muncie and was admitted to practice in the same year, in 1855 being elected prosecuting attorney. He served in the legislature, and as a lawyer he took high rank in the county.

Thomas J. Blount, who died September 29, 1890, while still a young man, was admitted to the bar April 29, 1873. Though he had only a common school education, he began a career of much promise. An injury received early in life brought misfortune to him when he was in his prime, and he died respected by bench and bar and the entire county.

Thomas J. Sample was one of the attorneys named in the "Indiana Annual Register and Pocket Manual" for 1845 as residing in this county, the other names appearing alongside of his being: A. Kennedy, Walter March, Levi L. Hunter, J. S. Buckles, Joseph Anthony, John Marshall, James H. Swaar, Warren Stewart, W. H. Withers, Joseph Underwood, J. H. Mellett, William Brady, J. H. Haynes, S. W. Harlan. Judge Sample, as he was best known, was a native of Maryland, lived for some years in Connersville and then in Yorktown, this county, where he was a merchant with O. H. Smith, and while selling goods took up the study of law. Admitted to the bar in 1842, he came to Muncie in 1843, and was engaged in practice for many years.

In the death of Carlton E. Shipley, July 31, 1905, the Delaware county bar lost its oldest member, he having been admitted to the bar fifty-three years previous to his demise. He had lived in Muncie with brief exceptions since 1843, had been a clerk and school teacher, read law with J. S. Buckles, was one of the early district attorneys of the common pleas distriet, and besides practicing law with a success merited by his active and comprehensive learning, he often took part in enterprises that have become important in the county's welfare.

February 5, 1902, occurred the death of Judge Orlando J. Lotz, aged fifty-one years. His service on the circuit and appellate bench marks him as one of the most distinguished jurists of the Delaware county bar. He was the first judge of the forty-sixth judicial circuit, serving from March, 1885, until 1892, when he was elected to the appellate court, a position he adorned until his death. His rank in his profession and as a citizen is happily summarized in the following expressions written at the time of his death. Judge Lotz was the "possessor of a good heart, a clean and vigorous intellect, an honest intent, a clean record"; was "a close reasoner, a stiff but fair fighter in party politics, a hard student of the law, a profound observer of passing events, an excellent judge."

The attorneys and law firms in Muncie in 1881 were:

Blount & Templer (Blount died in 1891).
W. Brotherton.*

* Deceased.

Buckles & Ryan (J. S. Buckles dead).
W. H. N. Cooper.
R. S. Gregory.
John A. Keener.*
George H. Koons.
Lotz (O. J.) & Kilgore (C. W.) (Lotz dead—Kilgore retired).
McMahan & McCulloch (McMahan dead).
C. L. Nedsker.
Nellett (J. E.) & Dunn (both left years ago).
C. W. Noore.*
W. W. Orr.
T. F. Rose (retired).
J. F. Sanders.*
C. E. Shipley.*
S. D. Spooner (left here several years ago).*
R. C. Summer (left here several years ago).*
T. S. & J. T. Walterhouse.
L. F. Wilson (left here years ago).*
W. H. Younce, at Eaton.*

Ten years later, in 1891, there were many additions to the personnel of the bar. Several of those named in the preceding list had died or removed from the county or taken up other lines of business. Some thirteen still continued among the active attorneys. The list for 1891 follows:

A. W. Brady.
William R. Brotherton.
W. H. N. Cooper.
G. W. Cromer.
J. F. Duckwall (retired).
Ellis (Frank) & Walterhouse (J. T.).
Gregory & Silverburg (A. C.).
R. C. Griffith.
W. H. Hickman.
John A. Keener.
George H. Koons.
W. P. Koons.
J. G. Leffler.
C. L. Nedsker.
J. F. Neredith.
C. W. Noore.
Charles Nation.
W. W. Orr.
T. F. Rose.
Ryan (J. W.) & Thompson (W. A.).
J. F. Sanders.
A. L. Shideler.

* Deceased.

Spence & Cranor.
G. W. Stephenson.
C. B. Templer.
E. R. Templer.
J. N. Templer.
Rollin Warner.
J. S. Alldredge, Yorktown (retired).
Otho Dowden, Albany.*
Liberty Ginn, Wheeling.
R. N. Snodgrass, Reed.
W. H. Younce, Eaton.*

In the present year (1907) the list of attorneys reveals many changes and additions. Fully half of those named in 1881 have been summoned by death and their places taken by a younger generation. The rewards and activities of business and affairs have drawn not a few away from active practice, so that some of those enrolled in the present Delaware county bar never receive a case nor prepare a brief for a client. This is one of the changes in the legal profession noted by Ambassador Bryce in a review of changes in American life since he issued his "American Commonwealth." Lawyers are more and more drawn into business affairs, or combine business enterprise with legal practice.

The members of the legal profession of Delaware county at this time, 1907, are the following:

J. W. Baird.
Claude C. Ball.
    Ball (W. L.) & Needham (A. E.).
    Bingham (James), White (W. F.) & Haymond (W. T.).
    E. E. Botkin.
    J. W. Brissey.
    W. R. Brotherton.
    W. H. N. Cooper.
    G. W. Cromer.
    C. W. Dearth.
    Frank Ellis.
    Feely (Frank) & Redkey (H. S.).
    J. N. Fitch.
    Walter Gray.
    Gray (N. H.) & Kent (F. J.).
    Gregory & Lotz (W. J.).
    Griffith (R. C.) & Ross (J. A.),
    L. A. Guthrie.
    Sheldon Hickman.
    W. H. Hickman.
    George H. Koons.

* Deceased.

W. P. Koons.
J. O. Lewellen.
McClellan (F. F.) & Hensel (D. D.).
A. D. McKinley.
John McPhee.
J. F. Mann.
Mann & Lesh (Lincoln).
Ward Marshall.
C. L. Medsker.
J. F. Meredith.
R. W. Monroe.
H. G. Murphy.
Orr & Orr (W. W. & H. H.).
T. S. Owen.
R. W. Ross.
Ryman (W. L.) & Long (Harry).
Ryan & Ryan (J. W. & T. L.).
Shaw (F. A.) & Selleck (S. B.).
Silverburg (A. C.) & Bracken (Leonidas).
A. J. Smith.
N. N. Spence.
A. O. Stanley.
R. E. Stevenson.
C. A. Taughinbaugh.
C. B. Templer.
E. R. Templer.*
Thompson & Thompson (W. A. & W. H.).
A. M. Van Nuys.
H. E. Walk.
J. T. Walterhouse.
Rollin Warner.
O. G. Weir.
Ira Young.
A. M. Poland, Albany.
M. J. Fenwick, Daleville.
O. M. Rearick, Eaton.

Muncie Bar Association.

There have been several organizations among the lawyers of this county, though none with great permanence or vitality. In September, 1905, a meeting was held in Muncie which resulted in the formation of the Muncie Bar Association, which is now the principal organization of members of the bar in the county. Articles of incorporation for the association were recorded October 2, 1905, and Article I of the constitution names those who should be considered charter members. They are: Ralph S. Gregory, Joseph G. Leffler, Walter L. Ball, Edward M. White, William A. Thompson, James Bingham, J. Frank Mann, George H. Koons, Frank

*Deceased.

Ellis, Frederick F. McClellan. The first set of officers were elected February 24, 1906, namely: R. S. Gregory, president; George H. Koons, first vice president; Frank Ellis, second vice president; F. F. McClellan, secretary; E. N. White, treasurer. In May, 1907, the officers elected were: George H. Koons, president; A. C. Silverburg, first vice president; William W. Orr, second vice president; W. T. Haymond, secretary; Frank Ellis, treasurer.

Before the November election of 1906 the association passed resolutions favoring a constitutional amendment raising the requirements for admission to the bar to the same plane as the regulations safeguarding the practice of medicine and other professions. Along the line of these recommendations the principal objects of the association may be said to lie. In admitting members to its own ranks, it has endeavored to pass upon the qualifications of the applicants, and thus in a measure set a standard for the entire Muncie bar.

CHAPTER IX.

EARLY TRANSPORTATION AND COMMUNICATION.

The subject of means of communication has recurred again and again in this history of the settlement of the county. Ever since men began to live on the earth, the matter of getting from place to place and carrying things from place to place has been of vital importance; and the higher the development of society the more perfected become the methods of such communication. It would be impossible to conceive of our country in its present state of civilization without the facilities for movement and transportation which men have devised and improved during the last hundred years. It seems that the principal efforts of men are now bent upon the problems presented in the moving of material and persons from place to place. Transportation is the key to population and also to industry. Cities grow in population accordingly as they are conveniently situated with respect to transportation facilities, or as these facilities are supplied to them when needed. An agricultural district, however fertile, will be improved to the point of profitable production only when means are at hand or are provided by which the products may be readily and economically taken away to the markets. It is little wonder, therefore, in view of the importance of the general subject of communication, that special phases of the subject are at the present time the greatest vital issues, both economically and politically, before the American people. From this point of view the subject has only incidental pertinence to the history of Delaware county; but in studying the general theme of communication this county affords as many concrete examples as any other. The county has had its Indian trails, its paths blazed through the woods, its primitive state and local highways, its toll roads, its free pikes, its limited water routes, its railroads, and its electric lines, each accompanying a new degree of development and marking a new era in the welfare of the people.

Before civilization introduced scientific road-making, wild animals were the markers and surveyors of roads. The narrow, deep-worn and wavering path through the woods, indicating the route of the wild animal between its lair and the spring where it quenched its thirst, was the course which the Indian, and later the white man, took in going through the woods. Thus animals were the first road makers, and blazed the way for their immediate successors, the roving Indians. The latter would naturally extend and connect the trails into certain long avenues of travel across the country, which they would follow in making their pilgrimages from one hunting ground to another or for their war expeditions.

Several of these trails existed in Delaware county long before white man set his foot here. The Indian villages near Muncie, Yorktown and and on the Mississinewa were centers from which radiated numerous trails, several of which had been used so long, were so well marked, that they possessed the importance of "trunk lines" among Indian tribes and as such were widely known and used.

National Road.

After Rome had conquered a nation she made roads to that nation; so she was in easy communication with the remotest parts of her empire, and they with her. It is said that when Congress first met after the war for independence, under the new constitution, the lack of good roads was much commented upon by congressmen and citizens generally, and various schemes suggested to meet the want. The settlers of Kentucky and Tennessee on leaving Virginia had plunged into the wilderness and had followed Indian traces across the mountains to their new homes. With the acquisition of the Northwest Territory, extending the territory of the United States to the Mississippi, it was recognized that, in order to make this region an integral part of the nation, effective communication must be established between all parts. This necessity was emphasized when, owing to the absence of water communication over the mountains, the Kentucky settlements were practically isolated from the eastern states and threatened to secede from the Union because the government was about to allow Spain to close up the mouth of the Mississippi to American commerce. Before any definite steps had been taken by the government toward connecting the east and west by roads, the Louisiana purchase had widened our boundaries to the Pacific, and, with an energetic and far-seeing statesman like Jefferson as president, the matter of binding these vast areas closely together became a vital question. In the act of Congress, in 1802, by which Ohio was permitted to enter the Union, it was provided that two percent of the proceeds of the sales of the public lands within her limits should be held and applied in the construction of a public highway "from the navigable waters emptying into the Atlantic" to a point on the Ohio river and within the state of Ohio. A like provision was made in the act admitting Indiana to the Union.

The proposition for a National road first took practical shape in 1806, when an act passed Congress authorizing the appointment of three commissioners to lay out a road from Cumberland, at the head waters of the Potomac in Maryland, to the state of Ohio. This was the beginning of the old Cumberland or National Road, the only highway of its kind ever wholly constructed by the government of the United States, and a road of wonderful significance in the development of the west and the greatest and one of the most romantic highways of America. The National Road, though it was finally extended across Indiana, did not touch Delaware county. But it was none the less a factor in the county's history. The existence of this road, and the part it played in directing and distributing emigrants, should be thoroughly understood and constantly kept in mind in the discussion of the early settlement of the county. The detailed history of the "Old Pike" has been told, in a most interesting way, by T. B. Searight, under the title given. He generalizes the importance of the highway in the following language: "It was a highway at once so grand and imposing, an artery so largely instrumental in promoting the early growth and development of our coun_ try's wonderful resources, so influential in strengthening the bonds of the American Union, and at the same time so replete with important events and interesting incidents, that the writer of these pages has long cherished a hope that some capable hand would write its history and collect and pre- serve its legends. . . . From the time it was thrown open to the public, in the year 1818, until the coming of railroads west of the Alleghany mountains in 1852, the National Road was the one great highway over which passed the bulk of trade and travel, and the mails between the east and west. Its numerous and stately stone bridges with handsomely turned arches, its iron mile posts and its old iron gates, attest the skill of the work- men engaged on its construction, and to this day remain enduring monu- ments of its grandeur and solidity." For most parts of the west and a great part of the southwest, this was the most direct route to Washington city. For this reason all classes of people from this part of the country having business at the national capital made it their highway to and from Washing- ton. The stage coaches for the carrying of the mails and passengers were taxed to their utmost capacity, and their numbers were constantly increased. So great was the travel that it is said as many as twenty-five coaches could be seen leaving Wheeling at one time for Cumberland, and as many would leave Cumberland for the west. The freight traffic was even greater. Long and almost interminable lines of huge Conestoga wagons, drawn by four, six and sometimes by eight horses, with their loads of flour, bacon, tobacco, whisky, butter and other products, on their eastward way, or with loads of every imaginable kind of merchandise when bound for the west, might be seen at all times. Then, too, there might be seen similar trains of wagons laden with the household effects of those who were seeking new homes in the west. Thousands of cattle, horses and hogs were wending their way to the eastern markets. "From morning till night," is the description given by another observer, "there was a continual rumble of wheels, and when the rush was greatest there was never a minute that wagons were not in sight, and as a rule one company of wagons was closely followed by another." By day the eye could follow the route from horizon to horizon by the clouds of dust raised by the crowding caravans, and by night the camp fires blazed at brief intervals as far as one could see.

Here was the great avenue by which the western expansion that began after the war of 1812 advanced into all the fertile places of the west. For some years the National Road carried the travelers only to the eastern borders of Ohio, and thence they followed the course of the Ohio to their destination, usually continuing the journey by boats, but also by overland journeys. "It is estimated," says Mr. Searight, "that two-fifths of the trade and travel of the road were diverted at Brownsville [in southwest Pennsylvania, near Pittsburg] and fell into the channel furnished at that point by the slack water improvement of the Monongahela river, and a like proportion descended the Ohio river from Wheeling, and the remaining fifth continued on the road to Columbus, Ohio, and points further west. . . .' Before the era of railroads Columbus derived its chief business from the National Road."

In 1827 the National Road was completed through Wayne county, Indiana. The tide of migration, much smaller in volume, to be true, than when it passed over the mountains, was by this means brought within the state of Indiana before being dispersed to individual settlements. Herein we see the principal reason why so large a proportion of the early settlers of this county came from Wayne county. In 1829 Congress appropriated money for opening the road, eighty feet wide, east and west from Indianapolis, and in the course of the next few years about a million dollars was appropriated for continuing the road in Indiana. But before the road was completed through this state, and could assume such importance as it enjoyed along the eastern sections, the railroad era had come and the decline of overland travel was rapid. A rhetorical picture of this change was drawn by Mr. Yancey in Congress in 1846, when he spoke of the road as follows: "When the project of the Cumberland road was first conceived, it was needed as a great highway for the trade and produce of the fertile west to find an outlet on the Atlantic coast. The mountains intervened between the Ohio valley and the Atlantic coast. Steam, not then in such general use as now, had not rendered the upper Ohio navigable; railroads had not clamped as now with iron bands the trembling earth. The rich produce of the soil found its way to market over rough roads upon the lumbering wagons, and the traveler when jolted over them at the rate of sixty miles a day considered himself as doing a good day's work. How different now! The broad Ohio is navigable by hundreds of floating palaces, propelled against its current by fire-breathing engines. The mountains are pierced by railroads and canals. . . . Why, sir, men are behind the times with this old road. The spirit of the age is on. ward. Thirty miles an hour on land; a thousand miles a minute on Pro. fessor Morse's wires is deemed ordinary speed. On this road, my friend from Indiana (Mr. Owen), informs me that during parts of the year he has been able to make but two miles an hour on horseback."

State Geologist Blatchley of Indiana relates what became of the Indiana division of the road. "In 1848 the road was turned over to the respective states through which it passed. In 1850 the Wayne County Turnpike Com. pany was organized and took over, under a charter granted by the state, that portion of the road, twenty-two miles in length, within that county. The company then graveled the road and operated it as a toll road until 1890-94, when it was purchased by the several townships through which it passed and made free from tolls. From Wayne county westward the road passed through Henry, Hancock, Marion, Hendricks, Putnam, Clay and Vigo coun. ties. That portion in Henry county was secured by a private corporation, graveled, and made a toll road about 1853. In 1849 the Central Plank Road Company, composed of prominent citizens of Marion and Hendricks counties, was granted that portion of the road extending from the east line of Hancock county to the west line of Putnam county, for the purpose of constructing a plank road. With the granting of it to these several corporations the old National Road as a public institution, fostered by the nation or the state, ceased to be. It had fulfilled its high purpose, and was superseded by bet. ter things which owed to it their coming." As a final tribute to this old high. way it "carried thousands of population and millions of wealth into the west, and more than any other material structure in the land served to harmonize and strengthen, if not save, the Union."

So we saw, during the twenties and thirties, a constant stream of popu. lation flowing along the Old Pike by way of Wayne county. Very early in the history of Delaware county, probably at the time the county was organ. ized, there was a well defined and well traveled road leading from Richmond northwest into this county. This was not a way that had been marked by surveyors and legally "made," but was blazed through by the settlers, each party that came that way adding some little improvement—cutting down a few trees, wearing away the undergrowth, dropping logs in the low places— by which this became a highroad.

Erie Canal.

One other route by which the population of the east found outlet to the new west calls for mention here, though it was of very much less importance to the settlement of Delaware county. In 1825 the Erie Canal, after eight

years in building, was opened to traffic, and the waters of Lake Erie flowed across the state of New York into the Hudson river. The land-bound commerce of the Atlantic seaboard found, in this direction, outlet to the eager west, and, borne along the same channel, the grain harvests of the inland were brought to the markets of the world. It was no uncommon thing for fifty ark-like boats, loaded with passengers and freight, to depart from the eastern terminus of the Erie canal in a single day, passing to the west at the rate of four miles an hour. Before the waters were turned into the "Big Ditch" the toilsome urging of creaking wagon had not carried a fraction of the commerce that passed along this waterway.

The Erie canal not only gave a tremendous impetus to western expansion and development, but it partly changed its direction. Before 1825 the trend of westward emigration had been down the Ohio valley. The great water courses were fringed with settlements, when the inland country was still an unbroken wilderness. The regions bordering the riverways and great lakes were populous before a tree had been felled for a settler's cabin on the fertile prairies and woodland of northern Indiana and southern Michigan. A map of the highways of traffic of the United States in the year 1825 shows a network of routes along the Ohio valley, but very few north of the watershed into the great lakes. The homeseekers who traveled across Lake Erie to its western end would, on their arrival at Detroit, find one generally used road to the west. That led southwest to Monroe, up the valley of the Maumee, past Defiance, Ohio, through Fort Wayne, Indiana, thence northwesterly around the lower bend of Lake Michigan to Chicago or farther west. Fort Wayne, built on the site of the old Indian trading post, Kekionga, already mentioned, had been a recognized station and meeting point for a century, and was, in 1825, the converging point for several other roads leading from different points along the Ohio river. This northern road undoubtedly had its influence on the settlement of counties as far south as Delaware, but it was small as compared with the National Road. In the northwestern counties of Indiana, however, the larger part of first settlers came in by way of Fort Wayne. Since the land office at which was entered most of the land now comprising this county was located at Fort Wayne, that town had an important relation to the early settlers. Many who came to the county by way of the southern route were compelled to make the journey of seventy miles to Fort Wayne in order to secure land certificates. It is related that to avoid this trouble the settlers often employed some one who was familiar with the procedure at the land office and who became a sort of agent for the settlers in negotiating their land entries, making the trip frequently between this county and the seat of the land office.

Of the shorter roads—branches of the two principal routes just described—first of all should be mentioned what was known as "the government road," which is the oldest road defined by white men in Delaware county. It was laid out in the early twenties in order to provide a route by which the Delawares, who had ceded their land at the treaty of St. Mary's, might be moved to the west. Its course approximated very closely the present line of the Big Four Railroad, running from Greenville, Ohio, through Randolph county at Union City, passing in the vicinity of Smithfield and leaving the county at the present site of Daleville.

CHAPTER X.

TURNPIKES AND RAILROADS.

About the time the last public lands were entered and Delaware county became "settled up," the economic needs of the people called for improved facilities of transportation; at the same time the material resources of the county had increased far enough to warrant such public improvements. The closest kind of relation existed between the welfare of the farmer and the kind of roads over which to carry crops to market. The condition of the early roads and their effect on the farmer are described by Prof. E. Tucker in a former history.

"In making the roads," says this writer, "men drove through the woods, cutting out brush and poles when necessary, to admit the passage of the wagon. . . . And when actual roads, intended for traveling by wagon, began to be made, it was done simply by removing some of the largest trees, so as to give room for the wagon to pass, and building bridges, not merely over the streams, but across the swamps also, of poles or logs laid crosswise of the track. Sometimes earth was thrown upon the bridge thus made, but oftener the poles or the logs were entirely bare. And the wagons would thump and bounce in passing over that wonderful highway. . . . Pork and grain had to be hauled to Cincinnati, and instances were frequent in which pork brought only $1.50 net in the market. Some of the early settlers of Wayne county tried in vain to sell as good wheat as ever grew for twelve and a half cents a bushel to pay their taxes." With prices so low and the roads so wretched, there were times when it did not pay to haul the farm products to market. Even when prices for grains were high, and farmers' wagons followed in close succession on the way to market, the roads were such that men and teams both were exhausted by the time they had gone twenty miles. It is not strange, then, that the problem of transportation was the most vexatious and the one that received the most consideration among the first generation of citizens.

Canals, turnpikes and railroads were discussed and planned for in every part of the middle west during the forties. In 1842 a charter was granted the Muncietown and Fort Wayne Railroad for a line seventy-five miles long between those two points. But it was nearly thirty years before a railroad was constructed over this route. In a Muncie paper of December, 1843, is a discussion of the proposed turnpike road from Muncie northwest to the Wabash river at Lagro. The building of railroads was earnestly pleaded for in press and in public meeting, but shortly before the beginning of the railroad era in the actual construction of lines through the west there was inaugurated another movement designed to meet the urgent necessity for better transportation. This was the "plank road idea," an innovation which, according to a recent contributor to the Indiana Magazine of History, originated in Russia, thence found its way to Canada, and from there into the northern United States. "In a country," continues this writer, "where timber was not merely abundant, but an actual incumbrance, the conversion of this timber into a solid road as smooth as a floor was a captivating proposition, and the fever caught and spread. In no place was there better reason for it spreading than in Indiana, and accordingly for nearly ten years (through the fifties) we had the plank road era. The promise of immediate returns was, presumably, sufficient to attract capital, and the state very wisely handed over the new movement to the capitalists. From 1848 we find laws authorizing corporations to take possession of the existing roads, to convert them into plank roads, and to erect and maintain toll houses for revenue along the same."

The first laws with reference to gravel roads are found in 1858. Plank roads had only a brief vogue, and yet were a very useful institution while they lasted. It was found that these roads endured the stress of weather and heavy travel only a few years, and unless expensive repairs were undertaken the warping and working loose of the planks soon put these highways in a condition of almost impassability. About the close of the fifties legislation on plank roads ceases. Another reason for the decadence of plank roads was the appearance of the long awaited railroads west of the Alleghanies. With the construction of the Bellefontaine and Indianapolis Railroad through Delaware county its farmers found that their produce could be shipped almost from their doors, and that a haul of a few miles at most was all that was necessary to place their grain and stock in easy reach of market. So the former agitation for long commercial thoroughfares ceased, and thereafter the improvement of roads became largely a matter of local concern and usually was undertaken by private capital.

Toll Roads.

The first toll road in Delaware county was constructed by the Cambridge City, Simons Creek and Muncie Turnpike Company during the early fifties. This connected Cambridge City in Wayne county with Muncie.

But the era of gravel pikes, with their toll houses and sweep poles, such as are familiar to the majority of people in Delaware county, did not really begin until the late sixties. By that time conditions had vastly changed in the county over those that existed when the road question was first agitated.

The county was no longer a pioneer region, with its resources largely unde-veloped, and the people dependent on their constant industry to obtain means of living and the conveniences of civilization. Notwithstanding the economic drain caused by the war, all parts of the country were prosperous, and the foundation of solid wealth had been laid beyond the power of temporary reverses to destroy. Accordingly, it seems that the principal avenue in which many citizens of Delaware county turned their energies and capital during the latter part of the sixties wa- the construction of gravel turnpikes. As a result we find, in 1880, when the agitation for free gravel roads was at its height, a Muncie editor referring proudly to the "eleven grand" turnpike roads radiating in every direction from Muncie, bringing people to market from all parts of the county, and removing the usual obstacles to trade of muddy roads. A brief history of each of these roads follows:

Muncie and Middletown: Muncie and Middletown Turnpike Company organized June 29, 1866, directors being James W. Heath, Asher Storer, J. E. Wilcoxen, William J. Hurst, James A. Tomlinson. The following year an extension of the road was authorized. The road was eight and a third miles long, extending southwest from Muncie into the south part of Salem township.

Blountsville and Morristown: Chartered in December, 1866, by thir-teen persons resident of Henry, Delaware and Randolph counties. Road to run from Blountsville, in Henry county, touching the southeast corner of Delaware county, to Morristown, in Randolph county.

Range Line road: Articles of association filed May 16, 1867. The road was made three miles long, extending from the Middletown and Muncie road south on the range line, to the northeast corner of section 24, Salem township.

Middletown and Range Line: This road was built from the northeast corner of section 24 on the east line of Salem township, west four miles, then south to the county line. The right of way was granted in June, 1867, and the articles of association were filed the same month.

Muncie and Wheeling: This road, for which right of way was granted by the county commissioners in June, 1867, extends in a northwesterly direc-tion through the northern part of Center, the western part of Hamilton and the northeast corner of Harrison to Washington township, and thence north to Wheeling. It is about thirteen miles in length.

Middletown and Daleville: The company was organized and the right of way granted in June, 1867, for a north and south road four and one-quar-ter miles long, running from the Daleville pike, at the northeast corner of section 7 in Salem township, south over the line into Henry county.

Daleville and Bell Creek: Right of way granted in June, 1867. Con-structed from Daleville east to Middletown avenue.

Muncie and New Burlington: Constructed by a company organized in 1867, a total length of ten and three-quarters miles, from Muncie southeast to New Burlington.

Muncie and Yorktown: The company was granted right of way in

January, 1868, and the pike was laid from the west edge of Muncie along what is called State avenue to the bridge over Buck creek at Yorktown.

Jackson Street: This road, for which right of way was given in January, 1868, was made a toll road from the Calvert street bridge at Muncie to the west line of the county, a distance of ten and a quarter miles.

Muncie and Bethel: The Bethel pike runs from the northwest corner of Muncie in a northwesterly direction ten and one-half miles to the west side of Harrison township. The right of way was granted in March, 1869.

Muncie and Eaton: This pike, beginning at a point between sections 34 and 35 of Center township, and extending north about eight miles to the Mississinewa river at Eaton, was built by the Studebaker Turnpike Company, and is generally known as the Studebaker pike. The right of way was granted in March, 1867.

Muncie and Granville: Constructed nine and one-half miles in length northeast through Center, Hamilton, Delaware townships to Granville.

Centennial: This pike, so named because right of way was granted in June, 1876, begins on the Granville pike on the north side of Muncie and runs east along the south side of sections 2 and 1 in Center township, continuing in the same direction into Liberty township.

Junction: Right of way granted March, 1868. Commenced on east side of county near Windsor, thence west along State road to intersection with New Burlington pike.

Smithfield and Albany: Right of way granted April, 1869.

Mississinewa and Albany: Right of way, April, 1869.

Mississinewa Valley: Right of way granted April, 1869.

Muncie and Smithfield: Right of way granted April, 1869, for road extending from New Burlington pike, about a mile east of Muncie, across the Helvie bridge, and, with several turns, to a point north of Smithfield.

Blountsville and Smithfield: Right of way granted July, 1869. Road extended from southwest corner of section 23 in Perry township north to junction with Winchester and Muncie road.

New Corner: This turnpike company filed articles of association in December, 1870, for the purpose of constructing a road from the west side of Hamilton township, at a point on the south side of section 7, in a northwest direction, by angling route, to New Corner.

Free Roads.

The gravel pikes of Delaware county were of tremendous advantage to the material welfare of the county. They brought city and country together, and, as elsewhere stated, were specially beneficial to the city of Muncie. These roads began the work of consolidating the people and their interests, which the later development of interurban railroads has brought, seemingly, to the highest state of perfection.

But within twenty years after the beginning of the turnpike era in Delaware county there appeared a change of sentiment regarding those roads. It is a popular belief of long standing that the highways are free and public, and only in return for a great general benefit will the people allow an individual or corporation to tax the use of such highways. Accordingly, during the late seventies and early eighties Indiana experienced an agitation for free pikes, resulting finally in a law by which each county, when the people so willed, could purchase the pikes and open them to all, toll free.

The question first came to vote in Delaware county in April, 1882, at which time 2,252 votes were cast against free roads and 1,514 in favor of the purchase. This did not settle the matter, however, and the following year a special election was appointed to decide. A warm campaign was indulged in by the advocates and opponents of free pikes. One of the strongest supporters of the free-pike movement was R. S. Gregory of Muncie. In a speech made before the election he declared that according to the sworn reports of the directors of the toll roads the 107 miles of pike in the county had, in the past five years to June 30, 1883, received in tolls, $83,714.68, or $778.68 to each mile. Of this the officers received as salaries $13,281.84, or $2,656.57 each year, and expended in maintaining the roads $30,000, leaving $53,625 to be divided among stockholders and officers. "There are 45 miles of free gravel roads," asserted Mr. Gregory, "and an assessment of one cent per hundred dollars has kept them up for one year, at a cost of $1,000 for 45 miles. Now, the Granville, Studebaker, Central, Wheeling and Bethel pikes, which aggregate the same distance—45 miles—collect annually $8,-697.02 in tolls, or $7,697.02 more than it takes to keep up the same length of free gravel roads."

Though public sentiment in favor of free pikes was strong at that time and in subsequent years has grown until the toll road would hardly be tolerated, yet the vote taken on the question in 1883 was so evenly divided that the county commissioners could not regard the decision as compelling immediate action, and in fact the complete abolishment of the toll-gate was delayed for nearly twenty years. The vote was taken October 20, 1883, when 1,901 ballots were cast in favor of purchasing the toll pikes, and 1,778 against, free roads winning by a majority of 123. As an example of the opposition expressed in certain parts of the county to free roads there was a movement in the following year among several townships for secession from the county. Washington, Union and Niles talked annexation to Blackford county, while Perry and Liberty developed a similar current of opposition. The amount required to buy the pikes was assessed against the townships. The residents of the north tier of townships would be benefited in only a small measure by the pikes of Delaware county, and if they used those of Blackford county they would be compelled to pay toll, so it was natural that they should object to paying for free roads in their own county, which they would use infrequently and in addition be burdened with tolls every time they used the roads of the adjoining county. Another cause of grievance originating about the same time with the free-pike question was the building of the court house at Muncie. The buying of the pikes and the building of a new court house were undertakings that were discussed with a great deal of ardor among the people of Delaware county, and they continued to be tender subjects until they were quite obscured in the excitement of the gas boom.

RAILROADS.

In some reminiscences contributed to a former history, Thomas S. Neely stated his recollections of the agitation for railroad connection in Delaware county as follows: "At the time of the agitation of the railroad question over the country I thought we ought to have a railroad connection, but did not know where, only that we ought to have an outlet. The canal outlet had failed in reaching us, and railroads were beginning to excite the people. I got up a paper and carried it around among the people, but it failed to excite any particular interest. Dr. Anthony laughed at me, and said it was foolishness to talk about such a thing. A meeting, however, was called at the court house, and brought out a large crowd. Several persons addressed the meeting, myself among them. No one had any idea where the road was to be built, or to what point. Some suggested Fort Wayne in order to connect with the canal. I was not favorable to that project, because it would freeze up. Others suggested Connersville, Indianapolis, Bellefontaine, etc. I was most in favor of a connection to the southwestward, to join the Madison and Indianapolis Railroad, then just completed and put in running order. We were finally solicited by parties both from Fort Wayne and from Bellefontaine, and finally agreed to join with the Bellefontaine folks. The manner in which the question was settled was indeed novel. At a meeting at the Ohio state line, where Union City is now located—there was no Union City then—after a number of speeches had been delivered from a box, it was decided to put the question to the test, and all who were favorable to Bellefontaine were directed to take one side of the door as they filed out, and those favorable to other points, the other side. It was found that the Bellefontaine folks had two-thirds majority over all. O. H. Smith was made the first president of the road. Thus was formed and permanently located a road destined to become one of the most important roads in the northwest."

The interesting part about this statement is the division of opinion among the people as to what points should be connected by the railroad. Indianapolis, as the capital, had obvious advantages, while Fort Wayne's later importance as a center of trunk lines was foreshadowed in the claims thus early advanced for a line from Muncie to that point. For the route that was finally selected there was much appropriateness in the title "Great Central Railroad to the West," for the Indianapolis and Bellefontaine was a section of a line of transportation that penetrated the heart of the country west of the Alleghanies.*

One of the results of the session of the Indiana legislature in 1847-48 was a charter for the first railroad line planned through east central Indiana, and named the Indianapolis and Bellefontaine Railroad. The co-operation of the citizens of the counties along the line was assumed as essential to the success of the enterprise, and special provisions in the charter directed what should be done in each county. From that time on the building of the road was the principal theme of conversation. Every official action whether taken by the local boards of directors or directed by that distant power of capital in the east was discussed in the press and by the people. On learning what the road would cost per mile, many shook their heads and doubted that it would ever pay. When construction actually began, interest increased, an interesting proof of their interest being shown in the eagerness with which the people sought information about all details of the railroad. The "T-rail" was just coming into favor with railroads at that time, superseding the old "strap rail" with which such of the settlers were familiar as had been in the east after railroad construction began, and a Muncie newspaper devoted half a column to an explanation of this new form of rail, and a section of one was also exhibited in one of the local stores.

In July, 1848, three directors were elected from Delaware county as local representatives on the railroad board, namely, S. P. Anthony, who became the active agent of the railroad in this county; David Kilgore and James Truitt. At the same time John Black, of Delaware township, was appointed appraiser of the real estate to be subscribed in stock to the railroad

---

*Indiana Signal, September 30, 1848: By an advertisement in to-day's paper, it will be seen that a new and direct route of communication from central and western Indiana, with our eastern cities, is about being opened, by means of a railroad from Indianapolis to Bellefontaine, at which latter place it intersects the road from Sandusky to Cincinnati, now doing so much to divert the trade of the West to the North. By means of the road now being constructed from Pittsburgh to Bellefontaine, the entire trade of this fertile region, the products of which have been sent South, may be secured to Philadelphia. It is quite certain, that if it be not thus secured, it must inevitably go to New York and Boston.

By reference to the map, it will be seen that the line is almost a direct one from Philadelphia, by Harrisburgh, Pittsburgh and Bellefontaine, to Indianapolis, the capital of Indiana,—the total difference being six hundred and seventy miles. The distance from Pittsburgh to Bellefontaine is two hundred and five miles, from Bellefontaine to Indianapolis, one hundred and thirty-five. From Indianapolis to Madison, on the Ohio river, a distance of eighty miles, there is a road completed (and yielding a profit of fourteen per cent.), the stock of which is mostly owned in New York and Boston. From Indianapolis to Terre Haute, on the Wabash river, the distance is seventy miles; and a company is now constructing a road between these points. Thus it will be perceived, that there are now four railroad companies, actively engaged on this great Central Western or "Backbone" route from Pittsburgh to Terre Haute,—thus making the entire railroad distance from Philadelphia to St. Louis only eight hundred and twenty-five miles. All must see in what a commanding position in regard to the Western trade the completion of this route must place Philadelphia.

company. It was decided that the railroad within Indiana should be constructed in three sections—from Indianapolis to Pendleton; Pendleton to Muncie; Muncie to the Ohio line.

In April, 1849, the enthusiasm of the people for a railroad was put to a practical test when a vote was taken on whether the county should tax itself to produce twelve thousand dollars to be subscribed for stock in the proposed railroad. Many persons thought the proposed subscription an enormous sum, burdensome to the people and unwise as a matter of civil policy. It was understood that the tax should not exceed one dollar on the hundred valuation, only half of it to be collected the first year. The vote on the question whether the county should be taxed for railroad stock resulted in some figures that tell at a glance the division of sentiment in various parts of the county. Here is the tabulated vote:

Township—	For	Against	Township—	For	Against
Salem	6	73	Union	7	43
Mt. Pleasant	106	7	Perry	27	28
Harrison	8	55	Liberty	111	8
Washington	4	4	Delaware	92	8
Monroe	18	48	Niles	6	8
Center	176	53			
Hamilton	33	10	Total	594	344
			Majority	250	

Clearly, the townships that would not be traversed by the proposed railroad were not altogether willing to tax themselves for its building. In the case of a few townships it would seem that the citizens cared little about the question either pro or con. Salem, for some reason or other, showed the most vigorous opposition, though the road was to cross the township. Center gave the largest majority for the measure, but not the largest percent of her total vote, Mount Pleasant and Liberty both surpassing in that respect.

Happily, the railroad was built in a little more than contract time, and the people who had lived in the county a quarter of a century and never known any better means of transportation than a heavy wagon and an ox or horse team, were soon gratified in knowing that an iron road bound them with the outside world and swiftly moving trains were ready to carry every production of the soil and shop to the market where it was most needed. It was provided that the first installment of the money subscribed by the county should be paid when the road had been cleared and grubbed continuously from Indianapolis to the east line of this county. This payment was made in May, 1850. In June of the same year the grading contract between Yorktown and Muncie was let, and during the summer tracklaying proceeded between the capital and Pendleton. October 8, 1850, a celebration, in which all the surrounding country took part, marked the completion of the road to Pendleton. In July it had been decided that the Muncie depot should be located on land owned by C. F. Willard, south of the public square. In

February, 1851, the second installment of subscription by Delaware county was paid, this marking the completion of the grading and bridging to the east line of the county. In June, 1852, the final installment had been paid, at which time the line was supposed to be completed, ready for cars, from Indianapolis to Muncie. The pioneer William Jackson thus described the completion of the road: "On the 17th of June, 1852, there was a grand rail- road celebration here, made in honor of the completion of the Bellefontaine Railroad from Indianapolis to Muncie. A train of cars was made up here, and run down to Indianapolis and back. The cars were open flat cars, and had been provided with plank seats, etc. A large crowd of people came in from points on the line between Indianapolis and Muncie. Before they ar- rived, however, and during their stay, a very heavy rain set in, which some- what dampened their clothes and bodies, but not their ardor, as the celebra- tion was a very enthusiastic one. Many were soaked through and through, and the ladies and children presented a sad and ludicrous sight."

During the winter of 1852-53 the road was completed to the Ohio line. The name Indianapolis and Bellefontaine was retained several years, and it then became known as the Indianapolis, Cleveland and Pittsburg Railroad. When the road was officially consolidated with the Ohio line in 1859, its property in Indiana, comprising not only the road bed and right of way but buildings and rolling stock, was appraised at only $4,300 per mile, the 20.36 miles in Delaware county aggregating a value of $87,548. In 1868, after consolidation with the Cleveland, Columbus and Cincinnati, the name became the Cleveland, Columbus, Cincinnati and Indianapolis Railroad, which soon became better known as "The Bee Line." Doubtless, few people remember the exact time when this appellation was superseded by "The Big Four," the name now borne by the first railroad built within the county. June 26, 1889, was the date of the completion of the transactions by which the Bee Line was consolidated with the Indianapolis and St. Louis and the Cincin- nati, Indianapolis and Chicago railroads, thus creating the Cleveland, Cin- cinnati, Chicago and St. Louis, or the "Big Four Route." Only recently the Big Four became part of a still greater consolidation, and is now known as one of the New York Central Lines, though still retaining the familiar designation to distinguish it from other lines of the system.

The stock of the Indianapolis and Bellefontaine, originally bought and held by Delaware county, was transferred in December, 1853, as a bonus to the then nascent Fort Wayne and Southern Railroad, an equal amount of the latter's stock being given to the county in return.

Lake Erie and Western Lines.

Since the construction of the first railroad, the construction of other roads through and into Delaware county has been marked by many vicissitudes. The names of the different roads have been changed so many times that probably few persons could recall them all in order, and changes of management and ownership have been equally frequent. Comprised in what are now the Lake Erie and Western (a part of the New York Central system) are the roads that were built thirty-five years ago and were then known as the Fort Wayne, Muncie and Cincinnati, and the Lafayette, Bloomington and Muncie.

The road from Fort Wayne to Muncie has existed in the words of charters for over sixty years. Several Delaware county citizens were connected' with the company which proposed to construct the road during the fifties. But no practical progress was made until the latter sixties. The late David T. Haines of Muncie was more closely identified with the building of this north and south road through the county than any other local party. He was secretary of the old Fort Wayne and Southern Railroad Co. from 1853 until its failure in 1855. He continued as custodian of the archives, stocks, bonds and books of the company until 1868, when they were turned over to John C. Parker, who attempted to build the road from Jeffersonville to Muncie. After the failure of this project Mr. Haines assisted in organizing the company that built the road from Fort Wayne to Muncie, of which he was secretary and treasurer, and later became vice president of the road until it was sold to Charles H. Dalton and others. He was elected an official in 1868 of the company that constructed the road from Connersville to Fort Wayne. The various railroad companies that projected roads to run from Muncie in a southerly direction to Cincinnati were finally consolidated as the Fort Wayne, Muncie and Cincinnati, and Mr. Haines became secretary and a director of this line. He was one of the committee that bought the iron for the road and the first six engines. Practically he had personal charge of the construction of the road, and it was largely due to his exertions that the company was able to complete the work at the time specified in order to receive the subsidy promised by Delaware and Wells counties. He continued with the company until the sale of the line in 1872. The freight office of the Fort Wayne road was opened in Muncie in February, 1869. Somewhat later this road became known as the Fort Wayne, Cincinnati and Louisville, and in 1889 it was popularly styled "The Muncie Route." In June, 1890, the road was transferred to Calvin Brice and associates and made a division of the Lake Erie and Western.

It is profitless to follow the intricacies of ownership and control of this north and south route. The main point of interest for the history of Delaware county is that it was constructed about 1870, and from that date became a definite influence in the development of that part of the county through which it passed. In Union township the advent of this road fixed Eaton as a permanent town, incidentally causing the decline of Granville

on the east and Wheeling on the west. The opening of a depot at the south
edge of the township was the most important event in the history of Shideler,
a little village that has continued as a shipping point and small commercial
center ever since. Royerton was likewise stimulated to growth by the coming of the railroad. The Fort Wayne road increased the importance of
Muncie as a central town of the county, and was one of the very large
factors that determined the commercial and industrial prestige of the county
seat during the years preceding the gas boom.

The road from Muncie to Lafayette was completed in January, 1876,
the first train to Lafayette carrying forty Muncie citizens, making the trip
February 1. The county had voted in August, 1869, a subsidy of $150,000
for the construction of this road. This was at first known as the Lafayette,
Bloomington and Muncie road. From Muncie it was extended eastward
through Albany and finally completed to Sandusky, and took the name of
Lake Erie and Western.

Thus by the early eighties Delaware county was intersected by three
different lines of railroad, all centering in Muncie and radiating from there
in six directions. Too much emphasis cannot be placed on the part played by
these early railroad lines in distributing population and starting towns and
industries. The first railroad in 1852 found two towns in the county already
established—Muncie and Yorktown—and it immediately put those towns,
especially Muncie, on a new basis and started their development. Furthermore, the railroad was the cause of the founding of the town of Selma, at
the same time destroying Smithfield's prospects; and revived the village of
Daleville, which had nearly lost its identity since the pioneer days. Twenty
years later the Fort Wayne route gave the main impetus to the growth of
Eaton, Shideler, Royerton, Cowan and Oakville. Then a few years later
the original line of the Lake Erie, besides contributing to the growing importance of Muncie, gave Albany its much needed railroad communication,
and gave occasion for the establishment of such stations (each with some industrial and commercial features) as Reed's, Cammack, DeSoto.

These were all the railroad lines Delaware county had until within the
past ten years. The history of these later lines belongs to another chapter
and to another period of development.

CHAPTER XI.

BEGINNING OF CENTERS OF POPULATION.

The grouping of population and the formation of village centers, being the result of natural growth, are more interesting than the organization of townships and the marking of boundary lines, which is an artificial process. Every town has an individual history, like that of Muncie, and so requires a special article to describe it. But it is impossible to indicate in a general way the beginnings of a typical village community, and mention the causes and effects that characterize the history of all such centers. The process may be described thus: A fertile and well situated region receives its share of the immigration then overflowing the country. Assuming that they are pioneers, it will be almost a necessity that most of them till the soil, even though combining that with another occupation. Or, if a timbered region, those engaged in the lumber industry would be subject to the same centralizing influences. If the settlement was on a much traveled thoroughfare, one or perhaps more of the pioneer houses would be opened for the entertainment of the transient public. On the banks of a stream some one constructs a saw mill or a grist mill. At some convenient and central point a settler with commercial instincts will open a stock of goods such as will supply the other settlers and immigrants. A postoffice comes next, the postmaster very likely being the merchant or tavern-keeper. A physician, looking for a location, is pleased with the conditions and occupies a cabin near the store or inn. A carpenter or other mechanic is more accessible to his patronage if he lives near the postoffice or other common gathering point. If the schoolhouse of the district has not already been built, it is probable that it will be placed at the increasingly central site. And the first church is a natural addition. Already this nucleus of settlement is a village in embryo, and in the natural course of development a variety of enterprises will center there; the mechanical, the manufacturing, the commercial and the professional departments of human labor will be grouped together for the purpose of efficiency and convenience. By such accretions of population, by diversification of industry, by natural advantages of location and the improvement of means of transportation, this community in time becomes organized as a village, and, with continued prosperity, as a city.

Sometimes the development is arrested at a particular stage. The village remains a village, the hamlet ceases to grow, and we have a center of population without special business, industrial or civic development. Then there are instances in this county of retrogression. A locality that could once be dignified with name of village has disintegrated under the stress of rivalry from other centers or from other causes, and is now little more than a place and a name.

The centers of Delaware county illustrate all these processes. As a general observation it may be said that during the early years, when communication was primitive and isolation quite complete even between localities separated by a few miles, the tendency was toward centralization in numerous hamlets and small villages. But in keeping with the economic development for which the past century was noted, and especially because of the improvement of all forms of transportation, the barriers against easy communication with all parts of the county were thrown down, and the best situated centers grew and flourished at the expense of the smaller centers, which gradually dwindled into comparative insignificance. Nothing has done more to accelerate this movement than the establishment of rural free delivery and the extension of telephone service into the country districts. The post-office was the central point of community life, and remoteness from its privileges was a severe privation. Rural delivery has made every home a post-office, puts each home in daily contact with the world, and while it is destroying provincialism and isolation, it is effecting a wholesome distribution of population. The telephone has been equally and similarly beneficial. And the introduction into Indiana of the system of public transportation of school children to and from school removes another powerful incentive to village life. When weak districts may be consolidated and a large, well graded and modern union school be provided convenient and accessible to every child in the enlarged school area, families no longer find it necessary "to move to town in order to educate their children."

SMITHFIELD AND SELMA.

Reference to original land entries of Liberty township shows that William Blunt Sr., Wilder Potter, David Branson and others located along the White river during 1822-1823. What is said to have been the first mill in the township was constructed on the river in section 22 about 1828 by David Stout, and shortly afterward another mill was located in the same vicinity. In a few years the north bank of the river exhibited a wide clearing, on which were half a dozen or more houses, and already it was distinguished as a "local habitation" with a name. A merchant opened a stock of goods, and on one of the early thoroughfares from the east leading through this locality, it is likely that one or more houses were regularly opened for the entertainment of travelers. Thus Smithfield became a village, and some years later, when it was platted by the proprietors, David Stout and William Duncan, these men may have had some visions of its growth to a town of size and commercial importance. Smithfield played its part in the early history of the county, but in the fifties the river and the high road lost their commercial importance as compared with the railroad whose line passed a mile and a half to the north. A railroad station was established, a store was opened by Joseph Babb, and within a short time the activities of the town on the river began to decline, and Selma, fortified along the iron highway, attracted merchants, doctors, churches and schools, and the various interests which have constituted it one of the recognized centers of the county. For many years, however, Smithfield continued to have a store and blacksmith shop, and a grist mill run with water power.

YORKTOWN.

Along the course of White river and the old State road are to be found some of the oldest towns of the county. After Smithfield and Muncie, the next deserving attention is Yorktown. Samuel Casman, the Delaware half-breed, entered the land on which most of this village is situated, and when he disposed of it to Oliver H. Smith, the latter platted a village. The site selected was on the west side of the river, along the State road. Another advantage at the time was the proposed canal which was planned to pass through this locality. The first house is said to have been built about 1834, by Joshua Turner. In the third house erected, John Longley opened a stock of groceries, and on his removal O. H. Smith and T. J. Sample put up a store, about 1839, and were the principal merchants for some years. On the west side of the village were two taverns, one being known as the "Blue Ball Tavern," from the sign that hung suspended before it. Joseph Van Matre kept this place, which he built about 1830, and conducted it in a manner to make it famous among travelers. He and his wife lived there until they passed away, and then after standing half a century the house was torn down. The second house erected on the village site was used at various times for residence, church and schoolhouse. Thus the principal interests needful to make a village community were soon supplied. Dr. John C. Helm located there soon after the platting of the town, and Dr. Godwin was another early physician. Before Mr. Smith platted the site, a postoffice was kept by William Jones a mile and a half west, but soon afterward it was moved to Yorktown. As early as 1830 the waters of Buck creek near its junction with White river had been tapped by a race, and a saw mill built. This, the first industrial enterprise, was established by William Hardwick, who about 1832 added machinery for grinding corn, and continued to operate the mill until his death. O. H. Smith got control of it and converted it into a woolen mill. A. and D. M. Yingling finally secured the property, and before the boom days of Yorktown the Yingling Woolen Mill was the principal manufacturing enterprise.

DALEVILLE.

The vicinity about the White river in the extreme west side of the county has been known as a center of settlement for about seventy years. In the early thirties what was known as "the hydraulic" was begun by the state at this point. This was intended as a feeder to the Wabash canal. A dam ten feet high was constructed across the river at this point, and some of the stones and timbers were to be seen in the bed of the river as late as ten years ago. The canal was cut on the north bank of the river, extending along low hills in many places nearly a mile from the river. At the head of this canal, on the opposite side of the river from where Daleville now stands, a town said to have had two or three hundred inhabitants and known as Mount Summit grew up. The canal enterprise failed, however, and the village disintegrated. Some of the old buildings stood for over half a century, but the owner of the land, John Bronnenberg, had long since plowed across the streets that had been laid out when the village was started. In the early sixties some private capitalists proposed to make use of the disused channel by completing a canal to Anderson, using the water to run mills and factories. About sixty thousand dollars was expended, but constant breaks in the masonry near Chesterfield caused a final abandonment of the enterprise. Some of the masonry still stands, though the old cut is well nigh obliterated and when observed often becomes a matter of curious speculation to account for its origin.

The village of Daleville takes its name from the Dale family. Campbell Dale had entered land in that locality in 1827, and his sons platted the village. Where the principal north and south street of the village crosses the Muncie road, a two story frame building had been erected about 1845 and used for a tavern by Abraham Pugsley. One or two mercantile enterprises had been started here at an earlier date, but the town had no real permanence until the railroad was built in the early fifties.

ALBANY.

It is said that the land on which the village of Albany was later built was first located by Andrew Kennedy, in 1827. After making some improvements he sold to William Venard, who bought the land of the government, the date of his entry being October 3, 1832. In the following year he subdivided the land into town lots and founded the village of Albany, which has since grown and extended its limits over a considerable part of two sections. So far as known, Albany was a site without any business enterprise for several years. Granville Hastings had opened a stock of goods in section 16 at the locality variously known as Clifton, Sharon and Zehner Mill, in 1834, and it was two years later before Uriah Pace started a little store in Albany.

Other early merchants of the village were John Mitchell, William Krohn, Jacob Powers and the Bergdolls. Dr. Isaiah Templin was the first physician to locate there. As late as 1880 Albany had but six mercantile firms, besides the various trades and four or five physicians. The history of Albany as the progressive town next in size to Muncie in the county is contained within the last twenty-five years, for previous to that period the interests were few and no important industries had yet been established.

EATON.

Eaton, whose chief claim to fame outside its own county lies in its being the pioneer gas town of Indiana, had its origin as a center of population in a milling enterprise that was located on the river in what is now the south edge of town. This mill, the first in the township and one of the first in the county, was built by Francis Harris in the early thirties; some eight or nine years later was sold to the firm of Carter and Johnson, who discarded some of the primitive features of the grist machinery and put up a combination saw and grist mill. The Carter brothers, Charles and George, later owned and controlled the property, and in time a new flouring mill and saw mill succeeded the earlier plants, the Carter mill becoming one of the industrial landmarks of Eaton and the north side of the county.

In the vicinity of this mill, previous to 1870, some four or five families had grouped their homes. The Younts, Young and Carmichael families were the principal ones thus distinguished as pioneer residents of the community which has since grown into the town of Eaton. In 1870 the Fort Wayne, Muncie and Cincinnati Railroad was completed through this point, and almost immediately population and the general village interests began to increase. A census was taken in May, 1873, at which time 158 persons lived in the locality, and as a result of this census and the expressed desires of the people a petition was presented to the county commissioners asking that this community be incorporated as a town. July 5, 1873, the vote taken in accordance with the instructions from the commissioners showed that 28 were in favor of incorporation and none against it. Eaton was incorporated September 10, 1873, the first town in the county beside the county seat to acquire this form of local government. The first officers chosen to administer the affairs of the town corporation, at an election September 20, 1873, were: Adam Foorman, Wilson Martin, Nathan Baisinger, trustees; John Foorman, clerk, treasurer and assessor.

GRANVILLE.

Granville, in section 31 of Niles township and on the south bank of the Mississinewa, is one of the oldest villages in the county. It is the successor of Georgetown, which was located a short distance further up the river, Price Thomas having hewed the logs for the first house on that site in 1833.

This village enterprise failed, however, and a more vigorous community grew up where John Gregory divided a part of his land into town lots in 1836 and founded Granville. To this point it is said the inhabitants of Georgetown floated their houses down the river and erected them again on the new village site. James A. Maddy was the first merchant at the place, though he sold goods for Wilson Stanley, the owner. This store was opened in 1836, and was located in a log house on the banks of the river. David Shideler was also a merchant here. For many years Granville kept pretty well on a par with its neighbors, Eaton and Albany, but the railroad changed conditions and gave the latter insuperable advantages that the quiet river village could never overcome.

WHEELING AND NEW CORNER.

Washington township contains several sites of population centers that have undergone many fluctuations in the course of history. Outside of the recorder's office, very few people have any practical knowledge of the site once known as Elizabethtown, which was situated on the north bank of the Mississinewa river in section 12. Joseph Wilson, the original proprietor of the town, platted the site because it was believed to be the central location and the natural selection for the county seat of a county which was to be formed from part of Delaware and the land situated to the north. The name was given in honor of Elizabeth Wilson, whose grandson is Mark Powers, of Gaston. A village was started, merchants and blacksmiths and other mechanics located there, town lots brought fancy prices, and during the thirties Elizabethtown had more importance than some of the present day towns that were not then on the map. But the boundaries of Blackford county, when formed in 1839, did not even include Elizabethtown. This humiliation was more than the natural vigor of the town could endure, and in a few years little remained to mark the site of this ambitious enterprise.

William McCormick, one of the pioneer settlers of the township, about 1833 purchased land in the northeast corner of section 14 and later laid out a village there. One of the oldest roads in the county is Wheeling avenue, as it is now called, leading from Muncie to this point, and this highway was the first regular mail route to this part of the county. The mail was carried by horseback as far as Logansport, and later a hack service was installed and continued in use until the railroad was built a few years ago. William McCormick's house was the first postoffice, which went by the name of Cranberry postoffice until it was changed to Wheeling.

New Corner, which is now the enterprising Gaston, but which at an even earlier date was known as Snagtown, dates back to February, 1855, when David L. Jones laid the first plat on part of the northeast quarter of section 33. This village necessarily had little prosperity beyond the rural hamlet stage until the coming of the railroad many years after the laying of the plat.

NEW BURLINGTON.

The road between Muncie and Richmond, one of the earliest and most traveled highways of the county, passed through Perry township, along the line of the New Burlington pike. Houses of entertainment, taverns or inns as they were called, were numerous along this route, and occasionally a village grew up around such a house. Also, merchants found the traffic of the highway to their advantage, and country stores offered their wares to the passing public at short intervals. Where the road crosses section 8 of Perry township, George Ribble had platted a village in the thirties, and at that point was located the first postoffice of the township, John Newcomb offered the first stock of goods for sale in 1838, and a year or so later Charles Mansfield opened a tavern that became popular and much frequented by travelers along the road. Mansfield soon succeeded to the merchandise stock, and some time later sold all to John Kyger. Benjamin Pugh was the first postmaster, Dr. S. V. Jump and George W. Shroyer being his successors, the latter having been the principal merchant for many years. These sum up the chief interests of New Burlington during its early history.

With the building of the railroad through Perry township, New Burlington lost most of its prestige. About two miles west was located a little station known as Medford, the postoffice being called Phillips.

Another center of Perry township is Mount Pleasant, in the southwest corner, which consisted largely of a group of homes about the United Brethren church, and made no pretensions to commercial or industrial enterprise.

Monroe Township Centers.

After the building of the railroad through the center of this township a station was established about the center of the township and named Mc-Cowan's, which has come to be known best as Cowan. Charles McCowan, after whom it was named, was one of the early settlers of the township, and a man of remarkable industry, as a result of which he accumulated a competence, and at his death gave six thousand dollars for the building of a church and graded school building at McCowan's station. Around these institutions a village community was formed, a postoffice was established, and within a few years there were two stores, two saw mills, a tile factory, and the usual interests of such a place.

For a number of years a postoffice called Macedonia was kept at a store in the southeast corner of section 14, but in November, 1890, it was discontinued because no one would perform the duties of the office. Afterward the people of this vicinity got their mail at Luray, and Macedonia practically ceased to exist.

Oakville is another community that was grouped about a railroad station. It was a little community with one store and postoffice in 1880.

Richwood postoffice on the west side of the township belongs in the list of those little communities that existed chiefly because of the postoffice and have ceased to be since the rural route superseded the postoffice.

ROYERTON.

Royerton dates back to about 1870, when John Royer divided forty acres of land into town lots, reserving sites for schoolhouse and church. He already had a store and postoffice at that point, and with the impetus of the railroad the commercial interests and one or two mills were maintained.

SHIDELER.

About the same time Isaac Shideler, who had been active in promoting the first railroad from Fort Wayne and had then given land for depot site at the north edge of Hamilton township, revived the town of Shideler, and with the building of a depot the village may be said to have begun. Mr. Shideler was proprietor of the store and the postmaster at this point.

Other Centers.

Before the days of the rural free delivery a great many centers, named and located on the map, had little else to distinguish them or give them importance except the postoffice. As long as there was reason for the existence of a postoffice, to which the people of the surrounding neighborhood would regularly come for their mail, the same place would offer attractions for a country store and blacksmith shop and perhaps thus become the nucleus of a larger center. With the discontinuance of postoffices of this class by the rural free delivery, a great many of these centers are disappearing, and deserve mention largely because they existed in the past. A list of such places follows:

Culbertson's Corner, in southwest part, and Cologne Postoffice in the northwest corner, respectively, of Washington township.

In Salem township are Tabor, once a postoffice and site of a church and school community (a familiar name was "Sockum"). Crossroads, near the south line of the township, had some commercial distinction in early years, a store having been opened there about 1832, though it failed of success, and in 1838 the Moffett brothers opened another.

In Harrison township is the little place called Bethel, or, more recently, Stout, from the name of the merchant for a long time located at that point, Isaac Stout. This is on the south side of section 20, and not far away was the placed named Harrison, designed as a village by Job Garner, who conducted the first merchandising enterprise of the township at that point.

CHAPTER XII.

MUNCIE.

In Center township, the White river, after pursuing a sinuous course from its head waters in Randolph county, makes a broad bend that marks the northernmost limit of its course, from that point following a generally southwest direction until it meets with the Wabash in southwestern Indiana. From this bend it is only a few miles over the watershed to the great Wabash valley, the waters of the Mississinewa and those of White river diverging at this point, not to mingle within the same banks until they have flowed several hundred miles in widely separate paths. On the north side of the bend the land begins an almost abrupt ascent toward the high ground of the watershed. On the south, half encircled by the river, lies the large bottom which the current has overrun many times in the history of the stream and has finally made into an alluvial plain.

Three quarters of a century ago, the region thus described was, according to current testimony, one vast hazel thicket, among which rose many varieties of forest growth, the beech and oak, the dogwood and hackberry, while along the river were many areas of marshland with its own peculiar growth. It was nature's wilderness, and probably only a few winding trails penetrated its density and indicated the passage of wild denizen or human beings. By treaty with the general government, probably the St. Mary's treaty of 1818, a tract containing 672 acres, lying on both sides of the river at the bend, was reserved and at the time of which we are now writing was held by a Delaware Indian, a widow, named Rebecca Hackley; hence was called the Hackley Reserve.* So far as known, the land had been put to

*In 1901 the C. I. & E. Railroad sought by condemnation a right-of-way across White river, which the Whitely Land Company had refused to grant. The attorneys for the railroad, in course of the proceedings, introduced a very unexpected and novel plea that the land company did not own the river bed, offering in support of this contention the following bit of history, going back to the very beginning of Muncie:

Quoting an article from the treaty of 1819—"To Rebecca Hackley, a half-blooded Miami Indian, is granted one section of land, to be located at Munseytown, on White river, so that it shall extend on both sides to include 320 acres of the prairie, in the bend of White river, where the bend assumes the shape of a horseshoe."

The Indian woman, with superstition characteristic of her race, refused to accept that part of the land covered by water, hence the plea of the attorneys for the railroad that " . . . in pursuance of said treaty (above mentioned) 320 acres of land lying south of said river was surveyed . . . and 320 acres of land lying north was likewise surveyed; that in the survey of said land the river was excluded. That, including said river, there is now 672 acres in said section of land. That no use, although there may have been a little patch of ground where the widow Hackley or other members of her household cultivated some Indian corn and vegetables. To describe the situation of this reserve by modern landmarks: Its southeast corner was near Washington and Elm streets; the southwest corner is now in the river near the old dug road nearly north of the Jefferson school; the northeast and northwest corners being one mile north of the two corners mentioned, the tract being parts of sections 3, 4, 9 and 10. The south line of the reserve passes through the center of the court house.

While the first land entries were being made in the south and southeastern parts of the county, Goldsmith C. Gilbert (whose career has been sketched) was trading with the Indians on the Mississinewa. The story goes that his store was burned down by a drunken Indian, who had been excited to riotous conduct by the Gilbert brand of whiskey, and with the money collected as damages from the tribe because of this outrage Mr. Gilbert shortly afterward purchased from the widow Hackley the reserve on White river. Like several other notable purchases in American history, the amount originally paid for this land ($960), though it was higher than the price paid for government land, bears small proportion to its present value.

This sale was transacted about 1825, and about the same time two cabins were built in a clearing where is now the court house square. One of these Mr. Gilbert used for a residence, and the other for a trading post. Thus trade was the starting point of Muncie. At one end of the historical vista we see the trader's cabin, set in a little open space among the trees and hazel brush; its rough log walls sheltering and protecting a miscellaneous stock of the necessities of pioneer life; while idling about were some Indian bucks, buying so much as their purse or credit permitted or exchanging the results of hunting and trapping for the few staples and the liquor that civilization had taught them to appreciate. A varied panorama intervenes between this primitive view and the present. At the other end a thousand interests are crowded together to represent the products of a twentieth century civilization. Near the site of the old trading post is the stone court house; on all sides are stores and dwellings, each one a splendid structure as compared with the old log cabin and every one constructed long after the old store had been demolished. All around, homes, factories, schools, and churches, along paved streets and avenues, occupy the ground then thicketed with hazel and other wild vegetation. A lonely cabin in the wil-

plaintiff is informed that and believes that the Indians would not receive a river or water for land ceded to them, and that they did not do so; that the United States has never received any consideration for the land constituting the bed and banks of said river; that it has never parted with its title thereto, unless by the treaty and surveys aforesaid, and unless said grant carried title to the thread of the stream.''

derness at the bend of the river: a city of brick and stone and wood, where thousands of people live and unite their industry and social activities—is it possible to conceive a greater contrast?

The county institutions are a prize eagerly sought by various localities when a new county is organized. Other conditions being equal, the county seat will easily surpass all other centers in a county, and it is probable that in the country at large the county seats are usually the principal towns in their respective counties. For this reason, in the history of many counties we are treated with the spectacle of a lively county-seat fight, wherein two or more towns, each aspiring for the honor, contend for the prize with the inducements of money, the arts of politics, and even, as has been known, with the harsher means of open warfare.

The location of the county seat of Delaware county on land donated by G. C. Gilbert, Lemuel Jackson and William Brown has been described in the civil history of the county. Muncie has never had an important rival for this honor, and has continued the home of the county government for eighty years. With the establishment of the county seat at this point, and the donation of some fifty acres of land for the site of the town and county institutions, the history of Muncie may be said to have really begun. Besides being the center of the civil government, it quickly became the commercial center, where the residents of the outlying country resorted to obtain their supplies of provisions, to have implements repaired and horses shod, to get an occasional letter or paper, and also hear and discuss the current local news and politics.

Unfortunately, there is little contemporary information regarding Muncie's early history. For the most part it is necessary to rely on reminiscences of men who were here at the time, but who, at the time of recording their memories, had to look back over a long period of years, during which many details dropped away and the exact succession of events was often lost.

Muncie in 1837.

The earliest description that we have of Muncie is one that appeared in the first issue of the Muncietonian in 1837.

Muncietown—The seat of justice of Delaware county, situated on the south bank of White river, on an elevation of about thirty feet above the bed of the river. It was laid out in 1827, by four different proprietors, in the form of an oblong square. The four principal streets are sixty feet wide, the others forty-five, all crossing each other at right angles. It contains, at present 320 inhabitants, a postoffice, a printing office, four physicians, six mercantile stores, three taverns, three groceries, one grist mill, one saw mill, one distillery, one carding machine, one cabinet-maker's shop, two tailors, two hatters, one shoemaker, six house joiners, one bricklayer, and plasterer, two chair makers, two tanners, two blacksmiths, one gunsmith, one wagon maker, one painter, one saddler's shop, four milliners, one school mistress, one minister of the gospel, one judge, four attorneys, one sheriff, one clerk of the court, two magistrates, one school commissioner, one county surveyor and recorder. A superb court house with a cupola etc., 45 feet square, and 28 feet high, is to be built, and is now under contract. The contemplated Central Canal will pass through this place, and the connecting link, either by canal or railroad, between the Central and Whitewater Canals, will in all probability terminate at this point, as the Board of Canal Commissioners have reported favorable to such termination. The State Road from the Ohio State line to Indianapolis passes through this place—a State Road from Richmond to Logansport—a State Road from New Castle, in Henry county, to Fort Wayne—all pass through this town. There is also a State Road leading to Pendleton, and Delphi. Muncietown is about 61 miles N. E. from Indianapolis N. lat. 40 deg. 7 min. W. lon. 8 deg. 9 min.

Around the public square, as soon as it was laid out, there began to appear the various features of community life. On the north side Mr. Gilbert kept his store and his tavern for the accommodation of travelers. A general store, kept by Samuel Watson, stood on the northwest corner of Washington and High streets, while on Walnut street stood a blacksmith shop and about the same time the postoffice. Of course a certain amount of manufacturing was one of the important foundation stones of the new town. The pioneer manufacturer was Goldsmith C. Gilbert. Perhaps he was influenced in purchasing the reserve by observing the millsite afforded in the bend of the river at this point. In 1828, the year following the location of the county seat, he dug a mill race, blasting it part way through rock, and the next year constructed the "Old Mill," as Muncie's first grist mill was called. It was fit only for "cracking corn" at first, but later was supplied with a burr for grinding wheat. About the same time a sawmill was built just north of the grist mill; later a distillery was erected, and also a woolen mill, the latter being located at the point where the race enters the river. Mr. Gilbert started all these establishments, which comprised the manufacturing interests of the town for several years.

Even in a pioneer community death is not an unknown guest, hence Muncie had scarcely begun to grow when a place was set aside for the interment of the dead. The first cemetery was on the north side of East Main street, east of Beacon street, and the second on the north side of Adams west of Franklin. When the present cemetery was laid out the bodies were disinterred from the old grounds and placed in the new.

Even with several factories, Muncie could not produce all the necessities of life, many of which had to be brought in from the larger centers. Cincinnati was the trading metropolis, and among those who used to cover the distance between these places with team and wagon was Boyd Linville.

Sometimes he could make the trip in a week, but more frequently in two weeks. The road to Richmond, which was the route used in this traffic, was very circuitous to avoid the bogs and other obstructions, and transportation was beset with tremendous difficulties.

With the help of an early newspaper and some reminiscences formerly published it is possible in a measure to reconstruct the Muncietown of seventy years ago. The brief description above quoted from the Muncietonian is a summary of the principal features, but this outline can be filled out somewhat by a study of the advertising columns, which are the important and almost only local items published by the old-fashioned newspaper. The business and professional interests of the little village in June, 1837, as represented by advertisers, were the following:

Eli Green, brick maker, layer and plasterer; William Scott, tanner and currier; Thomas C. Anthony, lawyer; John Smith, whose chair factory was located at Jackson and Liberty streets; A. R. East, who had just been appointed school commissioner of the county vice T. C. Anthony resigned; W. G. Renner, lawyer; Mrs. Ellen O. Minshall and Miss Louvina Long, milliners; Joseph Anthony, lawyer; Eleazer Coffeen, who had claims against various persons of the county; G. W. Garst, W. C. Willard, John A. Clark, physicians; Edward S. Keasbey, who manufactured hats at the corner of Main and Mulberry; Anderson Carter and Davis Williams, tailors; Stephen Cox, grocer at Main and Franklin; James Hodge, cabinet maker at Franklin and Washington; Walton and Harlan, saddlery on Main street; Watton and Cummerford, chair makers at Jackson and Liberty streets; Edward Benbow, wagon and plow shop, Main and Mulberry; Asahel Spencer, gunsmith; Israel Shoemaker, boots and shoes; Minus Turner, grocer on Main street; the Exchange and Green Tree hotels; Kirby and Willard's general store; James O. Leas, general store; Bloomfield and Jack, general store; Joseph Lefavour, general store; C. F. Willard and Samuel P. Anthony, drugs; while the following additional persons published "estray notices," which were very common in those days and characterized that state of development when fences are rare: William Williams, Joel Triplet, William Jones, Jesse Delaney, Benjamin Prickett, Ichabod Dille, Major Nottingham, John Marshall.

This summary is no doubt accurate, so far as it goes, though there are probably some important omissions. Apparently, the most important occupations and forms of trade were represented, so that there was no occasion for anyone to want the necessities nor even some of the luxuries. That the women of the community were not denied their most particular fashion is proved by the presence of two milliners. Doubtless the ladies felt that the pioneer lot was somewhat relieved when they could put on beribboned bonnets to visit neighbors who lived on the other side of the square. Mrs. Minshall, one of the milliners, was the widow of the Dr. Levi Minshall who had been one of the early physicians and had died only a short time previous to the date of this advertisement. Stephen Cox, who advertised as a grocer, had a dilapidated cabin at Main and Franklin, and is said to have made a specialty of "wet goods," of which he himself drank as freely as he sold to customers. He was charged with the practice of pouring into the barrel as much water as was drawn off in liquor through the spigot—perhaps a safer custom than the western one of maintaining the strength of the barrel by additions of vitriol, though a time must have come when the diluted contents were too weak even for a pioneer thirst. The "Great Western," a saloon that stood on the southwest corner of Main and Mulberry about the same date, was also noted for the mean quality of its whiskey.

Post Coaches.

The first paper tells what the means of communication were, in a card announcing the arrival and departure of mails, the mail from Richmond on the south and from Peru on the north arriving twice a week, and that from Indianapolis, Winchester, and Connersville, once a week. What was termed "a much needed public accommodation" was a "four horse post coach" to run semi-weekly between Indianapolis and Greenville, Ohio, via Noblesville, Andersontown, Muncietown and Winchester, the contract for which was opened to bid in this paper (June, 1837).

By 1840 Delaware county had a population of nearly nine thousand. It is estimated that only about 400 were located at Muncie at this time. The village was growing, however, and about this time occurred the first movement toward incorporation, so far as is now known. In a letter, dated January 7, 1842 (now in possession of Mrs. Julia Williamson), John A. Clark, writing to G. C. Gilbert, then in the legislature at Indianapolis, states that a meeting had just been held "for the incorporation of Muncietown," and that "we have raised a remonstrance." "I [Clark] am not as yet apprised of whether we will get a majority against it or not, but Alsop Edmond and all your Slickville friends are in favor of no incorporation." James Russey was reputed to be the head of the corporation movement. The attempt did not succeed, since Muncie did not become a corporation for more than ten years.

Muncietown Becomes Muncie.

For nearly twenty years the county seat was known as Muncietown. Likewise in those days Anderson was called Andersontown. The abbreviation of the name was probably dictated by several reasons, sufficient to cause the state legislature to give the name its present form. There was some local affection for the old name however, since a correspondent in the Muncie Democrat, May 10, 1845, spoke regretfully of a late act of the legislature that changed the name to Muncie.

Muncie and the County in 1848.

Some interesting records of the past are contained in Volume I No. 15 of the Indiana Signal, published at Muncie June 24, 1848. John C. Osburn was editor and proprietor, his name being the first to catch the attention of the reader. The newspapers of that time devoted much space to exchange matter, short stories, moral essays, etc., but, overlooking these, one finds much direct representation of the affairs that concerned Delaware county people sixty years ago.

First, was the agitation for free schools. Indiana had then no free schools in the modern sense, and the question was soon to be put to vote whether the people favored free schools or not. This subject is discussed elsewhere in the chapter on education.

"All letters," reads an editorial notice, "must be *postpaid* to receive attention." It would be unnecessary to instruct anyone now to prepay the postage on a letter. In 1848 the postal system was still in its beginnings. It cost anywhere from five to twenty-five cents to send a letter, but it was largely optional whether the sender or the receiver should pay the postage. Hence the wisdom of the editor's little notice, who was thus safeguarding himself from paying postage on letters that had little pertinence to his business and perhaps contained criticism of his paper.

Many persons have never seen an old-fashioned letter, and the following describes one that was written over sixty years ago. Written on paper about twelve by six inches, the two ends were folded to meet in the center; then a fold from the left up to about two inches of the right side, which was then turned over in the same manner as the flap of a present-day envelope, being fixed with wax, on which was often stamped the sender's initial letter or other character. On the opposite side was a plain face for the address and postmark. The circular postmark on this particular letter bears on the outer edge "Muncietown, Ind." and in the center "Jan. 7" [1842]. No postage stamps were used, but the sending office had a stamp with the word "paid," after which was written in figures the amount, which, in this case, was ten cents, that being the rate for a letter between Muncietown and Indianapolis.

Political discussion claimed a large share of newspaper space. At the date of this issue the presidential campaign was just joined, by the nomination of Gen. Lewis Cass by the Democrats, and of Zachary Taylor, the hero of the Mexican war, by the Whigs. Over half of the news space in the Signal was devoted to these candidates, with natural preference for Taylor, since the editor was a Whig.

It is more material interests that are reflected in the price list of "Muncie produce markets." It is worth quoting, as follows:

Flour, per cwt.	$1.75	Beeswax, per lb.	$ .18
Wheat, per bu.	50@.55	Lard, per lb.	.05
Corn, per bu.	.25	Butter, per lb.	.08
Oats, per bu.	.20	Eggs, per doz.	.04
Beans, per bu.	.70	Flaxseed, per bu.	.55
Potatoes, per bu.	.25	Ginseng, per lb.	.25
Feathers, per lb.	.20		

While the Signal of sixty years ago did not contain a column or more of amusement notices, as can now be found in the local press, there was one announcement that meant more, socially, to the people of Delaware county from the oldest to the youngest than any single event of this more lively and spectacular age. The announcement, of the "celebration of Independence day," went on to state that the citizens of Muncie and vicinity would meet in a grove near town on the morning of July 4th and participate in the following exercises:—"Prayer, by Rev. Mr. Ash; Declaration read, by T. J. Sample; oration, by R. B. Abbott, A. B."—The Pendleton band was expected to be present, and vocal music was also on the program. These exercises over, a procession would be formed under the direction of James L. Russey, marshal, and John Brady and William Perkins, assistant marshals, to march thence to the public square, "where a dinner will have been provided by the Muncie Sewing Circle, to be partaken of at one dollar per couple: the proceeds of which will be applied to the erection of a new Methodist church in this place." Of those in charge of arrangements are some familiar names:—James S. Ferris, Samuel W. Harlan, John Jack, James Nottingham, William G. Ethell, F. E. Putnam, Job Swain, James Hodge, Joseph Martin, George W. Garst, Joseph E. King, Samuel F. Brady, William N. Jackson, Charles P. Sample, John Dungan, Albert Heath.

We also get a glimpse of local political leaders, in the column of candidates' cards. Josiah P. Williams, Charles Mansfield and Jonathan Wachtel aspired to be county commissioners. James Hodge was candidate for state senator, also Joseph S. Buckles and Warren Stewart. Samuel Orr and George W. Garst desired the office of representative. John A. Gilbert and Warner Mann were candidates for associate judge of Delaware circuit court. For the office of clerk Samuel W. Harlan announced his candidacy.

Only one of the legal notices calls for attention. The county auditor invited bids for the "building of a house [of brick] for four offices, on the public square in Muncie, to be completed by the first Monday of December next."

A perusal of this paper explains the transportation facilities, when mails arrived only twice weekly from Indianapolis and other points, when a regular twice-a-week hack line ran from Muncie to Cincinnati, and all passenger traffic was by horse traction. The dawn of a new era, however, is seen in a notice for election of directors for the Indianapolis and Bellefontaine Railroad, which in a few years was built and is now the line of the Big Four road. Sixty years ago the state capital was as distant to the people of Muncie as St. Louis is now, for it was never less than a day's journey there, and a very fatiguing one at that.

From the two columns of "Business Directory" we can partly reconstruct the business and professional interests of that day. Nearly all the business houses were on Main street, and in the vicinity of the public square. At the west end of this street were A. M. Klein, clock and watch maker, and W. G. Ethell, printer, glazier and chairmaker; at Main and Chestnut was J. Walling, saddle, harness and trunkmaker; at east end and south side of Main street were Patrick Justice and J. R. Lockwood, tanners, shoemakers and harnessmakers. Central Hotel, kept by S. Hoon, and Eastern Hotel, by Joseph Anthony, were on Main street, the latter at the east end and the Central on the southeast corner of Main and Walnut. Between these was the Trimble House, kept by John Trimble. Many of the business establishments designated their position with reference to the Central or Eastern hotels. Thus, B. Buckley, a shoemaker, was two doors south of Central Hotel; Nottingham and Meeks, cabinet makers, were nearly opposite the Eastern; G. W. Greene, tailor, was opposite the Trimble House; John Jack and J. L. Russey, dry goods and groceries, were one door east of Central Hotel; Charles F. Willard, merchant, was north of Central Hotel and east of square. Other business men and their locations were: Mark Walling, tanner and currier, north of Jack, Russey & Co.'s grist mill; George Liston, chairmaker and turner, on Washington street, near woolen factory; Charles Rickert, plowstocker and carriage maker, one door west of Neeley's blacksmith shop; Joseph Stradling, wagon, carriage and plowmaker, corner Main and Mulberry; Edward G. Keasbey, hatmaker, Main street; John and S. F. Brady, saddle, harness and trunk makers, adjoining postoffice, which stood on Main and Jefferson streets; Milton and R. M. Rogers, wholesale and retail hardware, one door east of Russey and Jack's store; P. Tuthill, shoemaker, four doors west of Eastern Hotel; Elisha Spear, shoemaker, one door east of Willard's store; T. S. Neeley, blacksmith and plow dealer, Main street; William S. Collis, sash and blind manufacturer, Liberty and Jackson streets; James Hodge, dry goods and groceries, Chestnut and Main; Jonathan Wachtel, chairmaker, west end Main street; Josiah P. Williams, grocer, Main street, corner opposite court house; W. W. Moore's bakery and confectionery, one door east of postoffice, north side Main street. Physicians' cards appeared of B. F. Paris and A. F. Esterbrook, "botanic physicians and surgeons"; J. E. Moler, two doors east of Galliher and Burt's store, Main street. The only lawyers whose cards appear were Thomas J. Sample, east end of Main street; Joseph S. Buckles, in court house; Joseph Anthony, near Eastern Hotel.

(Indiana Signal, October 28, 1848.) Besides the erection of several dwellings, and one or two business houses, the past summer, there is now in the course of erection a splendid fire proof county building, designed to be occupied by four of the principal county officers. A few weeks ago and the foundation stone was not yet laid, and now there stands a brick building nearly ready for the covering. But a few weeks more will elapse, ere it will be ready for the reception of those who are to occupy it. All of this has been thus speedily performed by our enterprising citizens, Messrs. Russey, Jack, and Wysor, who are the contractors.

There are in this village eight Dry Goods Stores, (though one would scarcely have believed it, had they taken our advertising columns as a criterion by which to judge,) all doing good business; four Groceries and Bakeries; three Public Inns; three Furniture Warehouses; three Blacksmith's shops; one Tin Manufactory, and Stove Depot; two Tanner and Curriers; one Hatter; four Waggon and Carriage Makers; three tailors; three Shoemakers; three Chair Manufactories; one Clock and Watch Repairer; one or two House and Sign Painters; one Tinker; one Grist and Saw Mill; one Woolen Factory; one Seminary with two or three good Teachers; two Churches; two Apothecary Shops; a plenty of Lawyers and Physicians; several Masons, Carpenters and Joiners, and one Sash and Blind Manufacturer,—all of which are well supported, and in a county too, that is not as yet blessed with any internal improvements. The population falls but little short of 1500.

The account of Muncie in 1848, as given above, describes the town just before it entered upon the period of growth and enlargement consequent on the building of the railroad. Four years afterward the railroad was completed. This new force changed many of the old fashions of living. Previously it had been the habit of the editor to excuse a late issue of his paper by saying that bad roads had prevented the arrival of paper from Cincinnati, or the merchant had a like plausible reason why his shelves were bare of staples. The daily passing of freight trains put an end to the condition that made such excuses necessary. The railroad brought a daily mail, and along with it came the telegraph, so that the mental horizon of this town was extended to the furthest limits of the world.

Incorporation.

Muncie grew during this period, largely because of the railroad. During the decade of the forties the county increased in population just two thousand; during the next decade, by five thousand. From a town of about four hundred it contained about nine hundred within two years after the completion of the railroad. Numerous additions were made to the town plat during this period, and the spirit of progress was felt by all.

One result of it was the incorporation of the town. A movement that had failed ten or twelve years before, now had hardly a dissenting vote. This time it was comparatively easy to obtain the signatures of more than a third of the voting population, and a petition asking for corporation was presented to the board of county commissioners in September, 1854. The board, satisfied the sentiment for corporation was strong, ordered an election for the voters of the proposed town to decide the question. On September 30, 1854, 57 voters wrote the word "yes," 42 the words "for corporation," and 4 the word "no" on their ballots. The board decreed that Muncie was henceforth a corporate town, and in the following spring trustees and other officers were elected.

February 24, 1864, a petition, signed by more than a third of the voters within the corporate limits of Muncie, was presented to the town trustees, asking that board to take such steps as were necessary to secure incorporation of Muncie as a city. The following November the board directed the town marshal to take a census as preliminary to city organization. The marshal made returns showing that Muncie had a population of 2196, more than double the number in 1854. February 2, 1865, the voters went to the polls to decide whether city organization was desired, and when the ballots were counted only one was against it and 293 signified assent to the proposition. Before retiring from office the town trustees divided Muncie into four wards. The limits of these original wards were as follows: First ward—all the city west of High street; Second—all between High street and Jefferson street; Third—all between Jefferson street and Monroe street; and Fourth —all east of Monroe street.

The first mayor, aldermen and other officers of the City of Muncie were elected on February 25, 1865. John Brady was chosen to the executive office of the city. Joseph F. Duckwall was elected clerk, William H. Stewart treasurer, Jacob Dodson city assessor, Joshua Truitt city engineer, and John T. Robinson marshal and street commissioner. The first ward returned as its representatives in the council, Mark Walling and James Truitt. William B. Kline and Franklin Shafer were elected from the second ward; the third ward chose John L. Little and Isaac Meeks, while that portion of the city lying east of Monroe street elected William Brotherton and Lewis S. Smith.

California Forty-Niners from Delaware County.

The discovery of gold in California created quite as much excitement in Delaware county as in other similar sections of the country. Many left their settled pursuits and homes for the adventurous life of the west coast. Probably no complete record of all the Forty-Niners could be found, but some old papers preserve the record of a company of twenty-eight who left the county for California on October 1, 1849. They were: James H. Wysor, J. H. Jemison, T. E. Burt, Elisha Spear, David B. Dowden, from Muncie. Stephen Hamilton, father and son, Thompson Walling, Archibald Hamilton,

Samuel Martin, Crockett Ribble, Thomas R. Points, from the district along White river. Charles Carter, William Adsit, Samuel Peck, Dr. S. Hathaway, Daniel Dilley, Reason Imes, John Sherry, James Hinton, George Carter, Peter Shideler, Thomas Beird, Wesley Carroll, Benjamin Lewis, William Green, Isaac Ferguson, Dr. Davis, all from the Mississinewa. It is known that two other Delaware county men, Russey and Woods, met death while mining.

Probably the majority of these returned to the county within a few years, all enriched by strange experience if not by gold. One of them, however, failed to return, and as nothing of his fate was learned, his disappearance became one of those mysteries that sometimes shadow family histories. The final solution of the mystery revealed the most interesting romance in the county's annals. The substance of the strange story, as told in the Daily News of June 18, 1884, under the title of "A Modern Enoch Arden," is as follows:—

Thompson Walling, one of the '49ers, married Susanah, daughter of George Shafer, in 1841, and lived for some years on a farm in this county. In the excitement of '49 with $500.00 loaned him by Volney Willson, he started in company with Henry Wysor, Stephen Hamilton, Jr., Theo. Burt, Elisha Spear, Dr. Hathaway, Charles Jeminson, Chas. McLaughlin, Samuel Martin and a number of people from along the Mississinewa, for California.

The company met with varying success, and some of them returned with the start that proved the foundation for later fortune, but young Walling remained, as did poor Russey, who fell a victim to the red man's malignant hatred.

Walling's fortunes varied. Year after year passed, and he was heard of as having a stake, and anon as having lost his all, and at last came rumors that he had forsaken the mines and was meeting with varying success at the gambling table, also that misfortune had led to dissipation which, together with the determination to not return empty handed, kept him until 1852, when he made a stake of $3,000 by a good mine investment and sent $500 home to his wife. Part of these rumors only were true and all were probably greatly exaggerated.

Meantime, his wife had given him up as dead, obtained a divorce, married twice, and was twice left a widow, and since 1882 had lived on her forty acre farm near Muncie.

Never in all this time had she any word from the absent wanderer, nor had any one any hope of his existence save Mr. Volney Willson, his old time friend, who, broken down by the rheumatism by this time, amused himself by sending numberless letters throughout the west in quest of him long since lost to his friends. At Weatherby, a village postoffice, in Oregon, at the beginning of the present year, the postmaster, Mr. Weatherby, for whom the village had evidently been named, and who was himself a "forty niner" and had not seen his family for twenty years, became homesick, sent for his family, and while he was absent on his long postponed mission, a deputy postmaster distributed the morning mail. Suddenly a postmark

_Muncie, Indiana,—startled him. He looked at the superscription. It was directed to the postmaster. As deputy he had a perfect right to open it. It was from his home. A sudden thrill pervaded his frame and with trembling fingers he broke the seal and perused the missive. It was a letter of inquiry from Mr. Willson as to himself. Emotions which he had not experienced, perhaps, for years, came over him in a torrent, and hastening to answer it, he wrote to Mr. Willson a long letter, detailing his trials, his hardships and his despair of ever returning to his old home until at last he gave up hope and supposing all who were once near and dear to him had long since died, gave up to remain in his new home. The letter was answered, telling the story of waiting, and of fond hopes blasted, and also of the living wife, twice the wife of others, but again alone, and in return came a letter saying that in all the years, the wanderer had known none who could take the place of Susanah, his early love. Whether he had yielded again to the tender passion did not transpire, but no ties, apparently, bound him to the west, and a series of letters resulted in the determination to come home and throw himself upon the mercy of his wife, and renew old ties, if such might be.

In pursuance of this design, Mr. Walling arrived in the city Tuesday morning, and visited Mr. Willson, his brother Marc, and his old friends of the "forty-niners" and before the day was half gone, his son, Joseph, now a man grown, arrived with a buggy to take him home.

Who can imagine his feeling as he drew nigh the home of her whom he took for better, for worse, forty-three years since, and whom he had not seen for thirty-five years? We draw a veil over the meeting. Suffice it to say that it was affecting in the extreme, and that the wife of '49 welcomed her recreant husband, and that a portion of the old love at least was awakened, and when a News man casually dropped in upon them, at a late hour that night, he found them rehearsing the incidents of thirty-five years.

CHAPTER XIII.

THE PUTNAM DIARY.

F. E. Putnam came to Muncie, according to his own words, "October 19, 1838, and first clerked for Charles F. Willard at $20 per month, with board, washing and mending." He began business for himself in 1842 and with that event he began a daily chronicle of his personal, business, and general affairs, which he continued, with unusual faithfulness, until a few days before his death, nearly sixty years later. Through the kindness of his daughter, Mrs. Olcott, the sixteen books containing this diary were entrusted to the editor for examination, and as a result the following extracts have been chosen which have pertinence to a general history of the county. Naturally the greater part of the record is devoted to weather conditions and personal matters and minor events that would be out of place in this publication, and yet his outlook from day to day, as expressed in these books, is a record of quaint and continued interest, and one that deserves a cherished place in the family possessions.

The diary fills a very valuable place in the chronology of Muncie, from 1842 to 1882, during which time no newspaper files exist to supply historical data. The diary is not drawn upon during the years following 1882 since the newspapers have furnished the material for these years. The only omission in the diary is the book for the years 1853-57, and with this exception there is a fairly complete contemporaneous record of the principal happenings of town and county during the long period when Mr. Putnam was one of the merchants of Muncie.

1842.

Mar. 21—Commenced selling goods this day.

July 4—Guns fired. Band played on court house square. Supposed to be 1200 people in town.

Dec. 27—Lots of pork in town; selling for $1.25 (per bbl.).

"In closing this year, I deem it very necessary that some general remarks should be made in regard to the present state of our once prosperous country, that the rising generation (if their eyes should chance to meet this 'my log') may warn themselves of the effects of bad government. . . . There never was known a more fruitful season since the fall of man, and why the cause of hard times? No tariff for the protection of 'our home' manufacturers—No uniform currency for the American people excepting depreciated paper, which will not pass two hundred miles from home; State Legislature doing nothing to relieve their people, the general government doing all they can, and the President (Tyler) vetoing (six times already)—our character lost abroad, our confidence broken at home, repudiating the prevailing sentiment of some states, and how can we have good times! Indiana state scrip worth 50 cents to the $1 and dull at that; wheat 25 cents, corn 10, oats 8 1/3, butter 4 cents per lb., eggs 3, apples 25 cents per bushel, and all other things in proportion, no market abroad and none at home, everything prostrate, all are seeking office and not many getting except the favored few."

1843.

March 31—Thus ends month of March, having been one of more severe cold weather, more snow and more continued frozen ground, than any previous since the memory of our oldest residents. . . . It is also remarkable for the visible comet. . . . It is also remarkable as no sugar has been made and sold. And still further remarkable for the sus_ tention of men's moral character as well as private by the circuit court of Delaware county. And also for the reduction of prices on goods. . . .

1844.

Jan.—An exhibition of mesmerism in Muncie, mentioned in the diary indicates the time when this phase of the occult was beginning to be culti_ vated.

Jan.—Burial of G. C. Gilbert.

1846.

June 13—Grand organization of the militia, volunteer company of sixty raised with Gen. Kilgore as Captain; T. J. Sample and J. S. Garver, first and second lieutenants.

1847.

May 2—Hung court house bell (see mention of this bell elsewhere).

May 12—Death of Dr. John Allen Clark.

June—Butter, 6 cents; wheat, 60 cents; flour, $2.25 per hundred.

June 26—Great mass meeting for railroad purposes. Great cry and little wool.

Dec.—Small-pox begins in Muncie, a man being taken at Hoon's (site of Patterson Block) with the disease.

Dec. 31—Death of Andrew Kennedy (of smallpox) at Palmer House in Indianapolis.

1849.

July 28—California fever raging strong—little else doing.

Oct. 1—J. H. Wysor, J. H. Jamison, Theophilus E. Burt, Stephen Hamilton Sr. and Jr., Arch Hamilton and company, including Thompson Walling, David B. Dowden, Samuel Martin, and others, left for California.

Characteristic and frequently repeated notes refer to the wretched condition of roads, which were invariably bad in the spring and early winter; to chills and fever and ague; to transportation of goods overland from Cincinnati.

Dec.—J. L. Russey, J. P. Martin, Josh Lockwood, Warren Stewart start for California.

Dec. 10—John Russey died this morning.

1850.

Some social events:—Jan. 7—Lecture at court house to-night.

Jan. 8—Cotillon party at Jo Davis's (supper at Neely's).

Jan. 10—Musical concert at court house.

March 18—Mr. Wachtel died this morning.

Aug. 4-5—Death of William F. Brady.

Aug. 16—Heard of David Gharky's death.

Sept. 17—Daguerreo car left town (traveling photographers made the pictures of Muncie people in those days).

1851.

July 7—George A. Spilker died.

Sept. 12—Raised depot (for the railroad then under construction).

Oct. 9—Railroad celebration at Chesterfield.

Dec. 12—A plank road meeting at the court house.

1852.

May 13—J. W. Rupey elected depot clerk. Three railroad presidents in town.

May 28—Cars close to town.

May 29—Dinner at Hoon's and Davis's for railroad hands.

May 31—Passenger cars up for the first time.

June 17—Warm and cloudy in the morn with heavy showers in the eve. Railroad celebration and lots of people in town, say 7000, five trains down and six up, and one to York and back. Sample made reception speech and Smith replied.

1853.

Jan. 17—First session of court of common pleas.

Feb. 1—Cars commence running through to Cincinnati.*

1858.

Dec. 15—County sold first bonds for the erection of jail.

Dec. 18—Provisions of all descriptions very scarce. Chickens and turkeys quite plentiful. Eggs in demand at 12½ to 15; butter, 16 cents a pound; potatoes, none to be had; no apples, dried fruits scarce and high; coon 75 cents.

1859.

July 4—The Glorious old fourth came in very cold, almost ice cold, with the firing of cannon, crackers, ringing of bells, shouting and playing by the band. . . . People commenced arriving about seven o'clock and continued until sundown. Procession formed about ten by soldiers of war of 1812 and Mexican, and then came citizens, led by the Muncie "Sax Horn Band," when we marched to the fair ground under the marshalship of David Nation and Job Swain. . . . The president, Thomas J. Sample, announced the order of the day to be, music by the band, prayer by chaplain, F. A. Hardin, music by the choir, reading of the Declaration of Independence by Dr. George W. Edgerle, music by the band and choir, tune Hail Columbia, and sung by the multitude, oration by Clark N. Anthony, dinner in pic-nic, toasts regular and volunteer, music and speaking generally—which were all faithfully and energetically carried out.

Oct. 1—Mr. John Jack died this morning.

*An omission of book from 1853 to 1857.

Oct. 8—Patrick Justice died this forenoon.

Dec. 11—Presbyterian church dedicated. . . . Large turn out, $361.50 raised with but little trouble.

Dec. 20—Free schools commenced yesterday, and Mr. Jones, Zimmerman and myself joined in visiting the school, establishing rules and order in the school.

Dec. 21—Visited lower school district this morning. Eighty scholars in the lower room and forty in the upper room. Mr. Johnson principal, Misses Helen Jack and Mary Kurtz, assistants.

1860.

May 18—Report of nomination of Lincoln and Hamlin gives general satisfaction.

June 25—Report of the nomination of Douglas by the "Rump" convention confirmed . . . also of Breckenridge and Lane by the National Democracy. Douglas faces long, no excitement or enthusiasm, and the Douglas Democrats don't have much to say.

Sept. 9—Preaching at the Universalist church last night, and the church dedicated by Sylvanus Cobb to-day.

Sept. 27—Joshua R. Giddings made a first-rate speech at the court house this evening.

Nov. 6—Election day for the president of the United States, the largest vote ever given in the town was given to-day—634. Everything passed off quietly.

Dec. 17—Schools opened to-day and free. Schools tolerably full—three teachers in Seminary building and seven in the other.

1861.

April 13—Bombardment of Fort Sumter said to have commenced yesterday morning.

April 15—Great prospects for war, a fight appearing inevitable. Meeting at court house this evening—Judge Brady, Walter March, Tom Brady, Newcomb and others spoke.

April 16—Volunteer company made up and Tom Brady captain [later Gen. Thos. J. Brady]; drum, fife and music all day.

April 17—War excitement and enlisting the order of the day.

April 18—Volunteers left for Indianapolis this morning, escorted by band. large crowd at depot.

April 22—The star spangled banner flung to the breeze on court house square by order of Judge Buckles. . . . Flags going up all over town.

July 2—Volunteers from this place, Capt. Luther Willson, and Selma, Capt. Williams, left for Indianapolis to-day.

July 4—The greatest number of people that ever visited Muncie here to-day. The military were out in full force, "Scott Rifles," "Ellsworth Rifles," Horse companies, etc.

July 5—The Fourteenth Indiana Regiment passed through here to-day on their way to Virginia—basket dinner prepared for them and they were pleased.

Aug. 20—Captain Brady and his company left for Indianapolis this morning.

Aug. 21—Capt. Alfred Kilgore's company left for Richmond this morning.

Sept. 21—E. C. Anthony's company left for Indianapolis.

Sept. 26—Fast day by act of Congress and proclamation of President and Governor, and very universally kept and especially in Muncie, business suspended.

Nov. 11—Dr. George W. Edgerle died this afternoon.

1862.

March 7—Last day of free schools. (Free schools began in December, so it will be seen the sessions were very brief.)

May 16—Rev. W. S. Bradford died to-day. [Bradford was Captain of Co. F, 57th Ind. Vols.]

July 16—A large company of our town boys left for Indianapolis for services to the government for 30 days, making everything look dull.

July 19—Indiana invaded by the rebels (under Morgan) last night.

Aug. 4—Good deal of excitement on account of volunteering for T. S. Walterhouse's company; speeches by Judge W. A. Bickle and Judge Joseph S. Buckles.

Aug. 8—John Trimble died to-day, he being among the first settlers of this town and county. T. S. Walterhouse elected captain and David Nation first lieutenant of company just formed.

Aug. 11—Great excitement on account of grand procession from the Mississinewa river in wagons with volunteers for Capt. John H. Ellis and Taylor.

Aug. 22—Volunteering for Dr. Henry Kirby's and Kilgore's companies.

Sept. 22—Reported death of G. H. Richardson, teacher and member of 19th Regiment. [Richardson was superintendent of the Muncie public schools when he enlisted. He was killed at South Mountain only a few days after his enlistment. G. W. H. K.]

1863.

April 7—Passenger depot burned last night, supposed accidental.

April 30—All business houses closed for the day and fast day was strictly observed.

May 12—Joseph Walling Sr. died night before last and buried to-day.

June 24—Corner stone of Masonic Hall laid by Dept. G. M. Caleb B. Smith and a very large assemblage of Masons, said to be over four hundred.

Aug. 21—55th Mass. Regiment went through and were fed here to-day.

Oct. 8—Very large crowd in town caused by Union meeting. The Home Guards out in large numbers.

Oct. 29—Some little secession fuss in Monroe township at a religious meeting.

Dec. 4—Grand dance at opening of Walling's Hall last night.

News of the army movements from day to day, the passing of the various regiments through Muncie, a trainload of rebel prisoners, a visit from an escaped Libby prisoner, the frequent event of a father, relative or friend bringing home a soldier's corpse for burial, fairs and sociables for the benefit of the army, and many similar notices indicate the progress of the great war, though these references are so brief and so detached that it would be impracticable to record more of them than are here set down.

1864.

April 19—20th Indiana passed through on their way to Washington.

April 20—8th Indiana veterans returned this evening looking fine.

April 25—The government calls for 20,000 One Hundred day men—great excitement among the boys, volunteering fast.

July 4—John A. Klein died this morning.

Nov. 21—Edward G. Keasby, formerly captain in the Florida War, died.

Nov. 24—Thanksgiving day appointed by the President in all the states—meeting in Methodist church morn and eve. Men turned out and chopped wood for the poor, subscription in cash $140.

1865.

April 10—Glorious news from General Grant. General Lee surrendered with his North Virginia army. Great rejoicing, firing of cannon, guns, crackers, burning boxes, barrels, etc., marching in all shapes, people drunk and happy.

April 15—Abraham Lincoln, president of the United States, died this morning at . . . o'clock from pistol shot from the hand of an assassin at his private box in Ford's theatre last night. By order the business houses were closed at one o'clock to-day. The assassin of President Lincoln is reported to be Booth.

April 19—The day appointed by governor as a day of fasting and prayer. The day very strictly observed, preaching at the church, all business houses draped in mourning.

Aug. 8—John S. Hutchings died Sunday and buried to-day by the Masons and Odd Fellows.

Oct. 21—Remains of Lieut. George Olcott Willard arrived from near Atlanta, Georgia (Oct. 22). Buried in honors of war.

1866.

Oct. 3—Henry C. Wachtel died to-day.

Nov. 10—Great excitement over the robbery of George H. Baxter's bank safe. which he found broken open and completely robbed of bonds, money, etc., loss about $16.000.

1867.

Jan. 8—O. S. Fowler, the phrenologist, in town.

Feb. 22—Last day of free school.

Mar. 11—Dramatics to-night (probably one of the early private theatricals mentioned elsewhere in this work; these "dramatics" continued, in the n e sa s church, to be mentioned, and they were probably rehearsals)U iv r li t

April 3—(Judge) Joseph Anthony died yesterday.

May 22—Jeremiah Wilson died yesterday.

May 25—Barnum, Van Amberg and Frost menagerie here.

1868.

Jan. 9—Moses L. Neely died to-day.

March 23—Commissioners granted donation of $100,000 to railroad (the road from Fort Wayne).

May 30—Soldiers' graves decorated (probably the first formal observance of that now annual custom).

June 2—John A. Gilbert died this morning.

June 5—James Truitt, an old citizen of the county, died to-day.

Oct. 10—Perhaps the grandest day in every respect Muncie ever had. At five o'clock A. M. Hackleman's Battery announced General Fremont's arrival, and from that time until after one o'clock P. M. there was a con- stant stream of people in every conceivable conveyance until they numbered upwards of thirty thousand, being by much the largest number ever here. Speaking at the fair grounds by Fremont, Morton and others.

Oct. 22—Absalom Perdieu died to-day.

Nov. 3—Splendid triumph of the Republican party in the election of Grant and Colfax.

1869.

Sept. 1—Second day of Fair. Balloon ascension and lady velocipede riding.

Sept. 4—Junction of the Newcastle road with the Bellfontaine this P. M.

Sept. 19—William Buffington died to-day.

Sept. 29—Garret Gibson Sr. dead.

Oct. 17—Passenger cars on the Junction Railroad arrived to-day.

Nov. 6—Dr. William C. Willard, one of the oldest practicing physicians of the county, died to-day, aged about 60 years; much respected for his eminent medical ability.

1870.

July 4—Old Settlers meeting at the Fair ground largely attended con- sidering everything. Speeches made by Asahel Thornburg, John Simmons, Job Swain, James Hodge, John Richey, Samuel Gregory, William G. Wil- liams, Thomas J. Sample, William J. Moore, Warren Stewart, and others. The oldest lady present, Mrs. George Turner, having been in the county over fifty years.

Oct. 10—First train from Indianapolis to Fort Wayne to-day.

1871.

Jan. 26—Dr. Samuel W. Mitchell died this morning.

Nov. 16—Dr. Jer. Dynes of Smithfield buried to-day. James Carter of Eaton died this morning.

Nov. 23—Charles F. Willard died last night. Came to Muncie in Feb- ruary, 1831. (Was a partner of F. E. Putnam.)

1872.

April 8—John C. Helm died this morning.

May 30—Decoration day and very generally observed, for the first time.

June 11—Muncie improving more this, than any former year, and (improvements) are of a substantial character—Wysor's opera house, Brady and Mellette printing office, Mark Walling's dwelling, Hummel's front part three-story.

June 18—Last night property of J. A. Maddy, Huffer Bros., Charles F. Willard and Volney Willson, on Walnut street, burned, a total loss.

June 25—James E. Wilcoxon died this morning.

Aug. 8—The laying of the cornerstone by the Odd Fellows of their new hall.

Aug. 30—John Wright died at the Jo Davis house this morning.

Sept. 3—Considerable building in town, Wysor's Opera House (at Main and Walnut), Odd Fellows, and Davis, Willard and Huffer are laying brick.

Sept. 21—John W. Burson died this morning.

Nov. 5—Presidential election between U. S. Grant, Republican, and Horace Greeley, Liberal Republican and Democrat. Total vote in Center township, 1110, 21 less than at state election.

Nov. 9—F. E. Putnam's house lit with gas this eve. (Several items had appeared concerning the erection of the gas works during this fall).

Nov. 13—Isaac Shideler died to-day.

Dec. 26—Samuel W. Harlan buried by Delaware Lodge No. 46.

1873.

Aug. 29—Charles Parker Sample died suddenly.

Dec. 15—Wysor preparing to open his opera house this evening.

1874.

Feb. 10—Women's Temperance organization chief topic of conversation. Great excitement.*

Feb. 23—Second crusade of the women against the rum holes. "Butcher Smith" turned his (liquors) into the gutter.

Feb. 28—Seventh crusade; a tremendous outpouring of people from city and country.

March 1—Dr. George W. Garst buried to-day.

March 13—Seventeenth crusade. Topers getting scarce.

March 25—R. and I. Necks commenced tearing down the old Jere Howell tavern (built in 1838). Mrs. Livermore gave a grand lecture at the opera house last night and at the N. E. church this morning. Twelfth prayer meeting and twenty-sixth crusade.

April 10—Thirty-ninth crusade. . . . Whiskey spilled in the gutter by crusade.

May 5—Election for city officers. 46th all-day prayer meeting. Whiskeyites glad over the election, although it is no victory to them.

May 16—The Women's Crusade of this city laid the cornerstone of the house of R. & I. Necks on the south side of Main between Walnut and Mulberry, and deposited various articles in the sealed box.

May 22—(69th and last crusade).

July 12—John Wilcoxon died this morning.

. Oct. 2—Joshua R. Lockwood died last evening.

Oct. 21—The steam fire engine "Delaware Chief" on trial this evening.

*This was the "Women's Crusade," which swept over Ohio and Indiana. I now have in my possession a small handbill, which reads as follows: "Temperance War! The friends of temperance are requested to meet at Simpson Chapel, M. E. Church, at 3 o'clock this afternoon, to express their sympathy with the noble women who, in this state and Ohio, are resisting the whisky traffic, and to take steps to prevent the granting of licenses in this city."
Dated, "Muncie, Saturday, February 7, 1874." (G. W. H. K.)

Nov. 5—Rev. Robert Irwin Sr. died last night.
Nov. 18—Citizens Bank commenced yesterday.

1875.

Jan. 9—Public library opened this morning, free.
March 2—Asher Storer, an old citizen, buried to-day.
May 26—James W. Heath died last evening.
Sept. 9—James Collier, an old citizen, died this morning, and George H. Baxter, another old resident, died this afternoon.

1876.

Jan. 29—River very high, higher than it has been since January, 1847.
May 29—The old Jo Davis House (which had been damaged by fire previously) disappearing fast, down to top of first story.
July 4—The 100th anniversary of our American Independence. All the bells of the city commenced ringing at ten o'clock, firing of all kinds of powder, noise and confusion all night. Grand parade.
July 22—Samuel P. Anthony died this morning; eighty-three years old and one of the oldest citizens as well as the wealthiest.
Sept. 3—The Episcopal church opened and preached in for the first time, by Rev. Root. Church on North Walnut street.
Sept. 15—Jacob Calvert, an old citizen, died on his farm near town to-day.

1877.

March 20—James L. Stephenson died this morning.
April 22—Joseph A. Walling died this morning.
April 29—Job Swain, one of our oldest citizens, died this morning.
June 26—Calvin Breese, an old settler, buried yesterday.
Nov. 11—Rev. Wm. M. Stryker, the second pastor of the Presbyterian church in this city, preached with us to-day—first time since 1852.

1878.

Jan. 25—William McConnell, one of the old settlers of the county, died yesterday, aged 77.
Oct. 10—Abraham Buckles, an old citizen of the county, buried to-day, aged 80 years.
Oct. 20—The Times printing office burned this morning.

1879.

Jan. 24—David Kilgore died at his residence this morning—an old settler, formerly called the "Delaware Chief."
March 2—Thomas Madden, an old citizen of Delaware county, about 95 years old, died yesterday.
May 4—Adam Shafer, another old settler, of Hamilton township, died yesterday.
Aug. 14—Thomas Kirby died this morning.
Oct. 22—Commenced laying iron on the L. E. & W. R. R. (on 20th) and are up to Liberty street this evening. (This was the so-called Toledo road, from Muncie northeast to Albany, for which a tax had been voted by the county a short time before.)

1880.

Jan. 21—Passenger trains commenced running east on the L. E. & W. road Monday morning (Jan. 19).

Sept. 8—Fred Douglas, the colored orator, spoke in the opera house this afternoon.

Dec. 3—Boyce block (Jefferson and Main) nearly completed.

1881.

Jan. 13—Calvin P. Streeter, an old citizen, who came to Muncie in 1836, died last evening.

Feb. 19—Washington Trout, an old citizen of Harrison township, died yesterday.

March 24—Commenced tearing down the old Keasby property on the southeast corner of Main and Jefferson streets, once occupied as a dwelling and postoffice kept by Edward G. Keasby years ago.

CHAPTER XIV.

MUNCIE AND VICINITY AT THE BEGINNING OF THE LAST QUARTER CENTURY.

In 1880 Muncie city had a population of 5,219; all of Center township had 6,681. Muncie was a city in civil status, but still had the population of a quiet town. South of the Big Four Railroad track were a few scattering houses. The town had made no growth west of the river, and in fact hardly extended west of Council street. None of the half dozen suburbs and additions that now border the north bank of the river had been planned. Taking the court house as a center and striking a circle with a radius of half a mile, the area thus limited would have included, in 1880, nine-tenths of the population and commercial and manufacturing resources of Muncie city. At the present time, to include a proportionate amount of the city, it would be necessary to lengthen the radius nearly four times, or nearly two miles.

In 1890 Muncie city had a population of 11,345, having doubled in ten years. In the same period Center township had increased to 12,879. It is interesting to note that the entire county had a population, in 1880, of 22,926; in 1890, of 30,131. The increase in the county was, in round numbers, seven thousand; in Muncie city it was six thousand, showing that the increase in population during this decade was confined almost entirely to Muncie.

This is one way to tell the story, a graphic way—of Munice's growth from a town to a city. It is a favorite method of computing the growth of cities, but is misleading so far as a proper estimate of the city's resources and improvement are concerned. Population may remain almost stationary, yet a community may advance in material development, in public spirit and civic improvement, in education and general culture and morality to a degree that the general census tables would never indicate.

For citizens of Delaware county, the story of progress during the last twenty-five years should have never-failing interest. The city was merely the center to which were turned the resources of the entire surrounding district, and for that reason the history of the surrounding country is told together with the story of Muncie's progress from a town of five thousand people to a city of thirty thousand. Before beginning a chronological narrative of the history of the city and vicinity during the past quarter century, it will be well to take a brief resume of Muncie at the beginning of that period.

Municipal Status in 1880.

Muncie has long outgrown the institutions and improvements which she possessed in 1880—save one, the city hall at the corner of Jackson and Mulberry streets. This old building, now headquarters of the fire department, seems to demand some mention at the outset. The land on which it stands was bought in 1872 from Kirby brothers, but it was two years before the brick building was completed, in which were quarters for the fire department, council room, and city calaboose. The cost, up to May, 1874. was $5,402.64, but by 1878 nearly fourteen thousand dollars had been expended on land and improvements for the city at that corner. In the meantime, the original building having been found to be inadequate, several thousand dollars were expended in additions, after which the building appeared practically as at the present time. The city hall as thus completed became and remained for some years an important center of city affairs. The public library and reading room were located there until their removal to the present library building. The fire department, the police department, the mayor's and clerk's office and all departments of the city government had their quarters there.

The following sentences from the mayor's report of May, 1878, are a general description of Muncie's status at that time: "The fire department . . . is in a sufficient and satisfactory condition, and is believed to be acceptable to the city and public. From the report of the city board of education it is proper to say that the whole system of our common schools, embracing the academy, appears to have been well and safely controlled. All our school property . . . is free from debts of any kind, and the treasury with means to further provide educational facilities. . . . In this connection I desire to call your attention to the public library as one of the departments of general education . . . In the past, some efforts have been made to establish a board of health. . . . But thus far without success. Many fears are entertained that our sanitary condition as a city is not what prudence would dictate nor safety require. . . . Necessity makes it a duty that your attention should be called to the city prison. Decency and common humanity requires that persons of both sexes should not be confined in the same room. Our present situation is such that a temporary separation only can be maintained. . . ."

In 1880 the annual disbursements for the principal departments of the city, expressed in round numbers, were:

Fire Department $1,150
Streets and Alleys 5,100
Cemetery 2,800
General Sewerage 3,500
Library 800
Street Lights 62

These reports are chiefly noteworthy as indicating what Muncie city did not have in 1880. There was a fire department, but it was a volunteer service, and while a Babcock fire extinguisher, a steam fire engine, a team of fire horses, fire cisterns, etc., were among the equipment, the department had little of the efficiency and completeness that are now demanded. The schools and the public library were sufficient for the time. However, of the improvements and conveniences that are none the less prized because so generally supplied, Muncie had only a beginning in 1880. The streets in the business portion were graded and graveled, but were uneven and covered with ruts, muddy and sometimes hardly passable in bad weather. There was considerable flag-stone sidewalk, but at the sides as well as in the center the streets were unattractive in appearance and many of them inconvenient as thoroughfares. Though much money was expended each year for drainage, nothing approaching a sewerage system had been begun. Cesspools and underground vaults were in common use, the rains passed off by surface drainage, and, as the mayor pointed out, the sanitary condition of the city called for serious consideration and action on the part of the authorities.

Gas and Electricity.

From the condition of the streets our thoughts naturally pass to the methods of lighting them. Muncie has had a variety of experience with street lighting. The oldest resident can doubtless remember when the heavenly luminaries were the only sources of light by day or by night. The fitful rays of a tallow candle sometimes stole from the houses around the square and made more prominent the gloom of the streets, or a wandering lantern lighted the footsteps from store to home. Some years later came the kerosene oil lamp. These served as beacons to guide one from point to point rather than really to illuminate the streets. In 1862 it was first proposed to light the streets with gas, inducements being offered by the town for the location of a plant for manufacturing gas. But the primitive methods of lighting continued for many years. Again and again the city council considered the matter, but not until 1874 was a definite course decided upon, and even then no gas works were built. Five years passed, and in July, 1879, the firm of Miller and Kuhn, from Pennsylvania, offered to build a coal gas plant, to erect cast-iron posts for street lights, and to furnish gas for city purposes at $1.65 a thousand feet. The city granted a franchise, and the company pushed the work with such energy that the plant was in operation before the contract time (Nov. 1, 1879). The lighting of the gas was an important event to the little city, being described by the Muncie Times as follows: "Last Saturday evening, Oct. 18, 1879, at half past 6 o'clock, the illumination by the Muncie gas works took place. The 'gas tree' erected at the southeast corner of the public square consisted of a gas pipe standing perpendicular, to the height of about fifteen feet, and from it protruded numerous prongs, arms, limbs and various unique contrivances. A large star adorned the top of the pipe, and immediately under it were the words 'Muncie Gas Company.' The evening being very blustery, the wind blew out the lights occasionally, and while it was not the success it might have been, it was a beautiful scene. The streets were crowded to witness the burning of the first gas from the new gas works, and Messrs. Miller and Kuhn start out under auspicious circumstances, there being sixty consumers on that evening." In 1882 the city was illuminated by eighty-three street lights, and gas was also used in the library and city building. Electric lighting was still in experimental stages, no one dreamed of natural gas, and so it was considered that Muncie had a modern and satisfactory system of public lighting.

The inestimable advantages of water works had not yet been afforded Muncie citizens. There was a well or cistern in every yard, and we have noted the fact that the fire department used fire cisterns located in various parts of the city.

Telephone.

One convenience had been just introduced into Muncie about 1880, and was an object of curiosity rather than practical use, when compared with its prevalence and efficiency at this day. Telephonic communication is now so familiar that it is rather difficult to appreciate the point of view from which the editor of the News regarded the introduction of telephones into Muncie, as described in the following extracts from that paper:

(Muncie Daily News, January 22, 1880.) The telephone exchange that has been spoken of through the columns of the News at various times recently, is now a certainty, and at no distant day the people of Muncie can sit in their parlors or offices and converse with their friends in another portion of the city with almost as much satisfaction as if they were conversing face to face. As many are aware, the enterprise is being managed by Messrs. Wilcoxon & Son, J. M. and W. H. Long, and through their efforts the success of the undertaking is due. All the materials to be used in the construction of the exchange have been ordered, and the work of erecting it will be commenced about the first of the month. The following are those who have already subscribed and will use it for at least one year:

L. E. & W. R. R. depot.
C. C. C. & I. R. R. depot.
R. S. Hall, Haines House.
J. A. Heinsohn, Kirby House.
N. F. Ethell, News Office.
E. W. Brady, Times Office.
Yost Bros., Livery Stable.
Weeks & Kimbrough, Livery Stable.

T. H. Kirby's grocery.
Adamson & Goddard's grocery.
Muncie National Bank.
Citizens' National Bank.
James Boyce Flax Mill.
James Boyce Shoe Store.
George H. Andrews' Drug Store.
Dr. G. W. H. Kemper.
Dr. G. D. Leach.
Dr. Robert Winton.
G. W. Stephenson.
A. L. Kerwood, Clerk's Office.
W. T. Davis, Hub & Spoke Factory.
City Building.
Templer & Gregory's Law Office.
Blount & Templer's Law Office.
J. E. Mellett.
Putnam & Kirby's Store.
Putnam & Kirby's Lumber Yard.
F. E. Putnam's residence.
J. M. Long's Store.
L. Wilcoxon & Son, flouring mills.
A. A. Milligan, residence.
Charles N. Wilcoxon, residence.
George Stephenson, residence.
J. M. Long, residence.
John Kirby, residence.
L. Wilcoxon, residence.
J. H. Long, residence.

Judge Buckles and Mr. D. Cammack have the matter under consideration and if necessary arrangements can be made, will also have a line
connecting with the exchange run, the former to his residence in the
country and the latter to his mill five miles west of the city.

(Muncie Daily News, March 8, 1882.) It is two years this month
since Muncie began enjoying the privileges and benefits of the system of
telephones, the wires of which span our streets at all points.

The company owning and operating the Muncie Bell Telephone Company is composed of the same gentlemen originally introducing the enterprise here, namely: Messrs. Lloyd Wilcoxon, J. M. Long, Charles Wilcoxon,
manager, and Harry Long, secretary.

The instruments used are the Bell Telephone and the Blake Transmitter.
This is considered one of the most successful forms of the telephone for city
exchange purposes and has proved highly satisfactory here, as a general
thing. There are now in use sixty-two instruments, on forty-six lines, in
this city, several instruments being in use on one circuit in a few instances.
It is estimated that an average of five persons use each telephone. This
gives us an aggregate of three hundred and ten people who are continually
accommodated by this convenience, whereby the calling of the Exchange
places them in direct communication with any of this number, including
public buildings, schools, stores, factories and residences.

Compared with many systems of city telephone lines and exchanges we may consider ourselves eminently well fitted and suited in the comfort, convenience and real reliability of our "Hello" contrivance, which is increasing its new work of wires almost every day.

Commercial and Manufacturing.

Muncie had considerable prominence as a business and manufacturing center at the beginning of the eighties, though it was mainly such importance as belonged to a county-seat town of five thousand people. Boyce's bagging factory, employing about a hundred persons, was the leading manufacturing enterprise of the city at that time. There were flour mills and saw mills, planing mills, a foundry and machine shop, and several factories for making special implements. Two national banks and one private bank, besides the various mercantile stores, were the principal features of the commercial district.

The business district had few commendable buildings. On the public square stood the old court house. North of it, the building now used as the Muncie Trust Company's home was the most conspicuous, and nearby was the Times building, which had recently been rebuilt. Walling Hall stood on the west side, and Masonic hall at the southwest corner. Where the modern Wysor block now stands was a three-story brick building, using the old Wysor opera house. The best block in the city at the time, and in fact the first modern business block, was the Boyce block on the north side of Main between Mulberry and Jefferson. This was built in 1880, and was a distinct improvement on all the business buildings of the city at the time; in fact, was so far in advance of the times that many prophesied that its owner could never make it profitable. Across from this block was the Kirby House, with its mansard roof, at that time the most conspicuous building in the city. South Walnut street contained no buildings of note, "Rat Row," at the corner of Jackson, already being in disgrace as a business block. The city hall on Jackson and the high school building on West Adams were then new, especially the latter, and were pointed out with considerable pride by citizens as examples of first-class public buildings. None of the modern churches that are now so conspicuous had then been built, the railroad depots were eyesores to the citizens, and architecturally Muncie was at the beginning of her career.

It is common to refer the beginning of Muncie's modern era as dating from the discovery of natural gas. This is true in general, but a study of the city and county's affairs during the three or four years preceding that discovery leads one to believe that an unusual era of prosperity had already begun, and would have resulted in a remarkable degree of development even without the aid of gas. It will be remembered that the Civil war was followed by several years when the entire country advanced under tremendous pressure of enterprise and confidence. Then in the seventies came a disastrous panic, affecting every section of the country and retarding improvement of every kind. Confidence was restored and business and industry revived from this condition about the close of the decade, so that at the time now under consideration Muncie and the surrounding country had joined in the general progress being made everywhere. Building improvements are a fair index of local prosperity, and a summary of the amount expended during the year 1883 in this respect indicated an unusual state of prosperity in the county. It was estimated that $118,000 was the amount expended for this class of improvements in Muncie during the year, consisting of 160 buildings and additions. And at the same time similar expenditures in the county outside of Muncie amounted to two hundred thousand dollars, Union, Monroe and Liberty townships and the town of Albany being credited with the largest amounts.

With regard to the distribution of the population of Muncie in 1884 much interest attaches to the figures obtained in the school enumeration made in April of that year. This showed a total population of 5,820, 1,788 of whom were of school age. For school purposes the city was divided into four districts. The first district, lying north of the Big Four tracks and east of the Ft. W., C. & L., contained 1,189 persons, or 178 families. Between the Fort Wayne tracks and Franklin street were 1,864 people, or 414 families. West of Franklin street to the limits were 1,340 people, or 312 families. While south of the Big Four Railroad, which comprised the fourth district, was a population of 1,427, or 316 families.

Water Works.

Several large public enterprises were undertaken by city and county during the years preceding the discovery of gas, but to Muncie the matter of most vital interest was the building of water works. The issue of water works was raised early in the eighties, and has never ceased to be a live one in all the succeeding years. In the early years the people were by no means a unit as to the wisdom of building water works, and the discussion over the subject did not lack interest, nor was logic wanting to either side in advancing arguments for or against the movement. The plan to establish municipal water works, only a short time after it was broached, brought out a very spicy article from Mr. N. F. Ethell. While expressing his opposition to the movement, he adds some comments concerning the status of Muncie's development and his opinions concerning the future that are particularly interesting to the present-day reader, aside from the bearing they had on the question under consideration. His article follows:

(Muncie Daily Times, January 19, 1882.) If the citizens of Muncie want water works it is, right now, the easiest thing in the world to take steps to have them. Petitions for signatures are placed in the advertised places and a hundred signatures, as we understand it, will be sufficient to authorize the council to call an election to decide the question. The votes cast, if there be a moderately full expression of opinion by ballot, will be the basis for the future action of the council, and if we may judge from their actions, they will plunge headlong into the work, if given the smallest encouragement. Not a long time will be required to have a vote taken, money borrowed, the preliminaries arranged, and then a small army of men will be tearing up our streets, laying mains, piping houses, putting in hydrants, erecting stand-pipes, placing engines in position, and arranging for the new order of things. In a year or two, if the people wish it, we can have it to say to strangers, with a smile, "We have water works." That, no doubt, will be a satisfaction, and we can put out our fires by the new system instead of the old (probably not so well) ; we can have hydrant water to drink instead of well; we can sprinkle our yards so easily in dry times; and we may save a few cents in the year on insurance, and so forth. All nice enough, but then come the long years of heavy taxation, and groans innumerable from every side wearing off the smile of satisfaction, and probably leaving us to say "We paid dearly for our whistle."

A good system of water works will, some day, be a good thing for Muncie—if Muncie shall ever become a city of any size. But will that time ever come? Is there any prospect of our increasing in size—of growing large enough to justify the establishment of water works at enormous expense. Just now there is but little doubt that we are standing still, if not, in fact, retrograding. There are today a dozen empty yawning business houses on our two principal streets, and a number of dwelling houses in various parts of our city wanting tenants. Some of our citizens are leaving us for more energetic and thriving towns, and some of our manufacturers are "going west" to points where they can obtain assistance, and have a chance to grow.

The outlook is not very cheering for an increase of population or of business, and if we do not grow we won't feel the need of water works.

Is it not well for our people to pause and ponder, before taking this momentous step—a step which they may always regret? If we must have water works, however, let due deliberation be had. Let the people see or know of some other plans than the one submitted for consideration. The only plan proposed is hardly understood and should be before them for many months. And while this consideration is being had let us hasten to get out of debt and accumulate some money in the treasury, so that we may not be compelled to borrow every cent required to place the works. It will be the easiest matter to get started into a lavish expenditure of money; but who can tell where the end will be? It is certainly cruel to think of plunging into a vast debt when our treasury is empty and our city retrograding.

If Muncie were growing in population and business; if we had thriving manufactories in our midst and more coming in ; if our streets were thronged with vehicles conveying manufactured articles to the cars to be shipped to various parts of the country; if strangers were flocking in to become residents and to make investments of money; if the value of our real estate and other property were advancing; if the people could feel and know that there was a "boom" of some kind going on and that everybody was encouraged and happy and full of snap and energy; if all our workmen and mechanics were constantly at work as they would like to be; if our people were united as one man in a full fixed determination to build up our industries; if all these things were so and visible, then it would be well, perchance, to plunge into the water works business with a grand halloo and whoop it up along with the balance of the good things going on. Or even if the great bulk of the good people of Muncie were satisfied—thoroughly convinced—that water works were a full necessity and must be established, now and at once, why then, let the thing be done. Not otherwise.

It is plain to every passably observant person that the entire people are not ready to plunge into this vortex of debt. It is doubtful if a bare majority are so ready. There does not seem to be a general uprising for water works. Some want them—as many don't want them. A few, for this or that reason—reasons personal to themselves—want them badly. For equally as good reasons as many do not want them. We are not as yet a united people in this matter. The truth is plain to everyone that the time is not ripe for water works, at least not for the system and plan now before the people—with no specimens of other systems or plans to choose from. And would it be right for a bare majority to force a large unwilling minority into a long course of taxation?

In the past, and not very far in the past, the people have been badly bored by hasty or thoughtless action, and have suffered for it, and are likely to so suffer for a long time to come. Too easy acquiescence in the acceptance of things as they drifted, or as they were quietly guided by scheming and unseen hands, has wrought mischief in the past, and the people have repented bitterly their good nature or carelessness. The revolution in the school board—a revolution brought about by two or three shrewd co-workers—is one example. It was done because the people were not watchful enough or careful enough of the first or initiatory steps. Of course the infernal hullabaloo set going by this event in our history should not be considered as a comparison with so good a thing as water works. But it is an example of what carelessness may do. The question is, are we ready to go to the expense of water works now, and just as we are commencing to build a $150,000 court house, $50,000 of which the citizens of Muncie will have to pay? It is a serious question, and should be so treated, and our worthy Councilmen should be loath to ask or urge the people to do that which may bring upon themselves a load of trouble that the people will not forget or forgive.

A water works ordinance was passed by the city council April 14, 1884, but on January 19, 1885, was repealed and a new ordinance passed, giving the mayor and clerk power to sign a contract for the erection of water works. The building of a municipal system was considered inadvisible or impracticable, and the contract was to be made with a private company. The contract was signed between the city and S. A. Wilson, A. L. Johnson,

T. F. Rose and S. M. Highlands, who were to organize the Muncie Water
Works Company. The plant was to cost not less than $100,000, and water
was to be furnished the city at $5,000 annually. A direct pressure system
was to be built, capable of furnishing "an ample and constant supply of
good, pure water for fire, domestic and manufacturing purposes." Equipment to be brick building, two pumps, etc., with capacity of at least two
million gallons per day; at least seven miles of water pipes to be main.
tained, with eighty-five hydrants for fire. At any time after twenty years
from the completion of the works the city was to have the right of purchase,
either on terms of mutual agreement or as fixed by a board of three. The
works were to be completed on or before January 1, 1887. The company,
thus empowered, went to work at once, and by the following spring the
streets were well torn up by the trenchers and pipe layers.

Opposition to the contract made with the company by the city was
still apparent. Many citizens had doubts and misgivings similar to those
expressed by Mr. Ethell several years before. The council came in for
a good share of criticism. In response to these objectors, Mr. T. F. Rose,
a member of the water company, prepared a statement, in May, 1885, which
is in effect a history of the water works up to that time, as also a defense
of the action of the council and water company. Mr. Rose's article, in
part, is as follows:

(Muncie Daily News, May 9, 1885.) The common council began to
agitate earnestly the subject of water works as early as the summer of 1881,
before any of the members of the late council were elected. That council
employed a competent engineer, Frank Doran, of Richmond, Indiana, and
on the 6th day of December, 1881, he furnished a complete plan and specifications with costs for "water works amply sufficient to meet the requirements of the city until it has a population of 20,000." This was a plan for
the works to be erected by the city and is substantially the same in size and
capacity as the franchise granted to the company now erecting the works,
except the pumping house will be located east instead of west of the city.

The subject of water works was discussed from time to time, by the
council and city papers, until the adoption of the constitutional amendment
prohibiting cities from incurring indebtedness in excess of two per cent of
the taxable property. Our city tax duplicate at that time showed a value
of about $2,000,000, which made the plan impossible.

During the summer of 1883 J. D. Cook, of Toledo, Ohio, whose
eminent qualifications and abilities as a water works engineer will not be
questioned, was employed to prepare plans, specifications, estimates and costs
of water works for our city. All who have taken the trouble to examine
the information furnished by Mr. Cook will not say the common council
acted unadvisedly. On the 17th day of January, 1884, the plans were submitted and shortly afterwards the council passed an ordinance establishing
water works for the city of Muncie, to be erected by private parties and

directed the city clerk to advertise for bidders. There were filed with the water works committee four propositions for the erection of the works.

The proposition finally accepted, after some changes, was presented some four or five months prior to its passage, and I can say in justification of the committee and council, a candid and careful consideration of the terms and requirements of the contract were discussed from time to time and fully understood by all. The proposition accepted was the best proposed, all who have examined will admit.

We learn from the records the expense of maintaining the present fire department will average over $5,000 per year, not including new fire cisterns every year or so, with the cost of an occasional fire engine thrown in. An estimate by the secretary of the Fire Insurance Board states that there is $2,500,000 worth of property insured annually in this city; with an efficient water works the rate of insurance will doubtless be reduced so as to save to the citizens from $3,000 to $4,000 annually. Then, as a financial problem, has not the city council acted for the best interest of the city, to say nothing about the free use of water for public buildings and schools, flushing of streets and sewers, the increased fire protection, sanitary facilities, encouragement to manufactories, and beautifying our city by clean streets, green lawns, graceful fountains and beautiful flowers, all of which have a money value in the sale of property and the comforts of homes.

The water works company prosecuted its work with such expedition that on July 31, 1885, it notified the city council that the works were completed and ready for use. On October 19, following, the council directed the use of the water works according to contract.

Streets and Sewers.

At every council meeting during 1884 the improvement of streets and alleys was new and important business. The city was awake to the necessity of improving the streets and creating a more sanitary condition than had existed in previous years. The beginning of sewer building, the organization of a board of health, and many other public improvements had their origin in the years just before the "big boom." The Jackson street sewer, the first large sewer, which was built in the spring of 1884, did not prove very satisfactory to the people because of faulty construction. It was called "cloaca magna" and denounced as extremely unsanitary and no improvement on the old methods of surface drainage.

Electric Lights.

The year 1885 marks the beginning of electric lighting in Muncie. In February of that year Mr. J. H. Wysor, while building a skating rink on North Walnut street, negotiated for the use of "Brush's electric lights" to be placed in the building; whether they were installed and were the first used in the city is not known by the writer. October 19, 1885, the council granted James Boyce permission to erect poles for electric lights in his mills, residence and storerooms. Mr. Boyce soon had a dynamo in operation, and on December 19, 1885, the Boyce block and H. Klein's jewelry store were illuminated by electricity, which was quite as much of an event as the first exhibition of gas lighting had been some six years before. Mr. Boyce soon extended wires to other business houses, and from this time the use of electricity for lighting made rapid progress.

CHAPTER XV.

NATURAL GAS.

In the spring of 1886 the farmers of Delaware county prepared their fields and sowed them with grain, as had been done for many years. Under the sun and rain of summer the soil grew and matured the crops, and with the coming of fall the ripened harvests were stored away in anticipation of a similar year to follow. Sturdy industry, average contentment, and material well-being were blessings possessed by the majority of homes throughout Delaware county, and the continuance of such prosperity was the most that was hoped for by nine persons out of ten.

And yet, before the year was out, all was changed. An awful force had struck the land, almost in a single night, and with the knowledge of a fluid wealth beneath their feet, men forgot the fruitful soil which for years had returned its regular reward to human toil. Beneficent Ceres was scorned, and men, in panic, worshiped Gas. Where had been the waving fields of green and gold, the earth was scarred by the burrowing drills, and skeleton derricks were strung in ghostly procession across the landscape. Quiet bucolic scenes became a roaring workshop of Vulcan and his devotees. An active gas field produces an awesome if not terrifying effect when first seen, and it is not surprising that many of the eastern visitors, on making their first visit to the gas fields and witnessing the tremendous power of a roaring gas well, fled in terror from the scene. The inert earth, which men have so long regarded as their surest stronghold against the tempests of the sky and the rage of the sea, all at once seems filled with the breath of life, and heaves with its exhalations as though preparing to revolt and overthrow the puny works of mankind. The pursuits and ambition of man changed in keeping with the new forces of the earth, and with the discovery of natural gas was ushered in a new era for Delaware county.

Old settlers used to speak of the "Indiana coon belt," a geographical description that referred to the area of big timber and flat and often swampy land in eastern Indiana. One of the best known products of this region was the coon, though the phrase "coon belt" received several additional meanings which were thought of when the term was used. It is a noteworthy coincidence, told the writer by an old resident, that the natural gas belt corresponds in area quite nearly with the "coon belt." Whether there is any scientific connection between the two, is an inquiry that has not been pushed with any profit.

Natural gas having played such an important part in the development of this county, it seems that a brief statement concerning the nature and origin of this fluid wealth will not be out of keeping in a history of Delaware county. A few years after the discovery of gas and while the development of the fields was at its height, a large party of scientists visited this section of the state for the purpose of observing and studying the gas field. As a result of his observations, one of the party, H. C. Hovey, contributed to the Scientific American an article in which he describes in untechnical language the origin of this gas.

"Knowing that marsh gas and natural gas," to quote the substance of his article, "are nearly identical, the fair inference is that they share a similar origin. Stir the sediment at the bottom of a marsh, and inflammable bubbles arise. The gas they contain comes from decayed vegetable matter. So it is with the larger accumulations in beds of lakes and seas. The Spanish navigators found an area equal to continental Europe filled with an enormous mass of seaweed, single specimens being hundreds of feet long and their stems huge vegetable cables a foot in diameter. Imagine some ancient Sargasso sea to have had its mass of algæ caught in a bed of calcareous mud where it underwent slow decomposition. What a measureless quantity of gas would have been manufactured and afterward imprisoned in the surrounding limestone formed from the mud. The time would plainly come when, the work of decomposition being finished, no more gas could be made;· but what had been created would stay there until in some way released. . . . The fact is at first hard to comprehend that natural gas, instead of being collected in a cavernous reservoir, is stored up in what appears to be solid limestone of the Trenton period. But this is true in the Ohio and Indiana gas fields. In the latter the Niagara limestone is always surface rock, being about 400 feet thick. Next below come nearly 600 feet of Hudson River and Utica bituminous shales, that appear to roof over and confine the true gas bed. The Trenton limestone is next to the shale and yields gas almost as soon as struck. Microscopic examination proves all gas rock to be porous, no matter how solid it may seem to be. . . . The elevation of the Trenton rock is another important indication. At Muncie and Anderson it lies entirely above sea level, and therefore there is no danger from salt water. Where it lies from 200 to 700 feet below sea level, no gas is to be had. This partly explains the fact that although the Trenton rock underlies perhaps fifty counties in the state, the productive gas region, as thus far developed, is limited to six or eight of them: Delaware, Blackford, Madison, Grant, Hamilton, Howard, Tipton and Shelby."

In March, 1890, there died at Eaton George W. Carter, the discoverer of the Indiana gas field. His name deserves lasting remembrance in Delaware county for this pioneer work. The discovery, or rather the reopening, of the first gas well in Indiana, was described in the state geologist's report published about January, 1887. Dr. A. J. Phinney, of Muncie, furnished the information about the well, the substance of which is here given.

In 1876, at Eaton, a well was sunk to the depth of 600 feet, the hole being two inches in diameter. As the company was exploring for coal, no attention was paid to the flow of "an ill-smelling gas" which was obtained, at that depth, in sufficient quantity to produce a flame two feet in height. Gas was not thought at that time to possess any economic value. With the discovery and development of natural gas fields in Ohio, those formerly interested in the Eaton well became convinced that gas would be found in paying quantities there. Among those most sanguine of success were George W. Carter, of Eaton; W. W. Worthington and Hon. Robert Bell of Fort Wayne. These gentlemen, with some enterprising citizens of the town, organized a company, and gave A. H. Cranell the contract for sinking the well. The hole had a diameter of eight inches the first 250 feet, and five and one-half inches for the remaining distance; height of the derrick was 72 feet. The bore was sunk 890 feet to Trenton rock, and after penetrating that 32 feet a satisfactory flow of gas was obtained.

Development of Gas Territory.

Shortly after the successful completion of the Eaton well, and before the close of the year, gas well No. 1 had been bored one mile east of Muncie, and at a depth of 898 feet gas was obtained with a pressure of 325 pounds to the square inch. In January, 1887, pipes were laid on Walnut street from the gas well and gas began to be used for heating the boilers in the electric light plant and in stores for light. The Kuhn and Highlands well near the gas works in south Muncie was opened January 14th, and the natural gas was used for the manufacture of coal gas. A few weeks later it was claimed that the Muncie Gas Co. was furnishing natural gas instead of coal gas to its customers. This was of course in violation of their contract, which had been made before natural gas was thought of, and in February the city council resolved to obtain an injunction restraining the company from any such substitution.

The gas field was developed with amazing rapidity. The sinking of wells suddenly became a profitable business of itself, and the demand for boring tools and experienced men to handle them was much greater than the supply. The farmers who had sufficient capital were eager to put down wells on their farms, or to lease their land to one of the many development companies that were formed about that time. Gas companies opened wells in all the smaller towns and supplied the fuel for lighting, heating and manufacturing purposes. On September 18, 1887, a well was opened at Selma, and in a short time pipes were laid throughout the village for lighting. In November, 1887, the Muncie Natural Gas Co. reported nine producing wells, from which it supplied 1004 customers, through nineteen and a half miles of mains and pipes, the entire cost of their plant being $78,-148.88. By July, 1888, it was claimed that Delaware county had 35 producing wells. In January, 1889, a total of 39 wells was reported in the county, distributed as follows: Muncie, 25; New Corner, 1; Nixon's, 1; Eaton, 2; and one each at Albany, Shideler, Boyceton, Selma, Daleville, Yorktown, Cowan, Oakville, Anthony, DeSoto. At the same time Madison county had 28 wells; Grant county, 27; Randolph county, 9; Jay county, 17.

It soon became the boast that Muncie had no coal or wood yards, that twelve dollars a year paid for all the gas needed for fuel and light. Gas supply is unlimited, there is enough to last a thousand years, a well may be placed on every forty acres or even less and will continue to produce gas for all time. Such was the optimism developed at a time when nearly every day marked the increase of the gas output by millions of cubic feet. For several years the people indulged in riotous extravagance with nature's gift. It has been said that Americans are the most wasteful people on earth, and that they can afford to be because their natural resources are as yet beyond the limit of development. Certainly that was true of the natural gas belt twenty years ago. It was a glorious period, buoyant and enthusiastic, and the ambitions of men were as irrepressible as the roaring gushers themselves. Even now when men who were at the center of affairs during those days talk of the gas boom, they admit that they pursued a reckless policy but they speak with less regret than with pleasant recollection of a time when men were stirred to the utmost of endeavor and the very air was vibrant with a new-born enthusiasm.

The gas was allowed to burn night and day. At noontide as at midnight, the roaring flambeaux that stood by the roadside and at the crossroads in the country consumed gas by thousands of feet, but never once was there a thought of checking it. The horizon was aglow with the flames from thousands of gas lights, and some farmyards were so brightly lighted that the chickens never knew the proper time to roost. One morning at two o'clock, while driving in from the country, Dr. Kemper observed a hen with her brood picking up insects within the circle of light shed by a roadside gas torch.

There was almost no limit to the methods devised for consuming gas without adequate returns or practical use. When a party of visitors from outside the gas belt came to town, it was a part of their entertainment to open one of the strongest gushers in the neighborhood and allow its roaring flame to leap heavenward until, in the words of the local chronicler, "it singed the beard of Jove." Only those who have witnessed one of those burning wells can have an adequate conception of what a magnificent spectacle it is. As a manifestation of nature's power it rivals heaven's thunderbolts and all the forces of the air, and approaches the terrific effects of the volcano. Occasionally, when the gas was ignited before the removal of the derrick, the heat was so great that the derrick and every part of the surrounding structures were consumed so quickly that they seemed to have been blown away by the flames. Yet another diversion for the entertainment of visitors may be mentioned. Gas pipes were laid under the water in White river, and the gas allowed to escape through the water. Being ignited at the surface, the flames spread out over the water, giving the appearance that the river was on fire. In fact, the water became so hot, after such a unique spectacle, that the fish perished and the vegetation along the banks was cooked.

Such were the principal facts connected with the discovery and exploitation of natural gas in Delaware county. As already stated, it heralded a new era in the country. In many portions of America it is an easy and familiar custom to divide time and events into two general divisions—"before the war" and "after the war." But in addition to this history-marker, the people of Delaware county, as also in other parts of the gas belt, are very sure to designate the occurrence of events as either before or after the discovery of gas, so that, for purposes of local history, it would be an easy and apt means of placing events in their proper connection by adding the words "before gas," or "after gas." The history of Muncie and other centers of the county after the discovery of gas will be taken up in succeeding pages, where the story of natural gas is closely involved with the material prosperity of these communities.

CHAPTER XVI.

NATURAL GAS MAKES A CITY OF MUNCIE.

Perhaps Muncie people did not immediately realize what the gas discovery meant for their material prosperity. But by the spring of 1887 the spirit of change, progress and enterprise was thoroughly active. On March 18 the Daily News announces in black type the arrival of the Muncie Boom, and as a concrete example says that Joseph Stafford intended laying out the eighty lots of the Winton place into streets and village property. Already, it was reported, a syndicate of capitalists, representing two millions of dollars, had purchased real estate to the value of $150,000 in Muncie and vicinity. A few days later Col. Dan Meade and Nicholas Ohmer bought $60,000 worth of suburban real estate. The events of the next week or so proved beyond doubt that Muncie and vicinity were in the throes of a speculative real estate movement, and that values were no longer based on real worth but on the air-blown estimates of the future.

In April real estate transfers involving large sums were of daily if not hourly occurrence. People began to talk of Muncie as the "Birmingham of the North," the older citizens began to dream of a metropolis, with multitudes of people thriving on the products of mill and factory, and to all it seemed that Muncie was at the threshold of an era of wonderful growth. Every time a new flow of gas was started, the hopes and plans of the citizens —and the prices of real estate—were given increased buoyancy. The following is one of the parodies provoked by the boom, and part of the contents of the article that followed it, as printed in the Daily News (April 6)—

> "Tell me not in mournful numbers
> That the town is full of gloom,
> For the man's a crank who slumbers
> In these bursting days of boom."

The boom is on.

Everywhere, on the corners, in the stores, and through the country you can find people casting their weather eye toward desirable pieces of property and asking, "what's the price?"

We thought it was warm last week but now it is hot and still heating. Nearly fifty men were here yesterday representing syndicates with immense capital, and large tracts were purchased.

Some business and residence property in the heart of the city is moving at good figures and the influx of strangers makes houses scarce, and rent is growing higher.

The deals yesterday were the largest in the history of the county, and confidence with which outside capitalists take hold of the property is a good indication that the boom is not one of mushroom growth, but one which has come to stay. Property in many instances can be purchased today for the same money it could three, four or five years ago. This shows that prices are not inflated and valued relative.

With the establishment at this place of factories, machine shops, car works, etc., Muncie cannot help but boom and become a city of 30,000 inhabitants in the next few years.

A few days later Muncie was the subject of an article in the Indianapolis Journal, in which Muncie was described as follows:

"Six natural gas wells has Muncie. It is a thriving city of eight thousand people. Though small, it is metropolitan. Here are the essential conveniences of the largest American cities, without their dust, disease and foul air. The Muncie citizen orders his groceries by telephone, his residence is lighted by artificial gas, his place of business by electric light, having choice of both systems, the Brush and Edison incandescent, his meals are cooked by natural gas; there is a good fire department and the Gamewell fire alarm system; he has three railroads, and will soon have an electric line of cable street railway; there is a first-class system of water works; there is a good system of sewerage and clean macadamized streets; he sends his children to public schools that have no superior in the state, and they have the reading of a free public library of 6,500 selected volumes. Muncie already has taken rank as a manufacturing point, and of her eight thousand population more than a thousand are employed in her manufactories. Two factories from Cincinnati are soon to remove to Muncie, and negotiations are pending with a number of establishments in Pennsylvania and Ohio which are desirous of coming to the Indiana gasopolis."

One more quotation from the enthusiastic newspapers of the time will suffice. From quiet, matter-of-fact statement of current news, the local papers had quickly adopted a style in harmony with the enthusiasm of the hour, and ordinary news is quite lost among the big leaders describing the opening of new wells, location of factories, etc. Indeed, it is necessary for the historian to modify, in the light of known later facts, many of the confident assertions of the press at that time. The following is quoted from the Muncie Daily News of April 12, 1887:

The boom breezes were much stronger and more regular yesterday than it has been at any time yet. Many of the gentlemen who were here last week and went home over Sunday came back with reinforcements. The men who came for the first yesterday found the supply of gas much larger than they had been led to suspect. Speculators expected to find in Muncie an Indiana village like Portland, Anderson or New Castle, with a sickly natural gas flame as a curiosity. Instead of that they see a city with all the improvements of a place of 20,000 people. They see a city with a solidly built business centre—long rows of handsome edifices with shining plate glass fronts. Handsome public buildings in all parts of the city. A court house finer than ones possessed by Cincinnati or Indianapolis. They see a city of 7,500 with $150,000 invested in public school buildings. A city with $15,000 invested in a fire department and a corps of firemen as good as there is in any city in the state. A city with $3,000 invested in the most approved fire alarm system. Visitors standing in front of the Kirby last evening heard the bell ring and in sixteen seconds saw a magnificent team of horses dashing down the street drawing the same fire machinery they would see used in New York City. The visitors were incredulous and thought the alarm came from the engine house, but investigation proved that a key was turned one-half mile away, which informed every citizen of Muncie where the fire was located, rang gongs which awakened the firemen, opened the stall doors of the horses and the great doors of the department.

Our surprised individual said to the writer: 'Why this is not a Hoosier village, but an Indiana city."

One of the results of the boom was to arouse the spirit of enterprise and nerve men to engage in undertakings which they would regard as impossible during ordinary times. One evening, while the speculative fever and general enthusiasm was at its height, a number of men were sitting in the Kirby House discussing various features of the boom. Among other things, one expressed his desire for a ground floor office, something that could not be had anywhere in Muncie at that time. Several others were of like mind and said they would pay handsomely for such an advantage of location. In the group was James Boyce, who turned to the first speaker and asked how much he would pay for such a room. "There is a lot and just in the right location," pointing to the corner where the Commercial Club building now stands. One said he would give sixty dollars a month for such a room, but it was useless to discuss it, for no building was there and none could be put there as soon as needed. "Gentlemen," was Mr. Boyce's reply, 'if you will rent the rooms, I will have a brick building there in a week's time!' It was in the nature of a wager, and the business men hardly thought it possible for Boyce to fulfill his promise though they were quite willing to accept their part of the bargain. It is indicative of the spirit and energy of the time that Mr. Boyce succeeded. On Monday, April 18, he contracted with D. C. Mitchell to erect on the corner of Main and Jefferson, a one-story brick building, 96 feet front and 24 feet deep, six rooms, with plate-glass windows, and all to be completed by the following Saturday evening. Here is a paragraph from the News:—"Building by gas light. One of the most novel sights ever witnessed in this town or any other was the work on the new Boyce building last evening. Ground was broken yesterday morning and this morning some of the walls are one story high. The workmen were at their places all night, and by the aid of flaming gas torches are able to work as readily as they can in day." Saturday evening Mitchell turned over the keys of the completed building to Boyce. This was long known as "Real Estate Row."

For a time building and real estate were the principal interests of the city. It was announced early in April, 1887, that "Rat Row," corner of Jackson and Walnut streets, would be replaced with a three-story business block, and other buildings were projected. If the newspaper reports of the transactions are to be believed, the amounts invested in local land by outside capitalists ran into the hundreds of thousands every week. On April 11, for instance, Goshorn brothers of Cincinnati bought William Walling's farm and John Luick's farm, paying $52,000 for the two tracts. On the same day T. H. Kirby sold 66 acres of suburban property at $275 an acre. April 22, thirty acres on Walnut street pike sold for $650 an acre, and a corner lot sold for $5,500 that two weeks before had brought $3,500. April 27 the Kirby tract of 41 acres west of town sold at $475 an acre; six days before, the price was $250 an acre. These are a few examples selected from the long list of transactions published every day. Shorn of the exaggeration natural to the occasion, they represent a phenomenal rise in real estate values.

Board of Trade.

February 24, 1887, was organized the Muncie Board of Trade as a corporation "for promotion of any and all undertakings calculated to advance the interests, improvement and general welfare of the city of Muncie." The first officers were: J. A. Goddard, president; S. A. Wilson, first vice president; T. F. Rose, second vice president; J. R. McMahan, third vice president; W. M. Marsh, treasurer. The Board of Trade was the first of several similar and successive organizations that, each in turn, worked for the welfare and industrial development of Muncie. The scope of the work to be done by the Board is shown by the names of the committees—Manufactures, public improvements, ways and means, local roads and streets, projected railroads, completed railroads, public affairs, etc. The Board of Trade had its origin in a citizens' meeting of February 1st, to devise means to attract manufacturers and utilize the gas supply. At that time the following committee were appointed: James Boyce, S. M. Highlands, J. N. Templer, George Kirby, A. L. Johnson.

The charter members of the Board of Trade, men who thus actively identified themselves with the progress of Muncie after the gas discoveries, though most of them had been for years working public-spiritedly along the same lines, were as follows:

James Boyce,	George Kirby,
Webster S. Richey,	J. A. Heinsohn,
W. L. Lacey,	J. C. Greisheimer,

F. L. Wachtell,
Thomas McKillip,
Carl Spilker,
T. F. Rose,
Samuel A. Wilson,
J. E. Burson,
C. E. Adamson,
W. M. Marsh,
John M. Kirby,
Joseph A. Goddard,
Fred W. Heath,
F. Leon,
J. W. Templer,
John F. Sanders,
C. F. W. Neely,
A. A. Wilkinson,
J. R. McMahan,
J. W. Perkins,

J. R. Meeks,
S. M. Highlands,
C. N. Wilcoxon,
J. H. Smith,
J. W. Ream,
Edward Tuhey,
C. P. Franklin,
C. H. Anthony,
John F. Wildman,
B. F. Bratton,
W. L. Little,
John M. Bloss,
E. P. Smith,
T. A. Neely,
Joshua Truitt,
W. P. Jenkins,
A. L. Johnson,
Frank Ellis.

It is surprising how quickly the boom of 1887 died out. The enthusiasm was too great to last. No one could be found to confess that it was gone, the newspapers said not a word about it, though their pages once more took on somewhat of the appearance and routine news matter they had had in the previous year. But as one who was most active in the movement said, "The boom broke in a single night." However, it must not be understood that this marked a real calamity and permanent cessation of the development of Muncie. So far, the sudden activity and progress of the city was artificial, was speculative, and consisted mainly of real estate transfers that might enrich individuals but added no real wealth to the community. The real and effective resources (gas) had hardly been touched. It took time, and careful planning on the part of the citizens, to establish manufactories and make Muncie a big center of industry. That was accomplished in the course of a year or so, and then the real boom came, compared to which this first speculative flurry was insignificant.

Muncie was progressing during this time and was laying the foundations for permanent development. Yet, if one could judge entirely by the newspapers of the time, there was almost a complete cessation of enterprise during the political campaign of 1888, and there was no revival until the following spring. But while the city may not have added greatly to its business interests during that time, it is certain that much had been done for the enduring welfare of the city. The manufactories that have remained longest and proved the foundation of the industrial city were established here during the first two years. Many of the interesting details of these years must be included in the chronological summary, but the larger facts may be sketched.

Manufactories.

As already stated, Muncie had a splendid nucleus of manufacturing enterprise before the gas boom, though it is true that most of the industries employed only a few persons and therefore did not contribute materially to the making of a "factory city." The principal factories of Muncie before the boom, as enumerated by the News on July 23, 1885, were as follows: James Boyce, flax bagging and handles; J. W. Little, feather dusters; Wysor, Haines & Co., machine works; A. L. Johnson & Co., hardwood lumber; Johnson & Hitchcock, skewers; Wysor, Kline & Co. and C. N. Wilcoxon, roller flour mills; E. P. Smith, Mock Bros. and Joseph Prutzman, tile and brick; Bandy Planing Mill Company; New York Spoke Works; J. H. Smith & Co., bent wood work; Garrard & Patterson, bed springs. Roller skates, then much in demand, were made by T. A. Neely, Bishop & Long, Becktel & Johnson, Coleman, Streeter & Co., and Victor Skate Company. Besides all these, Muncie's manufactured products included curry combs, reed organs, furniture, hubs, wringers and scrubbers, cigars, boots and shoes, leather, brooms, barrels. Several manufacturers made goods on their own patents. It is a matter to be recognized in this history that the list of Muncie's inventors is a long one.

The list of names just given should be regarded somewhat as an honor roll, since they had located in the city before it was able to offer extraordinary inducements to manufactures. Hardly had the news of the discovery of gas in eastern Indiana reached the east when the movement of manufacturers to this region began. For some kinds of manufactories, notably glass making, natural gas was the pre-eminent fuel; but even aside from this adaptability, the extreme cheapness of gas proved an alluring bait to a host of manufacturers who located in this part of the state about that time. Many towns, through their commercial clubs or boards of trade, increased the inducements by offering sites and a gas well already developed, so that the company might use its ledger space for ground rent and fuel for recording additional profits.

One of the first enterprises to locate in Muncie was the Kinnear Manufacturing Company, carved wood being their specialty. The company was incorporated in July, 1887, with capital stock of $30,000. This was largely a local concern, its directors being C. E. Tuthill, B. F. Kinnear, A. L. Kerwood, George Kirby and T. F. Rose. They conducted a successful business for several years.

In the same month (July) the Ball Brothers, of Buffalo, New York, began their negotiations which resulted in the location of their great glass factories in Muncie. The plans of the enterprise were published July 28, and the building of the plant on Meridian street in Galliher's addition was begun at once. Their gas well was opened September 9, and in a short time the enterprise was in operation.

The oldest, as well as one of the largest, of the manufacturing enter-prises whose history belongs within the gas regime, is the Indiana Bridge Company, which was incorporated shortly after the gas discovery, with capital stock of $30,000. It is worth noting that the officers of this concern were all local men, who were identified with Muncie long before natural gas was thought of. They were: T. F. Rose, president; J. C. Johnson, treasurer, and George F. McCulloch, secretary. Natural gas wells were sunk on their premises east of town, and by March, 1887, they had com-pleted one large brick and stone building and were building another.

Many people remember that Muncie once had a rubber works. The Muncie Rubber Company was incorporated September 21, 1887, by J. W. Nutt, C. T. Petchell and J. D. Mitchell, and the contract for the building was let in the following November.

About the time natural gas was discovered in Indiana, the new Inter-State Commerce bill went into effect. Just how much influence on the manufacturing growth of Muncie this may have had cannot be stated accurately, but it was asserted at the time that the new law had paralyzed the nail and glass business in the Virginias, and that this was an additional incentive for such industries to move to the natural gas belt. It is certain that a big rush of glass makers followed the discovery of gas. After the coming of the Balls, the next important enterprise of this kind was the Hemingray Bros., who in January, 1888, announced their decision to move part of their glass factories from Covington, Kentucky. The location chosen by this firm, which has continued as one of the big industries of Muncie, was on Macedonia avenue, east of the Ball plant.

In January, 1888, the Muncie News gave a list of the factories that had been located since the gas discovery. The total number of employes connected with these enterprises was given as 1,400, mainly skilled work-men, but it is evident that these figures were not the result of actual counting, but rather an estimate based on future growth of each factory to its promised capacity. The plants named, with the number of employes, were the following: Kinnear Manufacturing Company, 100; Brooks Creamery, 20; Balls Bros. Glass Company, 300; G. Jaeger Paper Com-pany, 200; Muncie Rubber Company, 100; Hemingray Glass Company, 500; E. P. Smith & Co., 50; Thompson Enameling Company, 125.

The year 1888 was one of marked activity in Muncie's factory develop-ment. Many of the older firms, including the bagging mills, handle factory, bent wood works, and the Indiana bridge works, continued in flourishing condition, while the new plants were rapidly nearing completion. The pulp works, southwest of town, began operation during the summer, and for the first time the farmers of the county had a commercial demand for their straw, the pulp mill paying three dollars a ton for it when delivered. In May, largely through the efforts of the Board of Trade, a large nail factory, hitherto located in Greencastle, Indiana, was obtained for Muncie, being renamed the Muncie Nail Works. Mr. Charles Darnall was president. One hundred and fifty lots were obtained for the plant in the Galliher subdivision.

Without disparaging the efforts of other men, it may be said truthfully that Mr. James Boyce was as indefatigable in the work of building a city here during the gas boom as he had been during earlier years, when he was the principal manufacturer of the city of five thousand people. In 1888 Mr. Boyce platted a suburb on his land across the river on the east of town, giving it the name of Boyceton. Here, it was announced in June of that year, Maring, Hart & Co. would locate their window glass works, moving them from their former location in Bellaire, Ohio. The securing of this enterprise for Muncie was attributed entirely to Mr. Boyce's efforts.

Another enterprise brought in during this year was the C. H. Over Glass Works. All these glass works were to begin operation in the fall, so the outlook was very bright for industrial Muncie. At the close of 1888, in the report of the state geologist, was published a list of the factories at Muncie using natural gas for fuel. This included practically all the larger enterprises, and as the statistics concerning each may be considered fairly reliable, the report is summarized here:

Muncie Pulp Company; capacity, 20 tons daily; 80 employes.

Muncie Combination Manufacturing Company; capital, $25,000; 25 employes.

Ball Glass Works, fruit jars, green and amber bottles; two furnaces, nine pots; value of daily product, $700; 125 employes; weekly payroll, $1,200; sand from Millington, Illinois; lime from Fostoria, Ohio, and soda ash from England.

Hemingray Glass Company, bottles; one furnace, fourteen pots; 100 employes; weekly payroll, $800.

C. H. Over, window glass; two furnaces, sixteen pots; weekly capacity, 1,400 boxes of glass; 84 employes; weekly payroll, $1,400.

Maring, Hart & Co., window glass; two furnaces, twenty pots; capacity of 7,680 50-feet boxes of glass monthly; 120 employes.

Muncie Nail Company, steel and iron nails; daily capacity, 500 kegs of nails; 200 employes; monthly payroll, $10,000.

Many of the details of Muncie's growth, the establishment of factories, and other interesting facts must be omitted here and mentioned in the chronological chapter or under special titles. The street railway had its origin early in the gas boom, but the history of that can best be told in one article. The rapid development of the city was also reflected in the building of churches and schools and these too must be described elsewhere. However, as one studies the events of those years, one is convinced of the fact that Muncie grew disproportionately during the first few years. The splendid energy of the citizens was directed for the most part to the making of a big manufacturing center. Factories, more factories, seemed to be the aim of all the organized efforts put forth at this time. This being true, the other interests of the city could not possibly keep pace with its industrial advancement. The population of the city increased threefold within a few years, a dozen immense factories came in, and while bringing with them great possibilities of wealth, also introduced a complexity of good and evil conditions that the city was unable to cope with for some years to come. Liberality was naturally a characteristic of city and citizens at a time when a cordial invitation, together with a fat money bonus, was extended to the manufacturing interests of the world. But partly as a result of this liberality and open-handedness and partly because of the absorption of all classes in business affairs, Muncie soon came to have the reputation of being a "free and easy town," where the good people were too busy to concern themselves greatly with moral conditions. So, for a number of years, Muncie's history is marked by social evils and statutory crimes that in the aggregate make a record from which any city might well wish to be free. It was not "an outbreak of crime," such as occurs in all cities from time to time, but the record forms almost a continuous story from day to day extending over several years. Criminality in Muncie was due to the conditions, as stated, rather than to any sudden infection of depravity. For a long while hardly any attempt was made to regulate the saloons, and the "quart shops," low dives and other haunts of vice flourished without check. These conditions were tolerated by the city government and by the better classes largely, it would seem, because such evils were deemed to be a necessary part of industrial prosperity, and also because the moral forces and organizations had not increased apace with the material expansion of the city. While it seems necessary to call attention to this feature of Muncie's history, a detailed account of the criminal record happily has no place here; those whose morbid desire leads them in quest of such accounts, need only turn over the pages of the local newspapers of that period.

By the close of 1890 Muncie's factories produced an amazing variety of products, chief among them being fine window glass, bottles and miscellaneous glass articles, nails and iron work, wood pulp, architectural iron, brass and novelties, caskets, bent wood, hubs and spokes, handles, coil hoops, etc., etc. Johnson's sawmill, Truitt's sawmill, Bandy planing mill, Muncie foundry were all enterprises that had helped make Muncie before the boom, and were still doing flourishing business. In the spring of 1891, however,

Muncie lost one of her oldest and most important factories. The Muncie
Bagging Co., largely the enterprise of Mr. Boyce, had existed here nearly
twenty years, notwithstanding the fact that its raw material was imported
from abroad and that its principal market was in the south. But at this
time it was considered wise to move it to the east.

With the first years of the '90s' came the "big boom," not alone at
Muncie but throughout the county and the gas belt. The recoil that followed the first burst of enthusiasm in 1887 did not materially affect the
prosperity of the city and country, and in the meantime capital had come in
and development work had proceeded so far that the second advance may be
said to have been. "all along the line." It possessed real substance, both
money and energy, and exhibited its strength and influence in every part of
the county.

Citizens Enterprise Company.

While it would be impossible to describe Muncie's development during
these years without reference to the Citizens Enterprise Company, it is also
true that the story of that company is the most characteristic feature of the
city's industrial history and represents very correctly the interests and activities and the strenuous enterprise of the time. The Citizens Enterprise
Company was organized August 14, 1891, at a meeting held in the city
council chamber and attended by representatives of all the important interests of the city. The board of directors that were chosen were: George
Kirby, George L. Lenon, O. J. Lotz, Frank Leon, James Boyce, J. A. Goddard, A. L. Johnson, W. M. Marsh, C. H. Church; with an advisory board
consisting of A. L. Kerwood, George W. Spilker, J. R. Sprankle, J. A.
Heinsohn, J. H. Wysor, J. F. Darnall.

The object of the company was to promote the industrial interests of
the city and especially to secure additional factories. For this purpose a
large sum of money was needed, and remarkable energy was shown in raising the amount. Committees were appointed for every ward in the city,
to solicit subscriptions; the property owners in Center township outside of
the city were even called on for assistance. As a result of the vigorous
campaign, the committee reported $103.000 secured by September 28th.
By the end of October the amount had crept up to $140,000. For a time it
seemed impossible to get any further. Finally, at a public meeting, the
reserve was broken by a single subscription of $12,000, which was followed
by a scene of remarkable enthusiasm and good will, during which the liberal
donations soon increased the total to more than two hundred thousand dollars—the exact amount was $211,050. The company was in reality a public-
spirited stock company, the capital stock being divided among a large number of stockholders. The first assessment on this stock, amounting to ten
percent, was called for on January 1, 1892, and during the existence of

the company only three other assessments were made, amounting to fifty percent in all, from which was realized, by the end of 1894, the sum of $9,685.48. When the last assessment was levied, it was found that several subscribers refused to pay their share, and the collectors for the company had extreme difficulty in performing their tasks. The matter went to the courts, where it was finally decided that the subscriptions to the company's stock represented valid claims upon the subscribers and were collectible by law. In 1895 suit was brought by some of the subscribers to annul the charter of the company, and when this was defeated in the circuit court the decision was considered one of the most important that had been handed down in the history of the county. The company continued to exist until January, 1897, having accomplished, especially during the first two or three years, work of inestimable value to Muncie.

With the expenditure of the ninety odd thousand dollars raised by subscriptions, the Enterprise Company brought into Muncie two million dollars represented in factories and capital. The Ohio Wagon works was the first enterprise secured $3,500 in the form of a loan being given it by the Enterprise Co. The works burned down, and the Enterprise Company collecting the insurance, lost only $114 by the transaction. The R. E. Hill Mfg. Co., knitting mills, was the next concern, contracted for in March, 1892. The company met reverses, finally passing to the Muncie Underwear Co. The Common Sense Engine Co., the third industry, passed through several court judgments, but for three or four years was called one of the important factories of the city. The Midland Steel Company, secured by the Enterprise Company in April, 1892, was the best achievement of the latter organization. The White River Iron and Steel Company, which was brought from Anderson, had misfortunes after locating here, but in 1895 was still in operation, under the name of Park Iron and Steel Company. The Whitely reaper works, also secured by the Citizens company, was an important industry, of which great results were expected, but the plant was destroyed by fire, and never resumed its original size and importance as an independent manufacturing concern. Of the other factories secured by the Enterprise Company, there were in operation in April, 1895, the following: Gill Bros. Glass Pot factory, Bell Stove Co., Tappan Shoe Co., Consumers Paper Co., Muncie Electrical works (secured in July, 1893, and at first badly managed), Muncie Wheel Co. (which was double its original size by 1895), the Muncie Iron and Steel Co. (a home company), Whitely Malleable Iron Castings Co., Patton Hollow Ware works. The location of the Indiana Iron works was due partly to Col. A. L. Conger and partly to the Enterprise Company. It was secured in 1892 and in 1895 was a large industry, employing several hundred men.

Referring to the work of the Enterprise Company, a booklet on Muncie, "past, present and future," issued about the middle of 1892, states that "the class of factories [secured by the Enterprise Co.] has been of the best and most permanent kind, such as any city might well be proud of; 2600 factory hands added in six months, this means an increase of 9,000 people. In view of all these facts it is not an idle prophecy to state that before five years Muncie will be a city of 50,000 people." And so it might have been but for contingencies that are not within the power of men to foresee.

Panic of 1893.

Mere mention of the year 1893 brings to mind financial panic and business depression, which was quite general all over the United States. But in Muncie occurred a combination of conditions such as probably no other city in the land experienced. This city, because of its flourishing factories, the splendid resources of natural gas, and the remarkable enterprise of the citizens, was in better condition to weather a financial panic than most places in the country, and it is evident from a study of events that Muncie suffered more from other causes than from the panic proper.

As having a slight influence on industrial confidence, it should be mentioned that the first admissions that the gas supply was weakening were made early in 1893. Only in the preceding year the extravagant prediction had been made, by calculations based on conditions at Pittsburg, Penn., that the gas supply in Indiana would last "seven hundred years." Nevertheless, Delaware county had all along refused the transportation of any gas beyond its boundaries, there being a strong public opinion on this point. Therefore, the Chicago pipe line companies had made little progress in encroaching on the gas supply of this county.

Some intimations of the business crisis were felt in Muncie during the summer of 1893, but nothing serious occurred until the suspension of the Citizens National Bank in August. The splendid support given by the citizens to this institution, as told on other pages, did much to restore confidence, and as a matter of fact it can be said that the Citizens National affair was of only superficial importance, and indicated nothing alarming in the financial condition of the city.

Locally, Muncie suffered more from the smallpox epidemic that lasted from August into November, than from any other cause. The retail business and the general activities of the city were almost suspended during this time, and smallpox proved a strong ally of hard times in the attack upon the city's credit and resources.

Reference to the chronological record of this period will show individual examples of the results of the panic. There were one or two mercantile failures, several of the factories suspended temporarily or reduced their working force, and the feeling if not the actual fact of business stagnation was certainly present throughout the latter months of 1893 and through 1894.

A blow was struck from another quarter early in 1894. One of the chief acts of the second Cleveland administration was the Wilson tariff bill, providing for many important reductions in the tariff rates. Among these, the duties on glass were reduced almost half. The glass manufacturers at Muncie were not long in feeling the adverse effects of the measure. In February, 1894, the reason assigned for the shut-down of the Over glass works was the Wilson tariff bill. In the following fall, the results of the tariff reduction were seen in the horizontal lowering of wages of window glass workers nearly twenty-five percent.

Notwithstanding all these adversities, Muncie passed through the panic without permanent injury to her resources from that cause alone. The manufacturing interests by 1895 showed an increase in number of employes in nearly every establishment, and were in a fairly prosperous condition, as indicated by a careful statistical summary given by the News. Again it is needful to state that figures concerning industrial plants are almost invariably approximates, and cannot be relied on for literal exactness; yet the tables given by the News and summarized here are probably as close an estimate on this subject as can be made at any time:—

Name—	Number employes	Payroll monthly
Indiana Iron Works	800	$35,000
Indiana Bridge Co	160	6,500
Midland Steel Co	400	22,000
Florence Iron and Steel Co	300	12,000
Park Iron and Steel Co	65	2,500
Muncie Iron and Steel Works	135	4,500
Muncie Wheel Works	150	5,000
Muncie Pulp Co	100	4,000
Muncie Glass Co	200	7,000
Hemingray Glass Co	160	6,000
Muncie Casket Works	35	1,500
J. H. Smith & Co. Bending Works	140	6,000
Patton Hollow Ware Co	125	7,000
Nelson Glass Co	165	8,000
Ball Bros. Glass Factory	1,000	35,000
Common Sense Engine Co	175	7,000
Port Glass Works	125	6,000
Consumers' Paper Co	50	2,000
Whitely Malleable Castings Co	250	15,000
Bell Stove Works	40	2,000
Boyce Handle Factory	30	1,500
Maring, Hart & Co., Glass	250	12,000
Tappan Shoe Co	150	3,000
Gill Bros. Pot Factory	40	2,000
Muncie Underwear Co	90	4,000
C. H. Over Glass Works	225	16,000
Whitely Reaper Works	100	5,000
	5,680	$241,500

Many minor concerns increased the total of employes nearly five hundred, so that by this showing at least half of Muncie's population was identified with and dependent on the manufacturing interests.

Postoffice.

Besides manufacturing, Muncie had many other interests and there were numerous changes that reflect the growth of the city during this period. By many students of statistics, it is claimed that one of the best indexes of a community's business prosperity is the postoffice. There are some figures at hand that are of considerable interest in this connection. Muncie postoffice was elevated to the rank of second class on June 13, 1887, while John E. Banta was postmaster. For a number of years the postoffice had been located in the Times building at the corner of Washington and Walnut streets. But soon after the completion of the Anthony block (which for some years was the finest business block in the city) the postoffice was moved to that building (February 13, 1888) and equipped with entirely new furniture. The receipts from stamps, etc., during the month of December, 1887, were $991.17, and for the last three months of that year were $2,617.60. So steadily were the revenues kept up during the following year that on January 1, 1889, free delivery was begun, with three carriers. During the first month of free delivery the reported receipts at the postoffice were $1,041, the largest known for any month up to that time, not even excepting the holiday month of the year (December). During the first month of the new system the carriers delivered 18,800 letters, 4,114 post cards, 12,823 newspapers and periodicals, 65 registered letters—total number of pieces, 35,802. In November, 1889, the number of letters delivered had increased to 25,386, with a corresponding increase in other classes of matter. The total receipts for the last six months of 1889 were $7,328.39. An interesting contrast is shown between the figures representing the gross receipts of the office for the year ending June 30, 1885, and the year ending June 30, 1892. The receipts were, for these respective dates, $6,621 and $19,151. Thus during this seven year period covering the growth of Muncie from before the gas discovery to the height of its boom, the postoffice receipts showed an increase of three hundred percent, corresponding very closely to the numerical increase of population. Probably most of the people who admire the present beautiful postoffice building are unaware of the fact that, had it not been for the panic and the consequent paring down of all appropriations in 1893, Muncie would have had a postoffice building at that time. A bill appropriating $150,000 for this purpose passed the senate, and a provision setting aside $50,000 was placed in a House bill, but the measure failed at that session and the following year the national treasury was shut tight by the panic.

Municipal Improvements.

In the line of municipal improvements there are many developments during this period. In September, 1891, for the first time in ten years, a street commissioner was elected, his duties having been performed by the city engineer for a decade. The city engineer, in recommending this division of duties, tells some interesting facts concerning the streets of the city:— In 1882 Muncie graded all new streets out of the public fund of $2,811.75; in 1890 the total expended on streets for material and labor was $8,489.90. In 1882 there were fifteen miles of streets, no paved sidewalks and but one little sewer. "Now," Sept., 1891, 'we have five miles of sandstone walk, five miles of brick walk, and two miles of cement walk; also over forty miles of graded streets and over ten miles of completed sewers.''

As late as 1887 complaint was made about cows running about the streets and destroying lawns, resulting in the passage of an ordinance prohibiting that bovine privilege. About the same time another feature of town days was abolished in the removal of the hitch-racks from the public square. This brought out a protest from the farmers, and the merchants were active in the agitation to provide suitable places for hitching teams. Though the city now has many miles of first-class sidewalk, of flags, brick or cement, very little of it goes back of twenty years ago. In January, 1888, the council, after much discussion of the subject, particularized how sidewalks should be constructed; namely, the walks should be of sawed sandstone, six feet wide, the gutters of dressed limestone slabs, while grass should be grown between walk and curb. Though cement is now one of the most popular materials for sidewalks, and used entirely in many towns, its use has been sanctioned only a few years, as is evident from the fact that in 1890 James Boyce was forbidden by the council to lay a "new-fashioned" concrete walk on East Jackson street and ordered to make it of brick.

In street lighting the city took some important steps during these years. In 1888 the council gave a contract to the Natural Gas Company for lighting the streets until December 1, 1889, at $120 per post annually. This method was by no means satisfactory. By the fall of 1890 both people and council were discussing the subject of street lighting. 'Away with torches that blaze and glare on nice clear nights and blow out leaving the city in darkness when needed the worst." It was estimated that the natural gas, with the extensions of the system then demanded, would cost the city $5,000 annually, while the cost of an adequate and modern system of arc electric lights would cost only six or seven thousand dollars. Nothing was done immediately, but when the legislature passed an act in 1891 regulating the use of natural gas and forbidding the burning of flambeaux, the fear was expressed that the law would apply to the flaring jets by which Muncie was lighted and that when the law went into effect in June the city lamplighters would lay themselves liable to prosecution. In the county at large were thousands of such flambeaux, around the farm houses and along the roads, all of which must be shut off by the new law, and one editor could foresee the event of Muncie being left in total darkness, when the citizens would be compelled to carry lanterns about the streets. The editor exaggerated the prospect, but he increased the weight of public sentiment for electric lighting. September 28, 1891, the council resolved to build its own electric light plant. The plant, located at North Elm and Wysor streets, was completed in the following February and the city's streets began to be lighted with one hundred arc lights.

In 1897 the Commercial Club boasted that the city had a complete sewerage system, costing $285,000. As already mentioned, the building of sewers had only begun during the eighties. It was not until September, 1889, that the council let the contract for the big outlet sewer, extending from near the L. E. & W. R. R. bridge to the Jackson schoolhouse, the cost to be $90,000. Connected with the sewage question was that of the disposal of garbage. The council in June, 1891, discussed the bad condition of the city dump in the rear of Wysor's mill, and finally recommended the building of a garbage furnace and the burning of the material collected by the scavenger wagons. But nearly two years passed before such a furnace was erected on North Walnut street.

Muncie's Suburbs.

Most remarkable of all the features of Muncie's growth was the development and upbuilding of suburban additions. In nearly every case these were the natural result of the establishment of factories and the building of homes and a few stores within convenient distance. Such suburbs, with the factory as the center and cause of its being, were likely to continue and grow as long as the factory remained. The glass works, the steel mills and other big industries that have been in Muncie since the discovery of gas, are surrounded by homes and the necessary stores and institutions of a town center. While the expansion of the city was at high tide, confident real estate men projected several additions to Muncie that, with the partial collapse of the boom and also because there was little reason for the extension of the city in those directions, have now reverted almost to their original condition as meadows and woodland.

The beginning of Muncie's suburban growth is told, with the flavor of contemporary observation, by a reporter in the Daily News of February 29, 1888, describing his walk from the West Side to the river on the east.

The first place visited was West Side, the new suburb across White river on Jackson street. Two years ago the Calvert homestead was the only residence in the neighborhood. Now there are dozens of new houses and contracts have been let for the erection of fifty more. One pleasing feature about West Side is that nearly all the residents own their homes. They buy a lot and build themselves a house. None of the land is in the hands of speculators. Lots can be purchased at reasonable rates. Hundreds of lots are offered for sale and it is a fine place to live.

The writer then tramped across White river to the Yorktown road. There the work of the surveyor was to be seen and many lots are sold and will be occupied by neat buildings in the spring.

Making a bee line from here the Middletown road was soon reached and we were at Winton Place. This subdivision was primarily designed by the late Dr. Robert Winton. The doctor had grand ideas about Winton Place, which, unfortunately, he was never able to consummate. Nevertheless he left Muncie a rich heritage in the beautiful avenues of maples. The doctor intended that this should be the popular driveway of the city. His original plans have been accepted by the city as a subdivision, and many lots have been sold. Mr. George Stafford has given a contract for the erection of about twenty houses in this subdivision.

A few hundred feet to the south the writer came to Ohmer avenue. This avenue is a new thoroughfare. Commencing at Middletown road it goes directly east, crossing Walnut street; from there, it extends to Macedonia avenue. The avenue extends from there to the Burlington road. It will be 100 feet in width the entire length, will be graded and finished as a drive.

Without going the entire length of this long drive, we went south on the Fort Wayne Railroad. In a few paces we came to the rubber works. A little further along we came to the pulp works. At both of these manufactories work is progressing very satisfactorily.

From here we went north northeast, angling across lots to the "glass district." All the way across the work of the engineer was everywhere to be seen. Every inch of ground was laid off for lots, streets, alleys and parks. Along here was also to be seen the line of the long switch which is to connect the "glass district" with the Fort Wayne Railroad. Besides the stakes. are to be seen foundations of houses, lumber for houses and other indications of municipal growth. All along also were the red stakes which denoted that the lots had been sold.

Arriving at the "glass district" the crops of last year are not to be seen. The immense red buildings of the Ball Bros. Glass Works are looming up on the hill. A torch from their gas well stands as a sentinel of the work. To the east is a derrick, where a well is being put down for the Hemingrays.

Work has already progressed considerably at the Hemingray works. Yet the few large frame buildings and extensive foundations give no idea what the factory will be. The works will cover eight acres of ground.

Four and a half years later, in August, 1892, the suburban growth has extended to the north side of the river. Whitely was just beginning, while to the west, bordering Wheeling pike, the new place called Riverside was coming into notice as a residence district. Numerous improvements were being undertaken along the pike and Hudson avenue, the Neely place of eighty-five acres being cleared for buildings. The West Side was already a place of cottages and factories. Avondale, in October, 1889, was said to have grown from two or three houses to one hundred, two years later was mentioned for its beauty and size, while in August, 1892, it had improved streets, street-car transportation by way of Ohmer avenue, and had a school population that taxed the facilities that could be provided. Congerville, with its two iron mills, engine works, architectural iron works, nut and bolt factory, and many houses, was a new but very promising part of the city. Industry, the name given to the suburb that had grown up around the glass factory, was at that time denominated an unlucky suburb because of the numerous fires that had visited the factories there, but it was then and has continued to be one of the largest additions to Muncie. Boyceton, on the east side of the river, with Maring, Hart and Co.'s factories, had been projected by Mr. Boyce several years previously, and a number of houses had been erected by him for the benefit of the residents.

Fire Department.

The upbuilding of these suburbs brought the subject of fire protection into sudden prominence. The Muncie News in December, 1889, calls attention to the inadequacy of the fire department. The fire department was the same in force and equipment as when Muncie had seven thousand people, when there was no West Side, no Boyceton, no Avondale, no Anthony, no Galliher addition. There was only one station, water mains had not yet been extended to the outlying districts, and every time the engine company responded to a call from a suburb the team was exhausted by the long run.

In 1892 Muncie was afflicted with many serious fires. Altogether there were 77 alarms for the year, against 43 for 1891. The total loss for the year was $418,616. Fourteen fires were beyond the reach of the water service. That this was a most serious condition is shown by the further statistics that these fourteen fires resulted in sixty percent of the total fire loss for the year. However, the frequency of disastrous fires in the factory district had aroused the council to action, and during the summer of 1892 it was decided to add a new fire station, to be located on Mulberry and Willard streets, to serve the factory district. In December of the same year the Muncie Glass Co. opened a third station, which, however, was a private equipment and had no connection with the city department. In 1896 Chief Shepp reported the total value of the two stations and apparatus as $24,236, with annual expenses for 1895 about $8,750. Though the population and extent of the city had doubled within the preceding ten years, the value of the fire apparatus and the expense of operating had not increased correspondingly. In 1896 there were eleven miles of water pipes, 189 fire hydrants, and nine cisterns. In 1895, 118 alarms resulted in a loss of $77,907.

CHAPTER XVII.

PROGRESS AND CHANGE IN THE SMALLER CENTERS.

It is doubtful if a single adult resident of Delaware county during the years following the discovery of gas was unaffected by the spirit of development and the new energy that seemed to actuate all things. The county was very rapidly changed from an agricultural basis to an industrial—the greater wealth no longer came from the soil but from beneath it. Every landowner hoped for a share of the new wealth. Promoters were busy in every locality, organizing the citizens into associations for the development of gas wells, or the laying out of town sites, or erection of manufacturing plants. It would be impossible to say how much money was gathered in by promoters and speculators who had no further interest in the welfare of the county than to control a promising enterprise long enough to reap a golden harvest, then leaving the investors a bag to hold. One of the conspicuous characters of this sort produced during the boom was one Col. John H. Grover, who, during his popularity, was called the greatest land organizer and village promoter in the country. In two or three years, after having made the circuit of the county, he departed without having accomplished anything to cause his name to be permanently identified with the county except as a promoter of enterprises that ceased to exist as soon as he withdrew his enthusiasm and persuasive influence. As an example of his work in the county, in February, 1893, he got together the farmers and villagers about Royerton, and organized the North Muncie Land Co., with half a dozen well known citizens of that vicinity as officers or directors. The plans were to build a city and manufacturing center, which would be an adjunct and worthy rival of the city of Muncie.

EATON.

At Eaton, where gas was first discovered, it was early planned to promote the industrial and commercial growth of the town, with natural gas as a basis. The beginning of this era was regarded with pleasure by several men who had known the place as an unnamed locality in the wilderness. David Brandt, who died a few years ago, had been the proprietor of the store at "Hen-peck" in the forties and later had transferred his enterprise to the site of Eaton, and another resident at this period and one who took an active part in the development of industrial Eaton, was John W. Long.

who had been born on land that later became platted for the Eaton town-site and when a young man had carried the chain in laying out the village. In 1891 Eaton secured its glass works. In August, 1892, the Eaton Land and Improvement Co. was organized, and at once proceeded to acquire the Long farm east of town, containing the limestone quarries. The Paragon Paper Co. was also organized in 1892, with Herman Bergoff president, and the building of the paper plant began in the fall. The Old Fort Manufac-turing Co. was another concern secured by the enterprising citizens about that time. The Eaton Bank Co. was promoted in 1893 mainly by Fort Wayne people, and the bank building was completed during the summer of 1893. In December, 1894, the Farmers State Bank began business, and about a year later the Bank of Eaton was organized. In 1893 Emil Baur came to Eaton and took charge of the Eaton Window Glass Co. He has since been an energetic factor in maintaining Eaton's industrial interests, and is the leading manufacturer of the town. He and Joel Hamilton organ-ized the Eaton Manufacturing Co., which absorbed the Old Fort Manufac-turing Co. Mr. Baur is now president or proprietor of the Baur Window Glass Co., the Baur Gas Co. and the Eaton Manufacturing Co. Besides these, the largest industries of Eaton at the present time are the Western Flint Glass Co., of which John Poorman is president; the Carter Brothers, manufacturers and grain dealers, who represent the oldest established busi-ness connection in the town, the Carters having been engaged in milling here for more than forty years and also connected with the Brandts in mer-cantile affairs. The paper mill which has been idle since it was sold to the box board trust, has recently been reconstructed by A. B. Trentman and S. B. Fleming, preparatory to resumption of operations in the fall of 1907.

ALBANY.

The town of Albany probably benefited more from the gas discovery than any other town in the county outside of Muncie. As elsewhere stated, Albany had very little to distinguish it during the early eighties, and yet it was one of the oldest villages in the county. Fifty years ago, according to an old gazetteer, B. F. Cary was postmaster, L. Blake was the miller, Cary and Wingate, Allegre and Manning, and Ezra Maynard were proprietors of the general stores, and there were three doctors, one of whom also signed himself as a lawyer and justice of the peace.

But during the early nineties Albany began to grow apace. In June, 1893, the editor of the Muncie News speaks of the rapid increase of the town in population and wealth. He observes improvements in every di-rection, "150 dwellings in process of construction." In October, 1892, the Albany Land Co. was organized by citizens and farmers, with capital stock of $250,000; D. J. Manor, president; Robert Maxwell, vice president; L.

R. St. John, treasurer; Col. J. H. Grover, secretary.; J. R. Stafford, Joseph LeFavour, Ed Hannan, Willis Richey, David Black, directors. The growth of the town was anticipated by the platting of a large area east of the railroad, whereas the old village all lay west of the tracks.

One of the earliest manufactories was the Albany Paper Co., which began making strawboard in February, 1893. About the same time the foundations were being laid or other preparations made for the establishment of the Buckeye Window Glass Co., the Adams and Becknell furniture factory, the Industrial China Co., the Indiana Lounge Co., the Model Flint Glass Co., etc. In consequence of this industrial boom and the activity of the Improvement Company in the booming of the site east of the original town, the Lake Erie and Western, in 1894, moved its depot, freight office and telegraph office to the new suburb half a mile east of town. The townspeople protested vehemently against this and used every means in their avail to persuade the railroad people of their mistaken policy. They even tried a boycott against the railroad by hauling their goods overland from Muncie and also tried to get a new railroad line. However, it was not until 1903 that the station was returned to its old location within the town.

Up to nearly the close of the century Albany showed a steady increase in property valuation, but during the past six or seven years has gone back, according to the records of the assessors. In 1896 the total valuation, in round numbers, was $360,000. By the following year it had risen to $511,-000, and in 1899 was about $550,000. In 1906 the figures for total taxables are given as about $422,000, and in 1907 there was a decline to a little less than $400,000.

Albany has many civic improvements that have gradually been added during the past fifteen years. The Albany Water and Light Co. furnishes electric lighting and water. About ten years ago fire destroyed the Speicher block and threatened the entire business section. There was no fire protection, and the loss was nearly fifty thousand dollars. Since that time fire apparatus has been procured and an efficient organization perfected to protect the town from fire. Among the principal business enterprises at the present time may be mentioned the Albany Paper Co., the Albany State Bank, of which Isaiah Dudleston is president, the Delaware Mills, the Albany Automobile Co., the Stoner Cement Post works, etc.

WEST MUNCIE.

Of all the enterprises produced during the early nineties by enthusiastic promoters, whose designs seemed to embrace the entire county, which they would cover with populous cities and immense industries, West Muncie was started with the brightest promises and had perhaps the briefest career of substantial distinction. Probably not more than half the citizens have any remembrance of West Muncie, and what little remains of that interesting town is now considered part of Yorktown rather than of Muncie. In 1892, however, the Western Improvement Co. kept West Muncie constantly before the public, and hardly for a day did there fail some notice of that booming city. The Novelty and Brass works were located there, flour mill and many factories were to be built, New York avenue was to be graded, a lake was to be made by damming Buck creek, and twenty-five acres converted into a beautiful resort and park. A postoffice was established there in February, 1893, with Charles Perry as postmaster, and when the Yorktown depot was burned in the winter of 1892-93 it was decided to locate the new one on the east side of the river in West Muncie. In February, 1893, the West Muncie Strawboard Co. was incorporated, and this company established the only permanent industry in the town.

Without tracing the detailed progress and decline of this town further, the "fate of West Muncie," which was "designed as a rival of the city of Muncie," may be told by a writer for the Morning News, March 24, 1898, who told the story in this way:

West Muncie, which is on the Big Four railway, five miles west of the city of Muncie, started several years ago as a rival of this city, is now a sad monument of a boom town, with empty houses crumbling into ruins. Officials of the Big Four railway were the chief promoters, assisted by Muncie capitalists. In addition to being designed as a manufacturing center, West Muncie was also intended for a summer resort. A dam was constructed and quite a lake was formed in the stream known as Buck creek. A steam launch was purchased as a pleasure craft, with a number of smaller boats and canoes. This body of water was picturesque, and a grove nearby was inviting. A fine hotel, modern in every respect, containing seventy rooms, was built near the edge of the beautiful grove and the railway company expended $3,000 in a depot. This depot is standing idle, never having been used for the purposes contemplated. The hotel also stands as a monument of a boom which "died a-bornin'." A family resides therein, and it is also used for postoffice purposes, although very few letters or papers come that way. A large two-story brick block with plate glass windows has stood empty all these years. Other business houses are ragged and tottering, with broken doors and shattered window panes. A few of the dwellings are occupied, but others are falling into decay. The large dam has broken away, and the lake has long since disappeared. The big dancing pavilion and boat houses are almost ready to fall down. The town once had a newspaper, but it long since passed to the newspaper cemetery, while its editor and publisher is now in a printing office at Peru.

DE SOTO.

In December, 1892, DeSoto entered the circle of booming towns. A land company was organized, controlling four thousand acres in that vicinity, and it was intended here, as in other places, to locate some big manufacturing plants. The title of the promoting company was the East Muncie Land Co., and in January, 1893, it claimed to have secured a paper box factory and to have several other plants in prospect. Of course a gas well was sunk to provide fuel for manufacturing. The company within a year or so passed into the hands of a receiver, and in the spring of 1896 the property was sold to Adam Madill for $1,350, about the amount expended in sinking the gas well. Several Delaware county citizens lost money that they had invested in the enterprise. At the present time a large part of the active citizens of DeSoto are employed in the Kitselman wire works in East Muncie, and the substantial town interests are hardly more than they were in March, 1883, when it was reported that the village had three stores, depot, warehouse, a blacksmith shop, shoe shop, two sawmills, two carpenters, a doctor, the population consisting of thirteen families.

GASTON.

The thriving village of Gaston, known in earlier history as New Corner, was a country village, remote from railroad connections, until a few years ago. As a trading center for a very rich agricultural district, and under the leadership of some very enterprising men, it has, nevertheless, been a center of importance for many years. Its early history has been given elsewhere. Fifty years ago, according to an old directory, its population was 35. One physician, one sawmill, two churches, one school, one store (Jesse Miers, proprietor), several mechanics, comprised the leading interests. David L. Jones was owner of the sawmill and W. F. McInturf was postmaster. In 1885 New Corner was still a trading center, with the principal activities in the hands of the following: W. R. Bryan and Frank Woodring, general stores; Frank Miller & Co., store; D. E. Boulette, shoe store; J. W. Hammen, postmaster; Reason and Knight, drugs; Case & Co., tile factory; Drs. Clemens and Munsey, physicians. By this time the manufacturing had increased to two sawmills and a gristmill.

In the chronological records found elsewhere in this work will be found notices of several interesting events that have occurred in Gaston during the last ten or fifteen years. The citizens have long agitated the railroad question, and Washington township was usually found ready to vote subsidies for the companies that proposed building. As long ago as 1892 it was deemed almost a certainty that a division of the Panhandle would be built through this vicinity, and in the fall of that year the citizens of "The metropolis of Washington township," as it was called, forwarded a petition to Washington asking that the name of their town and postoffice be changed to "Gas Center." The change was not made for some time, however, when the name Gaston was selected. In the summer of 1901 the Cincinnati, Richmond and Muncie (now the C., C. & L. R. R.) was completed through the county, and Gaston was finally given railroad connection. However, the C., I. & E. R. R. was the first to put a regular train schedule into effect, and for a time the station at Stockport, two miles east of Gaston, received much of the traffic that later returned to Gaston. With the establishment of rail-road connection, new life was given the town. In May, 1902, the Gaston Banking Co. was organized, with Mark Powers as president. Mr. Powers is also president of the Gaston Canning Co., which is one of the most valu-able manufacturing concerns in northwest Delaware county, especially to the fruit and truck interests of that rich agricultural region. Several of the business concerns of Gaston have had a continuous existence for many years. The Huber Bros. flour and sawmill was established about thirty years ago, and W. R. Bryan & Bro.'s general store dates to 1883. The Gaston Tile fac-tory is another important industry.

<h2 style="text-align:center">SELMA.</h2>

Selma was also affected by the gas boom. Here the Selma Citizens' Co. organized in the spring of 1892 to further the interests of the town. This company was probably similar in aims and methods to the Enterprise Com-pany of Muncie. But in June, 1893, the Eureka Land Co. was organized, controlling a thousand acres around the town, its intentions being mainly to boom the town for speculative purposes. For the past twenty years Selma has been one of the centers of the gas and oil industries. Some of the lead-ing events of its recent history have been described in the record by years on other pages. The town is still the principal oil town of the county, and a large part of the inhabitants are connected in some capacity with the pro-duction of oil either independently or as employes of the Indiana Pipe Line.

Within the present year Selma has obtained town incorporation. May 21, 1907, by a vote of 75 to 10, the inhabitants voted in favor of incorpora-tion. The commissioners considered the report of the election on May 25, and an election of village officers was ordered for June 8. The first set of officials chosen at that time to direct the affairs of the corporation were: L. S. Clark, clerk; Eldon Cannaday, treasurer; Dr. Charles Jump, trustee of first district; A. J. Bailey, trustee of second district; Allen Howell, trustee of third district; George Ross, trustee of fourth district; and James Greene-walt, trustee of fifth district.

<h2 style="text-align:center">GILMAN.</h2>

The maps of Delaware county show a platted district on the west line of the county, under the name of Gilman. So much of this town as lies in Delaware county is purely a product of the boom during the nineties, and aside from the platting of the land nothing was done to making a town on this side of the county line. The Gas Center Land Co., a corporation in Marion county, laid this plat of 1,129 lots in June, 1893.

CHAPTER XVIII.

CHRONOLOGY OF THE LAST QUARTER CENTURY.

It is said that Lincoln had in his law office a large cabinet provided with numerous drawers and pigeonholes, with a label over each to designate the particular subject or class of the contents. But over the largest of these receptacles, and the one containing the largest number of papers, was the following inscription: "If you can't find it elsewhere, look here."

Perhaps the chief design of the following chapter was to provide some such "omnium gatherum" of the numerous details that could not well be given space elsewhere in this history. It is evident that many events, because they are detached from the main course of affairs, must be recorded in the form of annals rather than be narrated. Such a chronology as follows also has the advantage of ready reference. The principal events in the history of the county during the last twenty-five years are recorded in this way, though many of them receive more ample consideration on other pages. Had it been possible, the record would have been extended back fifty or even seventy-five years, but years of research would not produce as complete a record of those earlier periods as is given for the last quarter of a century, simply because no materials are in existence for such a compilation. Provided the value of this chronology is realized, it is hoped that local historians might continue the record thus begun, thus preserving a daily epitome of the changes and occurrences in the life and affairs of Delaware county. Incidentally this record serves as an index to the most important facts during the past quarter century, and indicates the date when a full description of the topic will be found in the files of the newspapers preserved in the public library.

1882.

July—Weller's sawmill burned.
July 23—Cornerstone of Baptist church laid, on E. Adams street.
Sept. 4—Boyce's flax mill suffers $15,000 loss by fire.
Sept.—Council street opened and graveled from Charles to Middletown pike.
Oct. 4—Wysor's opera house (on Main and Walnut streets), remodeled and opened with Denier's Humpty Dumpty Company.
Oct. 21—Death of T. S. Walterhouse, well known lawyer.
Oct.—Smallpox ravages in Granville.
Nov. 8—Williamson's flour mill at Yorktown burned.

1883.

March 1—Muncie Telephone Co. sells to Central Telephone Co. of Chicago.
March 6—Cammack's sawmill, at Cammack, burned.
March 31—Death of Judge Walter March, a profound lawyer and jurist.
Oct. 1—Order reducing postage from three cents to two takes effect.
Oct. 20—County votes to have free gravel pikes.
Nov. 18—Standard time adopted by the railroads.
Dec. 3—Failure of B. Smith and Son.

1884.

Jan. 14—Death of John Brady, pioneer; business houses of Muncie close
    for funeral.
Feb. 6—Citizens' National Bank moves from Main street to corner of Jack-
    son and Walnut, into former quarters of Claypool's bank.
March 1—Delaware County Tile and Brick Makers' Assn. organized; E. H.
    Case, president.
March 17—Death of Henry Hamilton, who came to the county in 1834.
April 1—Oakville swept by cyclone; four killed and many injured; only four
    houses left standing.
April 18—Death of Price Thomas, aged 75; came to county in 1832, lived
    near Granville over 50 years.
May 10—Frances E. Willard lectures at opera house in Muncie.
June 7—Death of E. C. Anthony.
July 11—New steam fire engine arrives in Muncie and is tested.
Aug. 30—Death of Mrs. John Brady.
Sept. 19—Earthquake shock disturbs Muncie people.
Oct. 17—Death of Dr. Henry C. Winans, prominent physician; an ener-
    getic member of Board of Health of Muncie.
Nov. 28—Minnie Maddern (now Mrs. Fiske) plays "Caprice" at Wysor's
    to a small audience.
Nov. 6—Minus and Fanny Marshall Turner celebrate golden wedding.
Dec. 8—Death of Peter Dragoo, aged 91, who came to Delaware county in
    1832.
During 1884-85 Muncie was a center of the roller skating craze which
then prevailed all over the country, and which during the last few years has
been revived, though not to such an extent as twenty years ago. Patterson's hall was a popular rink. The Royal Rink, at Jackson and Elm streets,
was opened for the "skatorial art" in April, 1885. Traveling shows introduced fancy roller skating as a drawing card. Muncie claimed to stand second in the manufacture of the roller skate. C. J. Becktel, J. F. Shafer and
others in the city were inventors of skates of improved devices.

1885.

Feb. 12—Death of Mrs. Jane (McClellan) Van Arsdol, aged 96, a member
    of the first group of settlers who located on White river five miles
    east of Muncie in 1820.
July 23—Cornerstone of present courthouse laid; during celebration come
    tidings of Gen. Grant's death.
April 21—Death of William Felton, aged 84, who came to Perry township
    in 1838.

May 22—Muncie Business & Manufacturing Assn. formed by committee, its object being the erection of buildings for purpose of manufacturing and promotion of manufacturing in Muncie and vicinity. Formal organization took place June 3, first board of directors being J. H. Smith, James Boyce, A. F. Patterson, T. A. Neely, J. M. Kirby.

July 30—Death of Dr. Robert Winton.

Aug. 13—Golden wedding anniversary of William J. and Sarah (Wilcoxon) Moore; former lived in county since 1830 and latter since 1832.

Oct. 24—Performance of Gilbert and Sullivan's "Mikado" at Wysor's.

Nov.—Polo becomes a favorite sport in Muncie.

1886.

[The items for 1886 are taken from the Putnam Diary, since newspaper files for the year are missing.]

Jan. 12—Fire destroyed the old frame dwelling put up by James Lease about 1839, on Main street, between the property of Mecks & Co. and J. A. Wachtel. The first trial of our water works.

Jan. 31—Samuel D. Chipman, an old citizen of this place, died this after-noon.

Feb. 5—Episcopal church occupied for the first time since completion.

March 11—Minus Turner, one of the earliest settlers of Muncie, died this morning.

March 23—Daniel Pitenger, an old citizen of Delaware township, died to-day.

May 12—Quite a number of our citizens went up to Portland to-day to see the oil well just bored out; come back somewhat excited.

June 4—The old C. F. Willard corner on the northeast corner of Main and Walnut torn down to-day for the purpose of rebuilding. It was one of the oldest brick buildings in Muncie, and the first building I entered when I came to Muncie, October 19, 1838.

Oct. 3—An excursion train to Eaton again this evening to see the natural gas burn.

Oct. 11—Preparing to bore for gas or oil or both.

Nov. 11—The persons employed to bore for oil have this morning "struck" gas, and everybody is on the way to see for themselves—and it is true, after boring over 800 feet; and it is this evening "lit up" and speaks for itself.

Nov. 20—An organization of a company with $100,000 capital for the purpose of furnishing gas to the city for lighting and manufacturing purposes last night and much confidence expressed in final success of enterprise.

Dec. 29—Laying pipe for the natural gas—completed to Weller's Mill.

1887.

Jan. 14—Death of John Marsh, aged 76, at Las Vegas, N. M.; cashier of Citizens' National Bank.

Feb. 11—Blind Tom performs at Wysor's Grand.

Feb. 23—Citizens' Well No. 3 at Muncie strikes gas at 885 feet.

April 9—Muncie Well No. 7 "shot," and becomes biggest well of all; 5,000,-
    000 feet daily.

April—Ohmer avenue surveyed. Galliher farm reported sold for over $100,-
    000, and Boyce buys Volney Willson place east of town for $27,-
    000.

April—Muncie postoffice shows receipts of $8,200 for four previous quar-
    ters; promising second class office and free delivery.

May—National Hotel, after a fire, being rebuilt; Winans building, Jackson
    and Walnut, in course of construction; J. A. Goddard removing
    old buildings at Walnut and Adams.

May—Belt Line railway surveyed; and street railway is discussed.

May 11—Excursion from Cincinnati and intermediate points brings 1,200
    visitors to Muncie and its gas fields; many other excursions about
    this time.

June 29—Death of Martin Galliher, aged 88, an early merchant of Muncie.

July 1—C. U. Telephone Co. inaugurate "five cents a talk" service.

July 12—Death of Terrell Summers in Salem township, aged 69, who came
    to Richwood's settlement in 1832.

Oct.—M. E. church of Muncie buys corner on Adams and High streets.

Oct. 5—Courthouse opened for official business.

Oct.—Standard Oil Co. establishes supply station in Muncie.

Nov. 17—Co-operative Fuel and Gas Light Co. of Muncie, capital stock
    $25,000, organized, first set of directors being: T. A. Neely, W. F.
    Watson, W. L. Richey, A. L. Kerwood, J. W. Ryan, Samuel Mar-
    tin, W. H. Wood.

Nov. 17—Muncie complains of dark streets, despite abundance of natural
    gas.

1888.

Jan. 31—Anthony block completed.

Feb. 6—Muncie, Heat, Light and Power Co. organized. Stockholders:
    James Boyce, Samuel Martin, W. F. Watson, T. H. Kirby, G. W.
    H. Kemper, Arthur Meeks, W. H. Wood, J. R. McMahan, W. S.
    Richey, Charles Boyce, A. L. Kerwood. James Boyce elected
    president, the company absorbing his electric light plant.

Feb. 7—David Swing lectures in Muncie.

Feb. 13—Co-operative Gas Co. strike big gusher on west side of Muncie.

March 3—S. C. Cowan & Co.'s Boston store and Bliss and Keller's cloth-
    ing store opened in new Anthony block.

March—Streets in wretched condition because of trenching and pipe lay-
    ing.

May 10—Contract let for building of High Street Methodist church.

May 26—An incandescent gas lamp is exhibited in Muncie; first local use
    of present day "mantle."

May—Southeast corner of Jackson and High streets to be occupied by
    "Larph" block; name composed of initial letters of Lenon, An-
    thony, Rice, Perkins, Heath, the builders.

May—Delaware County Building and Loan Association, capital $900,000,
    organized. Officers: J. M. Kirby, president; D. H. H. Shewmaker,
    vice president; C. A. Spilker, treasurer; J. W. Ryan, attorney; W.

R. Moore, secretary. Other directors were J. L. Streeter, Ezra Searls, W. H. Long, J. W. Perkins.

May—Muncie House Building Association organized; Joseph Hummel, president; A. W. Chapman, vice president; C. H. Church, treasurer, and J. N. Templer, attorney.

July 4—Cornerstone of M. E. church at Muncie laid.

July 14—Agitation for public park in Muncie begun.

July 14—Presbyterian church of Muncie celebrates semi-centennial of founding.

July 16—Society for prevention of cruelty to animals organized in Muncie; J. A. Goddard, president.

Aug. 14—First roll of pulp comes from Muncie Pulp Works.

Aug. 28—Muncie Free Kindergarten Association arrange to open free kindergarten in South Muncie.

Sept. 21—Numbering of Muncie houses according to ordinance completed.

Sept. 21—Fred Douglass, colored statesman, speaks at Royal Rink.

Oct. 2—Death of A. M. Klein, pioneer Muncie jeweler.

Jan.—Kinnear Manufacturing plant sold at receiver's sale to George Kirby.

Nov. 6—Delaware county gives big majority for Harrison and Morton.

Dec. 16—Floral and horticultural halls at fair grounds burned.

1889.

Jan.—Murphy temperance meetings in Muncie at Royal Rink. Hundreds sign pledge.

Feb. 12—Revival of the boom by presence of eastern capitalists to form Muncie Natural Gas and Land Improvement Co. Successive articles in New York World extol Muncie as "natural gas center of Indiana," spoke of boundless supply of fuel, the city's improvements and advantages, and the presence of three railroads and a belt line and 18 factories. The articles were inspired by and served as advertisement for the above named company, with its reputed two million dollars' capital, of which ex-Gov. Leon Abbett, of New Jersey, was president; E. G. Rideout, of New York, vice president and manager; J. M. Woods, assistant general manager; William Harris, of Union City, treasurer, and S. C. Goshorn, of Muncie, secretary. Excursions were run from New York to the "new Eldorado," where the company had about two thousand acres of land.

Feb. 17—Dedication of Church of God, Third and Chestnut streets, Muncie.

May 28—Recital in new M. E. church on first pipe organ in county.

July 25—J. H. Smith & Co.'s bent wood works destroyed by fire.

Aug. 2—John R. McMahan, lawyer and well known citizen, dies.

Aug. 4—Salvation Army opens first campaign in Muncie.

Aug. 5—Construction work on street railroad begins on Main street in Muncie.

Aug. 9—Ground broken for shoe factory.

Aug.—Adams Chilled Plow Co. and Chamberlain Mfg. Co. constructing plants on the west side.

Nov. 13—Dickens' "Bleak House" presented at Wysor's Grand.

1890.

Jan. 11—Boyce block ruined by fire, nearly twenty firms being burned out; total loss, $100,000.

Jan.—Muncie Architectural Iron works secured for Muncie; Muncie Brass and Novelty Co. buy Chamberlain Mfg. Co.'s pump works.

Jan.—Russian influenza or la grippe becomes epidemic in United States, including Delaware county.

Feb. 14—Muncie city council and Big Four R. R. compromise matter of opening High street; new depot to be erected.

March 3—Citizens' National Bank moves to Anthony block.

April—Muncie Board of Trade, after suspension of activity, revived for a short time.

July 4—Galliher grove on south side of Muncie opened as recreation park, under name of Heekin Park.

Aug. 23—American Association for Advancement of Science visit Muncie and witness wonders of natural gas; three hundred scientists and men of affairs in party.

Sept. 10—Work on Big Four depot at Muncie begun.

Sept. 5—Black letter headlines announce formation of new development company, commanding $10,000,000, to boom Muncie, by building factories, making and improving streets, and linking southern iron fields to Hoosier gas belt.

Oct. 5—English Lutheran church, Howard and Liberty streets, dedicated.

Oct. 9—Third and Ninth regiments of cavalry hold reunion in Muncie.

Oct. 10—Muncie Homestead Company begins building fifty houses on the south side.

Oct. 13—Pres. Harrison, while en route, is given a reception at the Muncie depot, and thousands hear him speak.

Oct. 25—An Edison phonograph is on exhibition in Muncie, being the first local demonstration of an invention that, in improved forms, is now in many households.

Oct. 27—Death of William F. Jones, 77 years old; was director and secretary of the Fort Wayne and Southern Railway in 1848, in 1852 moved to Muncie, where he was alderman and mayor (1877-78).

Oct. 27—Muncie stirred by confession of witness, who claimed that T. J. Blount was murdered by employes of Richmond asylum.

Nov. 4—First election under Australian ballot system.

Nov. 20—Mrs. Maria Woodworth begins meetings in Muncie Church of God.

Dec. 6—Street cars run on Walnut street to Ohmer avenue; three of the old-fashioned steam motor cars in use in the city.

Dec.—City hospital proposed by Alderman Kilgore.

1891.

Jan.—Agitation for 6 o'clock closing of shoe and clothing stores in Muncie.

Jan. 10—Fifty houses completed by Muncie Homestead Co.

Jan. 12—The Commercial Club and its building first talked of in public print.

Jan. 16—Death of Isaac Meeks, who was born in West Virginia in 1829 and lived in Delaware county since 1839.

Jan. 27—Meeting to promote Commercial Club held in courthouse.

Feb. 3—Sweigert's notorious gambling headquarters forced to close and gamblers disperse.

Feb.—Arrangements being made to manufacture ice in Muncie.

Feb. 10—Muncie Commercial and Social Club organized; James Boyce, S. C. Goshorn, John W. Little, J. H. Smith, George L. Lenon, first directors. Old Board of Trade rooms temporary headquarters.

Feb. 12—Joshua Truitt's sawmill, one of oldest in county, burned.

Feb.—Trade unionism gaining foothold in Muncie.

March 20—Contract let for iron bridge over West Jackson street, to take place of foot bridge formerly in use.

March 27—Death of Samuel Haines, one of Muncie's early merchants.

March 30—W. D. Whitney makes proposition to city council for city hospital; accepted May 4.

April 19—Death of Dr. Stephen Hathaway; in Muncie since 1844.

April 21—Death of Dr. Milton James, prominent as physician, in Democratic politics..and in affairs of city; his wife a daughter of Andrew Kennedy.

April 21—Fourth annual exhibit of Muncie Art school.

April 28—Madame Fanny Janauschek, the Bohemian tragic actress, who died in 1904, plays "Meg Merrilies" at Wysor's; "a classical entertainment" is the verdict of the Daily News.

May 2—Ohmer avenue car line is completed.

May 6—County asylum destroyed by fire.

May 18—Death of Samuel Ambrose Wilson, in banking business at Muncie for thirty years.

June 4—Death of Judge Eleazer Coffeen.

June 6—Jacob H. Wysor purchases corner of Mulberry and Jackson streets as site for new opera house. The old Wysor opera house was on the southwest corner of Main and Walnut streets.

June—People's National Bank organized, with $100,000 capital.

June 23—Indiana Music Teachers' Association meet in Muncie.

June 29—Trades Council organized in Muncie—representing a dozen unions, with united strength of one thousand men.

July 21—Death of Robert A. Gordon, oldest resident of the county; came here in 1819 with family of Andrew Broderick, and carried chain for the government surveyors in the survey of the county; afterwards did much railroad contracting.

July 4—Muncie celebrates with unusual elaboration and gaiety.

July—Kirby House exchanges its mansard roof for full fourth story; elevator also installed.

July 25—Dr. R. J. Gatling. inventor of famous gun, in Muncie investigating its resources; but eventually fails to locate an ordnance factory in Indiana.

Aug. 5—Work begins on Wysor Grand.

Aug. 8—Boys find two skulls east of Muncie; old settlers conjecture them to be the remains to two traders who passed through town one day in 1851, and whose wagon was found the next day, but nothing of the men.

Aug. 10—Barnum and Bailey in Muncie.

Aug. 14—Citizens' Enterprise Co. formed.

Aug.—Muncie Shoe and Leather Co.'s plant sold at auction by receiver.

Sept. 3—Death of "Aunt Patsy" Branson, aged 94, widow of Isaac Branson, who settled on Buck creek in 1828.

Sept. 7—Muncie's first Labor Day celebration.

Sept. 16—Death of George Shafer, aged 91, who had lived on his place two miles west since 1822.

Sept. 18—Highlands mill at Eaton burned.

Oct.—Western Improvement Co. prepare to boom Yorktown.

Oct. 28—$100,000 fire destroys Ball Bros. stamping department.

Nov.—Muncie City Hospital, S. Council street, completed; Dr. W. D. Whitney, the promoter and superintendent of the institution.

Dec.—Duplicate whist first comes into vogue.

Dec. 14—Senator Voorhees introduces a bill to provide Muncie with a post-office building; the appropriation was not secured, notwithstanding several efforts made about this time.

Dec. 18—Asahel Thornburg celebrates ninety-ninth birthday. Born in Tennessee, a soldier in war of 1812, voted for nineteen presidents, and lived in Liberty township since 1825.

Dec.—North View a new suburb just north of river; houses under construction and gas mains being laid.

1892.

Jan. 3—Death of Duncan Williams, a resident of Hamilton township since 1836.

Jan.—Delaware County Republican Club organize for the presidential campaign.

Jan. 20—Death of Boyd Linville at New Burlington, aged 82; one of the pioneers.

Jan. 23—Dr. A. B. Bradbury instantly killed at Hedricks crossing east of Muncie by Big Four train.

Jan. 29—Muncie Woman's Club celebrates sixteenth anniversary.

Jan. 31—United Presbyterian church in Muncie burns.

Feb. 9—Muncie electric light plant, completed, drives darkness from the streets with one hundred arc lights.

March—Ball Bros. stamping mill resumes operation in rebuilt quarters.

March 20—Adam Wolf, well known merchant, banker and business man, dies, aged 84; in Muncie since 1855.

March—"The sight of one of the ungainly motors ploughing through the business streets of Muncie is something that the majority of our citizens are not altogether satisfied with."—Daily News comment in urging the installation of an up-to-date electric car system for Muncie.

March—Agitation for renumbering Muncie's streets by the Philadelphia plan, with Walnut and Main the dividing lines.

March 27—Patriots' day celebrated in Muncie, Gov. I. J. Chase being the orator.

April 1—Death of George Elliott, Muncie jeweler since 1855.

April 12—Walker Whiteside plays "Hamlet" at Wysor's.

May 5—Ezra Kendall plays "A Pair of Kids" at Wysor's.

May—Tappan Shoe Co. organized to establish factory in abandoned plant.

June 8—Building of Common Sense Engine plant begun. Contract let for new Presbyterian church at Charles and Mulberry streets, to cost $42,300.

June 18—Hemingray and Over glass factories burned to the ground, a spark from a switch engine starting the fire; loss of nearly a quarter of a million dollars.

July 1—Great Homestead strike inaugurated; Muncie Rolling Mill Co. signs union scale.

July 5—Muncie Daily News changes to a morning edition of eight pages.

July 5—Fifty new houses to be built in Congerville to accommodate the newcomers in the factory district.

July 7—Work begins on the $65,000 paper mill at Albany.

Aug. 5—Contract for Broadway bridge over White river let for $15,500.

Aug. 6—Announcement that Whitely machine works will move to Muncie from Springfield, Ohio. "Whitely" the name of a new suburb to be formed across the river and east of the Fort Wayne tracks.

Aug. 15—Council resolves to build a garbage furnace in Muncie.

Aug. 19—Citizens' Street Railway Co. organized, with $250,000 capital; directors, W. N. Whitely, O. S. Kelly, W. A. Scott, all of Springfield, O.; A. L. Conger and K. B. Conger, of Akron; J. S. Talley, of Terre Haute, and George F. McCulloch, who was named in the articles of incorporation with the understanding that he should resign in favor of Mr. James Boyce. Council granted their petition for construction and operation of electric lines by this company.

Aug. 20—Fortieth annual fair brings out record-breaking crowds.

Aug. 23—Auction of Whitely lots; excursions run from neighboring cities to bring in purchasers; a "love feast" in evening at Wysor's.

Aug. 25—Reunion of 69th Reg., I. V. I., in Muncie.

Aug. 26—Muncie Nail works burned, with loss of about $50,000.

Aug. 27—Sale of lots being pushed in Heekin park.

Aug. 31—Architectural Iron works burned; loss of about $40,000.

Sept. 1—Cornerstone of Muncie Presbyterian church laid.

Sept. 2—Campaign of '92 opened in Muncie at Wysor's, where "Col." Charles W. Fairbanks was principal speaker.

Sept. 6—Boldt's glass factory suffers loss of about $15,000 by fire.

Sept. 15—Wysor's Grand Opera House, after a year in building, is opened to music and drama with Thomas W. Keene in Richard III.

Sept. 16—Reunion of the "Iron Brigade" in Muncie.

Sept. 29—Midland Steel mills begin operation.

Oct. 11—Ohio Wagon works destroyed by fire.

Nov. 2—John Wanamaker, postmaster general, makes political speech at Wysor's.

Nov. 8—Election day; Cleveland elected president, but Delaware county gives a large plurality for the Republican ticket.

Nov. 14—Death of John F. Sanders, lawyer.

Nov. 26—Lake View Hotel, in West Muncie, completed.

Dec. 28—Courthouse is damaged by fire that starts from leaking gas pipe; many records and documents in the court room lost, and loss is about $25,000.

Dec. 30—Whitely inaugural ball a brilliant social event, Gov. Chase being among the distinguished company that celebrate the beginning of Whitely factory suburb.

1893.

Jan.—Strike of L. E. & W. switchmen interferes with factory operation in Muncie.

Jan. 16—Council passes the first of many ordinances providing safety gates at railway crossings in Muncie; the railroads did not comply for several years.

Jan. 27—Eastern Indiana Jersey Cattle Breeding Association organized; Lewis Moore, president; James Boyce, vice president; M. S. Claypool, secretary; J. G. Bowers, treasurer.

Feb. 5—Muncie Cycling Club organized.

Feb. 16—Population of Muncie estimated at 19,763 by Charles Emerson, publisher of directory.

Feb. 22—Lake View Hotel, West Muncie, opened by reception and grand ball by Muncie lodge of Elks.

March 7—Citizens' Street Railway Co. begin construction of line from Whitely, through town on Walnut and Main streets, to the West side. Miss Minnie McKillip inaugurates work by casting the first shovel of dirt at Wysor and Monroe streets.

March—City council resolves to pave business district with asphalt; the resolution is not carried out for several years.

March 2—Metropolitan police bill passes both houses of the legislature, extending the system to Muncie. A. W. Chapman, Vernon Davis and W. E. Hitchcock were appointed first commissioners by the governor. They in turn appointed James Miller first chief of police; patrolmen: George Ball, William James, John Galligher, William Cole, Adam Deems, John Seldomridge, Curt Turner, George Benadum, Van Benbow, Hamilton Beall, Brinton Alstadt.

March 9—Chicago, Indiana and Eastern Railway incorporated.

March 31—Muncie Coil Hoop Works, on Westside, destroyed by fire; loss, $10,000.

April 9—Citizens' Electric Street Railway Co. steal march on protesting property owners by laying track down Walnut street to Main and thence to High early Sunday morning, when injunctions cannot be issued; the city police do not interfere.

April 10—Muncie Handle works destroyed by fire.

April 18—Garbage furnace on North Walnut street finally completed.

April 19—Helen Modjeska, supported by Otis Skinner, plays "As You Like It" at Wysor's Grand.

April 29—Center township gives majority of 628 in favor of tax for subsidy to Chicago and Southeastern Railroad and the C., I. & E., provided they are completed within certain limit (which they are not); Salem township gives 41 majority against tax for former road.

April 29—Death of Dr. Solomon Snell, for twenty-four years in Muncie.

May 5—Cowan has a fire that destroyed washing machine works of William Neff.

May—Strike of union carpenters ties up building operations in Muncie.

May 13—"Muncie's new electric street railway system is now in operation." In fifty days from starting of work on March 17, the line was completed from Main street north on Walnut, by the Wheeling pike to the fair grounds, and out Wysor street to Broadway in Whitely. At the power house, just completed on North Walnut, a reception was held; there was music; speeches were made by G. F. McCulloch, secretary of the company; Mayor Brady, Supt. Cotschal. The mayor started one engine, Miss Clara Koons the other, while Miss Fannie James switched on the current. Invited guests made several circuits of the line to the fair grounds. One who rode remembered the time when he had "hilled beans near where the power house stood."

May 18—Muncie Military Band organized; Charles McDonald, president; Charles Davis, director.

May 15—Death of George W. Robinson, well known city official.

May 19—Dunkards' convention at fair grounds.

May—C., I. & E. R. R. begin building line from Fairmount to Muncie.

May 25—Ground broken for Malleable Iron works on Wysor's Heights.

May 26—Street cars begin running to Whitely.

June 3—Farmers purchase "home-made' harvesting machines at Whitely. Dinner is served under the trees of Wood's park to purchasers and friends by officers of the company, followed by a parade through the city.

June 10—Muncie's streets without signs and houses without numbers, so that it is impossible for strangers and even residents to find their way.

June—The financial stringency of 1893 is felt in the country at large, and flourishing Muncie has intimations of its effects.

June 16—An electric motor supplies power for the Morning News press.

June—Bell Stove works, west of Muncie, began operation.

June 17—Whitely Malleable Casting Co. incorporated by B. H. Whitely, Elmer J. Whitely, Thomas Liggett, D. W. C. Bidwell, R. R. Armour, A. L. Johnson, G. F. McCulloch, A. F. Patterson, John Whitely.

June 19—City decides to furnish market place for farmers' produce.

June—Consumers' Paper Co. building a factory on west side to manufacture strawboard.

June 30—Glass factories and iron mills close for summer, and anxiety is felt, though not generally expressed, as to whether they will reopen in the fall.

July 1—Electric cars are running out Howard street to Westside.

July 6—Lime kiln, on Granville pike, just north of the river, a famous old landmark, being destroyed.

July 12—Fire partly consumes a house on North Walnut street in which Volney Willson taught school during the forties, and which was also used as store and dwelling.

July 13—Receiver appointed for Common Sense Engine Co.

July—West Muncie, with its Lake View Hotel and "Delaware Lake," has a brief reign as popular resort before hard times.

July 28—Muncie is infested by "bums and thieves": products of hard times.

Aug. 4—Temporary suspension of Citizens' National Bank. President Kerwood assures depositors that assets are ample; the cause assigned being inability to realize quickly on good paper. Nearly fifty of the most prominent citizens of Muncie, representing collective responsibility of $3,000,000, signed a guarantee of deposits in the Citizens' National, the Farmers' National, Delaware County National and Merchants' National Banks. This and other acts by individuals significant of the buoyant confidence of Muncie people in general. Comptroller Eckels, on hearing of the action of Muncie citizens in guaranteeing their banks, said: "That is patriotic, unselfish and good citizenship. That is the kind of stuff men should be made of. . . . If the intelligent and patriotic citizens in all sections of the country, who know that their banks are safe and honestly conducted, would band together in that fashion, it would improve the credit of the country and put a stop to bank failures in most instances."

Aug. 7—President Cleveland's famous message demanding repeal of silver purchase act and repletion of gold reserve.

Aug. 12—Arthur W. Brady appointed receiver of Citizens' National.

Aug. 12—Tappan Shoe factory closes for lack of business; also Darnall Nail works, and other plants reduce force of employes.

Aug. 24—Morning News reduces size from 7-columns to 6-columns.

Aug. 28—Street car franchise granted for 35 years. Many citizens express opposition to length of grant and free bestowal of public streets on private corporation.

Aug. 29—New chemical engine, long needed by fire department, is tested; a patrol wagon also a recent acquisition of police department.

Aug. 31.—Muncie branch of Gas Belt League, for promoting welfare of the city and gas belt, organized, officers being: W. A. Sampson, T. H. Kirby, F. J. Claypool, C. E. Everet, Charles Emerson, and James Boyce.

Aug.—Severe drought does much damage in Delaware county.

Aug.—Muncie has smallpox epidemic on south side; for six weeks no street car runs south on Walnut street.

Sept. 6—Darnall Nail works and Midland Steel works resume operation.

Sept. 7—Proclamation from Muncie health board on smallpox epidemic. warning against public meetings and congregating on streets and insisting on vaccination. Fifty-two cases since beginning of epidemic. Churches, Sunday schools and public school suspended, and quarantine against Muncie is declared in surrounding towns. Pest house built in Congerville.

Sept. 13.—"One might be led to believe, observing the quietness of the streets, that Muncie is a village. . . . Just as soon as this temporary panic is allayed, those 20,000 people will spring to work with an earnestness that will soon substantiate the claim that Muncie is the chief city of the gas belt."—News editorial. From this time there is a noticeable absence of enthusiastic accounts of building. factory progress, etc.

Sept. 13—Citizens' Electric and Muncie Street Railway Companies consolidate, new company being incorporated with $300,000 capital, $100,000 preferred stock bearing interest at seven per cent. Directors: J. Smith Talley, J. W. Landrum, of Terre Haute; Edward

Wells, Burlington, Vt.; G. F. McCulloch and Charles Miller, of Muncie.

Sept. 16—The "dummy" street car line being changed to an electric line; F. G. Brownell, superintendent of the old line, turns over management to new company.

Sept. 18—Muncie resolves to borrow $5,000 to fight smallpox scourge. In one week trustee of Center township issues one hundred relief orders to the poor of Muncie, indicating how the financial panic, the epidemic and general decline of prosperity affected the city, that only a short time previously was flourishing.

Sept. 30—The News finds encouragement in the business outlook, a revival of industry, and beginning of relief from smallpox.

Oct. 4—Leon & Metzger, clothiers, established in Muncie before the war, and with stores in several other cities, fail.

Oct.—Isaac J. Williams, stockman, wins five prizes on sheep exhibited at World's Fair.

Oct. 9—Muncie Iron and Nail Co. accept a receivership, their assignment being caused by failure of one of the stockholders.

Oct.—Central Union Telephone Co. said to have over 250 customers in Muncie.

Oct.—Over Glass factory resumes work; also Common Sense Engine works, the receivership having been dismissed.

Nov. 1—Electric cars begin running to Avondale.

Nov. 4—Smallpox quarantine, after lasting eight weeks, is raised, by permission of the state board of health. General jollification, assembling of people on streets, blowing of horns, burning of red fire. On following day church bells call the people to divine service, and on Nov. 6, the public schools are opened. Mercantile business revives at once, and the country people, so long barred from town, bring in their produce and trade at the stores. Quarantine established Sept. 11; 146 cases and 20 deaths. The city fought the disease unaided until the last four weeks, when the state gave aid ($3,400). Total cost of epidemic to city was $40,000.

Nov. 14—Opening of Walnut street electric line to Congerville (New York avenue).

Nov. 22—Citizens' National Bank, after a suspension of three months, reopens its doors. Charles M. Turner, a native of Muncie, succeeds W. M. Marsh, who has been connected with the bank as cashier for eighteen years.

Nov. 19—Methodist Protestant Church on East Jackson street dedicated.

Nov. 20—Electric line installed on East Main street to Macedonia avenue, taking place of old "dummy" system.

Nov. 23—Samuel McCreary, who came to Washington township in 1838, with Philip Woodring, Ezra Maynard and Nathan Maynard, dies near Gaston, aged 92.

Nov. 23—A. J. Buckles awarded a congressional medal of honor for gallantry at the battle of Wilderness.

Nov.—The first autumn in which football flourishes as a popular sport in Muncie.

Dec. 8—Agitation for first long-distance telephone.

Dec. 21—Regular service begun over Powers and Council street electric
    lines to Avondale.

In 1892 building permits in Muncie were issued to the value of $314,703.
In 1893, the corresponding figures, exclusive of suburbs, were $147,622.
This remarkable decrease may be attributed to the carpenters' strike in May,
the smallpox epidemic in the fall, and the general financial panic that was
felt throughout the latter half of the year.—Fire losses in Muncie for 1893
were $34,106, more than half of the total being insured. Total alarms were
eighty-eight. The running expenses of the city of Muncie during the year
1893 were $101,217.36.

1894.

Jan.—Muncie Muck Bar Co. succeeded the Darnall Nail works.

Jan. 11—Court house is lighted by electricity.

Jan. 16—Citizens' Enterprise Co. elect James Boyce president, W. M. Marsh
    vice president, George L. Lenon treasurer, and G. F. McCulloch
    secretary.

Feb. 3—Over Glass factory shuts down because Wilson tariff bill cuts duty
    on window glass nearly in half.

Feb. 15—Lake View Hotel at West Muncie attached by sheriff.

Feb. 17—Patterson Glass works at West Muncie sold by receiver to George
    L. Lenon.

Feb. 19—Muncie Commercial Club organized "to promote the commercial
    and manufacturing interests and general welfare of the city of
    Muncie." C. M. Turner, president; Thomas McKillip, vice presi-
    dent; Frank Claypool, secretary; E. M. Smith, treasurer, and T. F.
    Rose, A. W. Brady and C. M. Turner, executive committee.

Feb. 26—City council orders "standard asphalt pavement" of Walnut street,
    from North to Willard; Washington street, Walnut to High; High,
    Washington to Jackson; Jackson, High to Mulberry; Mulberry,
    Jackson to Main; Main, High to Madison. Contract let in April,
    the cost in round numbers to be $80,000. The question of paving
    had been a live one in Muncie for several years. The graveled
    streets in the business center were as inadequate for the service de-
    manded as had been the old-time mud streets of the early forties.
    Deep ruts, thick mud and sloppiness had been favorite themes
    with the press when civic criticism was in order or news items were
    scarce.

March 13—Chicago and Southeastern Railroad (Midland) begins grading
    from Anderson to Muncie.

March 26—Plant of Consumers' Paper Co., built during hard times, is com-
    pleted and begins the making of strawboard.

March 27—Police assist the progress of a delegation on their way to join
    Coxey's Army of the Commonwealth.

April 11—Mlle. Rhea plays the "New Magdalene" at Wysor's.

April 12—Two hundred and seventy-three telephones in operation in Mun-
    cie: hard times caused nearly forty instruments to be taken out in
    past six months.

April 13—Ground broken for plant of Patton Hollow-ware Mfg. Co., in
    Boyceton. (This concern was short lived).

May 8—"Gen." Aubrey's army of thirty-four commonwealers of the Coxey type camp at Muncie, having marched in from Anderson. Citizens soon dismiss them, without having contributed much money to their cause.

May 6—Whitely Reaper and Mower works destroyed by fire; out of reach of the city water mains, and there was no insurance for the loss of over $100,000.

June 8—Coleman H. Maitlen, former sheriff, resident of county since 1832, dies in Muncie, aged 74.

June 24—Presbyterian Church at Charles and Mulberry streets dedicated, after two years in building; cost about $48,000.

June 27—"Minnetrista" (winding waters) name given to Ball Bros. residence addition north of White river.

July 5—Great Pullman strike delays Muncie mails.

July 17—Street paving begins on Mulberry street.

July 19—The Muncie Fencibles (the name of the local militia company) reach home after doing guard duty at Hammond and East Chicago during the railroad strike.

July 31—Citizens' League is organized in Muncie to begin crusade against lawlessness, especially Sabbath breaking.

Aug. 8—Mississinewa river, according to report of committees sent to investigate, is black and foul from the refuse of the pulp works at Albany.

Aug. 22—Annual reunion of Fleming family, headed by Gov. Fleming, of West Virginia, held in Muncie.

Aug. 18—Four squares of asphalt pavement completed in Muncie, Dr. A. C. Jones being the first to drive a vehicle over it.

Aug. 20—Whitely Malleable Castings works at Wysor's Heights begin operations.

Aug. 30—Apollo Club, after several years of inactivity, reorganized.

Sept. 1—Market house, corner of Charles and Walnut, reopened, three days in the week. Truck farmers offer fresh provisions, and the ringing of a bell is signal for the beginning of the market day.

Sept. 5—A 22½ per cent reduction is made in wages of employes of Window Glass Workers' Association, as a result of the tariff reductions and general business depression. Maring, Hart & Co. and Over factories in Muncie start soon afterward.

Sept. 15—The Street Railway Co. and the Asphalt Paving Co. dispute the possession of the streets and a pitched battle is barely averted; the paving people tear up a portion of the tracks and a riot occurs, order being restored when the court issues a restraining order against interference with street car traffic.

Sept. 23—Laying of cornerstone of Christian Church at Elm and Jackson streets.

Oct. 8—Cornerstone laid for M. E. Church at Gaston; a brick building to cost $5,000.

Sept. 26—Many citizens of Washington township and elsewhere meet in old M. E. Church at New Corner (George W. Cromer, chairman) and express their approval of a tax of 2 per cent on their tax valuation as a subsidy for a railroad that will make a town out of the little hamlet at that place.

Oct. 16—The Vanguard, a labor paper, started in Muncie by Oran Hall.

Oct. 27—Muncie Electrical works sold by receiver to a new company that has these officers: W. S. Richey, president and treasurer; R. F. Platt, vice president; A. S. Richey, secretary.

Oct. 30—Formal opening of Whitely Malleable Castings works and the public sale of lots at Wysor's Heights. Liberal advertising brought many strangers to the city, and the opening of the new addition and its principal industry was an important event.

Nov. 3—Ex-President Benjamin Harrison makes a speech, closing the campaign, on the court house square.

Nov. 6—Republicans are victorious in county and state election.

Nov.—7,210 feet of asphalt paving cost Muncie $91,626.48, which was distributed among the benefited parties for payment, the city, the street railway company, the corporations and the citizens bearing the expense.

Nov. 13—Opening of long-distance telephone in Muncie. Officials and private citizens, through forty transmitters at the Kirby House, talk to New York, Terre Haute, Pittsburg, Cleveland, Cincinnati, Chicago and other cities.

Nov. 17—John E. McKendry, pioneer manufacturer of Muncie, proprietor of heading factory of East Main street, retires from business.

Dec. 1—Farmers' Insurance Co. of Delaware County organized; Enoch Drumm, of Harrison township, president; Lewis Moore, Hamilton township, vice president; Perry V. Stewart, Salem township, elected secretary-treasurer, but resigned, and J. R. Shoemaker, of Daleville, elected to his place. One director chosen for each township.

Dec. 12—Muncie Democrats choose Edward Tuhey postmaster.

Dec. 19—F. E. Putnam resigns office of secretary of Delaware Lodge No. 46, F. & A. M., after forty-six years of nearly continuous service.

Dec. 22—Muncie is favored with a performance of "A True American," with pugilist John L. Sullivan as the star.

Dec. 31—Muncie Free Kindergarten Association organized.

1895.

Jan. 15—"Ben Hur" given in pantomime at Wysor's Grand largely by home talent; called a "magnificent production."

Jan. 16—Spiritualists formally open their hall at Howard and High streets. Mrs. Wallace Hibbits conducting the meeting; the hall is dedicated on Feb. 10.

Jan. 28—New directory shows Muncie has population of 22,285, a gain of 2,500 despite the hard times.

Feb. 2—Albany loses its furniture factory by fire; buckets and small hose only implements for fighting fire.

Feb. 6—Neely residence, in Riverside, over forty years old and one of the landmarks, burned.

Feb. 23—Death of Eliza Adams Willard, widow of Dr. William C. Willard, aged 77; had lived in Muncie since 1836.

Feb. 25—Whitecap outrages at Granville.

March 8—Streets of Muncie being marked in accordance with ordinance of May 30, 1892.

March 11—Nicholson bill, regulating saloons and sale of liquors, receives the governor's signature.

March 25—Col. R. G. Ingersoll lectures in Muncie.

March 25—J. C. Wood & Co.'s sawmill and skewer factory and the plant of American Skewer Co., Hoyt avenue, burned; loss $30,000.

March 26—Reunion and encampment of the Indiana Department G. A. R. in Muncie begins.

March 30—The Vanguard has a new editor, George E. Holbrook. The Chicago, Indiana and Eastern R. R. graded their line to a . seven miles north of Muncie before hard times struck the country. For nearly two years nothing more was done, until the spring of 1895, when the enterprise was once more revived and efforts made to complete the line to Muncie. Special efforts were put forth to build the road as far as Matthews, which as yet existed only as a "paper town."

April 2—Failure of Findlay Rolling Mill Co., which operated as a branch the plant of old Muncie Nail works.

April 15—Muncie city council decides to pave forty-seven blocks, at a cost of about $80,000.

April 15—The Free Kindergarten Ass'n opens its first school in Avondale, in a five-room building on Ohmer avenue; 26 pupils the first day.

April 17—Buck Creek flour mill, one mile southwest of city, owned by Enoch Witt, and a popular institution among the farmers of that section, is burned.

April 17—Commercial Club elects A. W. Brady president, J. F. Wildman vice president, F. J. Claypool secretary, and Hardin Roads treasurer.

April 20—James Miller resigns as chief of police; William H. Fortner his successor.

April 22—Farmers' Bank of Eaton files articles of incorporation; $30,000 stock.

April 27—Works of Architectural Iron Co. destroyed by fire; loss about $20,000.

May 2—"Jahr Markt" at Wysor's Grand for benefit of kindergartens.

May 7—Suicide of Yost Dippel. 93 years old, an old resident of the county.

May 12—First Christian Church of Muncie dedicated.

May 19—Congerville Baptist Church dedicated.

May 22—Death of Chamillia Trout, widow of Washington Trout, a resident near Gaston since 1844.

June 2—Muncie Saving and Loan Co. plan a business block on southeast corner of High and Adams streets.

June 4—Muncie citizens alarmed when they discover that the water company turns river water into the mains to supplement the supply furnished by the wells.

June 4—George W. Spilker places provision in his will to donate property valued at $10,000 to the city for library purposes.

June—The first "bloomer" bicycle girl appears in Muncie.

June 1—Death of John S. Cecil at Selma, aged 78, member of a pioneer family that settled in the county in October, 1831.

June 8—Postal Telegraph-Cable Co. granted right to place poles and wires along the highways of Delaware county.

June 9—Harvest prospects gloomy on account of drought.

June 12—A. L. Johnson Lumber Co. organized; A. L. Johnson, president; J. C. Johnson, secretary and treasurer.

June 14—A. L. Johnson, J. C. Johnson and Thomas Morgan plan building of five-story modern business block, Walnut and Charles streets, where old Presbyterian church stood.

June 14—Total valuation of real and personal property in the county is $18,000,000, over $8,000,000 of it being in Muncie and Center township.

June 28—Muncie Cemetery Association formed to plan a new cemetery; first board of managers: J. C. Johnson, C. A. Willard, J. A. Goddard, W. A. Sampson, Hardin Roads, A. J. Meeks, A. W. Brady.

July 2—Saloon-keepers comply with Nicholson law by closing at 11 o'clock and removing screens and raising blinds; card, billiard and pool tables taken out.

July 4—Saloons shut tight, and bartenders have a holiday.

July 4—William G. Ethell, resident in Muncie 1838-67, dies in Anderson, aged 74.

July 6—Sale of Indianapolis *People* and other sensational papers stopped in Muncie in accordance with new law suppressing such publications. Reporter of "Muncie Topics" columns in said paper arrested.

July 9—Death of Joseph Davis, aged 88, who came to Muncie in 1845; in overland freighting business before the railroads, and later in merchandising and hotel business.

July 26—C., I. & E. R. R. running trains to Cumberland, only fifteen miles from Muncie. Will Center township offer inducements for road to come to Muncie?

August—Muncie buildings planned or in course of construction: Boyce's two-story block, north side of Main to Elm; Johnson business block, Walnut and Charles; Muncie Savings and Loan Co.'s three-story, High and Adams; Bishop's three-story block, Walnut and Howard; Seitz, three-story, Walnut near Charles; F. T. Roots, three-story, Charles street; J. J. Shields, two-story, East Main., etc., etc.

Aug. 11—Death of Elizabeth Griesheimer, near Yorktown, aged 88, closing a married life with John G. of sixty-seven years' duration.

Aug. 19—City council describes business and residence limits of Muncie, saloons being restricted within the former.

Aug. 24—People's Home and Savings Association incorporated, first directors being: J. J. Hartley, J. E. Reed, J. R. Hummel, C. L. Bender, W. W. Shirk, C. M. Turner, E. H. Tansey, C. L. Medsker, and James Boyce, first president.

Sept. 3—Selma in danger of destruction from a fiery gas well in center of town.

Sept. 6—Old Settlers' meeting at fair grounds. Lloyd Wilcoxen, Judge Buckles, James Maddy, Henry Wysor, James Charman, C. E. Shipley, David T. Haines, Mrs. Mary Edmonds (Muncie's first white child), and Scott Richardson (first male child in county) being among the pioneers still living.

Sept. 7—Pioneers' Association of Delaware County organized. Jacob Heath, president; J. W. Dungan, vice-president; N. N. Spence, secretary-treasurer; N. F. Ethell, historian secretary; township vice-presidents: James Tomlinson and Mrs. A. C. Smith, Center; William A. Jordan and Mrs. D. W. Cecil, Perry; Wilber Duncan and Mrs. Sarah Lewellen, Liberty; Gabriel Payton and Barbara Lake, Delaware; Calvin Crooks and Mary J. Wright, Niles; David Brandt and Mrs. Joseph Kirkwood, Union; Matthew McCormick and Mary Moore. Hamilton; Miles Herrold and Mrs. John Losh, Monroe; Josiah Cromer and Mrs. George Young, Salem; J. Harvey Koontz and Mrs. Samuel Parkison. Mt. Pleasant; Jacob Cecil and Mrs. James Peterson. Harrison; Thomas McCreary and Mrs. Benjamin Lewis, Washington.

Sept. 8—St. Lawrence Catholic Church dedicated.

Sept. 15—Location of postoffice decided at 417 South Walnut street. Bid of George A. Stafford accepted for building a three-story brick structure in which office to be located.

Sept. 20—Yorktown in midst of diphtheria epidemic.

Oct. 8—Citizens' National and Farmers' National banks of Muncie consolidate under name of Union National, to be located at Walnut and Jackson streets, on site of Citizens' National. Officers: C. M. Turner, president; Carl A. Spilker, vice-president; Edward Olcott, cashier; J. C. Abbott, assistant cashier.

Oct. 10—Death of John Ross, at Selma, aged 78.

Oct. 25—Mock Bros.' brick yard at Muncie burned.

Nov. 1—Ely Window Glass Co., a reorganization of Gilman Window Glass Co., incorporated to operate the plant at Gilman; directors: Otis E. Duncan, O. S. Jacobs, D. W. Joy, of Ohio; Charles Ely, of Gilman; J. W. Hamilton, of Eaton.

Nov. 2—Development of oil wells in Delaware county attracts attention.

Nov. 15—Cornerstone of addition to News building laid at 13 minutes past 12 a. m., inscription being: "Erected 1895. The Muncie News, established 1872. The Evening News, established 1878. The Morning News, established 1892. Chas. F. W. Neely, Pub."

Nov. 22—Y. P. S. C. E. and W. C. T. U. join with the Good Citizenship League to fight saloons.

Nov. 22—An investigation of the fire department of Muncie results in the discharge of three firemen.

Dec. 8—Henry Harrison McGinnis, a Muncie high school graduate, paints some pictures that call forth an editorial comment in the News.

Dec. 14—Diphtheria continues at Yorktown, and schools and churches suspended.

Dec.—In the visit of a Washington township farmer to attend court in Muncie is an echo of the discussion and trouble caused by the removal of the hitch-racks from the public square years before. At that time this farmer had vowed he would never again patronize Muncie merchants, and he had kept his word even to the extent of refusing to come to Muncie until forced to attend court at this time.

1896.

Jan. 6—"Trilby" presented at Wysor's Grand.

Jan. 13—Muncie district telegraph service inaugurated.

Jan. 15—Royerton gets a depot and telegraph office.

Jan. 22—Carl A. Spilker elected president of Union National bank; W. W. Shirk, vice-president; Cory Abbott, cashier.

Feb. 19—127 oil leases on record at the court house for territory in Delaware, Niles, Union and Hamilton townships.

Feb. 22—Muncie postoffice moved to new building on South Walnut street, where modern equipment, including lock boxes, is installed; space for office, 38 by 98 feet.

March 5—Mr. and Mrs. Robert Mecks celebrate golden wedding anniversary.

April 13—Fire insurance expert reports on inadequacy of Muncie water supply, inefficiency of machinery and equipment of water works, and the inability of a fire department designed for a city of 5,000 to protect a city of 25,000 population.

April 12—Death of James Carmichael, aged 76, pioneer, at New Burlington, in which vicinity he had lived since 1827.

April 19—Death of E. B. Bishop (at Dayton, O.), for a number of years a prominent citizen of Muncie.

April 28—Death of John Milton Thomas, aged 68, for fifty years a resident of the county.

May 24—Death of A. C. Mellette, at Pittsburg, Kan.; an early editor, lawyer; publisher with T. J. Brady, of Muncie Times; twice governor of South Dakota.

June 21—Death of George L. Lenon, aged 47, born near Smithfield, this county; prominent in business and a very public-spirited citizen.

June 23—Eastern Indiana Normal University organized.

July 13—Emmett M. Smith resigns from presidency of Delaware County National Bank; John C. Johnson becomes president, and W. E. Hitchcock, vice-president.

July 24—James A. Mount, candidate for governor, opens campaign of '96 in this county with speech at Muncie.

July 29—Albany Journal now published by C. L. Lockhart and T. L. Martin.

Sept. 3—Second annual picnic of Pioneers' Association.

Sept. 12—W. A. McNaughton opens department store in new Johnson block.

Sept. 16—Demolition of an old log house on West Gilbert street recalls pioneer incidents.

Sept. 19—Prof. John M. Bloss, educator, returns to Muncie from Oregon.

Sept. 28—Council grants franchise to W. J. Kurtz, James M. Best and Dr. E. T. Griffith to operate a new telephone system in Muncie.

Oct. 1—Street railway company reduces wages and service.

Oct. 15—Delaware Club celebrates first anniversary.

Oct. 15—Roswell P. Flower talks sound money in Muncie.

Oct. 21—Bryan arouses Democratic enthusiasm by a visit to Muncie

Nov. 30—Benjamin Harrison adds to Republican enthusiasm in Delaware
county.

Oct. 30—Death of George W. Staytes, an old and popular resident of
Muncie.

Nov. 3—McKinley elected president, receiving over 3,000 plurality in this
county.

Nov. 9—Muncie Glass Co. buys Nelson Flint Glass works, at Sullivan and
Peirce streets, which had been idle nine months.

Nov. 28—Christian Endeavor convention in Muncie.

Dec. 18—Muncie Lodge No. 433. F. & A. M., Muncie Chapter No. 30, and
Muncie Commandery No. 18, dedicate new quarters on the fifth
floor of the Johnson building.

Dec. 30—Rhea as "Nell Gwynne" at Wysor's.

1897.

Jan. 1—Albany postoffice raised to third class; showing growth of that
town.

Jan. 19—Muncie chapter, Daughters of American Revolution, organized,
being the fourth chapter in the state.

Jan. 20—Citizens' Enterprise Co., after an existence of five years and
the accomplishment of a remarkable amount of material benefit
for the city and county, is dissolved and begins closing its accounts.

Jan. 21—Charles Baldwin becomes chief of Muncie police.

Feb. 26—A cinematoscope gives a "moving picture" exhibit at Wysor's.

March 2—C. F. W. Neely retires from the Morning News and is succeeded
by Charles H. Bundy.

March 3—Muncie Lodge, I. O. G. T., organized with fifty members.

March 6—White river rises to flood stages; water works and many factories have to shut down.

March 24—Death of O. M. Todd, former county superintendent of schools
and pastor of the First Presbyterian Church of Muncie.

March 31—Albany has $25,000 fire in business district.

April 15—William H. Fortner, former superintendent of Muncie police,
killed by Big Four freight train.

April 29—Death of Joseph S. Buckles, 78 years old, lawyer, judge and
man of affairs.

May 3—Albany votes to build water works.

May 19—Lloyd Wilcoxon, aged 76, and sixty-five years a resident of this
county, dies.

May—The independent telephone company begins operation in Muncie.

May—Agitation renewed for municipal ownership of water works, and
criticism of its service, cost and tax returns.

June 23—Death of Charles Rickert, aged 90, a resident of Muncie since
1839.

July 1—F. J. Claypool and C. R. Heath become publishers of the Morning
News.

July 13—Benjamin F. Smith, old resident of county, dies near Inlow
Springs, aged 73.

July 15—Mr. and Mrs. Simon Conn, north of Muncie, celebrate sixtieth
anniversary of wedding. "Sime" Conn one of the well-known
pioneer freighters between Muncie and Cincinnati.

Sept. 2—Old Settlers picnic at Westside park. James A. Bass elected
president; John Graham, vice president; N. N. Spence, secretary.

Sept. 16—Phoebe A. Gilbert, widow of John A. Gilbert, dies at age of 72.

Sept. 27—Common Sense Engine works resume after a shutdown of more
than a year.

Sept. 25—Announcement of 10 per cent reduction in insurance rates on
Muncie property; fires of several years before had raised the rates
inordinately.

Oct. 27—Tappan Shoe factory leaves Muncie.

Oct. 28—Mr. and Mrs. John S. Fudge celebrates golden wedding at
Albany.

Oct. 28—"The postoffice department has been experimenting in the matter
of free delivery of mails in-rural districts. and results are so favorable that it does seem possible for the system to be adopted at no
distant day."—Morning News editorial.

Oct. 29—Death of Joseph Prutzman, aged 71; in Muncie since 1859; a
soldier in the Civil war, and a manufacturer of brick.

Nov. 4—"Rural free delivery service in Delaware county will go into effect
next Monday." (Nov. 8) Four routes, to Daleville, to Selma, to
Albany and to Wheeling. This was part of the experimental
service instituted in different parts of the country by the postoffice
department. The beginning of the permanent system is later.

Nov.—The "Committee of One Hundred" and other temperance organizations conduct a vigorous campaign against liquor dealers in the
residence portion of Muncie—especially against the Maple Grove
resort.

Nov. 16—Rebecca Wright, pioneer woman, sister of John Brady and
mother of A. L. Johnson, celebrates 89th birthday.

Nov. 23—Delaware County Veterans' Association organized; A. L. Kerwood, president; W. H. Younts, vice president; W. W. Ross,
treasurer; A. C. Stouder, general secretary; Joshua Jester, recording secretary.

Dec.—General awakening to the fact that the gas supply is failing and the
necessity of saving gas. The News speaks of "what might have
been" had regulation been adopted sooner.

Dec. 17—Death of Mark Walling, aged 77, who lived in the county since
1832, was builder of Walling Hall, and conducted a pioneer tanyard near North Walnut street.

Dec. 21—Patton Hollow-ware Manufacturing plant sold by receiver to
parties who intend to manufacture plumbers' supplies.

1898.

Jan. 3—Curfew ordinance passed in Muncie.

Jan. 21—The sawmill, only industry of Cammack, burned and will not be
rebuilt.

Jan. 24—Death of Rev. James Sparr, aged 81, pioneer Methodist preacher.

Jan. 24—Operating expenses of Muncie electric light plant for 1897 were
$4,344.82. Adding interest on bonds and depreciation ($2,640)
makes each light cost $47.10. But criticism comes from various
sources on inadequacy of plant and irregularity of lighting.

Jan. 25—Death of Michael Highlands, aged 84, long resident and proprietor of woolen and flour mills at Eaton.

Jan. 31—First prosecution in Delaware county for violation of new compulsory education law; a father in Congerville fined and sent to jail.

Feb. 8—The pole is removed and toll house destroyed on Yorktown pike, and after forty years it ceases to be a toll road. The commissioners bought the Yorktown pike in March for the nominal sum of $1. Every pike in the county now free except the Muncie and Granville, and agitation begins for the freeing of that.

Feb. 11—"Egypta," an oriental drama, given by home talent at Wysor's.

Feb. 16—Destruction of battleship Maine in Havana harbor.

Feb. 19—Death of Rebecca G., widow of E. C. Anthony, aged 76.

Feb. 21—Death of John S. Fudge at Albany, and Charles W. Moore, a lawyer in Muncie since 1859.

Feb. 27—Peter Fay collects volunteers for possible war with Spain.

March—Midland (C. & S. E.) R. R. resumes building from Anderson to Muncie; grade completed to within four miles of Muncie, about Richwoods.

March 17—Francis Wilson and Lulu Glaser play "Half a King" at Wysor's.

March—Fair store moves from Boyce block to Anthony block, occupying former quarters of Boston store.

March 31—Morning News gets Associated Press service.

April 1—Samuel Cashmore become superintendent of Muncie police.

April 16—Contract let for building of Jefferson school, West Jackson street, to cost about $30,000.

April 22—President McKinley, in accordance with resolution of Congress demanding evacuation of Cuba, orders blockade of Cuba; amounting to declaration of war.

April 23—Muncie streets filled with people, martial music plays, processions march up and down, and patriotic speeches are made, while the first volunteer company is being recruited by John K. Ritter, Fred Puckett and others; officers of company are: Capt. Ritter, First Lieut. F. L. Wachtell, and Second Lieut. Puckett.

April 30—Eastern Indiana Normal University, after weeks of effort on part of promoters, is assured, when 302 lots in Normal City are sold; building to be begun at once.

May 25—Morning News begins using linotype machines, the first in city and county.

May 24—"Shore Acres," by James A. Hearne, at Wysor's.

May 24—George W. Cromer chosen candidate for Congress for 8th Congressional district.

May 29—Dedication of Whitely M. E. Church.

June 11—Death of Clinton Anthony, an eccentric and widely known pioneer, son of Joseph Anthony.

July 2—Death of James A. Maddy, aged 83; in Muncie since 1834, a well-known merchant and local official.

July 24—Rural free delivery routes being extended and placed on a permanent basis. The Muncie and Middletown route changed from star route to free delivery.

Aug. 13—Death of Andrew Black, aged 68, at Black's Mills, where he had
  lived since 1837.
Aug. 26—William Parish, of Muncie, private of Co. C, 20th U. S. V., and
  soldier at Santiago, dies in hospital at Boston and is brought home
  and buried in Beech Grove.
Sept. 3—At annual meeting of the Delaware County Pioneers, John S. Ellis
  elected president; Gabriel Payton, vice-president; N. N. Spence,
  secretary-treasurer.
.... 16—Dedication of Second Christian Church at Muncie, Eighth street
  near Hoyt avenue; also of M. E. Church at Mt. Tabor.
October 11—Citizens of Westside decide to form a town incorporation with
  name of Normal City, in honor of school then being built.
Oct.—Jefferson school, most beautiful of Muncie's public school buildings,
  is completed.
Nov. 26—Death of Mrs. Susan Jack, aged 84, widow of John Jack, pioneer
  Muncie business man.
Dec. 1—Residents vote for incorporation of Normal City. At town election
  Eli J. Tomlinson chosen clerk and treasurer; James Summers,
  George N. Higman and Sherman M. Lee, trustees.
Dec. 4—Death of Clarissa A. Shipley, aged 66, wife of Judge C. E. Shipley.

1899.

Jan. 18—At invitation of Muncie Commercial Club, gas belt men meet to
  plan an organization to prevent pumping of gas from local fields.
  Ohio Pipe Line Co. said to be taking gas from Red Key district
  at pressure of 500-700 pounds (legal pressure being 200). It is
  now generally admitted that the supply of gas is rapidly
  diminishing.
Feb. 4—Death of Capt. James H. McClung, veteran newspaper man, for
  ten years part owner and publisher of Muncie Times.
Feb. 4—The Magic Packing Co. is reorganized from the Magic City Can-
  ning Co.; George A. Sampson, president.
Feb. 5—Death of Sarah Hickman Kirby, aged 86, widow of Thomas Kirby.
Feb. 9—Death of Nicholas Shafer, an old settler, at Royerton.
Feb. 18—Death of William Walling, aged 80; came to Delaware county in
  1832, a farmer, tanner, and connected with many business interests.
March 4—Death of Josiah P. Williams, aged 84; since 1839 in Muncie,
  where he was an early grocer.
March 14—Death of Rev. John L. Smith, a pioneer Methodist minister of
  Indiana and Muncie.
March 18—Franchise granted by county commissioners to George F. McCul-
  loch for electric road from Muncie west along highway through
  West Muncie, Yorktown and Daleville to county line; road between
  Muncie and Anderson to be completed by Sept. 1, 1900.
March 22—Death of George W. Spilker, aged 71, a resident of Muncie
  since 1842; an early county official, and for thirty years a banker
  and prominent in affairs.
April 12—Theodore Thomas Orchestra at Wysor's, under auspices of
  Ladies' Matinee Musical.
May 11—Anchor Silver Plate Co. to occupy old shoe factory; incorporated

by Alfred E. Seliger, J. C. Abbott, L. and J. E. Johnson, W. E. Hitchcock.

May—Country residents about Muncie begin installing telephones in their homes.

June 5—Elks Carnival and street fair in Muncie all week.

June 25—Dedication of Yorktown M. E. Church.

July 19—Muncie Telephone plant (independent) sold to D. F. Allen and J. H. Hedgcock, of Frankfort. At this date company said to have . . . miles of wire and 500 subscribers.

. . . . —Citizens' Progressive Association, of Normal City, organized; Rev. M. Hobson, president; H. C. Martin, vice-president; Dr. E. E. Polk, secretary; Claude Stephens, treasurer.

Aug. 1—Rural free delivery becomes permanent. Samuel B. Scott is first regular carrier, going down Middletown pike through Monroe and Salem townships to Middletown and back, a total distance of twenty-eight miles.

Aug. 4—Cornerstone of new Universalist Church in Muncie laid.

Aug. 10—Death of Mrs. John Williams, aged 82, a resident of Muncie nearly sixty years.

Aug. 13—Morning News locates in new quarters on Adams near Walnut street.

Aug. 20—C. & S. E. (Midland) R. R. track completed to Muncie and construction train reaches Buck creek. Frequent failure of funds had caused repeated delays in construction of road.

Aug. 29—Eastern Indiana Normal University opened; F. A. Z. Kumler, president.

Sept. 2—Fifth annual meeting of the Old Settlers at Westside park.

Sept. 9—New county council begins its work by cutting down all estimates of expenditures for the various offices and departments of the county government.

Sept. 11—Cornerstone laid for Madison Street M. E. Church in Muncie.

Nov. 2—Beginning of development of the oil field about Muncie; oil is struck while drilling a gas well on farm of John E. Reed, four miles north of Muncie, this being among the earlier oil finds.

Nov. 9—Muncie Lodge No. 74, I. O. O. F., celebrates 50th anniversary; David T. Haines and Eli Jamison only survivors of founders of lodge.

Nov. 13—Muncie city council grants franchise to Muncie Interurban Co. (F. G. Brownell, superintendent) to enter city with line from Hartford City; this franchise was later sold to people who built the Muncie, Hartford and Ft. Wayne traction road.

Dec. 15—Death of David T. Haines, aged 81, resident of Muncie nearly fifty years; was secretary of the old Ft. Wayne and Southern R. R. Co. in the 50s, and secretary and treasurer of the company that finally built the road between Ft. Wayne and Muncie; was also an early merchant, hotel man and manufacturer.

Dec. 18—Silver jubilee of Father Schmidt's pastorate in Muncie.

Dec. 21—Appellate court affirms decision against the Muncie Pulp Co. for polluting the water of Buck creek.

Dec. 29—The first independent telephone enterprise in Muncie becomes defunct, when the Muncie Telephone Co., operating about 400 phones, is transferred to the Bell company.

1900.

Jan. 2—Albany fire department, recently installed, fights successfully a fire in the Bartlett hotel, caused by natural gas explosion.

Jan.—Total receipts of the Muncie postoffice for the last quarter of 1899 amount to $10,473.66.

. . . . destroys the power house of the street railway and Muncie citizens walk until temporary service is installed.

Jan. 26—Death of M. C. Smith, aged 75, ending a career marked by long and varied public service; was resident of Muncie over forty years, and until retirement was merchant at Main and High streets.

Feb. 1—City Transfer Co.'s barns on Mulberry street burned.

Feb. 1—Workingmen's Library and Reading room of Muncie Trades Council receives $500 from Andrew Carnegie, increasing total contributions to $1,885.

Feb. 4—Dedication of Madison Street M. E. Church.

March 11—Universalist new church building in Muncie dedicated.

March 23—Bursting boiler in Nickum sawmill, Harrison township, kills Thomas Sullivan, C. E. Van Buskirk, Marion Carey, Alonzo Van Buskirk.

March 31—Receipts of Muncie postoffice for preceding twelve months are over $40,000.

April—Muncie Trust Co. begins business.

April 9—Council decides to build fire station No. 3 in Avondale.

April 20—Death at Albany of Adam Sheller, aged 84, for sixty years a resident of the county.

April—Delaware County Mutual Telephone Co. organized to give telephone communication to farmers.

May 7—Arrest of C. F. W. Neely for complicity in Cuban postal frauds.

May 10—Center township votes, by majority of 22, a subsidy of $75,000 to the Cincinnati, Richmond and Muncie R. R., provided line is completed from Richmond to Muncie by Dec. 31, 1901.

May 17—Architectural Iron Works in Congerville destroyed by fire.

June 12—C. I. & E. R. R. voted a subsidy of $75,000 by Center township, one-half to be paid when road reaches Muncie; this line and the C. R. & M. endeavor to outstrip each other in building to Muncie.

July 9—John Casey chosen Muncie's fire chief.

July 31—Work of grading on C. R. & M. R. R. from Muncie south begins.

July 31—Washington township votes against a subsidy for the C. I. & E. R. R.

Sept. 4—Announcement that Petty Auditorium on East Adams street will be built.

Sept. 4—Washington township, especially Gaston, vote a $15,000 subsidy for the C. R. & M. R. R.

Sept. 21—Mass meeting in Muncie protest against proposed increase of gas rates by Muncie Natural Gas Co.

Sept. 25—Mr. and Mrs. William Driscoll killed by Big Four train on an unguarded crossing in Muncie.

Sept.—A general outcry is made against companies controlling the distribution of fuel and water. Muncie Natural Gas Co. and the Heat, Light and Power Co. propose to raise rates one-fourth. Municipal ownership is talked. Merchants prepare to supply citizens with wood and coal, "more wood and coal stoves being shipped in than in preceding twelve years." Gas companies delay putting the increased schedules into effect for one month. The water company also comes in for share of criticism, because of alleged bad quality of water and ineffectual pressure.

Sept.—The interurban line between Anderson and Muncie is opened.

Sept. 5—W. J. Bryan makes short campaign speech in Muncie.

Oct.—A flowing oil well on county infirmary farm causes many leases to be filed on land in that vicinity.

Oct. 8—Council committee finds that the new gas rates are too high.

Oct. 11—Roosevelt, candidate for vice-president, spends half an hour in Muncie, being the object of a remarkable demonstration of enthusiasm.

Oct.—Merchants in small towns along the interurban claim their business is decreased by the electric line.

Oct. 22—City council grants C. & S. E. (Midland) a right of way into Muncie.

Oct. 23—Death of John Williams, aged 82, who had settled in Hamilton township in 1838.

Nov. 5—U. S. census gives the population of the county at 49,624, and that of Muncie 20,942.

Nov. 6—Election of McKinley and Roosevelt, the county giving them a majority of 3,654.

Nov. 12—Kitselman Bros., wire fence manufacturers, install their factory in east Muncie.

Nov.—Population of White river by Consumers' Paper Co. causes antagonism between landowners and manufacturers.

Nov. 21—Plans announced for new union station in Muncie for Big Four, Lake Erie, and Ft. Wayne, C. & L. (controlled by Lake Shore); a brick and stone structure to be placed east of old station and connecting with it.

Nov. 27—State supreme court annuls the act of 1889 forbidding the transportation of natural gas beyond state limits.

Nov. 27—Death of James Watson, aged 96, veteran of four wars.

Dec. 5—Mr. and Mrs. James Williamson, on Granville pike, celebrate fiftieth wedding anniversary.

Dec. 10—Fire stations Nos. 2 and 3 reported completed.

Dec. 14—First of "elegant new interurban cars" runs into Muncie from Anderson, but cannot come further than High street because of grooved rails.

Dec. 24—Rev. Jacob W. and Mrs. Heath celebrate golden wedding at their Muncie home.

Dec. 27—First train over the C., I. & E. R. R. from Matthews reaches North View, and the first schedule is put into effect on Dec. 29, the Muncie station being on Wysor street. The subsidy of $37,500 is won with two days to spare.

1901.

Jan. 6—Death of Hiram W. Weir, aged 79, who came to Muncie in October, 1836, and was a farmer of Mt. Pleasant township half a century.

Jan. 11—Death of Louis Reese, aged nearly 81, for many years a farmer south of the city; had lived in the county nearly all his life, being a son of one of the pioneers.

Jan. 12—Death of David Scott, pioneer farmer of Harrison township.

Jan. 18—Death of Frederick E. Putnam, aged 83, pioneer merchant, public official, and prominent in many activities; in Muncie since 1838.

Jan. 30—Petty Auditorium opened with polo contest.

Feb. 2—Plans completed for building interurban to Union City.

Feb. 3—Death of Evan M. Weir, aged 76, who had lived in the county sixty years.

Feb. 8—Death of Stephen Hamilton, aged 75, farmer and old citizen of Hamilton township.

Feb. 14—Mr. and Mrs. William B. Woodring, of Gaston, celebrate golden wedding.

Feb. 26—Attempt to enact a law establishing state normal branch in connection with the E. I. N. U. at Muncie is abandoned.

March 5—George F. McCulloch is elected president and general manager of I. U. Traction Co.

March 11—Andrew Carnegie's offer of $50,000 for a library building in Muncie is accepted by the city council.

March 12—Commercial Club takes first steps toward building a club home.

March 18—Large part of Congerville is annexed to Muncie city.

March 25—Judge Marsh, of Randolph circuit court, gives a decision in the case of Muncie vs. Muncie Natural Gas Co., restraining the latter from increasing rates above those guaranteed by the original franchise grant to the company.

March 25—Golden wedding of Mr. and Mrs. Samuel F. Brady in Muncie.

May 1—Death of James Wingate, president of Albany State Bank.

May 11—Cornerstone laid for Normal City M. E. Church.

May—Park site of nearly one hundred acres in Whitely is offered to the city by G. F. McCulloch, provided $2,500 is raised for improvement of the grounds, the donor of the land giving an equal amount for improvement. The Commercial Club sets about to raise the required amount.

June 3—Death of Josiah Cromer, near Cross Roads, a resident of the county over fifty years.

June 20—Terrific hail storm does great crop damage in the county.

July 9—Muncie, Hartford and Fort Wayne Railway Co. incorporated to build the road promoted by F. G. Brownell; A. L. Johnson and W. E. Hitchcock among the incorporators.

July 9—Work of establishing rural free delivery service in all parts of the county is begun, ten new routes being proposed.

July 17—P. S. Heath and C. R. Heath sell controlling interest in the Morning News; Harry McElwee becomes president of new company.

July 12—Contract let for construction of union passenger station in Muncie. to cost $30,000.

July 29—After much delay and long negotiations for other sites, the city council chooses the southeast corner of Jackson and Jefferson streets for the new library.

Aug. 9—Morning News goes into hands of receiver, and in a few weeks ceases publication.

Aug. 11—First passenger train from Richmond over the C., R. & M. R. R. reaches Muncie, and a regular schedule is put into operation both north and south of Muncie.

Aug. 16—Death of Thomas S. Neely, aged 90, a resident of Muncie since 1839; at one time had a daguerreotype studio in Muncie.

Aug. 23—Death of John Rees, aged 71, resident of county since 1836.

Aug. 29—Death of Samuel and Benjamin Bergsdol, brothers, aged respectively 82 and 79, natives of Virginia, who had lived in Albany and vicinity since about 1832.

Sept. 14—Death of President McKinley.

Nov. 1—Garfield school in Heekin Park completed.

Oct. 15—New R. F. D. system begins with twenty-six carriers. Stout, Anthony, Rural, Hazel, New Burlington and Cross Roads post-offices discontinued. Nine routes start from Muncie.

Oct. 23—Serious strike at Eaton in Western Flint Bottle Co.'s plant.

Oct.—Samuel Payton, aged 84, of Eaton, is the only man still living in Union township who entered land there.

Oct. 27—Death of Isaac Scott, of Salem township, aged 75, a pioneer.

Nov. 4—Gas pressure fails in lines of Muncie Natural Gas Co. and Heat, Light and Power Co., and situation becomes serious for citizens and business men.

Nov. 7—Commercial Club plans incorporation, the erection of a club building, and an energetic campaign for civic betterment.

Nov. 8—Talk of reviving Muncie Artificial Gas Co.'s plant to full capacity to supply deficiencies of natural gas; plant had been operated since gas boom merely in order to retain the franchise.

Nov. 11—Council appoints a committee to investigate the low gas pressure.

Nov. 17—Through service inaugurated between Muncie and Indianapolis over the interurban.

Nov. 16—C. R. & M. depot, costing $15,000, opened in Muncie.

Nov. 19—Otis Skinner plays "Francesca da Rimini" at Wysor's.

Nov.—St. Lawrence parochial school on East Charles street, costing $20,000, completed.

Nov. 20—Death of Arthur F. Patterson, aged 79, who came to Muncie in 1850 and soon entered the hardware trade, afterward becoming identified with various business and banking enterprises; one of the last of the old-time prominent business men.

Nov. 26—An independent company seeks to enter the field occupied by the Central Union Telephone Co., which at this date has 625 business phones and 875 residence phones; the independent company has 529 promised subscribers who also use the old phone, and 329 who have no phones.

Nov. 26—Commercial Club resolves upon northeast corner of Main and Jefferson as site for their building.

Dec.—Completion of Cohen block, Walnut and Seymour streets, three story, costing about $45,000.

Dec. 16—Council grants George W. Beers and W. E. Hitchcock, representing a company to be known as the Delaware and Madison County Telephone Company, a franchise to operate a telephone and telegraph system in the city for 35 years; all wires in the business district to be placed underground. Much opposition had been shown to the independent company, many protesting against the expense and inconvenience of a double system.

Dec. 19—Council passes a resolution demanding that the gas companies furnish their patrons an adequate supply of gas, claiming that an ample supply still exists and that the companies must comply with the terms of their franchises.

Dec. 20—Death of A. W. Chapman, aged 64, president of the Muncie Savings and Loan Ass'n since 1889.

1902.

Jan.—First wire made in Muncie by the Indiana Steel and Wire Co. in Boyceton (Kitselman Bros. plant).

Jan. 3—Muncie Commercial Club incorporated.

Jan. 12—Dedication of M. E. Church at Eaton.

Jan. 14—An independent telephone company organized at Albany.

Jan. 20—Death of Nepthalim Ross, aged 83, a resident of the county over 70 years and of Muncie 32 years; his wife a daughter of Garret Gibson, a pioneer.

Jan. 20—An enthusiastic meeting at Gaston for establishment of a canning factory.

Jan. 26—After a long controversy arrangements are made by which all railroads entering Muncie shall have equal rights on the Belt line.

Feb. 5—Death of Orlando J. Lotz, aged 51, member of Muncie bar since 1874, judge of the 46th judicial circuit nearly eight years, and at the time of his death judge of the 4th district appellate court.

Feb. 6—Death of Lemuel King, aged 77, an early merchant of Muncie.

Feb. 6—Organization in Hamilton township of Union College Farmers' Club, Lewis Moore, president.

Feb. 18—Gaston Bank organized, on private and co-operative plan, with Mark Powers president and Merle Chenoweth cashier.

March 3—Council passes three important ordinances—franchise to Muncie, Hartford and Ft. Wayne Ry. Co.; a franchise to Muncie Electric Light Co. allowing them to lay pipes in streets for heating purposes; and one permitting the gas companies to increase their rates to 18 cents per thousand, current rates (12 cents per thousand) to continue until October, 1902; meters to be installed.

April 1—Muncie union passenger station opened and dedicated.

March 9—Normal City M. E. Church dedicated.

March 10—Mayor Tuhey vetoes gas ordinance of March 3.

March 19—Death of Mrs. Sarah M. Mock, aged 82, resident of county since 1846.

March 24—C. F. W. Neely convicted of complicity in Cuban postal frauds.

March 24—Council orders 25 cement alleys in wards 1, 2 and 3.

March 25—Mr. and Mrs. Obadiah Scudder celebrate 61st wedding aninver_
sary in Riverside; residents of county nearly fifty years.

April 1—Receipts of Muncie postoffice for year ending March 31 are
$50,478.58.

April 6—Death of William H. Neff, aged 54, who founded the washboard
manufacturing industry at Cowan.

April 17.—Death of James M. Gray, aged 73, an early merchant of Daleville.

April 28—Contract for construction of the Carnegie Library awarded Mor_
row and Morrow of Muncie, at $46,375.70.

April 29—Death of Mrs. Joseph Dungan, aged 72, a native of the county,
and who for 60 years had lived in her home on East Jackson street.

April 30—Death of Richard Berger, aged 72, in Muncie since 1860, and
long time alderman.

May 12—Death of John S. Reid, aged 76, who came to Muncie in 1850, and
built one of the first steam sawmills.

May 28—Dedication of Red Men's block, High and Jackson, which cost
$35,000.

May—Agitation for public hospital in Muncie.

June 2—Death of Samuel Lee, aged 88, who settled in Harrison township
in 1841.

June—Ground broken for Commercial Club building.

June 9—Elks' carnival begins in Muncie, under auspices of Lodge No. 245,
B. P. O. E.

May—Appropriation of $80,000 made by Congress for Muncie federal
building.

June 10—Death of Albert L. Wright, aged 56, a member of the city council,
and a resident of Muncie nearly fifty years.

June—Rapid progress in construction of M. H. & Ft. W. traction line
through county; power house at Eaton nearing completion.

July—Express and freight service inaugurated over Union Traction to Indianapolis.

July—Trustee Dragoo of Center township decides to introduce manual training in the Congerville school during the following year.

July—Plans announced for McNaughton block on Charles and Walnut
streets.

July 27—Death of John W. Little, aged 58, who came to Muncie in 1858,
was merchant, manufacturer of feather dusters, and in real estate
and loans, and prominent in city affairs.

Aug. 9—Muncie and Portland Traction Co. organized; G. O. Driscoll, of
Muncie, president; Harve Lefiler, of Muncie, vice president.

Aug. 14—Death of Joseph Stradling, aged 89, who came to the county in
1857 and was a successful farmer.

Aug. 18—Gas question again becomes acute; the companies threaten to shut
off supply on October 1, and council retaliates with motion to com-
pel the companies to furnish gas or lose their franchises.

Aug.—Construction of steam-heating system and laying of mains to various
buildings and public buildings begun.

Aug. 2—Dumping ground on North Walnut street, after being used thirty
years, is closed.

Aug. 27—County fair begins its golden jubilee, or fiftieth annual session.

Aug. 31—C. & S. E. (Midland) after years of litigation, strikes, delays of construction, is transferred from a receivership to the Big Four system.

Sept. 2—Mr. and Mrs. Mahlon Crampton, on Wheeling pike, celebrate golden wedding; residents of county since 1854.

Sept. 15—Council amends gas companies' franchises, permitting maximum rates of 22 cents per thousand during the following year and requiring free meters. Also grants a franchise to the Wabash Oil and Gas Co. to furnish gas at 18 cents per thousand until October, 1904. The established companies refuse to accept the amendment.

Sept. 26—A compromise is reached in the long contention between gas companies and the council, when the latter passes the proposed amendments making a price of 23 cents per thousand for one year after October, 1902, 25 cents per thousand up to October, 1904, and 27 cents per thousand thereafter.

Oct. 8—Death of Rev. Jacob W. Heath, aged 73, who had lived in the county since 1829 and was one of the most prominent of the early Methodists.

Oct. 12—High Street M. E. Church is re-dedicated, having been remodeled and improved at a cost of $7,300.

Oct. 24—Marc Hanna, Republican leader, makes campaign speech on court house square.

Oct. 24—Death of William K. Helvie, aged 76, of Yorktown, an old soldier and prominent citizen.

Oct. 28—Commercial Club indorse movement to secure a new city charter from the legislature.

Nov. 4—Death of Joseph Warfel, aged 84, prominent citizen of Yorktown and resident of county since 1840.

Nov. 3—Death of William N. Scott at Selma.

Nov. 20—Death of William N. Jackson, a settler of 1844 and an old soldier.

Nov. 22—Death of Dr. C. A. Budd, prominent dentist and member of the Muncie council and active in public affairs.

Nov. 26—Dedication of Roosevelt school in Congerville.

Nov. 28—Site selected for the Muncie postoffice at the southwest corner of High and Charles streets; four lots cost $20,000, of which $5,000 was to be raised by subscriptions from citizens.

Dec. 21—Death of B. S. Whitney, aged 67, who had lived in the county nearly all his life.

1903.

Jan. 5—William H. Wood resigns his office as city engineer, which he had held since 1882.

Jan. 18—Death of Uriah Suman, aged 77, one of Daleville's oldest residents and an authority on Daleville history.

Jan.—206 arc lamps cost Muncie, in 1902, $67.48 each, including all charges against operation and maintenance and interest.

Jan.—Muncie Natural Gas Co. and Wabash Oil and Gas Co. properties pass to a new company, known as Muncie Gas, Light and Fuel Co.

Feb. 6—First car over the M. H. & Ft. W. interurban reaches Muncie from the Eaton power house.

Feb. 9—Old landmarks on the northwest corner of Main and Mulberry being torn down to make site for the Neely three-story modern business block.

March 8—Death of David Cammack, Muncie's postmaster, aged 57; came to the county in 1879, later establishing the sawmill at Cammack's Station, and later became interested in Muncie manufacturing grain business, gas, and public affairs.

April 23-24—Muncie Music Festival in Petty's Auditorium the most ambitious and successful of Muncie's musical events; Miss Nannie C. Love director of chorus, and Mr. Alfred Damm leader of orchestra. On the second evening "Stabat Mater" was given, Victor Herbert's orchestra assisting.

April—Old residence at corner of Mulberry and Jackson, a landmark, being torn down to make room for new hotel.

May 1—Death of John W. Dungan, aged 79, a resident of the county since 1842, an early sheriff, a soldier, and stock farmer.

May—"City of Punctured Pavement" is a phrase branding the condition of Muncie's streets; street repairs and paving become live questions.

May 18—Council gives name "McCulloch Park" to the tract donated by G. F. McCulloch.

May 18—"Riverside City" votes 94 to 60 in favor of incorporation of town.

May 25—Muncie Brewing Co. start the new brewery.

May 25—Delaware Lodge No. 46, F. & A. M., celebrates 60th anniversary.

June 2—Washington township by a majority of 2, favors a liquor license for Gaston saloon-keeper.

June 28—Dedication of the First Christian Church, Elm and North streets.

June 30—The Union Traction Company of Indiana is leased to the new Indiana Union Traction Co. for a period of 999 years.

June 30—Death of Mrs. Samantha (Collier) Patterson, aged 70, a native of Muncie, and widow of A. F. Patterson.

July 1—Delaware county board of charities and corrections find conditions at the infirmary "a disgrace to the county."

July—Selma, the center of an important oil field, experiences a boom consequent on the development of numerous oil wells.

Sept. 7—Daleville has $60,000 fire, when Ideal Stove and Foundry Co.'s plant is destroyed, a concern which had been organized in 1896 as a co-operative stock company.

Sept. 7—Council gives I. U. T. Co. use of certain streets for fifty years, and provides that terminal station be built.

Sept. 7—Resignation of superintendent of schools, W. R. Snyder, who had been connected with Muncie schools twenty years, all but four as superintendent. The high school and Washington school building the only modern buildings when he began, and in the meantime the corps of teachers had increased to over one hundred.

Sept. 10—Death of Dr. E. J. Puckett, aged 69, a well known Muncie physician.

Sept. 12—George L. Roberts, formerly superintendent of schools at Frankfort, Ind., succeeds Supt. Snyder.

Sept. 29—Death of John W. Heath, who came to the county in 1829, when 10 years old.

Oct.—Neely building, Main and Mulberry, completed, and Merchants' National Bank occupies it as principal tenant.

Oct. 18—South Avondale Christian Church dedicated.

Oct. 17—I. U. T. Co. buys corner on Mulberry between Charles and Howard as site for terminal station.

Nov. 8—Dedication of United Brethren Church at Gaston.

Nov. 14—McNaughton store opened in new building.

Nov. 14—Women's apartment in county jail completed at a cost of $1,250;
this removed a defect that had long been criticised.

Nov. 24—Muncie defeats, by a vote of 1,843 against and 211 for, the special charter proposed by the state legislature at the winter session.
Only half the normal vote cast, and little interest was manifested.

Nov. 25—Dedication of the Hamilton school at Royerton, a model school,
and a result of the consolidation system.

Dec. 4—Death of Thaddeus A. Neely, one of Muncie's best known and
most active citizens.

Dec. 28—Death of David Brandt, aged 88, a pioneer merchant of Eaton,
where he had been in business more than fifty years.

The year 1903 was also noted for unusual building activity, many of
the buildings which now are considered the best examples of Muncie's architecture having been begun or completed in this year. The five-story Mc-
Naughton block, the Jones block, both on South Walnut street, were first
occupied this year; also the Neely block, besides a number of residences
and flat buildings.

1904.

Jan. 1—Muncie Public Library dedicated.

Jan. 6—Daniels and Overman flour mill at Daleville, built by Peter A.
Helvie in 1874, is burned.

Jan. 12—Muncie Music Festival Ass'n give the "Messiah" under direction
of Miss Love.

Feb. 3—The Apollo Club, which was reorganized in the fall of 1903. gives
a classic program at Wysor's, David Bispham being principal soloist. The Club's officers at this date were: J. B. Shick, president;
L. H. Colvin, vice president; F. W. Prothero, secretary; Dr. J. M.
Quick, treasurer.

Jan.—White river floods Muncie, breaking levee on Walnut street, wreck-
ing street railway bridge at High street and causing other damage;
highest waters since July, 1895.

Feb.—Much activity in oil field about Albany, several large wells having
been developed.

Feb. 23—Gaston M. E. Church dedicated.

Feb. 24—Mr. and Mrs. James M. Laboyteaux place $10,000 in trust for the
Delaware County Hospital Association.

Feb. 25—Mr. and Mrs. George Gibson of Muncie celebrate golden wedding.

March 5—Death of Lawrence L. Weller, aged 68, early manufacturer of
lumber and organs, and one of the organizers of the Citizens'
Enterprise Co.

March 16—Golden wedding of Mr. and Mrs. J. C. Bacon, the former of whom came to the county in 1852, and the latter being a native of the county.

March 16—Death of Simon Conn, aged 86, one of the pioneer teamsters between Muncie and Cincinnati; hauled the court house bell from Cincinnati.

March 26—Most disastrous flood in history of Muncie sweeps the city, submerging Whitely, Walnut Grove, North Side, Riverside and Westside, doing damage amounting to thousands of dollars, especially in that part of Muncie lying north of Race street; the fires in the furnaces of the waterworks were drowned out, factories had to close, and the railroad lines were damaged. The Yorktown bridge was washed away, and this and other damage to roads and culverts cost the county fully five thousand dollars.

April—Muncie postoffice receipts for preceding year are $62,780.49.

April 12—Commercial Club building, built at a cost of about $55,000, and the handsomest and best equipped in the state outside of Indianapolis, is formally opened.

April 19—Death of Mordecai Whitney, aged 74, an old soldier and farmer, who came to the county when two years old.

April—Removal of an old landmark at 317 North Mulberry street, a low brick house, the bricks for which were hauled, so it is said, overland from Cincinnati.

April 22—Death of Gen. Thomas J. Brady in New York; was a native of Muncie, was a lawyer, soldier, newspaper man, public official, and since 1881 had been in business in the east.

May 16—Apollo Club concert, with Schumann-Heink as principal soloist.

June 24—Death of Mrs. Mary Jane Edmonds, aged 78, the first white child born in Muncie, a daughter of G. C. Gilbert.

June 26—Death of Joseph T. Hardesty, aged 85, an old Muncie resident.

July 17—Death of Timothy C. Stewart, aged 74, who was born in the county and for years farmed in Mount Pleasant township.

July 19—Sewer diggers unearth timbers of old mill built at North Walnut and Wysor streets in the '30s·

Aug.—First large concrete bridge in the county built over Buck creek at Yorktown, replacing the iron bridge carried away by the spring flood.

July 23—Selma is crowded on account of the oil boom, many people living in tents; insufficient machinery of government to uphold law and order, and illicit sale of liquor, gambling and the presence of undesirable persons give Selma somewhat the character of a border town.

Aug.—Contract let for the construction of a five-story hotel at the corner of Jackson and Mulberry; the first name proposed was Hotel March.

Aug. 9—Daleville and Salem township anti-saloon people win a victory and saloon license is refused.

Aug. 15—M. E. Church at Smithfield is burned, and because of the numerous oil derricks and tanks the venerable village is threatened with annihilation. Within a year Smithfield has been transformed from

a "Hoosier Sleepy Hollow" into a boom town; an oil derrick was
erected on the very ground occupied by the church.

Aug. 29—Factory No. 12 of the American Window Glass Co., built by
   C. H. Over in the '90s' burned, at a loss of over $50,000; had not
   been operated during the last two years, but used as storage ware-
   house.

Oct. 4—Aerial truck a new acquisition by the Muncie fire department.

Oct. 9—Death of Jesse Nixon, in Union township, aged 80, a resident of
   the county nearly all his life.

Oct. 22.—Death of David Heal, aged 81, for seventy-five years a resident
   of Washington township; a local official and a highly esteemed and
   successful business man.

Oct. 24—Council finds garbage disposal a vexing question; for the preceding sixteen years ashes had been almost unknown in the city and
   it now became necessary to devise additional means to dispose of
   them.

Oct. 25—Election in Gaston results 103 to 73 in favor of incorporation.

Oct. 27—G. F. McCulloch retires from active management of the Muncie
   Star and the morning papers of Indianapolis and Terre Haute,
   after having raised the combined circulation of the three dailies
   to 150,000; the Star was first issued May 29, 1899, and on Oct. 27,
   1904, its circulation was 27,602.

Oct.—As a result of three murders within the past five months, besides
   many lesser crimes, a crusade is started to abolish the "wine rooms"
   and other resorts of vice and gambling in the Muncie red light
   district.

Nov. 5—People's National Bank, recently organized with Edward Tuhey
   president, opened for business at northeast corner of Main and
   Mulberry, in quarters vacated a short time before by the Merchants'
   National.

Nov. 8—Roosevelt and Fairbanks elected, Delaware county giving them a
   majority of nearly five thousand.

Nov. 28—Dedication of Selma public school for the consolidated districts of
   the township, this being the best school building in the county
   outside of Muncie.

Nov. 14—The county commissioners refuse to consider a remonstrance
   against the incorporation of Gaston on the ground that the election
   was not valid.

Nov.—Muncie Gas, Light and Fuel Co. prepare to manufacture artificial
   gas.

Nov. 26—Delaware County Educational Ass'n, after an existence of many
   years, votes to discontinue.

Nov. 29—Muncie is said to be a "closed town" as a result of police activity
   in cleaning up resorts.

Dec. 6—Secretary of the State board of health declares that Muncie's
   water supply is rendered poisonous through the admixture of river
   water, which is contaminated with oil, salt water and other im-
   purities.

Dec. 13—Death of John C. Johnson, aged 61, president of the Delaware
   County National Bank; one of Muncie's most prominent business

men since 1884, a stockholder or official in half a dozen large corporations, influential in public affairs, and his death was felt as a
grave loss to Muncie. Factories, stores, street car traffic and
other business affairs were suspended ten minutes during the
funeral.

Dec.—The Smithfield oil boom has declined, the derricks are being removed,
and the wonted quiet of the place is resumed.

Dec. 18—Selma has a disastrous fire, starting in the Hotel De Long and
destroying $25,000 worth of property; no fire or police protection,
a bucket and blanket brigade fight the flames. The situation was
aggravated by the presence of many prospectors and loafers
brought together by the oil boom, who committed much looting
and outrage and spread terror among the peaceful citizens of the
town. As a result, during the following days, there was a general
closing up of gambling and liquor resorts, the vicious element was
driven out, and an active campaign waged by the county prosecutor assisted the reform sentiment of the town in purging the
town of Selma.

Dec. 19—Death of James W. Hannan, of Gaston, aged 78, an early teacher
in the county.

1905.

Jan. 10—Death of James Q. Mitchell, aged 73, an old soldier and a contractor.

Jan. 15—Riverside U. B. Church is dedicated.

Jan. 18—Death of Jacob H. Wysor, aged 85; had been active in business
and manufacturing affairs since 1840, and was one of the city's
largest property owners.

Feb. 4—Dayton and Muncie traction line completed to Selma from Winchester.

Feb. 2—Death of Jasper North, aged 83, nearly fifty years a resident of
the county.

Feb. 4—Death of William Dragoo, former county official, and resident of
the county from pioneer days.

Feb. 15—A party of fifteen, known as the "Canopic Party," from Muncie,
leave for tour of Holy Land, Egypt and Europe; party returned to
Muncie June 27.

Feb. 20—Franchise granted to William F. Warner, over the mayor's veto,
to construct an electric light plant and sell electricity at the maximum price of 10 cents per thousand kilowatts.

Feb. 22—Death of John Heffner, aged 75, a resident of Muncie forty-eight
years, and known as the "merchant policeman."

March 3—Daleville petitions for incorporation, having 799 inhabitants in
limits; petition is granted March 10.

March 4—The Delaware county bar banquet and show honors to the three
oldest lawyers—C. E. Shipley, John W. Ryan, J. N. Templer.

March 17—K. of P. building on Washington street, north side of square, is
dedicated by Welcome Lodge.

March 20—Death of William E. Decker, aged 78, who drilled the first gas
well in the Muncie field.

March 21—Press Publishing Co. purchases Muncie Times and Muncie Herald, evening papers, and after March 26 issues the Evening Press.

March 22—Citizens' Electric Light Co. incorporated with capital of $200,-
000 to use the franchise given to W. F. Warner, who becomes president of the new company; H. J. Keller, vice president; C. R. Hathaway, secretary; C. E. Hinkley, treasurer.

March 25—Police raid the "Old Home" wine room, Washington and High streets, making 65 arrests, 63 of them pleading guilty; in number of prisoners, the raid was without precedent in the history of the county.

March 28—An election in Daleville on subject of incorporation results 90 for and 90 against, with one vote in doubt; the election was really a contest between the saloon and the anti-saloon forces, the former desiring incorporation.

March 30—Plans are published for the six-story Wysor block, Walnut and Main, on site of the old opera house block.

April 26—Death of John M. Bloss, aged 66, soldier, educator and leading citizen.

May 16—John Seldomridge succeeds Samuel Cashmore as chief of police.

June—Miss Nannie C. Love resigns position as supervisor of music in Muncie public schools, a position she had held twenty years.

May   1—Under the terms of the towns and cities act passed by the legislature in 1905, Muncie obtained a new municipal government, and several new officers and boards begin service on May 1.

June 10—Death of Edward Beuoy, aged 77, a pioneer of Washington township.

June—A new garbage furnace, which had been contracted for by the city council in December, 1904, and which was erected on the south side at Eighteenth and Hackley streets, at a cost of nearly $18,000, fails to satisfy the tests, and the board of works, which in the meantime had come into control of this department of the city's affairs, refused to accept the furnace. In July the operation of the old furnace on North Walnut street was resumed. Twelve hundred dollars was paid for the site of the new furnace.

July 31—Death of Carlton E. Shipley, aged jurist and lawyer, aged 78, who came to Muncie in 1843, and had been a member of the bar over half a century; was the oldest practicing lawyer of Delaware county at the time of his death.

Aug.   1—Work of construction begun on the Muncie and Portland traction line.

Aug.—State statistician gives figures showing that cost per hydrant in cities having municipally operated water works is $12.23; with private plants the cost per hydrant is $49.22. Muncie pays $41.94 per hydrant.

Aug. 10—An experiment of oil-sprinkling of streets is made in Normal City, one of the first applications of a practice that has since become quite generally adopted.

Aug. 13—Mr. and Mrs. Canty Benbow celebrate their 60th wedding anniversary at Macedonia in Monroe township, where they had lived since pioneer days, beginning married life in a log cabin.

Aug. 16—Regular service begins over the Dayton and Muncie traction line from Muncie east.

Aug. 18—Board of works refuses to accept the new garbage furnace.

Aug. 19—Delaware Lodge No. 46 resolves to build Masonic temple costing over $50,000.

Aug. 19—Preparations for building of terminal station at Charles and Mulberry streets.

Sept. 6—The county council pass favorably upon an appropriation for a passenger elevator in the court house.

Sept.—The auxiliary pumping station of the Muncie water works on Buck creek in Monroe township is completed, and water is conveyed from that stream to the main plant.

Sept. 11—Death of Henry Mecker, aged 78, a resident of Muncie 71 years.

Sept. 17—Dedication of the Second Baptist Church on East Jackson street.

Sept. 28—Cornerstone laying of Selma M. E. Church.

Oct.—New arrangement of rural free delivery service begins, with twelve routes, from Muncie.

Sept. 24—Dedication of the Seventh Day Adventist Church, Mulberry and Ninth streets.

Sept. 24—Death of Elisha Langdon, aged 83, a resident for over half a century, and once owner of the National Hotel and a grocer.

Oct. 5—Annual report of the state board of charities declares that the Delaware county infirmary is "slovenly kept," that inmates are ill-clothed and fed; finds commendable conditions at the Orphans' Home but advises a new building; and reports good management and good conditions at the county jail. With regard to the infirmary the county commissioners reply that the data on which the report was made were gathered more than a year before, and that in the meantime many improvements had been made and that the conditions mentioned had been remedied.

Oct.—It is claimed that the water pumped from the new station on Buck creek contaminates and discolors the water for domestic use.

Oct. 30—Death of David Reese, aged 93, on farm south of Muncie, where he had lived since pioneer times.

Nov. 9—Cornerstone of the Masonic temple on West Main street laid by Delaware lodge with imposing ceremonies.

Nov. 11—Opening of Delaware Hotel on Mulberry and Jackson streets, Robert H. Adams being the first guest. A fireproof, steel, brick and stone structure, costing $200,000, and one of the most complete and modern hotel buildings in the state; T. F. Rose, owner.

Dec. 12—Sub-station of the Muncie and Portland traction line is completed at Albany.

Dec. 16—Death of Mrs. Mary (Truitt) Moore, aged 83, who had lived 77 years in the county.

Dec. 18—Mr. and Mrs. P. W. Franklin celebrate golden wedding, having lived in the county since the '30s.

Dec. 23—Board of works finally accepts incinerating furnace at $11,700, a reduction of $6,000 below original contract price. The final test of the furnace, though not satisfactory, is held to meet the requirements of the contract.

1906.

Jan.   1—Normal and Industrial Institute for colored boys and girls is
       opened on South Walnut street, under the auspices of the city
       school authorities; its continuance is brief.
Jan. 22—McKinley school, 14 rooms, brick and stone building, the most
       modern school in the city, is opened.
Jan.   1—B. E. Cannon, first regular instructor of manual training, starts
       classes in the Garfield and Lincoln schools.
Jan.   2—City court, another product of the municipal legislation of 1905,
       is inaugurated, with Frank Gass as first judge.
Jan.   5—A $25,000 fire in Lane furniture store, 315 South Walnut street.
Jan. 14—M. E. Church at Selma is dedicated.
Jan. 15—Big storm does much damage in county, especially in the oil field;
       wrecks the Muncie electric light plant, so that service is tempo-
       rarily suspended.
Jan. 19—Plant of the Muncie Pulp Co., in southwest Muncie, built during
       the gas boom, is bought by L. A. and Cary Franklin, after having
       been sold at auction.
Jan.—Muncie postoffice receipts in 1905 were $71,874.71.
Feb. 12—A meeting at the Commercial Club plans the Art Association.
Feb. 19—Death of Mrs. Mary Eiler, aged 96, probably the first Catholic
       to become a permanent resident of the county.
Feb. 24—Death of Robert Meeks, aged 84, who came to the county in 1839,
       and to Muncie in 1844.

CHAPTER XIX.

CITY AND COUNTRY IN THE TWENTIETH CENTURY; THE RESULTS OF THREE-QUARTERS OF A CENTURY OF PROGRESS.

It is not intended to bewilder the reader with statistical tables. Figures are referred to, but seldom read. However, figures must be used in estimating the growth of material wealth of a community, and in the following table, that shows the total valuations of property at various periods in the last sixty years, is contained a succinct summary of progress that could in no other way be compressed into such small space. It is believed that such a table as follows has never before been published, and so far as assessor's figures may be assumed to represent real values, this is the best obtainable data for measuring the county's growth. The figures for 1843 are especially noteworthy, since they go to prove what has been elsewhere asserted, that largest numbers of settlers and the most advanced degree of material development during the first twenty years were found in the townships crossed by White river and the course of the old State road. Thus, Perry, Liberty, Center, Mount Pleasant and Salem are the townships that have over one hundred thousand dollars worth of assessable property in each. The smallest valuation is obtained from the largest township—Harrison. And yet, in 1907, Harrison ranks well among the leading townships and has passed some of the early leaders. There are only two townships at the present time that have not a greater valuation than had the entire county in 1843.

	1843	1860	1880	1897	1907
Salem	$134,157	$434,230	$ 709,000	$1,121,910	$ 1,623,520
Mt. Pleasant	144,112	369,380	820,000	980,475	1,618,210
Harrison	74,949	280,145	533,000	842,460	1,353,845
Washington	82,906	281,435	427,000	747,840	1,181,795
Monroe	97,039	310,920	559,000	885,345	1,262,380
Center	239,236	441,390	1,171,000	2,543,225	3,354,625
Muncie	(In above)	604,185	1,795,000	6,917,905	11,167,235
Hamilton	78,746	278,130	1,795,000	920,315	1,393,130
Union	84,367	306,615	514,000	765,870	964,465
Perry	110,978	355,885	502,000	633,165	1,011,075
Liberty	108,576	406,830	833,000	975,105	2,026,925
Delaware	97,179	350,330	564,000	642,575	1,260,990
Niles	85,039	280,495	466,000	731,715	977,535
Albany	......	....	....	511,640	437,515
Eaton	......	....	....	336,060	639,515
Normal City	......	....	....	....	235,095
Riverside City	......	....	....	....	311,725
Gaston	......	....	....	....	176,210
Total	$1,137,284	4,787,543*	9,378,000	19,572,955	30,995,780

*This includes about $90,000 valuation of the Bellefontaine Railroad.

For 1907 the figures represent net total taxables—the total taxables returned by board of review, less mortgage deductions, increased by value of corporate property by state board. The value of additional assessments by state board in different townships—amounting to $194,955—should be added to "net total taxables."

The most impressive fact to be deduced from a study of these tables is the remarkable and almost sudden increase in material wealth during the years after 1880. The beginning of this increase is shown in the following table, containing the county's taxable property for 1886 and 1887, with the amount of increase and decrease for each township:

Table showing county's taxable property for 1886 and 1887, with amount of increase and decrease for each township:

Township—	1886	1887	Increase	Decrease
Salem	732,980	708,735	......	24,245
Mt. Pleasant	771,165	778,265	7,100	......
Harrison	589,555	592,520	2,965	......
Washington	479,105	476,300	......	2,805
Monroe	557,075	557,925	850	......
Center	959,255	988,810	......	445
Muncie City	1,915,240	2,027,965	112,725	......
Hamilton	561,025	571,820	10,795	......
Union	562,345	555,980	......	6,335
Perry	488,720	491,790	3,070	......
Liberty	838,050	824,375	......	13,675
Delaware	643,360	588,330	......	55,003
Niles	462,310	461,185	......	1,125
Total	$9,590,185	9,614,000		
Net increase 1887 over 1886....				$33,815

Corresponding figures ten years later—for 1896 and 1897—follow, showing total valuations and total gains:

Townships and Corporations—	Total Val., 1897.	Total Val., 1896.	Total Gains.
Salem	$ 1,121,910	$1,113,565	$ 8,345
Mt. Pleasant	980,475	943,735	36,740
Harrison	842,460	821,440	21,020
Washington	747,840	722,555	25,285
Monroe	885,345	867,610	17,735
Center	2,543,225	2,426,875	116,350
Hamilton	920,315	879,500	40,815
Union	765,870	743,255	22,615
Perry	633,165	632,990	175
Liberty	975,105	959,025	16,080
Delaware	642,575	611,475	31,100
Niles	731,715	691,650	40,065
Albany	511,640	360,740	150,900
Eaton	336,060	310,435	25,625
City of Muncie	6,935,255	6,633,275	301,980
Total	$19,572,955	$19,718,125	$554,830
Net Gain	854,830		

In four years, subsequent to 1887, values had risen in every township, and in Muncie especially the totals were double those of 1887. The following table, giving taxable property for August 1891, epitomizes the history of the county during those expansive years after the discovery of gas. The table gives for each township the acreage, the value per acre, the value per acre with improvements, and the total value of taxable property, both real and personal:

Township—	Acreage.	Value per Acre.	With Improvem'ts.	Total Value Taxable Property.
Salem	21,745	$ 34.55	$ 39.81	$ 1,183,520
Mt. Pleasant	21,174	29.24	32.41	918,815
Harrison	26,268	23.06	25.44	854,230
Washington	23,308	22.36	25.25	740,175
Monroe	19,324	33.79	38.96	937,280
Center	18,062	40.03	56.34	1,543,290
Muncie	489	847.01	1,216.58	4,924,393
Hamilton	18,693	31.85	36.88	887,235
Union	18,938	23.41	27.36	784,354
Perry	18,879	23.33	26.46	619,779
Liberty	21,978	26.48	30.32	913,199
Delaware	18,687	24.43	29.20	782,300
Niles	18,905	23.70	26.09	619,815
Totals or Average	245,456	$ 30.01	$ 34.40	$15,708,485

County's Financial Status.

It is a matter for historical record that the fiscal affairs of Delaware county are now in excellent condition. For many years this was a poor county. It will be remembered that the various townships were hardly able to support decent public schools until after the middle of the last century; and, as shown in the educational chapter, voted against the proposition for free schools. Then came the Civil war, which entailed great burdens on the county as well as the nation, and the county treasury was drawn upon for large sums to aid those families that had sent soldiers to the front at the sacrifice of their sole means of support. For some years after the war the county was meeting expenses that would now be merely nominal, but were then considered burdensome. It is recalled how strong was the opposition to the purchase of toll roads and how determined a large proportion of the citizens were in resisting the building of the court house. But days of splendid prosperity soon came, and during the past twenty years the county has been wealthy both as a civil government and as regards its individuals.

At the present time Delaware county has $38,000 in outstanding bonds. Should no more be issued in the meantime, the county will be entirely out of debt on October 1, 1913. On April 15, 1908, will be paid the $13,000 still owing on the court house bonds, issued when the court house was built. The court house has cost about $350,000, including interest and subsequent improvements on buildings and grounds, and every year a considerable sum has been drawn from the annual income to pay off the bonds and interest falling due. The $25,000 outstanding in bonds represent amounts expended

for the building of bridges, at a time when the county was unable to under-
take such work with the current income. By 1913 these bonds will be paid,
and with all interest-bearing debts canceled the county government will be
able to extend the work of public improvement, in the construction of roads
and bridges and in drainage and similar undertakings, that are so essential
to the general welfare of the county.

Electric Communication and Transportation.

The history of a county like Delaware abounds with proofs that indi-
vidualism is yielding to social interdependence; that the world, whether our
scope of view be a county, state or nation, is coming to be all of a piece.
Once every little community could live by itself, make its own clothes,
wagons, tools, and all the articles necessary for its existence. But with the
coming of the railroad, telegraph, telephone, etc., closer relations were established and communities and states became dependent upon each other. There
is "no isolation now," and yet so quickly have the people accommodated
themselves to the revolutionized methods of living wrought by modern communication and transportation, that the wonder now is "how did people ever
get along without such necessities as the telegraph, telephone, railroads,
etc.?" But, quoting in answer a recent editorial in the Muncie Star, "It is
only a little over half a century since Indianapolis people who wanted to
communicate with New York had to do it by mail, and the mail went by
stage.

"And yet they congratulated themselves on the advanced stage of civilization they had reached, for their predecessors of little more than a quarter of a century had to build their own houses, make their own furniture,
make their own clothing and its material, raise their own crops and do practically everything in the way of household economics, from curing pork to
making soap. It would be a severe affliction if the telephone service were
cut off, and there would be tumult if the street car service should stop. But
these are trifles compared with what might be. Suppose that something
should shut the bakeries, or close up the dairies, or even cut off the ice supply! Verily, we have reached a stage where a man is not only his brother's
keeper, but also is kept by his brother. It is a rash man who says nowadays:
'What's Hecuba to me, or I to Hecuba? Like enough Hecuba is making
his shoe polish, or his cigars, or his underclothing, or something else that
he considers indispensable. We are getting around to the federation of
mankind without regard to governmental forms.'"

The telegraph was the first practical use of electricity in this county.
That came with the first railroad. Many years later, about 1880, the telephone was introduced in Muncie, as narrated on other pages, and within a
few years the first use of electricity for lighting purposes is recorded. The

extension of these utilities to all parts of the county, the use of the telephone by rural residents as a feature of modern country life, are made matters of record in other chapters. The application of electricity to transportation has had even more vital bearing on the dvelopment of town and country, and yet it is all so recent that people are only beginning to realize its significance.

In the early history of the county the overland road to Cincinnati was the commercial route over which the larger portion of the surplus products went to market and by which the stores in Muncie and other towns received their supplies. To a much less important degree even the Mississinewa river was used as a transportation route down to the Wabash. Canals were much talked of, but never materialized far enough to affect this county. The railroad was the next development in transportation. It displaced the long overland routes, and in many ways effected revolutionary changes in commerce and industry. The gravel roads radiating from the principal railroad centers were important factors along with the railroads in the developments of the second half of the nineteenth century. And last among the transportation agencies is the electric railroad, which has done more than anything else to knit town and country together and abolish the old-time distinctions between urban and rural residents. Competent observers now maintain that electric roads will soon supersede steam roads in the field of local transportation, both freight and passenger, and it is evident that this change is already well under way, especially as regards passenger traffic. It is impossible to estimate the significance of this form of transportation in relation to future progress, and this history will confine itself to a record of the principal facts concerning the growth of electric traction in Muncie and Delaware county.

The nucleus of electric transportation in this county was the Muncie street railway. Street railway talk began in Muncie almost coincident with the discovery of gas. May 26, 1887, the city council passed a street railway ordinance authorizing A. N. Campbell, W. W. Ball, L. W. Robertson and associates, under the name of the Muncie City Railway Co., to construct roads on the streets of the city and operate by horse power, cable or electricity, for a period of twenty-five years; four miles of the road were to be in operation by August 1, 1888; cars to run every thirty minutes or less between 6 a. m. and 10 p. m.; fare 5 cents. Nothing was accomplished by the original promoters on the basis of this ordinance, and they turned over their rights to another company, who in June, 1888, secured an extension of sixty days for their franchise on the proviso that actual construction work begin by August 15. The franchise expired without any action being begun.

A second franchise was passed April 12, 1889, this being an open franchise to any company that would accept its terms. A supplementary ordinance was passed June 11 of the same year, providing that the track should be three feet wide, and defining the route. The Muncie Street Railway Company prepared to build a line in conformity with this ordinance, and during the summer of 1889 laid rails on Main street as the beginning of the system. On September 26, 1889, two motors and cars arrived and a few days later they made their first trip down Main street. The event occasioned considerable satisfaction among the friends of progress at first, and for some time the newspapers referred with pride to their street car line. But this feeling was of brief duration, and among Muncie citizens in general at the present time there seems a general reticence in referring to the first street cars. Perhaps there was reason for their disappointment. The cars were propelled neither by horse power nor by cable nor by electricity. The "motor" that drew the cars up the narrow track on Main street was a form of pony steam engine, resembling the kind used in mining camps and for railroad construction work. The engineer usually had difficulty in starting his train when loaded, seldom could round a curve except by getting much headway, and had equal difficulty in bringing his train to a standstill when vehicles, persons and other objects got in the way of the engine at full speed. The inefficiency of the system may be imagined, and yet it was patronized and for a time fulfilled its purpose in providing transportation to the rapidly growing city. In July, 1890, the track was completed to the railroad on South Walnut street, and later was extended to Ohmer avenue and east to the glass works, making a circuit around the principal divisions of the city.

Along in the early nineties the dissatisfaction with this method of transportation developed into active opposition to the operating company and to agitation for a modern electric car system. The Daily News led in this agitation, and its columns were often spiced with such recitals of occurrences and mishaps on the car line as the following, which appeared in April, 1892: "Great excitement was created on our streets Saturday evening by the appearance of the new (?) Mogul brought out by the Muncie Street Railway Company. As it made its first trip up East Main street the people fled in all directions. Many of our oldest citizens thought the court house was coming up the street on wheels. As it puffed down Walnut street crowd after crowd hooted as it passed. It is large enough to be used as a switch engine on our belt railroad. The engineer had much trouble with it yesterday, as it would jump the track at almost every turn." Fifty-three minutes, so it was claimed, were consumed in making the trip around the circuit.

In April, 1892, the Muncie Electric Street Railway Company was incorporated, its first set of directors being David Cammack, John M. Kirby, D. C. Mitchell, R. C. Griffith and William L. Little. They filed a petition with the council in the following May that right of way be granted

them over the streets for the construction of an electric line under the provisions of the general ordinance of 1889. A new franchise was given the
company in December, 1892, and the following spring work was actively
begun in the construction of the electric line, which was formally opened
on May 13, 1893. The details concerning the opening and the gradual
extension of the lines to the suburbs will be found in the chapter of
"Chronology" for 1893 and succeeding years.

Interurban Lines.

In a few years the electric car lines of Muncie had increased to six,
reaching out to all the suburbs, and forming a traction system of no little
magnitude. Now followed the next important development in electric
transportation. Many other cities in the gas belt had similar local systems
of street railways. Why not link them together by interurban electric lines,
thus benefiting not only the larger cities but the intermediate country as
well? The enterprising men who made practical answer to this question no
doubt had in mind more important results than a mere extension of street
car service to the country, and probably foresaw that by this means country
and city would be knitted together and that local and suburban transportation business would in a few years pass from the steam railroad to the
trolley line. Anyhow, in the results as they can now be understood, the
interurban traction line shares with the telephone and rural free delivery
the responsibility for the remarkable changes that have occurred in rural
life during the last ten or fifteen years.

The interurban movement began in Indiana, with Indianapolis as its
focal point, less than ten years ago. And among the first companies organized to promote the movement was the Union Traction Company of Indiana,
with its head offices at Anderson. Its first officers were Phillip Mater, of
Marion, president; C. L. Henry, of Anderson, secretary and general manager, and George F. McCulloch, of Muncie, treasurer. The capital stock
was $5,000,000. July 1, 1899, the Muncie street railway lines became the
property of this company.

In October, 1900, the interurban line between Anderson and Muncie
was put in operation and soon afterward cars were run through from this
city to Indianapolis. Hardly had the first line been opened when the merchants in the small towns along the road began complaining that their trade
was falling off and that the large stores of Muncie, Anderson and Indianapolis were getting a class of customers who had previously spent all their
money in the home village. There can be little question that this condition
is one of the most important results of electric transportation. The convenience and speed of the electric car have built up the large centers and
decreased the importance of the small towns. It is now as easy for the

resident of the farthest corner of the county to reach a department store in Muncie as it was twenty years ago to go to the general store in the nearest village, perhaps a mile away. As a result some very great changes have been taking place in the county during the present century. While improved transportation service increases communication between the city and coun- try, making each more accessible to the other and increasing the desirability of the country for residence, at the same time it tends to concentration of industries and business that thrive best where population is greatest. Whereas the city store once supplied a trade within a radius of three or four miles, modern transportation has lengthened that radius to twenty or thirty miles. It is very plain, with only the results of these few years before us. that the era of many small commercial centers is being succeeded by a period when one central city will be the point of supply for an entire county.

While the line was being built to Muncie from the west, franchise was being sought for one between Muncie and Fort Wayne. The Muncie Inter- urban Co. was the company that first promoted the line north to Hartford City, but the franchises were afterward transferred to the Muncie, Hartford and Fort Wayne Co. The Muncie and Dayton line was also being promoted, construction work being pushed from Dayton toward the west. Another line that was being planned during the first two or three years of this cen- tury was the Muncie and Portland. Of these the Muncie and Hartford City line was the first to be put in operation. The power house was com- pleted at Eaton in 1902, and in February of 1903 the first car ran into Muncie. The construction of the Dayton and Muncie road was continued from the Ohio line, the road being completed to Selma early in 1905, and in August of that year regular service was begun between Muncie and the east. While this line was nearing completion the road to Portland was begun, and in the early summer of 1906 was opened to traffic.

At the present time, therefore, electric lines parallel the steam road in four directions from Muncie. The Indiana Union Traction Co. is the con- trolling corporation of three of these lines. All points along the Big Four Railroad, both east and west, and along the Lake Erie lines to the north and northeast, including the principal villages of the county, are linked to Muncie by steam and electric transportation. Another line will probably be opened in a year or so between Muncie and Alexandria, and for several years a company has been negotiating for rights of way to construct a line between Muncie and Newcastle.

Recent Steam Roads.

The voting of subsidies, granting of franchises, and other events in the construction of the several lines of railroad that in recent years have entered Delaware county, have been recorded in the preceding chronologies.

Union Station, Muncie.

Perhaps nothing more than what is there mentioned need be said concerning the road running southwest from Muncie, known as the Chicago and Southeastern, or the Midland, a part of the Central Indiana lines. Few railroads had such difficulties during the period of financing and building. The construction was begun before the crisis of 1893, and during the following ten years made hardly any progress at all because of lack of funds, suits, strikes and other troubles too numerous to mention. Finally the track was completed to Muncie, though it did not gain entrance into the city for some time after. The road at last was sold, it was understood at the time, to the Big Four, and has since been operated by other lines. The latest information on the subject is given in an official report from the Pennsylvania Railroad Co., which says: "The Pennsylvania system now has an entrance to Muncie from the southwest on the Central Indiana Railroad, which taps the Vandalia and the Indianapolis and Richmond branches of the Panhandle. The Central Indiana, however, is only jointly owned by the Pennsylvania company."

The Chicago, Indiana & Eastern Railroad, which was completed to Muncie from the north in December, 1900, has recently been purchased by the Pennsylvania, with which it already had traffic agreements. The first section of this road, between Matthews and Fairmount, had been built in 1895, was extended to Swayze in 1898, and to Converse in 1899 (a total length of twenty-eight miles). The following statement from the purchasing railroad gives the history and status of this road:

"After clearing up the indebtedness of the Chicago, Indiana and Eastern Railroad, which has been operated for some time by a receiver, the Pennsylvania company secured all the stocks and bonds of the road and has made it a part of the Logansport division of the Pittsburg, Cincinnati, Chicago and St. Louis Railroad (The Panhandle), thereby providing for the Pennsylvania system a second entrance into Muncie, Ind., an important shipping center.

"The Chicago, Indiana and Eastern is a short line, forty-three miles long, running from Converse on the P., C., C. and St. L. to Muncie. It taps many small towns, and because of its little equipment, which totaled only nine engines and twenty-eight cars, was unable to handle the business of the district.

"For about two years negotiations have been under way between the stock and bondholders of the road and the Pennsylvania company, to have the latter take over the road. The transfer has just been completed and an agreement entered into between the Pennsylvania company and the P., C., C. and St. L. whereby the latter road will operate the line, beginning this month (August)."

· With regard to the Chicago, Cincinnati and Louisville (originally the

Cincinnati, Richmond and Muncie), the chronological statements may be
completed by saying that in the spring of 1907 the road was formally opened
as the "Chicago Short Line," and a through schedule of trains between Cincinnati and Chicago adopted. This road, for the building of which the
original company was incorporated in February, 1900, was built in sections
and under various corporate names, but all were merged together as the
C., C. & L. on July 1, 1903. However, the desired entrance at Chicago was
not secured and the road put into operation as a through route until the
present year.

Other Transportation.

It would not be proper to leave the subject of transportation without
some reference to a class of facilities that have undoubtedly been an
influential factor in modern life, in such general use by individuals that the
convenience and transaction of the affairs of business and daily life have
been increased. It was less than ten years ago that the first automobile was
seen in Muncie. At the present time there are probably 200 in the city and
county. They represent an investment of many thousands of dollars, and
with the improvement of the machines themselves with each succeeding year
and the increase of good streets and highways, the automobile is becoming a
large factor in transportation. The history of the automobile in its relations to the welfare of the county cannot yet be written, but it cannot be
overlooked in a summary of modern conditions.

It may be said that the bicycle was the predecessor of the automobile.
The bicycle is now so familiar that it is difficult to recall the exact impressions they created when they first came into use. That they were regarded
as a distinct innovation may be inferred from the following editorial taken
from the Muncie Daily News of June 10, 1882:

The bicycle is rapidly gaining ground and becoming popular, not only in cities
where it is encouraged, through large clubs, backed by big capital, but in smaller inland
towns. Its convenience and rapidity of transfer, ease of management, graceful appearance and docility as a rider has made it deservedly popular, and the only thing which
is an obstacle to its general use for travel in short distances is its cost.

There are at present fifteen machines at use in this city, distributed among the
following named persons: Carl Sample, Hugh Cowing, Rolla Marsh, Bob Meeks, Chester
Foster, George Jones, Sherman Hathaway, Charley West, Geo. H. Andrews, Bent
Meeker, Luther Purdue, Willie Kirby, Frank Niekey, Kirby Heinsohn and Clifford
Andrews, with two more parties to hear from. The money invested in these machines
foots up to twelve hundred dollars.

Public Roads.

The results of the turnpike building that was carried on so extensively
in the county during the sixties and seventies are still seen in the county.
The toll-road system was the foundation on which the best public roads of
to-day rest. According to a recent report, there are 800 miles of public
highway in Delaware county, and 600 miles are improved with gravel. All

of these improved roads are township or abandoned toll roads. It is estimated that the total original cost of these roads was $600.000.

Oil Production in Delaware County.

It is said that during the oil boom of 1904 everyone invested his ready
money in oil stock and that a year later the investor still had his stock, but
it was in most cases worthless. Hundreds lost money in the speculation,
and with few exceptions the companies that were quickly formed to develop
the oil territory, lacking the necessary experience and sufficient capital, were
soon bankrupt and their property was being operated by a receiver. Those
who were most successful were the experienced oil operators from the eastern fields, who had large capital backing their enterprise and could prosecute
their development to the point of profit.

Some phases of the oil boom have already been noted, especially in the
field of which Smithfield and Selma were the center. It is remarkable how
quickly Delaware county took its place among the foremost oil-producing
counties of Indiana. Up to 1903 most of the wells were shallow, but in
that year some were pushed down to the "deep pay sand" and were found
to be very productive. As a result the county was the center of the oil
excitement during the next year. In 1903 Delaware county had but 74 producing wells; in 1904 it had 831 producing wells. The total bores in 1903
were 122; in 1904 they had risen to 952. For the entire Indiana oil field the
increase of production for 1904 over 1903 was 72,152 barrels, of which more
than 50 per cent was furnished by Delaware county. In this county the
wells bored in 1903 gave an average initial production of 20.07 barrels,
while those bored in 1904 had an average initial production of 44.4. Both
figures are much higher than for the oil field as a whole, the average initial
production in the oil district in 1903 being 14.2, and in 1904, 18.6.

In 1905 the bottom dropped out of the oil business, the principal causes
assigned for it being the low price of oil, the fact that companies were
unable to operate or invest enough money, and that production was falling
off. It is a striking comment on the decline, that in 1904 there were forty-
nine oil and gas companies and promoters of oil properties advertised in the
Muncie directory. By October, 1905, but thirteen of these were in existence.

There is still a large amount of oil produced in Delaware county, but
compared with the amount in 1904 it seems insignificant. A good many
more wells were pulled out during the last summer (1907) than were sunk.
Salt water has seriously interfered with the production and made the sinking of wells too hazardous to be undertaken by conservative investors.

Rural Free Delivery.

The building of interurban railroads, the establishment of rural free
delivery and the consolidation of district schools have been, it is safe to

assert, the three most important events in the recent history of Delaware county, when the number of people affected and the benefits conferred are considered. The advantages of rural free delivery are too well understood at this time to need restatement, although the system is only ten years old, and in that time has passed through the experimental stage and become one of the most beneficial of all the undertakings of the federal government. At the present time there are about thirty routes in the county, twelve of which lead out from Muncie.

Concerning the first routes established in the county, some interesting information is contained in a report from Perry Heath while he was first assistant postmaster general. It should be remarked that this county owes the early establishment of rural free delivery mainly to Mr. Heath's interest and recommendations in behalf of his home county. This report, issued in November, 1899, while the service was still in its infancy, gives the following statistics about the routes:

Albany, established Nov. 8, 1897; one carrier; population served, 500; length of route, 20 miles.

Daleville, established Nov. 8, 1897; one carrier; population served, 275; length, 16 miles.

Eaton, established Nov. 8, 1897; one carrier; population served, 250; length, 18½ miles.

Muncie, established Feb. 1, 1898; one carrier; population served, 500; length, 24 miles. Muncie extension route, established Aug. 15, 1898, serving 350 people.

Selma, established Nov. 8, 1897; one carrier; population, 500; length, 16 miles.

Muncie Postoffice.

It is nearly eighty years since William Van Matre became the first postmaster of old Muncietown. In that time there have been nineteen different incumbents of the office. It was a position that required only incidental attention to its duties during the terms of the first postmasters, and in the names of the first incumbents will be recognized some of the business and professional men of that time, who sold goods and took law cases while managing the simple responsibilities of sorting and delivering the small bulk of daily mail. Van Matre or any of his early successors would be amazed and confounded if they were confronted with the task of managing the present Muncie postoffice. It is probable that outside of the three or four largest cities of the east, there was not a postoffice in America in 1828 that did so much business as the Muncie postoffice in 1906. In point of receipts alone, to say nothing of the value of its services to the business and general public, this postoffice is one of the leading institutions of Muncie. As told on a previous page, the receipts increased from about $6,600 in 1885 to $19,000

Federal Building, Muncie.

in 1892. Since then rural free delivery has thrown out lines in all directions from Muncie as a center, and with the steady growth of the city's postal business the receipts passed the $40,000 mark some years ago, and during the past ten years fully half a million dollars represents the amounts taken in through the various departments of the office. Receipts are now about $75,000 annually; money order department about $60,000 annually.

As told in the chapter of chronology, an appropriation was finally secured for the federal building at Muncie, and in the spring of 1907 the handsome structure, illustrated on another page, was dedicated. Including the cost of the site, the Muncie postoffice cost about $90,000, and is the last and in some respects the best of the additions to the public and business architecture of Muncie.

The successive postmasters of Muncie since 1828 are given in the following table, showing name and date of appointment:

ESTABLISHED AS MUNCIETOWN.

William Van Matre	Apr. 10, 1828
Dickinson Burt	Aug. 20, 1829
Chas. F. Willard	May 6, 1835
Samuel W. Harlan	Apr. 6, 1837
Amariah Cubberly	June 2, 1837
Edward S. Keasbey	Oct. 20, 1837
John Ethel	Apr. 28, 1847
John Brady	May 14, 1847

NAME OF P. O. CHANGED TO MUNCIE.

John Brady	Dec. 29, 1857
Robert Richey	Mar. 30, 1861
Samuel J. Watson	Jan. 12, 1865
Henry C. Marsh	Aug. 10, 1866
John C. Eiler	Feb. 3, 1875
Robert I. Patterson	Feb. 7, 1883
John E. Banta	Feb. 14, 1887
Frank Ellis	Feb. 9, 1891
Edward Tuhey	Jan. 15, 1895
David Cammack	Mar. 3, 1899
David A. Lambert	Mar. 10, 1903
Robe Carl White	Mar. 13, 1907

[Table furnished through courtesy of Hon. George W. Cromer.]

City of Muncie.

In 1891, when Muncie was only beginning the system of public improvements, its general outstanding bond issue amounted to $44,000, including a bank loan of $6,000. About half of these bonds have since been paid off, but the issues in the meantime have increased the general bonded indebtedness to $93,000. In 1891 the school bonds outstanding amounted to $8,000. At that time the building of the splendid school houses that are so creditable to the school city of Muncie, had only begun, and more than half a dozen elegant and well equipped schools have since been erected.

Notwithstanding this heavy expenditure on the part of the school city, the outstanding school bonds at this writing are only $20,000, representing an issue of April, 1895. July 1, 1907, bonds to the amount of $20,000 were paid, leaving only one issue to be paid, some eight years hence.

Combining city and school bonds, the indebtedness of Muncie is now $113,000. Compared with other cities of Indiana, Muncie has less bonded indebtedness than any other city of its size.

At the close of the year 1906 Muncie had improvement bonds outstanding to the amount of $174,180.37. In 1891 the street improvement bonds outstanding were $67,795, and the sewer bonds, $50,000, making a total of $117,795. These improvement bonds are not obligations on the city, but are what are commonly known as Barrett law bonds, issued by the city under statutory authority as first liens against property for street and sewer improvement. All objections to their validity were waived by the property owners before they were issued.

Municipal Improvements.

The history of the important changes in the municipal affairs of Muncie has been followed in considerable detail through the preceding chapters, and it now remains to describe the present status of the city in its relation to the public.

In the past year the city has abandoned its municipal lighting plant, and the streets and public buildings are now lighted by the Muncie Electric Light Co., in accordance with a contract entered into July 2, 1906, for a period of ten years, the total number of lights to be not less than 260 and to be kept lighted from half an hour after sunset to half an hour before sunrise. For the arc lamp such as is in general use, the cost to the city is $57.50 per year for all night service for the first 260 lamps, and $45 per year for each additional lamp. For the 50-candlepower incandescent light, the cost per year is fixed at $24.50 each.

Judging from the experience of the past, the city will receive lighting service at a cost certainly not greater than under the municipal ownership regime. About 1900, when there was so much agitation for the improvement of the city plant, owing to the poor service that had been given the people during the past months, a table was compiled showing the average cost of each light since the establishment of the plant, depreciation charges and expense of new equipment being combined with operating expenses in figuring this cost. According to this table, the cost per light in 1893, when there were 102 lights in use, was $65. For following years: 1894, $61; 1895, $57; 1896, $53; 1897, $49; 1898, $50.

Much has been said on previous pages about the water works and the water supply. The original franchise to the water company ran for twenty years, and expired in 1906. When the time came to renew the contract, the subject at once became the foremost municipal question. It resolved itself into two main issues—quality and adequacy of the supply, and rates. The latter was, wisely, subordinated to the former, since the chief interest of the public is pure water. Pure water has always been more or less difficult to obtain, since it has been found that the deep wells of the water company have afforded an insufficient supply, especially during fires, when it was necessary to increase the pressure and introduce river water into the mains. The old criticism that the water from the hydrants "looks like cider" has an occasional application even at this time, despite many radical and expensive improvements in the equipment of the works. The last report from the department of public health says: "The city water has been analyzed at different times and the quality was much improved over 1905. There is still danger of its becoming polluted and causing disease."

However, the discoloring of the water is claimed to be nothing more than rust and a salt of magnesium that separates out from the deep well water and does not unfit the water for domestic use. This history must be content to leave the subject with the statement that both the service and the quality of the water have been much improved during recent years. A report from an expert brought to Muncie to investigate the water supply contains some history of the plant that may be quoted:

"In 1885 the present water works company built works in accordance with a report made to the city by the late Mr. Cook. An intake a short distance to the east of the city was established, whereby water was taken from White river and pumped into the distributing system which comprised about seven miles of pipes. Muncie at that time had a population of some 5,000 or 6,000 people. Shortly afterwards the development in this locality of natural gas caused the city to grow rapidly. Manufacturing industries sprang up in and near the city and some objectionable local pollution from a small tributary entered the White river above the original intake. In 1889 the company abandoned this intake, and moved a considerable distance up the river to the present White river pumping station, situated some 2.5 miles from the center of the city. At first the supply came from flowing wells, driven about 200 feet into the fissured limestone underlying this section of the country and from a filter gallery about 400 feet long on the bank of the White river. Additional wells were gradually driven. In all 18 wells have been sunk along the White river for a distance of some 7,000 feet. In round numbers they have a capacity of 2,000,000 gallons daily. An emergency intake in the White river was established at the new pumping station, and the growth of the town made it necessary for some years to secure a portion of the supply from the river at times of maximum rate of pumping. In 1900 the pumping station was enlarged and improved with the addition of new, triple-expansion pumping engines and there was erected a filter plant having a capacity of about 2,000,000 gallons per 24 hours. Developments in the local oil field in 1904 soon after caused the White river to become so impregnated with oil that it was not a suitable source of supply. Efforts were made by the company early in 1905 to increase materially its well water supply. Air compressors were established to increase the yield, but practically with no avail. In connection with the effort an unfortunate accident occurred in July, 1905, to the well pumping outfit, whereby it became necessary for some days to pump into the city the foul-smelling and bad-tasting White river water. This produced much indignation among some of the citizens whose general view since that time has been in opposition to the public water supply coming from other than underground sources.

"Your board then took hold of the matter and arranged with the water company that immediately they should build an auxiliary pumping station upon Buck creek, a tributary of the White river, draining some 35 square miles or more of the area lying to the south of the city. In October, 1905, this pumping station and about three miles of force main were completed. Since that time the public water supply of Muncie has consisted of the deep well water of the water company to its full capacity, supplemented by such amounts of filtered Buck creek water as were necessary to maintain the supply."

The city entered into a new contract with the Muncie Water Works Company, August 17, 1906, by which a new schedule of prices for water for domestic uses was fixed, which schedule may be revised at the expiration of each period of ten years; for the sum of $10,000 annually the city obtains water for 300 fire hydrants, for flushing sewer tanks, and for all public buildings, schools, drinking fountains, cemeteries and parks.

The past ten years has seen many improvements in the fire department, both in size and equipment and in efficiency. According to a report mentioned in a preceding chapter, the fire department had not been improved to keep pace with the growing city. In 1896 there were two stations, which, with apparatus, were valued at about twenty-five thousand dollars. The report of Chief H. R. Gallivan on Dec. 31, 1906, gives the valuation of the departments, excluding the buildings, as $27,289.75. The annual expenses for 1895 were about $8,750, while for 1906 the total expenditures were $18,590.35. The present equipment is reported as follows:

"Department consists of three houses, No. 1 house, corner Jackson and Jefferson streets; No. 2 house, corner Willard and Ebright streets; No. 3, corner Willard and Council streets. Force consists of twenty men and salaries are as follows: Chief, $1,200; assistant chief, $900; two captains, $780 each, and sixteen firemen at $720 each; one substitute for five months to work vacations, $300. We now have ten head of horses, had two to die, turned two over to the cemetery and purchased four new head during 1906. We have 6,500 feet of 2½-inch hose, 4,500 feet good, 1,000 feet fair, 1,000 feet bad and have purchased 1,000 feet new hose; also recommend the purchase of 1,000 feet of new 2½-inch cotton hose. Apparatus is in good state of repair and consists of one chief wagon, one combination chemical and hose wagon, one 75-foot aerial truck, two hose wagons, all in use; also one

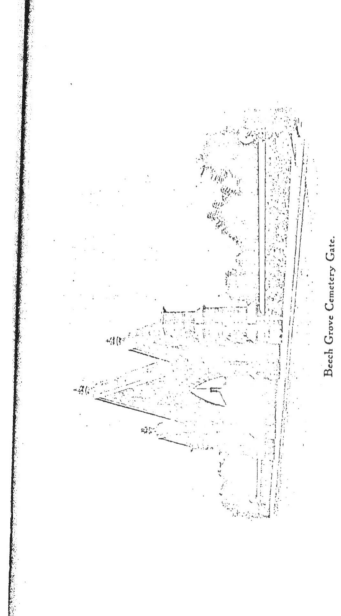

Beech Grove Cemetery Gate.

extra hose wagon and one Clapp & Jones first size engine that we do not use, but is always in readiness in case it is needed."

Cemetery.

It has been a matter of pride for a number of years that Muncie has one of the handsomest and best kept cemeteries in the state. It is a senti_ment commendable in every way that a community should desire the home of its dead to be made beautiful by the best methods of landscape gardening. Beech Grove is worthy of those who have passed away. Its stone gateway, its avenues, its park-like lawns, and the individual places of sepulture justify by their beauty and fitness all the care and expense bestowed upon them. During 1906 nearly fourteen thousand dollars were disbursed in the care and maintenance of this cemetery.

McCulloch Park.

McCulloch Park during the past five years has fully proved the wisdom of Mr. McCulloch in giving the city a recreation ground, and each summer finds its popularity increasing. Originally a part of the forest that covered the north banks of White river, it still retains many of the charms of the woods, especially in its native trees, which are the finest feature of the park. The park authorities have shown wisdom in leaving nature unadorned, and will do well to introduce a minimum of the artificial effects of landscape gardening. The principal facts concerning the history of the park are given in the report of the Board of Public Works, extracts from which are here given:

"On the 6th day of May, 1901, Mr. George F. McCulloch informed the Common Council of the City of Muncie by letter that he would make a gift of the grounds known as McCulloch Park to the City of Muncie, the only condition to said gift being that the City of Muncie hold the real estate in trust as a public park for the free use of all the inhabitants of the city. In his letter to the Council he further stated that he would give a further sum of $2,500, or any part thereof, the condition for said gift being that the people of the City of Muncie raise an equal amount. Said sums so given were to be used as a fund for the improvement and maintenance of said lands. The lands then conveyed to the City of Muncie consisted of about eighty-three acres. The Common Council on said date accepted the gift of the lands, subject to said trust. The offer of the trust fund was also accepted and the Committee on Parks was directed to take action to procure the sum to be subscribed by the people of Muncie, and said committee, together with the City Engineer, were ordered to prepare and report plans and specifications for the improvement of said land.

"Since the acceptance of said gift plans and specifications have been prepared which will require some time to perfect, looking forward to the beautifying and arrangement of all the lands and preparing it for the purpose for which it was intended.

"Not much work was done on the lands until in the year 1903. In June, 1903, the Common Council elected a superintendent. The Common Council of the City of Muncie had appointed a Park Commission, consisting of E. B. Ball, president; J. R. Marsh, secretary, and F. D. Haimbaugh, to look after the improvement and maintenance of the public park and co-operate with the superintendent thereof. About August 1, 1903, the work of building roadways and thoroughfares through the park was begun and from said date until the 1st day of December, 1903, the sum of $4,795.81 was expended in the improvement and maintenance of the park. During the year 1905 the sum of $2,442.71 was expended for maintenance of the park, and during the year 1906 the sum of $2,183.99 was expended for its maintenance. During the year 1905 the sum of $4,350 and during the year 1906 the sum of $2,825 were expended for the purchase of lands adjacent to McCulloch Park, and upon the purchase thereof were added to said park. The tax levy for 1904 and 1905 provided for a taxation of five cents upon each $100 of the taxable property of the City of Muncie to provide for the improvement and maintenance of the public parks. For the year 1906 the tax levy had no such provision and the improvement and maintenance of the parks of the City of Muncie are now paid out of the general fund.

"By a reference to the total amount of taxes collected we find that the amount paid out for public parks during the years 1905 and 1906 was a little less than the amount collected as provided for in the tax levy.

"Since the original conveyance of the eighty-three-acre tract the city of Muncie has added thereto until McCulloch Park now consists of about ninety-five acres. McCulloch Park has been improved and beautified by building about 130,000 square feet of roadway and walks, tennis courts, baseball grounds, cement walks, planting of trees, shrubs and flowers, placing of swings and benches and the sodding and sloping of lands."

During the summer of 1907 a part of the high ground of the park has been inclosed as a deer and elk park, and now contains a herd of those animals.

With the intention of establishing several small parks or "squares" throughout the city, the Council appropriated $6,000 recently for the purchase of the northwest corner of Howard and High streets. Other plots will also be secured in carrying out this design.

Streets and Paving.

Much has already been said about the streets. A number of years ago it was decided to pave the streets with asphalt, and the citizens took much pride in their many blocks of asphalt pavement. However, a few years ago, when the streets began to wear out and repairs and resurfacing became necessary, the city and the citizens were confronted with some problems only less troublesome than the original matter of paving. In a city the size of Muncie it is impracticable to maintain a repair plant for the asphalt streets, and no satisfactory method of repairing the breaks and holes in the pavement has been devised. Recently the asphalt com_panies have shown no eagerness to enter into contract with the city for repaving, failing to respond to the advertisements for sealed bids on the work. The subject is now the leading one before public consideration, and as the matter is as yet unsettled, this history can do no more than state the present indefiniteness with regard to paving, quoting as an example of current discussion the following editorial which contains some references to past and present conditions:

"One burning thought in connection with the warm discussion in Muncie over the kind of paving to be used in some of the streets soon to be improved is that cheap streets in the beginning are expensive in the long run. If substantial roadways, the kind that are durable under proper care, are laid, we will not hear constant complaints or protests against the cost of public works as regards these thoroughfares after the improve_ments are finished. The trouble with Muncie's experience in this direction has been that too much money has been sunk in temporary improvements and that, when first-class pavements have been constructed, the paving has been abused and neglected. Muncie's streets right now are in the worst condition in many years and the property owners and residents will sooner or later recognize of a necessity that they must improve and improve per_manently. The work must be done once for all time and, when done, prop_erly guarded and protected. The city officials will hear varied and divers recommendations as to the kind of paving to be put down, but it will be im_possible for them to please every one. Hence the best thing for them to do under the circumstances is to look as far ahead into the future as possible and have built the pavement or pavements that will be most satisfactory in the years to come regardless of individual disapproval or censure."

Some figures with regard to the streets, submitted by the engineering department in its report for year 1906, will be of interest. There are seven_ty-four miles of streets within the corporation. Of these nearly sixty miles are improved, 3.25 miles with asphalt pavement. It will be recalled that only a few years ago the City Council objected to the "new-fashioned" con_crete sidewalk. At the present time there are nearly fifty-five miles of cement sidewalk, while brick and sandstone walks total about sixteen miles in length. A feature that does much to add to the appearance of a city, not to mention its value from a sanitary standpoint, is paved alleys. Es_pecially in the business section Muncie has much to be proud of in this respect, there being about three miles of cement, stone or brick alleys. At the present time Muncie has nearly twenty-seven miles of sewers, all of which have been constructed during the past twenty-five years.

Architecture.

With regard to the architecture of Muncie, owing to the fact that the business section has been practically made over during the last ten years, it may be termed distinctively modern and even elegant so far as that quality consists with utility. The old and the new, permanence and progress are well illustrated in the building. On one hand are the high school and court house, dating back a quarter of a century. While the Wysor, the Johnson, the Vatet blocks are the best types of modern office and business blocks, all constructed within the last decade. The Anthony building, the first high-grade structure on Walnut street, though still an excellent building, has long yielded precedence. During the last three or four years, the first-class buildings that have been constructed would make a long list. Along Walnut street could be named the Wysor block, the McNaughton block and the Goddard wholesale building. A number of structures have been erected on or near Mulberry, including the traction terminal station on Charles (the finest terminal in Indiana outside of Indianapolis), the Building and Loan block and the Ware building, in the same locality, the Star building on Adams street, the Delaware hotel. On East Main street are some noteworthy contrasts. The Kirby House on the corner of Jefferson was erected in 1871 and was the largest building in town at the time. Across the street from it stands the Boyce block, built in 1880, which was the first high-grade business block, and was built in advance of the business demands of the town, as was then believed. Opposite from these older structures is the elegant Commercial Club building, which cost about $55,000, and which is the best building for its purpose in Indiana outside of the capital. With the exception of the old city hall, the public architecture of Muncie is commendable. The school buildings, with one or two exceptions, are particularly creditable as homes for the children during the most important period of life. The Jefferson building excels in a certain dignity and chaste beauty that are not inconsistent with its essential purposes, and the McKinley and other buildings might be mentioned for special merits. The library and the federal buildings probably possess more individuality in their architectural outlines than any other buildings, and yet each is well adapted to its purposes.

Manufacturing.

Muncie is still an important manufacturing city, though the days of cheap natural gas are over, and a brief review may be taken of industrial interests during this century. The United States census for 1900 enumerated 347 industrial establishments in Muncie, of which the combined capital amounted to nearly eight million dollars. There were 6,294 wage earners, and more than three million dollars each year went to them in salaries. The value of the products for 1900 was estimated at over twelve million dollars. The two chief interests were the steel and glass industries, the former of which paid nearly a million in wages, and the latter nearly nine hundred thousand dollars. All of these are impressive figures, and prove that manufacturing is the largest interest of the city.

More recent figures are furnished by the state statistician, whose report covers 1905. Evidently his data was somewhat different from that obtained by the federal bureau, and comparisons between the two sets of figures are probably misleading. According to the state statistician, Muncie had, in 1905, 102 manufacturing establishments, against 90 in 1900. In 1905 the invested capital in these concerns amounted to nearly five millions, the value of the products was six and a half millions, and the 3,074 wage earners divided a million and a half in salaries. From 1900 to 1905, the invested capital increased thirty-five per cent, but it is noticeable that the number of wage earners decreased 20.1 per cent, the amount of wages decreased 22.6 per cent, and the value of the products decreased 8 per cent. Among eight Indiana cities with more than twenty thousand population, Muncie's factories increased in number 13.3 per cent, standing fourth in the list; but the increase in value of products was but eight per cent, placing Muncie seventh in the list of cities.

General Progress.

It is a very common habit for people, in fixing their attention on the ideals of the future or counting the milestones that have long been passed, to fail to perceive the progress that is being made at present. They forget to measure the increase of culture, the diffusion of knowledge, the accumulation of comforts that every decade brings. Some features of present-day life are so familiar that they are unnoticed as instruments or results of progress, and yet they will be so regarded in the future. Among the many changes of the past few years, we have spoken of those produced by the interurban service. The population from the county mingles with that of the town with scarcely any obvious distinctions, and as the conveniences and comforts of life become more general, so the tastes of people are refined. Amusements have changed much in recent years. The prevalence of theatricals of all kinds, the "five-cent shows," are developments of this period that undoubtedly mark the beginning of important changes in the future. Music is everywhere, produced mechanically, and while it is not the highest grade, it is responsible for the formation of tastes that were unknown to most people a quarter of a century ago.

The last five years have witnessed a moral movement in Muncie and the county at large, the results of which are distinctly beneficial. Reference has been made to the conditions that marked Muncie's early career as a manufacturing city. The ill-repute borne by the city in consequence is rapidly disappearing, if it has not already gone. The churches and both the organized and unorganized forces for civic righteousness have done much in the last decade. In the county at large, outside of Muncie, the most important public question is the liquor traffic, and several communities have been and are bitterly divided in this matter. In Muncie, opposition has been directed not so much against the liquor dealing as such, but rather against the vice and immorality that find protection behind the legal saloon interests. As a result of quickened public opinion and unusual police activity, it is conceded that wine rooms and the worst resorts have been abolished.

The works of charity have also advanced. In 1900 the Associated Charities of Muncie and Delaware County was organized as a general society to which are affiliated the many benevolent organizations. For the past five years a public hospital for Muncie and the county has been the object of much discussion and individual and organized effort. There has recently been renewed activity on the part of the promoters, and with the substantial contributions that have elsewhere been noticed, it is possible that such an important public institution will soon be built.

The improvement of the city with respect to cleanliness of streets and alleys, the planting of trees, and the renovation of unwholesome districts, has been actively prosecuted during the past five years. The smallpox epidemic of 1893 has ever since been a stimulus for sanitation to prevent such a recurrence. The bridges across White river are another case where steel and concrete structures are taking the place of the older type. The old covered bridge across the river on Walnut street which was one of the old landmarks, was removed about 1900.

Shiner's Point.

While speaking of this kind of changes, this history should not omit the district famous in Muncie as "Shiner's Point." This will soon be only a memory, for the old houses, heaps of rubbish, and other miscellaneous material that were the distinguishing features of the Point are being removed or destroyed. This became possible through the recent death of the owner of the land that has so long been known as Shiner's Point. His name was Rutherford Powell, and he was about eighty years old at the time of his death. A shiftless sort of fellow, he drifted into Muncie after the war and for ninety dollars bought of Henry Wysor the narrow strip of land along the river north of Washington street. His accumulations of rubbish gradually extended his property out into the river, and on the "point" thus made he built his houses. The wife whom he married after coming to Muncie finally left him, but he continued his quiet existence unchanged by the changes around him, and persisted in keeping the disorder and unsightliness of the premises until his death.

Jefferson School, Muncie.

CHAPTER XX.

EDUCATION IN DELAWARE COUNTY.

The first schoolhouse in Delaware county was built by the pioneers of Perry township in 1827. Seven years before, the first considerable group of settlers had located in this township, that being the first permanent settlement in the county. The fact that these first settlers and many of their successors came from Wayne county, which has always been one of the educational strongholds of Indiana, may have had some bearing on the first attempts at education in the county.

That first schoolhouse, erected just eighty years before this writing, has long been an object of historical and sentimental interest for the people of Delaware county. Many years ago a Muncie schoolboy, who had listened many times to a pioneer's description of the schoolhouse, constructed a model of this first temple of learning in the county, and succeeded so well in reproducing the original that the miniature was part of Indiana's exhibit at the Philadelphia centennial, and drawings and cuts of the model have been used as a perfect representation of the first schoolhouse.

This school building was a fair type of the schoolhouses attended by the children of the pioneers. This one was twenty feet square, with ceiling eight feet high; built of round logs, fitted over each other by rough notching at the end; probably a puncheon floor, and a roof made of "shakes" split out with an axe, and bound down by long poles. Hardly a piece of iron in the shape of a nail went into the make-up. The door frame may have been smoothed and squared so the door would close tight; but it is likely that the door sagged as it swung on its wooden pivots or hinges. The cracks between the logs were chinked with mud or clay plaster most frequently. On the opposite side of the room from the door was the wide fireplace; its bottom a broad, flat stone or beaten clay, surrounded with a circle of stones or burnt clay extending up above the reach of the flames, and then continuing in a "mud and stick" chimney, the stick scaffolding supporting and giving shape to the hardened mud plaster in which it was embedded. From each of the other two sides of the room, about five or six feet from the floor, one of the horizontal logs had been cut out for the greater part of its length, and the opening thus left was the "window." To admit light and at the same time exclude the cold winds, greased paper was stretched over this aperture, window-glass being one of the later importations in a pioneer community.

While the exterior form of the school buildings varied, the interior furnishings remained about the same throughout what may be termed the pioneer period, in fact, until after the middle of the last century. The rough walls of the room were unadorned except as the individual taste of the teacher might seek to relieve its dreariness. The seats were primitive. They were nothing more than a split log with the flat surface up, and resting on legs driven into holes on the under side, or the timber for the seat might be a plank with some attempt at smoothing the top surface. But there were no backs to these benches. There were no desks in the modern sense of the term. Around two or three sides of the room was fixed a broad board, with a slant convenient for the writer, and on this the pupils, or as many of them as this rough form of desk would accomodate, did their 'copy book" writing. A piece of slate was used for all calculations, and paper was only used for penmanship exercises.

Of school apparatus there was none. Even the first forms of black-board were not introduced for some years. Graphite pencils were also unknown. A "pen knife" was then a necessary part of the teacher's equipment, for he used that instrument in a way to suggest the name, that is, to make for each scholar a pen from a selected goosequill. Paper was coarse and expensive, and the era of cheap wood-pulp paper tablets did not begin until comparatively recently.

Many pages might be written about these early schools. But nearly all were of the general type which prevailed in every county of Indiana during that period, and in fact in every state of the middle west. It is a tribute to the character of the pioneers that, within so short a time after reaching a new locality, they concerned themselves with providing some kind of school facilities for their children. Coming from whatever sections of the Union, most of the settlers understood the fundamental importance of education and, as a matter of course, included schools among their foremost plans for permanent settlement. A site was selected, a clearing was made, the standing trees would quickly be converted into some such building as has been described, and as soon as a teacher could be found the children of each pioneer home would begin attendance, often finding their way to the schoolhouse along a path indicated by blazed trees.

The building of the first schoolhouse in Perry township does not necessarily fix the date for the beginning of education in the county. The writer has not found any traditions that some of the pioneer mothers of Delaware county turned their spinning wheels and taught the children of the neighborhood at the same time, but it is probable that this happened in some individual homes at least, and in the majority of households the mother and father did what they could in assisting the children to learn the rudiments.

Pioneer Education.

These voluntary endeavors to provide literary instruction were the basis and principal support of all the common schools in Indiana until about the middle of the century. The first schoolhouses were built not because the laws of the nation, state or county commanded the people to build them, but because the people themselves chose to take this initiative and in spite of the fact that for many years little or no financial support was received from the civil authorities for the maintenance of schools.

The first constitution of Indiana, adopted in 1816, provided for educa. tion. Yet in an early day the cause advanced slowly. There was no school law under the territorial government, nor any state law on common schools until 1824. Nearly all the schoolhouses built both before and for some time after that date were erected by voluntary efforts of neighborhoods; and all schools were supported by agreement between teachers and patrons. The one definite provision for education made by the national government, in planning the disposition of the public domain, set aside section 16 in every township for the maintenance of public schools. When Indiana became a state the care of these school sections was entrusted to the state govern. ment; so that, while the other sections of the township were entered at the government land office, this section 16 was disposed of by local officials se. lected by the state, and the proceeds turned over for the support of schools in that particular township. Indiana and Michigan pursued very different policies with reference to this common school fund. In Michigan the pro. ceeds from the sale of the school sections were turned into a common state fund, and the income distributed to each locality according to the school population. Evidently many of the school sections proved of little value, while others sold for a high price, thus causing a wide divergence between the amounts derived from the various townships. In Indiana, since the proceeds of the school section were devoted to the benefit of the schools in the township where the section was located, the inequity of the system proved one of the greatest weaknesses of the common school system during the first half of the century. One township would receive a disproportion- ately large income for its schools, while perhaps the one adjoining, because section 16 had sold for only a few dollars, had no income for the support of schools except the local tax.

In 1824 the general assembly passed an act to incorporate congressional townships and provide for public schools therein. The act provided for the election in each congressional township of three persons of the township to act as school trustees, to whom the control of the school lands and the schools generally was given; and for the building of schoolhouses. Every able-bodied person in each school district who was over twenty-one years of age must work one day in each week, or else pay thirty-seven and one-half cents in lieu of a day's work, until the schoolhouse was built. Almost every session of the legislature witnessed some addition to or modification of the school law. Provision was made for the appointment of school examiners, but the examinations might be private, and the examiners were quite irresponsible. Under such circumstances it could not be expected that competent teachers be employed. Often the most trivial questions were asked a teacher, and this was called an examination. In many instances there was no examination at all—the teacher was simply engaged to teach.

A free school system was not provided for until after 1850. Each district had complete jurisdiction over its school affairs, deciding every question concerning the building of a schoolhouse, and the regulation of local school affairs. The taxes for building the schoolhouse and for the support of the teacher was raised by the authority of the district, and the amount of tuition to be assessed against each child attending school was fixed by the local board. There was no considerable state school fund until after 1837, so that the annual distribution of school money by the state had little effect on the individual schools. With local taxation kept down to a minimum amount by nearly all the counties, the school system of Indiana soon became a reproach to its free institutions. It was during this depressing period of educational backwardness that the word "Hoosier" became a term of derision, denoting the uncouth and ignorant countryman that the inhabitant of Indiana was supposed by most easterners to be.

Literacy in Delaware County.

In 1840 one-seventh of the adult population of Indiana could not read nor write, and many of those who could were densely ignorant. While one out of seven was illiterate in Indiana, the proportion in Ohio was only one out of eighteen. Ohio raised $200,000 in 1845 for common schools, while Indiana had no means of raising such tax. In the matter of literacy, Indiana stood sixteenth among twenty-three states in 1840; in 1850 she was twenty-third among twenty-six states, "lower than all the slave states but three," as Caleb Mills expressed it. The following table contains some interesting figures showing the population of Delaware county and some of its neighbors in 1840 and in 1850, and the number of illiterates over twenty years of age in the same years:

Counties—	Pop., 1840.	Illiterates.	Pop., 1850.	Illiterates.
Delaware	8,843	366	10,976	1,069
Grant	4,875	321	11,092	1,238
Henry	15,128	495	17,668	1,218
Jay	3,863	395	7,051	422
Madison	8,874	332	12,497	1,135
Wayne	23,290	42	25,900	1,065

It is seen that there was a rapid increase in most of the counties named in the number of illiterates between 1840 and 1850. Wayne county was the center of the Quaker settlements, where education was one of the chief concerns, and in 1840, with only 42 persons who could not read or write, this county had a remarkable record. But during the following decade, it is presumed, the inadequacy of Indiana's provisions for common schools deprived thousands of children of the most rudimentary education, and the number of illiterates in Wayne county as well as elsewhere increased many times. A like increase out of proportion to the total population is shown in Delaware county.

With such alarming statistics before them, the people of Indiana were soon awakened to their educational necessities by such agitators as Caleb Mills, whose memorials to the legislature form a most important contribution to the history of education in Indiana. Finally, on May 20, 1847, a state common school convention met in Indianapolis. Many prominent men were present, among them Oliver H. Smith of Delaware county, and their deliberations determined that: Common schools must be free; that the time had come for action by the state; that the revenue already provided must be increased by taxation until sufficient to maintain at least three months' free school each year.

Free Schools.

One of the results of this convention was that, at the general election of 1848, a question of public policy was referred to the voters, whether a law should be enacted "for raising by taxation an amount which, added to the present school funds, should be sufficient to support free common schools in all the school districts in the state not less than three nor more than six months each year." This was the question of free schools. At the election 78,523 votes were cast in the affirmative; 61,887 against it. Fifty-nine counties gave majorities in favor of free schools; thirty-one voted against them. Delaware county showed herself adverse to the establishment of free schools by a vote of 715 for them and 808 against them. It is interesting to compare the attitude taken by the neighboring counties with reference to the same proposition. The vote follows:

Counties—	For Free Schools.	Against.
Randolph	1,389	573
Jay	503	187
Blackford	245	87
Henry	1,072	1,404
Madison	488	1,182
Grant	880	424
Wayne	2,492	1,420
LaPorte	1,712	207

It will be noticed that La Porte, one of the counties on the northern line of the state, and settled largely by New England people, gave a heavy majority for free schools, as did all the northern Indiana counties. To explain satisfactorily the results of the vote in Delaware county and vicinity seems impossible, except that the sentiment for free schools seemed weakest in those counties whose percentage of illiteracy had been greatest.

The following legislature provided for a general tax for the support of common schools, and then referred the law to the people for approval. This question was in concrete form and touched the people more nearly since it provided for increased taxation. The voters of Delaware county showed themselves averse to any such taxation by giving a majority of 286 against the law. In the state at large the law was approved by a vote of 79,079, against 63,312, sixty-one counties voting for the measure and twenty-nine against it.

But before this law became effective for the improvement of the schools, a new constitution was adopted by the people, and pursuant to the provision that a general system of education should be established the school law of June 14, 1852, was passed. This marked the passing of the district system of schools and the beginning of the era of actual free schools. It abolished the congressional township as limiting school organizations, and made the civil townships into school corporations. Cities and incorporated towns were made school corporations distinct from the townships in which located.

Delaware County Seminary.

In the scheme of education that prevailed before the adoption of the new constitution, the place now taken by the township high school was taken by the county seminary, which was supposed to offer instruction intermediate between that of the common school and the state university. The Delaware County Seminary during its existence gave instruction to hundreds of boys and girls who otherwise would never have received any of what was then considered the "higher education," and many of the best known people of the county were students in that institution. To "graduate from the Seminary" was equivalent to graduation from the high school of this time, and because schools of that grade were not so numerous and their privileges not so free and attainable as those of the high schools now, attendance at the Seminary was doubtless esteemed as the highest educational advantage.

The County Seminary was established in 1841, its first trustees being B. F. Haycock, Samuel G. Campbell and John Jack. A square was donated by George W. Garst, upon which a building was constructed and many other citizens contributed generously. One of the first teachers was Volney

Willson. For several years the Seminary was little better than a common school, but with the advent of James S. Ferris as principal in 1847, the school was advanced to the rank which its name implied. Associated with him was Russell B. Abbott, and both are still gratefully remembered by some who were pupils during the late forties. Mr. Ferris resigned in the summer of 1850, and was succeeded by G. W. Hoss, a graduate of Asbury University. Other teachers were Pierre L. Munnis and Marshall White. In later years, before the development of the high schools, there were several private academies that gave many young people the education which they needed above that offered by the common schools. Luther W. Emerson, George H. Richardson,* E. J. Rice and William Richardson are those who are specially mentioned in this connection.

The following is a list of the students attending the Delaware County Seminary during the spring session ending May 22, 1846:

FEMALES.

Almira Davis,
Martha J. Davis,
Elizabeth Dragoo,
Mary Russey,
Cynthia R. Harlan,
Melissa A. Turner,
Sarah E. Taylor,
Mary E. Taylor,
Elizabeth K. Jackson,
Mary A. Perkins,
Margaret Griffin,
Edith Dragoo.
Clarissa Griffin,
Ethelinda Cooper,
Samantha Cooper,
Sarah A. Stewart,
Cynthia J. Brown,
Josephine Norris,
Emily Comerford,
Eliza Hoon.
Nancy J. Martin,
Henrietta Williams,
Seloma Coffeen,
Sarah Docherty,
Melvina Swain,

Mary E. Neely,
Martha J. Neely,
Emily E. Jack,
Mary F. Willard,
Emily C. Willard,
Anna Halstead,
Clara A. Jackson,
Frances C. Sayre,
Martha A. Janes,
Hannah A. Janes,
Mary M. Rockinfield,
Phoebe A. Davis,
Margaret A. Conn,
Juliet Minshall,
Elizabeth Sutton,
Nancy E. Nottingham,
Narcissa Simmons,
Mary E. Barnes,
Rachel A. Salisbury,
Mary J. Salisbury,
Psyche A. Jewell,
Irene Jewell.
Nancy M. Fisher,
Margaret A. Cunningham.

MALES.

Oliver J. Norris,
Harvey M. Perkins,
Nathaniel F. Ethell,
James Johnson,
Henry C. Sayre,
Richard Halstead,
George H. Harlan,
John M. Russey,
Wallace Hibbits,

William Coffeen,
Martin R. Harlan,
Alfred Rhodes,
Samuel Janes,
Ithamer W. Russey,
Henry C. Hodge,
Thadeus Halstead,
John Hoon,
Minus B. Marshall,

* Killed at the battle of South Mountain, Maryland, September 14, 1862.

James M. Davis,
Thomas J. Brady,
Eliltu H. Swain,
John A. Klein,
Evender C. Kennedy,
William A. Maddy,
Golesberry S. Maddy,
Martin V. B. Comerford,
Othniel Gilbert,
Orlando Swain,
Horace Williams,
Thomas Gilbert,
Charles D. Sayro,

Henry Wachtell,
William Slover,
James W. Sansbury,
John T. Walling,
Mark Anthony Stewart,
William A. Jewell,
Robert Irwin, Jr.,
William R. W. Irwin,
Thomas B. Jewell,
John Heal,
David R. Armitage,
Peter Saunders,
James Shipley.

School Supervision.

For many years there was lack of uniformity among the various townships in school affairs, resulting from the absence of anything like a central county supervision. It was not until 1873 that an important step was taken toward unity in school management, by the creation, in that year, of the office of county superintendent, a county board of education and of township institutes. Previous to that time the county examiner had exercised such general supervision as was permitted, and his reports show that he seldom interfered with the local school bodies.

Until 1837 the trustees of each congressional township had examined applicants for teaching positions. From 1837 to 1853 the circuit court appointed three persons as examiners; this appointing power was transferred to the county commissioners in 1853. In 1861 the number of examiners was reduced to one, with service term of three years. Those who held this position after the law of 1861 were E. J. Rice, William Richardson, Fred E. Putnam, Thomas J. Brady, Arthur C. Mellette, Ralph S. Gregory and O. M. Todd. Mr. Todd was in the office when the county examiner was abolished and his duties assumed by the county superintendent. Mr. Todd was the first to hold the office of county superintendent.

With the law of 1873 the county board of education was made to consist of the township trustees, the presidents of school boards of towns and cities and the county superintendent. The county superintendent was elected by the township trustees, for a term of two years, and the trustees and the superintendent have complete oversight of the schools of the county. By the same law the township institute became an effective instrument for securing unity in school work and raising the standards of the teaching body.

O. M. Todd served as county superintendent under the new law for six years. Albert W. Clancy was elected by the trustees in June, 1879, and held the office two terms. June 4, 1883, J. O. Lewellen was elected to the office, and by re-elections served until 1897. Since 1897 Mr. Chas. A. Van Matre has held the office of superintendent. In 1899 the term was lengthened to four years.

Early Schools in the Various Townships.

Since the first schools in Delaware county were subscription schools, organized and maintained by voluntary association and contribution of the settlers, it seldom happened that formal record of the schools was kept, and their history was usually preserved only in tradition and the memory of those who had been connected with them as pupils or parents of pupils. Quite often the formation of a school was not effected in strict accordance with the rules of the state, and owing to the fact that during the first ten years of this country's history no income was derived from the state fund, there was little incentive to follow the prescribed formalities. Doubtless some voluntary efforts resulting in the holding of school terms have escaped the attention of the annalists who have recorded the facts concerning the first schools, and now, since even the pupils of these schools have passed away, it would be impossible to determine and to honor with mention all those early schools.

The building of the first schoolhouse in the county has already been mentioned. This was built on land owned by Aaron Richardson, one of the first settlers of Perry township, and was only a short distance east of the site now covered by New Burlington. The Van Arsdoll, Reese and many other pioneer children attended this school, and among the first teachers was Aaron Richardson. Another schoolhouse is said to have been erected about 1829, and several other schools are mentioned in the years that followed. Nothing more than the fact, however, is recorded, and in some instances the name of a teacher.

"The first school in Muncietown," according to the local historian, John S. Ellis, "was taught in a log cabin that stood at or near the southwest corner of Main and Walnut streets, during the winter of 1829-30 by Henry Tomlinson, a native of North Carolina, who had come here a short time previously from Preble county, Ohio. The families represented in this school were about eight in number, sending some twenty pupils. It was maintained by subscription, the patrons agreeing to pay and paying so much for each and every scholar. Such was the custom of those days. As a consequence the schools were not continuous, occupying about three months during the winter, with an occasional summer term." The subsequent history of Muncie schools belongs in a separate article.

Mt. Pleasant township having been among the first settled, it is natural to look there for early schools. Yet, so far as known, the first school was taught there in 1831. In this case the teacher became in later years one of the county's best known men. His rise to prominence had already begun, in fact, and the year following his work as teacher for the pioneer families then gathered in Mt. Pleasant he went to the legislature, and a few years later was elected judge of the circuit court. David Kilgore had only recently come to the county, fresh from his law studies, and during the summer of 1831 he gathered some of the pioneer children in a deserted cabin and gave them, so far as can be ascertained, the first formal instruction imparted in this township. In 1832 a hewn-log building was erected for school purposes, which was long known as the Reed schoolhouse, being near No. 6 or Liberty schoolhouse. During the '40s several schools were formed and buildings erected, among them the Antioch school, Nebo school, Mt. Pleasant school, Shepherd school and a school in Yorktown.

In Salem township, in section 21, where David Van Matre had made settlement as early as 1826, the first school of the township was taught in 1828-29. The teacher was Elza Watkins, who did not become permanently identified with the county, but who was long remembered as having been a man of unusual culture and intellectual ability, and equipped beyond the average for the task of directing the young minds of pioneer children. Before the next winter a schoolhouse was erected on the farm of John Van Matre, and as successor of Mr. Watkins James Perdieu taught the second term of school. Rev. Abner Perdieu was also one of the early teachers of the township. A school was taught in 1833-34 on the site where afterward was located school No. 7, three miles east of Daleville, the lot having been donated by Henry Miller.

Of the early schools in Delaware township, Mr. Ellis has given a very interesting account in his history of the county. Joseph Godlove, one of the original settlers in section 4, taught the first school in his kitchen. "As to whether he had any other rooms in his house than the kitchen we are left to guess," remarked Mr. Ellis, who then continues with the following description of school custom. "It was a common practice in those early times for the school teachers to board by turns with the patrons, and in order to equalize matters he was supposed to board the most where the greatest number of pupils were sent from. While this arrangement was just, it was not always pleasant, as the teacher had some choice as to his boarding house . . . The week the teacher was to board at our house was always looked forward to with much interest. Mince pies were baked, 'crulls' were fried, the best applebury was opened, and a general talk had between the mother and children as to proper conduct in the presence of the teacher. And, oh! how proudly the mother would sit, the bright knitting needles flashing in the firelight as they were dexterously plied by her nimble fingers, while she listened to Mary and John rehearse their lessons to the teacher. . . .

"In the year 1836 the cabin which William Venard first settled, near the center of what is now the town of Albany, was converted into a schoolhouse, and a three months term of school taught by a man whose name has been forgotten. In the following year (1837) the first building erected expressly for school purposes was built on the farm of Adam Keever, some two miles south of Albany. This was a hewn-log building, much superior to the buildings in which the schools had been held formerly. This house became noted as being the first representative of the free school system in Delaware township, for in the winter of that year the term began and the public money, or 'congressional fund,' belonging to the township, was appropriated to pay the teacher. But unfortunately this fund proved sufficient only to meet the expenses of one-third of the term (one month) and the remaining two months' salary was made up pro rata by subscription, as was usual in such cases."

In Liberty township, because the settlers had not been able to maintain a school up to the year 1831, John Moore, who lived in the western edge of the township, sent his son down to Wayne county to receive instruction from one of the many excellent schools there. A short time later Mr. Moore converted a deserted cabin on his farm into a schoolhouse, and the parents of the neighborhood children having subscribed for a teacher's pay a two months' term of school was taught by Samuel Collier from Muncie. Near the old settlement of Smithfield a cabin was made into a schoolhouse and Anderson R. East taught there during the winter of 1832-33. In the northeast part of the township a school was taught by Amos Meeks in 1839.

In Monroe township a cabin on the land of Robert Gibson served as the first schoolhouse, where the Gibson children and others of the neighborhood gathered during the winter of 1830-31 to receive instruction from William Abrams. Deserted cabins were used for schoolhouses until 1838, when the first schoolhouse was erected in this township.

A cabin on the farm of Thomas Reeves in Hamilton township was the first schoolhouse, so far as known, and of the man who posed as teacher and exemplar to the few children who came to him during the winter of 1838-39, nothing is left to record except his name—Joseph Custer.

It seems that the majority of the pioneer teachers were men. Unruliness was characteristic of early schools, and it was thought necessary that a strong man should sit at the teacher's desk to subdue the restive spirits of the "big boys." However, in the earliest school known in Union township, taught in 1836, the teacher was Miss Susan Hanley. She taught in a cabin on the farm of Junius McMillen, in the east part of the township, and besides the McMillen children her scholars came from the homes of Wilson Martin, William Essley, Philip Stoner, Aaron Mote and Francis Harris, the teacher's salary being estimated at one dollar and a half a scholar. In the following year a log schoolhouse was built on the farm of Aaron Mote, and during that winter a man, William Campbell, was employed as teacher. Over in the western part of the township, in section 18, the first term of school was being conducted in the Green schoolhouse, on land owned by Havilla Green, Robert Wharton being the teacher.

As the first settlers of Niles township were grouped in the southwest corner. so, naturally, the first term of school was taught there, in a cabin on section 32, erected by John Sutton several years previously. This term was held in 1837. A year or so later, schools were taught on sections 28 and 19. The first building erected for special use as a school was on the farm of Walter Mann in section 36, in 1839. About this time school districts were formed, and a schoolhouse erected in each one.

In Harrison township it is thought that the first school was taught in a building erected for that purpose, on the southeast quarter of section 29, during the winter of 1834-35.

Washington township, as will be remembered, was early settled, but mainly by traders, so that it is not surprising that nearly ten years elapsed before the first effort was made to maintain a school. It was in the house of the pioneer William Heal, in section 11, that Mrs. Olive Heal, his wife, taught the first school for the benefit of her own and her neighbors' children in the winter of 1833-34. No schoolhouse was built until 1839, and Ezra Maynard was the name of the first teacher who occupied it. In the meantime, besides Mrs. Heal, school had been held in the Methodist church by William Wharton in 1838. In 1840 the second schoolhouse in the township was built at Wheeling, and as settlement proceeded other schools came into existence.

All these early schools, it will be understood, were subscription schools, and the history of each and of all was very similar. Of co-ordination and systematic methods of instruction there was nothing until long after the pioneer period had passed, and, as already indicated, little was done in this direction until the general law of 1873. To add anything of importance to the early history of education in Delaware county, further than what has been given, seems impossible. The pioneer schools seldom varied from the type that has been described. But to the men and women whose memory goes back to those old schools, there is an individuality of association, a distinctness of details, and a fondness for their recollection that no words of description would satisfy.

Consolidated Schools.

Until within the past decade half the school population of Delaware county was dependent on the ungraded district school for all the educational advantages offered them during childhood. Outside of Muncie, few schools had passed beyond the one-room one-teacher stage. So far as educational efficiency is concerned, the old district school merits little praise. It has a place of affection in the minds of all who attended one in youth, many associations dear to Americans cling about this institution in its primitive forms, and the "little red schoolhouse" has produced men and women of such sterling character, high-minded ability, and lofty patriotism, that their names and deeds will always exist as ready arguments for those who desire a defense of the old-fashioned education. But while the district school may not have failed in its essential purposes, it never measured up to the educational standards of the present day. Grading and classification, and specialization in teaching, which were never possible in the district school, are fundamental in the modern system of education. In towns and cities, where population is relatively dense, the grade principle is easily introduced, but in the country the advantages of classification were seldom obtained until a means was discovered for bringing the children of several districts, or a whole township, to one central school.

For a number of years some of the Delaware county towns have main_ tained schools ranking above the ordinary district school. Selma had, in 1868, erected a two-story brick building, containing four rooms, and costing $6,000, and in two of the rooms had established a school for the children of the town and district, employing two teachers. With the in_ crease of prosperity and population brought about by the gas boom, Albany and Eaton each developed the district school into the graded system, with two or more teachers dividing the responsibilities of instruction between them.

Jacob H. Koontz and David Kilgore were most actively concerned with the establishment of a free public school in Yorktown. After the law of 1852 enabling the people to vote taxes for public schools, the people of the township voted a small levy for that purpose, and then, a few weeks later, re_ considered their action and voted against the levy. Determined that York_ town should have a school, these two citizens secured about six hundred dollars by popular subscription, and, a lot having been donated by O. H. Smith, a one-story frame building, containing two rooms, was erected, and a public school for six months each year conducted. The subscribers to the school fund were afterward reimbursed for their contributions. In March, 1884, Yorktown completed and dedicated a new school building, H. W. Zuckle being principal at the time.

In 1880 there were, outside of Muncie, graded schools in Selma, York_ town, Daleville, Albany. In 1895 the graded schools of the county, outside of Muncie, were at the following points: Daleville, Cross Roads, York_ town, Cammack, Gaston, Cowan, Congerville, Whitely, West Side, Roger_ ton, Shideler, Eaton, Selma, Albany. At the present writing, in the fall of 1907, there are, in the county, outside of Muncie, Eaton and Albany, twenty-one graded schools, a number of them housed in handsome, modern buildings, with the best of educational facilities and the teachers in many cases are university graduates.

Such remarkable developments in education are not the result of in_ crease in population nor in material wealth, but have been produced by an entirely new movement in education. Marvelous as have been the changes wrought by the rural free delivery and the interurban traction service, they are not greater in permanent benefit to the rural communities than the new system of education that now prevails over half of Delaware county.

The experimental stages of the movement and a forecasting of results that has since been more than verified, were described in an editorial in the Muncie News, Dec. 24, 1897, at which date, as is evident, nothing had yet been accomplished in this county, outside of the towns, toward grading schools. The article reads as follows:

In these columns a few days ago reference was made to a suggestion of county superintendent of public instruction as to the advisability of consolidating the district schools of townships, partly because some of the schools, being sparsely attended, cost more than is required per capita for larger schools. This consolidation of the district schools in the center of the township has been tried in one or two instances and found to work admirably. In Webster township, Wayne county, there were formerly three school buildings, at this time there is but one, and it is answering every purpose of the three and it has been fully demonstrated that much better work is being done at a less expense. The school is located in the village of Webster, which is about the center of the township. Children who live a considerable distance away are carried to and fro in hacks, which are maintained by the trustees. Superintendent Wineberg says that the new system is working admirably and it is being gradually adopted in several other townships. A number of schools have been abolished in Perry, Dalton and Jefferson townships, same county, and it will not be long until there is but one in each. It was first thought the new scheme would be productive of no good and would only result in great inconvenience to children and greater expense to the townships. The experiment was made, and as it has proved a success it is thought its adoption will take place all over the state within a few years at the furthest.

The Wabash Plain Dealer says that the superintendent in that county has been investigating the subject and found to his surprise that some of the district schools had not more than ten pupils enrolled. As the teacher of these ten pupils receives $35 or $40 a month, it makes tuition come high. This superintendent thinks that many of the districts could be consolidated and graded schools be built up without discommoding pupils, and resulting in better schools at less cost. It is possible that in some localities or under some conditions the consolidation plan would not work well, but it is believed that in most localities it could be applied advantageously. Certainly one centrally located, well conducted graded school in a township is better than several feeble and sparsely attended ones.

Only a few weeks after the appearance of this editorial, Superintendent Van Matre, with Trustees Thornburg and Hollinger, investigated the Wayne county consolidation, and were so far convinced of the feasibility of the system as applied to conditions in Delaware county, that consolidation of schools has since been a fixed policy with the county superintendent and with many of the trustees, and as a principle has consistently gained ground since that time, only two or three individual cases showing reversion to the old system.

Practically, Perry township has the honor of having the first consolidated school, though all the requirements of such a school were not met. In the fall of 1898 the pupils of district 7, numbering seven in all, were conveyed by wagon to school No. 8. No grading was attempted, and the districts were not formally consolidated. But the experiment demonstrated the practicability of transporting pupils at the expense of the district, showing that the results were better when two small schools were combined and the expense less. The trial in Perry township was all that was done in 1898, but since that year consolidation has made rapid headway and has long since proved its value and passed beyond experimental stages.

The arguments for consolidated and graded schools were generally expressed in two categories, as follows:—

Defects of small district schools—

> Some inexperienced teachers must be placed in small district schools.
> Too many grades under one teacher.
> Classes too small to create enthusiasm.
> Proper classification impossible.
> No advanced work.
> Cost per pupil above average.

Advantages of graded schools—

> High school work in reach of all.
> Better classification.
> Ready and frequent promotions.
> Teachers prepared in special lines.
> Discipline easier.
> More life and enthusiasm.
> Economy in equipment.
> Social life of child extended.

The first thorough consolidation of districts was accomplished in Hamilton township, while William Campbell was trustee. In the fall of 1899 districts Nos. 1 and 4 were abandoned, two one-horse wagons were used to transport the ten or twelve children from each district to the school at Royerton (No. 8). It is of interest to note that schoolhouse No. 4 had been built only two years before this consolidation took place. At that time Royerton had a new two-room building, and when the new pupils came the old school building was used to accommodate the primary grades. Three teachers were employed. This was the first school in this county to adopt the principle of consolidation with graduation and centralization.

The next school consolidation was effected in Salem township, Superintendent Van Matre's own district. The Cross Roads school (No. 10) was already graded, having been made so in 1891, had two teachers and a two-room building. In 1900 the seven pupils in district No. 11 were hauled to Cross Roads and distributed among the grades, the most distant pupil living not more than five miles. This accession to Cross Roads did not necessitate another teacher nor did it increase to an appreciable extent the burden of instruction or extension of facilities in the school; yet the advantages accruing to the No. 10 pupils from the consolidation were all that the advocates of the new system had claimed. In 1901 another district in Salem was dissolved, when the seven pupils of Pike's Peak school (No. 2) were conveyed, some to the Daleville school (a four-room school) and some to a neighboring district school.

In 1901 Hamilton township made another great advance in consolidation. Districts Nos. 2, 5, 7 and 10 were all abandoned and the children conveyed to Royerton (No. 8), this making six schools that were merged with No. 8. The Royerton school, which by this time had four rooms and four teachers, drew its patronage from an area of twenty square miles. Seven wagons were used for conveyance of the 129 pupils, transportation costing $8.75 a day or about seven cents per pupil.

Liberty township was the third township to try consolidation. District No. 4 had been abandoned some time previously and the pupils had gone to Selma, the pupils providing their own conveyance, but in 1901 the 24 pupils of Nos. 10 and 4 were conveyed to Selma (which had a four-room school).

Consolidation in Center township also dates from 1901. District No. 10 of Hamilton, mentioned above, was a joint district, and when it was abandoned those pupils living in Center were given to No. 7 in Center (Riverside school). At the same time a partial consolidation of districts Nos. 3 and 9 was made with the Riverside school, a few of the pupils of No. 9 being hauled in order to give them the benefit of gradation. This was discontinued after two years.

The fall of 1902 found consolidations in five other localities. In Monroe township the first consolidation was district No. 6 with No. 5 (Cowan). In Center the Boyceton school (No. 11) was combined with Whitely (No. 14). In Perry the first real consolidation was effected. Petitions from four districts, Nos. 7, 8, 2 and 6, were filed with the trustee, and at the beginning of the fall terms four wagons were installed to carry the pupils of these districts to school No. 9. In the same year the Selma school in Liberty was increased by the granting of petitions from districts Nos. 2 and 3 that these schools be discontinued and their pupils conveyed to Selma.

In Union township Trustee Stradling had abandoned district No. 8 about 1899, but at that time sentiment was against the discontinuance of the old school districts and nothing in the way of real consolidation was done until 1902. By this time public opinion had so changed that no objections were made when district No. 6 was combined with No. 7.

1903-04.

Consolidation in this year was notable for the reversion of several districts to their original form. Despite the patent advantages in consolidation, the new system has everywhere made progress slowly. There is a sentimental attachment for the old district schools that becomes a formidable obstruction in the movement to establish fewer and better schools. The old school at the crossroads, within walking distance of every house in the district, was good enough for the preceding generation, why should the children of today be removed from their familiar home surroundings and conveyed four or five miles to be among strange associates? The district school was a central point in the community, and almost without exception in this part of the middle west was the pioneer institution. It preceded the church. There the settlers met to vote and perform civil business; there the problems that confront a new social organization were discussed and solved; there the people met for social enjoyment, and there they came together for religious worship. The schoolhouse was the focal point of pioneer life, and it is not strange that the descendants of the pioneers parted with the institution so regretfully and often unwillingly. For this reason and for various specific and local causes, sentiment has usually been divided on the subject of district consolidation, and the effective work accomplished in this county is the result of persistent argument and progressive activity on the part of the township trustees and the county superintendent.

In 1903 the Pike's Peak school (No. 2) in Salem township was re-established with its original limits, the patrons having become dissatisfied with consolidation, and at the present writing this district still maintains a separate school. But to take the place of No. 2, the Davis school (No. 9) was added to the Cross Roads school, and also No. 7 (Center school) was abandoned and its pupils distributed between the Cross Roads and the Daleville schools. District No. 7 retained its boundaries and was re-established in 1905, and in the meantime as no wagon was used to convey its pupils, no real consolidation was effected.

In Monroe township in this year, No. 8 was abandoned, the pupils going to Cowan, and also the children residing in that part of district No. 10 lying within Monroe township were added to Cowan (No. 5). In Perry township there was a breaking away from consolidation, when districts Nos. 2 and 6 were re-established. In Liberty township the Selma school was still further increased by the conveyance of the pupils of district No. 1 to that point. The first consolidation in Niles township was effected in 1903 when No. 4 was combined with No. 9.

1904-05.

Salem and Perry townships were the points of activity this year. In Salem No. 8 was consolidated with Cross Roads, making the latter the center of four original districts. In Perry a change of sentiment occurred favoring consolidation, and Nos. 2 and 6, which in the previous year had withdrawn, were again united with district No. 9.

1905-06.

School No. 9 was rapidly becoming the central and principal school of Perry township. In 1905 two new districts, Nos. 3 and 4, were annexed to it, making six districts that had been consolidated within the past three years.

In Salem township a new division of districts was made, by which No. 7 was re-established and enlarged by the annexation of No. 8, which was taken from No. 10.

In Liberty township Nos. 7 and 11 began taking their pupils to Selma.

In this year the first schools were consolidated in Delaware township. The town of Albany already had a good graded school and drew to it a number of children from the surrounding country. In 1905 the Stafford school (No. 2) was consolidated with the Albany town school. In addition, district No. 4 was combined with district No. 9, though without grading, and No. 8 was combined with No. 11.

In Center township No. 1 was combined with No. 14 (Whitely), and also the wagon that had previously conveyed the pupils from the Center-Hamilton joint district to the Riverside school now brought them to Whitely.

1906.

This year is notable by Washington township entering the consolidation movement. The Gaston school (No. 10) was a natural center for graded school work, and in the fall of 1906 districts Nos. 8, 9 and 11 were combined with it. In the same year school No. 9 in Perry received the pupils of district No. 1, and the Selma school district increased its area by the inclusion of districts Nos. 6 and 8.

1907.

A new law became effective in the spring of this year, favoring the consolidation movement. This made it obligatory upon a trustee, when the average attendance in a district fell below twelve, to abandon the school and find education for the pupils in another district. This law has already affected schools in four townships. In Salem, district No. 12 had to be abandoned, the pupils now going to Daleville. In Monroe, No. 2 was abandoned and combined with No. 5 (Cowan). In Niles, the pupils of No. 7 have been combined with No. 9, and in Delaware township school No. 10 has been annexed to Albany.

Besides these schools that have been abandoned according to the new law, regular consolidation has been effected in several other instances. In Monroe township No. 4 has been consolidated with No. 5. This year has seen the complete consolidation of Liberty township into one district, with Selma school at the center. No. 9 was the last outlying school to come in, and at this date the thirty-six square miles of Liberty's area are all included in one school jurisdiction, and every child in the township has school advantages hardly inferior to the best city schools.

In the southwest corner of Delaware township the sentiment of the people has been for consolidation during the past seven years. The De Soto school (No 11) is the natural center for a consolidated district, and yet owing to the lack of building accommodations the trustee has never been able until this year to permit consolidation. At various times as far back as 1900 districts Nos. 8, 9, and 4 have petitioned to combine with De Soto. In 1907, in answer to another set of petitions from Nos. 4 and 9, the trustee granted consolidation and at this writing a new building is in process of construction in De Soto to accommodate the increased attendance at that point. No. 5 is also combined with De Soto, and in consequence of school-house No. 7 having been burned a short time before the opening of the school term, it has become necessary for the pupils of that district also to attend at De Soto.

Some of the results of consolidation may be briefly stated. It is less than ten years since the movement started in this county, and the consolidated districts now embrace nearly half the entire area of the county. Mt. Pleasant and Harrison townships are the only ones in which consolidation has as yet obtained no foothold. The other townships have areas under consolidation as follows: Liberty, 36 (square miles) ; Perry, 27; Hamilton, 25; Delaware, 23; Salem, 22; Monroe, 14½; Center (exclusive of Muncie), 12; Washington, 10; Niles, 10; Union, 6. Out of a total area of 395 square miles, outside of Muncie, 185½ square miles are consolidated, practically one-half the county. Evidently consolidation has passed the experimental stage in this county. The conveyance of pupils has been proved practicable and less expensive than the wages of a separate teacher. The increased efficiency of the central school is in itself the best vindication of the system.

Representative Consolidated Schools.

Royerton had the first modern school building for the accommodation of the pupils of the combined districts. In 1903 a four-room addition was built to the two-room school which had first served the district. The building, which stands on the south edge of the village, is the best public structure in Hamilton township and in every way a credit to the school architecture of the county. It is a two-story brick building, with large corridors on the second floor which are converted into an auditorium seating three hundred persons. In the basement is a lavatory, a modern steam heating apparatus is a welcome change from the stove to which many pupils had been accustomed in the old district schoolhouse, and in convenience, comforts and sanitation the Royerton school is equal to most city schoolhouses. The cost of the building was $17,500. The Royerton high school has a recognized efficiency in second education, having been recently commissioned by the state university. The school has seven teachers and is maintained eight months in the year. The average daily attendance of pupils in Hamilton township is 309, all but five square miles belonging to the consolidated area. The daily cost per pupil, including transportation, is about 16 cents. Going back about twenty years, we find that with a school term of six months, the average cost per day was between ten and twelve cents per pupil. In 1884 a teacher's pay averaged $1.85 a day, while now it is $2.93. Taking these things into consideration, the average daily cost per pupil under the new system is very little more than it was twenty years ago, while even the most prejudiced would have to admit that the advantages offered by the Royerton school are far and away superior to those afforded in the best district schools. Some of the teachers are university graduates, all have had special training for their work, and the classification of pupils in grades makes the teachers' work more easy and more efficient.

The handsomest school building in the county, outside of Muncie, is that which was built in Selma in 1904. As already mentioned, Selma had a four-room building erected many years ago before consolidation was thought of. With the enlargement of district No. 5, more room was necessary, and the structure which is now used for school purposes for all the children of Liberty township is a two-story, eight-room brick and stone building that cost about $23,000, and is thoroughly modern. This and other schools erected during the last few years have a special excellence of design that suits them to all the demands that may be made upon them in the future as in the present. This design might be called a multiple unit system, the unit being a two-story two-room building complete in itself, and yet capable of combination with similar units so that a house of four, six or eight rooms may be made as needed. Thus, the Selma school is really a combination of four structural units, joined by corridors that in themselves increase the floor space of the building and afford, on the second floor, an auditorium with seating capacity for 700. An automatic steam blast heating apparatus is another modern feature of this building. The average attendance at the Selma school during 1906-07 was about 310, of whom 269 were transported at public expense. For the entire year there were but 68 cases of tardiness.

In Perry township, Center school, in the center of the township, was originally a district school. In 1899 a high school department had been

Consolidated School at Royerton.

established in a store building at New Burlington, but this arrangement was not satisfactory to the people in the east side of the township, and the result was the addition of a one-room building to the Center school to be used for high school purposes. There was no consolidation as yet, but the enlarged Center school was the nucleus around which consolidation was effected. In 1902, when the four districts were combined with Center (No. 9), the room which had been used for high school purposes was partitioned into two rooms, making three rooms for the accommodation of the grades. These rooms were used until the construction of the present building, which was finished about January, 1906. The Perry schoolhouse is built of cement blocks, is a two-story, four-room building, with an auditorium and cost about $12,000, being equipped with mechanical furnace and all the conveniences. There are four teachers. The enrollment is 212, of whom 203 are conveyed at public expense. The average attendance during the past year was 168. The other school in the township, the only district not consolidated, has an enrollment of 57.

The DeSoto building, already mentioned, was constructed in 1907, at a cost of $13,000, and is a two-story, brick, four rooms, and with the auditorium feature. Two other township buildings should be mentioned. In 1902 Center township erected the Roosevelt school in Congerville, a two-story brick, six rooms, costing about $14,000. Properly speaking this is a district school, built to accommodate the large school population in Muncie's suburb. However, the old joint district on the south edge of the township has been added to the Congerville school, and one wagon conveys the pupils from that neighborhood. The Longfellow school in Whitely is another handsome township school, erected by Center township in 1905, a two-story, eight-room brick building on a fine campus near McCulloch park, and costing about $25,000. The Whitely school, at the beginning of the consolidation movement which resulted in several districts being annexed to it, was located in a four-room frame building two blocks east of the present site.

MUNCIE SCHOOLS.

An account of the Delaware County Seminary and of the establishment of the first school on the site of Muncie has been given. Besides these facts, little of interest can be said about Muncie schools for a number of years. A belief that school facilities were not up to the standard during the forties is evidenced in the following excerpts from a criticism that appeared in the Muncie *Journal* March 21, 1846: "The town of Muncie has, I believe, about 800 inhabitants . . . which would give 133 children between the ages of 6 and 14 who should be constantly in school. From 6 to 16 constitute one-fourth of the population. This would give two hundred. Now deduct 25 per cent for necessary detention and you have 150 children in your town which should be at school. What are the facts as to the number actually attending school? Not 60, including those from the country and over 16. . . . Look at your sister county, Randolph. The seminary at Winchester has over one hundred students. And yet the population of Winchester is less than that of Muncie."

Muncie schools were under the direction of the township trustee until 1853, and were supported only by the townshhip school fund and general tax. Under such conditions free public schools were not possible, and "pay schools" were the rule with the exception of a few weeks each year. In June, 1853, a special school tax was voted down, but in the fall of the same year the proposition to levy a special tax carried. At this time Muncie had two schools, one of them in the seminary building, and the other, becoming too large for the schoolroom, was moved, about 1854, to the Methodist church.

During the ten years from 1855, while Muncie was a town corporation, the officials under whose direction the schools were improved were F. E. Putnam, Wm. F. Jones, Edward G. Keasby, who were on the board most of this period, George W. Spilker and Robert Winton serving brief terms. These trustees, in their report for 1859, said that in the spring of 1855 they "had found the corporation without schoolhouse or real estate, with the exception of one lot." In that year the trustees bought the old seminary building, and in the spring of 1856 commenced the erection of a new schoolhouse, which, until torn down to make room for the modern building, was the south room of the Washington school. A. J. Finch was principal in the Washington building and O. S. Howe in the seminary building. With an enumeration of nearly four hundred, even then there was not sufficient room. It is said that when a family was largely represented in school, the younger members were told to go home and remain until there should be more room or the older ones had completed their course. With the repairs and additions to the seminary, these two buildings served for school purposes until Muncie became a city. Until a few weeks, three months at most, of free school was afforded, each family contributing its share to support school for additional time.

Arthur F. Patterson, John A. Husted and Stacy A. Haines were the first school board under city government in 1865. They found the Washington school in good condition, capable of accommodating about three hundred pupils, but pronounced the seminary building unfit for use. In the meantime the school enumeration had increased to nearly eight hundred, with an enrollment of over six hundred, so that the Washington school could not accommodate more than a third of the children in the city. It was finally decided to remove the seminary building and build a two-story brick structure on the site. At a total cost of nearly $8,000 a schoolhouse, 33 by 65

Prof. George H. Richardson
Resigned his position as principal of
Muncie Schools to enter army,
and was killed at South
Mountain, Maryland,
Sep. 14th 1862.

feet, and two stories, was completed by December, 1866, and thenceforth
was known as the Jefferson school. This location, when first occupied by
the seminary, was thought to be out in the country. Many persons are still
living who were pupils of the city schools about this time, and will be interested in recalling the names of the teachers; they were: Charles R. Paine,
superintendent; Julia Gilbert, grammer room; Sophia Gilbert, intermediate,
all in the Washington school; while in No. 2, or Jefferson school, the teachers were Thomas Marshall, Josephine Gilbert, Abraham J. Buckles, Miss
Sarah M. Kemper. Including several assistants, there were twelve teachers
altogether, and the entire length of the free-school term was 60 days.

Two conspicuous figures now become identified with Muncie's educational affairs, and so influence and mold them that the schools became largely
representative of their ability and personality. A change in the superintendency was made in the summer of 1867, and Hamilton S. McRae was
chosen to that position and Miss Mary Emma Montgomery became principal
of the high school. At the same time the school board resolved to inaugurate
a free-school system worthy of the name, extending the term to ten months
or 200 days.

These changes were epochal in the history of Muncie's schools. Mr.
McRae, who was born in Indiana, January 2, 1833, was an organizer as well
as educator, and gained a place of lasting esteem because of his work in
Muncie. A few years after coming to Muncie he married Miss Montgomery,
the principal of the high school, a woman whose many excellencies of character and versatile ability brought her into prominence in various movements
connected with education. She was best known, after her marriage, as Mrs.
Emma Mont. McRae. Her activity in woman's club work is told on other
pages. Mr. McRae was superintendent of Muncie schools until 1883, and
four years later, in April, 1887, he died at Marion. He was buried in Muncie
and the honor in which he was held by all classes of citizens was shown in
many ways at the time. Besides his activity in the schools, he has been
given the credit for organizing the Muncie public library.

During the decade from 1870 to 1880 notable progress was made in
every department. The number of school buildings increased from two to
four; the number of teachers from ten to fourteen; the enrollment from
about nine hundred to nearly thirteen hundred; the amount paid teachers
from $4,655 to over eight thousand, while the value of school property
increased from $20,000 to over $80,000.

In the first year of Mr. McRae's superintendency the high school was
moved from the Washington building and quartered in the basement of the
Universalist Church. In 1873 another extension became necessary, when
a room was rented for the children living south of the railroad. From this
as a beginning came the Jackson school. Two rooms, afterward forming

the north end of the Jackson school, were built and opened in February, 1876, and in 1878 the south half of the building was completed. This was No. 3 school building, and was located on the south side.

Plans for the erection of the high school building, on the square surrounded by High, Adams, Charles and Franklin streets, were made in September, 1878. This four-story brick building, with ground dimensions of about 90 by 75 feet, is now the oldest school building of the city, and the only one in use before natural gas made a city out of the town. The building was completed some time during 1880, and is now the oldest public building in the city.

The progress of the schools during a quarter of a century afforded some interesting comparisons, which were stated by Mr. W. F. Jones in an address delivered in June, 1882. "In 1855," said he, "the city of Muncie had enumerated only 396 school children. At that time we had no school-house. . . . In 1880 we had scholars enrolled for the schools in Muncie, 1,790; we now have four large fine brick school buildings, of the value of $80,150. In 1880 we paid for tuition to our children $8,050. Our entire expenses for that year for all purposes in connection with our common and high school departments were $24,611.21."

The enrollment in the public schools in September, 1882, as given by the Daily News at the time, totaled 868, distributed in the four schools as follows:

High School:—Mrs. McRae's room, Mary Moore 1st Principal, Ella Blease, 2d Principal, 128; Primary, Lola Truitt, 60; Eva Kessler, 57. Total, 245.

Washington School:—D. H. H. Shewmaker, Principal, 51; Room 3, Kate Philips, 58; Room 2, Senora Silverburg, 52: Room 1, Lizzie Willard, 92. Total, 254.

Jefferson School:—May Hathaway, Principal, 37; Room 3, Alta Stiffler, 45; Room 2, Kate Kealy, 39; Room 1, Bessie Gilbert, 56. Total, 177.

Jackson School:—Harry Bowman, Principal, 21; Room 3, Flora Carpenter, 33; Room 2, Mrs. Monroe, 33; Room 1, Mary Hockett, 105. Total, 192.

A sketch of educational affairs in such a city as Muncie must be almost a continuous record of improvements, extensions, especially in buildings and facilities. During the fifties when the board built the brick building at Vine, Adams and Charles streets that was afterward called the Washington school, a distinct step had been taken in advancing the educational interests of Muncie. But less than thirty years afterward the agitation began for the removal of this part of the building (then only the south wing of the entire school building) and the erection of a modern structure on the site. However, the construction of the Washington school, which was the first of the modern school buildings that are now a matter of pride to the city and a distinct addition to its architecture, was not begun until June, 1889, after Muncie had begun its remarkable progress consequent upon the gas boom.

In the meantime Mr. McRae had resigned as superintendent of schools. He was followed by John M. Bloss, for a short term, who himself deserves prominence in the history of education both in Indiana and Delaware county. In June, 1887, W. R. Snyder, who had been principal of the high school, became superintendent. Under his progressive control the schools had a great growth. By the close of 1890 the city had eight school buildings and forty teachers, besides the Catholic parochial school. In that year a two-room addition to the Avondale school was completed, and in July construction of a four-room frame building was begun on the Jefferson school grounds. In January, 1891, an addition of four rooms was completed for the Jackson building.

Besides the existence of several art and other classes that were sometimes called "schools," several educational beginnings should be noted. The Muncie Business College was established about 1890, with J. W. Howard in charge, and its work and patronage continued in a flourishing condition from the start. A rival business college, known as the Ball Business School, was soon after established. In March, 1880, Mrs. N. C. Smith and Mrs. Theodore Riley started what afterward became known as the Industrial School, which existed for many years and accomplished results in practical benevolence that are immeasurable. It was a kind of mission Sunday school at first, meeting in Mrs. Smith's home and then in the mayor's office, but its scope expanded into a day school, and for many years its annual reports were a record of worthy benevolence which few of the more pretentious organizations could surpass. Mrs. Smith remained superintendent for years.

The Kindergarten movement was begun during the superintendency and largely at the suggestion of Mr. McRae. At a meeting of interested persons on March 19, 1879, the Kindergarten Association of Muncie was formed, to support a kindergarten, to which each member of the association had the privilege of sending one pupil. The first officers of the association were Mrs. Mary Kirby, president; Mrs. W. S. Richey, secretary; Mrs. Martha Little, treasurer. Miss Fannie C. Colcord was the first teacher obtained, and she opened a school with twenty-five members at the home of G. S. Maddy on March 31, 1879. On the completion of the high school building a room on the first floor was set aside for this purpose.

By January, 1892, there were 2,219 pupils in Muncie schools, against 1,419 in 1887, at the beginning of Mr. Snyder's term. In 1886 there were four buildings and 20 teachers, and in 1892, nine buildings and 45 teachers.

After the construction of the Washington school in the early nineties, it became a necessity, as a result of increase of wealth and population, to erect a large new schoolhouse every few years. In 1895 the Avondale school burned. It was the third schoolhouse erected within a few years for the accommodation of a rapidly growing school population, and the school board resolved to erect a building that should be ample for its purposes. In March, 1895, they obtained permission to issue $20,000 in bonds for the erection of a building at Sampson and Ohmer avenues, to be 106 by 100 feet in ground dimensions, a two-story stone and brick building, with basement and attic, of the most modern type. The contract was let in May and the building completed without delay. This was the Lincoln school.

The Blaine school was erected before the Lincoln, the school bond issue of $20,000 which was recently paid off having been made in July, 1892, for the erection of this building. Since 1895 the school city has built and equipped the Jefferson school building; purchased the grounds, built and equipped the Garfield and the McKinley school buildings; remodelled the Lincoln school building; installed new heating and ventilating systems in the Washington and the Lincoln buildings; installed system of sanitary closets in the Washington, High School, Lincoln and Jackson buildings; and planted trees, graded and improved the school grounds generally. All of these improvements, and interest on bonds, together with all necessary repairs, have been made and paid for without increasing in any way the indebtedness of the school city. The school property of Muncie, which is in a sense the material results of sixty years' progress, represents a total valuation of $354,200, as set forth in the following table:

	Grounds.	Buildings.	Contents.	Insurance.
High School	$ 40,000	$ 25,000	$ 5,000	$ 20,000
Jefferson School	12,000	32,000	5,000	20,000
McKinley School	10,000	40,000	5,000	16,500
Washington School	12,000	22,000	4,000	11,000
Blaine School	3,000	20,000	4,000	11,000
Jackson School	5,000	15,000	2,000	12,400
Harrison School	3,000	3,000	2,000	2,700
Lincoln School	3,000	25,000	5,000	16,000
Garfield School	5,000	32,500	5,000	16,200
Old McKinley School	5,000	1,000	500	1,000
East Jackson Street	3,000	......	.....	......
Willard and Blaine Streets	200	......	.....	......
	$101,200	$215,500	$37,500	$126,800

The growth of Muncie is reflected in a comparison between the figures given in a preceding paragraph for 1892 and those for 1906. In the latter year the school enrollment was 4,370, nearly double what it was fifteen years before. There has been a steady increase each year, but especially marked since 1904, in which year the enrollment was 3,635. In 1892 forty-five teachers composed the teaching corps. Ten years later these had increased to 98 teachers and three assistants, and in 1906 there were 111 teachers and three assistants. Besides, there has been growth in many other directions. Reference is made elsewhere to the introduction of manual training in the public schools, Mr. B. E. Cannon having charge of this work in the sixth, seventh and eighth grades, and the work for the girls of the same grades being under the direction of Miss Nina Walldorff.

The Eastern Indiana Normal University was incorporated May 14, 1896. J. O. Lewellen, president; L. J. Hooke, vice president; F. D. Haimbaugh, secretary; J. A. Quick, treasurer. The promoters of the enterprise set aside ten acres on the West side, one mile from the court house, and endeavored to dispose of the lots of the townsite, the income thus derived to be applied to the building and support of the institution. Those interested did not at first succeed, but in the spring of 1898 the matter was revived, and a vigorous campaign begun for selling three hundred lots at three hundred dollars each. The sale was continued up to April 29, when, by the help of one man who bought twenty lots at the last minute rather than see the undertaking fail, the ninety thousand dollars was raised and active preparations begun to open the university. A three-story building, of stone and white pressed brick, with handsome colonial front, was completed in the spring of 1899, and in the following fall the school was opened. The school was the center of a new town—Normal City—which was incorporated and which it was hoped would build up around the college.

The Indiana Business College was established in 1857, and incorporated under the laws of the state of Indiana in 1903. At the time of its incorporation, only three schools were included in the organization, namely, Marion, Kokomo, and Logansport. The headquarters of the association were then at Marion. Since its organization, the institution has grown very rapidly, and now includes schools at Muncie, Marion, Anderson, Kokomo, Lafayette, Logansport, Richmond, Columbus, and Indianapolis, making a total of nine schools. The head offices are now located at Indianapolis, and the officers are: J. D. Brunner, president, Indianapolis; Chas. C. Cring, general manager, Indianapolis; R. F. Cummins, vice president, Bluffton; J. T. Pickerill, business manager, Muncie; A. N. Hirons, principal, Muncie; W. H. Carrier, secretary, Lafayette.

Four years ago when the Muncie school was established the fall term opened with but two students in attendance. Last year the total enrollment in the Muncie school was about three hundred, and the present year bids fair to be even better. These figures show the rapid growth the institution is making. The institution also maintains an employment bureau, which finds employment for its graduates. This department is separate and apart from the school, and is located at Indianapolis in the American Central Life Building.

MUNCIE PUBLIC LIBRARY.*

Muncie was incorporated as a city February, 1865, with a population of 2,196. At a meeting of the Council January 13, 1873, several improvements were decided upon. Among them was the establishment of a public library and reading room. A meeting of the citizens was called by Hamilton S. McRae, superintendent of public schools, at the court house, for the evening of May 30, 1874, for the purpose of discussing the practicability of organizing a public library. Those who were present at this meeting become the stockholders of the society. They were Hamilton S. McRae, Walter March, William B. Kline, William Brotherton, Carlton E. Shipley, Thomas J. Brady, Erville B. Bishop, James Boyce, Marcus C. Smith, William Glenn, James N. Templer, Stanton Hussey, Frank Ellis, N. F. Ethell, David H. Case and John W. Ryan. All of these took two shares each, except David H. Case, who subscribed for five shares. After much discussion it was deemed impossible to support the library by private subscription and a committee was appointed which was to appeal to the city council to raise the subscription by taxation. This committee, consisting of H. S. McRae, M. C. Smith and J. W. Ryan, met with the city council on July 31, 1874, and secured the passage of an ordinance subscribing 1,500 shares of $2 each to the capital stock of the association; 375 shares had already been subscribed to by individuals.

The first books of the public library were those collected from the old county, township, Philalethian Society and Workingmen's libraries, consisting of about 2,195 volumes. The county library was in an upper room in the old court house, and books could be rented by the day or year. The Township library was located on East Main street, west of the Neely house, and Wilson R. Smith was librarian. Smith later became sheriff and removed to the jail, from where the books were circulated.

At a meeting November 6, 1874, "On motion William Glenn and E. B. Bishop were appointed a committee to meet the Common Council of Muncie at its next meeting and arrange for the use of the east room in the second story of the city building for library purposes." (From minutes of Secretary.) On December 12 the committee reported that it had secured the use of the rooms for one year, free of rent. Furniture was purchased at a cost of $145, 5 book cases, 1 table, 1 reading stand, library desk and a 25 foot counter, were also secured.

In the Mayor's address before the Common Council, May 13, 1878, among other things he says: "In this connection I desire to call your at-

*By Miss Artena M. Chapin, Librarian.

Muncie Public Library.

tention to the public library as one of the departments of general education.
Its cost to the city is hereinafter shown; its real value, time alone can
determine. From our librarian's report, I find periodicals, including dailies,
weeklies, monthlies and quarterlies upon her table, numbering fifty; number
of books issued for the year ending March 31, 1877, is 11,979; and for the
year ending March 31, 1878, is 17,120, being a gain on the last year in circulation, of 5,141; and for library reading by persons without cards of membership and the use of books in the library for reference, about 1,500, making
the equivalent to a reading of 18,620 books. This extensive reading by the
people cannot fail to have an influence for good, present and future, to the
people and the city. Through the efforts of the friends of education, our
public library has been selected as the repository of the Congressional publications for this Congressional district. From that source we have received, during the past year, many very valuable books. Our library now
needs room and shelving for about five hundred volumes that are now idle
for the want of such accommodations. In view of these facts, I recommend
to your consideration the adoption of some means in connection with the
library board, to place our library where it will be easy of access, free from
all objectionable surroundings, with proper room for the reading and storing
of its valuable treasure, believing that a generous public will sustain your
efforts."

Mrs. Harriet L. Patterson served as Librarian for six years, at a salary
of $250 "with the privilege of selling stationery in the Library rooms
only," and in her final report made in January, 1881, she says that in February, 1875, the books from the county and township libraries were given in
trust and sent to the public library; that the library committee about the
same time, purchased Henry Marsh's circulating library of over 1,300 books,
and the library of the Workingmen's institute was donated. The first book
in the catalogue was donated sometime during 1874 by Miss Lucy Trueworthy. The first donation in 1875 was made by Thomas Kirby. June 1,
1875, the library was opened to circulation. Up to that time there had been
entered on the accession catalogue 2,190 books.

The following concerning the opening of the library, is taken from
The Muncie News for June 3, 1875:

"On last Monday night the evening's exercises were opened by placing
Rev. O. M. Todd in the chair. Rev. Guthrie then delivered a very fine
prayer, and was followed by the regular address of the evening by Mr.
Todd. He was succeeded by Mr. J. W. Ryan, who read an historical sketch.
Then came Glenn March, Charley Kilgore, Charley Marsh and George
McCullough. Mrs. Patterson then delivered a short address, after which
the meeting adjourned."

Up to the time of moving into the present library building there was a case in the reading room containing many geological specimens. These specimens belonged to Mr. Charles Kilgore, who claimed them again at the time the library was moved. Interest in the library seems to have been active, for almost every issue of the paper contains some assurance that the circulation department will be opened as soon as possible; also notices of library attendance and of gifts appear almost every day.

The Secretary's book shows no record of a meeting between July 2, 1878, and January 1, 1881. At the meeting of January 1, 1881, a motion was made that a committee be appointed to make investigations as to a proper library building. January 12, 1881, Mrs. Caroline R. Fleming was chosen Librarian, at a salary of $200, "with an allowance of $40 for an assistant, janitor and such other help as may be found necessary."

Some talk was circulated among the members of the City Council in the early part of 1881 to the effect that the Kirby House livery stable would be purchased for the fire department and the public library be moved to the rooms occupied by the fire department. But nothing definite was done.

The library possesses a little blank book about 6x3 inches in which are written a list of paper bound books in the H. C. Marsh circulating library. The books number 146, and added is a list of periodicals, and also of donations. It also contains the expense book of the library beginning January, 1875, presumably the first one used. The expense for the quarter, January to March, 1875, was $4.72. This little book is also a record of receipts for stock purchased. It notes receipts and expenditures through October, 1902.

The Library is also fortunate in having the reports of the Secretary from the beginning, which show the progress of the library step by step. The growth was steady and each report makes apparent an increased interest.

When it began to be generally known that Andrew Carnegie was willing to assist various towns to equip a public library Muncie, always alert to take up anything which might benefit the town, was among the first in Indiana to agitate the question. It was discussed for some time by the members of the Library Board, but this Board having heard that the Commercial Club was considering the subject, decided to turn it over to their committee. The committee prepared the following letter, which was sent immediately to Mr. Carnegie:

Muncie, Indiana.
Feb. 27, 1901.

Andrew Carnegie, Esq.
Dear Sir:—
    We have been appointed a committee of the Commercial Club of this city, to ask for assistance in providing a public library for the city. We hope it will be convenient for you to investigate the conditions, which we believe will make the project worthy of a place in your splendid scheme of public benefactions.

We have a population of 29,000, city and suburbs. It is a manufacturing city, and has grown from a substantial county seat with a population of about 6,000 in 12 years to its present size. It has also, by public spirit, developed in a permanent and progressive manner. We already have a fair beginning for a public library. If we had a building worth $50,000 it could be liberally maintained and would be a perpetual fountain of intelligence and worthy of your noble efforts.

We would be glad to furnish any additional facts as to this project that may be desired.

Yours Respectfully,
(J. C. JOHNSON,
(JAMES A. DALY,
(HARDIN ROADS.

The answer was as follows:

Andrew Carnegie.
5 West 51st Street.
Hardin Roads, Esq.
Muncie, Indiana.
Dear Sirs:—

Yours of Feb. 27th received. If the city of Muncie will furnish a suitable site and agree to maintain a free public library at a cost of not less than $5,000 per year, Mr. Carnegie will be glad to give $50,000 for a building. Respectfully yours, JAMES BERTRAM, Secretary.

This reply was turned over to the city council, and at a meeting on March 11, 1901, was presented by Dr. Allen Budd, and with it the following resolution:

"Be it resolved by the Common Council in the City of Muncie, in the County of Delaware and State of Indiana, That the generous offer of Andrew Carnegie, stated in the letter of James Bertram, his private secretary, to Hardin Roads, dated March 8, 1901, to give said city $50,000 for a free public library, upon condition that said city provide a suitable site, and agree to maintain such free public library, at a cost of not less than $5,000 per year, be and the same is hereby accepted. Be it further

"Resolved, That the Mayor of said city be, and he hereby is instructed to express to Mr. Carnegie the appreciation of said gift by said city and this Common Council, and transmit to him a copy of the resolution, and request information with respect to such further proceedings as may be necessary to make such gift effective."

On March 25 the City Council passed a resolution guaranteeing a perpetual maintenance for a free public library, the annual income to be as required by Mr. Carnegie, i. e., 1-10th of donation. At this meeting a committee was appointed to investigate suitable building sites, and on July 29 it reported and recommended the purchase of the Shirk property, corner Jackson and Jefferson streets, which was valued by its owner at

$13,000. The recommendation was accepted and the committee authorized to purchase the property. Mr. George W. Spilker had previously given his home for library purposes, and this residence was now sold for $6,000 and the amount applied toward the new ground. Wing & Mahurin, of Fort Wayne, were chosen as architects, and the contract was awarded to Morrow & Morrow, of Muncie. The committee contracted with various firms for furniture, decorations, etc., as shown by the list given below, which shows the total cost of the building ready for use, to be about $56,000:

Morrow & Morrow, general contract, including all additions to same.....................................$46,970.85
Sutherland Mfg. Co., electrical fixtures.............. 2,500.00
Mandel Bros. art glass.............................   750.00
Mandel Bros. decorations........................... 1,500.00
Architects 2,000.00
Cement side-walks 350.00
Sundries 330.00
                                                   _____
    Total $55,900.85

The building was dedicated Jan. 1, 1904, with appropriate exercises, the Mayor of the city, Mr. Charles W. Sherritt, formally turning over the keys to the library board.

In January, 1903, the library was reorganized under the Mommert law of 1901. The Board required by law consisted of T. F. Rose and Mrs. Nellie M. Stouder, appointed by the city school board; L. W. Cates and Miss Belle Thomas, appointed by the City Council; A. L. Johnson, Miss Nettie Wood and C. M. Carter, appointed by the Circuit court judge. All of these were new members excepting Mr. Rose and Mrs. Stouder, both of whom had served for a number of years on the old board.

In accordance with an amendment made by the Legislature in 1903, the Township Trustee, J. W. Dragoo, and his appointee, G. A. Ball, became members of the Board in May, 1903.

During 1903 Miss Artena M. Chapin served as librarian, with an assistant part of the time, the library being open every day except Sundays from 9 A. M. till 9 P. M., closing one hour at noon and evening for meals.

Beginning Jan. 1. 1904, the library was open every day, continuously, from 9 A. M. until 9 P. M., except Sundays. On Sundays and holidays the reading room is open from 2 to 5 P. M.

On Jan. 1, 1904, the library contained 19,291 volumes, and during the year 1903, 35,077 books were circulated, an average of 118 per day. On Jan. 1, 1907, the library contained 22,750 volumes, 1,800 of which were added during the year. The statistics for 1906 showed that 77,765 books were circulated, making an average of 254 per day. In the reading room are 114 magazines and 12 newspapers. During 1906, 15,078 persons used the reading room. All persons living in Muncie and Center Township may have the privileges of the library and any others may have the same privileges by the payment of two dollars per year.

In the Monograph on Indiana Public Libraries issued for the Chicago World's Fair, Mr. Dunn gives statistics of libraries, and Muncie's library was 6th in number of volumes, and 9th in circulation, it then having 8,266 volumes, and a circulation of 10,000. The last report of the Indiana Library Commission (1904-06) shows Muncie fifth in number of volumes and second in circulation, the only public library having a greater number of books borrowed being the Indianapolis public library. In this report the Muncie library contained 20,859 books and had a circulation for the year of 66,525. A comparison of these figures is interesting as indicating the larger use of the library. In 1893 the circulation was 1.2 times the number of books in the library, and in 1905 it was 3.28 times. In 1893 the number of books borrowed was an equivalent to one book to every 1.13 persons in the town (population 11,345—census of 1890); in 1905 the circulation equaled 3.22 books to each person in the town (population 20,942—census of 1900). These statistics are very gratifying, showing, as they do, that while the funds of the library have not permitted a great expenditure upon books the interest has increased and the use of the books become much more widespread.

After the library had been open about a year it was found that the accommodations for the reference department were too small and it was decided to move the children's books down stairs, and to use the room formerly occupied by the Juvenile department for the reference books. This was done, a room being fitted up for the children with shelves and delivery desk, at a cost of about $700. The children's books were all removed to this room, which has been made the most attractive in the building. Here they are apart from the rest of the library and have a freedom which could not be allowed them while upstairs. Each Saturday afternoon there is a story-hour for the children, during which a story is told on some current topic or of some book which it is desired to bring to their attention. Recently a Children's Literary Club has been started. The club is conducted entirely by the children, a committee chosen among themselves having elected the officers, and formed the constitution. Another committee arranges the programs, which consist of discussions and papers on literary subjects.

Early in 1906 were started three Branch stations, one in Avondale, one in Congerville, and a third in Whiteley. The object in establishing these stations was to reach the people (especially the children) who lived at too great a distance to come to the main library. They have come to mean

merely an extension of the children's department, for so few adults came
that it did not seem practicable ,to send books for them. The books, during
school months, are kept in the respective school buildings, and one morning
each week, an assistant from the building goes there and distributes them.
During the summer the little libraries are kept in stores, whose use is
kindly donated by the proprietors; almost all of the children who use
these books were never in the habit of patronizing the main library. It is
hoped that when they reach the age to care for adult books they will continue in the habit of reading which they thus have formed, and will borrow
from the main building.

As is the case in every public library the per cent of fiction reading is
the largest part of the whole. And whether this is to be deplored, as some
librarians think, or whether it is merely as it should be, as other librarians
contend, it is always gratifying to find that through the instrumentality of
the library its patrons have been lead to more serious reading than is
found in the average novel. The annual report of the library for 1906
shows a gradual decrease in fiction reading for the past four years as follows:

1903—Fiction read....... .87   1905—Fiction read....... .84
1904—Fiction read....... .85   1906—Fiction read....... .79

The next largest class of books read is the magazines, current numbers of which are allowed to circulate whenever there are duplicates, and
otherwise as soon as the succeeding number is received. Duplicate copies
of about a half dozen of the most popular magazines are subscribed for
and these are bound in cloth binding and circulated as books. We find
that these magazines give as much satisfaction as the new fiction, to many
of our readers.

The library is advertised through the local press, the Muncie *Star* allowing us part of a column each Sunday.

The library is fortunate in having donations from some of its friends;
these include two water-colors by Alden Mote, and an oil painting of a view
of Muncie by J. O. Adams, the gift of T. F. Rose; a reproduction of "The
Lion Hunt," by Rubens, bequeathed to the library by Mrs. T. F. Neely;
some valuable relics from Dr. G. W. H. Kemper, besides the donation of
a number of medical periodicals and other books. Generous gifts of books
have been made by different citizens, and two clocks, made and donated
by Mr. Charles Willard, add much to the appearance of the library.

The library encourages the public school teachers to use its books by
putting forth every effort to have those needful in their work. An arrangement was made three years ago whereby the library buys eight copies
for the supplementary work and the school board furnishes the extra

copies. These eight copies are sometimes borrowed entirely by the teacher, who sends her pupils to the library to consult them. The reference work for the schools is heavy in the school months, and many lists are prepared to aid the pupils in their studies.

The largest part of the reference work, however, is done for the clubs. The programs are received in advance whenever possible and the subjects investigated so that they may be ready for use when needed.

The members of the Library Board at present are:

T. F. Rose, President, term expires Jan. 1, 1909.

Rev. Dr. C. N. Carter, Vice-president, term expires Jan. 1, 1910.

Mrs. Nellie N. Stouder, Secretary, term expires Jan. 1, 1909.

Dr. G. W. H. Kemper, Treasurer, term expires Jan. 1, 1908.

Nettie Wood, term expires Jan. 1, 1908.

A. L. Johnson, term expires Jan. 1, 1909.

C. E. Lambert, term expires with office as Township Trustee.

G. A. Ball, term expires Jan. 1, 1909.

The members of the Library Staff are:

Artena N. Chapin, Librarian.

Margaret E. Streeter, Reference Librarian and Cataloguer.

Helen Hurd, Desk and Periodical Assistant.

Gertrude Clark, Children's Librarian.

CHAPTER XXI.

THE DELAWARE COUNTY PRESS.

In the pioneer community of seventy years ago the newspaper seemed to serve its principal purpose in publishing the legal notices and the business cards of lawyers, doctors and merchants. Where there were no newspapers, notices of sheriffs' sales, estrays, elections and other legal business were laboriously penned on board or paper and affixed to the logs of the conspicuous buildings or to trees along the traveled thoroughfares. Until a county reached that degree of development where it could support at least one newspaper, its most important legal notices were often published in the nearest metropolis. In Wayne county, from which so large a bulk of the immigration came into Delaware county, there was a paper as early as 1820, and the well known Richmond *Palladium* dated from 1831. Also a newspaper was published in the state capital from its establishment.

Thus, in a sense, the pioneers of Delaware county were not without the benefits of the newspaper press. But the first newspaper in this county was not issued until the spring of 1837, ten years after the county was formed. This was the *Muncietonian*. The only number preserved in the Muncie library files, and perhaps the only one in existence, is Vol. 1, No. 2, dated June 15, 1837. The first number had been issued several weeks previously. No copy has been preserved. But the Richmond *Jeffersonian* in its issue of May 23, 1837, referred to the first issue of the *Muncietonian*, and also quoted some descriptive and statistical matter concerning Muncietown (found elsewhere in this history). It appears that only three or four issues of the *Muncietonian* appeared. The proprietors of the sheet, D. Charky and J. White, found it impossible to continue the publication, and probably used the plant, so far as it was used at all, for the small amount of job printing needed in the village and surrounding country. It is said that the double two-story log building in which this paper was published was situated where in after years the brewery stood, on Ohio avenue near the cemetery.

David Gharky.

David Charky, the proprietor of the *Muncietonian*, was an eccentric individual, and had had a rather remarkable career. Born in Pomerania, Prussia, in 1775, he came to America at the beginning of the 19th century, and was a pioneer settler along the Ohio river, at the new town of Portsmouth. At the close of his life he was moved to collect data for his biography, leaving it partly in the form of continuous narrative and partly as diary. This was afterwards published, according to his desires, by one of his sons, the title page bearing the following: "The life of David Charky, as written by himself; also, a record of the Charky family; a description of Muncietown, Indiana; of his adjoining possessions; of his lands in Bates county, Missouri, together with his last will and testament. Printed by John Gharky, Portsmouth, O., 1852." A queer old book, interesting to Muncie citizens for some facts relative to early history.

He lived in Portsmouth "until March, 1830, when I resigned my office and went to Muncietown, Indiana. In March, 1830, I bought a corner lot of Lemuel Jackson, with whom I lived. He entered a half quarter of land for me in Indianapolis. April the 12th I bought and entered 327 acres of school land. In May I entered into partnership with Lemuel Jackson and we built a sawmill. . . . August the 27th the mill began to saw and would have done very well, with good attendance, provided it had not been built on a sandy foundation." He soon went back to Portsmouth, where he lived until June, 1836. "I came to Muncietown with the liver complaint; boarded with Justice [Patrick], dug out my medical spring which cured me, and I went back to Portsmouth in the fall and bought A. J. Bingham's printing establishment. In May, 1837, John White printed three numbers of the *Muncietonian.*" He elsewhere says that he sold the printing establishment to Jones for $450 in spring of 1842. He continued to reside at Muncie for the greater part of his remaining years, as his diary shows, but died in Portsmouth August 9, 1850.

One clause of his will, which was made in 1846, reads as follows: "I request that two acres of my ground, on the highest part of my big mound, situate on lots No. 15 & 26, of school section 16,...... be set apart as a graveyard, with the Gharky street leading to it, for the only use and behoof of the Gharky family; and to be recorded as such; and in either of these places I wish to be buried, provided my decease will be in reach of either of them, within three hundred miles distance." The "big mound," once so familiar a feature of topography in southwest Muncie, has almost entirely disappeared, save a few hillocks near the railroad that will also be cut down to the general level as soon as convenience demands it. Gharky street and Mound street should always remind Muncie citizens of the glacial mound once owned by this pioneer citizen.

Elsewhere in the little volume is a description of his Muncie land. "My tract of land adjoining Muncie contains 260 acres of high, dry and fertile land, well timbered and well watered; with an improvement of 50 acres under fence, nine of which is sown with grass, and the rest ready for any sort of grain. Two state roads, one leading to Indianapolis and the other to Pendleton, run directly through it. Upon this land there are a mound 55

feet high, overlooking the town and its vicinity, of a very rich soil, now con-
tianing grass; a number of springs near the double cabin, and a medical
spring on lot No. 7, near which there is a mound 300 feet long and 30 feet
high.........."

The next paper in Muncie and Delaware county was the *Muncietown Telegraph*, whose publisher was John S. Garver. It is probable that the printing
outfit was the same employed to print the few numbers of the *Muncietonian*.
The machinery and other equipment of such a pioneer printing establishment was so primitive and the capital it represented was small even for
those days, and the loss of interest on the investment was insignificant and
the space required to store the plant could be found in the corner or attic of
one of the small houses that then adorned Muncie's main street. The owner
of the outfit, if he found no patronage for his paper, could, without detri-
ment to the public good and perhaps to his personal advantage, close up
shop, and apply himself to such avocations as fishing and hunting or to the
more usual pioneer industries.

The *Muncietown Telegraph*, which was a stanch advocate of Whig
principles, then triumphant under the first Harrison administration, was issued from March 15, 1841, to March 19, 1842, a little more than a year. The
plant was then sold to Joseph G. Jones, who changed the name to the *Village
Herald,* and continued under the same political banner. The issue of the
Herald was rather irregular, and the last number is said to have appeared on
November 5, 1842. The only numbers preserved in the library files are Nos.
6 and 7, the first dated June 4 and the latter dated June 25.

The *Muncietonian Yeoman,* the fourth of Delaware county's newspapers, lasted through ten issues, beginning on August 5, 1843, and ending October 7 the same year. Levi L. Hunter and Obadiah Coffeen were the
editors.

The term "political organ" was more applicable to the newspapers of
this period than to the modern press. As political sentiment and discussion
engaged the daily activities of the people to a degree of greater earnestness
if not greater enlightenment than in the twentieth century, so the newspapers
reflected a more strenuous partisanship and devoted more space to political
affairs. It was quite common for the members of one of the parties to form
an organization to publish a paper during campaign and then suspend.
Local news was given scant attention in the old papers, and to reconstruct
the history of the locality from that source alone would prove an almost impossible task.

The newspapers which have been mentioned so far had all been conducted under Whig auspices. But only three days after the extinction of
the *Muncietown Yeoman,* there appeared the first number of the *Delaware
County Democrat.* This paper was an avowed advocate of Jeffersonian

Democracy, and for two years or more was the only newspaper in the county. The files of this paper as preserved in the Muncie library end with the issue of December 29, 1845, which is probably the last number published. Isaac Norris was editor until November 30, 1844, and from then on Joseph S. Buckles, one of the young lawyers and a prominent local politician of that time, directed the paper.

Shortly after the *Democrat* ceased publication, a successor, of Whig politics, appeared in the *Muncie Journal*. It is impossible to speak with certainty, but it seems likely that these successive papers all used the same plant, with such improvements and additions as were made necessary from time to time. The first number of the *Muncie Journal* is dated January 10, 1846, and the file closes May 22, 1847. Warren H. Withers was editor.*

For some months Muncie was without a paper. Then, early in 1848, when politics became lively with the opening of the Taylor campaign for the presidency, John C. Osburn started the *Indiana Signal*. No. 6 of Volume I is dated April 27, 1848, this being the first number preserved. The last number of the *Signal* came out January 23, 1850. Osburn then sold the plant to Estabrook and Jones, and with A. F. Estabrook as editor they began the issue, reviving the name of the first paper of the county, of the *Muncietonian*. The file runs from February 2 to December 31, 1850. In politics this paper was "independent" on men and measures, but "advocating Republican principles."

The files of the oldest Delaware county newspapers preserved in the public library close with the last number of the *Muncietonian;* there is a lapse of twenty-five years of which the newspaper record has not been kept. The *Whig Banner* was the last paper to uphold Whig principles in the county, continuing from 1851 through the presidential campaign of 1852.

The *Muncie Messenger* was probably the successor of the *Banner*. Rev. J. B. Birt and his son, James H., were the first proprietors. In 1856 J. R. S. Bond, formerly editor of the Clermont (Ohio) *Courier* took control and was succeeded in June, 1857, by Joseph F. Duckwall, also of Clermont county, Ohio. Mr. Duckwall, one of the most prominent of the old-time editors, was also one of the first in this part of the state to turn the influence of a newspaper to strenuous advocacy of the new Republican party and for abolition of slavery. However, the *Messenger* was short-lived, the plant being removed to Anderson in the fall of 1858.

Just before the suspension of the *Messenger* several well known men started the *Delaware County Free Press*. After two years of successful management, Messrs. James H. Birt, H. H. Wachtell and Enoch Davis, who,

* Mr. Withers after leaving Muncie moved to Fort Wayne and became editor of the Fort Wayne Times. He was a lawyer by profession, and at one time was judge of the circuit court at Fort Wayne. He died in October, 1882.

early in 1860, sold the paper to C. B. Smith and John Q. Thompson, who changed the name to the *Eastern Indiana Courant*, with the intention of making it more than a local or county paper. In a few months Joseph F. Duckwall, by obtaining the interest of one of the partners, had again become a force in the Muncie newspaper field and directed the editorial policy of the *Courant*. When, soon after, he became sole proprietor, he resumed the original name of *Free Press*, and throughout the period of the Civil war and until the latter part of 1867, he conducted the *Free Press* as a tranchant champion of the Republican administration and the war for the Union. Alfred Kilgore was the next proprietor, and he not only changed the name, making it the *Guardian of Liberty*, but continued the brief existence of the paper under the banner of the Democratic party.

Muncie Times.

The oldest newspaper man in the county, though no longer active in the work, is Nathanael F. Ethell, who has been a resident of Delaware county the greater portion of seventy years, and who in 1860 began the publication of the *Delaware County Times*, which (later as the *Muncie Times*) was the first paper in the county to have a continuous existence of more than a decade. Mr. Ethell, who was born in Licking county, Ohio, in 1834, was brought to Muncie in 1839, and gained his education in the local schools and at the state university. After several years in civil engineering and railroad construction work, he became city editor of the *Daily Atlas*, at Indianapolis, and on January 1, 1860 (?), issued the first number of the *Delaware County Times*. The first home of the *Times* was a small building on the west side of the public square, and the second in a brick building near the corner of Main and Walnut. Mr. Ethell* had entire management of the *Times* during the first seven years, and for the next two years had M. D. Helm as an associate. Thomas J. Brady, then practicing law at Muncie, bought the *Times* in 1869, and in the following year his law partner, A. C. Mellette, also took a hand in the management of the *Times*. Both were able men, and under their direction the *Times* soon became one of the most influential Republican papers east of Indianapolis. Besides raising the paper's standard editorially, they gave Muncie its first improved newspaper equipment, discarding the old-fashioned Washington press and using steam power to turn the cylinder press. From the third floor of the Odd Fellows block on the north side of Main street, they moved the plant, in 1873, to a new two-story brick building on the corner of Washington and Walnut streets (where for a number of years the postoffice also was located). October 20, 1878, the plant was ruined by fire, but was soon restored by Mr. Brady, and in a short time the

*Mr. Ethell married Millie A. Turner, daughter of Minus Turner, one of Muncie's pioneers.

Times plant was known as one of the most complete in Indiana. About the time of the fire Mr. Mellette retired from the newspaper business. He took a prominent part in Republican politics, and later became the first governor of the state of South Dakota.

For a quarter of a century the *Times* continued to be the leading Republican evening paper, the name being eventually changed to the *Evening Times*. W. E. Sutton was the last editor of the *Evening Times*, and during the latter years the paper was published at 112 East Adams street. The *Weekly Times* is still published, as a Republican paper, and, in this form, can claim the honor of being the oldest paper with a continuous existence in Delaware county.

For a time in its early history there was published the "*Sunday Morning Times*," Vol. 1, No. 3, being dated Jan. 15, 1882. At this time John C. Eiler, for a long time one of the leading Republicans of Muncie, was publisher.

May 28, 1887, was issued the first number of the *Muncie Daily Times*, Wildman and Ferrier being proprietors. They frankly stated in the salutatory that "we do not know that any 'long felt want' has existed that this paper has come to fill; but we hope to create for it a want by publishing a paper that will be abreast with the industrial and intellectual status and advancement of the city." And so the *Daily Times* continued for nearly twenty years, with various changes of publishers and proprietors.

Democrat and Herald.

In 1870 Samuel Shafer established the Muncie *Democrat*, a paper representing the minority party in the county and destined to many vicissitudes of existence. In 1871 Mr. Shafer went to Ohio, and the *Democrat* in a few months was suspended, the material being stored, so it is said, in corn sacks, and kept until needed by the Democratic central committee. In December, 1873, a Tennessee gentleman, Col. J. D. Williams, came to Muncie, and purchasing the old outfit, began the issue, on January 15, 1874, of a new *Democrat*. Under this management the *Democrat* improved and held its own for several years. In August, 1877, Walter L. Davis, another familiar name in Muncie's newspaper annals, who had been connected with the *Democrat* as city editor, became a partner with Mr. Williams, this firm continuing until January 1, 1879. Thereafter changes occurred in quick succession. L. A. Kirkwood, who had published the Muncie *Observer*, bought the *Democrat* and made it the *Democratic Observer*. Other changes occurred, and in September, 1880, Davis and Williams (W. L. Davis and C. A. Williams) became owners. In February, 1881, A. C. Stouder and L. A. Kirkwood bought the plant and merged the paper with the *Observer*. W. L. Davis then became connected with the *Daily News*.

The Muncie *Democrat* continued to exist until 1885. In the summer of 1885 it closed its thirteenth volume, with L. A. Kirkwood as publisher, who had resumed the name *Democrat* instead of *Observer*.

The successor of the *Democrat* was the *Muncie Daily Herald*, the first number of which was dated March 15, 1886. The first publishers were Davis and McKillip, and the office was in the Mitchell block on South Walnut street. The founder of the *Herald* was Thomas McKillip, who came to Muncie in 1882, and in 1885 purchased the plant of the Newcastle *Mercury*, removing it to Muncie, and on October 2, 1885, issued the first number of the Muncie *Democrat-Herald*. W. L. Davis retired from the *Democrat-Herald* and the firm became Hilligoss & McKillip on August 9, 1889.

In 1891 a half interest in the *Herald* was bought by F. D. Haimbaugh, who is now the dean of the newspaper profession in Muncie, none of those who were publishers or editors in 1891 being still active. Mr. Haimbaugh is independent, vigorous and public spirited in the conduct of a newspaper, qualities that characterize both his business management and his writing.

At the present time the *Herald* is continued as a weekly Democratic paper.

Evening Press.

March 21, 1905, the Press Publishing Co. purchased the Muncie *Times* and the Muncie *Herald*, the evening papers, and consolidated them under the name of the *Evening Press*, the first number under that name being issued March 26. The weekly issues of the *Times* and the *Herald* have been continued, as mentioned. F. D. Haimbaugh, the editor of the *Herald*, continued with the new publication as business manager, and W. E. Sutton, of the *Times*, as editor. September 3, 1907, another change was made, at which time Mr. William M. Butler, an experienced newspaper man, who has had a varied career in this line with leading papers in Indiana and elsewhere, bought the McCulloch stock and assumed the position of editor, Mr. Haimbaugh continuing as business manager. The *Evening Press* is an independent newspaper, and is rapidly being improved to the high standards of an influential metropolitan paper.

Muncie News.

That the exigencies of a political campaign have often called a newspaper into existence has been alluded to, but most of such papers have a brief life. Of more permanence and greater interest, however, is the case of the *Republican*, a paper started by a joint-stock company early in the famous Greeley-Grant campaign of 1872. W. P. Kline, Walter March, H. C. Winans, G. W. Stephenson and others were said to be the principal movers in the enterprise. The office was in a small frame building on the north side of the square. The campaign over, the plant was passed over to Hamilton and Kingsbury, and the name changed to the Muncie *Liberal.*

In 1873 Mr. N. F. Ethell again becomes an active factor in newspaper circles, by his purchase of the *Liberal.* He changed the name to the Muncie *News,* and during the following twelve years he won his largest share of success in the newspaper field as editor and publisher (alone much of the time) of the *News.* That the *News* was the successor of the *Republican* is indicated by the fact that the first issue of January, 1876, was numbered as Vol. IV, No. 31, marking its beginning in the year 1872. At the beginning of 1876 the *News* was published in the Odd Fellows building on Walnut street, under the firm name of Ethell and Turner. Mr. Ethell's progressive conduct of the paper is shown in a change effect May 10, 1876, when the *News* became a semi-weekly, the first in the county. C. M. Turner retired from the firm in the following July, and Samuel Leavitt of New York City became city editor.

During these days the *News* remained true, in large measure, to the principles under which it originated. It supported, and while a weekly devoted much of its news space, to the grange movement and to the advocacy of greenback principles. In 1876 it proclaimed its allegiance for Peter Cooper as head of the Independent National ticket. The issues of the *News* at that time, as can be seen from an examination of the files preserved in the public library, are quite filled with reports from the various grange organizations that were then flourishing in nearly every locality of Indiana and other states.

May 20, 1878, the *News* began a daily issue. The *News* was the first daily newspaper in the county, and for many years held an assured lead as the best patronized daily paper of the city. From his greenback allegiance, the editor had returned to his original stand with the Republican party, and throughout the years of its existence the *Daily News* was an exponent of Republican principles, yet seldom with offensive partisanship and invariably edited with ability and independence.

After making the *News* a strong and successful paper, Mr. Ethell finally, on November 9, 1885, sold the *Daily News* to Charles F. W. Neely. A. H. Harryman then became local editor. Under the new management the *News* continued to improve. The best evidence of this came four years later, when a two-story brick building, 35 by 62 feet, was constructed near the Anthony block, and the entire plant was installed there in January, 1890, at which time it was the most complete and efficient newspaper office and printing plant in the city.

The files of the Daily *News* have afforded the larger part of the material for this history of the county during the past quarter century. In the chronological record will be found several items concerning the history of the *News*, and only the main features of its career need be sketched here. The *News* became an 8-page paper on December 1, 1891, and for the follow- ing ten years kept pace with the improvement of the city by additions of equipment and news facilities that marked it as a metropolitan daily. After Mr. Neely sold his interests, the Muncie News Co. was organized, the prin- cipal officers of the company being P. S. and C. R. Heath and F. J. Clay- pool. In July, 1901, the Heaths sold their controlling interest in the com- pany, and within a few weeks the *News* was in the hands of a receiver. The plant was eventually purchased by George F. McCulloch, and for a time the name of Muncie *Daily News* was carried on the *Morning Star*, though the latter was not successor to the *News* nor was there a consolidation of the two papers.

Muncie Morning Star.

The Muncie *Morning Star* was founded May 29, 1899, George F. Mc- Culloch having the principal financial interests in the enterprise. The paper is one of the three *Star* papers published in Indiana, all morning issues, the other two being at Terre Haute and Indianapolis. Mr. McCulloch continued in the active management of the *Star* until October 27, 1904, having in the meantime given the three papers a combined circulation of about 150,000, that of the Muncie *Star* being over 25,000. The *Star* still occupies the field as the leading morning daily of eastern Indiana, and with Associated Press service, special correspondents, and first-class mechanical equipment, fur- nishes its readers all the important news of the world selected with reference to Muncie and this section of Indiana. The Muncie *Star* building at Mul- berry and Adams streets, is one of the modern business blocks of the city, and the presses, linotypes and other machinery are of the highest type of efficiency and power.

The Observer.

R. T. Winters, who has been connected with Muncie journalism a num- ber of years, with the *Times*, *Herald*, *News* and *Star*, is proprietor of "The *Observer* (Always Republican)", published at 111 North Mulberry street. September 28, 1907, it closed its fifth volume, during which time it has occu- pied a useful place as a weekly newspaper, characterized with a certain indi- viduality and independence of opinion that recommended it to a considerable patronage.

Other Papers.

Besides the earlier papers already mentioned, there have been numerous cases of newspaper ventures where considerable ability and worth were indi- cated by the journal, but as permanent and successful enterprises, failed. The Muncie *Telegraph* was started in 1870 by S. W. Swiggett and Son, of Cincinnati, intended to become popular as the family and fireside paper, and devoted to Republican politics. In April, 1871, the original owners sold the paper to William Chandler and J. W. Perkins. Mr. Chandler retired in August, 1872, and Mr. Perkins, with A. J. Wells, continued the enterprise until January, 1873, when the end came.

The Muncie *Mule* had a breezy and jolly existence of about six months. It would be difficult to describe its hybrid character; the copies that still exist prove that it did not attempt to fill the place of the standard-gauge newspaper. It was a small four-column folio, and ran from the latter part of 1875 until sometime the following year. The original members of the firm were Ed Smith, Charles Alf Williams, D. J. Hathaway and Will H. Williams, all men of some note in Muncie, whose ability and success in life were not to be measured by the career of the *Mule*—"a phenomenon in journalism," as one of them called it.

The Muncie Weekly *Advertiser* was an advertising medium, with periodical issue and carrying enough news to make it read. A. C. Stouder was proprietor, and it was started about 1880. Vol. 2, No. 18, is dated June 4, 1881, and Vol. 4, No. 5, is March 11, 1882. The *Saturday Pink*, which was first issued December 5, 1885, was also an advertising sheet. Some time later A. C. Stouder started another publication, called *The School and Home*, "a strictly moral and educational journal. . . . conducted on a plan that is calculated to lift the reader above the light trashy reading of the day." The first number was issued in December, 1888. Mr. Stouder was one of the early editors of the *News*, and had a varied experience as printer and newspaper man.

During the nineties a Rev. Sly conducted the *Bimetallist* for about a year, and the publication continued under another proprietor a few months until F. D. Haimbaugh bought the plant and discontinued the publication. The Muncie *Tribune* lived about a year under the proprietorship of George Stoll.

In the towns outside of Muncie the newspaper history is naturally brief and disconnected. About May, 1888, the *Eaton Gas Light* was established by M. A. Fisher. Charles Jester, who is still proprietor of a job printing office at Eaton, and has issued the Eaton *Advertiser* as an advertising sheet, published the *Gas Light* for a time. In 1892, during the boom, it was reported that the Eaton Land and Improvement Co. purchased the plant. J. W. McCarty is now proprietor of the *New Gas Light,* which is issued every Friday.

The *Gazette,* at Gaston, was established about 1897 by C. W. McIntosh and son, well known citizens of the town, who still continue the publication as a bright and newsy weekly, offering an advertising medium and the local news of the northwest corner of the county.

CHAPTER XXII.

MEDICAL HISTORY OF DELAWARE COUNTY.

By G. W. H. Kemper, M. D.

Dr. Dickinson Burt was the first physician to locate in Delaware county after its organization in 1827. The exact date of his location in Muncietown is not known,—it was prior to 1829, for the official records show that in addition to his medical duties, he was our second postmaster,—his commission bearing date August 29, 1829. The postoffice was at his home on the west side of Mulberry street near Gilbert street.

The number of physicians multiplied as the population increased, so that the medical and surgical wants of the early pioneers were not neglected. These men were subjected to numerous hardships,—riding on horseback, over mud roads, or along by-paths long distances by day and by night. These rides were made in all kinds of weather,—beneath the piercing rays of a summer sun, or in frozen zero weather, or through drenching rains.

"This undecorated soldier, of a hard, unequal strife,
Fought in many stubborn battles with the foes that sought his life.
In the night-time or the day time, he would rally brave and well,
Though the summer lark was fifing, or the frozen lances fell;
Knowing if he won the battle they would praise their Maker's name,
Knowing if he lost the battle then the doctor was to blame.
'Twas the brave old virtuous doctor,
'Twas the good old faulty doctor,
'Twas the faithful country doctor—fighting stoutly all the same."*
  * Carleton.

The author of this paper located in Muncie, August 18, 1865, and I esteem it an honor to have known personally a large number of the physicians who are named in this paper. The physicians whom I met at the time above indicated, were men of good attainments, and ripe experience,— a majority of them were elderly men, not only those located in Muncie, but those residing at other points in the county.

All physicians at that time were making country calls on horseback,— a few only were using buggies or carts in the summer season while the roads were in better condition. I made my country calls invariably on horseback during the first three years of my practice, and also a part of the time for several years later. As the roads were improved, vehicles became more common, until gradually the doctor with saddle-bags, merged into the physician riding in a phaeton, and still later, as at the present day, in an automobile,—a veritable evolution as I have witnessed from equestrianism to electricity!

The physicians who practice in Delaware county today and ride along its roads and streets in buggies, can little appreciate the hardships that these early practitioners endured before our gravel roads were made. Visits made on errands of mercy were often accompanied with peril, as it was no uncommon thing for the horses to mire in creeks and swamps. A thrilling experience in this line lingers in the memory of the writer. The hardships these men endured told upon their physical strength.

The various preparations of medicines have markedly improved during the past half century, or even a quarter of a century. Concentrated medicines as fluid extracts, specific tinctures, tablets, etc., enable us to carry a large list of remedies in a small space, which is a great improvement over the cumbersome saddle-bags required in former days to carry roots and leaves for the preparation of infusions and decoctions.

Many of our valuable instruments in common use at the present day were but little known or unused forty years ago. About the year 1866, I bought a hypodermic syringe, which I believe was the first one to be used in Delaware county. I think Dr. Robert Winton owned the first fever thermometer in this county. Two were then thought to be necessary,—one for the mouth, and a curved one for the axilla. Neither of these were self-registering, and it was necessary to read them while in situ. These useful but crude instruments soon gave way to the neater thermometer, so accurate and essential at the present day.

After sleeping in his grave for three and a half centuries, if Martin Luther could come forth, he would find the tenets of theology the same, and the doctrine that "The just shall live by faith," proclaimed as when he fell asleep. And if Sir William Blackstone, after more than a hundred years have passed, should enter a court room of his peers today, he would find them conducting trials by jury; the standard of law unchanged, and the principles of justice that he laid down, still in vogue.

If the physicians whom I met in Delaware county forty-two years ago were to rise from the dead and appear in our midst today, they would be startled at our speeding automobiles, but no less surprised at our new advances in medicine and surgery, as well as our strange medical terms, for, if they were to hear medical men conversing about antiseptics, Listerism, antitoxins, serums, and germs, they would not comprehend their meaning. Should they attempt a surgical operation according to the rules of their day, they would be liable to answer to the charge of malpractice.

Such have been the rapid advancements in the healing art in less than half a century!

County Medical Society.

The first practical steps toward organizing a medical society in Dela. ware county were taken on April 18, 1865, when some of the physicians of the county met in Walling's Hall (west side of public square), in the city of Muncie, to take preliminary steps for the formation of a permanent so- ciety. At that meeting, Dr. S. V. Jump occupied the chair, and Dr. N. W. Black was chosen secretary. A committee was then appointed, com. posed of Drs. Morgan, Winton, and Craig, on permanent organization. The adjournment was until Monday, the first day of May, following, when the meeting convened in Dr. Winton's office,—112 West Adams street. The physicians present were Drs. Armitage, Black, Craig, Hoover, Lewellen, Morgan, Skiff, Wheeler, Willard, Winton, W. H. Williams, and J. A. Williams. At this meeting the committee on permanent organization made a report and the plan of organization was read by sections, discussed, and adopted. The committee was continued, and empowered to revise the constitution and by-laws, and have the same published. Under this organ- ization the following named officers were chosen: President, Dr. S. V. Jump, Vice President, Dr. W. J. Morgan; Secretary, Dr. N. W. Black; Treasurer, Dr. William Craig; Censors, Drs. Robert Winton, W. C. Wil. lard, and J. H. Powers.

At a meeting held June 5, 1865, Drs. L. J. Bonnels, J. C. Helm, S. E. Mitchell, and H. C. Winans were admitted to membership. At a meeting held July 3, 1865, Dr. Henry Kirby was admitted, and at a meeting held in September, 1865, Drs. W. J. Andrews and G. W. H. Kemper were ad- mitted to membership.

The Delaware County Medical Society has been reorganized several times since its first organization in order to conform to the requirements of the State Medical Association, but the Society has never failed to exist, and the present one is virtually a continuation of the original Society. So far as the author can ascertain, Dr. W. J. Andrews, of Newark, N. J., and Dr. G. W. H. Kemper, of Muncie, are the only persons living who became members in 1865.

The record of the physicians of Delaware county has been a creditable one; few moral delinquencies have existed. They have been industrious as shown by the numerous contributions to medical literature contributed by our citizen physicians. Our death rate has not been excessive; our health officers have been competent, and our surgeons have successfully performed nearly all the operations known to surgery.

After considerable research and correspondence, I am able to give a few personal facts of some of the early physicians. My limited space requires that I must be brief. All that I shall mention in this list have "gone on that unreturning visit which allows of no excuse, and admits of no delay," save one,—Dr. Harvey Mitchell, who remains with us as "The Last Leaf."

Early Physicians.

Dr. Dickinson Burt (1829) was the first physician to locate in Muncietown or Delaware county. I have no information concerning his individual history or the exact date of location. Dr. Burt was the second postmaster at Muncietown and filled that office from August 29, 1829, to May 6, 1835. It is supposed that he left soon after the expiration of the term of his office. Nothing farther is known of his history.

Dr. Levi Minshall (1829) was the second physician to locate in Muncietown. He was born in Virginia, March 4, 1804. He was licensed to practice at Dayton, Ohio, in 1829, and came to Muncietown in the same year and at once began the practice of medicine. An old citizen who remembers Dr. Minshall's first appearance in Muncietown, says that he came here from Dayton, Ohio, riding a very large iron gray horse, and wore a suit of broadcloth, a circumstance that created almost a sensation among the primitive people living here at that time, as homespun jeans was the regulation apparel, and broadcloth was reserved for the rich and nobility. He was a man of scholarly attainments and soon gained a prominent place in the community as a physician and a citizen. One of the interesting incidents of his early practice in the country when visiting the sick, was that he would ride up and down White river in the water to avoid bears and wolves that roamed about in their native freedom in the woods in the territory which now comprises Delaware county. He died at Muncietown, March 6, 1836, aged 32 years. His remains repose in Beech Grove cemetery.

Dr. Ezra Stiles Trask came to Muncietown at an early period in its history. He removed from here to Marion in the year 1833. Dr. William Flynn, of Marion, under date of January 19, 1907, writes me as follows: "Dr. Ezra Stiles Trask was the third physician to locate in Grant county. He came to Marion in 1833, and lived here about six years. He did not practice medicine as a regular employment. His principal occupations were the buying, gathering, preparing and selling ginseng, horse trading, and sports of various kinds. The doctor was a man of many accomplishments,—being a graduate of Dartmouth College,* and a favorite professional pupil of Professor Mussey, of that school, and of Cincinnati. He

* Possibly this is an error. Mr. Ernest M. Hopkins, Secretary of Dartmouth College, writes me February 8, 1907, as follows: "He was not a graduate of the College, or any of the Associated Schools. We have no early records about men who were students here but who did not graduate. I am, therefore, unable to say whether or not Dr. Trask ever attended the College."—K.

acquired, early in life, a fondness for alcoholic beverages, and his death can be traced to his pronounced habits of dissipation. He was something of a politician, having served a term in the State Senate. He died in 1839, —leaving a most amiable wife and two very promising sons. The doctor was buried here, but no stone remains to point out his last resting place."

Dr. Samuel P. Anthony (1792-1876) was born at Lynchburg, Virginia, December 2, 1792. He pursued the study of medicine at Cincinnati, and then located in Clinton county, Ohio, where for three years he engaged in the practice of medicine. Then he removed to Cedarville, in the same state, where he practiced three more years. He located in Muncietown in 1831. He practiced here for twenty-five years, retiring about fifteen years before his death, which occurred in 1876. Dr. Anthony was very successful in his financial career, and accumulated quite a fortune. He reached a more advanced age than any of his colleagues,—dying at the age of 84. His last illness was short,—lasting only a few hours,—death being due, probably, to a cerebral hemorrhage.

John Allen Clark (—— 1847) was, probably, the third physician to locate in Muncietown. He was born in Ireland, and was educated, it is said, at the Dublin University. "When he was studying medicine he shaved off the hair of one-half of his head, and lived in a cave not far from his father's home in Ireland, and his food was carried to him by his sister. He did this so he could not go any place, but just give all his time to study."

Alas, for this early genius! He is said to have had a fair practice until he became very intemperate, and while he maintained an office on the north side of the public square, his headquarters were at Gilbert's distillery. He died in Muncie, May 12, 1847. (Diary of David Charky). A friend tells me that he was buried in the old cemetery, and his bones are still lying under some one of the fine homes near the Friends' new church.

Dr. William C. Willard (1810-1869) was born at Charlestown, New Hampshire, May 10, 1810. He received the degree of Bachelor of Arts at Dartmouth College in 1827, and afterwards pursued his medical studies at that institution. He was eminently the scholar of the early physicians of Delaware county. He located in Muncietown in 1836, and continued to reside there until the date of his death, November 6, 1869. Dr. Willard was quite a sufferer from rheumatism, especially during the later years of his life.

Dr. George W. Garst (1809-1874) was born in Botetourt county, Virginia, February 12, 1809. It is probable that he was not a graduate in medicine. He practiced medicine in Lynchburg, Virginia, and later in Wabash, Indiana, and removed from the latter place to Muncietown about 1837 or 1838. He died suddenly, probably of cerebral hemorrhage, at his home in Muncie, February 22, 1874.

Dr. John C. Helm (1812-1872) was born in Jefferson county, Tennessee, October 10, 1812. He received his medical education at Lexington, Kentucky. After graduating he located near Charleston, South Carolina, owing to anti-slavery sentiments he soon removed to Ohio. On the first of April, 1839, he removed to Yorktown, and from that place to Muncietown in 1848, where he continued to reside until his death, April 8, 1872. He was the first U. S. Examiner for Pensions in Delaware county. Dr. Helm possessed a fund of knowledge in collateral sciences, as well as medicine. He was prominent in local medical societies, and enjoyed the esteem of his medical brethren.

Dr. Jeremiah Dynes (1815-1871) was born near Lebanon, Ohio, April 2, 1815. He came to Smithfield, in this county, in the summer of 1840, where he located and practiced medicine for thirty-one years. A short time before his death, which occurred November 14, 1871, he removed to Indianapolis.

Dr. Daniel H. Andrews (1811-1856) was born in Washington county, New York, in June, 1811. He studied medicine in Cincinnati, under Dr. R. D. Mussey, and graduated at one of the colleges in that city. He located in Florida, where he practiced medicine until 1842, when he removed to Muncietown. He remained here, and practiced his profession,—ranking high as a surgeon,—until his death, which occurred March 12, 1856.

Dr. Stephen Hathaway (1819-1891) was born near Columbus, Ohio, August 1, 1819. He was a graduate of one of the medical colleges of Columbus. He located at Granville in 1844, where he began the practice of medicine. In 1849 he went to California, where he remained but a short time, and returned home, locating in Muncietown in 1850, where he resumed his practice. Dr. Hathaway was a lover of nature, and gave much attention to horticulture, having retired from practice about 1870. He died April 20, 1891.

Dr. Robert Winton (1820-1885) was born in Rossville, Ohio, November 20, 1820. He graduated at the Rush Medical College. He located in Wheeling in 1846, and removed to Muncie in 1856, where he continued to reside and practice medicine until his death, which occurred July 30, 1885. Dr. Winton enjoyed the esteem and confidence of his neighbors, and his friends were numbered by the thousands. He was an ardent lover of nature, and was quick to discover the beautiful wherever it existed. He lived and died a consistent Christian.

Dr. Samuel V. Jump (1822-1887) was born June 27, 1822, in Kent county, Delaware. He was a graduate of the Ohio Medical College, and located at New Burlington, in the spring of 1848. He remained here in active practice until the time of his death, August 13, 1887. His work was arduous, as he lived in this county while it was emerging from a primeval forest. He was a skillful physician, and a Christian gentleman.

Dr. George W. Godwin (1799-1865) was born in Baltimore, Maryland, December 1, 1799. He was educated in Baltimore, and graduated from one of its medical colleges. After practicing three or four years at some place in the east, he removed to Chesterfield about 1834. Fifteen years later, he changed his residence to Daleville, where he remained three months, and then located in Yorktown in the year 1850. He practiced medicine in Yorktown from 1850, to 1862, when he returned to Chesterfield, where he continued to practice until his death, which occurred April 20, 1865.

Dr. James H. Powers (1819-1882) was born in southern Indiana in 1819, but spent most of his early life in Greene county, Ohio. He graduated from the Starling Medical College in 1850, and located the same year at Albany. Here he continued to reside and practice medicine until the date of his death, which occurred March 9, 1882.

Dr. Harvey Mitchell (1825 ——) was born in Greene county, Pennsylvania, July 21, 1825. He graduated at Columbus, Ohio, in 1850, and the same year located in Granville. He removed to Muncie in 1864, where he continued in active practice until 1890, since which date he has led a retired life,—living in affluence at the present time.

Dr. Samuel E. Mitchell (1820-1871) was born in Miami county, Ohio, February 1, 1820. He practiced medicine in Virginia from 1845 until 1851, when he removed to Delaware county and located at Bethel, Harrison township. He arrived at his new home in May, 1851, where he began and continued an arduous practice until removed by death, January 26, 1871.

Dr. Benjamin F. Hittle (1808-1882) was born in the year 1808. He came from Greensburg, Indiana, to Yorktown in 1852, where he practiced medicine until the year of his death, which occurred July 26, 1882.

Dr. George W. Slack (1825-1886) was born in Bucks county, Pennsylvania, February 13, 1825. He came with his father to Delaware county in 1837. He graduated in 1854, at the Rush Medical College, and began, the same year, the practice of medicine at Yorktown, where he remained until his death, January 14, 1886. Dr. Slack took a lively interest in agriculture and horticulture. He was a Christian gentleman of the highest type.

Dr. William Craig (1818-1903) was born in Northumberland county, Pennsylvania, January 2, 1818. When but two years of age his parents removed to Clark county, Ohio. In 1837 he came to Muncietown, where he taught school, and studied medicine. He graduated from the Starling Medical College in 1849. He practiced for a short time at Wapakoneta, Ohio, and then removed to Winchester, Indiana, where he became a druggist. He came back to Muncie about 1855, practiced for a time, and then went into the drug trade, at which he continued until 1870, when he removed to California, where he remained until his death at Redlands, July 25, 1903.

Dr. Clark Skiff (1826-1888) was born in Clinton county, Ohio, January 16, 1826. He located in Selma in the year 1855, where he conducted an active practice until his death, which occurred October 12, 1888. Dr. Skiff was a modest unassuming physician, as well as the type of a Christian gentleman.

Dr. John Horne (1814-1883) was born in Scotland, February 14, 1814. He graduated in medicine at Cincinnati in 1840. He located in Yorktown about the year 1855, and remained there until his death, October 16, 1883.

Dr. James McCulloch (1813-1877) was born in Springfield, Pennsylvania, March 27, 1813. He graduated at the University of Pennsylvania, in 1847. For a time he practiced medicine in Lancaster, Ohio, and removed to Muncie in 1856. Dr. McCulloch was a modest, studious, and ethical physician. He was an upright Christian gentleman in the full sense of that term. He died at Muncie May 3, 1877.

Dr. Henry C. Winans (1829-1884) was born in Greene county, Ohio, December 31, 1829. He was a graduate of the Starling Medical College. He first practiced medicine at Xenia, Illinois. Here he was residing when the civil war began, and he entered the service as Surgeon of the 25th Illinois Volunteer Regiment. He was compelled to resign on account of physical disabilities, and came to Muncie in 1862, where he remained until his death, October 17, 1884. The last few years of Dr. Winans' life he suffered intensely from rheumatism and its results.

If space would permit, I would gladly extend this roll of honor, but I must desist. I will add a list of deceased physicians in chronological order as to dates of death:

Levi Minshall, March 6, 1836.
Ezra Stiles Trask, 1839.
John Allen Clark, May 12, 1847.
Isaac C. Helm, March 2, 1850.
Andrew J. Clawson, March, 1851.
Samuel S. Winslow, November 20, 1853.
Benjamin Paris, 1854.
Daniel H. Andrews, March 12, 1856.
Franklin P. Furry, July 14, 1858.
George W. Edgerle, November 10, 1861.
George W. Godwin, April 20, 1865.
John H. Rutter, February 15, 1866.
William C. Willard, November 6, 1869.
Samuel E. Mitchell, January 26, 1871.
Jeremiah Dynes. November 14, 1871.
John C. Helm, April 8, 1872.
John E. Van Buskirk, March 25, 1873.

William H. Williams, July 10, 1873.
William Andrews, December, 1873.
George W. Garst, February 26, 1874.
John A. Williams, May 13, 1875.
Samuel P. Anthony, July 22, 1876.
James McCulloch, May 3, 1877.
Norman W. Black, July 30, 1880.
James H. Powers, March 9, 1882.
Benjamin F. Hittle, July 26, 1882.
Oliver F. Anderson, June 23, 1883.
John Horne, October 16, 1883.
Henry C. Winans, October 17, 1884.
Robert Winton, July 30, 1885.
George W. Slack, January 10, 1886.
Samuel V. Jump, August 13, 1887.
Clark Skiff, October 12, 1888.
Andrew J. Green, January 5, 1889.
John H. Helm, May 2, 1890.
Francis M. Davis, April 5, 1891.
Stephen Hathaway, April 20, 1891.
Milton James, April 21, 1891.
David R. Armitage, August 23, 1891.
Allison B. Bradbury, January 23, 1892.
William W. Cornelius, July 3, 1892.
William R. Rogers, February 2, 1893.
Horace Winton, March 17, 1893.
Solomon R. Snell, April 29, 1893.
Evender C. Kennedy, August 26, 1893.
John S. D. Comstock, February 24, 1896.
John W. Pugh, September 24, 1896.
William J. Morgan, October 13, 1896.
Abner C. Jones, January 28, 1897.
Nathanael C. Dill, February 14, 1897.
Elijah D. Rutledge, July 4, 1897.
Seth Allen, March 15, 1898.
Martin W. Ricks, April 19, 1898.
John W. Sage, December 10, 1899.
Jesse M. Harris, January 15, 1900.
Joseph K. Shideler, March 28, 1900.
James S. Williams, May 4, 1900.
Robert Polk, April 19, 1901.
Daniel Schaub, June 8, 1902.
John E. Moler, July 24, 1902.
Henry C. Summers, November 4, 1902.
Isaac N. Addington, January 21, 1903.
Henry Kirby, June 22, 1903.
William Craig, July 25, 1903.
Elisha J. Puckett, September 10, 1903.
David R. McKinney, September 29, 1903.
W. H. Wheeler, September 14, 1904.

David N. Shively, January 3, 1905.
Augustus H. Shively, March 28, 1906.
Alfred L. Murray, June 7, 1906.
John B. Guysinger, October 21, 1906.
George W. Cassel, July 1, 1906.
John B. Summers, July 17, 1907.

Alphabetical List of Physicians of Delaware County from 1827 to 1907.

* Dead.   † Removed.   ‡ Soldier of Civil War.

* Adams, Aaron
† Adams, Bonnie O.
* Adams, Godfrey
† Adams, Mary E.
* Addington, Isaac N.
* Allen, Seth
Ames, George F.
* Anderson (Niles Tp.)
* Anderson, Oliver F.
* Andrews, Daniel H.
Andrews, George R.
* Andrews, William
† Andrews, William J.
* Anthony, Samuel P.
† Arlington, (Eaton)
† Annington, J. L.
* Armitage, David R.
† Armstrong, P.
Arnold, James W.
Atkinson, James M.
† Austin, Winser
Bacon, Casper L.
Baird, John V.
Baird, Mary A.
† Baker, Harry H.
Ball, Clay A.
Ball, Lucius L.
† Ballard, Albert M.
Barnard, Pliny C.
† Barnes, Robert A.
† Beam, Ulysses S. G.
† Beck, Isaac N.
† Beckwith, Edwin
Bell, John N.
† Berry, John L.
       —h D.
† Birchfield, James W.
† Bishop, Elias A.
† Blachley, T. L.
* Black, Norman W.

† Bland, Mary C.
† Bobbitt, William H.
† Bohannon, Charles L.
† Bonnels, L. J.
† Bowers, Joseph F.
Bowles, Herman S.
Bowles, Thomas J.
Boyden, Wilbur J.
† Brabham, William S.
*‡Bradbury, Allison B.
† Bragg, William N.
† Brandon, Oscar W.
Brandon, Winfield S.
† Brennan, V. Graham
† Broadbent, Oliver
† Bryson, William A.
Bucklin, George W.
† Bufkins, Ezra E.
† Bulla, Joseph M.
Bunch, Fred L.
Bunch, Robert A.
Bunch, Rollin H.
† Burcham, Henry C.
Burris, Samuel O.
* Burt, Dickinson
Burton, Thomas C.
† Cameron, John J.
† Carter, William J.
*‡Cassel, George W.
† Caswell, Glenn G.
Cecil, Aaron A.
* Chandler, George E.
† Chapman, Milo
† Chase, (Muncie.)
† Childs, Benjamin F.
† Christopher, William H.
* Clark, John Allen
* Clawson, Andrew J.
† Clemens, William D.
Coffman, John S.

* Comstock, John S. D.
† Compton, Joshua A.
  Cooper, Absalom M.
† Cornelius, A. Jackson
* Cornelius, William W.
‡ Cottrell, Daniel W.
† Cowgill, Alla
  Cowing, Hugh A.
* Craig, William
† Cullen, John C.
† Danner, John A.
† Davis, Elmer J.
*‡Davis, Francis M.
† Dawson, (Shideler.)
† Day, Benjamin F.
† De Long, Orville A.
† Derbyshire, John E.
  Dick, Peter B.
* Dill, Nathanael C.
* Dille, Edward
† Dillon, Jephtha
† Dodds, Thomas C.
† Doolittle, (Muncie.)
† Douglas, H. L.
  Dowell, John A.
‡ Downing, Jonathan R.
  Downing, J. Frank
†‡Downing, Samuel G.
† Dragoo, Christina
† Driscoll, William E.
  Drumm, Howard
† Dumon, John H.
  Dunn, William H.
* Dynes, Jeremiah
  Eastes, William T.
*‡Edgerle, George W.
† Egbert, William A.
  Ellis, Edwin W.
* Eskew, William C.
* Esterbrook, A. F.
† Ewing, Mrs. Herbert H.
  Fair, Herbert D.
† Fallis, Amos L.
† Farrow, W. R.
† Fenner.
† Fertich, George W.
† Fisher, John M.
† Flowers, Bartina J.
† Foster, E. Marvin
† Fowler, Elmer E.

  Franks, Hamilton P.
  Frazer, Charles
* Furry, Franklin P.
* Gandy, (Granville.)
* Garst, George W.
† Gernaud, J. E.
† Ginn, James F.
* Ginn, John C.
  Glasgow, Glen A.
† Gleason, George W.
* Godwin, George W.
‡ Good, Alonzo H.
† Graham, John J.
  Grant, William L. T.
† Gray, Frank P.
* Green, Andrew J.
  Green, Dwight M.
  Green, George R.
† Greenfield, Julia
† Greer, Lee H.
† Gregg, Elijah H.
† Griffin, Anna M. L.
† Griffith, Edward T.
† Griffith, J. Barton
* Guysinger (Granville)
* Guysinger, John S.
* Hall, John
† Halton, John
  Harbaugh, Cyrus A.
* Harris, Jesse M.
  Hastings, Aaron H.
† Hastings, Seth G.
* Hathaway, Stephen
  Hayden, John H.
* Helm, Isaac C.
* Helm, John C.
* Helm, John H.
† Heltman, Elmer W.
* Henley, Ambrose W.
* Henning (Niles Tp.)
  Henry, Thomas C.
† Hetsler, Orrie I.
† Hickman, Thomas L.
  Hill, Frank E.
† Hill, J. Stanley
* Hittle, Benjamin F.
† Hood, C. O.
† Hoover, J. Emery
† Hoover, (Muncie.)
* Horne, John

† Horne, William N.
† Hough, William A.
Houseman, Kate
Huber, George W.
†‡Hunt, John W.
† Hunt, Thomas
* Irwin, John
Jackson, Frank G.
* Jackson, Logan M.
*‡James, Milton
† Jeffrey, Homer S.
† Johnson, Thomas S.
(Missionary in India.)
*‡Jones, Abner C.
† Jones, Alfred F.
Julian, James F.
Jump, Charles A.
Jump, Samuel G.
* Jump, Samuel V.
Kearns, Thomas A.
Kemper, Arthur T.
‡ Kemper, General W. H.
Kemper, William W.
* Kennedy, Evander C.
Kilgore, Franklin T.
* Kilgore, Tecumseh
* Kirby, Henry
† Knotts (Granville)
† Kratzer,
† Krohn, W.
* Kyte, David V.
† Langtry, Sarah E.
Larimore, Joseph D.
† Lee, David F.
Leech, Garret D.
Le Favour, Joseph
* Lewellen, Wesley
† Little, Benjamin F.
† Littler, John M.
Loar, Laban T.
† McCaellehan, George
† McCray, William F.
* McCrillus, Charles C.
* McCulloch, James
† McIlwain, James R.
† McKeown, John
*‡McKinney, David R.
Mann, Eli B.
* Manor, Charles
† Manville, James H.

Mansfield, Thomas J.
† Manzer, Hiram B.
Martin, John S.
† Martin, Simeon
† Marsh, Henry M.
Marshall, Reuben
† Mask, John R.
† Mendenhall (Granville.)
† Mendenhall (Granville.)
† Metzler, S. N.
† Meyers, Edwin E.
Miller, Charles E.
† Miller, Elizabeth
Miller (Eaton)
† Minor, James C.
* Minshall, Levi
Mitchell, Harvey
* Mitchell, Samuel E.
Mitchell, Walter P.
Mix, Charles M.
Mock, Andrew R.
* Moler, John E.
Molloy, William J.
† Moore, Silas H.
† Morgan, Franklyn J.
* Morgan, William J.
† Morris, O. W.
Morrow, Benjamin B.
‡ Munsey, David O.
* Munsey, Jesse S.
† Munsey, Samuel
* Munsey, Skidmore
*‡ Murray, Alfred L.
‡ Murray, Albert P.
† Myers, Morton
† Neff, John W.
† Newlin, Edgar S.
† Norrel, John W.
† Nyce, George W.
Owens, Owen W.
† Orr, David
† Overholt, I. O.
† Painter, Lester H.
* Paris, Benjamin F.
* Paris, L. D.
† Paul, Philip D.
Payton, Lewis
† Perry, Martha A.
† Peters.
† Pielemier, Edward F.

*‡Pierce, William O.
† Philpott, Lewis W.
† Phinney, Arthur J.
Poland, Ulysses G.
Polk, Elmer E.
* Polk, Robert
† Pollock, Calvin
* Porter, Ezra
† Potter, George W.
* Powers, James H.
Powers, Ulysses G.
† Prior, Henry
*‡Puckett, Elisha J.
* Pugh, John W.
Quick, James M.
Quick, John C.
† Quickel, D. S.
† Quinn, James L.
† Ragin, Samuel
† Ramer, Buchanan
† Rawn, J. W.
† Raymond, Bardna
Rea, Clarence G.
† Read, Horace G.
† Reading, Lama Ewing
† Reasoner, Garrett
† Reasoner, Harmon D.
Reasoner, Osmer I.
† Rice, William G.
† Richardson,
Rickard, Claudia A.
Rickard, William A.
*‡Ricks, Martin W.
Ried, Samuel M.
† Riggs,
† Rogers, Leroy
*‡Rogers, William R.
† Roselle, Joseph H.
Ross, John C.
Ross, Nelson B.
† Runyan, James
† Russell, George A.
* Russell, William H.
* Rutledge, Elijah D.
† Rutledge,
* Rutter, John H., Sr.
* Rutter, John H., Jr.
† Sabin (Eaton.)
† Sage, Ira T.
*‡Sage, John W.

† Saunders, Benjamin
† Saunders, Charles B.
* Schaub, Daniel
† Schenk, Charles H.
Searcy, George H.
† Severns, Benjamin F.
† Severns, Ella
* Shafer, Henry B.
† Shafer, Ozro B.
Shaw, Homer N.
* Shepardson, Noah
* Sherwood, R. R.
* Shideler, Joseph K.
Shields, Edgar S.
† Shirey, Harlan M.
* Shively, Augustus H.
* Shively, David M.
*‡Shockley, John
*‡Shoemaker, David M.
† Shoemaker, Rollin C.
† Siggins, John J.
† Silvers, James M.
† Simmons, William D.
* Skiff, Clark
* Slack, George W.
† Slocum, Stewart
* Small, Noah W.
† Smith, Albert K.
Smith, Charles W.
† Smith, Frank
† Smith, Harry L.
† Smith, Monroe T.
Smith, William
* Snell, Solomon R.
* Snodgrass, Benjamin D.
† Snodgrass, Nancy E.
Spickermon, Harry R.
Spurgeon, Orville E.
Spurgeon, William A.
* Stackhouse. Urbin
† Stanley, John W.
* Stewart, Henry
Stick, Jesse
† Stiers, Francis R.
Stover, Charles J.
† Stout, O. M.
† Stradley, Ayres
* Stradley, D. N.
† Studley, J. W.
† Suman, William

* Summers, John B.
* Summers, Henry C.
Surber, Alva C.
* Swain, William R.
* Swayze, J. B.
† Taylor, G. C.
* Taylor, Samuel
* Templin, Isaiah
† Thornton, Thomas F.
Tidrick, Ruskin O.
Tindal, Edward F.
* Trask, Ezra F.
† Travis, John J.
Trent, Isaac N.
† Trowbridge, David L.
† Trueworthy, John W.
Tuttle, John R.
* Van Buskirk, John E.
† Van Camp (Granville.)
Vanderburg, James M.
† Van Horn, Claude B.
† Vanmatire, Milton
Vinton, Arthur E.
Wadsworth, William W.
† Wallace, G. Edward
* Waldo, Loring A.
† Walsh, Edward J.
* Waymer, John

† West (Granville.)
† Wheeler, W. H.
Whitson, John S.
† Whittaker, James T.
† White, Lindoll E.
Whitney, Emmer A.
Whitney, William D.
* Willard, William C.
† Williams, James R.
* Williams, James S.
* Williams, John A.
* Williams, William H.
† Williamson, John W.
Wilmuth, Clifford S.
† Wilson, Isaac
*‡Winans, Henry C.
Winans, Henry M.
* Winslow, Samuel S.
* Winton, Horace
* Winton, Robert
† Woods, Charles
† Woolpert, David C.
Wright, Carl H.
† Wright, Ivy E.
*†Wroughton, J. W.
† Youngs, Benjamin F.
† Zimmerman, G. W.
† Zoeller, Louis J.

NOTE.—I wish to thank physicians, friends, and the laity, who have so kindly and patiently assisted me in the preparation of the above list of names.—Editor.

CHAPTER XXIII.

'BANKING AND FINANCE.

Edited by C. H. Church.

Western banking, under state laws, during the first half of the nineteenth century was conspicuous for its many failures, as the result of loose regulations and excessive issue of "wild cat" currency, almost in direct contrast to the strict supervision and business methods now prevailing, which form the basis for ideal banking.

A notable exception to the general rule during that experience and deserving special mention was the State Bank of Indiana, whose history the state may well be proud of, as its managers were men of sterling worth who made its career a notable success. It was chartered in 1834, and passing through many panics, never closed its doors or defaulted in its promises, going into voluntary liquidation in 1866. The State of Indiana invested some $800,000 in this enterprise and in about twenty-five years its net earnings amounted to $3,500,000.

It was so successful that a feeling of hostility was aroused against it, which was engendered and promoted by the politicians for their own selfish purposes. A strong fight was made by this faction against the renewal of its charter, as the time approached for its expiration, as they desired a charter to issue for a new state bank, which they could control.

In 1853 the legislature passed a free bank law and in 1855 renewed the charter for the bank of the State of Indiana, however, both of these bills had to be passed over the governor's veto.

In order to delay the last bill taking effect, the matter was carried to the supreme court, who sustained the act, and the bank was reorganized with the Hon. Hugh McCulloch of Fort Wayne, as president, and again commenced business in 1857, and successfully weathered all financial storms, which wrecked other banks, leading a prosperous career until the introduction of the national system in 1863, when itself and most of its branches became national banks.

While the state bank was undergoing reorganization the Muncie branch was established, being organized July 2, 1856, with a capital of $100,000, but did not open for business until January 2, 1857. John Marsh was its first president, with J. W. Burson, cashier, and with these, the directors were William Petty, Volney Wilson and Edwin C. Anthony.

As the national bank act imposed a tax of ten per cent on all state bank issues, making that part of the business practically prohibitive, the state branch went into voluntary liquidation, and the Muncie National Bank was chartered as its successor, and with the same officers, continued for many years as Muncie's most permanent financial institution, enjoying a very extensive business, and going into voluntary liquidation at the expiration of its charter in January, 1885. Mr. Burson continued as cashier until his death, September 21, 1871, when S. A. Wilson was chosen as his successor. Mr. Marsh resigned as president in 1874, when F. F. White was elected to the vacancy, and no material change occurred in its management during the remaining period of its existence.

The Burson Banking Company succeeded and continued in business several years in the same location.

The building in which the Branch Bank and its successors carried on business for over thirty years still stands on the northeast corner of the public square, now the home of the Muncie Trust Company, and is one of the landmarks of the city, having stood there half a century. It was built in accordance with the current ideas of the time concerning bank architecture; combining a banking house and home for the cashier.

Citizens' National Bank.

The Citizens' Bank was organized November 16, 1874, and reorganized as the Citizens' National Bank on March 15, 1875, with George W. Spilker as its first president, who held the office eleven years, being succeeded by A. L. Kerwood. John Marsh was its first cashier, with Arthur F. Smith, assistant cashier. John Marsh continued as cashier until his death in 1887.

For a number of years this bank was located in a building on the south side of the public square, but in 1884 moved to the corner of Walnut and Jackson streets, in the room formerly occupied by the Claypool Bank, where it remained until 1890, when it moved to its new quarters in the Anthony block.

During the panic of 1893, this bank with many others throughout the country was forced to suspend, and Arthur W. Brady was appointed receiver. The suspension was only temporary, as arrangements were soon made by which the bank was reopened with G. W. H. Kemper, president, and C. M. Turner, cashier, and all depositors were paid in full, and was succeeded by the Union National Bank.

Claypool Bank.

One of the financial institutions of recognized standing in Muncie, up to about twenty years ago, was the Muncie Bank, or popularly known as the Claypool Bank, established in 1871, by A. J. Claypool, of Connersville, and soon after Austin B. Claypool became associated in the undertaking, and later on, Marcus S. Claypool.

It continued to be known as a safe, reliable, private banking house during its continuance in business, until about 1884, when it was voluntarily discontinued.

In 1886 George W. Spilker, on retiring from the presidency of the Citizens' National Bank, in connection with his son, C. A. Spilker, established the Farmers' Bank, a private institution, conducting the same successfully several years, afterward converted to a national bank, and later on it was consolidated with the Union National Bank.

Delaware County National Bank.

The oldest banking institution in the county from the point of continuance up to the present time, is the Delaware County National Bank, which at this writing, has completed twenty years of prosperous business, and throughout has been under the same roof, the Willard block, on the northeast corner of Main and Walnut. It was organized April 14, 1887, as a State Bank, and opened for business the following day, with capital stock of $50,000, and the following stockholders: R. Sprankle, J. R. Sprankle, C. H. Church, C. A. Willard, John Kirby, Isaac Meeks, William Brotherton, W. A. McClellan, Jesse Nixon, W. F. Watson.

The first officers were: R. Sprankle, president; J. R. Sprankle, vice president; C. H. Church, cashier.

It continued business under prosperous conditions until 1892, when it took out a charter as a national bank, under its present title, with Emmet M. Smith, president, and C. H. Church, cashier.

In 1896, J. C. Johnson succeeded to the presidency, with W. E. Hitchcock, vice president. Mr. Johnson remained president until his death in 1904, when he was succeeded by Mr. Hitchcock; H. C. Haymond becoming vice president, with no change in the cashiership, C. H. Church having retained that position since the bank started in 1887 to the present time.

The organization of this bank dates from the discovery of natural gas in Delaware county, and the subsequent boom which came to Muncie, developing the city from ten thousand in 1887 to thirty thousand in 1907, and the Delaware County National Bank fortunately participated in all this prosperity, building up a large and extensive business, which still continues.

Its Board of Directors is composed of well known citizens of excellent standing in the business community, and are as follows: William E. Hitchcock, H. C. Haymond, C. M. Kimbrough, George A. Ball, John S. Smith, William H. Phillips, A. L. Johnson, George A. Stafford, C. H. Church.

The Merchants' National Bank.

The Merchants' National Bank was organized in 1893, with Hardin Roads, president; Fred Klopfer, vice president; F. A. Brown, cashier, these same officers continuing at present.

It enjoys a very prosperous business and is counted one of Muncie's most substantial financial institutions. Its location is on East Main and Mulberry streets, where it has elegant quarters.

The directors are men of substantial character, having business qualifications second to none, and who are as follows: W. C. Ball, James W. Meeks, Fred Klopfer, Joseph A. Goddard, A. L. Kitselman, J. C. Wood, Hardin Roads, Mark Powers, and J. M. Maring.

The Union National Bank.

The consolidation of the Citizens and Farmers' National Banks occurred in 1895, with C. M. Turner, president; C. A. Spilker, vice president, and Edward Olcott, cashier, who were its first officers, and succeeded to the business of both banks under the title of the Union National Bank, occupying the quarters in the Anthony block.

C. M. Turner soon retired to engage in the glass business, when C. A. Spilker was made president, with Edward Olcott, cashier. Later on T. F. Rose became president and C. F. Koontz vice president, Edward Olcott cashier, continuing as such officers at the present time.

This bank is having a successful career, doing its full share of Muncie's banking business, its managers and directors being men of high standing, amply qualified for the purpose. The Board of Directors are as follows: T. F. Rose, F. Koontz, William W. Shirk, Benj. C. Bowman, A. C. Silverburg, Wallace Hibbitts, G. W. H. Kemper.

People's National Bank.

The youngest financial institution in the city is the People's National Bank, having been organized only about three years. It took over the business of the Muncie Bank, a small institution started during the oil boom, ostensibly to provide an oil bank for the operators, but on the failure of the oil field decided to discontinue.

The People's National Bank is a well managed, growing institution, having a good corps of officers and directors selected from among our best business men, and have excellent prospects of success.

C. A. Willard is president, W. E. Black, vice president, with C. H. Ellis, cashier.

Its Board of Directors is as follows:

Edward Tuhey, C. A. Willard, Norman E. Black, C. S. Wachtell, Jos. Sheets, J. E. Davis, J. M. Motsenbocker, Richard McGauley.

The Muncie Trust Company.

The Muncie Trust Company, which has its quarters in the old Branch Bank or Burson building, at the corner of Walnut and Washington streets, was incorporated February 12, 1900, and was opened for business April 2, 1900.

Its officers, who have remained the same from the beginning, are: J. M. Maring, president; B. C. Bowman, vice president; H. N. Koontz, secretary.

This is primarily a trust and loan company, but a savings department is conducted. It also acts as trustee for corporations or estates; is a prosperous reliable institution, officered by men of the highest standing and integrity.

Savings and Loan Companies.

Among the strong financial institutions of Muncie, who have materially assisted in its growth and prosperity, are three well conducted building and loan associations, whose combined resources are practically $1,800,000, which represents that amount expended in homes for the people of this city, and in very many instances could not have been provided but for their assistance.

The oldest association is The Muncie Savings and Loan Company, organized in 1889, with only $150 deposited the first meeting night. It now reaches about $900,000.

The next one to organize was the People's Home and Savings Association; and next, The Mutual Home and Savings Association, all being in a prosperous condition, owing to conservative management.

There are three state banks and two private banks in Delaware county, in addition to those already mentioned; The Albany State Bank, at Albany; The Farmers' State Bank, and the Eaton State Bank, both at Eaton, the Gaston Banking Company at Gaston, and the Commercial Bank at Daleville, all prosperous, well managed, and a great convenience to the community where located.

An enviable record has been made by the banking fraternity of Muncie, as it is developed that since the adoption of the national banking system, a period of nearly half a century, not a dollar has been lost to a depositor, and the business has been conducted along such conservative lines that it has resulted in contributing large sums to surplus and dividends, thereby extensively increasing the value of the original investments.

Another significant feature is the growth and development of Delaware county within the past twenty years, which has not only been rapid, but phenomenal, as evidenced by the extraordinary growth of the city of Muncie, the building up and extension of the smaller towns of the county, the increased values in farm property, and also, the extensive increase of individual wealth. These facts are strongly confirmed by the various financial institutions of the county, whose combined resources aggregate over six millions, a very large proportion of which naturally gravitates toward the center of traffic, the city of Muncie, and is by the bankers, placed in the channels of trade and commerce, assisting in the general business and development of a city in which every citizen of the county is not only vitally interested, but proud of its prosperity and achievements.

CHAPTER XXIV.

MILITARY HISTORY OF DELAWARE COUNTY.

By A. L. Kerwood.

"The mystic chords of memory, stretching from every battle-field and patriot grave to every living heart and hearthstone in all this broad land, will yet swell the chorus of the Union when again touched, as surely they will be, by the better angels of our nature."
—LINCOLN.

THE WAR OF THE REVOLUTION.

When the war for independence was fought the region now known as Delaware county had not yet seen the dawn of civilization.

The only tribute we can pay the memory of those venerable heroes of the past, who gave us a country and a flag, is to glean the fragments of their history from official or family archives, and present them in durable form for the information of the present and of coming generations. The data we have is scant, but being mainly from official records, may be considered reliable.

History, that patient and persistent worker of the ages, has left upon record a pen sketch of some of the heroic men who marched from Pennsylvania, Virginia and the upper Carolinas to join the Continental Army under the command of General George Washington, at the city of Boston. "They were determined men, stern of mien, and very striking in their appearance. They wore coarse, fringed hunting shirts, belted with deerskin bands, trousers of rough cloth, flax, wool or skin made by the industrious women in the cabins, raw-hide shoes of the roughest kind, woolen hats of cloth, also home made; some three-cornered with sprigs of green for cockades; some like 'Scotch bonnets;' many with brimless crowns; they carried their blankets folded and strapped over their shoulders by thongs of deer-skin; pouches of the same held their day's supply of rock-a-hominy, (Indian corn parched and pounded coarsely between two stones), a handful was eaten, then a cup of water was swallowed to moisten; this, and what wild game their rifles brought down, had sustained them on the long march to Boston. Their arms consisted of their rifles, bits of lead, a powder-horn, home-made, sometimes a cow's horn, sometimes a gourd, a hunting knife, and the Spartan soldier was ready for the fray."

"William Blount, who is supposed to have been a soldier of the Revolution, and his wife, Mary (McCoy) Blount, were natives of Tennessee. They removed to Kentucky, but three or four years later came to Indiana, and located in Wayne county, on Whitewater river, two miles below Richmond. They built a cabin but only remained there four or five years, when they moved to the western part of the county on Martindale's creek, that being as far as they could go on account of the Indians. They subsequently moved to Henry county, and in 1820 removed to a farm seven miles above Muncie-town, remaining in the vicinity of Muncietown till their death. They had a family of eleven children—Andrew, John, William, Joseph, Amos, Thomas, Aaron, Rachel, Hannah, Mary and Elizabeth, all now deceased." The above facts we have taken from a history of Henry county, Indiana, published in 1884. Our own records show that on December 9, 1822, William Blunt, Sr. (it must be the same man), entered land in section twenty-eight in Liberty township. Some years later, by entry or purchase, he came to the possession of above one hundred acres of land just east of what was, at that time, the village of Muncietown. It was afterwards owned by the late Thomas Kirby, and the growth of Muncie in recent years, has spread far beyond the limits of the tract owned at one time by this venerable pioneer. When the board of directors of the Muncie Exploring Company made choice of the location upon which the first gas well in this vicinity should be drilled, one thought which prompted them was to pay a compliment to the memory of a broad-minded and benevolent gentleman, who did so much for the growth and benefit of Muncie. Little they suspected that by that act, they were also paying tribute to the memory of a venerable soldier who, we now believe, bore a part in the War of Independence. How long William Blount lived on these premises, and when he died, we are unable to tell; but we do know that he was buried in the east part of what is now the city of Muncie, and in ground which lies between Main and Washington streets. The records of the Interior Department at Washington show that there were *seven* William Blounts in the War of the Revolution, and that quite a good part of the number were from the South. We hope to be able to cut this Gordian knot, and some day, upon the pages of a permanent record, purchased by the Grand Army Post in this city, to see recorded the document which will place beyond any doubt the record of military service of this veteran pioneer.

William Daugherty, Sr., who was supposed to have been a soldier of the War of the Revolution, was among the very early pioneers of Delaware county. He came here from Clinton county, Ohio, in the year 1829, and in 1834, as shown by public records, he entered land in sections fourteen and fifteen, in Mount Pleasant township. From all we can learn of him we conclude he resided in Clinton County, Ohio, at, and possibly prior to, the year 1790. He was a very industrious man; cleared up a farm in the wilderness.

When 90 years of age he walked from his former home in Ohio to Delaware county. He died about the year 1845, being then 92 years of age. He was buried on the bank of White river below Yorktown, upon land now owned by David Campbell. He was of Irish ancestry, and may have been born in Ireland. The approximate age at date of death, would indicate he was about 23 years of age when the War of Independence commenced.

Based upon an application for a pension, made September 28, 1832, the records of the Bureau of Pensions at Washington disclose the fact that Sewel Gilbert, whose remains lie in Beech Grove cemetery, was born December 9, 1765. His residence at the time of his application was Springwater, Livingston county, New York, and his age was 67 years.

In 1780 he enlisted for a term of nine months as a private soldier under command of Captain Jotham White, and was credited to the state of Vermont. In 1781 he made a second enlistment for the same period, at Cavendish, Vermont, under Captain Green. Fifty years had passed since the close of his last term of service. His claim for a pension was allowed, though we are unable to state the rate at which he was paid. In 1838 he had removed to the West and resided somewhere in Ohio, place not stated. Some time during the ensuing five years he took up his residence in Muncietown. November 8, 1843, Mr. F. E. Putnam made the following entry in his diary: "Old Mr. Gilbert (Revolutionary pensioner), died; buried next day with martial honors." As shown by the records, he first enlisted in his sixteenth year, and he was 78 years old at the date of his death.

(From Delaware County *Democrat*, Nov. 11, 1843.) "Another old Revolutionary soldier dead. On the 7th inst., at the hour of 1 o'clock, at the residence of William Gilbert, died Suel Gilbert, aged 87 years, after a protracted illness of three weeks and two days. . . . ." He entered the army when but a youth of seventeen years, serving three years; was at the battles of Bunker Hill, Bennington, Castle Town, Crown Point, Ticonderoga, Fort Anne, Fort Edwards, Fort Miller, Saratoga or Queenstown Heights, at the capturing of Burgoyne; also at Falmouth, Mass., which was burned by the British. "This day, the 9th inst., we paid the last respect due to our old veteran. He was buried in military style and to the great credit of the citizens of Muncietown be it told, notwithstanding the inclemency of the weather, there was no lack on their part of showing that feeling which still burns in the breast of every American citizen toward those who fought" for their oppressed country. Although the day was unpleasant and cold, the ladies "came out en masse to show the respect due to one of the defenders of their country. After a very appropriate and elaborate discourse by the Rev. Robert Irvin, the procession moved on toward the graveyard under the solemn sound of martial music. The scene was affecting—twelve armed musketeers, commanded by Captain Liston, marched solemnly along to pay their last tribute at his grave. . . . As the old warrior lived, so he died; always in good faith with his neighbors, truly honest and a good citizen. May his ashes forever rest in peace.   Mr. Irvin closed the scene at the graveyard by prayer."

John McConnell, a soldier of the war of the Revolution, was of Scotch-Irish ancestry. His wife Barbara (Bowman) McConnell was of German descent. He had seven children all of whom have passed away. The old home was in Scioto county, Ohio, from which the family, or at least part of them, emigrated to Indiana. In 1832, one son, William McConnell, entered 80 acres of land in section 20, township 20, range 10, and the following year moved to what was then an unbroken wilderness. Presumably the parents came about the same time. Here at least these aged people resided for some years and here they died. John McConnell died January 6, 1847, at the age of eighty-three years, and his wife died in December, 1838, aged 63 years. They were first buried in ground now known as Forest Park. When improvements crowded in that quarter their remains were removed to Beech Grove Cemetery. There is no record of the command and services in this case, but there is a well-defined tradition that he was for seven years a regular wagoner in the Continental Army. That at one time when the train, taken by surprise, was attacked by the British, he made such heroic efforts that he and his team alone escaped the enemy and reached the Colonial camp, and then only after he was shot and severely wounded in the thigh. And thus another resting place of the heroic men of the Revolution is known.

John Quinn, a soldier of the war of the Revolution, was born in Scotland in the year 1759. He was married to Sarah Tapper in that country after which he emigrated to America and enlisted in the Continental Army. He was a very early settler in Delaware county, having entered land in section 2 in Delaware township, on the 24th day of November, 1832. He had three sons and four daughters. We are unable to furnish any details of his service, or just at what date he took up his abode at Yorktown. But about his having performed some kind of service there is no question whatever. In a census taken by the Government in the year 1840, the year in which he died, his name appears as one of the three pensioners then living in the county of Delaware. The other two in that list were William Williams and William Whicker. In the cemetery at Yorktown, upon a slab of sandstone sunk deep into the ground, we were able with some difficulty to make out the following inscription: "In memory of John Quinn, who departed this life in the year 1840, in the 81st year of his age."

Has the tomb of this old soldier ever borne the burden of a single flower in the land of his adoption and partly of his own creation?

Mrs. Cynthia A. Randal, of this city, with her gude Scotch face, hale and hearty at seventy-one years, is now the only surviving daughter of this venerable hero of the long ago. This warrior from the land of Burns was just old enough to vote when the thunder of the guns was reverberating about Bunker's Hill in Boston.

Benjamin Wallace, supposed to be a soldier of the war of the Revolution, was born in Ireland, and emigrated to the state of Virginia. The name of his wife (taken from a Bible published in 1829), was Sally. Milly Roleing, daughter of Benjamin and Sallie Wallace, his wife, was born the 17th day of May, 1772. This is not positive as to the last figure. Even under a strong glass it is hard to decipher, as the figure has been changed and badly blurred. This daughter of the Revolution was the grandmother of Comrade James H. Childs, late of Company "C," 140th Regiment Indiana Infantry, to whom we are under very many obligations for the tradition about his great grandfather. The story shall be furnished in his own words: "Roland Childs, my grandfather, married Millie Roleing Wallace, and my father, George Childs, deceased, was their son. My grandmother said the family went from Virginia to the state of Tennessee, then back to Virginia, and then to Indiana, and settled near Bethel. She told me that grandfather Wallace served seven years in the Revolutionary war. That at one time during his experience with the army, he did without a bite of food to eat for eight days, except a stalk of cabbage which he was fortunate enough to find. Benjamin Wallace lived but one or two years after they came to Indiana. My father came in 1837, and grandfather died some time between that and the year 1840, at the home of his daughter, named Newhouse, on what was afterwards known as the Daniel Connor farm. He was a farmer during his lifetime. His burial took place at what is called the Miller graveyard in Harrison township. I think from what I can remember, that I could come within a very few feet of pointing out the spot where he lies. The tradition of the family has always been, as long as I can remember, that he served under General Washington for the full period of seven years. He had one son (James Wallace) and three daughters, one of whom became Millie Childs, my grandmother." Comrade Childs, who is now in poor health, as the result of exposure and arduous service during the Civil war, besides at the village of Cammack. He married Miss Nannie S. Lee, who was born and raised in Mason county, West Virginia. She remembers her grandfather's name, George Lee, who was a cousin of General Robert E. Lee, the distinguished commander of the Army of Northern Virginia. She very much resembles General Fitzhugh Lee, a nephew of General Robert E. Lee.

William Whicker, the subject of this sketch, was born August 27, 1760, near Richmond in Hanover county, Virginia. His father was from England, his mother was French. Soon after his birth they moved from Hanover county to the southern part of Virginia where they received a large grant of land, recognized by both the English government and the

state of Virginia. Soon after locating on this land there was hostility with
the Indians. The country was sparsely settled and on account of this Indian outbreak, the entire colony moved further south expecting to return
when peace was restored. He located in Granville county, North Carolina,
and was living there at commencement of the Revolutionary war. When
but a boy fourteen years of age, he entered the service without enlistment
and remained with the Minute Men of Sumter and Marion until the fall
of 1777, when he and his brother James enlisted as privates and served two
months under Captain Hester, in the command of General Taylor. In
1778 he was still with the same company officer, and under command of
General Richard Caswell. In 1779 he enlisted for three months in the
company of Captain Pearce and was transferred to the command of General Davidson. He was first sergeant of the company. On the morning of
February 1, 1781, at McCown's ford, on the Catawba river, the defeat and
death of General Davidson scattered his three hundred men. Sergeant
Whicker was detailed to carry the news of General Davidson's death and
the defeat of the three hundred men to General Butler. He rode all day in
a steady, hard rain, catching his drinking water in the rim of his hat, and
reaching General Butler late in the evening. General Davidson's command
was utterly ruined in this engagement and William Whicker, for meritorious
service (he having again enlisted) was appointed a first sergeant in Captain
William Gillam's company under General Butler, then in command of the
South Carolina Militia. Sergeant Whicker was in five battles, among which
were McCown's Ford, Guilford Court House, Cowpens and Rugsley's Mills.
In the last engagement he lost a thumb, for which he afterwards received
a pension. Later in the war he again enlisted for three months, this, as
shown by the records in the War Department at Washington, being his fifth
enlistment. He was enrolled in Captain James Blackwell's company (in
which he appears as second in command), in Colonel Mebane's regiment of
cavalry. This regiment was made up of Colonial boys who furnished and
fed their own horses, and were ready for service wherever sent. They were
sometimes with Sumter and at other times with Marion. They were with
General Greene on his march to the north after the battle of the Cowpens.
They were also under the command of Generals Morgan and Gates. They
were fearless Rangers, ready for hazardous service at any call. At the close
of the war Sergeant Whicker married Sarah Bingaman, a daughter of a
German, who lived near Guilford Court House, and whose acquaintance he
made while stationed near that place with the command of General Butler.
He settled in Guilford county where he ran a boarding house and operated
a distillery until about 1820. He had four sons and two daughters. The
sons were Matthew, Asa, Luke and Berry. The daughters were Susan and
Elizabeth. About 1820 he moved to Lebanon, Warren county, Ohio, and

purchased a distillery there and a distillery at Waynesville, Ohio. His sons Asa and Luke located in Jefferson township, Fayette county, Ohio. His wife died about 1830. He then sold his interests in Warren county, Ohio, and went to live with his son in Fayette county. While there he secured his pension, applying October 4, 1832. He was then seventy-one years of age, almost blind from a cataract and finally lost his sight entirely. His son Asa became blind from the same cause. He moved from Fayette county, Ohio, with his sons Asa and Luke, and his daughter, Susan Fisher, to Delaware county, Indiana, in 1834, locating near Albany, where he died November 2, 1851, aged ninety-one years, two months and five days. Mrs. Fisher died November 15, of the same year. His son Asa died April 30, 1853, and his son Luke died June 9, 1853. All these are buried in the Strong Cemetery near Albany. His daughter Elizabeth settled in South Bend, Indiana, and his son Berry settled in Fountain county, near Attica, Indiana, in 1854. William Whicker drove from Albany, Indiana, to Cincinnati, Ohio, once a year to get his pension. He was liberal in his religion but was not a member of any church. He was a member of the Masonic order but never moved his membership from Guilford county, North Carolina. He had a good education for his times, and in one political campaign he stumped the state of Ohio. It is not clear just what campaign this was, but it is supposed to have been the Jackson and Adams campaign of the year 1824. It is believed also that he knew General Jackson personally, having probably made his acquaintance subsequent to the war of the Revolution, and that by reason of his admiration for the old hero, and perchance at his own request, he made his campaign for the venerable comrade. This is all that is known about the politics of William Whicker. The above sketch is compiled from information furnished by the War Department, Mr. J. Wesley Whicker, attorney at law, Attica, Indiana, great grandson, and the Society of the Daughters of the Revolution in this city.

William Williams, a soldier of the Revolutionary war, is supposed to have been born in Virginia, and from that state to have entered the Continental Army. Among the early events that occurred in what is now Liberty township, was the holding of the first election for President. At that time Delaware county had no distinct civil existence, being still within the territorial area of Randolph county. The election was held at the cabin of William Williams. The year was 1824, and the candidates were John Adams and Andrew Jackson. March 3, 1836, William Williams, Sr., entered land in section twenty-seven in Liberty township. He had but one son, William Williams, Jr., who was a teacher and Justice of the Peace. Mr. Michael Dunkin relates that in those early days there was a venerable Methodist preacher, who also did merchandising in the village of Smithfield. At one time this preacher, Rev. Benjamin Garrison, felt called upon to impart a serious warning and appeal to the old soldier, concerning his spiritual interests. The veteran listened patiently to the end, and then, after some time was taken to deliberate, he said: "Uncle Ben, d—d if I don't think the Methodists and the dog fennel will take the town." When the old man became feeble, the son built a round-log house for him and his wife, in which they ended their days. He died about the year 1842, and was buried only some 300 yards distant near the bank of White River, upon land now owned by a Mr. Eckenberger. In 1840 he was drawing a pension from the Government, being then one of three survivors of the war of the Revolution, then living in Delaware county. Who would have believed that the ashes of eight of these old heroes reposed within our borders?

SECOND WAR WITH ENGLAND.

"I hear the tread of pioneers,
    Of millions yet to be;
The first low wash of waves, where soon
Shall roll a human sea."

—WHITTIER.

James Abbott was born where the city of Cincinnati now stands, February 27, 1794. He was a son of Aaron Abbott, of English extraction, who was born near Boston, Mass., but reared in Warren county, Ohio. Shortly after the removal of the family to that county the colony was attacked with cholera, and Mr. Abbott was one of the few who survived the scourge. Soon after the birth of his son James, he died, and all previous records of the family were lost. James Abbott was reared in Warren county, and there learned the trade of cabinet-maker. While yet a minor he enlisted in the war of 1812, and in 1813 was in one of the vessels on Lake Erie during the battle between Commodore Perry of the Lawrence and the British fleet. His service did not extend over very many months, and after his return home he located at Lebanon, Ohio, where he worked at his trade, until his marriage June 19, 1825. After this event he removed to Miami county, Ohio, where he engaged in farming for about twelve years, when he removed to Indiana, in 1847, and became one of the early pioneers of Delaware county. He purchased a fine farm of one hundred and sixty acres near Granville, in Niles township, and there remained until his death, which occurred October 14, 1874. His wife died April 16, 1881, and both were buried in the Granville cemetery, where a modest stone marks their last resting place.

Mr. Abbott was a successful business man and became possessed of considerable property. Both he and his wife were members for many years of the Free Will Baptist church. In his early days he was a Whig, but upon the birth of the Republican party he joined that and supported its principles through life. He was the father of seven children: Aaron, John K., Ellen, William, James D., George and Sarah E.

Edmund Alldredge, a soldier of the war of 1812, was the son of a Revolutionary soldier whose ancestors came from Wales. His services continued throughout the entire war. He took part in the battle of Bunker's Hill, and brought with him as a souvenir, from its bloody field, a British powder-horn embellished by a brazen deer on one side. Edmund Alldredge was born April 2, 1784, near Wilkes Court House, North Carolina. It was from this mountain home that his father went forth to fight his country's battles. Like all pioneers at that early day the opportunities for education were limited, but he succeeded in acquiring a fair knowledge of the three R's and was all his life a wide reader. Hearing of the fertile country in Indiana, he set out on horseback and rode the entire distance. After numerous hardships he reached the No Name country south of Muncietown, containing not over a half dozen houses.

He entered a fine tract of land and secured a patent from the Government. He had made the acquaintance of an estimable young lady near Cincinnati, Miss Jane Mulford. Their marriage took place October 4, 1810, and the wedding trip was a journey on horseback from her father's house to the new home in the woods. The woods abounded in game, and he largely supplied the table with wild meats from the forest. They had ten children: Francis B., Elijah, Hiram, William, Isaac, Kezia, Mary, John, Elizabeth and Edmund Jr. When the second war for Independence was declared he joined the standard of General Harrison. The army suffered much, during the bitterly cold weather of the Michigan campaign, and he afterwards, in reminiscent mood, often said that no tongue could express the suffering of night picket duty along the great lakes facing the frigid gales that swept in from the north. Refusing promotion, he served in the ranks until peace was declared, when he returned to home and family. His oldest son did not recognize his father with his buckskin clothes, soldier equipments, and, as a trophy, an Indian tomahawk. He again took up the pursuit of farming and stock-raising, and prospered until the year 1833, when a terrible scourge of disease known as milksickness visited the family and neighborhood. Those who drank of the milk were attacked with a terrible malady, attended with sweating and nervous weakness that often proved fatal. In a little over one year he lost five of his family, including his faithful wife. The attack he suffered from was light, but he felt its presence in his system to the end of his life. With this bereavement and affliction he did not despair. A faithful Christian, a member of the M. E. church, he was fully sustained by the bearer of burdens for the "weary and heavy laden." Five years after the death of his first wife, he married Mrs. Fannie Breece, with whom he lived happily until her death, four or five years later. Two years later he married Mrs. Jane Armstrong, but the union proved an unhappy one, and resulted in his obtaining a divorce. Soon after he met, won and married Mrs. Jane Hundley, with whom he lived in great harmony until his death, March 30, 1858, at the age of seventy-four years. He was thrown from a load of hay, breaking the left leg above the ankle. Because of his age, medical skill failed, and he died two days later, declaring his unswerving faith in God's love and mercy. His last words to his son John were, "I am going to rest, having no fear of death." He was a worthy, honest man, absolutely truthful, and trusted and respected by his neighbors. In politics he was an ardent Whig, despising slavery and doing all in his power against the great crime, abolished five years after he passed away. His remains rest in the Heath cemetery, near his old home. Of his kindred, but two remain, Edmund F. Alldredge of Muncie and J. S. Alldredge of Anderson, Indiana.

John Applegate, a soldier of the war of 1812, was born September 23, 1794, near Maysville, Mason county, Kentucky. His father, Henry Applegate, was a soldier in the war of Independence, probably from Virginia. John Applegate entered the service from Kentucky in the year 1812. He served in the infantry, and was at the battle of Lundy's Lane and other engagements. While home upon furlough, he was married to Elizabeth Trafford, of Irish descent, who was born in 1796. He was discharged in 1815. He received land warrant for one hundred and sixty acres of land. This he sold. He had fourteen children, seven sons and five daughters, also two who died infants, unnamed. In the state of Kentucky his business was that of an overseer. He was an old Whig. He removed, first, to Rush county, Indiana, and then in the year 1836 to Delaware county. He purchased 160 acres of land now known as the Franklin Fullhart farm, a large part of which he cleared, and upon which he resided until the year 1842. He was the owner, also, of 80 acres on the north, and the same upon the east of the home place. He removed to Iowa, remained four years, came back and purchased part of the land he formerly owned. Again sold out and returned to Iowa in 1855, and lost his wife in 1856. He then came back to Delaware county, where he resided until February 2, 1862, the date of his death. He was buried at the Yorktown cemetery. He was a member of the United Brethren church.

Stephen H. Baker, soldier of the war of 1812, was born January 22, 1790. Died May 1, 1875, aged 85 years, and was buried in Beech Grove cemetery.

John Barton, a soldier of the war of 1812. So far as we can ascertain he was born in Tennessee, raised in the same state and from there entered the service. He probably served in the Southern Department, as he often related his experience with the Army while in the vicinity of Mobile, Alabama. He had ten children, six sons and four daughters. So far as we could learn, none of his descendants are now living in Delaware county, or other locality known to any one here. The old veteran died many years ago and was buried at Granville.

David Bell, a soldier of the war of 1812, was born in 1792, in the state of Maryland. Later he emigrated to Greene county, Ohio, where he married Lydia Kyle, and afterwards removed to Jay county, Indiana. He was the father of five sons and six daughters. He died February 1, 1850, aged 58 years, and was buried at the Bethel cemetery near Albany. We have no particulars of his service. To us this is cause for genuine regret. But he was a soldier, no doubt about that, and our word for it he was a good one. After his death the Government issued a land warrant to his heirs which called for one hundred and sixty acres of land. From an old pupil who was under his tutelage during six terms of "deestrict school," we learn he was for a long time a teacher. A typical "Hoosier School Master." He was small, bald-headed, and very active. His pupils imagined he had eyes in the back part of his head, so certain was he to detect them in any kind of mischief. "Full well the busy whisper circling round, conveyed the dismal tidings when he frowned." He was a disciplinarian of the strictest sort. Some suppose there was a clock-like system by which he was controlled, to be learned alone in the school of the soldier. He had an imaginary line separating the boys from the girls, and woe to the luckless wight who crossed the forbidden boundary. He had something more than rules, too. Back of his desk in full view of the school were two wooden hooks, which he kept filled with a variety of beech switches, exactly suited to the size of the pupil, and the grade of the offense.

'No lickin', no larnin', says I." Often there was a goose quill over each ear, and another in his fingers, which he deftly scraped and sharpened for use, as only an expert could. He was supplied with a stentorian voice, and abundant lung power. When he called "books!" the dullest youngster within a mile could hear the call. Verily the old soldier had an impressive way of teaching young ideas how to "shoot."

David Bell was a land surveyor, also, in the early days of this county. His father had been a sea captain. No wonder the teacher had systematic methods of business. He was a faithful and devout member of the M. E. Church.

David M. Bell, a son of the aged veteran, was himself a valiant soldier, he having served in Company D, Second Indiana Cavalry, from September 22, 1861, until October 4, 1864.

Martin Bobo, a soldier supposed to have been in the war of 1812, from the state of Ohio. Of his history, in or out of the army, we can learn nothing. Persons who knew him, while he lived in Delaware county, say that he had lost one eye; that he had quite an appetite for strong drink. Sometimes he had to hide his "supplies." This he always attempted to do with some care. At one time he had eyesight sufficient to hide his favorite jug in a dense patch of "jimpson weed" to keep his watchful enemies from finding where he had stored it, but alas! his vision was not good enough to enable him to find it. He was buried at Granville. Age and date of his death are unknown. No headstone.

Stephen D. Berry, Sr., a soldier of the Indian wars, and of the war of 1812, was born in the state of Virginia, in the year 1774. He early removed to the state of Ohio, from which he entered the army. He was married in Ross county, Ohio, to Jane Greenlee, who was born in Pennsylvania. They were the parents of ten sons and four daughters. He removed to Delaware county, Indiana, in the year 1837. Our records show that on November 12, 1836, a part of section nine, in Delaware township, was entered by one Stephen Berry. This was, perhaps, the old hero of two wars. Prior to his removal here he pursued the trade of a carpenter. In Indiana he became a farmer, and it is probably true of him, as of so many of those early pioneers, that he came where land was plentiful and cheap, and where he could found a home of his own.

The only facts about his service we have been able to gather, are that he received an honorable discharge and a warrant for land. He was a faithful and consistent member of the Baptist church. Church privileges were very crude in those days. Under the friendly roof of this "devout soldier" the services were conducted for years, until a schoolhouse was erected upon the corner of his farm, after which that was used as a place of worship. The venerable old man died in December, 1855, and was buried in the Black cemetery.

Isaac Branson, a soldier of the war of 1812, was born in Virginia in 1794, and was married June 9, 1818, to Martha Chipman in Kentucky, who was born February 15, 1798, in the same state. In the same year they settled in Highland county, Ohio, and in 1819 removed to Randolph county, Indiana. In 1828 they came to Delaware county and settled on Buck Creek within six miles of Muncietown. In 1858 they removed to Muncietown, where Mr. Branson died three weeks later. He was a successful dealer in land and owned many tracts, at various times, in this and adjoining counties. He was a good man; respected by all who knew him. There were no children born to this worthy couple, but to their credit be it said, the homeless orphan found no better friends. During their married life they furnished a home and supplied the wants of no less than fourteen children—some of them until they reached mature years. To the last, the venerable hero loved children. He was blind during the closing years of his life. He died November 8, 1858. Perhaps no pioneer of the county was held in greater esteem or had more true friends than the quaint, old-time lady whom so many people knew and called "Aunt Patsy Branson."

It was a humorous boast of hers that for forty years she cut her garments by the same pattern. She possessed a strong individuality, had a noble heart and was a true friend. She was remarkably active for one so well advanced in years, with a step light and ?? ??c almost as that of a girl. Through the long years of her widowhood sh.. ? ained cheerful and sunny in disposition, always recognizing the realitie life, but thinking of the brighter side. During her last years she was warded with a pension at the rate of $12.00 per month. Aunt Patsy d? September 4, 1891, at the ripe old age of ninety-three years. This ?? able couple are buried in Beech Grove cemetery.

Henry Brown, a soldier of the war of 1812, was said to have seen service upon a war vessel, but this brief statement is all there is of what, if within our reach, might be an interesting bit of history. He was buried at the Jones cemetery.

Patrick Carmichael, a soldier of the war of 1812, was born December 11, 1794, in the state of Kentucky. His ancestors were Irish. He probably entered the service when about 18 or 19 years of age, afterwards was married to Margaret Lee, on February 15, 1815, very soon after he came from the army. So far as known his wife was also born in the state of Kentucky. They were the parents of eleven children, as follows: Catharine, John, William H., Andrew J., Patrick L., Lewis R., Mary A., Nancy J., Sarah E., James M. and Tempy A. About the record of this old veteran there can be no question. During the later years of his life he drew a pension, something which can be fully relied upon as the basis of a soldier's history. He emigrated to Indiana at an early date, for the public records show that he purchased land in section twelve in Union township, and settled upon it in 1836. Here, in the unbroken forest, this hardy pioneer battled as courageously with his new enemies as when arrayed for the contest in the garb of the soldier. Here he ended his days, dying at a ripe old age. He was buried on the Eshenfelder farm, some two miles northwest of Eaton.

Of John Carroll, whose name appears upon a list of soldiers of the war of 1812, and whose grave is regularly decorated as such, we can only say that he once lived in the old village of Granville; that he was buried in the cemetery at that village, and that his grave has no tombstone.

Francis Ciscus, a soldier of the war of 1812, was born in the year 1786. The place of birth we have been unable to locate. Tradition says he spent many years upon the ocean. In an early day—possibly in the early thirties— he removed from some point in Pennsylvania to Delaware county, Indiana, and purchased eighty acres of land of Peter Bradshaw, a part of section

36, in Union township. Here he established his home and here he died, February 1, 1856. His wife, Catharine, died March 1, 1848. They had one daughter, who married Joseph Slonaker. This aged and scarred veteran of sea and shore often repeated to younger, but willing hearers, the thrilling story of his adventures and conflicts. He showed the evidence of severe wounds in the neck; his shoulder-blade was cut open by the blow of an Indian tomahawk, and there were marks of two bullet wounds in one of his lower limbs. At one time, while on military duty, he was taken prisoner by the Indians, bound, and closely guarded to . revent his escape. When additional supplies of ammunition were needed he was untied, disrobed and required to assist in molding bullets. He closely watched his chance and made a dash for liberty, hiding himself when pursued in a dense mass of heavy thistles, which the Indian dogs could not penetrate. Without a bite of food he cheerfully took up the weary march to reach the encampment. At one stage of his journey he was so near starved that he cut a slice from the body of a dead pony. Later he came upon the corpse of a dead soldier and secured his musket, with which he was fortunate enough to shoot a bear. This bit of good luck supplied him with provisions enough to last until he reached the camp. To the end of his life his hatred of the Indian was intense. He and his wife lie in the Laird cemetery on a bank overlooking the Mississinewa river, and from his tombstone this writer copied the inscription: "Precious in the sight of the Lord is the death of his saints."

The name of Henry Clouse comes to us as one who was a very old soldier. Some supposed he was in the war of the Revolution, but that theory is not sustained. He was probably in the war of 1812, or the Indian wars. There are no further details except that he died long since, and was buried at Bethel or Granville.

The sketch of Robert Sanders shows that when he reached the trading station of David Connor, near Wheeling, he found an old comrade of the Indian campaigns. Mr. Connor removed from Delaware county at an early date, and we can hear no further word of him. We presume he was a soldier under General Anthony Wayne.

William H. Daugherty, a soldier of the war of 1812, was born at or near Wilmington, Clinton county, Ohio, March 3, 1790. He was of Irish ancestry and his father, William Daugherty, Sr., was probably a soldier in the Revolutionary army.* But of the service of the younger Daugherty there is a reliable and honorable record. He was enrolled at Lebanon, Ohio, in August, 1812, for the period of six months, serving in Captain John Spencer's company of the regiment commanded by Colonel Shumait of the Ohio militia. He was located some time at Lower Sandusky, Ohio.

From that point he was ordered to Detroit, Mich., and thence to Sandwich, Canada. He then returned to Lower Sandusky and assisted in guarding prisoners of war to Chillicothe, Ohio. While upon this duty he was taken sick and prevented from active duty for some months. He was discharged from service at Lebanon, Ohio, in 1813, and in 1814 he married Miss Tauser Thornburg, in Clinton county, Ohio. He received from the government a warrant for eighty acres of land. About the year 1829 he emigrated to Indiana, and settled in Mount Pleasant township, near Yorktown.

His first wife having died, he later married Mrs. Deborah (Combs) Koontz, mother of Hon. J. H. Koontz, and the late L. D. Koontz. She died August 17, 1865. He also married the third wife, who outlived him. Mr. Daugherty was the father of four sons and seven daughters. He was all his life a farmer. It is said that he was somewhat pugnacious and knew well how to defend his own interests in a conflict. Like the brave people by whom he was surrounded in those early days, and with whom he mingled, he was made of good fibre, and bore well his part in the heavy duties of a frontier life. He died August 29, 1876, and his remains lie in the cemetery at Yorktown.

Samuel Darter, a soldier of the war of 1812, was born March 13, in the year 1795, in the State of Virginia, and married Letitia Parker, who was born in the state of North Carolina. They moved to Indiana at an early day and settled in the county of Fayette, where Mr. Darter became possessed of valuable real estate, consisting of a farm of 160 acres. Here he remained for some years and then removed to Delaware county, where he purchased land in Harrison and Mount Pleasant townships, in the latter of which he made his home until his death. Mrs. Darter died in 1856, and subsequently Mr. Darter married Sarah Beach, who departed this life in the year 1887.

He was a man of prominence in the community where he resided; he was a member of the Methodist church and was active in the promotion of the cause of religion. He was intensely radical in his political views, having been one of the original abolitionists of Indiana. He died August 29, 1872, aged 77 years 5 months and 16 days. He was buried in the Jones cemetery.

Martin Depoy, a soldier of the war of 1812, was born in the year 1776. He came at an early day from Greenbrier county, Virginia. March 26, 1836, he bought land in section three in Delaware township. Of his service we have no data. He died September 29, 1838, and was buried at the Strong cemetery near Albany.

Jacob Dickover, a soldier of the war of 1812, was born August 26, 1785, in Lancaster county, Pennsylvania. He was the son of Henry Dickover, of Lancaster county, concerning whose history some very interesting papers have come to hand, and are herewith published.

"Harrisburgh, Penna., March 11, 1898.

To Whom It May Concern :—

I hereby certify to the Revolutionary services of Henry Dickover, as follows :—

Henry Dickover enlisted as a private in Capt. John Wither's Company of Militia, of Col. John Ferrie's battalion of Associators in Lancaster county, destined for the Jerseys, mustered at Lancaster August 19, 1776. This command was in active service in the Jerseys in the summer of that year. The company was in service from August, 1776, until February, 1777.

For reference see Penna. Archives, Vol. 13. pages 333 and 305.

Yours with respect,

William Henry Eyle, M. D.,

State Librarian and Editor Penna. Archives."

Some of the descendants of Henry Dickover have the impression he was a Hessian, captured at the battle of Trenton, and sent to Carlisle, Penn., after which he enlisted in the Continental Army. He may have been a Hessian. But the records show he was mustered August 19, 1776, and the battle of Trenton was fought in December, 1776. If he were a Hessian prisoner, he was captured prior to August 19, 1776.

The records of the War Department in Washington show that, "his name appears on a muster roll, dated at Lancaster, August 19, 1776, which bears no special remarks relative to his service." Here, on the margin of this roll, would have been a very appropriate place for the fact of his having been a soldier among the Hessians. Jacob Dickover, one of the eleven sons of Henry Dickover, entered the service for the war of 1812, from the state of Pennsylvania. His record of service we do not have, but we do have the fact that he received a land warrant, and that during the last years of his life he drew a pension. In 1835 he removed from Wayne county, Indiana, to the county of Delaware. He bought one hundred and twenty acres of land one mile north of Selma, cleared up a farm, occupied it as a permanent home, and here he died March 23, 1876, and was buried in the Bortsfield cemetery. His age was ninety years, six months and 27 days.

He married Hannah Baney, by whom he had one son and seven daughters. His wife died April 14, 1877, aged 67 years one month and 28 days, and lies by his side. They were members of the United Brethren church. In an interview with Mr. Michael Dunkin, the oldest man in his region, he related some experience when a boy of ten years. His father had erected a two-story, hewed-log house. Mr. Jacob Dickover was the bricklayer who built the chimney, and young Dunkin was his helper. At one stage of the work he mounted a steep ladder, bearing a hod of mortar, at some outlay of sweat and muscular power. But it proved to be too thick. So the hod was returned, the mortar was tempered, as directed, by the use of "more water." The young man not only felt very anxious to get that hod of mortar exactly right, but another idea struck him with some force. He sincerely believed the four first letters of the name of the gentleman for whom he was doing duty, was a misnomer, and that when properly addressed, the full name should be Mr. Richard Over. And when he made the second trip with his burden he very politely said: "How will that suit you, Mr. Over?" The brick mason promptly suspended proceedings long enough to retort, with some warmth, "Why don't you call me by my right name?" One of the descendants of this aged patriot, a professional gentleman, very anxious that every crumb of historic detail should be carefully preserved, has said, that at one time his grandfather, in the line of his mechanical pursuits, was frequently called upon to aid in the erection of distilleries, and that as he grew older his conscience became very much quickened; so he determined to abandon the "camp of the Hessians" by starting a family altar, and here, daily, about this sacred spot, he sought supplies of grace to enable him to offset the evil influences of his earlier days. Samuel Dickover, son of Jacob, volunteered in Company "K," 19th Regiment, Indiana Volunteers, in October, 1862, and served through until the end of the Civil war, taking part in all of the engagements of his command after his enlistment. To him we are under obligations for the historical matter in this sketch.

William Dunkin, Sr., a soldier of the war of 1812, was born and raised near Dayton, Ohio, and from there he entered the service, having enlisted for two terms, of one year each. There are no records of his service now within reach. But of tradition there is an abundance.

He was in the Dragoons. He rode the same horse during the whole of his service. The horse was afterwards brought to Indiana. He died on the home farm near Smithfield, when he was 37 years old. He received great care at the last; no work was required of him for several years. He was handled like a baby in the winter season to prolong his life. The grim old warrior related many accounts of his military experience. Once while the command was located at Fort Harrison on the Wabash, the order came to "mount," instantly, which was done, and the Dragoons rode rapidly all night long, with one halt of fifteen minutes to refresh the men and animals. Upon their arrival at the destination, the horses were utterly exhausted. General Harrison had met and defeated the Indians, who were then in rapid retreat with the troops in pursuit. There are numerous stories of skirmishes with Indians, and of long and toilsome marches. William Dunkin drew no pension but received a land warrant for 80 acres of land for each enlistment.

The wife's maiden name was Hannah Smith, born and raised near Trenton, New Jersey. They had eight children, five sons and three daughters, of whom but two sons, Michael and William, are now living. William

Dunkin, Sr., first entered land in Ohio, and later he removed to Union county, Indiana, and then, in 1827, he came to the county of Delaware. Here he bought 160 acres of land upon which there was a log cabin, and a small clearing. He cleared much of this land and at the time of his death more than half of it was in a good state of cultivation. The village of Smithfield was laid out upon these premises. Mr. Dunkin was a member of the old Baptist church. When he came to Indiana there was no organized society here, but he remained firm in his belief, and died in that faith. At his death he and his wife were buried in the woods near Smithfield, but ... ...rs since they were removed to the Mount Tabor graveyard.

John L. Elliott, soldier of 1812, came from Lancaster county, Penn., to Clinton county, Ohio, and thence to Indiana, some sixty years ago. In Ohio he owned a farm. He was tall, raw-boned, muscular and stout—a splendid physique. He had one son who died young; also seven daughters, none of whom are now living. He settled at Yorktown, where he was by turns farmer and teamster. His team was a yoke of heavy cattle. The date of his death we cannot give. He was buried at Yorktown and no slab marks his resting place.

Here is another case of military tradition. But there are some touches in the story that any old soldier would be able to recognize. To a grandson, Mr. Belty Dragoo, he related how, at one time, the command to which he belonged stealthily crept upon a camp of the enemy in the night time and fired without any warning, killing several British soldiers. The volley had entered a group who were playing at cards, by the smoldering embers of a camp fire. One of the dead soldiers was found with fingers tightly clinched. When relaxed they showed a hand which read, "High, low, Jack and the game." We wonder if any testament-reader in the civil war ever had his thoughts disturbed by the frequent and boisterous use of those words?

John Ethell, a soldier in the war of 1812, was born in Fairfax county, Virginia, in the year 1778. After the war he removed to Licking county, Ohio, where he lived until he moved to Muncietown, in the year 1839, and resided there until the day of his death, in 1862. For his services he received a land warrant the same as other soldiers in that war. His occupation was chairmaking, which he followed here until his health became too feeble for work. His wife's maiden name was Mary Cunard. She was born in Loudoun county, Virginia. They had eight children, but three of whom reached maturity, to-wit: William G., Sarah and Nathaniel F. Sarah was the wife of Armstead Klein. John Ethell was at one time postmaster in Muncietown, keeping the office in his residence at the southeast corner of Main and Franklin streets. He was 84 years old at the time of his death. He died at the home of Mr. William G. Ethell, in the building at the corner of Monroe and East Adams, now belonging to the Episcopal church organization. He was buried in Beech Grove cemetery, and a soldier's headstone. furnished by the Government, marks the place of his burial.

Thomas Fires, a soldier of the war of 1812, was an Irishman, a cooper by trade. which occupation he followed in connection with farming, upon the same place, about four miles north of Selma. He had four sons and two daughters. Two of his sons enlisted in the Nineteenth Regiment, Indiana Volunteers. One of them was a fifer in Company K, and died at Upton's Hill. in Virginia. He was intensely patriotic during the Civil war. Lincoln and Loyalty, were his constant watchwords. We regret lack of time to investigate, as he deserves, the history and service of this old soldier. Persons who knew him say that he possessed a rather striking facial appearance. He was lantern-jawed, and had a very long chin. From its point, bushy whiskers protruded somewhat after the manner of an elongated shaving-brush. He was short on teeth; he worked his jaws with great rapidity and much regularity. The surplus power he constantly used to grind tobacco, which he chewed as a cow would chew her cud. When in full operation it was said to have resembled an automatic pump-handle. The only reservation he made was time to take his meals, his rest, and the conversation necessary to the common business affairs of life. All the rest he spent in grinding his favorite weed. He died about the year 1875, and was buried, probably, at the Spahr graveyard.

Silas Fleming was a soldier in the second war with England. He descended from a distinguished line of Scotch-Irish ancestors—some of whom emigrated to America in the seventeenth century and settled in Virginia and North Carolina. Sir Thomas Fleming, son of the Earl of Wigton, emigrated to Virginia in 1616. Many of the family followed him to the same colony, one of whom was Colonel William Fleming, and another, the father of James Fleming, who was born near Staatsville, Iredell county, North Carolina, in 1762. The records at Washington show that James Fleming served two terms of enlistment in the Revolutionary army. He married Elizabeth Mitchell of Virginia and emigrated to New Paris, Preble county, Ohio, in 1807, where he died in 1832.

Silas Fleming, son of James, was born near Staatsville, Iredell county, North Carolina, in 1789. He was a soldier of the war of 1812, from the state of North Carolina, though we do not know the period of his enlistment, nor the names of the officers under whom he served. If he came to Ohio in 1807, at the time of his father's removal, he would then have been eighteen years of age. He was married to Elizabeth Caughey, by whom he had twelve children, five sons and seven daughters, all of whom were born at New Paris, Ohio. Of the above, five daughters became residents of Muncie, and four of them died in this city. The first wife of Silas Fleming died about the year 1837, after which he married Lavina Purviance, and about

1856, removed to Bloomington, Ill. In 1870, while upon a visit to his sis_
ters in Muncie, Mr. Fleming was attacked with paralysis. Here he died
and here he was buried. He was by occupation a miller; a man of sterling
character and integrity; firm and upright in his dealings with all men. In
religious faith he was a Universalist. Of his daughters who were long
time residents of this city, there was Mrs. Sarah Richey, Mrs. Jane Ross,
Mrs. Amy Ireland, Mrs. Nancy Greene and the Misses Cynthia and Lucinda
Fleming. No wonder these good ladies were always ready with baskets
filled to aid in supplying hungry soldiers passing to or from the front during
the civil war. Their hearts were in such work.

Enoch Garner, a soldier of the war of 1812, was born June 10, 1780.
The place of his birth, his ancestry, the details of his service are all un_
known to this writer. Our public records show that in the year 1837 he
entered land in Harrison township. Part of section thirteen, township twenty-one, range eight. This land he cleared and improved, thus opening up
a homestead in the dense forest, and here he continued to reside until Jan_
uary 4, 1852, when he died, at the age of 71 years, 6 months and
13 days. He was buried at the Jones cemetery, on the Jackson street Turnpike. About the record of this old soldier there is no question. His aged
widow was still living in the year 1875, and drawing a pension. The Gov_
ernment adopted some very harsh measures against these worthy old ladies,
who chanced to be upon the pension rolls. It required them to appear before
the Clerk of the Circuit Court, personally, and execute their vouchers. It
could not be delegated to a deputy. Upon the tombstone of Mr. Garner is
the following very interesting bit of history: "Being a member of the
Christian Friends Church, for the last ten years of his life." A fire, which
destroyed the dwelling of the late Vincent Garner, son of Enoch Garner, is
said to account for the loss of all family records, which would have furnished
the details so much desired about this old soldier.

William Gilbert, a soldier and officer in the war of 1812, was born in
Rutledge, Vermont, in 1789. He was married to Anna De Lamater in
Whitehall, New York, in 1813. He enlisted in the state of New York, and
so far as known was enrolled as a private, afterwards being promoted until
he reached the rank of Major. His command and the officers under whom
he served are unknown to his family. He removed to Delaware County,
Indiana, in the year 1827, settling at Muncietown. He died in April, 1857,
and was buried in Beech Grove cemetery. His wife died in 1845, and lies
by his side. When the war was declared between the United States and
Mexico, Mr. Gilbert, then a resident of the place (Muncietown), had his
military uniform and officer's outfit, which consisted in part of a red silk
sash, a fur hat the shape of a half-moon, and two swords. One of these
swords was a steel blade, with handle of ivory and bronze, adorned with an

eagle's head. During the period of the Mexican war all men between the
ages of eighteen and forty-five years were required to enroll and muster for
regular drill, subject to call for duty when their services should be required
in the field.

Some companies were organized here, and this sash, hat and the two
swords were loaned to the officers who were in command. What became of
them it is now impossible to say. Certain it is they were never returned to
the Gilbert family. Major Gilbert never drew a pension. His son, now an
aged man living in Chicago, to whom we are indebted for these sketches of
the life of his father, is of the opinion he neglected to make proper application. Major Gilbert was very nearly related to Suel Gilbert, the Revolutionary soldier, he being a nephew of that venerable man, and it was at the
Major's home that the aged veteran passed away, in the year 1843.

William H. Green, a soldier of the war of 1812, was born April 12,
1779. He was of English descent and a native of the state of New York.
In an early day he removed from that state to Athens county, Ohio, and
from Ohio to Delaware county, where he purchased a tract of land in Niles
township, and became one of the early pioneers of that section. The tradition of the family is, that he was drafted for service and after enrollment
and muster-in he was sent to assist in guarding the Canadian border. His
first wife was Miss Amy Ingram, by whom he had seven sons and one
daughter. She died and was buried in Athens county, Ohio. He afterwards married Anna Simonton. Upon her decease he married, for his third
wife, Mrs. Nancy Duddleston, who bore him one daughter. Mr. Green
received a land warrant for eighty acres of land. He was always quite
reticent as to any experience he had in the army, and the traditions about
him are very scant. A fire which destroyed the old home, and all its contents, many years since, burned up some records which might have given
some facts about his history. He departed this life September 12, 1855,
aged seventy-six years and six months. His wife survived until October
25, 1882. They were both buried in the cemetery near Granville. Mrs.
Nancy Green drew a pension during the last years of her widowhood.

John Hall, a soldier of the war of 1812, was born June 19, 1793, in the
State of Pennsylvania. When quite young, and at that time living in Virginia, his parents both died, and at the age of thirteen years he went to live
with relatives in Ohio. He afterwards became a resident of Kentucky,
from which he is supposed to have entered the army. The discharge papers,
preserved by his descendants until within the two years last past, being now
lost, we are unable to furnish details of his service. Family tradition shows
him to have been sick at Norfolk, Virginia, and to have been discharged as
the result of disability. He was a patriot and lover of his country. He
was married to Elenora Butey September 19, 1838, in the State of Ohio,

and came to Indiana in the same year, where he resided until his death. He had two sons and three daughters, as follows: Daniel, John, Matilda, Eliza and Manorva, all of whom are dead except Mrs. Manorva Taylor, who yet resides on the old homestead. After their decease Mr. Hall and his wife were buried in the Mount Pleasant cemetery in Perry township. We are unable to give the date of their death.

George M. Harter, a soldier of the war of 1812, was born in the year 1786, in the state of Virginia, and emigrated from there to the state of Kentucky. In 1819 he removed to Ohio, locating at or near Troy. He married Mary Brush, and was the father of eleven children. The only fact known about his service by the members of his family is, that he was in the army for a period of nine months. He removed to Indiana about the year 1844, and died here May 15, 1865. His widow, Mary Harter, died May 20, 1875, aged eighty-nine years. They both rest in Beech Grove cemetery. Mr. Harter was a farmer and shoemaker.

Lawrence Heffner, a soldier supposed to have seen service in the war of 1812, was born in 1787 in the state of Maryland. We have no record of his service. He drew no pension nor received a land warrant. It is supposed he was called out in some emergency for a brief time only, and may never have been mustered. His descendants say that whatever the nature of his service, he was left with feeble health,—in fact, was always sick—to the end of his life. He died in Muncie, December 6, 1860, aged seventy-three years. His wife, Charlotte Heffner, died September 20, 1858, aged sixty-one years, four months and nineteen days. They were buried in Beech Grove cemetery.

John Holmes, a soldier of the war of 1812, was born in New Jersey, and from that state probably entered the service. Afterwards he came to Greene county, and later to Clinton county, Ohio. He married Patience Pugh, by whom he had seven children, five sons and two daughters. He was a farmer, of Quaker parentage, though himself and his family were members of the M. E. church. Mr. Holmes died in July, 1842, and was buried some two miles northeast of Eaton, Indiana. His widow survived until 1892, when she, too, died, and was buried at Eaton, for the reason that burials were no longer made upon the farm where the interment of Mr. Holmes was made. We have no details of the service nor the name of any officer under whom he served.

Clement Hurtt, a soldier of the war 1812, was born in 1795. He enlisted as a private in Captain Ullery's company, in a regiment commanded by Colonel McCarty of the Second Division Ohio militia. The place of birth is not known. He had children, but their place of residence is unknown. Neither can we tell when he came to Muncie. He died here March 3, 1875, aged eighty years, and was buried in Beech Grove cemetery. He drew a pension on certificate No. 4,938. The number indicates he drew this pension for some time. He is supposed to have been in the battle of Lake Erie, as he often recounted its details. Eliza Hurtt, widow of Clement Hurtt, deceased, applied for a pension. Her claim was allowed and the certificate issued, but she died without receiving any money. We have no further details.

Sewell Hutchins, a soldier of the war of 1812, was born December 21, 1784, at Prince Frederick, C---- county, Maryland. His parents died when he was quite small. He ----ered the service from the state and place of his birth. He was married the fourth time. The maiden name of the fourth wife was Eleanor Simmons. Two children were born after they came to Indiana, of whom J. L. Hutchins, a soldier of the Civil war, alone now remains. He was a farmer and a member of the M. E. church in Smithfield, Indiana. He died at his home near that village, February 25, 1865, and was buried at Mount Tabor cemetery. We have no record of his service, but to his family, during his lifetime, he frequently related the account of hardships endured and battles fought during the war. His special reference to the broadsides delivered by some of the historic old war vessels under command of the brave Commodore Barney would lead one to suppose he might have been connected with that branch of the service.

Thomas Jackson, a soldier of the war of 1812, was born February 14, 1794, at Waterford, Loudoun county, Virginia. He was a son of Robert Jackson, who performed service in Captain John Hay's company, Ninth Virginia Regiment of Foot, during the war of the Revolution. Thomas Jackson was married to Amelia Conrad in May, 1822. He was a cabinetmaker by occupation. They had four sons and two daughters. Many years ago the family removed from Virginia to Ohio, thence to Greenup county, Kentucky, and later, in 1844, came to make their home at Muncietown. Mr. Jackson was one of the pioneers of this locality, where he spent the residue of a long and useful life. He died October 19, 1863, and was buried in Beech Grove cemetery. An effort was made to get his military history from the archives in Washington. The following is an extract from a letter sent to Mrs. Mock, his granddaughter, who made the inquiry: "The records show that many persons named Thomas Jackson served as members of organizations from the state of Virginia in the service of the United States during the war of 1812, but it cannot be determined whether or not any one of them was identical with the name of the man of that name referred to within." This is a good showing in patriotism for the name of Jackson but fails to furnish the details we ought to have about this very worthy old veteran. William N. Jackson, son of Thomas, was a member of Company "E," Nineteenth Regiment Indiana Infantry, and served during the entire period of its history in the field.

Gilbert Jones, soldier of the war of 1812, was born in 1788; place of birth unknown. He was enrolled in Captain Ledyard's company, Twelfth Regiment, Fourth Brigade, at Schenectady, New York, in June, 1812, and was honorably discharged at Sackett's Harbor, New York, in February, 1813. He served as a private, and was stationed at Sackett's Harbor during the period of his service. He died October 24, 1883, aged ninety-five years, four months and twenty days, at Rochester, Indiana. His remains were brought to Muncie and buried in Beech Grove cemetery.

Samuel Kyle, a soldier of the war of 1812, was born in 1780. The place of his birth is unknown. He had three sons and six daughters. He was a farmer and a member of the Methodist church. He owned a good farm in Niles township, where he died in the year 1852, and was buried at the Bethel cemetery.

Isaac Maitlen, Sr., a soldier of the war of 1812, whose place and date of birth we cannot give, came from the state of Virginia at an early day to Greene or Clark county, Ohio, and thence to Delaware county, Indiana, April 4, 1836. He entered land in section twenty-four in Niles township. He was the father of eighteen children. Eight sons and three daughters came to mature years, the other children dying in infancy. There is a touching story connected with his closing years. At one time he selected a beautiful knoll or piece of elevated land upon the home farm and remarked, "What a beautiful place for burial." Some time afterward he was caught by the limb of a falling tree which he and his father had felled in the forest and mortally injured. No doctor was nearer than Muncietown. Some kind neighbor killed a horse in the attempt to relieve him with surgical skill. But it was too late. He was unable to speak, but before he passed away he motioned for some small twigs. These he arranged in the shape of a coffin, and pointed to the spot he had selected. There he was buried. He died about the year 1839. His widow drew a pension from the Government until her death, about 1868, when she, too, passed away at the age of ninety-two years.

Isaac Martin, a soldier of the war of 1812, was born in 1780. He married Elizabeth Wilson, and about 1828 came from Miami county, Ohio, to Indiana, and entered or purchased land in Niles township, about one mile from Granville. Here he established his home, cleared his farm, and spent the last twenty years of his honorable life. He had eleven children, five sons and six daughters. He and his wife were members of the Mississinewa Baptist church, one of the earliest religious societies of the township. The meeting for organization was held April 1, 1836, at the house of Isaac Martin. There are no records accessible at present showing the facts of his military service. His death occurred February 6, 1847, when sixty-seven years of age. His widow survived until February 11, 1858, when she passed away at the age of seventy-one years. They were buried at the Granville cemetery, located upon the home farm now occupied by a grandson, Mr. Henry Williams.

James Mansfield, a soldier of the war of 1812, came from Wayne county, Indiana, in the year 1826, and settled on the west side of Buck creek. January 22, 1829, he entered land in section twenty-three, and in February, 1836, he also entered land in section thirty-four. Like all early owners of real estate, he proce   d to clear and improve, keeping pace with the growth of the region about him until some time prior to the Civil war, when he sold his possessions in this state and removed to Missouri, where, some years later, he died. We have no account of his service nor any family data.

Elias Matthews, a soldier of 1812, was born in the year 1785, in the state of Maryland, and from that state he entered the service. After the close of the war he came from Baltimore to the state of Ohio, and settled on a farm near Dayton. He died October 4, 1844, at his home in Montgomery county, Ohio, aged fifty-nine years, one month and twenty-eight days. His death was caused by a fall. Afterwards his remains were brought to this city and buried in Beech Grove cemetery upon the family lot of his son, the late Thomas J. Matthews. We are unable to secure details of his service or the officers under whom he served.

Isaac McClanahan was a soldier of the war of 1812, or of the Indian wars under General Harrison. We can get scant information about him. He was an Irishman, of robust build and had a defect in his speech. He was a pensioner, and would make the journey to Cincinnati, Ohio, to draw his money. He had an Irishman's taste for a "wee drop to wet the whistle," and often requested merchants to lend him a picayune, so he could go and draw his "tension." The small sum would not bear his expenses very far, but it would pay for the drink, and he probably walked to the place of settlement. As to date of his death and place of burial we know nothing. He was wounded at the battle of Tippecanoe.

William B. Pace, soldier of the war of 1812, was born in Fluvanna county, Virginia, in 1778. There he married Mary Thomas, after which, in 1814, they moved to Ross county, Ohio, and there engaged in farming. In 1828 they removed to Fayette county, Ohio, and remained there until 1841, when they came to Indiana and settled on a farm near the town of Albany. They reared a family of nine children, all of whom have passed away except Mrs. Julia Allegre, the youngest daughter, who survives, December 10, 1907, at the age of eighty-six years. Mr. Pace died in 1845 and two years later Mrs. Pace also passed away. Their remains rest in the Strong cemetery at Albany. Formerly the family were members of the Baptist church, but late in life Mr. Pace entered the Methodist Episcopal church. He was a kind father, a good man, esteemed and respected by all. There are no records available to show the details of his service, but the very interesting story of his return home is still well remembered by Mrs. Allegre, as she often heard it from the lips of her mother. A long time elapsed without any word from the absent soldier, and there were no tidings of his return. But one morning his mother said, "We will put on the pot of sweet potatoes to-day and cook them just as William would like them, for he is coming home to-day." And he did.

Archibald Reasoner was a soldier in the war of 1812. He was born in Virginia, and probably entered the service from that state. Here again there are no records, but a current tradition, that he enlisted and went to the army, where, while upon duty in the trenches, he was so severely exposed that he contracted rheumatism, from which he suffered to the end of his days. The same tradition relates that his father, whose ideas of soldierly honor were high, refused to take his hand upon his return home until he first presented an honorable discharge from the service. Some years later he came to Coshocton county, Ohio, and about the early forties removed to Blackford county, Indiana, where his last years were passed, part of the time, however, with his brother, William P. Reasoner, who then resided in Wheeling. He never married. He was so crippled with the disease that for years he could only walk with the aid of crutches. A lost discharge prevented his drawing a pension. Such business is managed differently in these days. He was buried at Wheeling.

Archibald Parker, a soldier of the war of 1812, was born in North Carolina in 1794. In 1811, at the age of seventeen years, he removed to Fayette county, Indiana. He was one of the early pioneers of Harrison and Mount Pleasant townships. While yet a resident of Fayette county, he married Elizabeth Patton. In 1828 he settled near Yorktown on White river upon land which he rented. In 1833 he entered a tract of land in section thirty-six, and here began the labor of clearing a farm which was afterwards owned by William Lee. He lived on this farm for several years, when he sold out, purchasing another farm in Madison county. Several years later he again sold out and removed to the state of Iowa. He died there in the year 1878. He was a man of strong character, and never behind his neighbors in the matter of improvements. It was he who presented the petition for the organization of Harrison township, and by him the name was conferred in honor of the "hero of Tippecanoe." We have no details of his service nor the officers under whose command he served. If he performed the duties of a military career as he did those of a sturdy pioneer, he must have been a good soldier.

Jacob Peyton, a soldier of the war of 1812, was born November 26, 1787. He married Lois Hutchings, who was born November 6, 1793. They had nine children, seven sons and two daughters. The family moved from Kentucky at an early day. On August 17, 1832, Jacob Peyton entered land in section thirty in Liberty township. He cleared a large part of the old home place now owned by Mr. Gabriel Peyton, who came to this county at the age of nine years. They settled first in Wayne or Union county, Indiana. The wife of Mr. Peyton died in 1861, in Delaware county, Indiana. He afterwards moved to the state of Iowa or Illinois, where he died. We have no details of his service.

William Peyton, a soldier of the war of 1812, appears among the very early pioneers of Liberty township, he having entered land in section seventeen on June 27, 1833. He had two sons, David and William, and seven daughters. He was a model of physical manhood. He was low in stature but very well developed, and very stout. Some writers would say, "he was well set up." It is said of him that at one load he carried seven bushels of wheat up two flights of stairs. In his earlier life he was a farmer, and cleared up much land. What a soldier he must have been! He was an old-time Methodist local preacher. In disposition he was like a ray of sunshine, and was brimful of good humor and innocent mischief. He had quite a reputation for attending meetings—class meetings, quarterly meetings and camp meetings. He was strong in the pulpit and popular with the people—a good preacher and a good man. He "allured to brighter worlds and led the way." When age crept upon him and he ceased to carry the heavier burdens of life, he removed from Delaware county and took up his residence at Roanoke, Indiana. We have heard a specimen of the mischievous pranks perpetrated by him late in life. From some kind of soft wood he carved a pipe, with bowl large enough to hold nearly a pint. This he put in his overcoat pocket, and called upon his merchant to "please furnish him with a pipe of tobacco." When the pipe came to view the merchant was so much amused at the old man's humor, he presented him an entire package of smoking tobacco, of the best brand, and, quite probably, his known favorite. When the end came he "ceased at once to work and live," having dropped dead without an hour's illness. He was buried at Roanoke. Soon afterwards the body was exhumed and sold to the Medical college in Fort Wayne for the purpose of dissection. Here his remains were recognized by an acquaintance, secured, and sent to Iowa for reinterment, where they rest in peace. "Aunt Polly" Brown, of Avondale, is the oldest living descendant of the old soldier, and one of the oldest persons now living in Delaware county. Mrs. Abner Wolverton, of Albany, is also a daughter.

Alexander Price, a soldier of the war of 1812, was born in the year 1797. He entered the army from Ohio, he at that time being a resident of Miami county. In the year 1834 he moved to Delaware county, where he entered land upon which he afterwards lived to the close of his life. The maiden name of his wife was Hannah Studabaker. He had three children, all daughters, Mary, Catharine and Elizabeth. He never applied for a pension nor received a warrant for land. His home was in Niles township, near the village of Granville. He died January 4, 1860, aged sixty-three years, eight months and twenty-eight days. His tombstone in the cemetery at Granville bears this inscription:

> 'His toils are past, his work is done,
>   And he is fully blest;
> He fought the fight, the victory won,
>   And entered into rest."

Robert Sanders was born in Pennsylvania in 1765. From there he moved with his parents to Culpeper county, Virginia, thence to Ohio, where he married Sarah McCormick, sister of Judge McCormick, one of the earliest residents of Washington township. From there he moved with his family to Fayette county, Indiana, remaining until about the 1st of December, 1826, when he came to Delaware county. Upon arrival at the trading station, established in 1823 by David Connor, who had entered the land now known as the McCormick farm, just west of the village of Wheeling, he found in the person of its owner an old comrade, who had been with him in the Indian campaign under General Anthony Wayne. He made a brief stop with his comrade and then rented his farm. Later he entered land joining it on the east, where he made his home for a number of years. He kept the first tavern in the township, which was located on the Government road; devoted much time to traffic with the Indians and clearing and cultivation of his land. October 21, 1829, he entered land in section three, township twenty-two, in Grant county, Indiana (the original deed from the Government being yet in existence). Upon this land he laid out the town of New Cumberland, September 16, 1833. He was one of the earliest settlers in Delaware county. When he came the Indians were still here in large numbers. Game abounded in great variety. Bears, wolves, deer, wild turkeys and many other kinds. He was the father of eleven children, viz.: John, Katharine, William, Mary, Nancy, Millie, James, Abner, Lavina, Coleman. and Joseph. Of these only Mrs. Lavina Reasoner is now living, at the age of ninety-four years. This heroic soldier, frontiersman and pioneer served for three years under General Wayne in his arduous Indian campaigns, enduring the hardships, encountering the dangers of this important service. He bore a part in several engagements and scouting expeditions in the vicinity of Fort Wayne, along the Maumee, St. Mary's and St. Joseph rivers, and in the region about Detroit, Michigan. When he settled here the neighbors were far apart, the nearest settlement being at Muncietown, about fourteen miles distant. He lived an exemplary life; he was a useful and honored citizen, respected by all who knew him. He died March 31, 1861. His final resting place is in the cemetery at Wheeling.

George Saunders, son of Theodore Saunders, of German ancestry, was a soldier of the war of 1812, and was born April 25, 1792, in Lancaster county, Pennsylvania. He afterwards removed to the state of Ohio, where he enlisted about May 1, 1813, at Troy, and soon after he was ordered to a blockhouse on Turtle creek, about ten miles from Piqua, for duty. The tradition in his family is, that he made two enlistments. Of these we have the data of one only. At one time he marched from Fort Wayne, Indiana, to Sidney, Ohio, when the roads and swamps were in a fearful condition. He assisted in the care of stores and in furnishing supplies to a body of fifteen hundred Indians of whom the Government had charge at Sidney. He was discharged at Troy, Ohio, in October or November, 1813. Afterwards he was married to Elizabeth Sills. He had twelve children, four sons and eight daughters. Two sons and three daughters died in infancy. His wife died in 1836. Soon after he moved to Delaware county and settled on land east of Muncie. He received warrants for two eighty-acre tracts of land. By occupation he was farmer, carpenter and pumpmaker. He cleared a farm which is now part of the estate of Mr. Thomas Wilson. Mr. Saunders died November 10, 1878, at the home of Elizabeth Barker, a daughter, in this city, aged about eighty-six years. His remains were interred at Black's cemetery in Niles township. This venerable soldier has quite a long line of descendants. This writer has a genealogical list made up ten years since, at the time of holding a Saunders-Wilson reunion in Delaware county, which then numbered two hundred and fifty-seven. Nowhere have we found a list so thoroughly and carefully compiled showing all branches of the family tree. Mrs. Mary Carpenter, the youngest and only living daughter, but two weeks since furnished many of the particulars of this sketch. She has since passed to the great beyond. In 1871, he then being seventy-nine years of age, Mr. Saunders applied for and received a pension, which he continued to draw until his death, at the rate of twelve dollars per month.

William Scott, a soldier of the war of 1812, was born in the state of Virginia in 1785. He removed to Fayette county, Indiana, in an early day, and later he came to Delaware county, settling in Delaware township, where he continued to reside until his death, June 15, 1860. He was buried at the Bethel cemetery, near Albany. We have no details of his service. He was a farmer. He had two sons and three daughters. He was a small and very active man; physically, tough as a pine knot.

Jacob Secrist, a soldier of the war of 1812, was, so near as we can learn, born near Sabina, Clinton county, Ohio. He came to Delaware county in the early thirties and entered land here. He cleared ten acres and erected a home. He returned to Ohio to secure funds with which to pay for his land, took sick, and was delayed so long that the time for payment expired. Some other man, knowing the date was past, made the entry under him and compelled the old soldier to surrender possession of the premises. He then entered the land now owned by Mrs. Samuel Stout, near Reed's Station, and there cleared up a farm. There he lived until his death in 1852. He was buried in the Jones cemetery. We have no details of his service. He had three sons, all of whom were soldiers in the Civil war. He also had five daughters.

Joseph Shannon, a soldier of 1812, was born near Baltimore, Maryland, in the year 1795. He was married to Elizabeth Artz, and in an early day removed to the state of Ohio. Some time in the thirties he came to Delaware county. He was a farmer by occupation. He reared a family of ten children, four sons and six daughters, all now deceased. From what state he enlisted we cannot tell. His descendants have a combination knife, fork and spoon which he carried while in the service. The letters "N. L." are inscribed in a monogram upon the horn handle. It would be interesting to know what they stand for. Could they be the initials of some British soldier? Mr. Shannon was a good man and useful citizen, one of those who did such noble work here in the early days. He died July 5, 1850, aged fifty-five years. His wife Elizabeth died November 23, 1859. They are both buried at the Leard cemetery in Union township.

Isaac Shellenberger, a soldier of 1812, was born in Pennsylvania in the year 1797, and came with his parents to Greene county, Ohio, when about ten years of age. He enlisted for six months and was enrolled in Capt. William Wrightmyer's company, Ohio militia, in Fairfield county, Ohio, and was honorably discharged at Detroit, Michigan, in March or April, 1815. He married Mary Jane Clark in Greene county, Ohio, and in October, 1845, came to Indiana, settling in Liberty township. He received a warrant for eighty acres of land and this he sold for eighty dollars in gold. He was under age at the date of his enlistment and took 'French leave." His application for pension, made April 4, 1871, was approved, and to the end of his days he was paid eight dollars per month. He had fourteen sons and daughters, part of whom died in infancy. Mr. Shellenberger died at the home of Mr. Stewart Cecil, and was buried at Mount Tabor cemetery, in Liberty township.

Henry Shults, a soldier of the war of 1812, enlisted for the war at Newport, Kentucky, in Captain Hawkins' company, Seventeenth Kentucky Infantry, and was discharged at Chillicothe, Ohio, in June, 1815. He received bounty and land warrant for one hundred and sixty acres of land. He was a broommaker by trade. He probably came from Ohio to Delaware county, but we have failed to learn when. He had six children, three sons and three daughters. He made his home at the Richwoods. April 21, 1871, when seventy-four years of age, he applied for a pension under the Act of February 14, 1871. Later he removed to the county of Huntington, where he died. Date of death and place of burial we do not know. His taste ran to the use of bright colors in dress. The flashy stripes of a vest he invariably wore gave to him the well-used name of "Jack of Diamonds."

Daniel Simmons, a soldier of the war of 1812, was born in the state of Virginia, and probably entered the army from that state. He emigrated to Ohio, where, in 1816, he married Catharine Hoover, who was born in 17͡8 in Bedford county, Pennsylvania. Thence he removed to Delaware county, Indiana, locating at Prairie Creek, where he remained until, in 1831, when he came to Muncietown. He was a miller by trade and worked at Goldsmith's mill. He was large, tall, stout and active; the true type of a pioneer. He had two sons and three daughters. William Simmons, a son, saw service in the Mexican war; he was a member of Company C, Nineteenth Regiment Indiana Infantry, and was killed at the battle of Gettysburg, Pennsylvania. Daniel Simmons died of erysipelas after four days' illness, in the year 1845. His widow, so well known among our people in her day as "Aunt Katy Simmons," hearty and sprightly, survived her husband many years. She never wore glasses, and her eyesight was good to the end. She was more than fifty years a member of the German Baptist church. Her education was meager, but she was intelligent and could relate many interesting reminiscences of her experience with the Indians, who surrounded her home in the early days. This venerable couple were buried in Beech Grove cemetery.

George N. Smith was a soldier in the war of 1812. He had eleven children, three sons and eight daughters. He died in the year 1845. No further details furnished.

James Stewart, a soldier of the war of 1812, was born in the state of Virginia in the year 1787. He married Sophia Chew, and lived for some years near Leesburg, Highland county, Ohio, when he came to Indiana and settled on land near Albany. He was one of the sturdy pioneers who came to this state when the forests were dense, the county new, and but sparsely settled, to carve a farm and a home out of the unfavorable surroundings. He was the father of three sons and six daughters. Particulars of his service there are none. He was rugged and strong, and, under the law then in force, could not have drawn a pension. He was a member of the M. E. church for forty years. This devout and venerable man passed to the future life January 19, 1872, aged eighty-five years, nine months and nineteen days. Sophia Stewart, widow of James Stewart, survived him until January 26, 1886, when she died, aged eighty-seven years, eight months and twenty-five days. She was a member of the M. E. church for fifty-five years. They lie side by side in Bethel cemetery, sleeping the years away.

David Thompson was born September 12, 1771, in Amherst county,

Virginia. He performed distinguished services during the campaign against the Indians of the Northwest under General Wayne, and received a letter from the captain of the company in which he served, showing his bravery and high standing. It is in the following words:

"The bearer hereof, David Thompson, has served as a Corporal in my company of riflemen, in the Army of the United States, from which he has obtained an honorable discharge. But in justice to the said Corporal, for many services he has rendered the public, I consider it my duty and am fully warranted to say that his conduct has uniformly met with my approbation, as well as that of all other officers who had an opportunity to know him. Corporal Thompson was employed in reconnoitering the Indian country, and paths leading to and from their several towns and villages, as well as being constantly in advance of the army during the campaign. While thus engaged he assisted in taking seven Indian prisoners—all warriors except one—from their towns and villages, in order to gain information for our army. In accomplishing this great object several skirmishes ensued, in which he behaved in a brave and soldier-like manner, and when the garrison at Fort Recovery, which I had the honor to command, was attacked and surrounded by nearly two thousand savages this Corporal Thompson made an escape through them with intelligence to the Commander-in-Chief, who was twenty-four miles distant from the place. For this service I now beg leave to return him my sincere thanks, and hope that all good people, who are friends to their country, may receive and treat with respect the said David Thompson, a reward which he has merited.

"Certified under my hand and seal at Staunton, in the State of Virginia, the 29th day of October, 1795.   ALEX. GIBSON,
                                    "Captain of the Tenth Legion."

His discharge is in these words:

"By his Excellency, Anthony Wayne, Esqr., Major General and Commander-in-Chief of the Legion of the United States:

"These are to certify that the bearer hereof, David Thompson, a Corporal in the Fourth Sub Legion, has served in the above Legion, and in Capt. Gibson's company, for the space of three years, and is, for the reason below mentioned, discharged from the said Legion, he having received his pay up to the 1st of January, 1795, clothing of all kinds, and all other just demands from the time of his enlisting in the Legion to the day of his discharge, as appears by the following receipt. * * * He is discharged, having faithfully served the full term of time for which he engaged. To prevent any ill use that may be made of his discharge by its falling into the hands of any other person whatsoever, here follows the description of said David Thompson: He is twenty years of age, five feet eleven inches tall, dark complexion, black hair and black eyes; born in the county of Amherst, in the State of Virginia; a farmer.

"Given under my hand and seal, at headquarters, this 19th day of August, 1795.   WILLIAM CLARK,
"Lieutenant Acting. Sub Legion, Major and Inspector to the Fourth Sub Legion.   ANT'Y WAYNE.
"To whom it may concern, civil or military."

After the treaty of Greenville, August 8, 1795, when the troops were disbanded, Mr. Thompson settled in the western part of Virginia (now West Virginia), and there formed the acquaintance of Miss Mary Swope, whom he soon afterwards married. She was born September 21, 1775, in the old fort in Monroe county, Virginia. In 1817, Mr. Thompson removed with his wife and ten children to Butler county, Ohio, and in 1823 to Henry county, Indiana. About 1842 they settled in Salem township, Delaware county, where both Mr. Thompson and his wife died. Mr. Thompson died October 22, 1847. Mrs. Thompson died March 9, 1844. They were buried at the Sharp graveyard, in Salem township. This fine old soldier was the father of twelve children, four sons and eight daughters. One of these sons is Mr. David Thompson, one of the oldest and longest residents of Delaware county, who, with his wife, yet remain to witness and enjoy the wonderful changes which have come to us in these later years.

Ephraim Thompson, one of the first residents of Delaware township, was a soldier in the early wars. He seems hard to classify. His record is very obscure, and his actual service and what we know is founded on what he repeated in his lifetime. No campaign is remembered and no battle described. To us he first appears as the owner of a parcel of real estate, suspended on a hillside, on the banks of a stream called Brush creek, in the county of Adams and state of Ohio. A cabin crowned the crest of the ridge; part way down was a rough, log stable, and at the foot a deep gulley, cut out by the descending floods of water. He was an Irishman, a raw product from Erin, a kind of military conundrum, whom war might batter and disfigure but never quite kill, floating down the stream of time. He probably had some serious disagreement with George the Third, King of England, and did not admire crowned heads very much at best. No heavy guns were fired when he sailed, and upon arrival at our shores he failed to assist the historian by keeping a true account of future proceedings. He had a wife, whom he called Margery. He also had two sons and one daughter. One of the sons he called "Robert Jeems." He had other property. There was a yoke of oxen, designated "Buck and Berry." Though much in the company of these pioneer bovines, it is hinted that upon certain occasions there was quite a good deal of disagreement. At one time the old hater of despotism caught one of these animals violating some of his very important regulations. He protested against these infractions of good order and discipline in vain. But he took prompt measures to prevent their repetition. He slipped the bow, released the pestiferous ox, pushed him over the bank of the gully, and landed him at the bottom. He then covered him with logs and brush, lighted a kind of Scandinavian campfire and burned him to a crisp as warning to all other oxen to be more prudent in their conduct. He had three names. His front name was Ephraim. This was pre-

sented to him as a souvenir of the day on which he was born. The other
two he earned. He had a scrap with some party having an athletic jaw-
bone, who bit off nearly an inch of his nasal appendage—smoothly, as if
cut with a knife. Afterwards he was called "Nosey" and "Bit Nose." This
disfigurement added quite a bit to the facial charms of the old Hibernian.
When he talked, especially when in an earnest or emphatic way, a kind of
whistle escaped through the nostrils at the same time he was making a
noise with his mouth. He liked a good racehorse. At times he had the
spare change to make such an investment. His presence at the races must
have been fully as entertaining as the main show. One might imagine his
movements, and the discordant sounds to which he gave utterance, when he
sidled up to his hopeful son, sitting astride the Rosinante, champing his bits
and waiting the signal, and urged him to "push 'em up, push 'em up. Robert
Jeems," but to attempt it here would be a task impossible. His first and
main dependence in horse flesh was a faithful old nag he called "Bawley."
When all other horses failed "Bawley" was true as steel. He would ride
this patient and sensible steed, hitched to the front wheels of his wagon, to
Youngsville, to bring home a barrel of liquor. The effort to transfer the
contents of the barrel to his stomach was often too much. Sometimes he
fell off and lay for hours beside "Bawley," who never got the least excited
upon such occasions. When the master "straightened up" they proceeded
to their place of abode. Fire destroyed his house and its contents. Ordinary
discouragements, however, never daunted him. Into the center of a mow,
filled with straw, he burrowed like a ground-hog and found warm and comfortable quarters. When he came to live in Delaware county we could
not learn, but no one who ever knew him doubted the fact of his arrival. The old warrior brought with him from beyond the sea a great fondness for the "Yule-tide" festivities. The season having arrived for his favorite ceremony, he paid a neighbor who owned a vacant house with a fireplace the sum of two dollars for the use of his premises until the "Yule-
log"* burned out. He and his invited guests cut and rolled in a back-log
of black gum. Whether the preparation was attended with an ancient
custom, which required much detail, we are unable to say. But there appeared no disposition to hurry along the business after exercises commenced.
When they continued for a week, the owner presented himself and tendered
the two dollars as an inducement for that interesting group to vacate the
premises. The log was then only just well marked. Eccentricity increased
with advancing years. He became a perfect recluse or hermit. Beside a
large log he constructed a rude hut or shelter. Here he lived; and here, all

* The burning of the Yule-log is an ancient Christmas ceremony, transmitted to
us from our Scandinavian ancestors, who at their feast of June, at the winter solstice,
used to kindle huge bonfires in honor of their god Thor.—Century Dic.

alone, he died about the year 1854, above one hundred years of age. "Thomp-son's log" was long a place of interest, pointed out to the wondering passer-by. He is supposed to have been buried at Union Chapel, or the Godlove cemetery.

Asaiel Thornburg, one of the earliest and oldest pioneers of Delaware county, was, so far as we can learn, enrolled for service in the war of 1812 from Greene county, Ohio; that he at once marched to Columbus, where tidings reached him that peace was declared and the war was ended. Be-yond the fact that he sat for three days at the treaty of Greenville, Ohio, we have no further incidents. The biographical material for a proper sketch—and from the records—was furnished for another department of this work and will appear among the historical accounts of Liberty town-ship.

Cornelius Vanarsdoll, of German ancestry, was a soldier of the war of 1812 and of the Indian campaign; was born in the year 1789, probably in Montgomery county, Ohio. He entered the army from that state. There is no doubt about his military record, as he drew a pension and received a warrant for land. He was a dispatch bearer or courier and most of this duty was performed on foot. He was in the battle of Tippecanoe and also many skirmishes with the Indians. The scene of one of his struggles with the red men was upon ground where, afterwards, he located and entered land for the home farm. He intended coming there at the close of the war, but the Indians were so bad he had to postpone it until 1820. He cut his initials in a rock near the camp as a mark to guide him upon his return. The early life of this rugged old pioneer and fighter was crowded with adventures and experience of a most exciting nature. At one period of his service the Indians used great cunning in their operations. Many sentinels were shot at a certain outpost. Vanarsdoll made the rounds at night and assisted in setting on foot a movement to stop the shooting of pickets. One of the men agreed to take the post of duty if allowed to follow his own plans. He was put upon guard at the fatal spot. In the night the sound of his gun aroused the camp and when approached it was discovered he had shot an Indian, wearing a hogskin and small bell on his neck. He once took dispatches from near Dayton to some point on the Aurglaize river. When the former camp was reached the troops were gone and only some smoldering coals marked the site of the campfire. Being completely exhausted, he dropped beside them and soon fell into a deep slumber. He became unconscious from severe cold and weariness, and was nearly dead when discovered by some comrades sent to search, who found him at the abandoned camp. He married Jane McClellan, by whom he had three sons and six daughters. This brave woman had some thrilling experience in her early married life. At one time the blockhouse was surrounded and attacked by Indians. She assisted in molding bullets. Her dress and apron caught fire and were nearly burned off her. When Mr. Vanarsdoll first settled on the land chosen by him he did not have the means to pay for it, even at the paltry price of $1.25 per acre. Finally he discovered that plans were on foot to displace him. In one day he walked to Wayne county and returned with the money. A neighbor then took the money, rode a swift horse all night, reached the land office at Fort Wayne, Indiana, and made payment in time to meet the party intending to do the old hero the great wrong just as he reached the door. This land was in section thirty-one, Liberty township, and was legally entered and paid for on the 25th day of October, 1830. His was the first white family from 1820 to 1823, when other settlers located near them. For the rest of his life the old warrior was farmer, blacksmith and preacher. He established the first society of the Christian church in his own home, and spent much time from home holding services. No pay was received for this and none was expected. Wild game, honey, nuts and ginseng were abundant. Mr. Cornelius Vanarsdoll, a son of the soldier and subject of this sketch, was born in 1822. There were no whites here then. He was dressed the first time by Indian Sally, who said, "My pappoose." The venerable patriot and pioneer preacher followed his calling for about forty years. He died April 24, 1868, aged seventy-nine years and two days. His wife survived until February 12, 1885, when she passed away at the age of ninety-six years, one month and eighteen days. They were both buried in Mount Tabor cemetery.

Matthew Whicker, a soldier of the war of 1812, was the eldest son of William Whicker, a soldier of the Revolution, whose sketch forms part of this chapter. We have nothing but tradition, outside of what we get in the records of William Whicker. But Matthew Whicker was probably born in Guilford county, North Carolina, entered the service during the second war with England from the same state, and later may have removed with his parents to the state of Ohio. At one time he resided near Albany, but afterwards returned to the state of Ohio, and there he died. We have no data of birth, particulars of service, nor the date and place of his death.

Samuel P. Wilson, a soldier of the war of 1812, was born in the state of Virginia in the year 1794. He came to the state of Ohio at an early period in its history; married; came to Delaware county, Indiana, in 1857, and died in 1874, aged eighty years. He had five children, two sons and three daughters, none of whom survive except one daughter, Miss Kate Wilson. Mrs. Elizabeth O. Wilson, widow of Samuel P., drew a pension from the Government at the rate of ninety-six dollars a year. She died in 1890, at the age of eighty-nine years. She was afflicted with rheumatism during many years. But she possessed a vigorous mind, took much interest in the current events of the times in which she lived, and was well informed respecting them. Captain Luther B. Wilson was an officer in the Nineteenth Regiment, Indiana Volunteers. S. Ambrose Wilson was a member of the same regiment, and was afterwards cashier of the Muncie National Bank. Mrs. Burson, the daughter with whom the aged lady spent the closing years of her life, was very active in deeds of kindness, and in many ways assisted soldiers and their families during the Civil war.

Lloyd Wilcoxon, Sr., was a soldier in the war of 1812. He was of English ancestry, and was a native of the state of Maryland, where he was born October 4, 1792, and where he resided with his parents until he was sixteen years old, when his father moved to Kentucky. After living there a few years they moved to Scioto county, Ohio, where he was engaged at the carpenter trade, and where he was married June 28, 1813, to Elizabeth Truitt. In 1833 he moved to Delaware county, and settled near Muncie, where he passed the residue of a long and useful life, dying in this city in June, 1866, at the age of seventy-three years. He and his wife are buried at the Moore cemetery, two miles east of Muncie. There is no question about his service, so far as family tradition goes, but it is impossible now to state positively from what state, the period of his service or any of the officers under whose command he served.

Phillip Wingate, a soldier of the war of 1812, was born in the state of Delaware in the year 1793. He was married to Sarah Wright, who died in 1821, and was buried near where she was born and reared. Phillip Wingate was married a second time in the state of Maryland, after which he moved to Highland county, Ohio, and settled near Leesburg, where he worked at his trade, a carriage maker, which he learned by serving an apprenticeship of five years in his native state. Then, in 1847, he came to Albany, Delaware county, Indiana, where he worked at wagonmaking. He died at the home of his son, James W., October 9, 1870, and was laid to rest in Bethel cemetery. Mary, the second wife, died July 20, 1851. She was buried also at Bethel. Phillip Wingate was the father of ten children, eight sons and two daughters. Like so many others whose records we do not have from the books, we cannot tell what was the experience of this soldier during the war, but there is a record upon the tombstone which marks his last resting place. It will tell its own story, and is in these words: "Lieutenant in the war of 1812."

The names of William Finley, James Manson and Hugh Winget were furnished with the statement that each were soldiers of the war of 1812. We have no details.

MEXICAN WAR.

Until the Civil war of 1861, only one national contest had engaged the attention of our people—the war against Mexico, in 1846-48. Delaware county took but small part in the conflict of arms, only about one dozen men participating, though at one time a company was recruited here and its services tendered to the state. On June 6, 1846, the Muncie *Journal* published the following call for the enrollment of volunteers:

"I, Wm. Van Matre, colonel of 69th Reg. of Indiana Militia, having received orders from Brig. Gen. of 22d Brig. to organize militia under my command, do hereby request that all citizens of Delaware county subject to military enrollment meet at Muncie on Saturday, 13th of June, to enroll themselves, form companies and elect officers.

"N. B. The object of the above call is that the Indiana Militia may be placed in a proper condition for any military requisition that the exigencies of our country may require."

On designated day was a large gathering and address by Gen. Kilgore. "At the close of his remarks, the general himself setting the example, some sixty odd came forward and enrolled their names as volunteers."

The company then elected David Kilgore captain; Thomas J. Sample, first lieutenant; John S. Sarver, second lieutenant, and William J. Brady, orderly sergeant. Great efforts were made to have the company accepted by the state. The "Muncie Guards" sent their messenger, Mr. Kilgore, to Indianapolis on horseback, but after an all night ride his arrival was too late; Indiana's quota was already filled. However, the organization was kept up for some time. A new requisition for a regiment of infantry was made by Governor Whitcomb in April, 1847, and the following May 22 the Muncie *Journal* mentioned the presence of two recruiting officers for the "Marion Guards." "Notwithstanding they were with us but a few hours, and no notice whatever of their coming was had, a number enrolled themselves and were sworn into the company." On the 21st of April, 1847, three men started on foot from Yorktown for Anderson to enlist for Mexico. They found already there nine others from Delaware county. The following are the names of the twelve: William T. Collins, Firman V. Carmichael, Abel Gibson, James Halstead, Joseph E. Hurt, Samuel Macum, James Moore, George W. Parkinson, William S. Reeves, Joseph Secrist, William Sutton and Alexander Williamson. Two others from Delaware county, William Simmons and Jesse Sheary, joined a regiment which was organized later. The twelve first named became members of Company "A" in the Fourth Indiana Volunteer Infantry. The following officers were chosen to command: Captain, John M. Wallace, of Marion; first lieutenant, Decatur Carey, of Grant county; second lieutenant, John W. Dodd, of Grant county; third lieutenant, Nineveh Berry, of Madison county; Willis A. Gorman was made colonel and Ebenezer Dumont, lieutenant colonel. To Mr. George W. Parkinson, a member of the regiment, a worthy citizen of Yorktown, and later an officer in the Eighth Indiana Infantry in the Civil war, now deceased, we are indebted for a very interesting sketch of the experiences through which his company passed.

The company marched to Edinburg, south of Indianapolis. There it took passage on the cars of the Madison and Indianapolis Railroad, which had just been completed to Edinburg. For most of the company these cars were the first they had ever seen. They went by rail to Madison, and by steamer to Jeffersonville, at which place the regiment completed its organization and was mustered into the service. After remaining at Jeffersonville about four weeks, the regiment went by steamer to New Orleans, stopped there two weeks, thence proceeding in two divisions, and in different steamers, on its way to the seat of war.

Soon after passing out upon the Gulf of Mexico the vessel upon which was embarked the right wing of the regiment, to which Company "A" belonged, exploded one of her boilers, apparently disabling the boat. Several men were killed, among them Firman V. Carmichael, one of the soldiers from Delaware county. Sixty-five of the men went to the shore in three boat loads. The first load carried the remains of their dead comrade to the land for burial. While they were performing that mournful service, the two other boats came, and those who were in them said that the whole body were coming on shore; but, for some reason unknown to those who had been landed, the steamer found means to go on her way, and left that company of sixty-five men to their fate! There they were, in the Louisiana swamps, without food and with no suitable water, and perhaps two days' journey from any settlement. But the boys would never say "die," and off they tramped for two days to Sabine City, at the mouth of Sabine river, fasting as they went. At that place they staid a week.

In some way a man went from Sabine City on horseback to Galveston to carry the news. An old schooner, the Lone Star, was sent to hunt them up, and at Galveston they rejoined their comrades. There they "boarded" the Robinson Crusoe for Brazos Santiago, near the mouth of the Rio Grande, and went on thence up the Rio Grande to Camp Mier, perhaps two hundred miles, and reported to General Taylor. He ordered them to Vera Cruz, and so back they marched to the mouth of the river, whence they were taken to Vera Cruz and sent forward into the heart of Mexico. At Vera Cruz had lately arrived the Fourth Ohio, five companies from Pennsylvania, and a cavalry company from Louisiana, Capt. Walker. Gen. Scott had taken Vera Cruz, fought Cerro Gordo, captured Puebla, and gone forward to fight the terrible battles around the capital city. But the Mexican forces had turned back, and were laying siege to Puebla, defended by the gallant Gen. Childs, with his handful of men.

Just then the little army from the coast came up, fought and won the battle of Huamantla, scattered the swarming foe, raised the siege, and saved the city and its garrison.

They went no further, but stayed in the vicinity of Puebla for several months, having some skirmishes and street conflicts but no heavy fighting. Peace was made, and the soldiers came home. The men from Delaware county arrived at Indianapolis the last of August, 1848. Except Carmichael, killed by the explosion, all the 'Delaware squad" survived.

William Sutton was nearly blind, and the severe sunshine made him worse, so that he could scarcely see at all, and he was discharged early; but all the others "went the rounds," and came home again safe and sound.

"We are enabled to announce the arrival of most of the Delaware volunteers. Messrs. Neff, Stone, Halstead, Reeves, Collins, Moore, Williamson and Gibson arrived here Sunday. As soon as it was announced that the volunteers were near town our citizens were on the alert, some mounted on horses and others on foot, to meet them, and Hoon's corner (now known as the Patterson block) and the street west to the suburbs of town were literally crowded with citizens." (From Indiana *Signal*, August 24, 1848.)

The two first above named were probably volunteers from the county of Randolph.

Alexander Armstrong, a soldier of the Mexican war, lived in Shelby county, Ohio. He had two sons and one daughter. In the year 1881 he came to spend the winter with the family of the late William K. Helvie, of Yorktown, Indiana. He died suddenly from heart failure March 13, 1881, aged sixty-eight years, and was buried in the Yorktown cemetery.

Thomas Curtis was a soldier in the Mexican war. He was buried at the Hawk cemetery. No details of his life and service at hand.

John Holbert, a soldier in the Mexican and Civil wars, was born in Hagerstown, Washington County, Maryland, February 17, 1822. He acquired a limited education, and afterwards learned the tailor's trade. In 1846 he removed to Butler county, Ohio, where he enlisted as a private soldier in the First Ohio Volunteers, in Captain John B. Weller's company, Second Rifles. Serving his term of one year, he was discharged at New Orleans, and returned to Butler county, Ohio, in the fall of 1847. He married Miss Mary M. Fadely, April 7, 1848. In 1850 he came to Delaware county and settled in Smithfield, where he continued to follow his trade, until the fall of 1862, when he enlisted in Captain William's Company K of the Nineteenth Regiment, Indiana Volunteers. In the engagement at Hatcher's Run, near Petersburg, Virginia, he lost his left leg, which was amputated in the field. In 1866 he was elected trustee of Liberty township, which position he filled for six years, when he was, in 1872, elected treasurer of Delaware county, and re-elected in 1874. At the close of his life Mr. Holbert removed to his farm a few miles out on the Centennial pike, and here he died, July 28, 1883, aged sixty-one years, five months and eleven days. He was buried in Beech Grove cemetery.

James Moore, a soldier of the Mexican and Civil wars, was born in the year 1823. He was a member of Company A, Fifth Regiment, Indiana Volunteers, and also of Company G, Eighth Indiana Volunteers. He died December 4, 1893, aged sixty-nine years, six months and fourteen days, and was buried in the Jones cemetery. We are not prepared with data sufficient for an account of the service of this soldier of two wars. We are told, however, that the storming of the fortress of Chapultepec furnished great opportunity for the exercise of his descriptive powers, and these he used with such persistence that some wag gave him the name of that historic place, and it remained with him all the rest of his life.

William Sutton, a soldier of the Mexican war, died July 19, 1863, aged thirty-eight years, three months and twenty-seven days. He was buried in Beech Grove cemetery. We have no data of his life or particulars of his service.

Alexander Williamson, a soldier of the Mexican war, was born in the year 1829 in the state of Ohio. He was a member of the Fifth Indiana Infantry Volunteers. After escaping the perils and dangers incident to the career of a soldier, he returned in safety to his home. Some years later he went to the Pacific coast, where he engaged in mining. Like many a man who has had army experience, he frequently related the details of his service to willing hearers. Upon one of these occasions, to a group of men who were his companions and camp associates, he spent part of an evening in fighting over again some of the scraps with the "Greasers." It happened there was a Mexican in the party at the time. Soon after one of the Americans present told Williamson "to keep an eye on the Mexican," as, when the relation of his war experience was under way, "the fellow had turned all kinds of color, and he might do him harm." Williamson thought but little of it and remarked: "I am the only man in camp who can speak the Spanish language, and I can get along with him." The day following, in an unguarded moment, when Williamson was watching the cloud of smoke he blew from a cigar, the Mexican stabbed him three times with a knife. It was one hundred miles to a doctor, but one was brought and did the best he knew to relieve the suffering soldier. But all was in vain. He died a few days later. Before he passed away he was permitted to see his murderer hung from the limb of a tree which stood not far away. He was buried in Jacksonville, Oregon, where he remained until the year 1896, when his remains were brought home and buried near the family monument in the Yorktown cemetery. At one time Mr. Williamson raised and commanded a company of miners, who rescued a train of emigrants which had been surrounded by Indians. The full details of his very interesting and thrilling experience in the West would exceed the bounds of a sketch of this kind.

THE CIVIL WAR OF 1861.

"Mark ye well her bulwarks. . . . That ye may tell it to the generation following."

Within twenty-four hours after the fall of Fort Sumter, the wires bore the following message to President Lincoln:

"EXECUTIVE DEPARTMENT OF INDIANA,
INDIANAPOLIS, April 15, 1861.
"To Abraham Lincoln, President of the United States:
"On behalf of the State of Indiana, I tender to you for the defense of the Nation, and to uphold the authority of the Government, *ten thousand men.*
"OLIVER P. MORTON,
"Governor of Indiana."

The call of the President issued on the same day for seventy-five thousand troops greatly stimulated the military ardor of the people, and volunteers came forward in great numbers to offer their services. Who that lived during those exciting days of the Civil war period can ever forget them? In the county of Delaware, which up to that time knew so little of war, some preparations had already been made. When the Government undertook to reinforce the garrison and send supplies to Fort Sumter, and the Star of the West was fired upon, the signs of the coming contest were evident to all thoughtful people. Then it was that the nucleus of our first organization was begun. It bore the name of "The Minute Men of Muncie." The company was drilled in "Scott's Tactics," by the only man then in this locality who had seen service and knew the duties and demands of a soldier's life.* An attempt was made to have the company accepted by the state, but that step was premature and nothing came of it at that time. The name was subsequently changed to the "Delaware Guards." At a meeting held in the courthouse on the night of April 16, 1861, at which Judge John Brady presided, the ranks were filled. Thomas J. Brady (afterwards brigadier general by brevet) was elected captain, who at once proceeded to the state capitol, tendered the company to Governor Morton, which was promptly accepted and ordered to report for duty immediately. It was later known as Company "D," Eighth Indiana Volunteer Infantry. Bright and early on the morning of April 18 the ringing of the bell at the courthouse called the Guards together; the company was formed on East Main, right resting at Walnut street. Here each member was presented with a testament. A beautiful banner, the gift of the loyal ladies of Muncie, was also accepted and unfurled at the front of the line. Then, led by the Muncie Cornet Band playing "Hail Columbia," and accompanied and cheered by hundreds of sympathetic and patriotic citizens, these raw recruits marched to the station on what was then the Indianapolis and Bellefontaine Railroad.

The scene at the station was one always to be remembered. There were many touching and tearful farewells by the loyal people who saw these first volunteers depart, and who were to be followed to the field by two thousand of her brave sons before the war ended.

*Lieutenant Joseph Kirk, who had recently closed a three years' term of service in the United States Army. His regiment was on the frontier and participated in the campaign under the command of General Albert Sidney Johnston against the Mormons in Utah.

The journey to the capital was one continued ovation. People at towns and villages crowded to see the strange spectacle of an organized body of men on the way to the field of strife. Cannon and anvils thundered their greetings; cheers were mingled with tears; bands played stirring national airs. The hearts of those boyish soldiers swelled with emotions of pride as they hurriedly passed to obey the summons to defend the flag so gloriously fluttering in the morning sunbeams.

Eighth Regiment Infantry (Three Months).

The Eighth Regiment, Indiana Infantry Volunteers, was organized and mustered into service for three months at Camp Morton in Indianapolis by Major Thomas J. Wood, on April 25, 1861, with William P. Benton as colonel. On the 19th of June it marched by rail to Clarksburg, in Western Virginia, via Cincinnati, Marietta and Parkersburg. Remaining here two days engaged in building fortifications, it marched thence to Buckhannon, thirty miles away, where the enemy were reported to be encamped. Upon arrival the enemy had abandoned the place and moved toward Rich Mountain. Here the Eighth was reviewed by General McClellan on July 4, and assigned to the Brigade commanded by General Rosecrans. Three days later the column under General McClellan, consisting of three Brigades, had marched to Roaring Creek, about two miles from Colonel Pegram's position at Rich Mountain. A reconnoissance made on the 10th showed the enemy in a very strong position, difficult to assail by a front attack. In the evening Rosecrans took to McClellan a young man named Hart,* whose father lived on the mountain two miles in the rear of the Confederate position. He proposed to guide a column of infantry, by a trail making a circuit to the right of eight miles, up the rocky slopes to his father's farm.

The Eighth regiment left its camp on the afternoon of the 10th, spent the night on outpost duty and at daybreak the following morning marched at the head of the brigade to make the ascent of the mountain and assail the enemy in his rear. The march up the mountain through dense thickets of chaparral was slow and toilsome. It took ten hours' climbing to reach the vicinity of the Hart homestead.

The Muncie company, "D," was deployed at the front and retained the position until near the spot where the enemy opened fire. Standing in full view of a mountain road, which crossed the farm at a right angle, the cap-

*David B. Hart, the guide who led the column, belonged to a historic family. His father, Joseph Hart, who owned the farm, and around whose home the battle was fought, was a grandson of John Hart of New Jersey, one of the signers of the Declaration of Independence. Upon the reorganization of the 10th Indiana, David Hart enlisted and was appointed Commissary Sergeant. He died at Nashville, Tenn., March 29, 1862. He had three brothers, Squire B., Alexander P. and George D., all of whom saw service in the Union army during the Civil war. The writer learned these facts about the Hart family while upon a visit to the old homestead and battlefield in 1893.

tain did not correctly understand the guide, and, upon reaching the road, turned to the right, while the movement should have been to the left. The march was at a quick step; before the mistake was discovered the regiment had moved its entire length in the wrong direction. Following closely came the Tenth Indiana Regiment, whose leading company took the left hand, and in a few moments received the first fire of the enemy.

The entire brigade, consisting of the Eighth, Tenth, Thirteenth Indiana, Nineteenth Ohio and Burdsall's Ohio Cavalry, pressed forward, the infantry becoming engaged with the enemy's line, posted behind fortifications. While the column under General Rosecrans was making the movement upon the flank of the Confederate line, a mounted courier dashed up the turn pike with dispatches from General McClellan. Passing the trail by which the troops, at break of day, had left the main highway, he pressed onward, and at a sudden turn in the road found himself face to face with the outpost of the enemy. Knowing the importance of the message he bore, the brave man undertook to make his escape. He was badly wounded, his horse was killed and he was a prisoner. Refusing to make known the purpose of his ride, because it might hazard the success of the marching column, he was charged with being a spy, and was about to be treated as such, when he pointed to his boot, now filled with blood from his wound. Upon removing the boot the dispatch was found, which fully explained his business and revealed the movement of the flanking column.

It also caused the hurried preparations at the top of the mountain, and explained the hastily constructed line of entrenchments manned with troops and cannon which confronted the column under General Rosecrans when it approached the Hart homestead. The ground was rough and rocky, the men were for the first time under fire, and the skirmishing combat continued for two or three hours. Then a charge by part of the Union line, aided by some heavy volleys by a portion of the force which had secured a good position, broke the enemy's line, leaving his killed, wounded and some prisoners in the hands of the victorious Federals. Reinforcements from Pegram's main position were near at hand, also a regiment was approaching from the direction of Beverly, but all were too late, and Rosecrans was in possession of the field and directed his men to rest upon their arms until the next morning. The march and assault was made in rain and storm.

The Confederates left twenty wounded on the field and sixty-three were surrendered at the lower camp. No reliable report of their dead was ever made. All the residue of Pegram's forces, after two days' wandering among the mountains, came in and surrendered to General McClellan. Rosecrans' loss had been twelve killed and forty-nine wounded. Of the latter were five from the Muncie company. The affair at Rich Mountain and subsequent movements were but minor events in a great war. But out of this brief

...! brilliant campaign came the promotion of General McClellan to the
command of the Army of the Potomac.

Two days after the battle the Eighth regiment marched to Beverly,
where it remained a short time. On the 24th of July it marched to Webster,
and thence moved by rail to Indianapolis, where, on August 6, it was mustered out of the service. The stirring events of the campaign furnished
some real service in these opening days of the great war. The Confederate
forces not killed or captured beat a precipitate retreat over the mountains.
McClellan was the hero of the hour. In congratulatory orders to his troops,
he announced that "they had annihilated two armies, commanded by educated and experienced soldiers, intrenched in mountain fastnesses fortified
at their leisure." The news thrilled the country and pleased the men who
were experienced their first "baptism of fire." But how like a holiday excursion were these few weeks among the Virginia mountains when compared
with the stern and bitter experiences which followed, when men remained
in the field for months and years, enduring, suffering, and thousands of them
dying in the contest.

Statistics.

Officers, 37; enlisted men, 747; total, 784. Died, 7; deserted, 15; returned, 762.

COMPANY D.

Captain--Thomas J. Brady.
First Lieutenants—Geo. W. Edgerle (promoted Assistant Surgeon), Joseph Kirk.
Second Lieutenants—William Fisher, Nathan Branson.
Sergeants—Andrew O'Daniel, George James, William Berry, Edwin Pugh.
Corporals—Samuel G. Williams, Thomas H. Kirby, Cyrus M. Newcomb, William
Hatfield.
Musicians—Thomas Dalrymple, Mile S. Smith.
Privates—James Adams, Emanuel Aldrich, John Bishop, Henry Bowman, John
H. Brown, Samuel Carmenes, Frederick Coppersmith, wounded July 11, 1861; Thomas
Cribitt, James Cummerford, George Darracott, George W. Eastman, Isaac W. Ellis,
James Ennis, Lewis Everett, John Fifer, Jacob Fry, Robert Galbraith, William Gates,
Joseph Gessell, John A. Gilbert, Uriah Harrold, Robert Harter, Joshua Horsman, John
Irwin, Louis Jordan, Daniel B. Kimball, Asbury L. Kerwood, wounded July 11, 1861;
Jacob Kinsey, John Kirk, Charles Kiser, John A. Klein, John B. Maddy, Richard M.
Martin, Alexander Miller, John H. Miller, Simon Miller, John Motes, Sylvester Peter-
man, Jeremiah Priest, Abel Pugh, James Pugh, George Raupp, Collier M. Reid, wounded
July 11, 1861; Andrew G. Ridenour, wounded July 11, 1861; John Ridge, Butler Sears,
John Shields, Francis Sheel, Joseph Shipley, Apton Single, John Stake, William Stevens,
Samuel Sullivan, George Taylor, John C. Taylor, John H. Walker, wounded July 11,
1861; William Watson, Francis Williams, Horace Williams, Jesse Williamson, Willis
Williamson, Nicholas Wise, Aaron V. Wright, Eli Younce.
Total wounded, 5.

Three Years' Service.

The Eighth Regiment was reorganized for the three years' service at
Indianapolis on the 20th of August, 1861, and mustered in on the 5th day
of September, 1861, with William P. Benton as colonel. Leaving Indianapolis by rail on the 10th of September, it proceeded to St. Louis, there
joining the army under General Fremont in the Department of Missouri. A
few days later the regiment marched toward the State Capital, reaching

Jefferson City on September 14, where it was assigned to the brigade commanded by Col. Jeff. C. Davis of the Twenty-second Indiana Volunteers. On the 22d the march was resumed for Springfield, which place it reached after fourteen days' march, and returned to Otterville in seven days. On the 17th of December the Eighth marched to Warrensburg and assisted in the capture of thirteen hundred rebels. Returning to Otterville, it remained in camp until January 24, 1862, when it marched for Springfield, joining the command of General Curtis on the route. From there the march was continued to Cross Timbers, Arkansas, and immediately the three days' battle of Pea Ridge was fought on March 6, 7 and 8, in which the Eighth bore an honorable part.

After remaining nearly one month in camp at Cross Timbers, it then moved in the direction of Forsythe, Missouri, over the Ozark Mountains, and then proceeded down the valley of White River and across the country to Batesville, Arkansas, halting nearly two months at Sulphur Rock. Leaving here June 22, it reached Helena, on the Mississippi river, on the 13th of July. The command endured much suffering on this arduous march by reason of scarcity of provisions, there being but a scanty supply with the command and but little in the country; very often the daily ration consisted of four ears of corn with a small allowance of meat. Some skirmishing with the enemy took place among the canebrakes of White river and there was an engagement fought at Cotton Plant. In August, while on an expedition from Helena, a skirmish occurred at Austin, Mississippi. On October 6 the Eighth was placed in the command of General Steele and proceeded by steamer to Sulphur Hill, near St. Louis, from which place it marched to Ironton, Missouri, on the 11th of October, and from thence marched and countermarched through the southeastern part of the state, until March 5, 1863, when the regiment embarked on a steamer at St. Genevieve to join General Grant's army at Milliken's Bend, Louisiana. Here it was assigned to Benton's Brigade, Carr's Division, of the Thirteenth Corps, then commanded by General McClernand. The regiment crossed the Mississippi river on the 29th of April and participated in the engagement at Port Gibson, on the 1st of May, losing thirty-two in killed and wounded; at Jackson on the 14th; at Champion Hills on the 16th; at Black River Bridge on the 17th; and from the 19th of May till the 4th of July was engaged in the siege of Vicksburg. In the assault on the enemy's work on the 22d of June the Eighth lost one hundred and seventeen in killed and wounded. On the 5th of July it marched to Jackson, which, being evacuated by the enemy, the Eighth returned to Vicksburg on the 24th of July, where it remained until the 20th of August, when it embarked on a steamer for Carrollton, Louisiana. From here a campaign was made through the Teche country under Gen. Banks. On the 12th of November the regiment embarked from Ber-

...ick City for Texas, and on the 17th took part in the attack and capture of a fort on Mustang Island, near Aransas Pass. On the 27th it was engaged in the attack and capture of Fort Esperanza, after which it marched to Indianola. Here on January 1, 1864, the regiment re-enlisted, 417 out of 515 being remustered as veterans. Prior to this date the Eighth had lost 28 killed in battle, 32 died of wounds, 137 died of disease, a total of 217.

The regiment arrived at Indianapolis April 22 and remained on veteran furlough in the state one month. Returning to New Orleans, it embarked on July 27 for Morganza Bend, and the following day marched to Atchafalaya, where it engaged the enemy and returned to Morganza Bend, from which point it embarked for Washington City, arriving on the 12th of August. From thence it marched to Berryville, Virginia, where it was assigned to the Nineteenth Corps, and participated in the campaign of the Shenandoah Valley, under General Sheridan. The regiment was in the engagement at Opequan on the 19th of September, the battle of Fisher's Hill on the 22d of September, and of Cedar Creek on the 19th of October. Leaving the Valley on January 6, 1865, it reached Savannah, Georgia, from Baltimore by steamer on the 16th of the same month. It remained on duty in Georgia until August 28, 1865, when it was mustered out of service.

On the 17th of September the Eighth arrived at Indianapolis, in command of Lieutenant Colonel John R. Polk, with 14 officers and 245 men, where it was finally discharged from service, after being publicly received in the capitol grounds by Governor Morton on behalf of the state.

The line of duty carried the men of the Eighth regiment over a wide field. Their marches and campaigns embraced the states of Virginia, West Virginia, Missouri, Arkansas, Mississippi, Louisiana, Georgia and Texas. Hard battles were fought in nearly all of these states, and the graves of those who fell by death or wounds upon the field, by sickness from exposure and hardships which severely tested the endurance of the bravest of men would make a long list. Only experience of a like nature can enable one to fully comprehend what these brave men endured in behalf of their country.

From first to last, the Eighth Indiana took part in the following engagements in their order:

Rich Mountain. Virginia, July 11, 1861; Pea Ridge, Arkansas, March 7-8. 1862; Cotton Plant, Arkansas, July 7, 1862; Austin, Mississippi, August, 1862; siege of Vicksburg, Mississippi, from May 19 to July 4. 1863; Fort Gibson (Magnolia Hill), Mississippi, May 1, 1863; Jackson, May 14; Champion Hill, May 16; Black River Bridge, May 17; assault on Vicksburg, June 22; siege of Jackson, July 9-16, 1863; Mustang Island, Texas, November 17, 1863; Fort Esperanza, Texas, November 27, 1863; Atchafalaya, Louisiana, July 28, 1864; Opequan, Virginia, September 19, 1864;

Fisher's Hill, Virginia, September 22; New Market, Virginia, September 23, and Cedar Creek, Virginia, October 19, 1864.

STATISTICS.

Officers, 72; men, 980; recruits, 177. Total, 1,229. Died, 233; deserted, 75.

REGIMENTAL OFFICERS—(FROM DELAWARE COUNTY).

Major—Thomas J. Brady; commissioned May 10, 1862; promoted to Colonel of the One Hundred and Seventeenth Regiment, September 19, 1863; was mustered out at the expiration of term, six months; re-entered as Colonel of the One Hundred and Fortieth Regiment, for one year, October 20, 1864, and was mustered out with the regiment, July 11, 1865; meantime he had been appointed Brigadier General by brevet, March 13, 1865.

Quarter Master—Nathan Branson; dismissed February 27, 1865.
Assistant Surgeon—George W. Edgerle, died November 10, 1861.

COMPANY A.

Captain—Thomas J. Brady; promoted to Major; Colonel of the One Hundred and Seventeenth Regiment; Colonel of the One Hundred and Fortieth Regiment; mustered out of service July 11, 1865.

First Lieutenant—George W. Parkison, resigned December 31, 1861.

Second Lieutenant—Andrew O'Daniel; promoted to First Lieutenant; Captain; killed in action at Vicksburg May 22, 1863.

Commissary Sergeant—John A. McConnell, veteran.

First Sergeant—William Watson, promoted to First Lieutenant; Captain; killed in the action at Cedar Creek, Virginia, October 19, 1864.

Sergeants—Matthew M. Hughes, promoted to First Lieutenant, Captain; James Nation, discharged, 1861, disability; Samuel C. Williams, appointed Sergeant Major, discharged for disability, 1862; Thomas Carman, mustered out September, 1864.

Corporals—James H. Adams, veteran, promoted to Second Lieutenant, mustered out as private, August 28, 1865; Jacob H. Kinzey, veteran; John C. Gaunt, transferred to Veteran Reserve Corps; Andrew Ridenour, killed at Vicksburg, May 22, 1863; George Eviston, discharged, 1861, disability; Thomas Corbitt, veteran, died at Savannah, Georgia, April 25, 1865; George Craw, killed at Vicksburg, May 22, 1863; William A. Gates, veteran, discharged April 26, 1865.

Musicians—Anthony Leakey, veteran, discharged November 28, 1864; George V. Tilson, veteran, mustered out with regiment.

Wagoner—William Coffeen, mustered out as private, September 4, 1864.

Privates—Josiah F. Adams, veteran; William G. Beath, veteran, captured at Cedar Creek, Virginia; Joseph Brown, veteran; John Carmin, veteran, Corporal, Sergeant; George Cummins, Richard E. Craw, Benjamin Drake, veteran, appointed Corporal; William F. Fisher, veteran; Andrew J. Gibbs; Henry Garrison, veteran; Emeriah Garrard, veteran; William R. Irwin. Quartermaster Sergeant, promoted to Second Lieutenant. First Lieutenant. Assistant Commissary Sergeant; Daniel Keen, veteran; James Landfair, veteran; David Lutz, veteran; Thomas Leakey, veteran; Esquire Miller, veteran; Geo. W. Needler, veteran; Samuel Newbold; William M. Parker, veteran; Lewis N. Rumsey, veteran; Daniel T. Reynolds, veteran; Joshua Richardson, veteran; Thomas H. Smith, veteran, appointed Corporal; David M. Wills, veteran; William P. Wagoner, veteran; John W. Windsor, veteran.

George Albin, died at Rolla, Mo., May 8, 1862.
Watson Adams, transferred to Eighteenth United States Infantry.
David B. Babb, discharged January 17, 1863.
Milton Brown, veteran, Corporal, Sergeant; mustered out August 28, 1865.
Joshua P. Bennett, died at Indianola, Texas.
Robert Clift, discharged October 17, 1862.
William Cooly, mustered out October, 1864.
William Collins, mustered out August 28, 1866, to date back to November 15, 1864.
William R. Corwin, died at Otterville, Mo., February 11, 1862.
David Craw, appointed Corporal; mustered out September 24, 1864.
William A. Craw, died at Cairo, Ill., August 16, 1863.
James Cummins, mustered out September 4, 1864.

James Cummerford, veteran, discharged December 4, 1864, disabled.
Samuel Collins, died at St. Louis October 31, 1862.
James Davis, died at Memphis, Tenn., July 19, 1863.
Francis Derin [record indefinite].
William Dick, discharged March 23, 1863; disability.
Larkin E. Daly, mustered out as a wagoner. August, 1865.
George W. Eby, killed at Vicksburg May 25, 1863.
Robert Galbraith, died at Keokuk, Iowa, December 31, 1862.
Ner. Gaunt, mustered out September 4, 1864.
Isaiah Gayman, mustered out September 4, 1864.
James Graves [record indefinite].
Luther Grosse [record indefinite].
John Haines, discharged 1861; accidental wounds.
William Hamilton, veteran; First Sergeant, Second Lieutenant; mustered out as Sergeant August 28, 1865.
Jacob Hatzler, mustered out September 4, 1864.
John Hensley, died at Syracuse, Miss., December 5, 1861.
John Hewey [record indefinite].
Dudley Holdren, died at Keokuk, Iowa, October 23, 1862.
George W. Hawk, veteran; mustered out June 14, 1865.
Richard Harpster, veteran; captured; mustered out June 12, 1865.
Amos Hatzler, mustered out May 26, 1865.
Daniel Hoffaker, discharged December 18, 1862.
Henry Jack, discharged 1861; disability.
Gabriel Johnson, mustered out September 4, 1864.
George Keen, discharged September 16, 1863.
John Ledler, discharged December 18, 1862.
Henry Lace, discharged December 26, 1862.
Columbus F. Lay, mustered out September 4, 1864.
John M. Little, discharged at Louisville September 16, 1862.
Josephus Lacey, Veteran Reserve Corps, discharged March 21, 1865.
Daniel Miller, mustered out September 4, 1864.
John Miller, died at Keokuk, Iowa, October 25, 1862.
Henry McDermitt, discharged 1862, for disability.
William A. McFarland, mustered out September 4, 1864.
Seth Nation, mustered out September 4, 1864.
James F. Neal, killed at Vicksburg May 25, 1863.
John Parkison, discharged, 1861, for disability.
William I. Parkison, died 1862.
George Paxon, discharged, 1862, for disability.
Thomas Paxon, discharged, December 30, 1862.
Price Powers, died at Jefferson Barracks, Missouri, July 23, 1863.
James R. Parker, veteran, mustered out June 14, 1865.
Joseph W. Rigdon, promoted to First Lieutenant; transferred to the Veteran Reserve Corps as Sergeant.
Hessle Stradling, died at Keokuk, Iowa, December 26, 1862.
Abner Saunders, discharged March 17, 1863.
Abner S. Saunders, discharged, 1862, for disability.
Joseph Sink, appointed Corporal; mustered out September 4, 1864.
Jacob Shafer, mustered out September 4, 1864.
John Slife, transferred to Veteran Reserve Corps July 7, 1864.
John S. Smiley, mustered out September 4, 1864.
Allen Stultz, died at Otterville, Mo., January 14, 1862.
Jacob Swain, mustered out September 4, 1864.
Israel Shafer, killed at Vicksburg May 27, 1863.
Henry Sheets, transferred to Veteran Reserve Corps July 7, 1864.
John Slack, killed at Vicksburg, May 22, 1863.
Daniel Studebaker, from Company E, mustered out June 14, 1865.
George Taylor, mustered out September 4, 1864.
William R. Tinker, discharged, 1862, for disability.
George W. Thompson, discharged March 17, 1863.
Miles Thornburg, transferred to Veteran Reserve Corps.

Sylvester Triplett, killed at Vicksburg May 22, 1863.
Joseph Walden, February 2, 1863.
Lewis C. Wilson, veteran; captured at Cedar Creek. Va., October 19, 1864.
William C. Walker, mustered out September 14, 1864.
Albert Whitman, died at Evansville July 26, 1863; wounded at Vicksburg.
John C. Walker, died October 18, 1863.

COMPANY E.

Privates—George W. Barrett, veteran; Joel Cummings, veteran; Henry R. Graham, veteran; William H. Skinner, veteran; Henry Shoemaker, veteran.
David Clements, died at St. Louis August 12, 1863.
William Cummings, transferred to Invalid Corps.
William Coffeen, mustered out September 4, 1864.
Joseph Foraere, discharged April 10, 1863, for disability.
Josiah Huggins, discharged January 16, 1863.
William Lemond, mustered out September 4, 1864.
Jacob Snyder, transferred to Company A; mustered out June 14, 1865.
Daniel Studebaker, transferred to Company A; mustered out June 14, 1865.
William Van Matre, mustered out September 4, 1864.
Cyrus Van Matre, discharged June 8, 1864, for disability.
Zachariah Windsor, discharged June 8, 1864, for disability.
Joseph Snyder, honorably discharged.
Jacob Snyder (Company E), transferred to Invalid Corps; died at St. Louis August 11, 1863.

COMPANY I.

Samuel Harris, absent since August 24, 1864.
William C. Scott, mustered out June 14, 1865.

TENTH REGIMENT (Three Months' Service).

Evender C. Kennedy.

TWELFTH REGIMENT.

COMPANY A.

Charles F. W. Gibson, transferred to Fifty-ninth Regiment and mustered out July 17, 1865.
Henry Thompson, mustered out June 8, 1865.
Caleb L. Wilcoxon, transferred to Fifty-ninth Regiment, mustered out July 17, 1865.

THIRTEENTH REGIMENT.

Mustered into service at Indianapolis, June 19, 1861. Jeremiah C. Sullivan, colonel. Officers, 71; men, 976; recruits, 192; total, 1,239. Officers died, 8; men died, 128; deserted, 103. Mustered out at Goldsboro, North Carolina, September 5, 1865; 29 officers and 550 men. Only five names from Delaware county have been found in this regiment.

COMPANY A.

Charles Brown, transferred to Thirteenth Regiment, re-organized; mustered out September 5, 1865. William J. Ranier, promoted to Second Lieutenant, First Lieutenant; mustered out November 19, 1864.
Enos Thornburg, killed at Chester Station May 10, 1864.
John Thornburg, mustered out July 1, 1864.

COMPANY H.

Private William Lewis, appointed Sergeant Major. First Lieutenant, of Company H.

THIRTEENTH REGIMENT (Reorganized).

COMPANY H.

First Lieutenant—William Lewis, mustered out September 5, 1865.
Sergeant—Eli Young, mustered out September 5, 1865.
Corporal—George Jones, mustered out September 5, 1865, as Sergeant.

SIXTEENTH REGIMENT.

Thomas Reamond, honorably discharged.

NINETEENTH REGIMENT (THREE YEARS).

The Nineteenth Regiment was organized and mustered into service for three years at Indianapolis on July 29, 1861, with Solomon Meredith as colonel. Leaving the capital on the 5th of August, it joined the Army of the Potomac at Washington on the 9th of the same month. On the 11th of September it was engaged in the affair at Lewinsville, losing three killed and wounded and three prisoners.

Subsequently it participated in the advance upon Falls Church, and then went into quarters at Fort Craig, on Arlington Heights. On March 10, 1862, it marched with the First Corps, under Gen. McDowell, to Fredericksburg, from whence it moved in May towards the Shenandoah Valley, and then to Warrenton. Remaining here until the 5th of August, it marched to Fredericksburg, and from thence on reconnoissance to Spotsylvania Court House. On the 10th it reached Cedar Mountain, where it remained until the army retired before the advance of the enemy. While on the retreat the brigade to which the Nineteenth was attached had a severe engagement with Ewell's command at Gainesville on the night of the 28th of August, the regiment losing 187 killed and wounded and 33 missing. Major Isaac M. May was killed in this action. At Manassas Junction, on the 30th, it was again engaged with but slight loss, after which it marched with the army to Washington, and thence to Frederick City, Maryland.

On the 14th of September the regiment participated in the battle of South Mountain, serving in the First Corps, commanded by General Reynolds, and losing 40 killed and wounded and 7 missing.

In the battle of Antietam, on the 17th, it was conspicuously engaged, going into the battle with about 200 officers and men, and coming out with but 37 officers and men; among the killed was Lieutenant Colonel Alois O. Bachman. After the battle the regiment lay encamped near Sharpsburg, where it remained until the middle of October. Colonel Meredith having received promotion as brigadier general on the 6th of October, Lieutenant Colonel Samuel J. Williams was advanced to the grade of a colonel.

Crossing the Potomac on the 30th of October, the regiment moved to Warrenton, from whence it moved to the Rappahannock, near Fredericksburg, and participated in Burnside's attempt to assault the rebel works at that place on the 12th and 13th of December. After this it went into winter quarters at Belle Plaine.

On the 28th of April, 1863, the Nineteenth marched to Fitzhugh's Crossing, below Fredericksburg, where it passed the Rappahannock on the following morning and engaged the enemy, losing four killed and wounded. The movement at this point being a feint to enable the main army to cross the river above, on the 2d of May General Reynolds recrossed the Rappahannock with the First Corps and marched to United States Ford, crossing over before day on the 3d and taking position in the line of battle near Chancellorsville, but was not engaged. On the 21st of May it marched to Westmoreland Court House, and assisted the return of a cavalry force sent in that direction, and on the 12th of June it commenced its march northward, crossing into Maryland at Edward's Ferry, and marching through Frederick City, reached the battlefield of Gettysburg just as the engagement was opening on the morning of the 1st of July.

It was the first infantry force to engage the enemy, and in a charge made by the First Division of the First Corps assisted in defeating the enemy and capturing Archer's rebel brigade. In the afternoon the regiment was engaged in the resistance made to the desperate charge made by the rebel army upon the First and Eleventh Corps, and was forced to fall back to Cemetery Hill. During the day the regiment lost 210 out of 288 that went into battle. On the 2d and 3d of July the Nineteenth occupied a position on Cemetery Hill, but was not actively engaged, though somewhat exposed to the enemy's fire; its loss after the first day was but two wounded.

On the 18th of July the regiment crossed the Potomac at Berlin, and proceeded to Rappahannock Station, where it arrived on the 1st of August. It then moved to Culpepper, where it remained until the operations against Mine Run in November, in which it participated.

At the close of the campaign the regiment took up winter quarters, and was not engaged in active duty until the following spring. During the winter of 1864 a portion of the regiment re-enlisted at Culpepper, Virginia, and these soon after spent some time in Indiana on veteran furlough.

Moving with Grant's army across the Rapidan on the 4th of May, the Nineteenth participated in the battles that followed, including those in the Wilderness, at Laurel Hill, North Anna and Cold Harbor.

At the Wilderness, on the 5th of May, Colonel Williams was killed, and soon after Lieutenant Colonel John M. Lindley was commissioned his successor. In the siege of Petersburg the Nineteenth was almost constantly on duty, and in the assault on the enemy's works on the 18th of June it bore a conspicuous part.

The losses sustained by the regiment from the crossing of the Rapidan to the 30th of July are reported as follows: Killed, 36; severely wounded, 94; slightly wounded, 74; missing, 16—total, 220.

The non-veterans left the regiment early in August, and on reaching Indianapolis were mustered out of service. The remaining members were afterward consolidated with the Twentieth Indiana regiment.

Statistics.

Officers, 73; men, 981; recruits, 218; unassigned recruits, 226; total, 1,498. Officers died, 7; men died, 260.

IRON BRIGADE.

In October, 1861, what was later known as the "Iron Brigade," was organized under Gen. Rufus King, composed of the Second, Sixth and Seventh Wisconsin regiments and Nineteenth Indiana, to which Battery B, Fourth United States Artillery, was soon after assigned. Many members of this historic company of artillerists were details from the infantry of the brigade. It was commanded then by Captain, afterwards General John Gibbon. What was later known as Stewart's battery met with the greatest aggregate of loss of any light artillery in the service during the Civil war. There is little doubt that more men fell at Stewart's guns than in any other battery in the Union armies. In proportion to its numbers this brigade sustained the heaviest losses of any in the war. The name of the Iron Brigade was a title well merited, and honestly earned, by hard fighting on many a hotly contested and sanguinary field. At Gainesville the four regiments lost: Killed, 148; wounded, 626; missing, 120—a total of 894 out of about 2,000 engaged. Yet this heroic body of troops which met Ewell's division was reported at the time as having had a "skirmish." October, 1862, the Twenty-fourth Michigan was assigned to the brigade. At Gettysburg the five regiments were engaged, losing 162 killed, 724 wounded and 267 missing—a total of 1,153 out of 1,883 engaged, 61 per cent.

The percentage of killed and died of wounds by regiments is as follows: Second Wisconsin, 19.7 per cent; Sixth Wisconsin, 12.5 per cent; Seventh Wisconsin, 17.2 per cent; Nineteenth Indiana, 15.9; Twenty-fourth Michigan, 15.2.

The Nineteenth Indiana sustained the greatest loss in battle of any regiment from Indiana. Credit has been given to the Twentieth Indiana, but it is believed unjustly, because the losses sustained from October 18, 1864, the date of consolidation, were credited to the Twentieth Indiana.

The Iron Brigade took part in the following engagements:

1862.

Rappahannock Station, Va.	Aug. 20-23
Sulphur Springs, Va.	Aug. 26
Gainesville. Va.	Aug. 28
Bull Run, Second.	Aug. 29-30
South Mountain, Md.	Sept. 14
Antietam, Md.	Sept. 17
Fredericksburg, Va.	Dec. 11-15

1863.

Fitzhugh's Crossing, Va.	April 29-30
Chancellorsville, Va.	May 1-5
Gettysburg, Pa.	July 1-4
Mine Run, Va.	Nov. 26 and Dec. 2

1864.

Wilderness, Va.	May 5-7
Laurel Hill and Spottsylvania, Va.	May 8-21
North Anna and Jericho Ford.	May 23-26
Tolopotomy, Va.	May 28-30

Bethesda Church, Va..May 31 and June 1
Cold Harbor, Va..June 1-6
Petersburg, Va., Siege of..........................June 17, 1864, to April 3, 1865
Petersburg, Va., Assault on...June 18
Mine Explosion, Va..July 30
Weldon Railroad, Va..Aug. 19-21
Tatcher's Run..Oct. 27-28
Weldon Railroad Expedition, Va..Dec. 7-11

REGIMENTAL OFFICERS.

Lieutenant Colonel—Samuel J. Williams, September 18, 1862; promoted to Colonel; killed at the battle of the Wilderness May 6, 1864.

Major—Isaac M. May, killed at Gainesville, Va., August 28, 1862.

Major—William Orr, commissioned August 4, 1864; promoted to Colonel of the Twentieth, on final consolidation; honorably discharged May 15, 1865.

Adjutant—John M. Rissey, commissioned April 7, 1862; resigned January 9, 1865.

Chaplain—Lewis Dale, resigned March 8, 1863. Thomas Barnett, commissioned April 10, 1863; resigned July 5, 1864.

COMPANY A.

Captain—Isaac M. May, promoted Major; killed at Gainesville, Va., August 28, 1862.
First Lieutenant—James L. Kilgore, resigned.

Second Lieutenant—Alonzo T. Makepeace, promoted to First Lieutenant—to Captain; honorably discharged March 12, 1865; paroled prisoner of war.

Sergeants—Julius Voit, promoted to Second Lieutenant, resigned December 18, 1862; Adam Gisse, wounded, promoted to Second Lieutenant, mustered out July 12, 1865.

Privates—David A. Babb, mustered out September 23, 1864.

George A. Ieldic, veteran, transferred to Twentieth Regiment; mustered out July 12, 1865.

Andrew Liable, veteran, transferred to the Twentieth Regiment; mustered out July 18, 1865.

COMPANY B.

Privates—Robert McMartin, prisoner at Andersonville nine months; mustered out July 12, 1865.
Isaac Smith, veteran, mustered out July 12, 1865.

COMPANY D.

First Lieutenant—William Orr, declined.

COMPANY E.

Captain—Luther B. Wilson, resigned; re-commissioned; honorably discharged April 4, 1863.

First Lieutenant—George W. Greene, promoted to Captain; honorably discharged March 12, 1865; paroled prisoner of war.

Second Lieutenant—John M. Rissey, promoted to Adjutant; resigned January 9, 1865.

Sergeants—Isaac W. Wittemeyer, promoted to Second Lieutenant—to First Lieutenant, left the army January 7, 1864; George C. Stewart, discharged in 1862, for disability; William Fisher, died October 6, 1861; John D. Perrong, wounded, transferred to Veteran Reserve Corps; Isaac Branson, wounded, promoted to Second Lieutenant—to First Lieutenant, mustered out October 26, 1864.

Corporals—Henry C. Klein, mustered out September 23, 1864; Andrew J. McLeroy, died March 31, 1862; George A. Reynolds, mustered out September 23, 1864; Edwin O. Birt, veteran, wounded at Petersburg, transferred to Twentieth Regiment; Oliver Carmichael, appointed Sergeant, wounded, transferred to Twentieth Regiment; George W. Van Matre, record indefinite; Thomas K. Michener, appointed Sergeant, killed at Gettysburg; Joseph Collins, discharged 1862, for disability.

Musicians—John B. Armstrong, discharged early, from disability; Spencer D. Richardson, veteran, wounded in the battle of the Wilderness, transferred to Twentieth Regiment, mustered out July 19, 1865.

Wagoner—Thomas I. Gilbert, mustered out July 28, 1865.

Privates—Clinton Anthony, wounded at South Mountain; William Archer, veteran, Twentieth Regiment as reorganized.

Abraham J. Bickles, veteran, wounded at the battle of the Wilderness, transferred to the Twentieth Regiment.

David Burgess, wounded.

Henry H. Clasmier, veteran, transferred to Twentieth Regiment.

Joseph X. Cochren, mustered out as Corporal; absent, wounded.

Joseph Collins, promoted to First Lieutenant, Co. F, One Hundred and Forty-seventh Regiment.

Andrew J. Collins, recruit.

John Collins, transferred to Company D, Twentieth Regiment.

David R. Dumont, veteran, transferred to Twentieth Regiment.

James I. Denton, wounded at Petersburg; transferred to Twentieth Regiment.

George F. Ethele, veteran, transferred to Twentieth Regiment; mustered out as Corporal.

Thomas J. Fison, veteran.

Andrew Goodpasture, wounded.

John Gump, veteran, transferred to the Twentieth Regiment.

Jacob Gump.

Joseph Gerrard, transferred to the Twentieth Regiment.

William K. Helvie, transferred to the Twentieth Regiment.

John P. Helvie, transferred to the Twentieth Regiment.

Jasper Hoppis, transferred to the Twentieth Regiment.

John F. Harter, veteran, transferred to the Twentieth Regiment.

David Holdren, veteran.

George W. Hulford, veteran, transferred to the Twentieth Regiment.

Henry C. Klein, transferred to the Twentieth Regiment.

John W. Kennedy, wounded in the battle of the Wilderness.

Perry Miller, transferred to Veteran Reserve Corps.

Joshua Needham, veteran, transferred to the Twentieth Regiment.

Isaiah Pruitt, veteran, transferred to the Twentieth Regiment—to Veteran Reserve Corps.

John Shockley, veteran.

Timothy Stewart, veteran, transferred to the Twentieth Regiment.

Benton Skinner, veteran.

Thomson Smelser, transferred to the Twentieth Regiment.

Isaac Smith, veteran.

George W. Taylor (band), wounded at the battle before Petersburg; transferred to the Twentieth Regiment.

Elihu J. Whiccar, veteran, wounded at the battle of the Wilderness; transferred to the Twentieth Regiment.

Nicholas Wise, wounded May 23, 1864; transferred to the Twentieth Regiment.

Nathaniel Yingling (band); transferred to the Twentieth Regiment.

William Beagle, discharged July 28, 1864.

William J. Brinson, died of wounds received at South Mountain.

William H. Burt, mustered out September 23, 1864.

Philip Cochren, wounded, discharged for disability.

Hiram Conkle, killed at Gettysburg, Penn., July 1, 1863.

William Crum, appointed Corporal, killed at South Mountain September 14, 1862.

George W. Collins, crippled at Fairfax Seminary, discharged, 1862.

Samuel W. Dusang, died November 13, 1862, wounded at Antietam.

Joseph Dusang, appointed Corporal, wounded at Antietam September 17, 1862.

Charles Daugherty, mustered out May 12, 1865.

William J. Frownfelter, died November 6, 1862.

John M. Fitzsimmons, veteran, died August 17, 1864, of wounds.

James X. Franklin, died September 16, 1861.

James J. Galbraith, died January 29, 1862.

George W. Goldwin, died November 5, 1861.

O. J. Gilbert, wounded at Fredericksburg, discharged 1863.

Thomas J. Gilbert, wagoner, discharged July 28, 1864.

James Haines, mustered out as absent, wounded July 28, 1864.

Barton S. Harter, killed at Antietam September 17, 1862.

William J. Haney, died November 21, 1862, from wounds at Antietam.

William B. Heath, died October 6, 1862.

Robert W. Heath, discharged for disability December, 1861.

Isaac Hughes, mustered out September 23, 1864.

David U. Hernley, died February 23, 1863.

William H. Jones, veteran, killed at the battle of the Wilderness May 5, 1864, as Corporal.

James R. Jones, wounded, mustered out July 28, 1864, as Corporal.

Joshua Jones, died September 28, 1862; wounded at Antietam.

William N. Jackson, mustered out October 19, 1864.

Ira Kendall, wounded at Laurel Hill; mustered out July 28, 1864.

John W. Kendall, record indefinite.

Valentine Kiger, transferred to Twenty-fourth Regiment, July, 1865; mustered out October 13, 1865.

William Keen, wounded at Petersburg; transferred to Twentieth Regiment; discharged August 20, 1865—disability.

Henderson Lawson, hurt by railroad train, August 8, 1861; discharged soon after from disability.

Amos W. Lee, wounded; discharged March 23, 1863.

James Love, died September 29, 1862; wounded at South Mountain.

Oliver Love, died June 9, 1863.

William McAfee, mustered out July 28, 1864.

John W. Modlin, killed in the battle of the Wilderness May 5, 1864.

Henry C. Marsh, Hospital Steward.

Isaac McConnell, discharged—early disability.

Jacob Miller, wounded; mustered out July 28, 1864.

John Nicholson, wounded at the battle of the Wilderness; mustered out July 28, 1864.

Thomas Parsons, died September 17, 1861.

Benjamin Parsons, died September 29, 1862; wounded at Antietam.

George Parsons, mustered out September 23, 1864.

Robert I. Patterson, wounded at Antietam; discharged September, 1864.

Jacob Pearpoint, killed near Falmouth, Va., in 1862.

William Redpath, wounded; mustered out July 28, 1864.

Jacob Redpath, discharged for disability.

Lyman K. Riggs, veteran; captured at battle of Wilderness; died in Andersonville Prison August 3, 1864.

James Richey, mustered out September 23, 1864.

George H. Richardson, killed at South Mountain September 14, 1862.

Moses Saka, killed at the battle of Gettysburg July 1, 1863.

John A. Shafer, died at Fairfax Seminary, Va., 1863.

John Shafer, died at Alexandria, Va., August 23, 1863.

Joseph Sheperd (band), transferred to gunboat service.

William H. Sheperd, died December 30, 1861.

Isaiah Shew, died October 16, 1862.

William Simmons, killed at Gettysburg July 1, 1863.

George W. Smith, mustered out September 23, 1864.

Daniel Smith, died December 18, 1861.

Isaac Sourwine, mustered out September 23, 1864.

Elbridge G. Stevenson, died September 12, 1861.

Alexander Stewart.

James M. Stewart, killed at Gainesville, Va., August 28, 1862.

Crittenden Storer, died October 6, 1861.

Jeremiah Smith (band), record indefinite.

Enos Thayer, wounded at the Wilderness, mustered out July 28, 1864.

Harbard S. Tomlinson, veteran, killed at Petersburg June 6, 1864.

Bartlett H. Trowbridge, died October 4, 1861.

Joseph Turnpaugh, wounded, mustered out July 28, 1864.

George Warrington (band), died October 6, 1861.

Alfred Warfel, died in the service.

Joseph Worrel.

Thomson Williams, veteran, captured at Yellow House, Va., died at Salisbury Prison, N. C., July 19, 1865.

S. Ambrose Wilson (band), mustered out in 1862 as Musician.

Hamilton Yingling (band), died August 6, 1864.

Albert Young, wounded at the Wilderness, transferred to the Twentieth Regiment, discharged April 12, 1865.

COMPANY K.

Captain—Samuel J. Williams, promoted to Lieutenant Colonel, to Colonel, killed at the battle of the Wilderness.

First Lieutenant—Benjamin C. Harter, resigned August 22, 1862.

Second Lieutenant—William Orr, promoted to First Lieutenant, Captain, Major, Colonel of the Twentieth Regiment on final consolidation.

Sergeants—William H. Campbell, promoted to Second Lieutenant, to First Lieutenant, honorably discharged October 14, 1863; Andrew J. Adleman, died January 12, 1862; Edmond Davis, discharged in 1862 for disability; Crockett T. East, promoted to Second Lieutenant, killed at Gettysburg July 1, 1863; Milton L. Sparr, promoted to Second Lieutenant, resigned April 23, 1863.

Corporals—Joseph P. Carder, promoted to First Lieutenant Twentieth Regiment, mustered out December 6, 1864; Mason Hitchcock, died September 22, 1861; Thomas Winset, appointed Sergeant, killed at Gettysburg July 1, 1863; Joseph M. Helvie, veteran, wounded at the Wilderness, transferred to the Twentieth Regiment; Elijah Bales, veteran, transferred to Twentieth Regiment, mustered out July 12, 1865; John W. Moore, veteran, wounded at Gettysburg, transferred to Twentieth Regiment, mustered out July 10, 1865; William H. Murray, wounded at South Mountain and Wilderness, promoted to Second Lieutenant, brevetted Captain, resigned September 14, 1864; John M. Hubbard, mustered out July 28, 1864, as Chief Musician.

Musicians—James M. Campbell, mustered out July 28, 1864, as Sergeant; James Fiers, died November 6, 1862.

PRIVATES.

Jacob V. Bush, veteran, transferred to Twentieth Regiment.

John W. Barnell, transferred to Twentieth Regiment.

John C. Barnes, transferred to Twentieth Regiment.

James H. Baughn, transferred to Twentieth Regiment.

Samuel C. Bowen, transferred to Twentieth Regiment, mustered out as Corporal.

Peter Casper, veteran, transferred to Twentieth Regiment.

Daniel Conrad, transferred to Twentieth Regiment.

Levi Chalfant, transferred to Twentieth Regiment.

Samuel A. Dickover, transferred to Twentieth Regiment.

Allen W. Galyean, transferred to Twentieth Regiment.

John Hawk, veteran, transferred to Twentieth Regiment.

Ezra Hackman, veteran, transferred to Twentieth Regiment.

Samuel Hackman, transferred to Twentieth Regiment.

John Holbert, transferred to Twentieth Regiment, wounded.

G. D. Harter, transferred to Twentieth Regiment.

John B. Knight, veteran, transferred to Twentieth Regiment.

James Kenton, transferred to Twentieth Regiment.

William J. Leagally, transferred to Twentieth Regiment.

Benjamin N. Moore, veteran, transferred to Twentieth Regiment.

James W. Moore, transferred to Twentieth Regiment.

Albert P. Murray, transferred to Twentieth Regiment.

Henry C. Marsh, transferred to Twentieth Regiment, Hospital Steward.

David S. Norris, wounded at Petersburg, transferred to Twentieth Regiment.

Elisha B. Odell, veteran, transferred to Twentieth Regiment.

David P. Orr, veteran, transferred to Twentieth Regiment.

William W. Payton, veteran, transferred to Twentieth Regiment.

Martin Phillips, veteran, wounded in battles of the Wilderness and Cold Harbor, transferred to Twentieth Regiment.

John Poland, veteran, wounded in battle of the Wilderness, transferred to Twentieth Regiment.

Adam Stonebraker, veteran, wounded, transferred to Twentieth Regiment.

Hugh M. Strain, wounded at battle of the Wilderness, transferred to Twentieth Regiment.

Jesse W. Trego, veteran, transferred to Twentieth Regiment.

John Thomson, wounded at battle of the Wilderness, transferred to Twentieth Regiment.

Elihu M. Thornburg, wounded at Petersburg, transferred to Twentieth Regiment.

Alexander Wasson, veteran, transferred to Twentieth Regiment.

David Whitney, veteran, wounded at battle of Wilderness, captured. Died in rebel prison.

Samuel L. Williams, veteran, transferred to Twentieth Regiment.

Abijah Williams, transferred to Twentieth Regiment.

Isaac Arnold, wounded at battle of Wilderness, Petersburg, transferred to Twentieth Regiment, discharged April 15, 1865.

Ephraim Ashcraft, mustered out December 28, 1864.

Joel L. Bales, discharged June 4, 1863, from disability.

George W. Bell, wounded at Gettysburg, mustered out July 28, 1864.

William M. Boots, wounded at Gettysburg, mustered out July 28, 1864, as a Corporal.

William H. Braden, discharged in 1862 for disability.

Elijah Brewington, captured at Gettysburg, mustered out July 28, 1864.

John T. Bromagen, transferred to Veteran Reserve Corps July 1, 1863.

Benjamin F. Bush, discharged April 16, 1862, for disability.

Milton L. Bock, wounded at battle of Wilderness, transferred to Twentieth Regiment to the Veteran Reserve Corps.

James Buchanan, transferred to Twentieth Regiment, mustered out May 29, 1865.

Wilson J. Baker, Quartermaster Sergeant, promoted to Assistant Commissary, mustered out September 23, 1864.

James H. Birt, record indefinite.

Henry I. Cain, veteran, killed at Petersburg July 30, 1864.

Ephraim Chidester, killed at White River, Arkansas, July 7, 1863, in the naval service.

Bennett Cline, discharged in 1862 for disability.

Henry C. Cline, discharged March 25, 1863, for disability.

Miles Conrad, discharged December 10, 1861, for disability.

William H. M. Cooper, discharged August 26, 1863, lost a leg at Gainesville.

George M. Crannels, discharged March 14, 1863, for disability.

Albert M. Craner, discharged February 21, 1862, for disability.

Burlington Cunningham, wounded at Antietam and Gettysburg, mustered out July 28, 1864.

Isaac D. Current, discharged August 23, 1863, for disability.

Joshua B. Cain, wounded at Spottsylvania Court House, transferred to Twentieth Regiment, mustered out September 8, 1865.

John M. Culbertson, record indefinite.

Nathaniel Carey, died June — 1864.

Francis B. Cottrell, wounded at the Wilderness and Cold Harbor, transferred to Twentieth Regiment, mustered out May 24, 1865.

Adam Day, discharged February 21, 1862, for disability.

Thomas J. Daugherty, appointed Sergeant, killed at Gettysburg July 1, 1863.

John W. Dotson, killed at Petersburg June 19, 1864.

Joseph T. Endsley, discharged November 1, 1861, for disability.

Lewis Fiers, discharged November 1, 1862, for disability.

George W. Fullhart, wounded at Petersburg, transferred to Twentieth Regiment, mustered out July 8, 1865.

Adam Friedline, died December 12, 1861.

Job Gaunt, discharged February 18, 1863; re-enlisted, killed at battle of the Wilderness May 5, 1864.

George C. Gates, discharged 1862, for disability.

James R. Goings, veteran, died March, 1864.

Milton N. Goff, promoted First Lieutenant, Company E, One Hundred and Forty-seventh Regiment; wounded at Chancellorsville; mustered out July 28, 1864.

Thomas W. Goff, discharged July 9, 1863, from wounds at Gainesville.

Samuel Gustin, discharged January 5, 1863, from wounds at Gainesville.

Samuel Gibson, wounded at battle of the Wilderness; transferred to the Twentieth Regiment; mustered out May 29, 1865.

Peter Goff, died 1864.

David Harness, discharged February 26, 1862, for disability.

John Hastings, discharged February 6, 1863, for disability.

Silas Hiatt, discharged April 10, 1864, for disability.
David C. Hamer, transferred to the Twentieth Regiment; mustered out.
Daniel L. Hawk, wounded at Petersburg, transferred to Twentieth Regiment, discharged April 9, 1865, for disability.
Benjamin C. Harter, First Lieutenant, resigned August 22, 1862.
Roswell Jackson, veteran, transferred to Veteran Reserve Corps; mustered out September 12, 1865.
Leander E. Jarnagin, killed at Fredericksburg December 13, 1862.
James M. Jenkins, transferred to Fourth United States Artillery.
Jacob Y. Jones, killed at ___ttysburg July 1, 1863.
James B. Jones, killed at ' ___ Harbor June 5, 1864.
Andrew Knapp, veteran, w___ ___ at Petersburg, transferred to Twentieth Regiment, discharged June 23, 1865, for disability.
John W. Knight, mustered out July 28, 1864.
Willson Knight, died November 2, 1861.
Franklin L. Keever, transferred to Twentieth Regiment; died at City Point April 14, 1865.
Andrew J. Lakin, discharged October 30, 1862, from wounds at Gainesville.
William B. Lacey, discharged May 1, 1862, for disability.
David W. Lennon, killed at Antietam September 17, 1862.
William H. Levell, wounded at Gettysburg; mustered out July 28, 1865.
James M. Levell, transferred to Twentieth Regiment; discharged June 17, 1865, for disability.
Permon McKinney, discharged October 8, 1861, for disability.
Harvey McNees, discharged August 15, 1863, for disability.
William K. Moore, wounded at Gettysburg, mustered out July 28, 1864.
James Miller, killed in battle of the Wilderness May, 1864.
Albert P. Murray, mustered out July 12, 1865.
David W. Niswanger, discharged April 1, 1863; wounded at Antietam.
Michael J. Owens, transferred to gunboat service February 18, 1862.
James G. Payton, died November 1, 1861.
William Phillips, discharged June 8, 1862, for disability.
Andrew N. Ribble, discharged December 6, 1862; wounded at Antietam.
Cornelius W. Ribble, died December 31, 1861.
George W. Ribble, died January 12, 1862.
Edward Rodman, mustered out July 28, 1864.
George F. Rowley, killed at Laurel Hill May 10, 1864.
Michael Ryan, killed at Petersburg June 18, 1864.
Charles Rodman, discharged December 20, 1862, for disability.
Josiah Saucer, discharged July 15, 1862, for disability.
Benjamin Shields, died October 8, 1861.
William M. Shoity, discharged December 19, 1861, for disability.
Absalom Shroyer, veteran, killed at Laurel Hill May 9, 1864.
John W. Skiff, discharged May 5, 1862, for disability.
Daniel Smith, died November 16, 1861.
Moses Stouder, died January 8, 1862.
Adam Smelser, wounded at Gettysburg, Wilderness; transferred to Twentieth Regiment; discharged June 2, 1865, for disability.
Isaac Van Arsdoll, killed at Gainesville August 28, 1862.
John W. Ward, died April 7, 1862.
John H. Widener, discharged May, 1862, for disability.
Mordecai Whitney, discharged, 1862, for disability.
James Wilcoxen, discharged June 28, 1863; wounded at Gainesville.
Philip A. Wingate, transferred to Fourth United States Artillery.
Franklin Whitney, killed at Laurel Hill, Va., May 9, 1864.

FIRST HEAVY ARTILLERY (THREE YEARS).

The Twenty-first Regiment was organized and mustered as an infantry organization for three years at Indianapolis on the 24th of July, 1861, with James W. McMillan as colonel.

The following week it was ordered East, reaching Baltimore August 3, where it remained until February 19, 1862, during which time it participated in Gen. Lockwood's expedition to the eastern shore of Virginia. The regiment sailed for Newport News, from which place it embarked, on March 4, on the steamship Constitution as part of the fleet of Gen. Butler in his movement against the city of New Orleans.

On the 15th of April it left Ship Island on the ship Great Republic, which laid off the mouth of the Southwest Pass during the bombardment of Forts St. Phillip and Jackson, after which, on the 29th of April, a portion of the regiment landed in the rear of St. Phillip and waded across to the Quarantine, while the balance went through Pass I.'Outre up the Mississippi to New Orleans. This portion of the regiment was the first of Butler's army to touch the New Orleans wharf on May 1, and marched up into the city, the regimental band playing "Picayune Butler's Coming, Coming."

The Twenty-first went into camp at Algiers, where it remained until the 30th of May, making frequent forays into the interior; it also captured many steamers in Red river, and the sea-going blockade-runner Fox, at the mouth of Grand Caillon, on the Gulf coast. On June 1 the regiment was landed at Baton Rouge, where it remained until the post was evacuated. On the 5th of August it participated in the battle of Baton Rouge, fighting for over three and a half hours against an entire brigade without faltering, and sustaining a loss of 126 killed and wounded. Adjutant Latham and Lieutenants Seeley, Grinstead and Bryant were killed in this engagement. After this the regiment went into camp near Carrollton, and on the 8th of September it surprised Walier's Texas Rangers at Des Allemands, killing twelve and capturing thirty or forty prisoners. The Twenty-first went to Berwick's Bay in October, where it remained until the latter part of February, 1863. During its stay in this region a portion of the regiment was temporarily transferred to gunboats and participated in daily fights with the ironclad "Cotton," and accompanied Weitzel's advance up the Bayou Teche, taking part in the fight at Cornet's Bridge and the destruction of the "Cotton."

Col. McMillan being promoted brigadier general, on the 29th of November, 1862, Lieut. Col. John A. Keith was commissioned his successor.

In February, 1863, the regiment was, by order of Gen. Banks, changed to heavy artillery service, and designated the First Heavy Artillery, and in July and October, under orders from the War Department, two additional companies—"L" and "M"—were organized and added to the regiment.

A portion of the regiment accompanied Gen. Banks up the Teche, and participated in the second battle of Camp Bisland. Subsequently the regiment, with the exception of two companies, was transported up the Mississippi, and took part in the siege of Port Hudson, in which it distinguished itself for the remarkable accuracy of its firing. The loss to the regiment during the siege of forty-two days was 28 in killed, wounded and missing.

On the 21st of June part of one company manned a light battery in a desperately contested little light at Lafourch Crossing, and on the 23d of June most of Company "F" was captured at Brashear City. In August three companies, under Major Roy, joined the expedition to Sabine Pass, and engaged the enemy at that place. During the winter of 1863 and 1864 a large majority of the regiment re-enlisted and were remustered as veterans at New Orleans. Soon after the veterans visited Indiana, when a grand reception was given them at Metropolitan Hall, Indianapolis, on February 19, 1864, at which addresses were made by Gov. Morton, Mayor Caven, Gen. Hovey, and Cols. James R. Slack and John A. Keith.

In the disastrous expedition of Gen. Banks up Red river in March 1864, Companies "G" and "H" bore an active part, after which the various companies of the regiment were stationed for duty at different points in the Department of the Gulf. In April, 1865, six batteries of the First Heavy Artillery, under command of Major Roy, participated in the investment of Mobile, the reduction of Forts Morgan and Gaines and Spanish Fort, and the capture of Mobile. At the close of active operations the different batteries were assigned to duty at Forts Morgan, Pickens and Barancas, and in the works at Baton Rouge and other points of river defense, with regimental headquarters at Mobile up to and after October, 1865, and was finally mustered out January 10, 1866.

STATISTICS.

Officers, 80; men, 1,283; recruits 1,332; veterans 448; unassigned recruits, 696; total 3,839.

Officers died, 10; men died, 382; deserters, 225; discharged, 1,208; number mustered out, about 941.

COMPANY I.

Henry Jarrels, mustered out January 13, 1866.

Francis H. Rodman, assigned to Company F and mustered out as Corporal January 10, 1866.

COMPANY C.

Lucas Brandt, mustered out as Corporal; Job W. Crabtree, Jacob Conkle, William M. Gardner, Jeremiah Gerrard, mustered out as Corporal; John Hamilton, mustered out as Corporal; Henry Hoagland, Walter F. Haines, William Love, James M. Pursley.

Joseph Berry, died June 27, 1864.

Martin Berry, died August 25, 1864.

David Collins, discharged January 7, 1865, by order of War Department.

William A. Crouch, died December 15, 1864.

Ossian A. Gilbert, mustered out July 31, 1864, as Corporal.

Ervin Graves, mustered out July 31, 1864, as Corporal.

Isaac Pingry, died July 17, 1864.

Philip Woodward, mustered out January 13, 1866.

COMPANY E.

Orson E. Hugh (Bugler), John A. Keller, J. W. Murphy.

Lucas Lennon, died at Baton Rouge, La., September 15, 1864.

E. C. Turner, died at Greencastle, Ind., January 11, 1865.

COMPANY F.

F. H. Benadum, mustered out January 10, 1866.

COMPANY H.

James R. Huff, at New Orleans, December 6, 1864.
William Rhodes, died at Fort Morgan, Ala., April 1, 1865.
Chauncey W. Searing, discharged February 20, 1865, for disability.

COMPANY I.

G. W. Ball; James W. Boling, mustered out as Corporal; Jasper Lucas, Reuben Lucas; Cornelius Tarvin; Albert N. Van Cleve, mustered out January 10, 1866.

COMPANY K.

Josiah Britton; George W. Coffeen, mustered out as Corporal; Cyril C. Jones, mustered out as Corporal; John A. Keener, William B. Sears, John S. Wilcoxon, Henry C. Wool.
John Kepley, record indefinite.
H. W. Little, transferred to Company F, May 9, 1864.
Edgar St. Cloud, record indefinite.
G. T. Ward, mustered out January 10, 1866, as Bugler.
Edward Winters, record indefinite.
Joseph Wool, mustered out July 20, 1865.

COMPANY L.

Edward W. Brady, mustered out April 10, 1865.
Carth J. Brady, mustered out January 10, 1866.

THIRTIETH REGIMENT (THREE YEARS.)

Mavel Fletcher, mustered out November 6, 1865.
George W. Marshall (Company H), mustered out November 25, 1865, as Sergeant.

THIRTY-SECOND REGIMENT (THREE YEARS).

Charles Kiser, mustered out September 7, 1864, as Sergeant.
George Roup, record indefinite.
Anton Single (Company A), mustered out September 7, 1864, as Corporal.

THIRTY-FIFTH REGIMENT (THREE YEARS).

George Albin, Sr., died at Nashville, January 9, 1865.
Patrick Tuhey (Company K), mustered out September 30, 1864.

THIRTY-SIXTH REGIMENT (THREE YEARS).

The Thirty-sixth Regiment was organized at Richmond and mustered for three years' service on September 16, 1861, with William Grose as colonel, and soon after left Indianapolis with 1,047 men, rank and file, reporting next day to Gen. Sherman at Louisville. It remained at New Haven, Kentucky, taking lessons in the school of the soldier until December 15, when it reached Camp Wickliffe, there being assigned to the Tenth Brigade, under command of Colonel Jacob Ammon. Like many other inexperienced but enthusiastic volunteers, the men of the regiment were impressed with the idea that the war might end and they have no part in it. But General Nelson, a thorough disciplinarian and competent commander of the division of which they formed a part, gave them the assurance that there would be enemies to meet upon the battlefield in great numbers after becoming skilled soldiers. The sufferings and sacrifices of this splendid regiment in the years following proved its truth. In February the regiment moved to West Point, on the Ohio river, embarking on the steamer Woodford—part of a fleet of transports—which carried the division down the Ohio and up the Cumberland to Nashville. The Thirty-sixth Indiana and Sixth Ohio were the first Federal troops that entered the city then being hastily abandoned by the rear guard of the Confederate army, under General Albert Sidney Johnston.

In March the Tenth Brigade led the advance in the movement of Buell's army to the Tennessee river. On Sunday morning, April 6, while break-fasting in camp and resting from the long march, the roar of the engage-ment at Shiloh burst upon their ears. About one o'clock the column got under way, the Thirty-sixth Indiana leading. In three and one-half hours the advance reached a point opposite the scene of the engagement. Amid great confusion and surroundings which might well dampen the ardor of volunteer forces in the first approach to the scene of conflict the Thirty-sixth moved with the soldierly bearing of veterans. The orders were issued to the colonel of the regiment by Gen. Buell in person, and were promptly obeyed. A few well-directed volleys caused the line of the enemy to give way, and as it was near dusk the firing soon ceased. It is perhaps but his-toric truth to say that no part of the Army of the Ohio under Gen. Buell took any active part in the Sunday evening fight near the Landing, except the Thirty-sixth Indiana. Upon the arrival of the regiment on the hill by the log house there were no troops in position, except Stone's Battery and the heavy guns three or four hundred yards to the right. In the battle of Shiloh the Thirty-sixth lost one officer and eight men killed; one officer and thirty-five men wounded—total, 45.

Encamping on the field, the regiment remained there until the move-ment against Corinth, when it marched forward and shared in its toils and dangers. After Corinth was evacuated by Beauregard the march was re-sumed along the line of the Memphis and Charleston Railroad in the direc-tion of Chattanooga. Later operations of the Confederate army under Gen. Bragg culminated in the retreat to Louisville. Here the Federal army met reinforcements and in a few days turned upon the Confederates, driving them from the state of Kentucky and concentrating under command of Gen. Rosecrans at Nashville. In all of these movements the Thirty-sixth In-diana had a part. The advance of the Army of the Cumberland from Nash-ville on December 26, 1862, was sharply resisted by the enemy, and the near approach to Murfreesboro by the heads of column developed the pres-ence of the Confederates in strong force. Early in the engagement on De-cember 31, 1862, the ranks of the Thirty-sixth were riddled by a volley from the enemy located in a dense cedar thicket near at hand, which the com-mander of the regiment understood was occupied by the Fifteenth United States Infantry. Here Major Kinley was desperately wounded. Captain A. D. Shultz, of Company "B," the Muncie company, fell mortally wounded. Every mounted officer in the regiment except the adjutant had his horse shot under him. In that hotly contested three days' struggle at

Stone River the Thirty-sixth lost 2 officers killed and 6 wounded; 23 enlisted men killed and 85 wounded; missing, 18—total, 134. The regiment then went into camp near Murfreesboro until May, when it moved to a fine camp on Cripple Creek, where it remained until the campaign against Chattanooga was begun. In the great battle of Chickamauga the Thirty-sixth had 1 officer and 13 enlisted men killed; 8 officers and 89 enlisted men wounded; missing in action, 17—total, 128. After the battle it returned to Chattanooga, and from thence moved to Whiteside and Tyner's Station, Tennessee, and while at the latter place a small portion of the regiment reenlisted in December, 1863, and February, 1864, and soon after visited Indiana on veteran furlough. In March it went into camp at Blue Springs, Tennessee, where it remained until the opening of the Atlanta campaign.

Early in May the regiment moved with Sherman's army toward Atlanta and participated in the marches, skirmishes and engagements of that memorable campaign. The losses from Dalton to Jonesboro, Georgia, were as follows: Three officers and nine enlisted men killed; two officers and fifty-two enlisted men wounded—total, 66. On September 3d, when near Atlanta, in pursuance of the orders of General Thomas, the non-veterans left the front and proceeded to Indianapolis, where they were mustered out of service.

The remaining veterans and recruits were then organized into a Residuary Battalion of one company, with Captain John P. Swisher in command. This company, after Atlanta, remained with the command of General Grose, mostly on duty at his headquarters. It participated in the battles of Franklin and Nashville, took part in the pursuit of Hood's broken army to the Tennessee river, thence, with the command of General Grose, to Huntsville, Alabama, and continued with the Third Brigade until July 12, 1865, when, by order of Gen. Sheridan, it was transferred to the Residuary Battalion of the Thirtieth Indiana Regiment, and made Company "H" thereof, moving soon thereafter, with the old Fourth Corps, to New Orleans, thence to Texas, and late in the fall of that year was mustered out and returned to home and friends.

STATISTICS.

Officers, 74; men, 949; recruits, 120; veterans, 21; unassigned recruits, 13; total, 1,177.

Officers died, 13; men died, 486.

The Thirty-sixth Indiana was engaged in the important battles of Shiloh, siege of Corinth, Perryville, Stone River, Chickamauga, Lookout Mountain, New Hope Church, Kenesaw Mountain, Nashville, etc. Its movements were chiefly through Kentucky and Tennessee, but its work was stern and thorough, and its brave men fully justified the honors conferred upon them, and the trust confided to them by their officers and by the State. They went forth, happy that they could take part in the contest against oppression and secession, and for the integrity of the Union.

Companies were represented as stated below, and the survivors returned to their native homes, thanking God for life preserved and for the salvation of the land from treason's bloody threats. The companies represented were, A, B, C, E, F, G, H, I and K.

COMPANY A.

George H. **Byrd**, transferred to Company H, Thirtieth Regiment, mustered out February 4, 1866.

William **Dowell**, transferred to Company H, Thirtieth Regiment, mustered out August 19, 1865.

Samuel **Farmer**, mustered out September 21, 1864.

David M. **Minnick**, transferred to Company H, Thirtieth Regiment, mustered out March 24, 1865.

Francis M. **Mohler**, died in ... on at Richmond, February 28, 1863.

William P. **Sherry**, transfer... o Company H, Thirtieth Regiment, mustered out March 29, 1865.

Luther D. **Van Matre**, transferred to Company H, Thirtieth Regiment, mustered out March 2, 1865.

COMPANY B.

Captain—Alfred **Kilgore**, resigned May 22, 1862.

First Lieutenant—Thomas H. **Kirby**, resigned February 1, 1862.

Second Lieutenant—Alfram D. **Shultz**, promoted to First Lieutenant and to Captain; killed at Stone River December 31, 1862.

Sergeants—Hugh A. **Stephens**, promoted to Second Lieutenant, to First Lieutenant, to Captain; Lindley **Thornburg**, discharged February 21, 1863, for disability; Lewis P. **Everett**, discharged May 13, 1862, for disability; Richard **Harris**, discharged May 27, 1862, for disability; Edward W. **Gilbert**, promoted to Second Lieutenant to First Lieutenant, Company I, mustered out with the regiment.

Corporals—Jonathan **Thomas**, promoted to Second Lieutenant, to First Lieutenant; mustered out as Second Lieutenant; William R. **Willard**, mustered out September 21, 1864, as Sergeant; Ephraim **Covolt**, mustered out September 21, 1864, as Sergeant; James T. **Broyles**, discharged December 16, 1862, for disability; Thomas Y. **Richey**, discharged April 26, 1862; John W. **Hazlebaker**, mustered out April 27, 1865; Jared W. **Hines**, mustered out September 21, 1864, as First Sergeant; George O. **Willard**, promoted to Second Lieutenant, to First Lieutenant, died August 6, 1864, of wounds.

Musicians—John H. **Stephens**, mustered out September 21, 1864; Mile S. **Smith**, mustered out September 21, 1864, as Principal Musician.

Wagoner—William S. **Driscoll**, discharged November 21, 1862, for disability.

PRIVATES.

George **Burcoy**, transferred to Company H, Thirtieth Regiment, August 13, 1864.

Nevil **Fletcher**, transferred to Company H, Thirtieth Regiment, August 13, 1864.

William **Hatfield**, transferred to Company H, Thirtieth Regiment, August 13, 1864.

James **Heath**, transferred to Company H, Thirtieth Regiment, August 13, 1864.

Sanford **Heath**, transferred to Company H, Thirtieth Regiment, August 13, 1864.

Joshua **Jester**, transferred to Company H, Thirtieth Regiment, August 13, 1864.

George W. **Kilgore**, transferred to Company H, Thirtieth Regiment, August 13, 1864, mustered out as Corporal.

George W. **Marshall**, mustered out as Sergeant.

Jacob **Mumford**, record indefinite.

Moses K. **Adams**, killed at Chickamauga, September 19, 1863.

John **Alfred**, mustered out September 21, 1864.

Harvey **Berry**, transferred to Company H, Thirtieth Regiment, mustered out June 10, 1865.

Joseph **Baney**, mustered out September 21, 1864.

Benjamin **Bartlett**, mustered out September 21, 1864, as Corporal.

Peter **Basinger**, missing at Chickamauga September 12, 1863.

John **Chandler**, discharged March 25, 1862, for disability.

John M. **Clevenger**, mustered out September 21, 1864.

William H. **Clevenger**, mustered out September 21, 1864.

William **Clevenger**, discharged October 27, 1862, for disability.

Reason **Craig**, died at Danville, Ky., November 12, 1862.

Marquis D. **Cree**, mustered out September 21, 1864.

Lemphi **Croy**, mustered out September 21, 1864.

John F. Cornell, transferred to Company H, Thirtieth Regiment, again transferred to Veteran Reserve Corps.

John Conner, died November 7, 1862.

John Cook, killed at Resaca, Ga., May 14, 1864.

John M. Driscoll, died February 26, 1862.

Simon Driscoll, died March 28, 1862.

William S. Driscoll, died December 23, 1862.

John W. Drennon, died at Nashville July 20, 1864, of wounds at Kenesaw.

Lemuel F. Eastes, record indefinite.

James Ennis, mustered out September 21, 1864.

Andrew Fisher, discharged April 5, 1863, for disability.

Benjamin L. Fletcher, died at Paducah, Ky.

Nevil Fletcher, discharged June 30, 1862, for disability.

John T. Fullhart, mustered out as Sergeant September 21, 1864.

John A. Gilbert, transferred to Company H, Thirtieth Regiment, August 13, 1864, mustered out May 15, 1865.

Michael Haines, died January 6, 1863.

David Harris, discharged May 27, 1863, for disability.

Christopher Hazlebaker, discharged July 16, 1863, for disability.

Tilberry Herbaugh, died February 17, 1862.

Walberry Herbaugh, died December 21, 1861.

Moses Hinton, mustered out September 21, 1864.

Jackson Hunt, died October 16, 1862.

Enos Hutson, mustered out September 21, 1864.

James Hutson, mustered out September 21, 1864.

William R. Hines, transferred to Company H, Thirtieth Regiment, August 13, 1864, mustered out November 25, 1865.

Robert V. Hurst, died in Andersonville Prison September 20, 1864.

John Y. Heath, killed at Chickamauga September 19, 1863.

John Johnson, mustered out September 21, 1864.

Robert Johnson, mustered out September 21, 1864.

George L. Janney, mustered out September 21, 1864.

John H. Janney, lost on Sultana on the Mississippi River.

William H. Jester, died June 21, 1864.

Philip A. B. Kennedy, mustered out September 21, 1864.

Charles Kiger, discharged for disability.

Crawford Kegeriss, transferred to Company H, Thirtieth Regiment, August 13, 1864, discharged October 2, 1864, from wounds.

James A. Lay, transferred to Fourth U. S. Cavalry May 5, 1862.

Marshall Lecky, discharged January 6, 1863, for disability.

John W. Little, mustered out September 21, 1864.

Lehu Love, discharged May 27, 1862, for disability.

George W. Lykins, mustered out as Corporal, September 21, 1864.

Robert D. Lake, killed at Stone River December 31, 1862.

Joseph Lybarger, died near Atlanta October 26, 1864.

John W. Maddox, mustered out September 21, 1864.

William H. McKinney, died February 14, 1862.

William McLain, mustered out September 21, 1864.

Ephraim McLaughlin, mustered out September 21, 1864.

Thomas McGriff, discharged May 17, 1862, for disability.

James T. Mix, mustered out September 21, 1864.

William H. H. Morris, mustered out September 21, 1864.

Daniel Mumford, transferred to Company H, Thirtieth Regiment, August 13, 1864.

Nathaniel Parshall, discharged November 21, 1863, for disability.

John H. Power, discharged January 24, 1864, wounded in action.

Alva C. Puckett, discharged April 17, 1863, for disability.

Charles L. Reynolds, mustered out September 21, 1864.

James G. Rainey, discharged June 30, 1863, for disability.

William F. Reynolds, mustered out September 21, 1864.

William H. H. Richey, discharged February 3, 1863, wounded in action.

Charles W. Riggs, mustered out September 21, 1864, as Corporal.

John P. Robinson, mustered out September 21, 1864.

Christian H. Runkle, mustered out September 21, 1864.

Jacob H. Kisling, transferred to Company H, Thirtieth Regiment, August 13, 1864.
Joseph M. Scott, mustered out September 21, 1864.
Abraham Shafer, mustered out September 21, 1864.
Alfred Smith, discharged July 16, 1863, for disability.
Henry Spilker, died April 28, 1862.
Joseph Stewart, died December 4, 1862.
Thomas R. Stephenson, died February 21, 1862.
George W. Stottler, mustered out September 21, 1864.
John D. Stradling, died September 5, 1863.
Joseph T. Sullivan, transferred to Company H, Thirtieth Regiment, August 13, 1864.
Jacob Sechrist, died at Nashville.
Daniel E. Taylor, died February 25, 1862.
George W. Taylor, discharged May 27, 1862.
James C. Thorn, transferred to Veteran Reserve Corps.
Samuel A. Thorn, died June 5, 1862.
John A. Thornburg, discharged January 16, 1862, for disability.
John Thornburg, mustered out September 21, 1864, as Sergeant.
Curtis Thornburg, discharged February 4, 1863, for disability.
Isaac H. Thornburg, mustered out September 21, 1864, as Corporal.
William S. Thornburg, mustered out September 21, 1864.
Jonathan W. Thornburg, discharged February 21, 1862, for disability.
James G. Taylor, transferred to Company H, Thirtieth Regiment, August 13, 1864.
John W. Taylor, transferred to Company H, Thirtieth Regiment, August 13, 1864.
John M. Tampset, transferred to Veteran Reserve Corps.
William K. Thomas, transferred to Company H, Thirtieth Regiment, August 13, 1864.
Winfield S. Van Matre, discharged February 21, 1863, for disability.
John B. Veal, discharged May 27, 1862, for disability.
Benjamin F. Vickroy, discharged February 13, 1863, for disability.
Benjamin F. Warrington, killed at Stone River December 31, 1862.
Thomas M. Watkins, mustered out September 21, 1864.
George W. Worrel, mustered out September 21, 1864.
Henry Wasson, mustered out September 21, 1864.
John Yingling.

COMPANY C.

Francis M. Buckles, died January 10, 1863.
Moses Saunders, died March 18, 1863.

COMPANY E.

George F. Andrew, discharged January 31, 1863, for disability.
William L. Andrew, died April 23, 1862.
John R. Ervin, mustered out September 21, 1864, as Sergeant.
Samuel Fisher, mustered out September 21, 1864.
William R. Hughey, died May 6, 1862, in hospital.
Daniel R. Irvin, died June 2, 1864; wounded at Dalton, Ga.
Jacob Keeny, mustered out September 21, 1864, as Corporal.
Isaac D. Keeny, Corporal, discharged September 21, 1864; wounded.
Lorenzo B. Reed, died October 3, 1863, of wounds at Chickamauga, Ga.
John W. Wills, discharged July 9, 1862.

COMPANY F.

William M. Goff, transferred to Company H, Thirtieth Regiment, August 30, 1864.
Aaron Hughes, transferred to Company H, Thirtieth Regiment, August 30, 1864.
Christopher Gordon, died at Indianola, Tex., September 21, 1865.
George W. Kilgore, transferred to Company H, Thirtieth Regiment, mustered out November 25, 1865, as Corporal.
William Sprang, discharged August 19, 1862.

COMPANY G.

Daniel Burcoy, discharged May 9, 1862, for disability.
John Snyder, transferred to Company H, Thirtieth Regiment, August 13, 1864, mustered out March 2, 1865.

Barney Snyder, transferred to Company H, Thirtieth Regiment, August 13, 1864, mustered out March 2, 1865, as Sergeant.

COMPANY H.

Giles B. King, died at Huntsville, Ala., October 31, 1862.

COMPANY I.

John H. Cecil, transferred to Company H, Thirtieth Regiment, August 13, 1864, mustered out March 24, 1865.

COMPANY K.

Peter A. Helm, mustered out September 21, 1864.
Jacob R. Helm, died at Nashville April 27, 1862.
William J. Helm, discharged February 7, 1862, for disability.
Thomas J. Mitchell, discharged June 27, 1862, for disability.
Aaron Rintzer, transferred to Company H, Thirtieth Regiment, August 13, 1864, mustered out March 29, 1865.
John Sanders, transferred to Company H, Thirtieth Regiment, August 13, 1864, mustered out March 2, 1865, as Corporal.
Joseph M. Slonaker, discharged November 28, 1862, for disability.

THE EIGHTH CAVALRY.

The Thirty-ninth Regiment was organized for infantry service at Indianapolis on the 29th of August, 1861, with Thomas J. Harrison as colonel, and early in September left for Kentucky. After encamping first on Muldraugh's Hill, near Elizabethtown, and next at Camp Nevin, on Nolin creek, and Camp Wood, on Green river, it marched with Buell's army to Nashville. From Nashville it advanced to the Tennessee river, and was engaged in the battle of Shiloh on the 7th of April, 1862, losing two killed and thirty-four wounded. Total loss, thirty-six. After the engagement at Shiloh it encamped on the field until the army moved toward Corinth, when the regiment moved with it, participating in the siege of that place.

Upon the evacuation of Corinth it marched with Buell's army through northern Alabama to Bridgeport, and from thence to Nashville. It then moved as part of the same force in the retreat to Louisville and joined in the pursuit of Bragg until he was driven from the state. Returning to Nashville in November, it marched with Rosecrans in the winter campaign to Murfreesboro, participating in the battle of Stone's River on the 31st of December, 1862, and the 1st and 2d of January, 1863. In this engagement the regiment suffered severely, especially in missing—the loss being thirty-one killed, one hundred and eighteen wounded and two hundred and thirty-one missing in action; total, three hundred and eighty. The Thirty-ninth remained in camp near Murfreesboro for some months following the battle at that place, and in April, 1862, it was mounted, and served in that capacity during the campaign of that year. On June 6, with the Second Indiana Cavalry, it met and had a sharp fight with the enemy under General Wheeler. Subsequently it took part in skirmishes at Middleton and Liberty Gap, and during the forward movement upon Chattanooga engaged the enemy at Winchester. On the 19th and 20th of September it participated in the battle of Cickamauga, and also took part in an expedition into East Tennessee. Authority being given to change the organization from infantry to cavalry, Companies "L" and "M" were organized in September, 1863, and on joining the command in the field the regiment was, on the 15th of October, 1863, reorganized as the Eighth Cavalry. In December the regiment was placed on courier duty between Chattanooga and Ringgold, and on the 22d of February, 1864, it re-enlisted as a veteran organization. In April the regiment visited Indiana on veteran furlough, and on returning to the field participated in the Rousseau raid into Alabama. One battalion of the regiment fought and routed a rebel brigade on the Coosa river, taking many prisoners, and again routed the enemy at Chehaw Bridge, Alabama.

It took part in the McCook raid around Atlanta, and was the only regiment that preserved its organization and made a charge on the enemy, thus opening the way for the escape of twelve hundred men of McCook's command. The regiment was next engaged in the Kilpatrick raid in Georgia, and at the battle of Lovejoy's Station led the charge of the left wing, riding over Ross' division of rebel cavalry, capturing all of his artillery and four battle flags. It was later engaged in the battles of Jonesboro and Flint river, and in several skirmishes that followed the capture of Atlanta.

In the campaign against Savannah and through the Carolinas it marched with Kilpatrick's command to Savannah and thence to Goldsboro. In this campaign it participated in the battles and skirmishes at Waynesboro, Buckhead Church, Browne's Cross Roads, Reynold's Farm, Aiken, Bentonville, Averysboro and Raleigh. In the engagement at Averysboro this regiment, under Col. Jones, charged and routed Rhett's South Carolina brigade of infantry, which outnumbered it ten to one. The Eighth Cavalry lost fourteen killed and fifty-nine wounded. A detachment of the regiment, left behind in Tennessee, fought Wheeler at Franklin, and also had a severe engagement with Forrest at Pulaski, Tennessee. While at Savannah, an order from General Sherman transferred the remaining veterans and recruits of the Third Indiana Cavalry to the Eighth Cavalry, the consolidated force bearing the designation of the latter regiment.

After the occupation of a portion of North Carolina by Sherman's army, and just before the negotiations were opened between Johnston and Sherman, the Eighth Cavalry whipped Hampton's entire force at Morrisville, and thus had the honor of fighting the last battle with the enemy in that state. The regiment remained on duty in North Carolina until the 20th of July, 1865, when it was mustered out of service, and soon after started for home. Reaching Indianapolis during the last week in July, it was present at a public reception given to returned troops in the capitol grounds, at which speeches were made by Lieutenant Governor Conrad Baker and

General Hovey, and, in a few days afterward, the regiment was finally dis. charged. The regiment during its term of service has borne on its rolls 2,500 men, and has had nine officers killed in battle. It has lost about three hun. dred in prisoners, and has captured from the enemy over fifteen hundred men, one thousand stand of arms, three railroad trains, fourteen hundred horses and mules, many wagons, fourteen pieces of artillery, four battle flags and destroyed many miles of railroad.

STATISTICS.

Officers, 53; men, 1,155; recruits, 776; re-enlisted veterans, 305; unassigned recruits, 126; total, 2,415. Officers died, 10; men died, 329; deserters, 56. Mustered out July 20, 1865.

COMPANY C.

James S. McLaughlin, missing in action November 28, 1864.

COMPANY G.

William I. Childs, John Curts, John F. Perdue.
John A. Shafer, died, date not stated.
Philip C. Adams, discharged June 5, 1865, for disability.
John R. Stewart, killed at Flint River, Ga., August 31, 1864.

COMPANY H.

Charles E. Wilkins, record indefinite.

COMPANY L.

John B. Allen, James W. Combs, F. W. Coppersmith, Joseph D. Coppersmith, Thomas J. Danner, Cyrus F. Dragoo, Abel Imbert, James A. Jester, Jesse Miller, Alexander McKinley, Darlin M. Tuttle, Jasper Van Matre as Corporal, Oliver H. P. Van Matre.
William Combs, mustered out June 16, 1865.
Marcellus Childs, mustered out August 9, 1865.
William P. Gilbert, mustered out July 9, 1865.
Asbury Newhouse, mustered out June 10, 1865.
Richard M. Rader, died in New York harbor April 25, 1865.
John L. Reynolds, mustered out July 20, 1865, as Commissary Sergeant.
Simon P. Swearingen, died at Nashville, June 30, 1864.

COMPANY M.

Joseph Stewart, John A. Smith, George W. Tuttle.
John B. Arnold, record indefinite.
George W. Nelson, mustered out July 6, 1865.
John W. Campbell, died of disease March 12, 1864.

FORTY-FIRST REGIMENT (THREE YEARS).

The Second Cavalry, Forty-first Regiment, was the first complete cavalry regiment raised in Indiana. It was organized in Indianapolis in September, 1861, with John A. Bridgeland as colonel. On the 16th of December it broke camp and moved across the country to Louisville, Kentucky, and thence to Camp Wickliffe. In February, 1862, it marched with Buell's army toward Nashville and from that point moved to the Tennessee river, reaching the field of Shiloh after the battle. On the 9th of April it had a skirmish with the enemy on the road to Corinth, and on the 15th of April engaged the rebels at Pea Ridge, Tennessee, losing a number in killed and wounded.

On the 22d it participated in a reconnoissance in force, driving the enemy three miles. During the siege of Corinth it was actively engaged, and immediately after the evacuation marched with Buell's army into northern Alabama, and on the 31st of May had a skirmish with the enemy at Tuscumbia, losing a few men in killed and wounded.

Moving into Tennessee the regiment fought the enemy at McMinville on the 9th of August and at Gallatin on the 21st and 27th of August, losing several in killed, wounded and missing. In September it marched into Kentucky, participating in the Bragg and Buell campaign, engaging the enemy at Vinegar Hill on the 22d of September, and at Perryville on the 8th of October.

On the 30th of November, while the regiment was at Nashville, a detachment under command of Major Samuel Hill was highly complimented by General Rosecrans, in special field orders, for having recaptured a Government train, defeating rebel cavalry, killing twenty of the enemy and capturing two hundred prisoners. During the winter of 1862 it was on duty near Nashville, and from there proceeded to Kentucky, where it remained a few months and then returned to Tennessee.

On the 11th of June, 1863, it fought the enemy at Triune, Tennessee, losing a number in killed and wounded. In the fall of 1863 it was on duty along the line of the Nashville and Chattanooga Railroad, and then moved into East Tennessee. On the 29th of November several men of the regiment were drowned in Caney Fork while on duty ferrying. On the 29th of December it participated in a sharp fight at Talbott's Station. While at Mossy Creek, Tennessee, the regiment re-enlisted on the 10th of January, 1864, and during the winter and spring was engaged in numerous scouts and skirmishes, losing a number of men. In May, 1864, the regiment moved with Sherman's army in its campaign against Atlanta, engaging in many skirmishes and battles, among which were the following: May 9, Varnell's Station, near Resaca; July 1, near Ackworth; July 28 and 30, near Newnan; August 30, near Atlanta. After the occupation of Atlanta the non-veterans were ordered to be mustered out, and on the 14th of September, 1864, the remaining veterans and recruits were consolidated into a battalion of four companies and placed in command of Major Roswell S. Hill. In November and December, 1864, the battalion was on duty in Kentucky, and in January, 1865, was transferred to the vicinity of Eastport, Alabama.

Joining the army of General Wilson, it participated in the raid through Alabama, engaging the enemy near Scottsville on the 2d of April, and at West Point, Georgia, on the 16th of April.

In the latter battle the regiment suffered severely, Major Hill having one of his legs shot off while leading a charge. Returning from this raid, it proceeded to Nashville, and was there mustered out on the 22d of July, 1865, and soon after was finally discharged at Indianapolis.

STATISTICS.

Officers, 55; enlisted men, 1,079; recruits, 340; veterans, 78; unassigned recruits, 176; total, 1,724. Officers died, 7; men died, 227; deserters, 105. Reorganized bat. talion: Officers, 18; men, 197; recruits, 9; unassigned recruits, 9; total, 233. Men died, 22.

COMPANY D.

Captain—Edwin C. Anthony, resigned March 15, 1862.
Nathaniel B. Coulston, veteran; transferred to Second Cavalry, reorganized.
William M. Lister, First Sergeant.
Thomas Mahan, Corporal.
Jephthah Strawn, veteran; transferred to Second Cavalry, reorganized.
Landry Van Matre, veteran; transferred to Second Cavalry, reorganized.
George Abbott, mustered out October 4, 1864.
George W. Bates, mustered out October 4, 1864.
John E. Beemer, record indefinite.
David M. Bell, mustered out October 4, 1864, as Corporal.
James Barrett, mustered out October 4, 1864, as Corporal.
Isaac Bracken, discharged November, 1862, for disability.
Samuel Biers, mustered out October 4, 1864.
Job Combs, discharged March 8, 1865, for disability.
Thomas Carter, mustered out October 6, 1864.
Richard Cray, transferred to the marine service.
Isaiah Duddleston, Corporal; mustered out October 4, 1864.
William Downs, mustered out October 4, 1864.
Samuel Drennon, transferred to the Veteran Reserve Corps.
Elijah Early, mustered out October 4, 1864.
James W. Ellis, mustered out October 4, 1864.
William J. Falkner, Corporal; mustered out October 4, 1864.
George B. Futrell, mustered out October 4, 1864.
Martin V. Fuller, mustered out October 4, 1864.
Stephen Flemming, Corporal; mustered out October 4, 1864.
Valentine Gibson, mustered out October 4, 1864.
Samuel M. Gregory, mustered out October 4, 1864.
D. M. Gregg, Corporal; mustered out October 4, 1864, as Sergeant.
Henry C. Godwin, mustered out October 4, 1864.
Ferdinand D. Goff, died at Louisville May 7, 1864.
George W. Goodman, discharged June 13, 1862, for disability.
Uriah Jarrold, mustered out October 4, 1864.
William Jaymond, mustered out October 4, 1864.
Henry Hernly, discharged for disability.
Thomas Hartley, captured at Atlanta; mustered out June 2, 1865.
William Jones, mustered out October 4, 1864.
George Jones, mustered out October 4, 1864.
Turner Johnson, mustered out October 4, 1864.
John S. Krohn, mustered out October 4, 1864.
Daniel B. Kimball, Sergeant; mustered out October 1, 1864, as First Sergeant.
John W. Keenan, mustered out October 4, 1864.
John Kirk, mustered out May 15, 1865.
Martin Mann, mustered out October 4, 1864.
William J. Michener, Corporal; mustered out October 4, 1864.
Fred J. McConnell, Quartermaster Sergeant; discharged August 1, 1862, for disability.
Wilson Martin, died at New Albany, 1862.
Lemuel O'Neil, mustered out October 4, 1864.
James D. Reynolds, mustered out October 4, 1864.
Robert Robe, mustered out October 4, 1864.
Andrew J. Reynolds, discharged October 29, 1862, for disability.
Joseph W. Slonaker, mustered out October 4, 1864, as Corporal.
Henry Stiffler, Corporal; mustered out October 4, 1864.
William J. Shrack, Sergeant; mustered out October 4, 1864.
Joel D. Starr, mustered out October 4, 1864.
William J. Sailors, mustered out October 4, 1864, as Corporal.

Horace H. Wade, mustered out October 4, 1864.
Owen N. Wilson, discharged April 15, 1863.
William Wright, mustered out October 4, 1864.
Eli Younce, mustered out October 4, 1864.
NOTE.—The names on roll in the army stood "Wilson, Wade, Wright (into) Younce"—and the Sergeant would call the roll that way, and Wilson would do that very thing as they went to quarters.

COMPANY F.

John W. Sherry, mustered out October 4, 1864, as Corporal.

COMPANY K.

Benjamin Sharp, discharged November 12, 1863, for disability.

FORTY-SEVENTH REGIMENT (THREE YEARS).

COMPANY G.

John Whitaker, veteran, mustered out October 23, 1866.

FIFTY-SEVENTH REGIMENT.

The Fifty-seventh Regiment was recruited in the Fifth and Eleventh Congressional Districts, chiefly through the efforts of Rev. J. W. T. McMullen and Rev. F. A. Hardin, and was mustered into service November 18, 1861, at Richmond, Indiana. On December 10, the regiment moved to Indianapolis, where it remained until December 23, when it moved to Louisville, Kentucky, and reported to General Buell. Here it was assigned to the Twenty-first Brigade, Sixth Division of the Army of the Ohio, then being organized at Bardstown. The command soon after moved to Lebanon to participate in the operations under General Thomas, which ended with the battle of Mill Springs. Thence to Munfordsville, it marched to Nashville. The campaign in Kentucky was severe, and, like all new regiments, the Fifty-seventh suffered a great depletion of numbers from disease.

The movement of Wood's division towards the Tennessee river commenced on March 29, 1862. The regiment was within hearing of the battle of Shiloh on the 6th of April, but did not reach the field until the 7th, when it became engaged in the closing operations of the day, having four men wounded. During the siege of Corinth there was much hard labor and exposure in the unhealthy swamps of that region. The losses caused by disease were greater than the average of losses in battle. One company reached the field of Shiloh with fifty-three men bearing arms. It reached Corinth with sixteen able for duty. In Halleck's army of one hundred thousand there were few really well men. From the poison of these Mississippi swamps the command gladly marched away to take part in a movement along the line of the Memphis and Charleston Railroad, towards Chattanooga. Until the retreat to Louisville the regiment was on duty at Floresville, Alabama; Tullahoma, Decherd and McMinville, Tennessee. During the campaign against Bragg, in Kentucky, it took an active part, being engaged at Perryville, where it suffered a slight loss. At the close of the pursuit of Bragg it marched to Nashville again, which place it reached about the 1st of December, 1862. At the battle of Stone River the Fifty-seventh was heavily engaged all day on December 31, 1862. It was in the left wing of the army, which so firmly withstood the rebel assaults on that historic day. It lost 75 men out of about 350 engaged. Col. C. C. Hines, who had succeeded Col. McMullen, and came to the command at Nashville in March, 1862, and Lieut. Col. G. W. Lennard, who succeeded Lieut. Col. Hardin, were both very severely wounded. During the remainder of the winter and the spring of 1863 it remained in camp at Murfreesboro, drilling constantly and doing very severe picket duty. By reason of his wounds, Col. Hines was unable for further duty, and was succeeded by Lieut. Col. Lennard. On the 24th of June the regiment broke camp and participated in the campaign against Tullahoma. Upon the evacuation of middle Tennessee by the enemy, it remained near Pelham, in the Elk river valley, until the 16th of August.

During the campaign which gave Chattanooga to the forces of the Union, General Wagner's Brigade, of which the Fifty-seventh was a part, operated on the north side of the Tennessee.

On the evacuation of that place, Wagner's Brigade crossed the river and took possession. Col. Lennard was assigned as provost marshal of the town and the regiment was placed on duty as provost guard. At the reorganization of the Army of the Cumberland, subsequent to the battle of Chickamauga, the Fifty-seventh was assigned to Sheridan's (Second) Division of the Fourth Corps, in which division it served to the end of the war. A few days before the battle of Mission Ridge it was relieved and rejoined the command, taking part in that memorable engagement, where it joined in the assault of the Ridge on the 25th of November, reaching the crest near the headquarters of General Bragg, and suffering a loss in killed and wounded of two officers and ninety men. The campaign in East Tennessee, for the relief of Gen. Burnside at Knoxville, was probably unequaled during the whole war for hardships and privations. Of these the Fifty-seventh suffered a full share. Much of the time the army lived "off the country." Often supplies were scanty and sometimes there were none at all. Many of the men marched the shoes from their feet and turned out barefooted upon the frozen ground. It was midwinter, and the cold so intense that nothing like it was known within the recollection of living men. There were no tents nor camp equipage of any kind whatever. Even shelter tents were ordered left at Chattanooga. Some had no overcoats; others had no blankets. The only protection from the wintry blasts was made from poles covered with boughs of cedar and dead leaves. There was but one axe to each regiment with which to prepare fuel. During the latter part of January nearly the entire regiment re-enlisted for "three years, or during the war."

At the end of the furlough of thirty days granted to all "veterans," the Fifty-seventh returned to the field, marching from Nashville to rejoin the command at Catoosa Springs, Georgia. It entered the campaign with 30 officers and 311 men for duty. The official reports were made to cover the entire operations of the army until the fall of Atlanta. Though under fire during most of the time from May 7 until September 2d, its principal engagements were as follows: Rocky Face Ridge, Resaca, New Hope Church, Kenesaw, June 18, 23 and 27; Peach Tree Creek, siege of Atlanta and battle of Jonesboro. At Resaca Col. Lennard, a brave and accomplished officer, was mortally wounded; June 18 Lieut. Beitzell was killed; June 23 Major Stidham was killed and Lieut. Callaway mortally wounded. At Jonesboro Lieut. Minesinger was mortally wounded. Joseph Hiatt and John N. Hatfield, both of Delaware county, were killed in battle, the former at New Hope Church, May 27, and the latter in front of Kenesaw Mountain on June 23. The loss during the campaign in killed, mortally and seriously wounded was one hundred and forty-six. Fifty prisoners and one stand of colors were captured by the regiment.

Soon after the fall of Atlanta the division was sent north to guard the lines of communication which were threatened by the enemy, finally becoming a part of the force with which General Thomas resisted Hood's invasion of Tennessee. The Fifty-seventh was engaged at Spring Hill, Franklin and Nashville. The losses in all these engagements, except at Franklin, were slight. Capt. Dunn was killed at Franklin; many soldiers lost their lives here, and a large number were taken prisoners, some of whom were afterwards lost on the steamer Sultana.

Out of a force of about three hundred engaged the loss in killed, wounded, missing in action and captured was one hundred and forty-five. After taking part in the driving of Hood's shattered forces beyond the Tennessee river, the regiment lay in camp at Huntsville, Alabama, some months, moving into East Tennessee as far as Bull's Gap in April, 1865. It then returned to Nashville and was transferred to Texas, where it remained until in December, at which time the final "muster out" of 23 officers and 168 men took place at Port Lavaca. On January 3, 1865, the survivors gathered at Indianapolis for the last business transaction connected with their long and arduous service. Here they received final payment and discharges from the Volunteer Army of the United States.

STATISTICS.

Officers, 50; men. 925; recruits, 449; veterans, 213; unassigned recruits, 15; total, 1,652. Officers died, 7; men died, 200; deserters, 54; mustered out, 23 officers and 138 men.

COMPANY C.

Captain—Robert B. Tenehan, commissioned January 1, 1865; resigned July 7, 1865.

COMPANY E.

Joseph A. Bowen, discharged February 12, 1863, for disability.
Lystra Haught, died at Corinth, Miss., May 26, 1862.
Elias E. tree, Corporal; veteran; transferred to the United States Engineers August 24, 1864; mustered out September 26, 1865.
Isaiah Cry. discharged July 22, 1862, for disability.
John N. Tatfield, killed at Kenesaw Mountain June 23, 1864.
Elmer L. Johns, veteran; died of wounds at Chattanooga July 1, 1864.
James H. Jones, mustered out April 4, 1865.
Lewis Jones, died at Tuscumbia, Ala., July 2, 1862.
Eli B. Cline, died at Nashville, Tenn., April 12, 1862.
Abram McConnell, veteran; transferred to Veteran Reserve Corps April 17, 1865.
Bethuel McConnell, veteran; mustered out as Corporal December 14, 1865.
Archibald S. H. Neff, discharged June 21, 1862, for disability.
Noel Russell, died at Nashville, Tenn.
Levi H. Shaffer, died at Hamburg, Tenn., July 4, 1862.
William Truitt, Brigade Wagonmaster; mustered out—time expired.
Thomas J. Updyke, discharged for disability November 18, 1862.

COMPANY F.

George C. Baker, veteran; mustered out as Corporal December 14, 1865.
Milton Carmichael, died at Louisville, Ky., November 27, 1862.
William T. Tiatt, veteran; mustered out as Corporal December 14, 1865.
Edwin A. Gregory, killed at Stone River, Tenn., December 31, 1862; the first of his regiment from Delaware County to be killed in battle.
Joseph Tiatt, veteran; killed at New Tope Church, Ga., May 27, 1864.
James D. Tiatt, discharged March 23, 1863, for disability.
Enoch Hiatt, discharged April 13, 1863, for disability.
Asbury L. Cerwood, First Sergeant, mustered out February 5, 1865.
Alonzo McLaughlin, lost an arm at Stone River; discharged 1863.
Martin McGeath, discharged June 21, 1862, for disability.
James F. Pettay, died at Nashville, Tenn., March 27, 1862.

COMPANY G.

Hiram T. Roberts, mustered out December 14, 1865, as Corporal.
Samuel Vounce, mustered out March 14, 1865.
Philip T. Vounce, died at Lavaca, Texas, November 24, 1865.

COMPANY I.

George Baney, discharged May 13, 1863.
Nathan Clements, killed at Peach Tree Creek, Ga., July 20, 1864.
Henry C. Clements, mustered out December 14, 1865.
David L. Cline, died at Lebanon, Ky., February 2, 1862.
George Fulton, discharged July 13, 1862.
George W. Gibson, mustered out December 14, 1865.
John W. Jackson, discharged July 3, 1862.
Goldsmith G. Norris, veteran, mustered out as Sergeant December 14, 1865.
Milton M. Norris, Selma, deserted July 29, 1862.
Ezra Searles, veteran, mustered out as Corporal December 14, 1865.
Parker Truitt, Corporal, died at Chattanooga December, 1863, of wounds.
Charles N. Thornburg, Corporal, discharged May 4, 1863, for wounds received at Stone River.
Asahel F. Thornburg, died at home June 28, 1862.
John W. White, veteran, commissioned Second Lieutenant June 1, 1865; mustered out December 14, 1865, as First Sergeant.
Hercules Wilcoxon, died at Murfreesboro, Tenn., January 25, 1863.

COMPANY H.

Lewis S. Horn, Second Lieutenant, promoted to First Lieutenant; resigned November 13, 1862, for disability.

COMPANY K.

First Lieutenant—Horace E. Williams, from Company D, Eighty-fourth Regiment,
Private—Nathan W. Dean, mustered out December 14, 1865.

SIXTY-NINTH REGIMENT (THREE YEARS).

The Sixty-ninth Regiment was organized at Richmond on the 19th of
August. 1862, with William A. Bickle as colonel. On the following day it
left for Kentucky, and on reaching Lexington moved in the direction of
Richmond. Kentucky. Near this place, on the 30th of August, it participated in the battle with Kirby Smith's rebel forces, losing two hundred and
eighteen men and officers, killed and wounded.

Though the men fought bravely the disciplined troops of the enemy
overpowered the regiment and captured it almost *en masse*. The captured
men were immediately paroled and sent to parole camp at Indianapolis.

Upon being exchanged the regiment was reorganized at Indianapolis,
and left that place on November 27, 1862, for Memphis, Tennessee, in
command of Colonel Thomas W. Bennett. On the 20th of December it proceeded down the Mississippi river with Sheldon's Brigade of Morgan's Division of Sherman's wing of Grant's army on the expedition to Vicksburg.
In the assault upon the enemy's works at Chickasaw Bluffs the regiment
took part, suffering but a slight loss. After the repulse at this place the
Sixty-ninth moved to Arkansas Post, where it was engaged on the 11th of
January, 1863, and after the capture of the post it proceeded to Young's
Point, and while stationed there over one hundred men died from disease.
In the latter part of February it moved to Milliken's Bend, and on the
morning of the 30th of March it was the advance regiment of Grant's army
in the movement against Vicksburg. On reaching Roundaway Bayou, opposite Richmond, Louisiana, in the afternoon, a rebel force was found and
dislodged. Crossing over to Richmond in boats, the regiment assisted in
building bridges for the passage of the main army.

It was during this movement that two thousand feet of bridging was
constructed in three days. Thus was a military road completed across the
peninsula from the river above Vicksburg to the river forty miles below
that city, over which the whole army rapidly moved. On the 30th of April
the advance crossed the Mississippi at Hard Times Landing, and disem-
barked at D'Sebron's on the opposite bank, from whence it marched to Port
Gibson, where, on the 1st of May, the battle of Thompson's Hill was fought.
In this engagement the Sixty-ninth lost seventy-one in killed and wounded.
On the 16th of May it was engaged at Champion Hills, and on the 17th of
May took part in the assault on the enemy's works at Black River Bridge.
It then moved to the rear of the rebel works at Vicksburg, participating in
the siege up to and including the assault on the 22d of May. On the 23d
of May it moved with Osterhau's division to the Black River Bridge, where

it was stationed during the remainder of the siege of Vicksburg, holding Johnston in check.

During all of these operations on the east side of the Mississippi river the regiment served in Osterhau's division, which opened every engagement prior to the investment of Vicksburg.

On the 6th of July the regiment moved toward Jackson with the same division, and at that place was actively engaged in the six days' siege. Returning to Vicksburg on the 3d of August, it was sent with the Thirteenth Army Corps to Port Hudson, and was afterwards transferred to the Department of the Gulf and sent to New Orleans. In September it moved to Berwick City, and there joined General Franklin's Teche expedition, and on its return was sent to Algiers, reaching there in November. It then embarked on steamship for Texas as part of General Bank's coast expedition, landing at Decrow's Point, Matagorda Bay, on the 1st of December, 1863. On the 13th of February, 1864, it sailed for Indianola, and on the 13th of March evacuated that place and started for Matagorda Island.

During the progress of this movement, while crossing from Bynio's Island to Matagorda Island, a boat swamped and two officers (Assistant Surgeon Witt and Lieutenant Temor) and twenty men were drowned. In April the regiment left Matagorda Island for New Orleans, and on arrival there was sent to Alexandria, which place was reached on the 27th of April. Here it met Banks' retreating army and was engaged in the fight near Alexandria, and in the retreat from that place to the Mississippi river supported Col. Lucas' Cavalry Brigade, which covered the retreat. The regiment then went into camp at Morganza, and from there participated in different expeditions sent out from that place. On the 7th of December it was sent to Dauphin Island, in Mobile Bay, and on the 14th of December joined Gen. Granger's Pascagoula expedition—a movement toward Mobile, intended to divert the attention of the enemy from other columns moving through the country.

Formation of Consolidated Battalion.

On the 23d of January, 1865, the regiment was consolidated into a battalion of four companies, of which Lieut. Col. Oran Perry was made the commanding officer. On January 31 the battalion embarked on steamship for Barancas, Florida, from whence, on the 14th of March, it moved with a division to Pensacola. It formed part of Steele's expedition through Florida and southern Alabama and was engaged April 9 in the assault on Fort Blakely, after which it guarded prisoners to Ship Island. For a time it remained on duty at Mobile. On the 5th of July, 1865, the battalion was mustered out of service at Mobile, and on the 7th left for home via New Orleans with 16 officers and 284 men. Arriving at Indianapolis, it was present at a public reception given to returned troops in the capitol grounds on the

18th of July, where it was addressed by Governor Norton. The regiment has left its dead in eleven states, and participated in the battles of Richmond, Kentucky, Chickasaw Bluffs, Arkansas Post, Thompson's Hill, Champion Hill, Black River Bridge, the sieges of Vicksburg and Jackson, and the capture of Fort Blakely, Alabama, which caused the surrender of Mobile. It returned to the state with 16 officers and 284 men.

STATISTICS.

Officers, 42; men, 962; recruits, 98; total, 1,102.
Officers died, 6; men died, 320; deserted, 61.

SOLDIERS FROM DELAWARE COUNTY IN THE SIXTY-NINTH.

Major—Thomas S. Walterhouse, resigned February 16, 1863.

COMPANY B.

Captain—Thomas S. Walterhouse, promoted to Major, August 19, 1862; David Nation, resigned February 18, 1863.

First Lieutenant—David K. Williams, resigned January 26, 1863.

Sergeants—Alvia M. Cowing, promoted to Second Lieutenant, killed at Richmond, Kentucky, August 30, 1862; John G. Ridge, promoted to Second Lieutenant, resigned February 5, 1863; John Linville, promoted to First Lieutenant, to Captain, mustered out January 25, 1865; Abel Gibson, promoted to Second Lieutenant, to First Lieutenant, resigned January 7, 1864; re-entered as Second Lieutenant of One Hundred Forty-seventh, mustered out with regiment; William P. Stewart, died January 18, 1864.

Corporals—Cyrus M. Newcomb, transferred to Veteran Reserve Corps, Benjamin R. Dragoo, discharged April 20, 1863, as Sergeant; James E. Reeves, discharged November 24, 1862; Jacob H. Wierman, discharged June 5, 1865; John A. Propps, died at Memphis Tennessee, January 1, 1863; Thomas N. McDonald, died at Cairo, Illinois, June 27, 1862; Sidney A. Jewett, mustered out July 5, 1865.

Musicians—Isaac Reeder, mustered out June 4, 1865.

Wagoner—George W. Huston, discharged April 20, 1863.

Privates—Zur. Acord, John F. Carnagua, Elijah Carman, Charles F. Eberstein, Daniel Fletcher, Erasmus Gum, Samuel H. Helvie, Charles B. Johnson, John Kiger, George Lutz, John S. Moore, John H. Nottingham, Mark Priest, Joseph Prutzman, William Reynolds, William C. Skinner, John Shroyer, C. A. Simon, as Corporal; Jacob Turner, William A. Turner, John H. Tom, John R. Tuthill, James M. Vanduzen, Henry Wells.

Emanuel Aldrich, discharged April 20, 1863.
William F. Byers, discharged March 20, 1863, for disability.
William Bryan, discharged May 20, 1863.
John Brown, killed at Richmond, Ky., August 30, 1862.
James H. Clark, died at St. Louis, Mo., June 21, 1863.
James H. Cray, discharged June 10, 1863.
William Carey, killed at Richmond, Ky., August 30, 1862.
Jonathan Clements, died at Memphis, Tenn., April 12, 1863.
Andrew Carmichael, died at Jefferson Barracks, Mo., February 8, 1863.
Nathan R. Dow, discharged November 6, 1862.
Moses Eby, discharged June 20, 1863.
John H. Emmett, discharged November 16, 1863, at Mound City, Ill.
W. H. Eby, died at Milliken's Bend, La., March 31, 1863.
John P. Fulton, died at New Orleans, La., December 28, 1863.
Theodore Fuqua, discharged April 20, 1863.
David N. Foorman, died at Lexington, Ky., September 10, 1862.
Garret Gibson, died at Memphis, Tenn., February 27, 1863.
Benjamin C. Goff, died at Milliken's Bend, La., April 1, 1863.
Porter Gibson, killed at Thompson's Hill May 1, 1863.
Samuel Gayman, discharged April 29, 1863.
Isaac Gibson, died at Young's Point, La., February 7, 1863.
William H. Hobson, died at Rogersville, Ky., September 10, 1862.
Robert Harter, mustered out May 27, 1865.

George Hale, discharged April 20, 1863.
William Hines, promoted to Second Lieutenant; resigned October 2, 1863.
Luther Helvie, died at New Orleans December 16, 1863.
Joseph P. Hipes, discharged February 15, 1863.
David Jetmore, discharged April 20, 1863.
David Kinsey, discharged November 6, 1862.
John Lacey, died at Jefferson Barracks, Mo., February 27, 1863.
Morris Lykins, discharged July 18, 1863.
James C. Lacey, transferred to Veteran Reserve Corps.
Stephen Losh, died at Jefferson Barracks, Mo., June 24, 1863.
George W. Losh, died at Milliken's Bend, La., April 12, 1863.
Willson P. Lacey, died at Young's Point, La., February 10, 1863.
James Mumford, died at Carrollton, La., August 25, 1863.
A. H. McClanahan, died at Muncie, Ind., September 14, 1863.
John W. Moody, discharged October 17, 1863.
William H. Martin, died at Jefferson Barracks, Mo., June 24, 1863.
Joseph W. Nottingham, drowned March 13, 1864, at Matagorda Island, Tex.
Elijah Noftsker, record indefinite.
David Nation, promoted Captain, resigned February 18, 1863.
Valentine Ogle, died at Yazoo River January 1, 1863.
Isaac M. Parsons, died at St. Louis, Mo., March 27, 1863.
Edward Petty, died at Young's Point, La., February 3, 1863.
William H. Propps, discharged November 24, 1862.
James Quinn, drowned November 29, 1862.
Levi Reeves, killed at Richmond, Ky., August 30, 1862.
Thomas Ruble, died at Milliken's Bend, La., April 9, 1863.
Simon Rector, died at Indianapolis June 24, 1863.
Henry Reynolds, died at Milliken's Bend, La., August 4, 1863.
James L. Richman, discharged April 20, 1863.
James Shockley, discharged February 15, 1863.
David Shockley, died at Vicksburg, Miss., August 7, 1863.
George W. Shroyer, discharged August 1, 1863.
Christian Slack, died at Memphis, Tenn., March 4, 1863.
Isaac Shaw, drowned March 13, 1864.
John W. Saunders, discharged May 4, 1863.
W. H. Stradling, died at East Pascagoula, Miss., January 5, 1865.
William Turner, died at Young's Point, La., March 3, 1863.
John R. Thompson, died at Milliken's Bend, La., March 29, 1863.
Larkins Turner, transferred to the Twenty-fourth Regiment June 15, 1865, as Corporal; mustered out November 15, 1865.
Martin Van Buskirk, discharged 1864.
Anthony Worley, died at Young's Point, La., February 11, 1863.

COMPANY G.

Jacob B. Trout, mustered out July 5, 1865.

COMPANY H.

Adam H. Cline, Obediah Stottler, John M. Shoemaker.
Reese Carter, discharged April 4, 1863, for disability.
Thomas J. Graves, killed at Jackson, Miss., July 16, 1863.
Abraham Mitchem, discharged March 5, 1863, for disability.
Charles T. Rainer, discharged October 2, 1863, for disability.
Augustus L. Sayford, killed at Thompson's Hill May 1, 1863.

COMPANY I.

Nathaniel Brown, discharged April 20, 1863, for disability.

SEVENTY-FIRST REGIMENT (THREE YEARS).

James W. Curtis, mustered out September 15, 1865.

EIGHTY-FOURTH REGIMENT (THREE YEARS).

The Eighty-fourth Regiment was organized at Richmond and mustered into the service on the 3d of September, 1862, with Nelson Trusler as colonel. On the 8th it left for Covington, Kentucky, and upon its arrival there was assigned to the defenses of that city and Cincinnati, then threatened by the invading force of the rebel Gen. Kirby Smith. The arrival of Buell's army caused the retreat of the Confederates, and on the 1st of October it started by rail for Point Pleasant, Western Virginia, remaining in camp at that point until the 13th, when it moved to Guyandotte. Here the regiment remained, occasionally employed in scouting duty, until the 14th of November. Upon that date it left for Catlettsburg, Kentucky, and after a brief stay at that place proceeded to Cassville, Kentucky, where it encamped until the 7th of February, 1863. The regiment then moved back to Catlettsburg, embarked on board a steamer and sailed down the Ohio to Louisville, reaching there on the 17th, and was assigned to the Second Brigade, Third Division, Army of Kentucky. It then proceeded to Nashville, where it encamped until the 5th of March, when it moved to Franklin and remained until the 3d of June. During this period it took part in several reconnoissances and skirmishes. On the 3d it marched with the division to Triune, Tennessee.

Joins the Army of the Cumberland.

On the 8th of June the Eighty-fourth was assigned to the First Brigade, First Division, Reserve Corps, commanded by Gen. Gordon Granger. On the 11th the enemy attacked Triune and were repulsed, the regiment taking part in the fight. On the 23d the regiment left Triune and marched in pursuit of the retiring forces of Bragg. The command marched to Middleton, thence to Shelbyville and Wartrace, where it camped until the 12th of August. On the 20th the march was resumed for Esteel Springs, where the regiment encamped a short time, and then moved to Tullahoma. Thence the march was taken up to Stevenson, Bridgeport and Chattanooga, where it arrived on the 13th of September. The Eighty-fourth went into camp at Rossville, five miles south of Chattanooga, and remained there until the 18th. It then moved to the front and took position on the left of the line of the Army of the Cumberland.

The Battle of Chickamauga.

In the battle of Chickamauga on the 19th and 20th of September, General James B. Steadman commanded the First Division, Reserve Corps, part of which was the brigade of General Whittaker, to which the Eighty-fourth belonged. Upon the afternoon of the 19th this division held the extreme left of our line and the key to Rosecrans' retreat. Repeated assaults were made by the enemy to obtain this coveted position, but they were repulsed.

On the 20th the enemy massed his troops and furiously assaulted Thomas. The noise of the conflict had penetrated the murky clouds which overhung the bloody field, and, reaching General Granger far to the left and rear, suggested the need of his troops where the battle was so hotly raging. He moved forward rapidly, in disregard of the enemy's effort to arrest his progress, and at the moment of greatest need reported to General Thomas with two brigades.

Saving the Army.

As the enemy moved down the northern slope of the ridge towards the rear of Brannan and Wood, Whittaker's and Mitchell's brigades of Stead-man's division, with a fury born of the impending peril, charged the foe and drove him over the ridge, and then formed line of battle from Bran-nan's right to the hill above Viditoe's, in front of Longstreet's flank. In gaining this position there was heavy loss; but if the issue of battle has ever given compensation for the loss of valuable lives, it was in this action, for the opportune aid of these two brigades saved the army from defeat and rout. The Eighty-fourth lost in this battle one hundred and twenty-five in killed, wounded and missing. Numbered with the slain were Captain John H. Ellis and Lieutenant George C. Hatfield of Company "B."

Leaving the battlefield on the night of the 20th, the regiment bivouacked in its old camp at Rossville, and the next morning crossed the Tennessee river and went on picket duty opposite Lookout Mountain, where it remained nine consecutive days and nights, keeping up a constant skirmish with the enemy across the river. The regiment then moved to Moccasin Point, where it remained until the 1st of November, thence to Shell Mound, where it encamped until the 26th of January, 1864, at which date it marched to Cleveland, arriving there on the 6th of February. On the 22d it started with a reconnoissance in force to Buzzard's Roost, and was in that engagement on the 25th. It then returned to Cleveland and remained in camp until the 3d of May, 1864. In the forward movement with Sherman's army towards Atlanta the regiment took part in the following engagements: Tunnel Hill, Rocky Face, Dalton, Resaca, Kingston, Pumpkin Vine Creek, Pine Mountain, Culp's Farm, Peach Tree Creek, in front of Atlanta, Shoal's Creek, Jonesboro, and Lovejoy's Station. With this record of valor, the regiment marched into the captured city of Atlanta.

On the 3d of October the command left Atlanta and marched to Chattanooga, meantime having been assigned to the Second Brigade, Third Division of the Fourth Army Corps, commanded by Gen. D. S. Stanley. From Chattanooga the regiment moved by rail to Athens, Alabama, and thence to Pulaski, Tennessee, arriving there on the 4th of November. On the 23d the command marched to Columbia, reaching Franklin on the 30th, where it participated in the battle at that place, at its close falling back to Nashville, where the army arrived December 1. In the second day at Nashville,

December 16, 1864, the regiment took part in a general charge upon the enemy's works, which resulted in carrying his strongly entrenched position and driving him in confusion from the field. The regiment lost in this battle twenty-three killed and wounded.

Joining in the pursuit of Hood, it crossed the Tennessee river, and was then ordered to Huntsville, Alabama, which place it reached on January 5, 1865. Here it remained until the 13th of March, when it moved to Knoxville, and from thence to Strawberry Plains, Bull's Gap and Shield's Mills, remaining until the 18th of April, when it returned to Nashville.

On the 14th of June the Eighty-fourth was mustered out of the service at Nashville, the remaining recruits being transferred to the Fifty-seventh Indiana Veterans, with which regiment they continued to serve until its final muster out at Lavaca, Texas, in November. The Eighty-fourth left Nashville on June 15 for Indianapolis, reached there on the 17th, was present at a public reception of returned heroes in the State House Grove on the 26th, who were warmly welcomed in behalf of the state of Indiana by Gov. Morton, Gen. Hovey, Gen. Wilder and others, and quickly departed to the peaceful pursuits of life. The regiment left for the field with an aggregate of nine hundred and forty-four officers and men, and returned with three hundred and twenty-seven men and twenty-two officers.

STATISTICS.

Officers, 43; men, 906; recruits, 78; total, 1,027. Officers died, 7; men died, 200; deserters, 53.

REGIMENTAL OFFICERS FROM DELAWARE COUNTY.

Lieutenant Colonel—Samuel Orr, resigned December 9, 1863.

Major—John C. Taylor, September 1, 1864, promoted to Lieutenant Colonel; resigned March 12, 1865.

Assistant Surgeon—Tecumseh Kilgore, August 5, 1863, transferred as Assistant Surgeon to the Thirteenth Cavalry; promoted to Surgeon, and mustered out with the regiment June 14, 1865.

Assistant Surgeon—Henry Kirby, November 22, 1862, promoted to Surgeon; mustered out June 14, 1865.

COMPANY B.

Captain—John H. Ellis, killed at Chickamauga September 20, 1863

First Lieutenant—George C. Hatfield, killed at Chickamauga September 20, 1863.

Second Lieutenant—William H. Spence, resigned October 8, 1863.

Sergeants—Frank Ellis, promoted Captain, mustered out June 14, 1865; Ralph S. Gregory, discharged December 4, 1863, for disability; Edward H. Hows, mustered out June 14, 1865; Daniel Burket, transferred to United States Engineer Corps July 25, 1864, mustered out as Corporal September 26, 1865; James M. Winsett, promoted to Second Lieutenant, mustered out June 26, 1865, as First Sergeant.

Corporals—Alfred A. Riggs, mustered out June 14, 1865; Amos W. Kirkwood, mustered out June 14, 1865, as Sergeant; Samuel B. Smith, mustered out June 14, 1865, as Sergeant; Emanuel J. McDermitt, mustered out June 14, 1865; Joseph Stiffler, mustered out June 14, 1865; William Needham, died at Nashville, Tenn., April 29, 1863; John M. Conner, mustered out June 14, 1865, as Sergeant; John M. Thomson, mustered out June 14, 1865, as Sergeant.

Musicians—Aaron Reading, died at Nashville April 16, 1863; Mowry H. Thompson, died at Cincinnati February 20, 1863.

Wagoner—William Switzer, mustered out June 14, 1865.

Privates—John Browning, Ethan R. Brown, William Boat, Henry Cline, William

Crow, Abraham Cemer, John C. Dunn, William Foorman, Thomas R. Gregory (as Sergeant), Anson Greenman (as Corporal), Samuel Gerrard, John H. Green, Thomas Klugh (as Corporal), William Lamb, Wilson A. Martin, John D. Morris, Donaldson Martin, John H. Null, Azariah Rending, Jehu Reynolds, Noah H. Reasoner, Henry Reasoner, David W. Reynolds (as Corporal), John Richey, Benjamin F. Ralston, Nathan N. Spence, David W. Slonaker, Andrew J. Shellabarger, Gen. George W. Smith (as Corporal), Elisha Wright, Sampson H. Williams (as Corporal).

    Isaac B. Babb, died at Stevenson, Ala., September 26, 1863, of wounds.
    John Brandt, died at Chattanooga, Tenn., January 24, 1864, of wounds.
    David H. Babb, transferred to Marine Brigade.
    George W. Clark, died at Catlettsburg, Ky., December 4, 1862.
    Harvey G. Childs, died at Murfreesboro, Tenn., October 13, 1863.
    Lewis Bantz, died at Covington, Ky., October 8, 1862.
    Newton Cochran, mustered out June 10, 1865.
    William Case, died at Chattanooga, Tenn., October 10, 1863, of wounds.
    John W. Coulson, died at Jeffersonville, Ind., December 20, 1864.
    John Carmichael, transferred to Fifty-seventh Regiment June 9, 1865; mustered out December 14, 1865.
    Benjamin R. Dunn, died at Chattanooga November 20, 1863, of wounds.
    Alexander B. Dillon, transferred to Fifty-seventh Regiment June 9, 1865; mustered out December 14, 1865.
    Aaron Edwards, killed at Kenesaw Mountain June 24, 1864.
    William Farmer, died at Cassville January 26, 1863.
    George W. Gregory, discharged July 8, 1864.
    Thomas H. Green, discharged September 10, 1863.
    Henry H. Green, died at Nashville April 9, 1863.
    Andrew Gustin, transferred to Veteran Reserve Corps January 16, 1864.
    Francis B. Gregory, promoted to First Lieutenant; mustered out June 14, 1865.
    Eli Gandy, discharged April 15, 1865.
    James Hoosack, killed at Lovejoy's Station September 2, 1864.
    George W. Harris, died at home November 5, 1864, of wounds.
    Elijah Huston, died at Indianapolis February 17, 1864.
    Nathaniel Jackson, killed at Atlanta August 14, 1864.
    John W. Jackson, died at Ashland, Ky., February 26, 1863.
    Oscar Keenan, transferred to the Fifty-seventh Regiment June 9, 1865; mustered out December 14, 1865.
    Tecumseh Kilgore, discharged November 15, 1863, as Hospital Steward.
    David Lenox, died at home July 1, 1864.
    William H. Long, mustered out June 14, 1865.
    Isaac Lowis, discharged January 16, 1863.
    George W. Lamar, transferred to Fifty-seventh Regiment; mustered out December 14, 1865.
    Meredith Lockhart, died at Chattanooga, Tenn., September 20, 1863.
    James L. Martin, transferred to the Veteran Reserve Corps January 10, 1865.
    Edward C. Mitchell, discharged October 14, 1863.
    Henry McCoy, transferred to the Veteran Reserve Corps.
    George W. Newhouse, died at Nashville October 8, 1863.
    George W. Nixon, mustered out June 30, 1865.
    Simeon W. Rader, discharged May 26, 1864.
    Joseph P. Reynolds, died at New Albany, Ind., May 30, 1863.
    Jonathan Redpath, died at Chattanooga June 30, 1865.
    John H. Rubart, died at Louisville, Ky., May 25, 1863.
    J. J. Richey, transferred to the Fifty-seventh Regiment June 9, 1865; mustered out December 14, 1865.
    Isaac Sharp, died at Nashville, Tenn., August 2, 1864.
    John Sanders, mustered out May 29, 1865.
    William R. Smith, discharged in September, 1863.
    John W. Smith, killed at Chickamauga, September 20, 1863.
    George W. Slonaker, died at Franklin, Tenn., May 11, 1863.
    James C. Secrist, died at Louisville, Ky., September 29, 1863.
    William M. Shrack, mustered out June 8, 1865, as Corporal.

Hiram B. Shideler, transferred to Fifty-seventh Regiment June 9, 1865; mustered out December 14, 1865.

Jacob M. V. Slonaker, transferred to Fifty-seventh Regiment June 9, 1865; mustered out December 14, 1865.

James W. Snider, mustered out June 8, 1865.

Jeremiah Thomas, transferred to Fifty-seventh Regiment June 9, 1865, Corporal; mustered out December 14, 1865, as Sergeant.

Jacob Taylor, transferred to Fifty-seventh Regiment; mustered out December 14, 1865, as Sergeant.

John W. Thorne, transferred to Fifty-seventh Regiment June 9, 1865; mustered out December 14, 1865.

Hugh W. Vincent, mustered out June 3, 1865.

John W. Wooster, transferred to United States Engineer Corps July 16, 1864; mustered out September 26, 1865.

Robert A. Williams, died at Nashville June 1, 1863.

Simon Windsor, died at Franklin, Tenn., May 29, 1863.

John F. Wright, transferred to Engineer Corps July 18, 1864; mustered out June 30, 1865.

John W. Wilson, died at Tullahoma, Tenn., August 25, 1863.

John H. Willson, killed at Buzzard's Roost, Ga., February 26, 1864.

Caleb Winget, killed at Dallas, Ga., May 31, 1864.

Philip Younce, died at Indianapolis February 17, 1864.

COMPANY D.

Captain—John C. Taylor, promoted to Major, to Lieutenant Colonel; resigned March 12, 1865.

First Lieutenant—James H. Orr, promoted to Captain of Company K; mustered out with the regiment.

Second Lieutenant—William A. McClellan, promoted to First Lieutenant, to Captain; mustered out with regiment.

Sergeants—Horace E. Williams, promoted to Second Lieutenant, to First Lieutenant, to Captain of Company K, Fifty-seventh Regiment; Orlando H. Swain, promoted to First Sergeant, Second Lieutenant, mustered out June 14, 1865, as First Sergeant; John Fifer, mustered out June 14, 1865; Thomas J. Applegate, discharged May 9, 1863; Robert M. Snodgrass, mustered out June 14, 1865.

Corporals—George W. Campbell, transferred to Engineer Corps July 27, 1864, mustered out June 26, 1865; Wesley T. White, mustered out June 28, 1864, for wounds; George C. Nixon, died June 3, 1864, of wounds; John W. Winset, mustered out June 14, 1865, as Sergeant; Andrew J. Collins, transferred to Veteran Reserve Corps September 1, 1863; John Pittenger, mustered out June 14, 1865; Bradley Landry, discharged July 2, 1863; James C. Stephenson, mustered out June 14, 1865, as Sergeant.

Musicians—Warren C. Gallahue, mustered out June 14, 1865; Isaac Randall, mustered out June 14, 1865, as Principal Musician.

Wagoner—Rufus W. Taylor, mustered out June 14, 1865.

Privates—George D. Applegate, as Corporal; Miles Conrad, Erastus H. Dowell, Henry H. Eppard, John Ginsber, William Goings, Jacob D. Hawks, Wilson Hutchings; Edward Harrold, as Corporal; Thomas Hunt; George Knight, as Corporal; Samuel A. Kelly; Amos R. Keen, as Corporal; Henry H. Langdon, Samuel Lamar, George W. Langdon, John Motes, Samuel McNairy, William H. Moore, Samuel Myers, Nicholas Finnegan, Smith R. Perdieu; William R. Pittenger, as Corporal; Stephen Price, Robert S. Ratcliff, Moses Ratcliff, David R. Reed, Benton Skinner, Elsey Stephenson, James L. Truitt, Jesse Thomas, William Welch, Granville Walden; Henry C. Wallace, as Corporal; Francis M. Winset.

William Applegate, discharged February 20, 1863.

Joseph Albin, died March, 1864.

Elza Bartlett, died August 3, 1864.

James Benadum, died September 28, 1862.

Alexander Brown, died October 9, 1863.

Henry Bancy, died May 31, 1862, in Andersonville Prison.

William Barrett, discharged.

Alexander Bolton, discharged September 12, 1863.

Lorenzo D. Bates, died October 8, 1863.

William H. Berry, transferred to Fifty-seventh Regiment; mustered out December 14, 1865, as Sergeant.

Hezekiah Campbell, transferred to Fifty-seventh Regiment; mustered out December 14, 1865.

Benjamin Campbell, died December 25, 1862.

Peter Crum, died September 23, 1863.

Zachariah Cecil, discharged May 20, 1865.

James H. Davis, died at Nashville July 3, 1863.

David Dick, died March 8, 1863.

James R. Ducket, transferred to Veteran Reserve Corps September 1, 1863.

Ephraim Emmons, died December 30, 1863.

Allen Eppard, died January 13, 1865.

William Fornero, discharged December 9, 1863.

William Groenendyke, discharged July 20, 1863.

William Gerrard, mustered out July 11, 1865.

Lewis Huston, died July 12, 1864, of wounds.

Calvin Hitchcock, discharged.

John H. Harlan, promoted to Captain, Commissary Sergeant.

John J. Hays, discharged December 14, 1863.

Williams Hays, died March 15, 1863.

James Iseley, mustered out May 29, 1865.

John Justice, mustered out May 29, 1865.

Elijah W. Johnson, mustered out May 29, 1865.

Ev C. Kennedy, promoted to Lieutenant One Hundred and Ninth U. S. Colored Troops, appointed Captain and Assistant Quartermaster in Regular Army; mustered out February 10, 1866.

Benjamin Luce, died October 4, 1863.

W. L. Lenon, died November 28, 1863.

Jacob A. Myers, discharged May 9, 1863.

Henry L. Miller, transferred to Veteran Reserve Corps; mustered out June 30, 1865.

William McKinley, died July 10, 1864, of wounds.

James R. Moore, died May 9, 1863.

Levi A. Miller, transferred to Veteran Reserve Corps September 1, 1863.

Adam Madill, transferred to Engineer Corps July 25, 1864; mustered out June 30, 1865.

David Mohler, transferred to Engineer Corps July 25, 1864; mustered out June 30, 1865.

John Patty, discharged February 14, 1865.

Reuben Pittenger, killed at Kenesaw June 23, 1864.

Isaac Reid, died July 28, 1863.

Albert Reed, died July 21, 1863.

James R. Reed, died October 25, 1865.

Jacob Shroyer, killed at Kenesaw June 23, 1864.

William Stephenson, mustered out May 16, 1865.

John W. Shroyer, transferred to Veteran Reserve Corps September 1, 1863.

James M. Sparr, transferred to Veteran Reserve Corps September 1, 1863.

Humphrey Triplett, died July 1, 1864, of wounds, as Sergeant.

Ezra Woodring, discharged April 5, 1864.

Nathan Ward, died.

Merit D. Willson, transferred to Veteran Reserve Corps September 1, 1863.

Horace B. Waters, transferred to Fifty-seventh Regiment; mustered out December 14, 1865.

Michael Young, killed at Kenesaw June 23, 1864.

COMPANY G.

Jesse Jackson, died at Nashville, Tenn., March 31, 1863.

COMPANY H.

Josiah Hodson, mustered out June 14, 1865, as Sergeant.

COMPANY I.

Captain—John W. White, commissioned June 1, 1865, mustered out December 14, 1865, as First Sergeant.

COMPANY K.

Captains—Henry Kirby, promoted to Assistant Surgeon, to Surgeon; mustered out with regiment June 14, 1865. James H. Orr, commissioned January 6, 1863; mustered out with regiment June 14, 1865.

First Lieutenant—Noble B. Gregory, killed at Nashville December 16, 1864.

Second Lieutenant—George S. Iams, resigned November 28, 1863.

Sergeants—Felix G. Cross, promoted to First Lieutenant; mustered out with regiment June 14, 1865. Amos L. Wilson, lost leg in battle of Nashville December 16, 1864; discharged June 7, 1865. Jacob Stahl, died January 23, 1865, of wounds. John H. Helm, promoted to Second Lieutenant; mustered out June 14, 1865, as First Sergeant. Reuben Patrick, discharged November 5, 1862.

Corporals—Isaac Rattreall, died October 12, 1862; John K. Carlyle, mustered out June 14, 1865, as Corporal; James McGinnis, record indefinite; George W. Evans, died October 25, 1863; George W. Brandt, died May 4, 1863; George H. Maddox, transferred to the Veteran Reserve Corps May 1, 1864; Isaac McDermitt, mustered out June 14, 1865, as Sergeant; James Racer, mustered out May 1, 1865.

Musicians—William Pickett, mustered out June 14, 1865; Lewis T. Willson, mustered out June 14, 1865.

Wagoner—Benoni R. Thomas, discharged March 19, 1865.

Privates—W. T. Allen, William A. Boyd; Isatus Boyd, as Corporal; Martin Bolimer, Alexander H. Clift, Robert B. Craw; Ebenezer T. Chaffee, promoted to Adjutant; Jacob Creek, Luther Hamilton, Clark Haywood, James Hamilton, George W. Holdren, David Little, John McMullen, Archibald S. H. Neff, William H. Phillabaum, William T. Ross, as Corporal; Daniel H. Sullivan; Edward Shideler, as Corporal; Ezra Stahl, as Sergeant Major; Peter Shideler; John W. Thornburg, as Sergeant; Laban Williams; A. H. Wasson, as Corporal; Joseph Wasson.

John R. Adsit, discharged October 28, 1864.

John W. Rattreall, discharged August 20, 1863.

Thomas Barrett, died March 26, 1864.

George Brock, transferred to Fifty-seventh Regiment; mustered out December 14, 1864.

James Buchanan, record indefinite.

Arthur N. Boyd, discharged March 7, 1865.

William Boliner, died at home March 1, 1863.

George W. Brady, transferred to Veteran Reserve Corps January 10, 1865.

Patrick Carmichael, died December 13, 1863, of wounds.

John N. Culbertson, transferred to Fifty-seventh Regiment; mustered out May 25, 1865, for disability.

John M. W. Culbertson, discharged May 18, 1863.

Freeborn Culbertson, discharged November 4, 1863.

Joseph A. Cross, killed at Kenesaw June 23, 1864.

Charles H. Clore, killed at Chickamauga September 20, 1863.

Soloman A. Dean, transferred to Fifty-seventh Regiment June 9, 1865; mustered out December 14, 1865.

Henry C. Davidson, promoted to Assistant Surgeon of Fifty-fourth Regiment; resigned March 23, 1863.

Nathan W. Dean, transferred to Fifty-seventh Regiment June 9, 1865; mustered out December 14, 1865.

William Everett, discharged August 5, 1863.

Moses Gunnion, died April 24, 1863.

Albert Gerrard, discharged December 6, 1862.

William H. Hightower, died October 16, 1863.

George W. Holdren, mustered out at the close of the war.

Benjamin F. Holden, transferred to Fifty-seventh Regiment June 9, 1865; mustered out December 14, 1865.

David L. Jones, discharged August 20, 1863.

John Jenkins, discharged October 23, 1862.

Benjamin Kitsmiller, died December 11, 1864.

Joseph Lovo, died January 1, 1863.

James J. Lucky, died December 7, 1862.

James W. Landon, died August 18, 1863.

Lewis C. Landon, record indefinite.

David Little, record indefinite.
Solomon McCormick, transferred to Veteran Reserve Corps; mustered out.
W. F. Melnturf, discharged April 9, 1864.
William Minton, discharged November 9, 1863.
George Neff, transferred to Fifty-seventh Regiment June 9, 1865; mustered out December 14, 1865.
Thomas M. O'Neal, transferred to Veteran Reserve Corps September 20, 1863.
Fantley H. Naylor, lost on the Sultana.
Thomas Pacey, missing at Chickamauga.
Daniel Phillabaum, died May 2, 1863.
David W. Roberts, killed at Tunnel Hill, Ga., May 9, 1864.
David C. Rowden, discharged October 19, 1863.
Henry C. Russey, discharged January 10, 1865.
David Sailors, transferred to Veteran Reserve Corps November 15, 1862.
John C. Turner, transferred to Veteran Reserve Corps February 15, 1864.
Jacob Van Gordon, died August 15, 1864, of wounds.
William W. Wade, died July 1, 1864.
James Wilson, discharged August 20, 1863.
Francis Williams, transferred to Engineer Corps July 29, 1864; mustered out September 26, 1865.
Benoni G. Wilson, transferred to Fifty-seventh Regiment June 9, 1865; mustered out December 14, 1865.
Isaac Wright, transferred to Veteran Reserve Corps March 23, 1864.

NINETIETH REGIMENT (FIFTH CAVALRY).

COMPANY C.

Henry McDermitt, mustered out June 15, 1865.
Samuel Mann, mustered out June 15, 1865.
William Nation, discharged November 12, 1862.

ONE HUNDRED AND FIRST REGIMENT (THREE YEARS).

Isaac Bales, died at Murfreesboro, Tenn., February 21, 1863.
Samuel Bales, discharged March 16, 1863.
Ephraim Howell, discharged February 14, 1865.
Rolla F. Howell, mustered out June 24, 1865.
William E. McDaniel, mustered out June 24, 1865.
John Yost, missing in action at Chickamauga, September 19, 1863.

Morgan's Raid Regiments.

The invasion of our state by the Confederate command of General John H. Morgan, in July, 1863, will always remain a prominent feature of our history. It aroused the martial spirit of the people, so that within two days after Governor Morton issued his call for troops, 65,000 men tendered their services.

Thirteen regiments were organized and mustered within less than one week and prepared for active service. The One Hundred and Tenth Regiment contained two companies from Delaware County. Company officers and men were furnished that regiment, as follows:

COMPANY E.

Captain—Albert L. Zimmerman.
First Lieutenant—Joseph Kirk.
Second Lieutenant—W. B. Williams.
Sergeants—John M. Russey, William L. Little, Samuel C. Spalding, William H. Current and John B. Pence.
Corporals—Sell L. Davis, William H. Scudder, John Kirby, Webster Smith.
Privates—James T. Austin, Robert Adams, Jacob Aughe, Henry Adams, Edward W. Brady, Samuel Brady, Thomas S. Benham, Spencer H. Benadum, Marion Bald-

win, Franklin Denadum, Robert Benoy, William Crouch, George Coffeen, Edward H.
Cowan, Joseph Clark, James M. Catterline, John A. Deal, John A. Douglass, David
Duffenbaugh, Lewis Ethell, Joseph Fox, Andrew J. George, George S. Howland, Sam-
uel R. Hutchinson, Mornay Helm, Daniel Huffer, Samuel V. Huffer, George Hazzard,
Adelbert Haines, Cyril Jones, George Kirby, Hall Little, David Lynn, John A. Lovett,
James McPherson, John Messick, Henry Matthews, Squire Miller, James Mack, Fred-
erick McClellan, Frank McClellan, John R. Mason, Elder M. Mitchener, Cyrus Neely,
Joseph Newman, George W. Nixon, Thomas Parker, William H. Powell, Samuel
Parker, Thomas Q. Parker, Samuel Rodman, Richard L. Richardson, Francis M.
Richardson, Patrick Ryan, Frederick E. Retz, George W. Reasoner, Henry Rodman,
Levin W. Shaffer, Stephen Streeter, John W. Scudder, Charles Sweeney, Joseph
Steele, Timothy Shannon, James Thomas, Leonidas S. Turne, Henry Vice, George W.
Watson, Henry Worrell, Ambrose Willson, Levi Wilcoxon, John Wilcoxon, William B.
Waldo, Albert Wright, William Winslow, John Youky.

COMPANY F.

Captain—James R. Nation.
First Lieutenant—William Wright.
Second Lieutenant—William Nation.
Sergeants—J. W. Thornburg, Noah Harrold, Isaac Sowerwine, William Graves,
N. E. Conn.
Corporals—John Needham, George Miller, Benjamin Brown, James J. Crouch.
Privates—Peter Asher, Isaac Arnold, Shem Bowers, George Bowers, Samuel
Brown, William Brown, David Brown, Charles Brown, George Besser, Michael Bowers,
Charles W. Clevenger, Jonathan Clevenger, John Clevenger, Albert Culbertson, John
Carmichael, Milton Davis, Isaac Downing, Taylor Gibson, William Gibson, George
Gibson, Walter Gibson, Richard Gibson, Ephraim Harrold, Milo Harrold, Valentine
Harrold, Aaron Hill, George Heath, James T. Harrison, Lewis Johnson, Charles
Johnson, James T. Johnson, J. N. McKinney, Abram Micham, Thomas Madden, Will-
iam Needham, Isaac Needham, James Powers, Isaac Rinker, John Simpson, John
Sherman, Thomas Shaw, George W. Stephenson, John W. Tuttle, Darlin Tuttle, W. S.
Thornburg, Thomas Thornburg, Reuben Thompson, Sherrod B. West, Charles H.
Weaver, Harvey White, William Windson, Christian Williams, James Wright.

ONE HUNDRED AND ELEVENTH REGIMENT—(MINUTE MEN.)

COMPANY A.

Captain—J. H. Koontz.
First Lieutenant—Alexander Miller.
Second Lieutenant—John J. Jones.
Sergeants—John T. Reynolds, George W. Kilgore, William F. Coppersmith, Wil-
liam Applegate, Gilbert S. Laudrey.
Corporals—Samuel Jones, James W. Reynolds, Henry C. Parkison, Isaac Neely.
Privates—James R. Applegate, David Antrim, Elliott Allen, William Combs,
James W. Curtis, Roark Cole, William Cock, Theophilus Davis, Cyrus Dragoo, Conrad
Dippell, Daniel Dragoo, Isaac Eppard, Jacob Erther, C. E. Gilbert, Andrew Gray,
William Gilbert, Sylvanus Hawk, William Harmon, William Horn, William N. Hens-
ley, John W. Howell, Isham Humphries, James A. Jester, Charles E. Jones, Alfred F.
Jones, John W. Jones, William H. Jones, Vachel Kendall, William R. Laudry, George
Liable, Stewart H. Literal, William Marker, Richard N. Miller, George McKinley,
William J. Morgan, Benjamin F. Neely, Matthias Pitser, Michael Fitser, William Pit-
ser, Samuel Parkison, William S. Fitser, John Paty, George W. Parkison, William J.
Patterson, Richard M. Rader, William Rader, Jesse M. Rollins, William H. Reynolds,
George W. Reed, John Shields, Joseph Stewart, John A. Swift, John Swift, Jacob Sta-
ley, William N. Stewart, Jesse Swift, Jacob Shimer, James Taylor, John W. Taylor,
John B. Turner, Darlin M. Tuttle, Jerry Van Note, S. S. Van Note, David Van Bus-
kirk, Hugh Walker, Jesse H. Williamson, Matthew S. Walker, William N. White,
Philip R. Weicle, James Williamson, Joseph T. White, F. E. White, Nathaniel Ying-
ling, Hamilton Yingling.

COMPANY D.

Captain—Christopher C. Ruggles.
First Lieutenant—Levi Clark.
Second Lieutenant—William H. Props.

Sergeants—Charles Carter, Owen M. Wilson, George Reynolds, Isaac Lewis, Matthew McCormick.

Corporals—Joseph M. Reynolds, George F. Black, Jacob Stiffler, John Mendwall.

Privates—James V. Abbott, Hiram Adams, Robert Brant, Allen T. Brandt, Lucas Brandt, William D. Barley, John Cohorn, Dennis Cabinall, Dillard Drake, Charles Ellis, Daniel Green, Jeremiah Gerrard, Benjamin Holdren, Daniel Haines, John Haines, Frederick Haines, Daniel Jackson, Peter B. Kennedy, Nelson Kirkpatrick, Calvin Keenan, Uriah Low, James Mitchell, William McCormack, John R. Mansfield, Robert Mansfield, James Northcut, Edward Purdue, David Pixley, Thomas Retherford, George Stafford, James R. Stafford, John Stafford, John Shideler, Joseph K. Shideler, John Sebring, William Smith, B. F. Slonaker, Frederick Stiffler, Jacob M. Slonaker, Jerry Thomas, Hiram Vincent, Lewis Vincent, William Walburn, Goldsberry Wilson, James Williams, Abijah A. Younce.

COMPANY F.

Captain—James P. Snodgrass.
First Lieutenant—Hiram H. Darter.
Second Lieutenant—Peter Trimble.
Sergeants—David Reed, James Moore, William Tinker, Jefferson Snodgrass, Samuel Finner.
Corporals—James Childs, James McLaughlin, James Smith, Lewis McLaughlin.
Privates—Thomas Antrim, William C. Antrim, Jefferson Antrim, David Antrim, Robert Baley, James Curts, Thomas J. Danner, Richard A. Danner, Sylvester George, Levi Hawk, Jacob Isley, Samuel Isley, George McLaughlin, John R. Miller, William McLaughlin, Jefferson McLaughlin, Samuel Noble, William F. Null, Green P. Reeder, James Reed, James M. Reed, George W. Resoes, Amos Ratliff, Samuel Reed, Samuel Stout, Barnet B. Stephenson, John Stout, David Shepherd, George W. Secrist, Matthew S. Swift, William G. Snodgrass, Joseph Thomas, Francis Van Buskirk, Samuel Welch, Samuel A. White.

COMPANY I.

Captain—Jacob H. Wysor.
First Lieutenant—Daniel W. Place.
Second Lieutenant—Joseph Edmonds.
Sergeants—Ozias L. Elliott, Frank Addington, Thomas Jones, Benjamin Place, Moses Butts.
Corporals—Henry Snyder, John Heffner, Peter Fogle, James Carpenter.
Privates—James Adams, James Andrews, Watson Adams, William Berry, John Berry, William J. Berk, John D. Bunch, William H. Brown, John W. Branson, Job M. Crabtree, George Coffeen, James Campbell, Wellington Cunningham, Patrick Dure, Jacob Dodson, John Dungan, Ezra Dick, Henry Dick, Levi Dick, John Decamp, Walter Everett, Michael Fahner, John M. Flinn, Squire Freeman, George Feathers, George Gordon, Ervin Graves, William Gordon, Robert Hines, Henry Hankins, George Huff, James Kinney, Henry Klein, Charles King, David Lee, Jerry Munsey, Squire Miller, Samuel Munsey, Thomas Moore, Laf McCormick, Samuel McCormick, James Cline, Reuben Prichard, George Parker, Samuel Parsons, George Robinson, Samuel Rodman, William Rich, Francis Shell, Jasper Snyder, Samuel Swear, Joseph Turner, Cole Wingate, Charles C. Willson, George Willson, Joseph Walling.

The regiments numbered 110 and 111 were not called into the field, and were mustered out July 15, 1863, two or three days after they were mustered into the service.

ONE HUNDRED AND SEVENTEENTH REGIMENT (SIX MONTHS).

Mustered into service at La Fayette, Ind., September 17, 1863, and mustered out in February, 1864.

STATISTICS.

Officers, 39; men, 958; recruits, 15; died, 95; deserters, 13.
Colonel—Thomas J. Brady; mustered out, time expired. Re-entered

service as Colonel of the One Hundred and Fortieth Regiment; brevetted Brigadier General March 13, 1865.

The field of operations occupied by the One Hundred and Seventeenth during the period of its service, was chiefly in East Tennessee, among the mountains, and for the most part in midwinter. As a consequence, the ordeal was a severe one, and the officers and men suffered accordingly. Their work, nevertheless, was well done, and deserving the commendations of the people.

ONE HUNDRED AND EIGHTEENTH REGIMENT (SIX MONTHS).

The One Hundred and Eighteenth Regiment was recruited mainly at Wabash and moved to Indianapolis and was mustered into the six-months service on September 16, 1863, with George W. Jackson as Colonel. Leaving Indianapolis same date, it proceeded to Kentucky, and was assigned to the command of General Wilcox, with which it marched into East Tennessee, reaching Cumberland Gap on the 3d of October. From there it moved to Morristown and thence to Greenville and Clinch River, where on the 3d of December, it took part in the engagement at Walker's Ford. Lieut. Col. Henry C. Elliott, in command of the regiment, reached the Clinch river about eleven o'clock in the morning. The stream was waded and the regiment sent forward and formed in line of battle on both sides of the road, advancing to relieve the Fifth Indiana Cavalry, then nearly destitute of ammunition. The retreat of the Cavalry was covered by the One Hundred and Eighteenth, which gradually fell back, though strongly pressed by a full brigade of the enemy moving in heavy force on both flanks of the regiment. At one time the enemy made a charge on the right, which was met and repelled with coolness, and soon after the regiment recrossed the river in safety.

Its loss was one killed and fourteen wounded. After this battle the regiment moved to Tazewell and other points in the mountains of East Tennessee, performing arduous duty and suffering many privations. In January, 1864, it marched to Cumberland Gap, and thence homeward by way of Camp Nelson. Reaching Indianapolis about the middle of February, it was finally discharged there and the men who made its rank and file returned to their homes. At the time of its muster in the regiment had 38 officers and 949 men; afterwards 30 recruits joined the command. Of these 81 died and 26 deserted.

COMPANY C.

Captain—Albert L. Zimmerman, mustered out—term expired.
First Lieutenant—Samuel C. Spalding, mustered out—time expired.
Sergeants—William J. Current, Robert H. Clift, William A. Crouch, Abner Saunders, Henry Lyon.
Corporals—George Reese, George W. Watson, William Nixon, George Reasoner, Alexander McKinley, Josiah Saucer, Morris Michener, Daniel Huffer.

Musicians—Charles Warner, John Brennan.

Wagoner—John Dickersort.

Privates—William Brown, Milton Burnett, Zachariah Blake, William Burke, Job Crabtree, James M. Clark, Jasper Culbertson, Elisha Conner, James Campbell, Reedy Cowgill, Andrew J. Driscoll, Dillard Drake, John W. Dewitt, John P. Dunning, Caleb T. Ellis, Henry Evans, William Emerson, Joseph Furcaere, Joseph Fox, Michael Fahner, Jefferson Fuson, Michael Friedline, Isaac Gibson, Charles Gibson, John Gibson, George W. Gibson, Peter Hester, Mornay Holm, Frederick Huber, George S. Huston, James Jernigan, Eli Jernigan, Silas Jenkins, Robert J. Jones, Thomas Karnes, Jacob S. Keller, Philip Larkins, William Lastutter, William J. Lee, Andrew J. Lyon William McCormick, John Messick, Elias Miller, Adam Michener, Dennis Martin, William T. Merrill, William R. Newhouse, Joseph Newhouse, Joseph Noble, Patrick Owens, James Parker, George Parker, Oscar Parker, William H. Painter, Orson Potter, William Rich, William H. Richer, John Shuman, James Summerville, Martin Smiley, William H. Scudder, William H. Steel, John W. Scudder, John Tuttle, John M. Thornburg, Theophilus Thornburg, Philip Woodward, William P. Waldo, Henry C. Worl, Samuel L. Warner, Noah Wirt, Joseph Ward, Simon Young.

ONE HUNDRED AND NINETEENTH REGIMENT.

The Seventh Cavalry, One Hundred and Nineteenth Regiment, was mustered at Indianapolis, October 1, 1863, with John P. C. Shanks as Colonel. On December 6, the command, numbering above twelve hundred men, marched toward Louisville, Ky., where upon arrival it was sent by way of Cairo to Union City, Tenn., and assigned to the First Brigade, Sixth Division, Sixteenth Army Corps.

On the 24th of December the Seventh moved with a force under command of Gen. A. J. Smith to cut off the retreat of Forrest from Jackson, Tenn. During that long and dreadful march, the thermometer standing below zero, the soldierly bearing and conduct of the officers and men of the regiment elicited the praise of the commanding General. At Egypt Station, Mississippi, the rebel rear guard was overtaken, where a sharp fight took place, the regiment sustaining slight loss in killed and wounded. Near Okalona, Miss., on February 22, a severe battle was fought, lasting all day. The Seventh Cavalry had 813 of its members in this engagement. The overpowering forces of the enemy drove the Federals from the field. When the rest of the division had fled, the Seventh Cavalry met and held in check the pursuing and exultant enemy, saved the train, and prevented our utter rout. Late in the evening it made a sabre charge, saved a battery abandoned by its support, was overpowered by numbers, and driven back, compelled to leave sixty of its brave men on the field. The entire loss was 11 killed, 36 wounded and 37 missing; total, 84. In a desperate fight at Guntown, Miss., on the 10th of June, 1864, the regiment bore an honorable part, losing eight killed, fifteen wounded and seventeen missing, and was complimented by General Grierson for its gallantry upon the field. On the 18th of August a detachment of the regiment was engaged in a fight at La Mavoo, Mississippi. On the 4th of October seven men of Company "F" were killed by guerillas near Memphis.

In November the regiment crossed into Arkansas and joined in a movement against the rebel General Price, then invading Missouri. At its close it
returned to Memphis by way of St. Louis.

On the 21st of December a cavalry expedition under General Grierson
moved from Memphis and on the 28th Forrest's dismounted camp at Vernon,
Mississippi, was surprised and captured, and a large quantity of rebel stores
destroyed, including four thousand new English carbines, and sixteen railroad cars loaded with pontoons for Hood's army. The enemy was attacked
at Egypt Station, his forces captured or dispersed, and a train of fourteen
cars destroyed. After this fight the Seventh Cavalry returned to Memphis.
Later the regiment was transferred to Louisiana, where, on the 21st of July,
1865, it was consolidated into six companies and supernumerary officers were
mustered out. From here it proceeded to the state of Texas, where it closed
a period of hard and efficient service. In the spring of 1865 a number of
its members, while returning from rebel prisons, were lost on the Steamer
Sultana.

MEMBERS FROM DELAWARE COUNTY.

COMPANY F.

Leander Downing, mustered out February 18, 1866.

COMPANY G.

Albert Culbertson, mustered out May 18, 1865.
Daniel G. Downing, mustered out November 17, 1865.
Samuel Downing, mustered out February 18, 1866.
William T. Downing, mustered out February 18, 1866.
John Hurley, honorably discharged February 4, 1865.
Silas M. Shoemaker, mustered out February 18, 1866.
Sanford H. Shoemaker, mustered out February 18, 1866.
Henry Stewart, record indefinite.

ONE HUNDRED AND TWENTY-FIRST REGIMENT.

The Ninth Cavalry, One Hundred and Twenty-First Regiment, was recruited during the fall and winter of 1863, and organized at Indianapolis on
March 1st, 1864, with George W. Jackson as Colonel. It remained in the
state under drill until the 3d of May, when, the mount not yet being completed, it proceeded by rail to Nashville, Tennessee, and thence to Pulaski,
where it remained on post duty until November 23d. On the 25th of September, 1864, a portion of the regiment, under command of Major Lilly,
was in an engagement at Sulphur Branch Trestle, Alabama, with Forrest,
losing one hundred and twenty men in killed, wounded and missing. When
Hood's campaign opened in Tennessee, the regiment fell back from Pulaski
to Nashville and was there mounted and sent to the front.

On December 17th, in an engagement with Forrest's Cavalry at Franklin, it lost twenty-six men and officers in killed and wounded and prisoners.
After defeat of Hood's army and its retreat from the state, the regiment went
into winter quarters at Gravelly Springs, Alabama, remaining there until

the 6th of February, 1865, when, under orders, it embarked on transports, and with its brigade organization, proceeded to New Orleans, arriving there on the 16th of March. Here the brigade was broken up, and the Ninth Cavalry turning over its horses, left on steamer and arrived at Vicksburg on the 25th of March. It remained on post duty at this point until the 3rd of May, when it was again mounted, and sent by detachment, into the interior of the state of Mississippi, to garrison various posts, on which duty it continued until the order for muster out of service was received.

On the 28th of August the regiment was mustered out at Vicksburg, and soon after proceeded up the Mississippi, homeward bound, and arrived at Indianapolis on the 5th of September. On the following day it was publicly received, with other returned regiments, and welcomed at a meeting held in the Capitol grounds, by speeches from General Mansfield, Hon. John H. Farquhar and others. Within a few days the officers and men were finally discharged and returned to their homes. On leaving the state the regiment was eleven hundred and fifty strong. It returned with three hundred and eighty-six men and officers.

On the Sultana.

On the 27th of April, 1865, by the explosion on board the steamer Sultana, the Ninth Cavalry lost fifty-five men. Those who were saved from the steamer reached Indianapolis early in May, and were there mustered out as paroled prisoners, under instructions from the War Department.

REGIMENTAL OFFICERS.

Major—James R. Nation, mustered out as Captain of Company G, June 5, 1865.

COMPANY C.

Solomon Bantz, discharged June 16, 1865.

COMPANY G.

Captain—James R. Nation, promoted Major.

First Lieutenant—Elihu H. Swain, mustered out and honorably discharged, May 15, 1865, for disability.

Second Lieutenant—John W. Watts, resigned March 4, 1865.

Privates—John H. Black, Spencer H. Benadum, John Barrett, Jacob Barrett, Jesse Chalfant, Gardner F. Collins; Clarkson Cates, as bugler; Samuel Disbennett, Robert Fadely, William Fertich, as sergeant; Eli Gandy; Samuel U. Huffer, promoted to Commissary Sergeant, to Second Lieutenant; Nelson Kirkpatrick, Jacob Keesling, George Keesling, as Corporal; Uriah Lowe, David Lee, John M. McCreary, David R. McKinney, as Quartermaster Sergeant; Francis M. Moore, promoted to Second Lieutenant, to First Lieutenant; Edward McKeever, Abner Myers, John F. McClellan, as Corporal; David Nihart, as Corporal; Aaron J. Oard, as Sergeant; Thomas Parker, Reuben Pence, as wagoner; Jacob H. Reese, Jacob G. Spradling, William G. Thornburg, Edwin Underwood, Samuel C. Williams, Richard Watts, John H. Will, William B. Wright, as Sergeant; Hiram Allison, mustered out June 17, 1865, as Corporal.

Peter Acker, mustered out July 11, 1865.

Samuel Brown, died at Vicksburg April 15, 1865.

Silas W. Black, mustered out September 27, 1865.

George W. Bowers, died in rebel prison.

Absalom Brown, mustered out July 21, 1865.

Charles W. Clevenger, lost on steamer Sultana, April 27, 1865.

Peter Cogshall, mustered out January 10, 1866.

John Cochran, died at Indianapolis April 24, 1864.
John C. Dragoo, died at Indianapolis January 11, 1865.
Jonathan R. Downing, mustered out July 8, 1865.
George Downing, mustered out July 8, 1865.
William H. Graves, lost on steamer Sultana April 27, 1865.
Daniel Gunnion, mustered out July 24, 1865.
Henry C. Hiatt, died in rebel prison.
Horton C. Hanna, mustered out June 17, 1865.
William C. Hooker, lost on Sultana, April 27, 1865.
Lewis Jones, died in rebel prison.
Philip Kessler, mustered out July 20, 1865.
Charles W. King, lost on Sultana, April 27, 1865.
Francis M. King, mustered out July 31, 1865.
Peter H. Kline, died at Pulaski, Tenn., September 8, 1864.
Henry J. Kline, mustered out June 17, 1865.
Thomas Maynard, died at New Orleans April 8, 1865.
John M. Maynard, lost on Sultana April 27, 1865.
John C. McCoy, mustered out June 23, 1865.
James S. Moore, mustered out August 18, 1865.
Samuel McCormick, mustered out July 24, 1865.
Isaac McConnell, mustered out June 10, 1865.
James C. Ollom, lost on Sultana April 27, 1865.
Robert Poland, mustered out July 24, 1865.
Reuben Pritchard, mustered out June 2, 1865.
Eben Porter, mustered out July 24, 1865.
William H. Peacock, mustered out June 17, 1865, as Corporal.
Wallace Rogers, mustered out May 3, 1864.
John R. Reasoner, lost on Sultana April 27, 1865.
Martin V. Rodepouch, lost on Sultana April 27, 1865.
John Reynolds, mustered out July 21, 1865.
Robert M. Smith, discharged July 21, 1865, by order of the War Department.
Elijah Signor, died at Pulaski, Tenn., July 1, 1864.
Jacob Smith, returned to One Hundred and First Regiment.
Frederick Stifler, mustered out August 15, 1865.
Asbury Shockley, died at Jefferson Barracks, May 10, 1865.
Martin Shoup, died at Eastport, Miss., February 7, 1865.
Jacob Shockley, mustered out July 1, 1865.
John W. Skiff, mustered out June 15, 1865.
John Tibbett, mustered out June 16, 1865.
Reuben Thompson, discharged May 15, 1865, as Sergeant.
Nathan Thornburg, lost on Sultana April 27, 1865.
Phillip D. Woodring, died at Cairo, Ill., April 8, 1865.
Thomas Williams, mustered out June 24, 1865, as Corporal.
Samuel Wilcoxon, mustered out August 19, 1865, as Corporal.
Andrew J. Wasson, died at Selma, Ind., July 1, 1865.
John H. Wasson, mustered out July 15, 1865, as Bugler.

COMPANY L.

Henry W. Larowe; George Linsacum, as Corporal; Henry O. Matthews, John H. Miller; John B. Reasoner, as Sergeant; Harrison Turner.
Burton Craw, died at Indianapolis February 29, 1864.
Henry Geer, mustered out September 11, 1865.
William P. Glaze, supposed lost on Sultana April 27, 1865.
Samuel Gresh, discharged May 30, 1865.
Samuel S. Reed, mustered out June 26, 1865.
James W. Turner, mustered out July 28, 1864.
W. H. Windsor, mustered out September 9, 1865.

ONE HUNDRED TWENTY-FOURTH REGIMENT.

The One Hundred and Twenty-Fourth Regiment was assembled at Richmond, and was mustered into service on the 10th of March, 1864, with James Burgess as Colonel. It left Indianapolis by rail on the 19th, reaching

Nashville the day following, and was assigned to the division commanded by General Hovey. The regiment reached Buzzard's Roost, Georgia, May 8th and took part in a demonstration against the enemy, losing one man killed and two wounded. It joined in the Federal advance towards Atlanta, frequently skirmishing with the enemy, finally taking position near Lost Mountain, where temporary works were constructed, the regiment moving forward in support of the lines under heavy fire of artillery and musketry. On June 23d it advanced close up to the works of the enemy at Kenesaw Mountain, and skirmished with his sharpshooters. Having crossed the Chattahoochee river, the regiment moved with its division on July 22d to the support of General Dodge, and aided in the repulse of the enemy.

In the battle of July 22d, before Atlanta, where the rebel corps of General Hardee attacked the Union forces on the left, the regiment, moving with the division to the support of General Dodge, aided in the repulse of the enemy. It shared in the labors and dangers of the siege of Atlanta, and at the close marched in the flank movement which gave possession of that city to Sherman's victorious army.

Following a brief rest in camp, it joined in the pursuit of Hood's army, northward to Gaylesville, Alabama, after which it was moved by rail to Nashville, where it arrived on the 9th of November. From there it marched to Pulaski and took part in the movement made by the army under General Thomas. Communications with our cavalry having been cut by the enemy, and the line of retreat being imperiled, our forces commenced to fall back. The regiment, with its brigade, covered the roads by which our army was marching to Franklin. At Spring Hill the enemy was encountered, and after a brisk fight, the regiment forced its way through, losing company "C," which was captured. It took part in the engagement at Nashville and joined in the pursuit of Hood's demoralized army.

On the 3rd of January, 1865, the regiment left Columbia, marching to Clifton, where it embarked and proceeded to Cincinnati, thence by rail to Washington City. Then embarking on transports it sailed for North Carolina, reaching Newbern on the 28th of February. Upon reaching Wise's Forks the enemy was met in strong force, and made an attack upon our left and center, but after a severe battle he was repulsed and retreated in confusion. The regiment took an active part in this battle. On the 31st of August it was mustered out of service at Greensboro. Leaving for home it arrived at Indianapolis on the 10th of September with 532 men and 33 officers under Col. John M. Orr.

COMPANY B.

Michael Carver, as Sergeant; Thomas T. Clevenger, as Corporal; F. M. Dick, as Corporal; Elijah Knight, Daniel Linder, Jonathan Rigdon.

COMPANY H.

Benjamin F. Bush, as Sergeant; James S. Hutchings, Corporal, mustered out as Sergeant; John S. King, Andrew H. McVees, as Corporal; Lemuel Daugherty, mustered out August 31, 1865; Richard Karns, mustered out July 15, 1865.

ONE HUNDRED AND THIRTIETH REGIMENT (THREE YEARS).

COMPANY H.

Alvah Johnson, mustered out December 2, 1865, as Corporal.

COMPANY K.

Samuel A. Fleenor, died in Georgia July 4, 1864.
Albert Newhouse, mustered out December 2, 1865, as Corporal.

ONE HUNDRED AND THIRTY-FIRST REGIMENT.

The One Hundred and Thirty-First Regiment was the last cavalry organization raised in the state. Mustered on the 29th of April, 1864, with Gilbert M. L. Johnson as Colonel, it left, dismounted, for Nashville, Tennessee. After one month in camp of instruction it proceeded to Huntsville, Alabama, where it did garrison duty until October 15, 1864. On the 30th of November, companies "A," "C," "D," "H," "F" and "I," under command of Colonel Johnson, proceeded to Lavergne, to watch the movements of Hood's army. Cut off from the line of retreat, they retired to Murfreesboro, reporting to General Rousseau, under whose direction they participated in the battles of Overall's Creek, Wilkinson's Pike and different skirmishes with the enemy, with a loss of sixty-five killed and wounded and two men missing, from three hundred and twenty-five present for duty. During the same period companies "B," "E," "G," "K," "L" and "M," under command of Lieut.-Colonel Pepper, participated, dismounted, in the battle of Nashville, immediately after which they were joined by the other six companies from Murfreesboro. Newly armed and remounted, the regiment was assigned to the Second Brigade, Seventh Division of the Cavalry Corps of the Military Division of the Mississippi, Colonel Johnson commanding the brigade. On the 11th of February it embarked for New Orleans, and from thence proceeded to participate in the operations against Mobile. After the fall of the city, the regiment marched with General Grierson on a raid of 800 miles through Alabama, Georgia and Mississippi, arriving at Columbus, Miss., May 22, 1865. Thence they moved to Macon, Miss., garrisoning that post, and the line of railroad sixty miles in extent, and taking charge of immense stores of captured commissary and quartermaster supplies and ordnance and ordnance stores.

It was mustered out of service on the 18th of November, 1865, and left for Indianapolis, reaching there on November 25, with twenty-three officers and six hundred and thirty-three men. After a sumptuous dinner at the Soldiers Home, it marched to the State House grounds, where addresses of welcome were delivered by Gov. Baker, Gen. Bennett, and responses by Gen. Johnson, Lieut.-Col. Moore and Capt. Wells.

Officers, 50; men, 1,107; recruits, 236; total, 1,393. Officers died, 3; men died, 133; deserted, 67.

Colonel—Gilbert M. L. Johnson, brevetted Brigadier General September 25, 1865; mustered out with regiment.

Major—Hugh A. Stephens, declined.

Assistant Surgeon—Tecumseh Kilgore, promoted Surgeon; mustered out with regiment.

COMPANY I.

John J. Berry, mustered out August 17, 1865.
Samuel Cowgill, record indefinite.
John II. Case, record indefinite.
John W. Cather, mustered out November 18, 1865.
O. L. Daugherty, mustered out November 18, 1865.
Albert C. Nelson, mustered out November 18, 1865, as Corporal.
Michael J. Owens, Sergeant, mustered out July 25, 1865.
James C. Swain, mustered out August 19, 1865.

ONE HUNDRED AND THIRTY-FOURTH REGIMENT.

This regiment was mustered into service for one hundred days, at Indianapolis on the 25th of May, 1864, with 41 officers and 908 men, Colonel James Gavin in command, and immediately proceeded by rail to the field of operations, which embraced Tennessee and North Alabama. The movements of this and other one-hundred-day regiments were designed to relieve the veterans from guard and garrison duty and permit them to rejoin their commands for the important campaign of the summer. The regiment performed its full share of the duties to which it had been assigned. Two companies were chiefly recruited from Delaware county.

It was mustered out in August, 1864, nineteen men having died during the brief campaign.

COMPANY A.

Captain—William H. Current, promoted to Major; mustered out as Captain.
First Lieutenant—George D. S. Reese, promoted Captain.
Second Lieutenant—William M. Winslow, promoted to First Lieutenant; mustered out with regiment.
Second Lieutenant—Cyrus G. Neely; mustered out with regiment.
Privates—John Abshire, Theodore M. Bernett, Robert C. Bell, Thomas H. Browne, John W. Booher, Johnson Branson, Daniel Brooks, John C. Bird, Alexander M. Current, John Clapper, Francis M. Campbell, William M. Carter, John W. Dewitt, George Daracott, Thomas F. Ditson, Lewis W. Davis, Henry J. Dicks, John T. Elliott, Lewis Ethell, Michael Friedline, David Frame, William Ford, Albert Gates, Perry Gunckle, James Gray, Clark Gibson, Richard Gibson, Jehiel R. Hull, Oliver Heath, Mornay Helm, George Hazzard, William A. Harlan, Thomas M. Hurt, Robert Hines, Nelson Jones, John W. Jones, Silas Johnson, George Kirby, Lewis H. Keener, Albert Ketchum, James S. Lane, Nathan Long, William Lynn, Joseph M. Lacey, William A. Lucas, William McAllister, John B. Maddy, David Munsey, Elias E. Matthews, John Messick, Lewis Moore, George McKinney, Daniel Mason, Nelson Myers, Cyrus G. Neely, promoted to Second Lieutenant; John W. Needham, Solon B. Parsons, James W. Pittinger, William Pittinger, Mark Powers, William Phillips, John Q. Reese, Zachariah Rozell, James Roch, William W. Ross, Webster F. Smith, John Stanley, Albert Study, John P. Shoemaker, Joseph R. Shoemaker, John Stonebreaker, John Shuman, Stephen B. Streeter, John W. Scudder, James H. Shaffer, William H. Stewart, William T. Seitz, George Sullivan, Jonathan Thornburg, Samandrous Thornburg, Robert Turner, Jacob Turner, Joseph Turner, John Turner, John Veneman, James J. Warfel, Dennis W. Worth, William P. Waldo, Charles L. Waldo, Edward Wilson, Joseph Walling, Albert L. Wright, Joseph Wilcoxon, Joseph Younce, George W. Wright, recruit.

COMPANY G.

Captain—Philip Cochren; mustered out with regiment.
First Lieutenant—James T. Broyles; mustered out with regiment.
Second Lieutenant—Levi W. Shafer; mustered out with regiment.

Privates—Hiram Adams, Robert Adams, Rankin H. Andrews, Benjamin Addison, William H. Broyles, John W. Broyles, Joseph W. Broyles, Asahel Brown, Jarrett Beal, William R. Bortzfield, Lewis Clark, Dennis Cavanaugh, Runy Carmin, Michael Crow, William R. Clift, John F. Chipman, Charles Carmichael, Andrew C. Clevenger, Francis R. Culbertson, Jonathan Clevenger, Jesse Drake, David Deffenbaugh, John Dynes, John Dickson, Francis Fox, Levi D. Fuller, Jefferson Fuson, Asahel Gibson, Minus Gibson, William H. Green, James Glaze, William Guinip, Martin Hinton, Valentine Harrold, Ephraim Harrold, Jonathan L. Harrold, Matthias House, Peter Hazelbaker, Charles Hamilton, Calvin Hitchcock, William Johnson, Joseph F. Janney, John W. E. Jones, Anderson Lee, James Levre, Samuel Manor, David J. Manor, James Q. Mitchell, John R. Miller, George McLaughlin, James K. Moore, Charles Mansfield, Joseph A. McCormick, John D. McCoy, John W. McKinley, William F. Null, Samuel Noble, Elijah Ogle, William W. Orr, James D. Orr, William H. Powell, Enos C. Powell, James Pixley, Joseph Reasoner, William L. Reasoner, James W. Roberts, Thomas J. Richardson, John W. Shockley, Eli W. Stanley, Solomon Shroyer, Joseph Shroyor, Joseph Snyder, David R. P. Slonaker, William H. Sherry, William O. Sherry, Samuel Spear, John H. Stafford, William H. Spence, John W. Shafer, William S. Shideler, John S. Shideler, Daniel Sweany, Henry Sweany, John Skinner, John Simpson, John Thompson, Darlin M. Tuttle, Hiram S. Vinson, Philip Vinson, Manaen Vinson, Isaac B. Wood, James W. Williams, Owen M. Wilson (First Sergeant), Chatless Weaver.

ONE HUNDRED AND FORTIETH REGIMENT.

The One Hundred and Fortieth Regiment was mustered into the service at Indianapolis on the 24th of October, 1864, for the period of one year, with Thomas J. Brady as Colonel. Reaching Murfreesboro on the 23d of November it was placed on duty in Fortress Rosecrans, where it remained during Hood's operations around Nashville, taking part in the battles and skirmishes in the vicinity of Murfreesboro. After the defeat of Hood's army, the regiment took up its line of march, arriving at Columbia on the 28th of December, and there rejoining the 23d Corps, being assigned to the Third Brigade, Third Division, under General Cox. On the 2d of January, 1865, the regiment commenced the march across the country to the Tennessee river, reaching Clifton, Tennessee, on the 6th. On the 16th it embarked on steamers and proceeded by water and rail to join the expedition against Fort Fisher near Wilmington in North Carolina. In the attack on Fort Anderson, the regiment was exposed to a severe fire from our own gunboats, and during the assault company "A" captured the garrison flag. On the 20th of February, the rebels were overtaken at Town Creek Bridge, where the regiment participated in their rout and capture, two companies of the regiment being the first troops to enter the enemy's works. On the 6th of March it took up its line of march for Kingston, and made the distance of eighty-six miles, through swamps, in five days, and started for Goldsboro on the 19th of March, arriving there on the 21st and remaining until the 2d of April. It was then detached from the brigade and placed on duty as commissary train guard between Goldsboro and Morehead City, and was so engaged until the 10th, when it was relieved.

Joining the brigade, it moved to Raleigh, arriving there on the 14th, where it remained until the 6th of May. It then marched to Greensboro, North Carolina, and there remained on duty until the 11th of July, 1865, where it was mustered out of service, and proceeded to Indiana.

Arriving at Indianapolis on the 21st of July, it was present at a grand reception given to returned regiments in the Capitol grounds, on the 25th, on which occasion addresses were delivered by Gov. Morton and General Sherman. On the 28th the regiment was paid off and discharged. Thirty-nine officers and ten hundred and sixteen enlisted men were mustered into the service. Of these one hundred and two died and fifty deserted.

OFFICERS FROM DELAWARE COUNTY.

Colonel—Thomas J. Brady, mustered out with regiment.
Quartermaster—John B. Routh, mustered out with regiment.

COMPANY C.

Captain—David Kilgore, resigned March 4, 1865.
First Lieutenant—Hiram H. Darter, promoted Captain; mustered out with regiment.
Second Lieutenant—Jefferson K. Snodgrass, resigned January 8, 1865.
Sergeants—Alexander McKinley, promoted to Second Lieutenant, mustered out with regiment; George W. Runyon, discharged May 29, 1865.
Corporals—Matthew Swift, mustered out June 22, 1865; Joseph Saunders, mustered out June 22, 1865; Lewis McLaughlin, mustered out July 11, 1865, as Sergeant.
Privates—Parkison Cales, mustered out July 11, 1865; George M. Dale, mustered out July 11, 1865; Philip Ebright, mustered out July 11, 1865, as Corporal.
Daniel Dragoo, died at Murfreesboro January 9, 1865.
Michael Fahner, mustered out July 11, 1865.
Burdon Fuqua, mustered out July 11, 1865.
Presley W. George, mustered out July 11, 1865.
Abel Gibson, mustered out July 11, 1865.
Charles Gibson, transferred to —— Regiment November 24, 1864.
William Grice, mustered out July 11, 1865.
Nathaniel Hayden, mustered out July 11, 1865.
Christopher Hazelbaker, mustered out July 11, 1865.
John Jackson, mustered out July 11, 1865.
Philip Lykins, mustered out June 8, 1865.
George W. Lykins, mustered out June 8, 1865.
George W. McLaughlin, mustered out June 8, 1865, as Corporal.
Daniel Miller, mustered out June 8, 1865.
John Marony, mustered out June 28, 1865.
Presley Montgomery, mustered out June 11, 1865.
Jacob H. Myers, mustered out June 11, 1865.
Charles Payne, mustered out June 11, 1865.
Thomas Reynolds, mustered out June 11, 1865.
Tandy Reynolds, killed on railroad at Yorktown, Ind., November 9, 1864.
Winfield S. Reed, mustered out July 11, 1865.
Jackson Rhoads, died at Columbia, Tenn., January 26, 1865.
Jonathan Rhoads, mustered out July 11, 1865.
Henry Sanders, mustered out July 11, 1865.
David Shepperd, died at Washington, D. C., February 5, 1865.
George W. Secrist, mustered out May 29, 1865.
William Sullivan, mustered out July 11, 1865.
John H. Trego, mustered out July 11, 1865.
John W. Tuttle, mustered out July 11, 1865.
Jeremiah Vance, mustered out July 11, 1865.
William H. Veneman, mustered out July 11, 1865.
Recruits—Charles A. Hazzard, mustered out July 11, 1865; Robert Wills, mustered out August 9, 1865.

ONE HUNDRED AND FORTY-SEVENTH REGIMENT.

The One Hundred and Forty-Seventh Regiment was organized at Indianapolis for one year and mustered into service on the 13th of March, 1865, with Milton Peden as Colonel. On the 16th it left Indianapolis for Harper's Ferry, Virginia, and on arriving there was marched to Charlestown, where it was assigned to one of the provisional divisions of the army of the Shenandoah. From that time until its muster out, on the 4th of August, 1865, it was engaged in doing guard and garrison duty at Stevenson Station, Summit Point, Berryville, Harper's Ferry and Maryland Heights. On the 9th of August it arrived at Indianapolis, with thirty-two officers and seven hundred and forty-three men for final discharge, and was publicly welcomed home, at a reception held in the State House grove, on the 11th, at which speeches were made by Lieut. Gov. Baker, General Harrison, and others, to which Colonel Peden responded. There were mustered with the command thirty-nine officers, ten hundred and twelve enlisted men and twenty-seven recruits; total, 1,078; died, forty-four; deserted, sixty-three.

COMPANY B.

Captain—Taylor Gibson, discharged June 19, 1865.

First Lieutenant—Matthew Jones, promoted to Captain, mustered out with regiment as First Lieutenant.

Second Lieutenant—Abel Gibson, mustered out with regiment.

Sergeants—Jonathan W. Thornburg, mustered out May 25, 1865, as Sergeant; William Saunders, promoted to Second Lieutenant, mustered out August 9, 1865, as First Sergeant; William Gibson, mustered out August 9, 1865; Silas Johnson, mustered out August 9, 1865; Milo Harrold, mustered out August 9, 1865.

Corporals—Asahel Brown; Joseph Fox, mustered out as Sergeant; William H. Sherry, mustered out as Sergeant; Isaac M. Jones, John W. Thornburg, Robert Goodwin, John Roblett, George W. Smeltzer.

Wagoner—Elijah Ledbetter.

Privates—Hiram Adams, Charles E. Bloom, Thomas H. Brown, Robert W. Bloom, Michael I. Boland, Peter A. Barley, Isaac Barker, as Corporal, William Bergdoll, William D. Barley, Isaac Brown, Charles Carmichael, Francis Campbell, James M. Cray, Dennis Cavanaugh, Luther B. Collins, Charles F. Corn, as Corporal; Freeborn Culberson, Alexander Darter, Charles Duddleston, William Driscoll, William Fox, Jefferson Fuson, Add. Givens, Richard Gibson, David Gennett, Joshua G. Hayes, Jonathan L. Harrold, Perry Heffner, Greenberry Jones, mustered out Corporal; Calvin Jackson, Quincy A. Johnson, Caldwell C. Johnson, Charles L. Korp, Edward F. Lovett, John J. Losh, Levi James, James McCormick, Joseph A. McCormick, William H. Needham, John M. Neff, Elijah Ogle, Edward Perdiue, Moses Richey, William Reeves, Henry Shaffer, as Corporal; Oscar L. Sweetman, Daniel Slonaker, James Shockley, Jacob J. Spears, John Simpson, William Triplett, Philip Turner, William P. Taylor, John S. Wilson, Michael S. Wigart.

Recruits—James M. Cochran, Joseph G. Cooper, Minus Gibson, James Howell, Wesley Jordan, Isaac R. Lotze, Valentine Perkins, John Allen, mustered out May 10, 1865.

Thomas M. Alderson, mustered out July 20, 1865.

Aaron Adamson, mustered out July 20, 1865.

William Abbott, mustered out June 28, 1865.

Hiram Branson, mustered out May 10, 1865.

Jonathan P. Bergdoll, died at Berryville, Va., June 23, 1865.

George Dick, mustered out May 10, 1865.

Absalom Edwards, died at Indianapolis March 8, 1865.

Franklin Gwinnup, died at Indianapolis, March 2, 1865.

Charles Groover, record indefinite.
Jonathan Harrold, mustered out July 17, 1865.
William Hitchcock, mustered out June 10, 1865.
Reason P. Harris, mustered out August 11, 1865.
Pharaoh Jordan, mustered out May 10, 1865.
Morris Lykins, mustered out May 30, 1865.
William Losh, died at home May 25, 1865.
David McConnell, died at Berryville, Va., June 16, 1865.
William Pittinger, died at home March 12, 1865.
John Russell, mustered out May 19, 1865.
John Ruble, mustered out May 10, 1865.
Green P. Reeder, mustered out June 19, 1865.
Robert P. Suber, mustered out May 29, 1865.
John Spence, mustered out July 20, 1865.
William Watson, died at home March 25, 1865.

COMPANY E.

Captain—James D. Hiatt, mustered out with regiment.
First Lieutenant—George W. Shroyer, discharged June 23, 1865.
Second Lieutenant—Milton N. Goff, promoted to First Lieutenant; mustered out with regiment.
Sergeants—Enoch Hiatt, Silas Stonebraker, Ephraim Heller, Joseph Barry, John Dewitt.
Corporals—George Barry, Amos Bortsfield, George W. Fulton, Lewis C. Reese, Cyrus Schlomridge, James Foster, Isaac W. Reese, Abram B. Combs.
Musician—Nelson Calkins.
Wagoner—Lewis Gunst.
Privates—Tobias Bickle, Luther R. Black, Leander Bloom, Jordan Clark, Luther Current, Alexander Current, Oliver Conrad, Samuel Collins, promoted to Second Lieutenant; William W. Cunningham, Henry J. H. Dick, Andrew J. Dixson, Thomas Durbin, Jasper Daugherty, Samuel Evens, David Evens, Samuel Hutchings, as Corporal; Levi Holloway, Silas R. Hiatt, Hickson Hunt, George L. Hale, William Jeffers, Robert A. Johnson, Levi Johnson, Henderson Knapp, Isaiah Lamb, John Landis, David M. Lewellen, William L. Loy, Joshua Leech, Richard Miller, as Corporal; Samuel Noble, Mark Powers, Solomon Reese, Albert C. Swain, Amos B. Spangler, as Corporal; Joseph Shaw, Martin V. Shoemaker, John R. Stonebraker, William Sudworth, James P. Shaffer, Theodore F. Turnbolt, Eli H. Thornburg, as Corporal.
Jonathan Brooks, died at Indianapolis March 13, 1865.
John Cline, mustered out June, 1865.
John Cortral, mustered out May 19, 1865.
Alexander Chalfant, mustered out May 7, 1865.
Zadoc Harwich, mustered out May 7, 1865.
Isaac McAlister, died at Indianapolis March 15, 1865.
George W. Vicroy, mustered out July 20, 1865.

COMPANY F.

First Lieutenant—Joseph Collins, discharged May 22, 1865.
Sergeant—Andrew J. Collins, record indefinite.
Corporals—Robert Johnson, Rhuna Carmine.
Musician—George W. Johnson, record indefinite.
Privates—Luther Burt, Robert Bartlett, Archibald Gothop, Henry Hamilton, Wallace Johnson, Samuel D. Kirkwood, Henry W. Foster, William Mahoney, Absalom McCurdy, Daniel Swaney, William Templin.
Joseph Mahoney, mustered out June 10, 1865.
John R. Miller, died at home March 10, 1865.

COMPANY I.

William Bechdolt, John F. Dishart, David A. Fisher, as Corporal; Hiram D. Harter, Henry C. Huffman, Martin Jones, mustered out June 13, 1865; Henry L. Rider, William B. Scott, Oliver P. White, Thomas Wright, Casper Zeph, as Corporal.

YORKTOWN GUARDS.

Captain, Jacob H. Koonts, promoted to Colonel. First Lieutenant, Collier M. Reed. Second Lieutenants, David Kilgore, promoted to Captain, entered service of

United States as Captain in One Hundred and Fortieth Regiment; James Reed, entered United States service; William Applegate.

DELAWARE COUNTY RANGERS.

Captain, David Nation. First Lieutenant, William H. Props. Second Lieutenant, Isaac Lewis.

UNION BLUES.

Captain, Lewis S. Horne, promoted to Lieutenant Colonel. First Lieutenant, James T. Broyles, promoted to Captain. Second Lieutenants, John S. D. Lewis, promoted to First Lieutenant; Daniel Hazelbaker.

HAMILTON TOWNSHIP GUARDS.

Captain, Philip Cochran. First Lieutenant, John W. E. Jones. Second Lieutenant, William Shideler.

ROSTER OF CAPTAIN KEASBY'S COMPANY (THIRTY DAYS).

Mustered in July 17, 1862; mustered out August 26, 1862.
Captain—Edward G. Keasby.
First Lieutenant—Lewis P. Everett.
Second Lieutenant—Christopher C. Ruggles.
Sergeants—Isaac W. Ellis, Samuel B. Taylor, James D. Orr, William Berry, Albert L. Zimmerman.
Corporals—Samuel Hutchins, Henry C. Klein, William Current, John H. Holm.
Wagoner—Levin W. Shaffer.
Privates—James F. Armstrong, Aaron V. Armitage, James Andrews, Isaac D. Battreall, John W. Battreall, William Bortsfield, John Boyce, William A. Boyd, Thomson M. Bracken, Charles Calvert, James J. Crouch, John C. Crouch, George Coffeen, Absalom Clark, John Clark, Job Crabtree, Samuel G. Campbell, John V. H. Cassady, George Darracott, Joseph Dunn, Benjamin Dragoo, Walter Everett, Thomas H. Ewell, John Farmer, Thos. Graves, Samuel Gibson, Barton S. Harter, Samuel U. Huffer, Adelbert Haines, John Haines, William Hines, Robert Hines, John N. Hines, William Hatfield, Jesse C. Housekeeper, Horton H. Hanna, Thomas Jones, Lewis Jones, John Jenkins, William Kiger, William L. Little, Philip W. Lewellen, John B. Maddy, John McClellan, Wesley McCuen, Isaac McConnell, Samuel McCormick, John McKinney, James A. Moore, James L. Moore, Cyrus G. Neely, Thaddeus A. Neely, George Nelson, James H. Orr, Isaac Pingrey, Thomas Parker, George W. Robison, Thomas J. Richardson, Mozart Randall, Henry Rodman, William Ross, Samuel M. Sullivan, James L. Streeter, John W. Shroyer, Jacob Shroyer, Solomon Shroyer, Andrew Smith, William Smith, William C. Smith, Patrick Sweeney, William Stradling, Henry Scudder, Monroe Spake, Jeremiah Thomas, Leonidas L. Turner, James L. Truitt, Joseph Vickroy, William Winslow, James Willson, S. A. Wilson, Amos L. Wilson, Solomon Warthamer, Henry Wachtel, Levi Wilcoxen, Hosea Williams, Laban Williams, Andrew Wein, George W. Watson, Wesley T. White, Jacob J. Warfel, John Walling, William Waldo, John L. Wood.

FIRST U. S. VETERAN VOLUNTEER ENGINEERS.

COMPANY B.

Corporal—George W. Campbell, from Company D, Eighty-fourth Indiana; mustered out June 26, 1865.
Artificer—Francis Williams, from Company K, Eighty-fourth Indiana, mustered out September 26, 1865.

COMPANY G.

Sergeant—Daniel Burket, from Company B, Eighty-fourth Indiana; mustered out September 26, 1865.
Artificers—Adam Madill, from Company D, Eighty-fourth Indiana; mustered out June 30, 1865. David Mobler, from Company D, Eighty-fourth Indiana; mustered out June 30, 1865.
Private—John W. Wooster, from Company B, Eighty-fourth Indiana; mustered out September 26, 1865.

Men who received bounty from Delaware County as three years' men, but whose company and regiment are unknown:

Watson Ammon, George W. Brock, William Barton, John C. Clark, John A. Clevenger, Richard T. Owins, John C. Fuson, Albert Gerrard, William Gray, Samuel

Gandy, Lemuel C. Neal, James Reese, Samuel Sasser, William Stevens, Henry J. Shepherd, James E. Trout, Abraham C. Williams, Henry Wolf, Isaac Wingate.

SECOND BATTERY.

Francis M. Haines, mustered out June 3, 1865.

THIRD BATTERY.

John O. Cottrell, mustered out August 23, 1865.
Daniel Cottrell, discharged August 21, 1865.
James P. Skinner, artificer; discharged December 5, 1863.

FOURTH BATTERY.

James P. Helvie, transferred to Veteran Reserve Corps; mustered out June 30, 1865.
John B. Campbell, mustered out July 20, 1865.

SIXTEENTH BATTERY.

Robert P. Hines, discharged May 20, 1862.
John Kelly, veteran; mustered out July 5, 1865.
Rufus Shideler, veteran; mustered out July 5, 1865.

TWENTY-SECOND BATTERY.

Wellington Cunningham, discharged May 29, 1865.

INDIANA LEGION.

(Delaware County Regiment.)
Colonel, Jacob H. Koontz. Lieutenant Colonel, Lewis S. Horne.

SPECIAL COMPANIES.

SCOTT RIFLES.

Captain, William B. Kline. First Lieutenant, Richard Berger. Second Lieutenant, David Nation, resigned August 30, 1861.

LIBERTY RANGERS.

Captain, Michael Dunkin. First Lieutenant, Robert White. Second Lieutenant, John Truitt.

DELAWARE RANGERS.

Captains, Edwin C. Anthony, entered United States service as Captain of Second Cavalry; David Jesse. First Lieutenant, Archibald Hamilton. Second Lieutenant, John W. Dungan.

UNION RANGERS.

Captain, Henry Kirby, entered United States service as Captain in Eighty-fourth Regiment. First Lieutenant, George Black. Second Lieutenant, James V. Abbott.

INDIANA GUARD.

Captain, James J. Stewart. First Lieutenants, William H. Shrack, entered United States service; George F. Andrew. Second Lieutenant, Andrew J. Reynolds.
Captain, C. C. Ruggles. First Lieutenant, Noble B. Gregory, entered United States service in Eighty-fourth Regiment. Second Lieutenant, George S. Iams, entered United States service in Eighty-fourth Regiment.

INDIANA STATE GUARDS.

Captain, James Orr. First Lieutenant, John R. Williams. Second Lieutenant, William Franklin.

NOBLE GUARDS.

Captains, James R. Nation, entered United States service as Captain of Ninth Cavalry; Calvin Skinner. First Lieutenants, William Wright, entered United States service; Jacob Bowers. Second Lieutenants, William Nation, removed from the county; Jonathan Thornburg, entered United States service; Taylor Gibson.

UNION GUARDS.

Captain, Martin Brandt. First Lieutenant, David Foorman. Second Lieutenant, William H. Props.

PERRY LEGION.

Captain, John B. Erwin, entered United States service. First Lieutenants, James D. Hiatt, promoted to Captain; George D. Reese.

MUNCIE SHARPSHOOTERS.

Captain, Jacob H. Wysor. First Lieutenant, Daniel W. Place. Second Lieutenant, Joseph W. Edmonds.

BETHEL HOME GUARDS.

Captain, John Jones, entered United States service. First Lieutenants, Hiram H. Darter, promoted to Captain, entered United States service as First Lieutenant of One Hundred and Fortieth Regiment; Joseph Thomas. Second Lieutenants, Peter Trimble, removed from the county; William R. Tinker.

THE BATTLE-LIST.

In the following exhibit we present a list of the battles and other engagements, in which regiments containing Delaware County soldiers took part:

1861.

Philippi, Western Virginia, June 3—Seventh Regiment.
Rich Mountain, July 11—Eighth and Thirteenth Regiments.
Carrick's Ford, Virginia, July 12—Seventh Regiment.
Lewinsville, Virginia, September 11—Nineteenth Regiment.
Cheat Mountain, Virginia, September 12 and 13—Thirteenth Regiment.
Elk Water, Virginia, September 12 and 13—Thirteenth Regiment.
Green Briar, Virginia, October 3—Thirteenth Regiment.
Chickamacomico, North Carolina, October 4—Twentieth Regiment.
Alleghany, Virginia, December 13—Thirteenth Regiment.
Rowlett's Station, Kentucky, December 17—Thirty-second Regiment.

1862.

Pea Ridge, Arkansas, March 6-8—Eighth Regiment.
Winchester, Virginia, March 22, 23—Seventh and Thirteenth Regiments.
Shiloh, Tennessee, April 6, 7—Thirty-sixth, Thirty-ninth and Fifty-seventh Regiments.
Siege of Corinth, Mississippi, April 11 to May 30—Thirty-sixth, Thirty-ninth, Forty-first, Fifty-seventh Regiments.
Pea Ridge, Tennessee, April 15—Forty-first Regiment.
Summerville, Virginia, May 7—Thirteenth Regiment.
Tuscumbia, Alabama, May 31—Forty-first Regiment.
Fair Oaks, Virginia, May 31 and June 1—Twentieth Regiment.
Port Republic, Virginia, June 9—Seventh Regiment.
Front Royal, Virginia, June 12—Seventh Regiment.
Orchards, Virginia, June 25—Twentieth Regiment.
Gaines' Mill, Virginia, June 27—Twentieth Regiment.
Glendale, Virginia, June 28—Twentieth Regiment.
Savage's Station, Virginia, June 29—Twentieth Regiment.
White Oak Swamp, Virginia, June 30—Twentieth Regiment.
Malvern Hills, Virginia, July 1—Twentieth Regiment.
Cotton Plant, Arkansas, July 7—Eighth Regiment.
Baton Rouge, Louisiana, August 5—Twenty-first Regiment.
Cedar Mountain, August 9—Seventh Regiment.
Austin, Mississippi, August 2—Eighth Regiment.
McMinnville, Tennessee, August 9—Forty-first Regiment.
Gainesville, Virginia, August 27.—Nineteenth Regiment.
Bull Run (second), Virginia, August 28—Nineteenth and Twentieth Regiments.
Richmond, Kentucky, August 30—Sixty-ninth Regiment.
Chantilly, Virginia, September 1.—Twentieth Regiment.
Des Allemands, Louisiana, September 8—Twenty-first Regiment.
South Mountain, Maryland, September 14—Nineteenth Regiment.
Antietam, Maryland, September 17—Nineteenth Regiment.
Vinegar Hill, Kentucky, September 22—Forty-first Regiment.
Perryville, Kentucky, October 8—Thirty-fifth, Forty-first and Fifty-seventh Regiments.
Fredericksburg, Virginia, December 11-13—Seventh, Nineteenth and Twentieth Regiments.
Cornet's Bridge, Louisiana, December—Twenty-first Regiment.
Chickasaw Bayou, Mississippi, December 28-31—Sixty-ninth Regiment.

Stone River, Tennessee, December 31, 1862, January 2, 1863—Thirty-fifth, Thirty-sixth, Thirty-ninth. Fifty-seventh Regiments.

1863.

Arkansas Post, Arkansas, January 11—Sixty-ninth Regiment.
Deserted Farm, Virginia, January 30—Thirteenth Regiment.
Milton, Tennessee, March 20—One Hundred and First Regiment.
Fitzhugh's Crossings, Virginia, April 29—Nineteenth Regiment.
Port Gibson (Magnolia Hill), Mississippi, May 1—Eighth and Sixty-ninth Regi-
ments.
Chancellorsville, Virginia, May 2, 3—Seventh, Nineteenth and Twentieth Regi-
ments.
Varnell's Station, Georgia, May 9—Forty-first Regiment.
Jackson, Mississippi, May 14—Eighth Regiment.
Champion Hills, Mississippi, May 16—Eighth and Sixty-ninth Regiments.
Black River Bridge, Mississippi, May 17—Eighth and Sixty-ninth Regiments.
Vicksburg (siege), Mississippi, May 18 to July 4—Eighth and Sixty-ninth Regi-
ments.
Port Hudson, Louisiana, May 21 to July 8—Twenty-first Regiment.
Triune, Tennessee, June 1—Forty-first and Eighty-fourth Regiments.
La Fourche Crossing, Louisiana, June 21—Forty-first Regiment.
Hoover's Gap, Tennessee, June 24—One hundred and First Regiment.
Liberty Gap, Tennessee, June 26—Thirty-ninth Regiment.
Gettysburg, Pennsylvania, July 1-3—Seventh, Nineteenth, Twentieth Regiments.
Jackson, Mississippi, July 9-16—Eighth, Twelfth, Sixty-ninth Regiments.
Buffington Island, Ohio River, July 19—Ninetieth Regiment.
Manassas Gap, Virginia, July 23—Twentieth Regiment.
Fort Wagner, South Carolina, September 7—Thirteenth Regiment.
Chickamauga, Georgia, September 19, 20—Thirty-second, Thirty-fifth, Thirty-
ninth, Eighty-fourth, One Hundred and First Regiments.
Zollicoffer, Tennessee, September 20—Ninetieth Regiment.
Blountsville, Tennessee, September 22—Ninetieth Regiment.
Henderson's Mill, Tennessee, October 11—Ninetieth Regiment.
Mustang Island, Texas, November 17—Eighth Regiment.
Mission Ridge, Tennessee, November 25—Twelfth, Thirty-second, Thirty-sixth,
Fifty-seventh, One Hundred and First Regiments.
Pursuit of Longstreet, Tennessee, November and December—Fifty-seventh and
Ninetieth Regiments.
Ashby's Gap, Virginia, November 27—Seventh Regiment.
Mine Run, Virginia, November 30—Seventh, Nineteenth, Twentieth Regiments.
Walker's Ford, Tennessee, December 2—Ninetieth Regiment.
Benn's Station, Tennessee, December 14—Ninetieth Regiment.
Talbott's Station, Tennessee, December 29—Forty-first Regiment.

1864.

Strawberry Plains, Tennessee, January 10—Ninetieth Regiment.
Mossy Creek, Tennessee, January 12—Ninetieth Regiment.
Dandridge, Tennessee, January 17—Ninetieth Regiment.
Egypt Station, Mississippi, February — —One Hundred and Nineteenth Regiment.
Paris, Tennessee, February — —One Hundred and Nineteenth Regiment.
Okolona, Mississippi, February 22—One Hundred and Nineteenth Regiment.
Sabine Cross Roads, Louisiana, April 1—Twenty-first Regiment.
Suffolk (defense), Virginia, April 10 and May 3—Thirteenth Regiment.
Wilderness, Virginia, May 5, 6 and 7—Nineteenth and Twentieth Regiments.
Tunnel Hill, Georgia, May 6 and 7—Eighty-fourth Regiment.
Wathel Junction, Virginia, May 7—Thirteenth Regiment.
Laurel Hill, Virginia, May 8—Seventh and Nineteenth Regiments.
Spottsylvania Court House, Virginia, May 8-10—Seventh, Nineteenth and Twen-
tieth Regiments.
Rocky Face Ridge, Georgia, May 9—Fifty-seventh, Eighty-fourth and One Hun-
dred and Thirtieth Regiments.
Chester Station, Virginia, May 10—Thirteenth Regiment.
Po River, Virginia, May 10 and 12—Seventh, Nineteenth and Twentieth Regi-
ments.

Yellow Tavern, Virginia, May 11—Seventh and Nineteenth Regiments.

Resaca, Georgia, May 14 and 15—Thirtieth, Thirty-second, Thirty-sixth, Fifty-seventh, Eighty-fourth, One Hundred and First, One Hundred and Twenty-fourth and One Hundred and Thirtieth Regiments.

Adairsville, Georgia, May — —One Hundred and First Regiment.

Cassville, Georgia, May 19—One Hundred and First.

Foster's Farm, Virginia, May 20—Seventh, Nineteenth and Twentieth Regiments.

North Anna, Virginia, May 25—Seventh and Nineteenth Regiments.

New Hope Church, Georgia, May 25—Twelfth, Thirty-sixth and Fifty-seventh Regiments.

Dallas, Georgia, May 27—Eighty-fourth and One Hundred and First Regiment.

Bethesda Church, May 30—Seventh Regiment.

Cold Harbor, Virginia, June 3—Seventh, Thirteenth, Nineteenth and Twentieth Regiments.

Guntown, Mississippi, June 10—One Hundred and Nineteenth Regiment.

Petersburg, Virginia, June, 1864, to April, 1865—Seventh, Thirteenth, Nineteenth and Twentieth Regiments.

Kingston, Georgia, June — —Eighty-fourth Regiment.

Lost Mountain, Georgia, June 17—One Hundred and Twenty-fourth and One Hundred and Thirtieth Regiments.

Kenesaw Mountain, Georgia, June 27 — Twelfth, Thirty-second, Fifty-seventh, Eighty-fourth, One Hundred and First, One Hundred and Twenty-fourth and One Hundred and Thirtieth Regiments.

Decatur, Georgia, July 19—One Hundred and Twenty-fourth and One Hundred and Thirtieth Regiments.

Peach Tree Creek, Georgia, July 20—Thirty-second, Fifty-seventh and Eighty-fourth Regiments.

Atlanta (siege), Georgia, July 21 to September 2—Twelfth, Thirty-second, Fifty-seventh, Eighty-fourth, One Hundred and First, One Hundred and Twenty-fourth and One Hundred and Thirtieth Regiments.

Atchafalaya, Louisiana, July 28—Eighth Regiment.

Newnan, Georgia, July 31—Forty-first Regiment.

Hillsboro, Georgia, July 31—Ninetieth Regiment.

Fort Gaines, Alabama, August 5-8—Twenty-first Regiment.

Fort Morgan, Alabama, August 5-12—Twenty-first Regiment.

La Mavoo, Mississippi, August 18—One Hundred and Nineteenth Regiment.

Yellow House, Virginia, August 19-21—Nineteenth Regiment.

Jonesboro, Georgia, September 1—Twelfth, Thirty-ninth, Fifty-seventh, Eighty-fourth, One Hundred and First and One Hundred and Thirtieth Regiments.

Lovejoy, Georgia, September 2—Thirty-ninth, Fifty-seventh, and Eighty-fourth Regiments.

Atlanta (capture), Georgia, September 2—See above.

Strawberry Plains, Virginia, September 15—Thirteenth and Twentieth Regiments.

Deep Bottom, Virginia, September 18—Thirteenth and Twentieth Regiments.

Opequan, Virginia, September 19—Eighth Regiment.

Chapin's Bluff, Virginia, September 19—Thirteenth and Twentieth Regiments.

Fort Gilmore, Virginia, September 20—Thirteenth and Twentieth Regiments.

Fisher's Hill, Virginia, September 22—Eighth Regiment.

New Market, Virginia, September 23—Eighth Regiment.

Sulphur Branch Trestle, Alabama, September 25—One Hundred and Twenty-first Regiment.

Huntsville, Alabama, October 1—One Hundred and Thirty-first Regiment.

Cedar Creek, Virginia, October 19—Eighth Regiment.

Griswoldville, Georgia, November 23—Twelfth Regiment.

Spring Hill, Tenn., November 29—Fifty-seventh Regiment.

Franklin, Tennessee, November 30—Thirty-ninth, Fifty-seventh, Eighty-fourth, One Hundred and First and One Hundred and Twenty-first Regiments.

Murfreesboro, Tennessee (defense), December 7—One Hundred and Fortieth Regiment.

Nashville, Tennessee, December 15 and 16—Fifty-seventh, Eighty-fourth, One Hundred and Twenty-fourth, One Hundred and Thirtieth and One Hundred and Thirty-first Regiments.

Vernon, Mississippi, December 28—One Hundred and Nineteenth Regiment.

Wilkinson's Pike, Tennessee, December — —One Hundred and Thirty-first Regiment.

Overall's Creek, Tennessee, December -- —One Hundred and Thirty-first Regiment.

1865.

Fort Fisher, North Carolina, January 14, 15—Thirteenth and One Hundred and Fortieth Regiments.

Fort Anderson, North Carolina, February 19—Thirteenth and One Hundred and Fortieth Regiments.

Fair Garden, Tennessee, February 19—Forty-first Regiment.

Town Creek Bridge, North Carolina, February 20—Thirteenth and One Hundred and Fortieth Regiments.

Wise's Works, North Carolina, March 10—One Hundred and Twenty-fourth and One Hundred and Thirtieth Regiments.

Averysboro, North Carolina, March 16—Thirty-ninth Regiment.

Bentonville, North Carolina, March 19—Twelfth and Thirty-ninth Regiments.

Mobile (siege), Alabama, March 27 to April 11—Sixty-ninth and One Hundred and Thirty-first Regiments.

Spanish Fort, Alabama, March 27 to April 19—Twenty-first and One Hundred and Thirty-first Regiments.

Scottsville, Alabama, April 2—Forty-first Regiment.

Morrisville, North Carolina, April — —Thirty-ninth Regiment.

Fort Blakely, Alabama, April 9—Sixty-ninth and One Hundred and Thirty-first Regiments.

Slover Hill, Virginia, April 9—Twentieth Regiment.

West Point, Georgia, April 16—Forty-first Regiment.

RECAPITULATION.

The following is the number of men in the different regiments set down to Delaware County:

Regiment.	Men.
Eighth Regiment (three months)	73
Seventh Regiment (three years)	2
Eighth Regiment (three years)	161
Twelfth Regiment (three years)	3
Thirteenth Regiment (three years)	5
Sixteenth Regiment (three years)	1
Nineteenth Regiment (three years)	291
Twenty-first Regiment (three years), First Heavy Artillery	51
Twenty-seventh Regiment (three years)	1
Thirtieth Regiment (three years)	2
Thirty-second Regiment (three years)	3
Thirty-fifth Regiment (three years)	2
Thirty-sixth Regiment (three years)	174
Thirty-ninth Regiment (three years), Eighth Cavalry	38
Forty-first Regiment (three years), Second Cavalry	41
Forty-seventh Regiment (three years)	1
Fifty-seventh Regiment (three years)	48
Sixty-ninth Regiment (three years)	118
Seventy-first Regiment (three years)	1
Eighty-fourth Regiment (three years)	330
Ninetieth Regiment (Fifth Cavalry)	3
One Hundred and First Regiment (three years)	6
One Hundred and Tenth Regiment (Morgan's raid)	153
One Hundred and Eleventh Regiment (Morgan's raid)	264
One Hundred and Seventeenth Regiment (six months)	1
One Hundred and Eighteenth Regiment (six months)	91
One Hundred and Nineteenth Regiment (Seventh Cavalry), three years	9
One Hundred and Twenty-first Regiment (Ninth Cavalry), three years	109
One Hundred and Twenty-fourth Regiment (three years)	12
One Hundred and Twenty-sixth Regiment (three years)	1
One Hundred and Thirtieth Regiment (three years)	3
One Hundred and Thirty-first Regiment (Thirteenth Cavalry), three years	8

One Hundred and Thirty-fourth Regiment (100 days)............................ 195
One Hundred and Fortieth Regiment (one year)................................. 47
One Hundred and Forty-seventh Regiment (one year)........................... 171
Second Battery (three years)... 1
Third Battery (three years).. 3
Fourth Battery (three years)... 2
Sixteenth Battery (three years).. 3
Twenty-second Battery (three years).. 1
Kensby's Company (thirty days)... 107
Hancock's Corps 1
Veteran Engineers 6
Bounty paid from Delaware County, Company and Regiment not named.......... 19

                                                                        2,563
    A considerable number of these names were repeated, as in cases of re-enlistment, but it is safe to say the whole number of men furnished by Delaware County will exceed two thousand.

Relief.

Full soon the families of the volunteers began to need aid, and the ladies at home took the business in hand and set on foot measures to raise money for the relief of the needy. In the early part of the war, before organization was fully developed, everything depended upon private, voluntary action, and right nobly did the citizens, male and female, take hold of the work. Supplies of food and clothing and money were raised and distributed. A "Ladies' Aid Society " was formed, and its operations were continued through most of the war.

By "socials" and sewing circles and fairs, by private collections, and by every other method which sharp-witted ladies could invent, the hearts and the pockets of the people, citizens and strangers as well, were attacked, and right splendidly did they respond to the earnest appeals thus persistently made. At one time, by a single effort, $500 were collected and sent to Mr. Hannaman, at Indianapolis, President of the Indiana Sanitary Commission. At one fair, held by the "Ladies' Aid Society," and continued through two or three days, the net avails were more than $700.

Supplies of all sorts, of necessities and delicacies were gathered from the citizens of the town and from the county at large, and sent forward to the State Commission or otherwise. The people seemed never to grow weary in this course of well-doing, but continued even to the end of the war, in this grand work of mercy and love.

Among the very many ladies prominently active in the work thus carried on in Muncie, a few, selected from the masses operating in this field, might with propriety be mentioned, though the whole people seemed to be moved as by a common impulse, to excel in forwarding the noble enterprise. We mention—not aiming in the least to underestimate the services of others —the names of Mrs. John W. Burson, Mrs. Judge March, Mrs. William B. Kline, Mrs. Carlton E. Shipley, Mrs. James A. Maddy, Mrs. John Marsh, Mrs. G. W. Spilker and numerous others entitled to equal credit for their share in the work. The presentation of these names, therefore, is not for the purpose of excluding others no doubt as prominently associated with the movement, but merely as instances now remembered, of the activity which everywhere prevailed.

Relief was given in a generous and liberal spirit both by the county and by townships, citizens and towns, in addition to that supplied by the people at large. The amounts, so far as can be obtained, both for bounty and relief, are as follows:

Bounty paid by county..........		$181,900.00
Relief paid by county............	$129,768.75	
Relief paid by townships.........	51,137.00	
Total relief................		$180,905.75
Aggregate		$362,805.75

a princely sum—showing, while citizens offered themselves willingly in the struggle to maintain the integrity of the nation, how nobly the authorities at home, and the people at large, assumed burdens, and contributed money, etc., for relief and support to the families of those who were absent in the service of the country, or who had died in her defense.

It may be proper to state that, up to 1869, the total amount expended throughout the State for bounty and relief, is computed to have been $20,-250,640.68. That sum has probably been largely increased since that date. Delaware County, for instance, has expended about $80,000 for bounty since 1872, under the action for equalization.

NATIONAL ACTION.

Probably in no war since the world began has the soldier been dealt by so liberally as in our civil war of 1861-65.

1. His wages were unusually large.

2. His supplies were abundant and generous.

3. Large bounties were given both by the nation, by counties, cities, towns and townships and by individuals.

4. Great sums of money were raised by taxation and by voluntary contribution, for the relief and support of soldiers' families.

5. Immense sums were expended by sanitary commissions, national, State and voluntary.

6. In many other ways, labor and money were applied to the comfort of the soldiers, as by hospitals, nurses, soldiers' homes, etc. Thus the nation showed, and the soldiers were made to feel, that her constant care was over them, to supply their wants, relieve their necessities, and support their loved ones. Much want and suffering existed, nevertheless; still, great and noble

efforts were put forth throughout the whole war to do all that could be done for help and comfort and for relief. The following is an account of the bounties given by the nation:

NATIONAL BOUNTIES.

Am't.	Authority,	To Whom.	Time.
$100	Act of July 22, 1861,...........	All Vounteers,....................	To July 18, 1864.
400	Gen. Or. No. 101, July 25, '63.	Re-enlisted volunteers...........	June 25, 1863, to April 1 1864.
300	Circular Oct. 24, 1863...........	Recruits in old regiments........	Oct. 21, 1863, to April 1, 1864.
300	Telegram, Dec. 24, 1803........	Recruits in any 3-years' organiza-	
		tion	Dec. 21, 1863, to April 1, 1864.
100	Act July, '64, and Circular 27.	Volunteers, 1 year..............	July 19, 1864, to July 1, 1805.
200	Act July, '64, and Circular 27.	Volunteers, 2 years.............	July 19, 1864, to July 1, 1805.
300	Act July, '64, and Circular 27.	Volunteers, 3 years.............	July 19, 1864, to July 1, 1805.
300	Gen. Order 287, Nov. 28, 1864.	1st Army Veteran Corps.........	Nov. 28, 1864, to July 1, 1805.
10	Letters Nov. 20 & Dec. 22, '63.	Colored recruits.................	April, 1801, to Oct. 24, 1863.
100	Act of Congress................	All colored volunteers...........	April, 1801, to Oct. 24, 1863.
100	Act of Congress................	Colored volunteers, new reg'ts...	Oct. 24, 1863, to Dec. 24, 1863.
100	Act of Congress................	All colored volunteers...........	April 1, 1864, to June 1, 1864.
800	Act of Congress................	Colored volunteers old reg'ts....	Oct. 25, 1863, to March 31, 1864.
100	Act of Congress................	Colored volunteers liable to draft.	Oct. 17 to Oct. 24, 1863.
300	Act of Congress................	Colored volunteers, new reg'ts...	Dec. 25, 1863, to March 31, 1864.
300	Act of Congress................	Colored volunteers, old regiments.	
		liable to draft..............	Oct. 25, 1863, to March 31, 1864.
300	Act of Congress................	Colored volunteers, new regi-	
		ments, liable to draft........	Dec. 25, 1863, to March 31, 1864.
100	Act of Congress................	Colored volunteers, 1 year......	July 19, 1864, to July 1, 1865.
200	Act of Congress................	Colored volunteers, 2 years.....	July 19, 1864, to July 1, 1865.
300	Act of Congress................	Colored volunteers, 3 years......	July 19, 1864, to July 1, 1865.

COUNTY ACTION.

In the general movement for bounty and relief, the people of Delaware County, by the Commissioners, Township Trustees,, City Councils, etc., took a full and abundant share.

In 1861, no bounties were needed.

In 1862, $25 were given to each volunteer then enlisting for three years, or during the war.

In 1863 and 1864, $100 were paid to each person so enlisting.

In 1873, the Commissioners provided for an equalization of bounty to all three-years men. Thus, under this action, every three-years man from Delaware County has received, or is entitled to receive, from the county as bounty, a sum equal to $100. Under the provisions made in 1872, the men enlisted in 1862 received $75, and the men volunteering in 1861, got $100, and so they all got equal bounty of $100 each.

DRAFT.

No draft was ever called for in Delaware County, except that in 1862, four townships seemed to have a deficiency of 24 men. Jay, at the time was short 103; Randolph, 49; Henry, 160; Wayne, 64; Allen, 597; Grant, 128; Madison, 177, etc. The people of Muncie, supposing their township was liable to the draft, raised by voluntary subscriptions, $8,000 or more, which was expended in hiring persons to enlist so as to avoid the draft. Perhaps twenty-five persons were thus hired to enlist. More careful examination showed that no quota was lacking from Muncie, even before these men had been hired. By this action, and by subsequent volunteers, no future draft was needed.

So ardent and patriotic was the spirit that prevailed, several gentlemen who were too old for the service, and some ladies also, hired persons to go as soldiers. One man sent two in that way, paying them $500 each. Indeed, we are astonished in looking back to those eventful days, at the vigorous and ceaseless enthusiasm which fired the public mind. Love for the cause, and overwhelming anxiety for its triumphant success, made labor easy and carried the people forward in an activity of enterprise and sacrifice without a parallel in our history, or equaled only, if at all, by that of the Revolutionary struggle.

Loss of the Sultana.

The steamer "Sultana," one of the largest on the Mississippi river, was built at Cincinnati, Ohio, in 1862. She was a regular St. Louis and New Orleans packet, and left Cairo April 15, 1865, bearing the news of the death of President Lincoln, to all points and posts on the river as far as New Orleans. She left the latter port on her fatal trip, April 21st, with about two hundred passengers and crew on board. In the graphic words of one who survived the wreck and published his experience, we quote the following: "But a still greater horror was in store for the ill-fated inmates of Cahaba. Lashed to the levee of Vicksburg was the strong and capacious steamer 'Sultana.' Her decks were covered with cots and beds for the ghastly skeletons called 'paroled prisoners.' Wherever it was possible to stow away a human being within her capacious guards, men who had fought starvation and cold, hunger and heat—men who had fought vermin and filth, despondency and death, were crowded in. . . . With her decks, above and below, crowded to discomfort, with weak-bodied, pinched, and sallow-faced men, the 'Sultana' steamed up the broad Mississippi. Every league of progress brought hope to her passengers; visions of a gray-haired mother whose heart has been bursting to know the fate of her boy; visions of a sister into whose eyes tears welled up at the mention of his name, came to the men and gave to them a new life. Memphis is reached; here a large amount of fuel is taken on and the boat goes steaming northward. Night settles down upon them, and when all but those to whom is given the care of the boat, and those to whom pain denies the boon of sleep, are lost in unconsciousness, a great flash lights up the darkness, and, mid crash and roar, mid falling timbers and mangled comrades, hundreds are thrown into the dark waters. The boiler has exploded, the boat is on fire and no help is at hand.

"Of the more than twenty-two hundred on board, more than three-fourths were lost." No one knows the true cause of the explosion. It may have been caused by careening of the vessel. It may have been the peculiar kind of boilers in use on the steamer. In just four of the great engagements

of the Civil War, was there greater loss of life to Union soldiers than re.
sulted from this explosion. They were Antietam, Gettysburg, Spottsylvania
and the Wilderness.

The disaster occurred about two o'clock in the morning of April 27th,
1865, in dark and misting rain, when some seven or eight miles above Mem.
phis, and near the cluster of islands called the "Hen and Chickens." In a
few moments the steamer was on fire, slowly burned to the water's edge as
she drifted downward with the current, and then sank upon the Arkansas
side of the Mississippi, three or four miles above Memphis. Fourteen hundred and forty-three were lost at once, and of the seven hundred and fifty-
seven rescued, nearly three hundred·died in the hospitals at Memphis in the
following twenty days. So that a careful estimate places the loss of life
caused by the explosion at about seventeen hundred and fifty, the greatest
loss of life from a marine disaster that ever occurred upon the Western
Hemisphere. One entire chapter of the thrilling sketch, 'Cahaba, a Story of
Captive Boys in Blue," deals with this sad event in our history, and the
Rev. C. D. Berry has published a volume, 'Loss of the Sultana and Reminiscences of Survivors," in which 138 of his comrades recite their recollections of that night of horror. The account by three soldiers from Delaware
County, all members of the Ninth Indiana Cavalry, are herewith published.

William H. Peacock.

"I was born in Tyler county, Va., May 28, 1845. · Enlisted in the service
of the United States at Muncie, Ind., on the 15th day of December, 1863, in
the 9th Regiment Indiana Cavalry. Was captured at Sulphur Trestle, nine
miles north of Athens, Ala., on the Nashville and Decatur Railroad, September 25, 1864, and confined in the Cahaba prison, Alabama. I was put
on board the Sultana with eighteen others of my company. The boat was
so crowded that there was not room for all of us on the second deck, so
five of us went up on the texas roof right in front of the pilot house. I
was the only one of the five that escaped. The first recollection I had of
the accident, I was falling, and had a cut on my shoulder, bruise on my
back and my right side and hip were scalded. This happened seven miles
above Memphis. I worked my way out from under the rubbish, and helped
get a good many of the boys out who were pinned down by it, until the fire
got so hot that I had to stop and look out for myself. I saw boys start out
to swim with all their clothes on, even their overcoats and shoes, but they
did not go far before they sank. The only clothes I had on was a pair of
drawers, a sock, a handkerchief (which one of the boys gave to me at
Vicksburg before he died), and a hat that I picked up about a mile from
the boat. I swam back to Memphis and was rescued by the gunboat boys
and taken to Fort Pickens, seven and one-half miles below where the steamer's boiler exploded. I, with the rest, had just got out of prison, and only
weighed ninety-one pounds. At the time of my capture I weighed one hundred and ninety-seven (197) pounds and had not been ·sick a day. My
present postoffice address is Cowan, Ind."

Lewis Johnson.

"I was born in Henry county, Indiana, November, 1845, and enlisted in the service of the United States at Henry county, Indiana, December, 1863, in Company G, 9th Cavalry. Was captured at Sulphur Trestle, Ala., September 25, 1864, and confined in Castle Morgan and Cahaba prisons. When the 'Sultana' exploded I was lying in front of the wheel house. I got up and walked across the boat, pulled off my clothes and jumped into the water. I was burned very badly on my neck and shoulders. I swam out to some timbers on the Arkansas side and got on a log. There were nine of us on it. We were there until eight o'clock, when we were taken in by a boat.

"Occupation, farming. P. O., Muncie, Ind."

Hiram Allison.

"I was born in Franklin county, Pennsylvania, December 4, 1830, and enlisted in the service of the United States at Muncie, Ind., December, 1863, in Company G, 9th Ind. Cavalry.

"Was captured at Sulphur Trestle, Ala., September 25, 1864, and confined in the Castle Morgan prison at Cahaba, Ala., until March, and then was taken to be exchanged at Big Black River, Miss. I got on the boat 'Sultana' at Vicksburg. She was crowded to her utmost capacity. Arrived at Memphis April 26, in the evening, where she discharged a lot of freight. * * * As near as I can tell we left about twelve or one o'clock that night. I was on the hurricane deck, close to the wheel house, lying down, and was just beginning to doze, when all at once I heard the crash. I jumped up the first thing and saw a great hole torn through the hurricane deck and fire coming through. I stood a few minutes and looked at my surroundings. I concluded to take to the water. I climbed down from the hurricane deck to the cabin deck and took off all my clothes but my drawers and shirt, and then glanced around the burning wreck and saw that I would have to go, so I jumped from the cabin deck into the water. I remained there for two or three hours and then came across a horse trough with a comrade on each end of it. I took the center. When I caught up with the two comrades they were both praying. When I got on with them I said, 'That was a terrible disaster.' They made no reply, but kept right on praying. I said no more to them, and when it was light enough for me to see they were gone. What became of them I never knew. I stayed on the trough till I got to some brush and logs on the Arkansas side; then I bid it good bye about five miles from the ill-fated 'Sultana.' I was taken to Memphis with others. I was put in the Overton hospital, remained there a few days, and then turned my face homeward. I was scalded on my legs and cut on the head. Postoffice address is Muncie, Delaware county, Ind. Occupation, carpenter and joiner."

How little these sketches, taken mainly and condensed from the report of the Adjutant General of Indiana, show of the real history of the men from Delaware county who saw service in the war! From first to last these regiments were to be found over the whole ground of the conflict,

A. L. Kerwood,

the complete battle list showing more than one hundred and fifty engagements. Many of them were heavy and long-contested battles and sieges. From these we name Rich Mountain, Pea Ridge, Shiloh, Corinth, with Butler at New Orleans, in the swamps of the Chickahominy, Cedar Mountain, Gainesville, second Bull Run, South Mountain, Antietam, Fredericksburg, Stone River, Chancellorsville, Gettysburg, Champion Hill, Vicksburg, Chickamauga, Lookout Mountain, Mission Ridge, the Wilderness, Spottsylvania, Cold Harbor, Resaca, Kenesaw Mountain, Jonesboro, Atlanta, March to the Sea, Franklin, Nashville, Winchester, Cedar Creek, Petersburg and Appomattox.

What do these formal and official descriptions of movements in the game of war tell us about hunger and thirst, of hardships and forced marches, of camp and bivouac without food or shelter? What of fierce and sanguinary battles, wounds, imprisonment and starvation? What do they tell us of hospitals and cots, of amputating tables, and the sufferings and groans of dying men? What of open trenches filled with the slain, or of the bodies of the dead and wounded heated and charred upon the burning battlefield, and denied a soldier's rough burial at the last? What of the holocaust of death when so many pale-faced prison survivors were blown into eternity, or drowned in the Mississippi river, by the explosion of the steamer "Sultana?" All these things were a possibility for every man who with uplifted hand swore to "protect and defend the Union of these United States against all her enemies and opposers whatsoever." They counted the cost. Hundreds of them paid the price.

Asbury L. Kerwood, author of the preceding military history of Delaware county, has been identified with the county by residence and varied business and civic activity for nearly half a century. About eighteen months before he was called into military service by the outbreak of the rebellion he had come to Muncie (in October, 1859) and become an apprentice to learn the saddler's trade with the firm of Brady & Osborn. This was the quiet pursuit that was interrupted by the war. His life as a soldier covered nearly four years, and his subsequent interest in the achievements of the war and in fellow veterans, especially his Delaware county comrades, gives him peculiar fitness for the authorship of this chapter. To his own experience and knowledge he has added painstaking care and diligence in the preparation of this department of the history, and in commending the reliable nature of the preceding articles the publishers also present an account of his life and military and public services.

Born in Preble county, Ohio, June 21, 1842, Mr. Kerwood is a son of Abia M. and Rebecca (Peden) Kerwood, both natives of Washington county, Pennsylvania, who in the thirties had joined the tide of westward emigration in its course down the Ohio valley and had found homes in the new country of western Ohio. Both branches of the family have been settled on the American side of the Atlantic for several generations, the paternal ancestors being of English stock and the maternal Scotch-Irish. Abia N. Kerwood was for thirty-two years a member of the North Indiana conference of the Methodist Episcopal church, spending the closing years of his life in Muncie, where he died in March, 1886. Living during his youth in the various homes established by his father during his ministry, the son Asbury received his education in the public schools of Preble county and in various counties in Indiana, and also one term at Liber College, in Jay county. At the age of seventeen he came to Muncie, as already stated, and lived here until April, 1861.

At the call for troops he enlisted for three months, and in a short time was in the Virginia field of operations. At Rich Mountain, Va., July 11, 1861, he was wounded, and August 6, 1861, was discharged at the end of his term. The following November he enlisted in Company F, Fifty-seventh Indiana Volunteer Infantry. Having never been absent from the command, his military experience during the next three years and a half was that of the Fifty-seventh Regiment. He was in the following engagements: Shiloh, siege of Corinth, Perryville, three days' battle of Stone River, Missionary Ridge, Rocky Face Ridge, Resaca, New Hope Church, Kenesaw Mountain (June 18, 23, 27, 1864), Peach Tree Creek, siege of Atlanta, Jonesboro, Spring Hill, Franklin and Nashville. He was discharged February 4, 1865, at Huntsville, Ala.

In October, 1867, Mr. Kerwood located at the little village of Wheeling, and was in business there until 1875, for part of the time being postmaster. At the Republican county convention of 1874 he received the nomination for office of clerk of the Delaware circuit court, and was elected in October and reëlected in 1878. The duties of this office brought him to Muncie, where he has resided ever since. In April, 1884, he was elected a director in the Citizens' National Bank, to fill the vacancy occasioned by the death of Henry Hamilton, and in April, 1885, succeeded George W. Spilker in the presidency of the bank. He continued as president of this institution until January 12, 1895, when failing health caused him to dispose of his interests and retire from business. Mr. Kerwood has been identified with the educational progress of Muncie, having been a member of the city school board, and served as its treasurer, by reëlection, for nine years. He was a director and treasurer of the Muncie Exploring Company, which drilled the first gas well in the Muncie belt after the discovery of gas at Eaton. His name is also connected with the history of the Citizens' Enterprise Company, he being a member of its first advisory board. In 1898 he

was elected on the Republican ticket as one of Delaware county's rep
sentatives in the legislature.

July 22, 1868, Mr. Kerwood married Mrs. Susan C. Craw, widow
Ephraim Craw, and daughter of William P. Reasoner. Mrs. Kerw
passed away April 15, 1895. Mr. Kerwood is a member of the High Str
Methodist Episcopal church, of Post No. 78, G. A. R., and of Mun
Lodge No. 433, F. and A. M.

CHAPTER XXV.

CHURCH ORGANIZATIONS OF DELAWARE COUNTY.

THE METHODIST.

High Street M. E. Church.

The history of Methodism in Muncie began in 1829, when Rev. Charles Downey held services in the two-story log court-house, or from house to house, after the old Apostolic custom. The Muncie circuit was formed in 1836, and the faithful few continued to worship God without a church home until 1839, when the first church was built. The ministers who rode the circuit, fording swollen streams, enduring many hardships, and suffering great privations to keep alive the Master's work, before the church was erected, were Rev. C. Downey, G. C. Beeks, Robert Burns, F. H. Carey and Wade Posey.

The members of High Street church sit in their comfortable pews, absorb the warmth and cheer that come from a modern steam-heated building, and listen to the quartet of trained voices, supported by the pipe organ, filling the entire building with a flood of triumphant music, without a thought of what it cost the pioneers to lay the foundations of this great church. We cannot estimate the cost by mere dollars and cents, but must consider the sacrifices made by the founders of Methodism to erect the two churches that preceded this one, for High Street church is the outgrowth of two other buildings.

The M. E. church that was erected in 1839 on the northwest corner of Washington and Elm streets was the first church to be built in Muncietown. There are still living some of the members of this first house of worship, and they love to tell about the grand revivals held there. The building was a frame structure 30x45 feet, costing $450. The windows were on the sides. The pulpit was in the north end, and was a square box sort of affair, with a door in each side, with two steps leading up to them, the desk in front, and a bench against the wall. The minister entered the pulpit and closed the door, thus separating himself from the people. On either side the pulpit were some benches. These were the amen corners. The seats were in four rows, a double row in the center, two aisles, and a single row next the walls.

The men occupied the west half of the building and the women the

Methodist Church,
Built 1839, the first church built in Delaware County
corner Elm and Washington Streets.
Cost $450.00.

Simpson Chapel, Muncie.

east half, and there was a door on each side so they need not even enter the church together.

There were tallow candles around the pulpit for light. Very few had hymn-books, and the minister lined the hymns. Mr. Job Swain led in the singing. During prayer every one knelt on the bare floor; no one thought of remaining seated during prayer.

The first quarterly conference of the Muncie Station was held in this church in October, 1851. The Sunday-school reported an average attendance of 50 pupils and seven teachers. This was the only Sunday-school in the county. The entire claims on the Muncie Station, including the pastor and presiding elder's salaries, was $434. Twelve ministers served as pastor of this church before a new building was erected.

In 1853 it was decided that the church was no longer a suitable house for the increasing membership. A lot was purchased on the northwest corner of Mulberry and Jackson streets. In April, 1854, plans for a two-story brick church with stone basement were submitted and accepted. The contract was let and work begun. Only the lower part was finished in 1854, and this was used until 1856, when the auditorium was completed, and Simpson Chapel was dedicated to the worship of almighty God on July 20, 1856. Bishop E. R. Ames preached the dedicatory sermon. The church cost when completed $4.467.80. Nineteen pastors served in this church.

In the fall of 1886 natural gas was discovered in Muncie, and the town had a phenomenal growth for twelve years. Many of the new people that came to live here were Methodists, and soon this church was no longer adequate for the growing membership, and the trustees began to look for new quarters. Up to this time nineteen ministers had served Simpson Chapel congregation as pastor.

High Street church and parsonage occupy two lots on the northwest corner of High and Adams streets. The lots were purchased for $6,000, and the building was erected in 1888. It is a modern church edifice, built of brick with stone trimmings, and the first cost was $26,000. It was dedicated on June 2, 1889, by Rev. C. H. Payne, D.D. Rev. C. U. Wade was pastor during the erection of this church, and for two years after. It has been remodeled since, in 1901, to suit the growing needs, at a cost of $10,000. The official board are now considering the advisability of making still greater improvements. The church now has a membership of nearly 1,500. In 1906 $4,026 was raised for missions and other benevolences, besides the pastor's salary of $2,200 and parsonage. Other running expenses of the church are $3,000 per year, so that it is necessary to raise $10,000 every year to carry on the work of High Street church.

Members of the church today who were members of the first church are: Mrs. Juliet Riley, Mrs. Mary Sample, Mrs. Edith Dungan, Mrs. Elizabeth Haines, Mrs. Rebecca Maddy, Mrs. Mary Meeks, Mr. and Mrs. P. W. Franklin and Mrs. Mary Streeter. Rev. C. U. Wade was the first pastor, and Dr. Clark Crawford is the pastor now.

The Sunday-school is one of the best in the State, having an average attendance of 500. John W. Dragoo, superintendent; Fred McClelland, assistant superintendent; Harden Roads, superintendent senior department; Mrs. Zula M. Valentine, superintendent intermediate department; Mrs. Olive Roberts, superintendent junior department; Mrs. Elmer Gamble, superintendent primary department; Mrs. Catherine Zihn, superintendent home department; Mrs. Mabel F. Lewis, superintendent messenger service; Ira J. McKimmey, director of orchestra. The W. F. M. S. was organized in Simpson Chapel January 23, 1872, during Rev. J. E. Ervin's pastorate; Mrs. Mary Marsh, first president. It had 40 members the first year and raised $41.75; in 1906 it has 163 members and 59 life members, and raised $940.50. Mrs. Sue Harrington, president. The Y. W. F. M. S. was organized in 1899 by Mrs. C. J. Hudson, and has 45 members. Mrs. Emma M. Ervin was the first president. Miss Zenobia Stewart is president in 1906. They raised $91 for missions last year. Standard Bearers, organized in 1906, have 42 active members and 16 contributing members; Mrs. Zeralda Stewart, supervisor, and Miss Mildred Lambert, president. They do the same work as the woman's society and are being trained to step into their places at the proper time. King's Heralds have a small band, organized in 1902 by Miss Elizabeth Wilkinson; Miss Daisy Colvin, president. Little Light Bearers are a band of 252 children under and up to 10 years of age. This is the largest band in the Northwestern Branch. Mrs. G. W. Bucklin is the superintendent. The W. H. M. S. was organized May 1, 1891, with Mrs. Maggie Driscoll president, and 13 members; $40 was raised the first year. In 1906 Mrs. Ida M. Watson was president; $545 was raised, besides other special work. This society has two auxiliaries, the Queen Esther Band, organized August 2, 1896, by Mrs. Elmira McCarty, and has 35 members, Miss Nellie Carmichael, president; the Mother's Jewels have 12 members; Mrs. Jessie Mitchell, president. There is also one of the best chapters of the Epworth League in the State, organized in 1889 by Rev. C. U. Wade. It has 150 members; J. M. Kirkpatrick, president. The Ladies' Aid Society is composed of all the ladies in the church. They furnish the kitchen in the church, buy all the carpets and keep the church clean. They have bought new pews, individual communion set, and in many other ways have aided the official board in keeping up the church. They also furnish many things in the parsonage and keep up some of the repairs. Mrs. W. A. Meeks is president.

List of ministers who preached on the Muncie circuit before they had a church: Rev. Charles Downey, 1829; Greenbury C. Beeks, Robert Burns, Francis H. Cary, Wade Posey. Those who served in the first M. E. church,

High Street Methodist Episcopal Church.

located on the northwest corner of Washington and Elm streets, were John H. Hull, J. S. Donaldson, J. L. Smith, J. H. Hull, Z. S. Clifford, Isaac Stagg, Luther Taylor, O. H. P. Ash, J. B. Birt, J. Colclazer, J. B. De Mott, Nelson Green. Those who served as pastors of Simpson Chapel, erected in 1854: Nelson Green, V. M. Beamer, H. N. Barnes, F. A. Hardin, A. Greenman, A. Marine, G. C. Becks, Benj. Smith, S. H. Rhodes, W. S. Birch, N. H. Phillips, J. E. Ervine, W. J. Vigus, E. F. Hasty, R. H. Sparks, Clark Skinner, F. T. Simpson, C. W. Lynch, O. Stabler, W. J. Vigus, C. U. Wade. Those who have served as pastors of High Street M. E. church, dedicated in 1889: C. U. Wade, G. H. Hill, D. J. Naftzger, A. W. Lamport, E. B. Randle, and Clark Crawford, the present pastor.

Madison Street, Muncie.

This church was organized in Heekin Park, June 2, 1895, by Rev. N. H. Phillips and John Richards. Besides these, the charter members were: John L. Crawford, Elizabeth Crawford, Mary A. Richards, U. Ticknor, Flora Ticknor, Charles N. Ticknor, John W. Max, James Hundley, Jessie Hundley, Sophie Miller, Matilda Miller, Anna Graham, Leah Hilty, Lena Crawford. The society did not erect a building for several years. The corner stone of their present church was laid in the fall of 1899, and on the following February 4, 1900, the church was dedicated by Dr. Lewis Curtis. The pastors of this congregation have been: N. H. Phillips, John K. Cecil, Herman G. Porter, I. W. Singer, Frank C. Morris.

Whitely.

In the fall of 1895, several years after Whitely had taken its place among the suburbs of Muncie, a Methodist Episcopal society was organized in a store room on Broadway. The church building, at the corner of Courth and A streets, was begun in the same year, and was completed in 1897, at a cost of $3,000. The charter members and oldest members of this church are: Dr. Charles Frazer, Anna Frazer, Mabel Frazer, W. R. Deaton, Emma Deaton, Emily Shaw, Lottie Johnson, Jennie Johnson, Celia Coat, Arthur Coat, Laurence Coat, Annie Pearson, Clarence Pearson, John Pearson, E. P. Hubbard, Sophia Hubbard, F. H. Hubbard, Rose Hubbard, Electa French, J. F. Maynard, Lora Maynard, R. R. Johnson, Cora Johnson, Emma Palmer, Cyntha Shafer, Henry Clinger, Aggie Clinger. The list of pastors is: George W. Wilson, C. W. Coons, R. S. Reed, John K. Cecil, Herman C. Porter, Charles W. Shoemaker, P. J. Albright, Gilbert E. Martin, J. Cook Graham.

Avondale.

The Avondale Methodist Episcopal Church was built during the summer of 1891, by Rev. C. U. Wade, then pastor of High Street M. E. Church. November 8, 1891, the church was duly dedicated and a society was formed, composed of the following: Charles W. Parr, Amanda Parr, John F. Hutchings, M. J. Hutchings, Myrtle Hutchings, E. G. Stevens, Lydia Stevens, Maggie Stanley, Nora George, Samuel Huston, Catherine Huston, Earl H. Bryant, Aggie Bryant, Catherine Cook, J. W. and Rebecca McKinley, John and Lydia Spangler, Sarah Twibble. In 1906 improvements were effected on the church building at a cost of $1,250. The pastors who have served this congregation with the dates of their pastorates have been: C. U. Wade, Nov. 8, 1891, to April, 1892; A. I. Ruley, to April, 1893; T. Sells, to April, 1894; C. A. Wilson, to Aug. 1, 1895; C. W. Coons, 1895; J. F. Bailey, to 1898; C. J. Everheart, 1899-1900; C. H. Shoemaker, to 1902; G. W. Martin, to 1903; J. P. Chamnes, 1904 to April, 1907.

Normal City M. E. Church.

The Methodist congregation in Normal City was organized June 16, 1900. The building of the church was begun December 11, 1900, and when finished cost $8,000. A parsonage was built through the untiring efforts of Charles J. Everson while pastor, and is one of the best in the city, costing $3,200. The church was built with extensive plans to meet the conditions resulting from the founding of the Normal University, it being designed to afford sufficient accommodations for the students. When the university failed it was seen that the church was larger than needed, and the members were unable to meet the financial obligations. Rev. Everson has borne the brunt of the labors in rescuing the church from bankruptcy, and since the commencement of his ministry the indebtedness has been reduced from $3,100 to less than a thousand dollars, and that is, at this writing, provided for. As stated, the parsonage has also been built in the meantime. Mr. Everson has served the church four years. Those preceding him were: J. K. Cecil, six months; W. A. Griert, two years and a half; P. J. Albright, one year. The charter members and oldest members now living are: Mr. George Birt, Mary A. Covalt, T. J. Cheeseman, Martha Higman, A. R. Hoover, Mary J. Hoover, Emily F. Martin, J. W. McDaniel, Barbara McDaniel, J. W. Mendenhall, Lucy Mendenhall, Philena Wilson.

Yorktown.*

In the year 1871 I came to this place and opened a small millinery store. The town was about one-fourth the size it now is, but was big enough to have two saloons and several fighting men in it. The Methodist Episcopal church stood upon the ground now owned by Sol Donovan and is occupied by a dwelling near Mrs. Mock's home. It was a very old frame building with leaky roof and smoky stove. A few faithful hearts kept the fire burn-

*The article on the Yorktown church, written by Mrs. Elizabeth A. Matthe and revised by the present pastor, contains so much incidental history that we feel justified in publishing it entire.

ing on the Lord's altar. Rev. Fish was the pastor. He lived in Middletown
and preached every three weeks in the afternoon. His salary was mostly
paid by Mrs. Dr. Hittle, who was a life-long Methodist.

The members of the class so far as I am able to remember them were
Mrs. Hittle, Thopolis Davis and wife, Mother Moore and family, Mrs.
Eliza Parkinson, Joshua Dickerson and wife, Mrs. Jane Bryant, Joseph
Burgess and wife, Samuel Bennett and wife, Mrs. Elizabeth Browning, Mrs.
Nancy Swift. The old members now living are Mr. and Mrs. Henry Over-
mire, Mrs. Elizabeth Matthe, Mrs. Esther Mock, Mrs. Mary Marker, Mrs.
Nancy Jane Swift, Mrs. Mary Yingling.

The names of the old ministers up to the present time are as follows:
1868, Revs. Rammel and Murray; 1869, Rev. John Pittinger; 1870, Rev.
John Cain; 1871, Rev. John Black; 1872, Rev. Fish; 1873, Rev. McDaniels;
1874, Rev. John Pierce; 1875, Rev. McCarty; 1876, Rev. McKaig; 1877-8,
Rev. Wolpert; 1879, Rev. Thos. Sells; 1880-1, Rev. Wayman; 1882, Rev.
Wolverton, who left the work; 1883-5, Rev. J. W. Miller; 1886-7-8, Rev.
Powell, and Rev. John H. McMahan came to finish out the work as a supply
when the work was divided; 1889, Rev. Reinhart came and stayed three
months and Rev. Melvin Pittinger took his place, remaining until 1892;
1892-4, Rev. William Peck; 1894-6, Rev. John S. McElwee; 1896-7, Rev.
Chas. W. Shoemaker; 1897-1903, Rev. Edgar L. Jones; 1903 to Oct. 1st,
1904, Rev. Herman G. Porter; Oct. 1st to 1906, Rev. L. A. Sevitts; 1906-8,
Rev. Walter W. Kent.

The names of the old trustees so far as we are able to find out are:
Wm. K. Helvie, Jas. Burgess, Sam. Parkinson (all dead) and David Campbell. The old church was dedicated in June, 1878, during Rev. McCarty's
pastorate, which stood until the present beautiful structure was built.

My parents had taken their membership to the Pike's Peak school house
a few years previous, where a small class had formed and where my sister
Taressa and self had become members under the pastorate of Rev. Leroy
Rammel. There was also a few Protestant Methodists here at that time who
held services once a month in the old church. Jason Miller was the pastor.
Father Warfel and wife belonged to that church.

The Presbyterians owned an old brick church that stood on the ground
that the old school house stands upon. The members of their class were:
Dr. Horne and wife, Dr. Slack and wife, Mr. and Mrs. Alfred Yingling and
their family. They had preaching once a month by Dr. Todd of Muncie.
Neither church had any Sunday school class or prayer-meeting.

Near this church stood the school house, which was a low, one-story
frame building, containing two rooms. Mr. Austin VanWinkle and Henry
Brandon were the teachers. Mr. VanWinkle superintended a small Sunday
school that met in this building. Very few parents attended. It was looked

upon as a kind of prelude to the day school. Mr. VanWinkle lived in the
country and on Sunday morning when the weather was bad he would not
come, hence there was no Sunday school for that day. I remember one
morning when he did not come the boys insisted that we have Sunday school
anyway. Jacob Koonts volunteered to lead the singing if I would open with
the lesson. I was very much disturbed about the prayer, but finally found
the Lord's Prayer in the Bible and we read it in concert.

The next spring, Rev. Fish was removed and Rev. McDaniels was sent
on the work. The Sunday school died out, with the close of the day school,
and the next winter a different teacher was employed who did not take up
this work.

The next spring, Bro. John Pierce was sent to the work and we were
put into the Muncie District. He resided in Muncie and preached at Mount
Zion, West Chapel, and Daleville, Yorktown. I think he also preached at
Florence Chapel, Anthony town.

By reason of the death of some of the members, the class had drifted
from Pike's Peak to Daleville. The next winter Mr. H. H. Shoemaker and
Julia Sparr of Muncie were employed as teachers in the school. They immediately opened the Sunday school in the old house, with Mr. Shoemaker
as superintendent and Miss Sparr as secretary. She had a sweet voice and
led the singing. One song I remember as being a great favorite with the
school was "Gates Ajar." The parents began to take more interest, which
resulted in a Bible class, taught by Mr. Shoemaker. Owing to the sickness
of his wife he was compelled to give up the school, and a Mr. Bodkin took
his place. He did not continue the Sunday school work.

In the spring of 1874 Bro. Pierce was removed and Bro. Carnes came.
He immediately took steps toward building a new church and prevailed upon
my parents to bring their membership back to Yorktown. He organized a
building committee and a board of trustees. David Campbell, Daniel Parkinson, Joseph Burgess and my father, William Helvie, were the trustees.

The members of the Pike's Peak church put their names here also.
There was Aunt Betsy Helvie, Esther Richmond and Mr. Bratton and
family. Hard work was done that year in subscribing for the new building.
The Protestant members joined with us, for all realized the need of strength
for the new building. There were Father Warfel and wife, Mr. Jester and
wife, Jiles Patterson and wife and Mrs. Carrie Spann. The old church and
lot was sold to David Campbell. One lot was bought of and another donated by Mr. Summers. In December the contract was let for the building
and everybody was happy.

The women of the town put their heads together and planned for a
new carpet for the rostrum and aisles. They succeeded in getting the
carpet for the platform, but objection was raised against the matting for

the aisles, as it was considered useless to put something for the men to spit upon. Finally Mother Moor offered to weave a rag carpet if the material was furnished. By much hard work we got enough together to make it. The next year Bro. McCarty was sent on the work. In June the new church was dedicated. The young men of the town, at the very last moment, bought the new bell. In the afternoon a Sunday school was organized, with William Fontick as superintendent. Prayer-meeting was decided upon and Joshua Dickerson chosen class leader. Mrs. Henry Overmire, Mrs. Davis, Mrs. Spann, Mother Moor and Father Warfel were the teachers.

The next spring (1876) Bro. McKaig was sent to us, and Dick Hall was made superintendent of the school. He organized the first teachers' meeting. He also introduced the Lesson Leaves, which caused some people to think we were not studying the Bible.

The next year Bro. Woolpert was sent here and remained two years and lived in Yorktown. During the year 1879 Bro. Sells was the pastor, living in Middletown. Bro. Wayman succeeded him in 1880, being on the work two years. We had left the town for some time, and upon our return we found that Dick Hall had died and James Cook had moved away, and the Sunday school had taken a vacation for want of a superintendent. Very little interest was shown in church matters, but one good sister suggested that we pray for the Lord to send us a superintendent. The result was that in 1883 Bro. L. D. Colvin and family moved to town and brought their letters to the church. We immediately organized a Sunday school, with him as superintendent, his son Frank as chorister, and Mary Overmire secretary. An organ was purchased and the school was well attended.

That year Bro. Miller was sent here and remained two years. In 1885 Bro. Wolverton was sent to us, but gave up the work in a few months. The local preacher filled out the year. In 1886 Bro. Powell became our pastor and remained three years. About this time we were feeling the need of a resident minister and commenced to talk parsonage. But this would mean a division of the circuit, and this my father greatly opposed, feeling sure that Yorktown and Mount Zion could not support a minister alone. The matter was brought to a climax by Middletown becoming a station and we were left without a pastor.

Bro. McMahan of Middletown was sent to us as a supply, but did not bring his family. Owing to the sickness and death of my mother nothing was done toward the building of the parsonage for several months. One thing was sure, the church board made no effort toward it.

About the last week in July Mrs. Sparr and several other ladies of Muncie desired to organize a W. C. T. U. and set a date for that purpose. The first time they came there was not enough to organize, but they made another date, and as some of our women were very desirous to have a society of that kind we organized with 18 members. Mrs. Syntha Pauline was president and Mrs. Nettie Goings secretary. Quite a number of our country friends were included in this company, among them being Mrs. J. H. Koontz, Mrs. David Campbell, Ida Aldridge and others. This was the first woman's organization in Yorktown, and while a great many of the members were inspired with the hope that it would banish the saloon from our village, some of us had a hope that through it we could build a parsonage. So in a short time a few of us met in Mrs. Colvin's parlor to discuss the situation and form plans whereby we could carry out both objects. Our plans were laid before the society and met no strong objection. We had Mr. Harvey Koonts write us a form to take subscriptions on and commenced the work at once. The church board fell into line readily and came down with their subscriptions and advice. Mr. Colvin, Mr. Warfel and my father were made a kind of advisory board and all helped willingly. Enough subscriptions were taken during the fall to insure the success and some time had to be given to let them secure the amounts. Rev. Reinhart was removed at the end of the first quarter and his place filled by Bro. Melvin Pittinger, who was most helpful. So the building slowly but surely was finished. Mrs. Flowers had organized a Loyal Legion, and through their efforts the means was raised to build the veranda. The next year Bro. Pittinger was returned to us and married a very sweet young wife and brought her to the little home we had worked so hard to get ready for them.

In 1892 Bro. Peck was sent to us and stayed two years. In 1894 Bro. McElwee was sent to us and remained two years. During his pastorate the Woman's Aid was organized and has not had a day's rest since. Then came Bro. Shoemaker for one year. He organized the Epworth League, with Miss Daisy Colvin president and Miss Melissa Helvie Jones as president of the Juniors. In 1897 Bro. Jones was sent here and remained pastor six years. During his second year Miss Harriet Kemper organized the Woman's Foreign Missionary Society with Mrs. Mary Williamson president. It has been one of the greatest blessings in showing us the need of those less fortunate, and is educating us to self-denial and helpful work. During the first year of Bro. Jones' pastorate he held a good revival, and on his return for a second year it became expedient to build a new church.

The wheels of prosperity were already rolling in our community. Factories had sprung up and the population was rapidly increasing. A new school building was builded and the little one-room frame building was too small to hold the Sunday school any longer. Everybody was ready to help, for steady labor and good wages warm the heart and awaken the spirit of generosity. The building committee consisted of W. T. Warfel, Thomas Bauer and others. The trustees immediately proceeded to take subscriptions and the following year the new church was dedicated. Bishop

Moore (who was then editor of the Western Christian Advocate) preached the dedicatory sermon and took the needed subscriptions.

Nearly all whose names are mentioned in this paper are now in the Glory Land, and it is with the sense of the fleeting of time that we realize that we are standing in the front rank of those who are numbered with the oldest members of the Church.

Mount Zion.

Mount Zion M. E. church, in the northwest corner of Monroe township, had its origin in the first religious organization of Salem township. Judge John Tomlinson, at whose house the meeting was held; Dolly Tomlinson. Ralph Heath, Mary Heath, John Lain, Sarah Lain and Ella Price were members of the first congregation. Dr. S. W. Heath, of Sioux Falls, S. D., has given the following account of the church:

"The class was first organized about 1835, and meetings were held at the homes of John Brown, John McClintock and Ralph Heath. In the year 1849 a log church was built on the farm of Jesse McKimmey, one-fourth of a mile north of the present church. The following is a copy of the subscription list to pay for plastering and seating the old log church: John Lain, $4 payable in stock; Harvey Heath, $1.14 in wheat; James Goff, $1 in stock, paid 73 cents in grain; Joseph Burges, $1 paid in corn; Robert Heath, $1 paid in grain; Manlif Halstead, $1 to be paid in stock or grain; Seth Nation, $1 to be paid in cash, or five bushels of corn; Thomas Heath, 87½ cents paid in cash; James McKimmey, $1.20 paid in wheat. One hundred and fifty feet of ceiling plank was left over and sold to Thomas Heath at 75 cents per hundred. The following subscribers paid $1 each in cash: John W. Heath, James W. Heath, Ralph Heath, Jesse McKimmey, John Ross and John Lain.

"In the year 1863 John W. Heath and Thomas W. Tuttle donated ground on which the present church stands, which was built at a cost of $1,200. In the year 1879 it was remodeled at a cost of $700. The changes consisted of taking out the two single doors and placing double doors in the center; the windows were remodeled and the two side aisles were changed to a central aisle, and a belfry and bell were added.

"My father, James W. Heath, drew up the subscription paper and so-licited for the building of the old log church, and the last act of the writer in the old Mt. Zion neighborhood was drawing up the subscription papers for remodeling the church and Thomas W. Tuttle taking one list and canvass-ing the south and east part of the territory, and I took the north and west part. Allen Perdieu headed the list with $35, and we had his father-in-law, Jesse McKimmey, down for $15, but when we called on him and explained the plan he said that $25 ought to be all the committee should expect of him.

That was certainly very liberal for a man living about four miles from the church and getting to attend only once in three months. Old Aunt Milley Heath in giving her subscription said it would do her no good, but might benefit her grandchildren. Ten years later, returning from the west and visiting the old neighborhood, as we were approaching the church the bell was tolling for the funeral of old Aunt Milley. This was the first time we had heard that bell tolling."

Daleville.

The early history of Daleville Methodism in Daleville and vicinity belongs with the Mount Zion, Yorktown and other congregations of that vicinity. The Daleville M. E. church was organized August 16, 1894, at the home of J. C. Dale. Strong opposition tried to defeat the purposes of those whose hearts were set on this church, but since its organization the church has been prosperous. At the first meeting H. N. Herrick was presiding elder, and Rev. Thomas Petty, a local preacher, was presiding pastor. The first members, all of whom are living, were Mrs. Allie Dale, Mrs. Julia Feely and Miss Minnie Hoover. Meetings were held in a hall for one year, two revivals and fifteen additional members being secured during that time. James and Maria Fish, Thomas Feely and Mrs. Martha Nelson are the oldest of those members. During 1895 a church was constructed on South Main street in Daleville, and was dedicated in January, 1896. Charles Shoemaker preached the sermon at dedication, and C. U. Wade was elder. The church building cost $2,500. The pastors, with the length of their service, have been: Thomas Petty, seven months; C. N. Shoemaker, one year; E. L. Jones, six years; Rev. Porter, one year; G. N. Martin, two years; Cook Graham, one year.

Wheeling.

The Methodists organized a class at Wheeling about 1835-36. For many years the society worshiped in a frame schoolhouse that stood on the ground now occupied by the Odd Fellows' hall, but during 1870-71 the present brick building was erected, being dedicated in the latter year. The charge has been included in different circuits, and the records of the church are fragmentary and not continuous. Of the oldest members now living are Mrs. Mary Milhollin, Mrs. Sarah Bryan, Amos Shaffer and wife. Of the pastors of later years may be named: George W. Green, George W. Martin, George H. Myers, Edward Dickson, Calvin J. Graves, Carlos A. Luse and John M. B. Reeves, the present pastor.

Before the Wheeling class was organized, it is said that the first religious meeting held in Washington township occurred in the home of William Heal, conducted by Robert Burns, a Methodist missionary. This was in 1830, and the class then organized consisted of William Heal and wife,

Thomas and Susannah Littler and Mrs. Martha Jobes. From this originated Olive Branch church, named in honor of Olive Heal. In 1863 the society moved from the log church to a new building situated within Grant county.

Pleasant Valley.

This class was organized about 1896, and worships in the little church it then built one-half mile west of Anthony. Mahlon Crampton, Charles Crampton, William Langsdon, Harvey McKinley are the charter members still connected with the church. The pastors have been George W. Green, Rev. Hunt, J. H. McNary.

Delaware Chapel.

The Methodist society now known as Delaware Chapel, whose church is located west of Albany, in the northwest part of Delaware township, had its origin in a meeting of organization held in Stafford's schoolhouse probably about 1863. Ralph and Jane Stafford, Jefferson and Rebecca Walburn, Joanna Williams, Mrs. Rhody Wright and Mrs. Susan Justice were the charter members. The oldest members now connected with the church are George Stafford, James E. Stafford, Mrs. Catherine Brammer, Jacob Peterson, Wilber Peterson, Mrs. Christina Black, Mrs. Sarah Parrett. The church, in which the society still worships, was erected in 1876 at a cost of $1,500. The pastors, so far as they can be recalled, have been: Rev. Black, Eli Rammel, G. B. Work, H. N. Herrick, R. J. Parrett, David Powell, D. C. Woolpert, W. E. Curtis, J. A. Ruley; S. L. Johnson, 1890-93; T. F. Frech, 1893; Eli Davis, 1894-98; J. B. Cook, 1898-02; C. M. Hollopeter, 1902-06; L. A. Sevits, present pastor.

Bethel—Albany Circuit.

The Bethel M. E. church was organized in 1836 at the house of Eli H. Anderson, the charter members being Eli H. Anderson and wife, John Wilson and wife, Thomas Vincent, John Dinsmore and wife. The oldest members now living are D. M. Bell and wife, Manaen Vincent and wife, William Shirk and wife, James R. Babb and wife, George Michael and wife. A hewed log building erected in 1839 served as the church home until it was burned a few years later, when it was replaced by another hewed log house. In 1859 the present frame building was erected, though it was completely remodeled eight years ago. The earlier pastors are not recalled, but beginning with 1890 they have been: S. L. Johnson, to 1893; T. F. Frech, 1893; Eli Davis, 1894-98; J. B. Cook, to 1902; C. M. Hollopeter, to 1906; L. A. Sevits, present pastor.

Muncie African M. E.

This society was organized April 12, 1871, and of the small number of charter members Martha Fry is now the only one living. The society was incorporated in November, 1871, and the following year a church building was erected. William Walker, Edward Pearce, John Davis, William Hawgreens, Thomas Hawkins, John Davis were the first trustees and officers. The first building, at 1018 East Jackson street, was remodeled in 1902 at a cost of $2,800. The pastors who have served this organization have been: Jason Bundy, H. H. Wilson, John Stanton, B. J. Coleman, Jason Bundy, H. E. Steward, G. H. White, T. E. Wilson, Martin Coleman, W. H. Taylor, E. A. Johnson, J. J. Evans, J. L. Craven.

Trinity M. E. (Colored).

This society was organized in 1895, at a meeting on High street. The names of charter members and oldest living members as given by the present pastor are: E. L. Benson, N. A. Pondexter, C. E. Maneall, L. A. Chandler, Mrs. Julia Downs, George W. Scott, Mrs. Hulda Gilmore, Enoch Fletcher, Susie Scott, Dora Benson, Elisha Benson. The building on East First street now occupied by the society was completed March 4, 1899, at a cost of $660. The names of the succeeding pastors are: John Downs, Joel Perkins, J. A. Smith, Fred White, G. W. Bailey, Henry Griffen, W. W. Heston, N. S. Johnson, W. W. Locke.

First Methodist Protestant Church of Muncie.

This society was organized in 1872, at 614 East Jackson street, the charter members participating in that organization being: Emanuel Rich, Mary Rich, Robert Gorden, Margaret Gorden, L. U. Buchanan, Susana L. Buchanan, Mary Campbell. The oldest members of the society now living are P. W. Patterson, Mrs. R. M. Patterson, Mrs. Sarah Nichols, Mrs. R. A. Calleson, Mrs. Belle Moles, August Maick, Mrs. Minnie Maick, S. D. Friar, Mrs. S. D. Friar, Simon Marshall, Mrs. Kate Marshall, Mrs. Sarah McIlvane, Mrs. A. Perdieu.

In 1868 the Evangelical Association had built a brick church 24 by 44 feet at 614 East Jackson street, and in 1872, when Rev. J. H. Luse, who at that time was pastor of the Luray circuit M. P., organized the Muncie society, this property was purchased for use of the new church. The society remained a part of the Luray circuit until the conference of 1873, when it was named the Muncie circuit. In 1875 Muncie was made a station, with S. A. Flood as pastor. Under the pastorate of Rev. J. H. C. McKinney in the spring of 1893 the old brick building, having served its time and purpose, was torn down and was replaced by the present new building, which was dedicated in the fall of 1893, having cost about $7,000.

The pastors who have served this church since Rev. Luse have been: B. F. Clark, S. A. Flood, H. M. Boyer, E. H. Moles, S. J. Jones, T. E. Lancaster, G. W. Boxell, W. W. Lineberry, J. H. Langley, Hugh Stackhouse, J.

M. Reeves, J. H. C. McKinney, N. H. Sly, S. S. Stanton, George H. Sisson, W. A. Corkle, E. S. Hawkins.

THE BAPTIST.

Regular Baptist Church of Muncie.

It is said that church services according to Baptist doctrine and principles were held in Muncie as long ago as 1835, when the Methodists had the only church building in town. Elder Robert Tisdale was best remembered of the traveling ministers of this denomination who occasionally held services in the little village by White river. It would have been a small congregation had the Baptists alone attended. But a religious meeting was an unusual event, and persons of all creeds came to hear the preacher's message. Among the pioneers who were Baptists by profession was Edward Keasby, the hat maker. His wife and Mrs. Martin Galliher were also of the same church. Rev. Samuel Hervey preached here about twice a month from 1844 to 1847, and he was probably the most influential of the early ministers in molding opinion toward church organization.

A church organization was not effected until 1859, though the minutes of the meeting of the council speak of "reorganizing" a church at this point. The formal organization took place September 11, there being twelve original members: Martin Galliher, Rhoda Galliher, Abraham Helvie, Ann Helvie, Ann Keasby, Harriet McClellan, Hester Newell, Martha Patterson, Thomas Wireman, James S. Whitman, Eliza A. Whitman and Margaret Davis. Early history shows that services were held once a month in charge of Elder Williams.

On October 14, 1860, a committee was appointed to purchase a lot on which to build a church. Previous to this time services had been held in the court house. On June 12 it was decided to build of brick a house of worship 34x48. The structure stood on the northeast corner of Jackson and Jefferson streets, with entrance from the south, and although plain and unpretentious, yet the spirit of God was ever present. The church was dedicated June 8, 1862. Sermon by Dr. Bailey, of Franklin. The cost of the building was $2,131. During this time accounts are given of preaching by Elder Gage.

The first regular pastor, Rev. J. Bloomer, accepted a call on September 12, 1863. He was here for only a brief period, and until November, 1865, the church was without a regular pastor. At this time Rev. J. C. Skinner was elected to serve as pastor. He resigned January 11, 1868, and in the year following Rev. James M. Bennett was chosen pastor. There are very few now living who came into the church prior to Mr. Bennett's pastorate—Mrs. Adah Helvie Bell, Mrs. Elizabeth Elliott, and perhaps a few others. Mr. Bennett resigned May 7, 1871. Rev. Virgil then supplied the pulpit for a short time. Rev. A. E. Edwards was elected pastor April 19, 1872. Rev. Abel Johnson, one of the pioneer preachers of northern Indiana, was called November 5, 1872. During his pastorate John D. Nock was elected deacon, which office he held continuously for about thirty years. There were at that time but two deacons, the other being Mr. Elijah Langdon.

Rev. J. L. Irwin was called May 9, 1875. During his pastorate Edward Nutting was chosen deacon. All of the constituent members were active up to and after this date. In August, 1878, Rev. W. A. Stanton became pastor. He was succeeded in May, 1881, by Rev. N. B. Rairdon, whose labors were very successful. He served four years, during which time the building was remodeled and the church became self-supporting. In June, 1885, following Mr. Rairdon's resignation in April, Rev. W. H. Dennis took charge. He served until June, 1886.

In March, 1887, Rev. L. A. Clevenger was called. As the house was crowded at every service, it became necessary to enlarge or remove. Trustees A. L. Johnson, N. J. Galliher, J. D. Nock, Clerk S. Goodin, Brethren O. N. Tyler and T. J. Allen were appointed a committee to buy a lot and build a new church, modern and roomy, as the growth of the church demanded. They recommended as a site the southwest corner of Charles and Jefferson streets. Here the new church was erected at a cost of $27,000. The cornerstone was laid on October 5, 1889, ceremonies conducted by Rev. S. A. Northup, of Ft. Wayne. The dedication followed on July 20, 1890, by Pastor Clevenger, assisted by Rev. Albert Ogle, of Indianapolis, and Rev. W. W. Everett, D.D., of Chicago. During Mr. Clevenger's term of service the membership of the church was doubled, and to his faithful, intelligent labors we are today indebted for many of our most valued, most valuable members. Mr. Clevenger resigned in May, 1891, and during the summer of this year the church was without a pastor.

Rev. S. S. Clark was elected pastor the following October. To the season of his labors we are also indebted for many efficient co-workers. Mr. Clark resigned in April, 1895. In September of the same year Rev. J. B. Tuttle became pastor. The parsonage was built during his pastorate. He remained until November 1, 1897. Rev. C. N. Carter took charge of the church January 2, 1898. The church was at that time entering upon the period of large prosperity which it is enjoying to a greater degree today. Among the most noteworthy achievements, humanly speaking, since that time was the fitting and opening, in April, 1900, of the institutional annex, so prolific in results and so influential in shaping the policies which are now the basis of important lines of work.

The large additions which were made to the church in 1900 cost about $18,000. The parsonage, built in 1897, was rebuilt in 1900.

First Presbyterian Church, Muncie.

Seventeenth Street Baptist Church, Muncie.

This society of Baptists was organized April 16, 1893, in the old Congerville school building. The charter members were John H. Dawall and wife, Jacob C. Lynn, William A. Reese, Sr., and wife, I. J. Langdon, William Reese, Jr., Margaret Reese, Polly Reese, Albert Russel and wife. All these are living except Mrs. William Reese, Sr. In 1894 a house of worship was erected, costing $4,500, at the southeast corner of Seventeenth and Jefferson streets. The pastors who have served the congregation have been: J. P. Green, I. W. Martin, John H. Schenck, John C. Hayes (supply), C. C. Martin.

THE PRESBYTERIAN.

First Presbyterian Church, Muncie.

This church, which next year will celebrate the seventieth anniversary of its existence, has numbered among its members many of the best-known families of Muncie, and its history, which has several times been written in full, is filled with personal references to men and women who have been actively identified with Muncie from the pioneer times. The following brief sketch of the church has been contributed by Miss Neely:

The pastors who have followed one another in this church since its organization have been: Rev. Robt. Irwin, pastor from 1838 to 1849; Rev. William M. Stryker, from 1850 to 1852; Rev. John F. Boyd, from 1852 to 1853; Rev. Charles A. Munn, from 1854 to 1857; Rev. John W. Drake, from 1858 to 1861; Rev. I. N. Shepherd, from 1861 to 1865; Rev. Edward Barr, from 1865 to 1867; Rev. O. M. Todd, from 1867 to 1871; Rev. George A. Beattie, from 1871 to 1878; Rev. David S. McCaslin, D. D., from 1878 to 1882; Rev. George A. Little, from 1883 to 1890; Rev. Frank Harper Hays, D. D., from 1890 to 1896; Rev. William Henry Oxtoby, D. D., from 1897 to 1903; Rev. Harry Noble Wilson, D. D., from 1903 to 1907; Rev. B. M. Nyce, from 1907—

The First Presbyterian church of Muncie was organized July 14, 1838. As most churches of that day in what was then the early west, its life was one of struggle from the start, yet its founders, firm in the faith that inspired them, never swerved from the path of duty, never gave up the noble purpose which filled their hearts, though sometimes tried as by fire.

It was five years after its organization before the church had a building of its own. That was a grand day when the struggling congregation held their first service in the new house of worship—the frame meeting-house. An incident connected with the building of this church shows how misfortune followed them. The contract for finishing the church was given to Silas Morgan. Seasoned lumber was not to be had—the flooring had to be kiln-dried and worked by hand. About the time Mr. Morgan was ready to use the lumber the kiln took fire and all burned. This caused a delay of one year in the work.

The frame church was dedicated July 15, 1843. P. D. Gurley of Indianapolis preached the dedication sermon. Candles were used for lighting this church, an official member snuffing the candles round twice during an evening service. The form of announcement was: "There will be services in this house tonight at early candlelighting." Rev. Robert Irwin, who is remembered here by many, was the first pastor. He was an earnest, faithful Christian. His work was done under great difficulties and many hardships. Through cold and heat, through storm and swollen streams, in weakness and in health, he kept steadily on. House-to-house prayer-meetings were kept up. The pastor's son, Rev. Robert Irwin, writing of these prayer-meetings, says: "Their value did not impress me then as now. I attended because my father took me; yet the early impressions then made have never left me; the simple exposition of God's word, the hearty singing of the grand old hymns, the earnest prayers of Godly men, and the cordial greetings after service, fixed their impress on my life."

In this letter, written a short time before his death at St. Charles, Mo., he says: "I do not remember very distinctly about the missionary efforts of the church, but I am sure so important a matter was not forgotten. At home we were taught to deny ourselves for the sake of the cause. We were offered so much each week if we would do without sugar, tea, coffee or butter so that the missionary fund might be enlarged. It was a valuable lesson, though not very easy at the time."

He further writes: "Before me is the first call presented by the Muncie church. It is a venerable document and is dated Sept. 4, 1843. It bears the autographs of the following officers of the church: Thomas S. Neely, Jonathan Wachtel, Thomas Barnes, William S. Slack, John C. Helm, John Galbreath, Edward G. Keasby, Joseph Wilson, Jr., Benjamin Sayre. The call contains the usual formula of the Presbyterian church, 'And that you may be free from worldly cares and avocations, we hereby promise and oblige ourselves to pay you the sum of one hundred and fifty dollars in half yearly payments during the time of your being and continuing to be the regular pastor of this church.' Living was cheaper then. I find, on my father's expense book, 'Beef 2¼ cents per pound, pork 3 cents, flour $1.50 per hundred, corn 25 cents, five turkeys for $1.00.' Sugar was high, 20 cents a pound. The revenue from marriage fees did not enrich very extravagantly —one dollar was the usual price. On one occasion father was called to go twenty miles to marry a couple. He was busy planting corn at the time and yet could not refuse to go. Promising my sister Caroline and her girl friend, Margaret Sayre (now Mrs. Margaret March), the wedding fee if they would complete the corn planting. He undertook the journey over almost impassable roads; was gone nearly two days and returned with a 95-cent piece as the fee. How the young ladies spent their fortune I will leave for Mrs. March to tell, for she yet remains with you, honored and beloved.

"Two entries in my father's journal may interest the ladies: 'June 21st, 1848, about 3 o'clock, I met with a number of our female members in the Presbyterian church to organize a sewing society. It was accomplished, but not without some opposition. A constitution was read and adopted and eleven females subscribed to it.' June 27th, 1849, the sewing circle presented two very neat and excellent chandeliers to the church. They cost $9.75. This being prayer-meeting evening, they were lit and performed most admirably, for we could read the hymn-books in *any part of the church.*"

Rev. W. N. Stryker succeeded Mr. Irwin as pastor; he was a good man and a fine scholar. The first parsonage—one-story frame—was built during his pastorate. Rev. J. W. Drake came next; the church prospered while under his care; he was a Godly man. Rev. I. N. Shepherd came to Muncie Nov. 13, 1861, preaching his first sermon the following Sunday, Nov. 17.

While the remains of President Lincoln were lying in state—Wednesday after his assassination—Mr. Shepherd, at special memorial services in the Presbyterian church, preached from the text, "Know ye not that there is a prince and a great man fallen this day in Israel?" This was in April, 1865.

Nov. 20th, 1865, Rev. E. Barr was unanimously elected pastor with a salary of eight hundred dollars a year and fifty dollars for moving expenses. March 3d, 1867, Mr. Barr told his church he intended to leave them and go to Lafayette.

The building now occupied by the church was built during Mr. Hay's pastorate. To his interest, zeal, judgment and industry are largely due the completeness of this structure. It was dedicated June 24, 1894. Dedication sermon by Rev. J. A. Rondthaler, D. D., of Indianapolis. The officers at this time were: Elders T. S. Neely, J. N. McClung, W. R. Snyder, George B. Best, George R. Green, J. C. Johnson, P. K. Morrison; Deacons W. A. Blair, S. L. Potter, J. W. Ream, D. K. Freeman, B. W. Bennett, O. B. Bannister; trustees, F. E. Putnam, W. L. Little, J. C. Johnson; superintendent of Sabbath school, J. T. Thorburn; musical director, George H. Andrews; organist, Clarence H. Carson.

First United Presbyterian Church, Muncie.

April 10, 1889, in the Board of Trade rooms in the Boyce block, this society was organized, after a sermon by Rev. J. T. Wilson. The following nineteen persons constituted the original membership: Peter T. King (a ruling elder), Mrs. Isabelle King, Miss Margaret T. King, Miss Mamie B. King, Peter K. Morrison, Mrs. Jane Wilson, Mrs. I. M. Wilson, Alexander

Giboney, Mrs. Mary Giboney, Miss Ella M. Giboney, Jesse E. Gartin, Mrs. Nannie J. Gartin, William Dunlap, Mrs. Mary Dunlap, Warren K. Moore, Andrew McComb, Mrs. Mary McComb, Alexander Halliday, Mary B. Dunlap. Of these Peter T. King is the only one remaining in the congregation, though most of them are still living.

In September, 1890, the society began the erection of a church building on Adams and Ebright streets, and the church was dedicated December 7, 1890, the total cost of the property being $8,000. January 31, 1892, the church was destroyed by fire, but was rebuilt the same year. In 1906 a parsonage was built on the north end of the church lot, at a cost of $3,200, giving a complete, comfortable and modern home for the pastor.

The pastors who have served the church to date have been: James T. Wilson, April, 1889, to July, 1890; Robert L. Hay, to April, 1892; George T. Scott, July, 1892, to April, 1894; John C. White, July, 1894, to August, 1898; R. G. Smith, July, 1899, to July, 1904; R. E. Lackey, to October, 1905; A. G. Hastings, who has been pastor since October, 1905.

THE CHRISTIAN.

The Jackson Street Christian Church.

The organization of the Jackson Street Christian Church dates from June 27, 1868. As early as 1848 Elder Benjamin Franklin held a meeting in a school house called the "Seminary," located at the present site of the Jefferson school, and at several other times before the organization was effected itinerant preachers paid visits to Muncie, and some converts to the Disciple's plea were gained, but these early records are incomplete. The present history begins with the summer of 1865, when the families of Jonathan P. Adamson and Andrew J. Slinger, then strangers, came to the town of Muncie. An incident happened about this time which illustrates the feeble status of the Disciples of Christ here. Mrs. Slinger, while attending a picnic at Smithfield, met a lady acquaintance from Muncie who mentioned a number of her friends, and then added that she had a neighbor, Mrs. Emily Adamson, whom she thought a splendid woman, but whose acquaintance she did not desire as Mrs. Adamson was a "Campbellite." Mrs. Slinger understood what this meant and lost no time in calling on Mrs. Adamson. In similar ways a few Disciples found each other and under the stress of severest opposition known to that day of intense religious prejudice the history of the Jackson Street Christian Church began its career.

Two itinerant Christian preachers from New Castle, David Geary and Aaron W. Moore, held occasional meetings. However, Dr. George W. Thompson of Union City did the important ministerial work of organizing the congregation and of giving it the start which has led to the great devel-

Jackson Street Christian Church "Disciples"

opment of the church. Most of the early meetings were held in the Louthian school house about two miles south of the city, but later they were held in the homes of the members.

After the organization in 1868 the congregation continued to meet in the private homes of the members, principally at the Adamson home on North High street. During the year 1873-4 Walling's Hall, just west of the present Court House, was used for a place of worship. But after one year the church found itself financially unable to pay the hall rent and the members were again compelled to hold their meetings in their homes or in the Court House. Finally, however, under the wise leadership of Dr. Thompson, the membership grew in numbers and financial strength until they were able to secure a church home. In 1875 a lot was purchased on the northwest corner of Jackson and Council streets at a cost of $500 and a church house built thereon at a cost of $3,739.14, exclusive of furniture. A part of the furniture was donated, the remainder cost $226.20. Dr. L. L. Carpenter, of Wabash, Indiana, preached the dedicatory sermon Sunday, November 21st, 1875. Mary J. Carmichael (now Mrs. Marcus Topp) was the first person baptized in the new church.

The following were among the names of those first identified with the organization of the church: Jonathan P. Adamson and wife, Emily; Amos Wilson, George Moore, Andrew J. Slinger and wife, Linda M.; Lizzie Louthian, Sally Mansfield, Martha A. Graves, Mrs. Matilda Rader, Hannah J. Pucket, Abigail Hines, Mrs. Rebecca Cumings, Mrs. Rebecca Carmichael, Mrs. A. J. Claypool, Harvey Wilkins, Elizabeth Frank, Sarah J. Wilkinson, Nancy Eber, Maggie Louthian (now Mrs. H. C. Haymond), George Louthian, Mr. and Mrs. C. S. Wachtell and Andrew McGalliard.

The first board of elders consisted of John Shoemaker, James Stewart and Jonathan P. Adamson. Messrs. Shoemaker and Stewart were members at Daleville, but served as officers here until other members were gained who could take their places. Mr. Adamson continued an elder until his death, June 17, 1889. His wife, "Aunt Emily," as she is affectionately styled, still survives and is the oldest charter member of the church.

Rev. Oliver Carmichael soon became a member, and while retaining his membership here has been prominent for many years as a minister of other Christian churches in the county. The preachers who regularly ministered to the congregation while worshiping in the building on West Jackson street were as follows: W. W. Witmer, Milton T. Hough, J. H. Vinson, Dr. W. A. Hough, E. B. Scofield, A. L. Orcott, J. L. Parsons, A. Martin, W. B. F. Treat.

The congregation grew so rapidly that before the year 1895 it was found necessary to provide larger quarters, so a lot was secured at the southeast corner of Jackson and Elm streets at a cost of $3,600, and a

commodious building was erected thereon at a cost of $20,000. The furni-
ture, including the pipe organ, cost $5,000 more. The building committee
consisted of Dr. W. A. Spurgeon, chairman; Robert N. Ball, C. S. Wachtell,
A. N. Waggoner and Robert H. Branch. The main auditorium of the
present building has a seating capacity of 400 and the Sunday school room
which opens conveniently into the main auditorium, has a seating capacity
of slightly more than that number. The building was dedicated on Sunday,
May 12, 1895. Elder Z. T. Sweeney, of Columbus, Indiana, preached the
dedicatorial sermon.   •

The Rev. W. B. F. Treat, who was pastor at the time of the removal
of the congregation from West Jackson street to its present location, continued to minister to the congregation until October of that year. Then
Rev. William D. Starr became the minister and served for three years. He
was succeeded by Rev. J. H. MacNeill, who served for three years. Rev.
T. A. Reynolds then served for four years, when in the fall of 1905 Rev.
William Huddleston Allen became the minister and is still serving the congregation. The congregation has grown so rapidly that within a short time
a still larger building must be erected. The present building cannot be made
to seat with comfort more than 850 people, whereas the membership of the
church numbers about 1,200.

When the church was first organized in 1868 it took the name of
"Church of Christ meeting in Muncie, Indiana." Soon after the congregation began worshipping in their building on Jackson and Council streets
they adopted the name "First Christian Church of Muncie, Indiana," and
this name was continued until 1905, although during a portion of that time
the title of the real estate owned by the church remained in the original
name. In 1905 the congregation adopted the name "Jackson Street Christian
Church of Muncie, Indiana."

It is one of the tenets of this brotherhood that any New Testament name,
such as Church of God, Church of Christ or Christian Church may appro-
priately be adopted by any congregation as a church name.

The official board of the church consists of thirty members; five elders,
including the minister; sixteen deacons and five trustees, the treasurer, the
clerk, the Sunday school superintendent, the president of the Senior Christian Endeavor Society.

The personnel of the official board is as follows: Elders, W. H. Allen,
minister; C. C. Pavey, W. R. Windsor, Prof. Ernest P. Wiles, Dr. James
N. Quick; Deacons, Charles C. Bryan, Charles D. Gray, Arthur B. Jester,
Charles W. Collins, N. A. Butterfield, E. J. Butterfield, C. S. Wachtell,
Horace G. Murphy, D. W. Stacy, G. W. Rowlett, W. P. Gilmore, D. N.
Miller, Walter Clark, I. B. Howard, C. F. Grunden and E. L. Addison;
Trustees, Robert N. Ball, J. A. Meeks, Dr. John C. Quick, P. V. Stewart

and C. S. Wachtell.   J. C. Bartling is church clerk, Robert Å. Ball is treasurer.   Horace G. Å urphy is president of the official Board and J. W. Allen is secretary.

. The Sunday school has an enrollment of more than 500 members and, as far as the room in the church building will permit, is modern in every respect. Clayton Bartling is superintendent.

It is the custom of the church to provide flowers for poor people or persons suffering from illness and for the funerals of deceased members. Mrs. E. L. Addison is chairman of the Flower committee.

The Senior Christian Endeavor Society has an enrollment of about 100 members. There is also a strong Junior Society. Å r. John W. Allen is president of the Senior Society and Å iss Olive Spurgeon is superintendent of the Junior Society.

The church also has a Ladies' Aid Society of more than 100 members, of which Mrs. R. Å. Ball is president. The society is very active in raising funds and carrying on the local missionary benevolent work of the church.

The Auxiliary to the Christian Women's Board of Å issions has a membership of about 100 members. Mrs. Sarah Allen is president. The activities of the organization are given to religious education and missions in both home and foreign fields. During the last year it raised more than $250 for those purposes. It has a permanent endowment fund of $500, known as the Å ary Å ansfield fund.

The Young Ladies' Å ission Circle has about 75 members. This society acts in connection with the C. W. B. Å. Å iss Grace Addison is president of the Circle and Mrs. Horace G. Å urphy is superintendent.

All of the missionary enterprises of the church are centered in a committee of six members from the official board and known as the committee on missions and benevolences. Prof. Ernest P. Wiles is chairman of this committee. On the fourth Sunday evening of each month a collection is taken for the benefit of poor and needy people in the city. The church has become a living link in the American Christian Å issionary Society. It gives $300 annually and supports a missionary in that field. It has also been given a life directorship in the foreign Christian Å issionary Society, the church having given more than $500 to foreign missions during the past year.   Horace G. Å urphy.

June 25, 1907.

First Christian Church, Muncie.

This church, whose home is at Elm and North streets, was organized February 15, 1892, in the Blue Ribbon hall. The charter members were: Jim Garrard, Savannah Garrard, William Fisher, Å aggie Fisher, Å adaline Pershing, Laura Selman, Anna Selman, Harvey Å. Cates, Cordelia Cates,

Julia Cates, Anna Coffin, Nancy North, Myra Miller, D. B. Miller, Eva Cates, Lew W. Cates, Dr. R. A. Bunch, Eli Hobbs, Isaac H. Gray, Hattie J. Gray, Massa Green, Eunice Green, Mrs. A. C. Blount, Elmira Thornbury, Edwin Wright, May Wright, James Newberry, Mrs. James Newberry, Albert C. Dudley, Sarah E. Dudley, J. C. Sharp, Mrs. J. C. Sharp.

The first church building had the outward appearance of a dwelling, two stories high, and was built in the fall of 1896. In 1902 was commenced the present building, and was completed and dedicated in June, 1903, the cost of the building complete being nearly $20,000.

The society was organized by Rev. J. R. Cortner, and the pastors who have followed him have been: W. T. Warbinton, D. L. Shoemaker, Daniel B. Atkinson, A. L. Platt, Frank P. Trotter, J. F. Burnett. At the time this information was given the church was without a pastor, but Daniel B. Atkinson was to commence his duties September 1, 1907.

White Chapel Christian Church.

This church was organized January 14, 1881, in Delaware township, three miles south of Albany, by Rev. John R. Cortner. For a house of worship they purchased the church formerly owned by the Methodist class, that had disbanded.

There were thirty-three charter members, viz.: Samuel Campbell, Pauline Campbell, Eliza Campbell, Levi Booner, Amelia Booner, Martha A. Jones, Catharine Jones, Benjamin Jones, Geo. W. Jones, William Goings, Adelia A. Goings, William H. Thornburg, Cynthia Thornburg, Henry Reasoner, Ella Reasoner, Madaline Pershing, Mary A. Godlove, Emma Godlove, Mary Garretson, Wm. K. Garretson, James Marquell, Louise Marquell, John Crites, Martha J. Jones, R. A. Bunch, William Walburn, Emery C. Cline, E. H. Dowell, John Friddle, Mary Friddle, Alice Baily, Lina Cline, Louisa Sutton. The oldest members now living are: Pauline Campbell, Eliza Campbell, Levi Booner, Amelia Booner, Adam Boots, Scott and Amanda Cline, James and Ellen Friddle, Ella Reasoner, Dortha Whitehair, John and Orila Burden, Henry and Esther Canter, Calvin and Elisabeth Jacobs, James and Louisa Markwell, Harvey and Elizabeth Pogue, Benjamin Selvey, Zachariah Shreves, Elisabeth Zehnor.

The present church building was purchased of the trustees of the M. E. Society at Albany, at a cost of $300, some time in the month of January, 1882, and was the third building on that same site. Prior to the organization of the church, services were held in the schoolhouse at Sharon by Rev. Thomas Brandon and Rev. John R. Cortner. After the organization of the church in January, 1881, Rev. John R. Cortner served the church as pastor until September, 1884. Those that have since served the church in that capacity are as follows: Rev. D. S. Davenport, 1884 to 1886; Rev. Gossett,

1887 to 1888; Rev. C. F. Byrkett, 1888 to September, 1889; Rev. G. W. Johnson, September, 1889, to September, 1891; Rev. O. S. Green, September, 1891, to September, 1892; Rev. C. F. Byrkett, September, 1892, to July, 1895; Rev. A. M. Addington, September, 1895, to September, 1896; Rev. R. P. Arrick, September, 1896, to 1900; Rev. I. V. D. R. Johnson, 1900 to September, 1905; Rev. E. G. Walk, March, 1905, to September, 1905; Rev. A. M. Addington, September, 1905, to the present time.

Christian Church, Albany.

The church was organized in a hall known as "Smith's Hall," in Albany, February 19, 1883, by the Rev. John R. Cortner, with 15 charter members, as follows: Ezra Bantz, A. J. Delong, Elisabeth Delong, John Crites, Elisabeth Crites, Levi Friddle, Martha Friddle, Isaac N. Flinn, Abner Wolverton, Rachel Wolverton, Rueben Bartlett, Catharine Bartlett, Joseph Hunt, Rachel N. Hunt, Christopher Star. The oldest members now living are: Levi and Martha M. Friddle, Rachel Wolverton, Reuben and Catharine Bartlett, Philip Cochren, Catharine Strong, William and Mary Champ, Miles and Catharine Miller, Edward Pace, John Brown, Stephen D. Frank, Clara Phillips, Samuel and Elisabeth Barkman, Harvey and Dora Meranda, Philip and Sarah Vincent, Joseph and Christie Wasson, George and Sarah Friddle, William and Ella Hobbs, Milton and Matilda Meranda, David and Elisabeth Slonaker, James and Comfort Burnside, James and Ann St. Clair, Joseph and Phebe Allen, Henry and Alice Marquell.

They built a substantial frame church house on the corner of Water and Manor streets in Albany on the present site. They have a very neat and commodious parsonage on the same lot. The entire value of the property is about $2,500.

Rev. J. R. Cortner served as pastor for three years; Rev. Clement Myers, Rev. W. L. Lundy, Rev. Geo. W. Johnson, one year each in the order named; Rev. C. F. Byrkett, for three years; Rev. F. F. Canada, one year; Rev. R. P. Arrick, for five years; Rev. I. V. D. R. Johnson, for three years; and Rev. A. M. Addington is now serving his sixth year. The church is in a very prosperous condition, free from debt, and pays all expenses by the free-will offerings of the members and the friends of the church.

Yorktown Christian Church.

This society was organized during the nineties, and their church building, which cost $1,300, was dedicated to worship May 1, 1892. The charter members of the organization were: Elijah Stevens, Mary Stevens, Alfred Jones, Lillian Jones, Joshua Jester, Eliza J. Jester, Sarah Crawford, Mrs. Cora Burk. The pastors who have served the congregation have been Elders

O. P. Snodgrass, Oliver Carmichael. Thompson, Webb, Cecil Franklin, E. L. D. Stamper.

Philadelphia Christian Church.

Articles of agreement were made in 1841 by the members of the Christian congregation at what is known as the Philadelphia church.. The charter members were the following: Vesta Halstead, Leonard Halstead, Martha Halstead, Charley Miller, Mary Miller, Martha McAlister, Lucinda Whitehead, Mary Jane Halstead, Jefferson McLenahan, Basha Hart, George Whitehead, David Wolf, Cornelius Vanarsdol, A. H. Kenedy, Abraham Yockey and Mary McCormick. Of these sixteen members the only one alive at this writing is Mary McCormick.

The first building, which was erected on the present site probably about 1842-43, was constructed of hewn logs, the labor of hewing and putting the timbers together being about the only expense connected with the building. The second and present building is of brick, constructed some years ago at a cost of about $1,200. The officiating ministers at the organization of this church were Rev. C. Vanarsdol, Andy McNees and James Lisk. As the early records are gone, only some of the later pastors can be given, namely: S. M. Stone, 1892; T. A. Spitzer, 1893; Wesley Grey, 1895; A. M. Addington, 1902; T. A. Spitzer, 1905; —— Bales, 1906; N. H. Thornburg, 1907.

Christian Church, Daleville.

The original society is said to have been organized at the barn of Major John Hupp, two miles east of Daleville, in 1845, but from another source of information it seems that the active organization was not effected until 1853, in the brick schoolhouse in Salem township, where the meetings were held after being transferred from the barn. Among the earliest members of the church were James and Drusilla Stewart, Jonas and Jane Shoemaker, Samuel and Mary Dusang, John and Maria Shoemaker, David and Amanda Shoemaker, John and Catharine Hupp. Part of the society after united with that at Middletown. In the late sixties a church building was begun in Daleville, and was dedicated in January, 1870. The original cost of this building was $3,000, and in 1903 it was remodeled into a modern church edifice at a cost of $6,000. The pastors who have served the congregation have been: David Franklin, Benjamin Franklin, Joseph Trowbridge, George W. Thompson, Robert Edmonson, John P. New, Jospeh Franklin, Daniel Franklin, Wesley Hartley, John Brazelton, —— Ludwig, Love H. Jameson, Walter Carpenter, Arthur Shoemaker, Burner, Bass, C. B. Coleman, A. L. Orcutt, Tine Carmichael, Harkins, Collins, Blankenship and F. D. Muse.

Hoffherr Chapel Christian Church.

Hoffherr Chapel, situated in Mt. Pleasant township, a mile and a half northwest of Yorktown, was erected in 1901 and dedicated to worship the first Sunday in April, 1902, by Elder Oliver Carmichael and J. H. Vinson, of Gas City, Ind. The building cost $1,500. The church society, which now has a membership of seventy, was organized May 8, 1902, the first officers and members being as follows: Elders, O. P. Snodgrass, A. F. Jones, James Jester; deacons, Joshua Jester and D. L. Humbert; members, R. H. Curtis, Marneva Reed, Elizabeth Jones, Maranda Kemp, Kate Jester, Eliza Jester, Rebecca Snodgrass. Oliver Carmichael, J. H. Vinson and T. A. Reynolds are the ministers who have conducted services at the chapel since the organization. The trustees at this writing are Joshua Jester, A. F. Jones and D. C. Childs.

Pleasant Run Christian Church.

The Hoffherr Chapel, mentioned above, is a branch of the older organization called Pleasant Run, and is now the most vigorous society outside of Yorktown in Mt. Pleasant township. Services under the Christian denomination have been held in the township for seventy years, but the organizations have grown and declined with the passing of the years. The Pleasant Run church record shows an organization as far back as 1858, with such names as Samuel Snodgrass, Daniel Van Buskirk, Thomas Cummings, William Reed and others among its leading members. During the war the society dwindled and finally broke up. In 1885 there was a reorganization, with the following as officers: Elders, George B. Snodgrass, A. F. Jones, James A. Jester, Jefferson K. Snodgrass; Deacons, Frederick Applegate, I. G. Snodgrass, John W. Jones. The church built up to 175 members, but it has since declined on account of deaths and removals and various causes, and in 1902 a large part of the Pleasant Run congregation organized as the Hoffherr Chapel. The present elders of the Pleasant Run church are: O. P. Snodgrass, J. A. Jester, A. F. Jones.

THE EPISCOPAL.

Grace Church Parish.

The first notice of any service of the church in Muncie is in a report to the General Board of Missions in June, 1839. It reads as follows: "The Reverend Mr. Fiske has officiated not only at Richmond, his proper station, but at Cambridge, Philometh, Muncietown, and at Eaton, Ohio; having at the latter place organized a parish." The next church service in Muncietown, so far as known, was held in the Presbyterian place of worship in November, 1859, by the Right Rev. George Upfold, D. D., Bishop of Indiana, assisted by the Rev. John D. Wakefield, D. D., rector of St. Paul's church, Richmond, Indiana.*

In 1870 services were held on week-day evenings by the Rev. George B. Engle, rector of Holy Innocents, Indianapolis, and still canonically resident in the diocese. Mr. Engle came to Muncietown at the invitation of Mrs. Caroline J. McCulloch and Miss Mary Burbank.

In 1875, through the efforts of Mrs. J. A. Heinsohn, a service was held in the opera house by the Rt. Rev. Joseph Cruikshank Talbot, D. D., LL. D., and an organization effected. The Rev. Jesse Richard Bicknell was appointed missionary, and services were held in the opera house and the council room in the city building. In March, 1875, a business meeting of the church people and others interested was held in the parlors of the Kirby House. A committee was appointed consisting of Charles A. Willard, John M. Kirby, A. R. Brown, A. H. Hamilton, J. E. Burson, J. A. Heinsohn and J. D. Williams to prepare a certificate of organization. Through the earnest work of the Rev. Jesse R. Bicknell a class of fourteen was presented to the bishop for confirmation; this was the fourth Sunday after Easter, May 14, 1876. Those confirmed were: John M. Kirby, Mary F. P. Kirby, Florence Shaw Brown, Wm. Shaw, Malvina R. Swain Spilker, Milissa Ann Turner Ethel, Clarissa Jackson Shipley, Fannie Shipley, Henrietta Holmes Hodge, Mary Caroline Smith, Letitia Smith, Harriet Galbraith, Anna Galbraith. During this same year the original church was built, at a cost of $650, on a lot the lease of which was donated by Mrs. John W. Burson.

In 1881 the lot on the southeast corner of Adams and Mulberry streets was purchased at a cost of $1,850 cash, and the church moved to its new foundation. During the three years' rectorship of the Rev. John W. Birchmore, the church was enlarged by the addition of a graceful nave, at a cost of $1,200, the old church forming a chancel and vestryroom. The church and sanctuary were at various times enriched by beautiful memorial gifts of altar and reredos, credence, bishop's chair, chancel rail, altar cross, vases, processional cross, font, prayer desk, organ, chancel books and music. The first gift to the church was the altar in memory of Mrs. Mary F. P. Kirby, wife of John M. Kirby. The baptismal font was a thank offering given by John M. Kirby at the baptism of his daughter Sarah, now Mrs. Wm. Church. The pipe organ was the gift of Mrs. Caroline McCulloch, a few years before her death. The prayer desk was carved by Miss Jeanette Love and presented by Miss Jeanette and Miss Nannie Love. The litany desk was given by Mrs. Samuel P. Anthony in memory of her parents, Mr. and Mrs. S. B. Bayless of Fort Wayne. Mr. George Olcott, brother of Mr.

*The following item occurred in one of the old Muncietown papers: ''Rt. Reverend Jackson Kemper, Bishop of the Diocese of Missouri, and Missionary Bishop of Indiana, preached at the court house in Muncietown, Tuesday, June 12, 1844.''—G. W. H. K.

Edward Olcott, was the donor of the bishop's chair and large front window in the present church. This window had been in the old parish church of Mr. Olcott's home town in Charlestown, New Hampshire. An oil painting of the Ascension of Christ was given by Mrs. J. R. Marsh and Mrs. R. J. Beatty. The altar desk, chancel books and markers were given by Mrs. Ada K. Over as a memorial to her son. The altar rail was given by Mr. and Mrs. Frederick E. Putman and Mr. and Mrs. Edward Olcott as a memorial to Mrs. Mary Kirby. The altar cross was the gift of Mr. and Mrs. Edward Olcott as a thank offering at the christening of their little daughter Mary. The credence was given as a memorial to her. A pair of brass vases were also given by Mr. Olcott in memory of his mother; and the silver communion service as a memorial to his brother, George Olcott. The processional cross was the gift of Mr. Willis Kutz. Mrs. Sarah Hartley gave the cover to the font; also the ewer and shell successively at the baptism of her children. The white brocade dossel cloth was the gift of the Guild of the Royal Cross, while the brass pole on which it rests was the gift of the Ladies' Auxiliary and the Guild of the Royal Cross. Mrs. Mark Claypool embroidered and gave one of the handsome altar cloths, while Mrs. Harriet M. Johnston and several of the other women of the church have embroidered and given altar cloths and book markers for the service.

Since the beginning of the regular services the following clergymen have had charge here: They are the Rev. Jesse R. Bicknell, the Rev. Mr. Root, while the church was yet a mission; and the following were the rectors after organization: The Rev. Mr. Allen, the Rev. F. D. Jaudon (1881 to 1882), the Rev. J. W. Birchmore (1883 to 1886), the Rev. R. Collison (1886), the Rev. F. W. Henry (1887 to 1890), the Rev. J. A. Antrim (1891), the Rev. F. O. Grannis (1891 to 1896), the Rev. H. M. Denslow (1896 to 1902), the Rev. W. K. Berry (1902 to 1906), and the Rev. F. F. Kraft, who is the present rector, having taken charge of the parish in September, 1906. During this time there have been 304 baptisms, 229 confirmations, 83 marriages, and 114 burials. During the last year there have been 3 marriages, 6 funerals, 12 baptisms, 16 confirmations. The church now has three societies: St. Martha's Guild, Saint Monica's Guild, and the Woman's Auxiliary. St. Martha's Guild makes a regular and generous contribution to the church work. Saint Monica's Guild is the sewing society of the parish and has made and given to the church the vestments for the choir boys. The Woman's Auxiliary was organized under the rectorship of the Rev. Mr. Henry and is a branch of the missionary society of the general church. Mrs. Caroline McCulloch was the first president of local branch of the Auxiliary, and continued to be so as long as she lived. Other organizations which have existed in the church, but which have been succeeded by the later societies, are the Ladies' Afternoon Social Guild, Order of the

Sisters of Bethany and Brotherhood of Saint Andrew. The Sunday school
has worked along with the church from the first and has always done credit.
able work. The good these church societies have done can scarcely be over.
estimated, and indeed it is certainly showing an honor to women's work that
Mr. McCulloch is to build the beautiful new church on the site of the old
one in memory of his wife and mother, two of the best workers of Grace
church parish. Probably the parish owes its existence more to Mr. McCul.
loch's mother than to any other person. At one time she was the only com.
municant in Muncietown, and the church today is the result of her efforts
when she started alone in the work.

In the spring of 1906 Bishop Francis, bishop of the diocese, announced
that Mr. McCulloch would build a church, parish house and rectory in mem.
ory of his wife and mother. A building committee was appointed consisting
of Bishop Francis, Messrs. Olcott, Marsh, Brady and Sampson, Mrs. Arthur
Smith and Mrs. Sarah Keiser, sisters of Mr. McCulloch, and Mrs. Harriet
Johnston, who immediately arranged for competitive plans. Several thou.
sand dollars was given to the building committee by Mr. McCulloch to defray
the expenses attendant upon the selection of plans. Plans were submitted
by Architects Wing and Mahurin of Fort Wayne, Abram Garfield of Cleve.
land, Sutcliffe of Chicago, and Alfred Grindel, formerly of Muncie, but now
of Indianapolis. The latter was successful in making a satisfactory set. The
plans as drawn by Mr. Grindel called for the erection of a church, parish
house and rectory of the Old English style. The three edifices will be of
Bedford stone, rock faced. The church, the central building of the group,
will be particularly beautiful. The nave will seat 350 people, and the morn.
ing chapel will accommodate about forty-eight. The chancel is very large
and will house a marble altar of striking design; the choir rooms and sacristies
will be connected with the church by an ambulatory which will afford the
choir an entrance to the chancel. The baptistry will be in the rear of the
church, near the main entrance. This arrangement will be in accordance with
the Episcopal teachings that baptism is the entrance to the church. The
parish house will be about 76x64 feet, and will follow in architectural style
the church and the rectory. This building will be used for Sunday. school
work, meetings of the various organizations of the parish, entertainments and
social events. In the basement of the parish house will be a fully equipped
gymnasium for the use of the younger social organizations. The rectory,
which will be at the extreme corner of the lot in Munroe street, will be of
stone, the upper story to be of half timber. In arranging the buildings it has
been Mr. McCulloch's wish that Old English lines be used in all the details.
In the belfry will be installed a set of chimes costing, it is said, about $5,000,
and a $6,000 organ will furnish the music for the church. The organ will be
built with a console in the morning chapel so that it can be played either from

First Universalist Church, Muncie.

there or from the main keyboard. The grounds surrounding the building will be made into lawn, intersected by cement walks leading to the entrances of the various buildings. The steps leading to all the buildings will be of stone. Grace parish is at the present time steadily growing, sixteen persons having been confirmed at the last visitation of Bishop Francis. It is believed that the erection of the new church buildings will bring out greater interest in parish work and force it to the front rank of Muncie churches.

THE UNIVERSALIST.

First Universalist Church, Muncie.

After some two years of occasional preaching of the doctrines of Universalism, instituted by Samuel I. Watson (a layman), he invited Rev. Benjamin F. Foster, a noted clergyman of Indianapolis, to come and hold a protracted meeting of about two weeks, in the court house. This resulted in his extending the "Right Hand of Fellowship" to the Universalist confession of faith to the following persons, who organized the First Universalist Church of Muncie on the following Wednesday evening of February 18, 1859:

Samuel I. Watson and Mrs. C. Watson, E. M. Watson, Alice Watson, A. W. Charman and Mrs. Jane Charman, James Charman, Samuel O. Budd, W. B. Kline and Mrs. M. Kline, John Richey, Peter Fullheart and Mrs. A. Fullheart, J. F. Fullheart, Miss E. J. Fullheart, Cynthia Fleming, Amy C. (Fleming) Ireland, Eliza Willard, Jane Spear, Mary Jane (Gilbert) Edmonds (first white girl born in Muncie), Mrs. E. Proud, Dr. W. H. McCormick, Mrs. C. A. McCormick, S. W. Harlan, R. Antrim, G. Goodman, W. H. Howell, L. B. Bonham, and A. B. Thomas. The oldest charter members living now are S. O. Budd, 77 past, and James Charman, 76.

At the corner of Jackson and Madison streets, the original building was dedicated September 9, 1860, at a cost of $6,000. This was remodeled in 1899 at a cost of $14,000. More recent improvements and the value of ground increase this by $10,000.

The church has been served by the following ministers: 1860, Henry Gifford, of Ohio; 1861, Josiah Davis; 1863, E. Case; 1866, Rev. W. B. Linell; 1867, W. C. Brooks; 1870, Marion Crosbey; 1873, J. J. Austin; 1874, Rev. Thomas S. Guthrie; 1877, J. L. and L. D. Crosbey; 1879, J. A. Dobson; 1881, W. C. Brooks; 1882, Thad. C. Druley; 1884, T. P. Abell; 1884, T. S. Guthrie; 1892, W. W. Gleason; 1893, J. F. Carney; 1897, Miss M. A. Brennen; 1902, J. H. Peardon; 1903, G. I. Keirn.

THE CATHOLIC.

St. Lawrence Catholic Church.

The spot where now stands the prosperous city of Muncie was occupied as late as 1828 by a few straggling cabins, and thickets of hazel brush, and was noted chiefly for its ague and mud. Missionaries in the earliest days occasionally visited the few Catholic families scattered here and there. The first priest visiting Muncie was Father Daniel Maloney, who came from Indianapolis. The first Holy Mass was celebrated at the house of Patrick Tubey, upon which site the magnificent Carnegie library is erected.

For nearly four years Father Maloney made monthly visits celebrating Holy Mass alternately at the homes of Patrick Tubey and Peter Mutch. Patrick Tuhey has long since gone to his eternal reward. Peter Mutch and his wife, both nearly ninety years of age, still occupy the home which was often the scene of the devotion of the Catholics of Muncie in the early missionary days.

Father Maloney today might have his choice of the Big Four Railroad or the interurban lines, but in his time, lacking these convenient modes of travel, he made his journey on horseback from Indianapolis.

Father Bessonies attended Muncie from Indianapolis in 1855 and 1856. Father Clark came to Muncie in 1857. He attended the missions of Winchester, Anderson, and Union City. He endeavored unsuccessfully to build a church in Muncie. The missionary visits continued, Fathers Seechrist, Shellamacher, Black, Vanderpoole, McMahon, Geoghan, Maloney and Doyle having care of this mission for short periods of time.

Father Fitzmaurice took charge in the early 60s and administered to the spiritual wants three years. Fathers Bleckman and Von Schwedler both attended Muncie from Union City. The Rev. Lawrence Lamour of Union City began the building of the church in 1869. The congregation at that time numbered 75 members, none of them possessing an abundance of this world's goods, but what they lacked in wealth, they supplied in zeal and persistence. They finally bought the lots in block 8 at the corner of Charles and Hackley streets, upon which the church was built. To Father Lamour belongs the credit of completing the church, a brick building, 35x60 feet in size. The church is named for his patron, St. Lawrence the Deacon. It was dedicated in 1873 by the Rt. Rev. Joseph Dwenger, at that time Bishop of Fort Wayne. The lots on which it was erected were bought by his predecessor, Bishop Luers. Father Joseph A. Marshall was stationed at Muncie from June to September, 1873. Father Crowley of Anderson succeeded Father Lamour and was zealously devoted to the care of the little flock in Muncie. He attended Muncie as a mission once a month and by collections paid off the indebtedness of the church all but $250, which remained when his successor was appointed. The present pastor, the Rev. William G. Schmidt, was ordained priest on December 19, 1874, by the Rt. Rev. Joseph Dwenger at the Cathedral in Fort Wayne and was then appointed pastor of Muncie, whose congregation comprised at that time about 45 families. He erected a small frame residence which served as a priest's

Catholic Church, Muncie.

house until 1899, when he built the present rectory at the cost of $7,000. The first parish residence was partially destroyed by fire on November 1, 1880.

Father Schmidt built a frame schoolhouse in 1881 wherein he taught from 1881 to 1882. He attended Hartford City in 1875, and Montpelier from 1875 to 1896. Sick-calls to Hartford City, Montpelier, and the surrounding country, were made by such modes of travel as horse-back riding, hand-cars, and similar primitive conveniences. The pastor describes one of these sick-calls made on a very cold winter night, the distance being from Muncie to Montpelier, in which he took his turn in propelling the conveyance, a hand-car, managed to keep from freezing, and spoiled with the grease used on the car one side of his new suit of clothes, a rare luxury in those days.

The present church edifice, a magnificent structure in the Gothic style of architectural beauty, cruciform in shape, and symmetrically perfect, was built by the Rev. William G. Schmidt, and dedicated by the Rt. Rev. Joseph Rademacher of beloved and blessed memory on the Feast of the Nativity of Our Lady, A. D. 1895. The altars and furniture are of fine oak, the high altar being a splendid Gothic creation in this wood, and a joy to the eye of a devout Catholic assisting at the Holy Sacrifice offered up to God on this Calvary erected by the devotion of the Muncie people. The cost of the church approximated the sum of $43,000. The money was raised by the efforts of Father Schmidt, ably seconded by the congregation. Its value today is about $50,000. The seating capacity of the church is 950.

After the new church was built, the old church was converted into two school-rooms which, with the frame structure erected in 1881, served for the accommodation of the parochial school pupils until 1901, in the spring of which year Father Schmidt began the erection of what is today one of the finest parochial school buildings in Indiana. The work progressed throughout the spring and summer of 1901 and in October of that year two rooms were prepared for occupancy in the new building. These rooms accommodated those children who had formerly attended in the "Old Church" school-rooms, which latter Father Schmidt tore down at this period. He rented for the first four to six weeks of the fall term two rooms in a neighboring building, formerly used as a blacksmith shop, and many of the children now attending school laughingly recall their school days in the "Blacksmith Shop." One of the Sisters having written her brother a description of her school-room at the time, received a humorous reply stating how he pictured his dear sister standing in the door of the "Blacksmith Shop" wistfully peering down the street in anticipation of the coming of the next horse.

As a reward for their happy endurance of the beauties and fresh air of the "Blacksmith Shop" the teachers and pupils of those two rooms received the earliest accommodation that could be prepared in the new building. The rooms of the rest were ready for occupancy by December, 1901. The building contains eight (8) splendidly-lighted, scientifically ventilated, and well equipped school-rooms, each 27x27 feet. Two spacious halls separate the rooms on each of the two floors occupied by the latter. A large auditorium occupies the third floor. The heating and other conveniences are of the most modern type, and not one of the upwards of 400 children who attend school is at any time exposed to aught dangerous to health from the opening hours of morning to the time the children are dismissed in the afternoon. The cost of the school approximated $20,000, while its value is about $25,000.

The school was first taught by the pastor, later by a lay teacher, then by the Sisters of St. Joseph, and since 1886 by the Sisters of St. Agnes from Fond du Lac, Wis. Ten Sisters form the Mission, eight of whom teach the school of eight grades followed by a modification of the ordinary high school and commercial college work combined with a view of affording a useful educational equipment in favor of children of a manufacturing town, some of whom are obliged to start early in life the task of winning a livelihood. The school is supported by a very small tuition fee and the proceeds of such entertainments as may be necessary for such balance as the tuition fees fail to cover. The Sisters attend to the entire care of the altars, making and washing the altar-cloths, albs, and all linens used in the sanctuary, attending to the sanctuary decorations and light, preparing the altar-breads, etc. The teachers reside in a frame building near the school-house. Father Schmidt contemplates the erection of a more spacious residence for the Sisters and hopes to accomplish it this year (1907).

The estimated value of the entire church property is: Ground, $15,000; improvements, $90,000. The balance of indebtedness on the same is $17,000.

The St. Vincent de Paul Aid Society established April 18, 1894, does a great good work among the poorer members of the congregation and even extends aid to cases of distress reported to them in favor of poor people not of our Faith.

The A. O. H. established May 1, 1892, and the Ladies' Auxiliary of A. O. H., besides extending charity to the sick, etc., among their members, are always ready and willing to assist any undertaking for the benefit of the church.

Other societies are the Catholic Benevolent Legion, the Ladies' Catholic Benevolent Association, the Sodality of the Blessed Virgin, and the Knights of Columbus.

For the young girls there is the St. Agnes' Sodality and the Children of Mary; for the boys, the Holy Name Sodality and the St. Aloysius' Society.

The younger children have organizations known as the Guardian Angel and Infant Jesus Societies.

The Rev. John Schmitz was assistant in 1899-1900. Later the Rev. L. R. Paquet, and still later the Rev. Z. Huot assisted the pastor for some time.

At the present time Rev. John H. Kohl is assistant.

The Rev. William George Schmidt, pastor of the St. Lawrence's congregation since his ordination in 1874, was born at Lahr in the Province of Nassau, Germany, February 5, 1852. Father Schmidt attended school for three years in his native country, and came to the United States when his father brought the family hither in 1861. They settled at Mineral Point, Wis., where his good father died on January 29, 1862. He attended school at Mineral Point for three years, and then became a student at Calvary College, Fond du Lac, Wis., in which institution he pursued his studies for a period of three years with the object of entering the priesthood. Subsequently he was engaged as a salesman in a mercantile house at Warren, Ill., and was occupied in a similar capacity later on at Dodgeville, Wis.

He then entered the seminary of St. Francis at Milwaukee, where he studied three and one-half years. He finished his theological studies at Mount St. Mary's Seminary, Cincinnati, Ohio, and was ordained by Bishop Dwenger on December 19, 1874. He assumed pastoral charge of St. Lawrence Congregation on January 28, 1875, and has been identified with the interests of the church in Muncie since that date. His mother resided with him from the period above mentioned until her holy death, October 31, 1889. On the occasion of the silver jubilee of his ordination, which was likewise that of his appointment to Muncie, the Catholics were seconded in their celebration by the foremost non-Catholic citizens of the town, many of whom, remembering the days of Muncie's sorrow when the small-pox caused dire suffering in the town, seemed happy, indeed, to give public expression to their appreciation of fidelity of the Catholic priesthood to suffering humanity at the risk of any sacrifice. The celebration was a great source of joy to the Catholics of Muncie chiefly because of the tribute of reverence paid by those outside of the fold to religion in the respect shown their pastor by all the citizens of Muncie. Father Schmidt is justly proud of his magnificent church—but the joy and delight of his heart, the theme of all themes interesting to him, is his Parochial School.

He is one of the priests of the Diocese of Fort Wayne, who, besides teaching his school himself in the first beginning, paid part of the expense of its maintenance out of his own meagre salary in the early years of the school's existence.

His congregation—it is a friend of his who speaks—appear to be like their "Little Father," quiet, reverent, and docile. No dissensions are heard of among them, and should a little misunderstanding threaten to arise, Father Schmidt's decision satisfies all parties, as his people have full confidence in his management of affairs, a trust born of the experience they have enjoyed in his long and edifying pastorate.

Albany.

Ten or fifteen years ago the members of the Catholic Church residing in or near Albany considered themselves sufficiently strong to effect a church organization, which was done in the spring of 1895. During that summer a church building costing about $1,500 was erected in the east part of the town. The charter members of the church were Mr. McGee, Mr. Hinkel, Andrew Tuttle, William Russell. At the present time there are only three Catholic families residing at Albany, and they attend service in Dunkirk. While the church remains in Albany and a semblance of organization, there is practically no parish. The three pastors who have held services there have been Rev. Constantine Manjay, Rev. William Hogan, Rev. John C. Wakefer.

THE FRIENDS.

Friends Society, Muncie.

The Quaker influence in the early settlement of southeastern Indiana has been referred to on previous pages. Nevertheless, though many Friends have lived in Delaware county from the early times, no regular meetings were held in Muncie until the seventies. It is said that Mrs. Mary H. Goddard was mainly influential in starting the movement that resulted in the formation of a meeting. William S. Wooten and other ministers came to Muncie occasionally, during 1875, preaching in the Methodist and Presbyterian churches, and as a result, on April 2, 1876, steps were taken for the organization of a Muncie meeting. Eighteen persons, six of them children, constituted the meeting, namely: Samuel Haines, Joseph A. and Mary H. Goddard, Calvin and Mary Haines, Margaret Burt, William and Deborah Carson, Harry Harrington, Lydia Harrington, William and Laura Jessup, Walter and Harvey Haines, Clarence Carson, William H., Grace and Anna Goddard. Mrs. Mary Burson gave, rent free, a small frame building on the north side of the square as a meeting house, but during a revival held by Nathan and Esther Frame, the first regular ministers, Walling Hall was used. The membership was greatly increased by the meetings, and in the summer of 1879 the contract was let for the building of the first church home, at the corner of Mulberry and Seymour (it was then Wall street).

Friends Church, Muncie.
Dedicated February 2, 1908.

The church was dedicated in February, 1880; it was a frame building, having cost about $1,800.

Following Nathan and Esther Frame, the ministers of the society have been: John Riley, Oliver White, Luke Woodard, Nevius Hodgin, William P. Angel, and Charles E. Hiatt.

In 1903 a lot was purchased at the corner of Cherry and Adams streets, and in 1906 was begun the erection of a modern church edifice, to cost about $30,000. It is one of the handsomest of Muncie's modern churches, though in its architectural lines and in its interior decoration and equipment a chaste simplicity characteristic of the church has been maintained. The building committee are: Joseph A. Goddard, Frank E. Osborne, H. H. Rayle, C. A. Ramsey, E. E. Elliott, and C. E. Hiatt.

THE UNITED BRETHREN.

Normal City United Brethren.

This society was organized in January, 1905. They bought from the Presbyterians the old church building standing at the corner of Calvert avenue and Adams street, and it was in this house that the organization took place. The church, though only two years old, now has 144 members, but those who were the first or charter members were George Calvert and wife Anna, Andrew Kane and wife and son, Rev. J. W. Gibson and wife, R. Bowden and wife, Rev. Ella Priddy and daughters Clara and Odessa. The church property was bought for $500, but recently the society have paid $400 for a lot at Jackson and Calvert and plan, at this writing, the building of a $10,000 church. Rev. J. Walter Gibson is the only pastor who has served this congregation, having organized the class and conducted it to its present success.

First Brethren, Muncie.

Elders D. F. Hoover, I. E. Branson, J. W. Rarick, and George L. Studebaker organized this church in Muncie, June 30, 1898, George L. Studebaker being chosen pastor of the congregation. The names of the charter members: George L. Studebaker, Mary E. Studebaker, Henry C. Brown (deceased), Bertha Brown, A. D. Bowman, Carrie Bowman (deceased), W. H. Cooper, Caroline Cooper, Phebe Yount, Lillie Yount, Silas Arnold, Fannie Arnold (deceased), Esta Arnold, Noah Witters, Mrs. Noah Witters, Charles Witters, Maggie Witters, Dora Nixon, Jessie Nixon, Ernest Nixon, Nora Acord, Viola Paul, Mary E. Dick, W. A. World, Mrs. W. A. World, S. M. Funk, Leola Fletcher, Catie Roeger, Dora Roads, George Gump, Harriet Gump. The church house and parsonage on Jackson and Council streets are valued at $6,000. George L. Studebaker has had

charge of the congregation since its organization. There are now about
ninety members. The following have been chosen to official position in the
church: Saylor G. Greyer, ordained to the ministry, and Henry C. Brown,
Ed Salters, D. O. Noomaw, Calvin W. Hooke (deceased), deacons.

Riverside Church, United Brethren.

This church of the United Brethren in Christ was organized Febru-
ary 17, 1903, in Jack Will's old bakeshop on Wheeling avenue, the constit-
uent members of the first congregation being the following: Emmit P.
Day, May Day, Samuel Fadely, Florence Fadely, Melville Fodge, Priscilla
Fodge, A. J. Shellenbarger, Moriah Stephenson, Harry Gamble, Jennie
Gamble, Olivet Hanking, Sarah Hanking, Nancy Hancock, C. C. McCrillus,
Kate McCrillus, Hazel McCrillus. William Mader, Sarah Mader, Orla
Mader, Ernest Snider, Minnie Snider, Ed Schmitts, Della Schmitts, William
Shellenbarger, Mary Shellenbarger, Emma Wills, R. G. Hammond, Hor-
tense Hammond, Lucile Hammond. The brick church on Wheeling ave-
nue, the only church home this society has had, and which cost about $7,000,
was dedicated January 17, 1905, by Bishop William M. Weekley, D.D. The
pastors have been R. G. Hammond, two years, H. S. James, one year, and
James B. Parsons.

Congerville U. B. Church.

The Congerville United Brethrens were organized in 1893, and their
church was erected in the same year, in the Congerville addition, corner of
Mulberry and Twenty-second streets, the building costing $2,000. The
charter members were: Rev. Mr. Tharp, Mrs. E. F. Crossgrave, Mr. and
Mrs. W. C. Bell, Mrs. Jennie Mathews, Mrs. Mary Williams.
The oldest members now living are: Mrs. E. F. Crossgrave, Mrs.
Martha Signits, Mr. and Mrs. W. C. Bell, Mrs. Jennie Mathews, Mrs. Mary
Williams, Mrs. Louvernia Williams, Rev. and Mrs. George A. Porter, Mr.
and Mrs. Isaac McDirmit, Mr. and Mrs. William Joseph, Mrs. Lilly Barnes,
Mr. and Mrs. Thomas Farrell. The pastors who have served the church
are: Rev. David Tharp, Rev. C. A. Love, Rev. F. M. Moore, Rev. Nettie
Valentine, Rev. H. S. James, Rev. James B. Parsons, Rev. S. B. Ervin,
D.D., Rev. J. W. Gibson, Rev. E. J. Scott, and Rev. G. E. Landen.

Selma.

This church, also known as Olive Branch U. B. Church, was organized
in 1856. The first church home, erected in 1856 at a cost of $1,200, was
used jointly by the United Brethren and Methodists, until the latter built
their own church. The charter members were Henry Will, J. W. Dickover, John Birtsfield, Joseph Greenwalt, David Gunckle, W. J. Moore. The
oldest members of the congregation now living are Matilda Birtsfield, Ed-

ward Schull, John Schull and wife, W. S. Dunkin and wife, Carl East and wife, Rev. P. E. Mott and wife, J. C. Barnes and wife, Lizzie Felton, Grant Whitney and wife, Mrs. Greenwalt, William Bergdoll and wife, Leslie Dickover. In 1896 the society erected a pretty little church costing $3,500. The church is located in the northwest part of town, opposite the high school building, and on the Muncie interurban road.

The pastors who have served the congregation during the past fifty years have been: A. R. Day, Daniel Stover, J. M. Krabrick, C. B. Small, Abraham Rust, George Maddox, Joseph Demundrum, F. M. Moore, John W. Utsler, M. O. Jarvis, C. E. Hunt, O. E. Evans, W. N. Sleeth, Nettie Valentine, J. B. Parsons, J. Ernest Paddock, C. A. Love, E. J. Scott, George E. Landen.

Beech Grove U. B. Church.

The history of this church as a United Brethren organization extends only to March 27, 1903, at which time the church building in Harrison township was sold to the Methodists of that vicinity for $250. The Methodists have repaired the structure at a cost of $500 and have since conducted services there, under the following ministers: Preston Polhemus, Clarence Hunt, Thomas A. Graham, C. M. Hollopeter, J. A. Ruby.

The Beech Grove U. B. Church was organized November 11, 1883. The members worshiped in schoolhouse No. 4 until 1888, when the church was built at a cost of $1,200. The charter members of the organization were: Alonzo and Lovina Morris, Thomas J. and Arminda Jackson, Isom and Emeline Wischart, Henry L. and Ellen Miller, Solomon and Malita McCormick, William F. and Anna Carpenter, Russell and Elsa Crammer, William and Armanda Cox, George and Elizabeth Shipley, Dica Jarret, Rebecca and Laura Ocker.

Maple Grove Brethren Church.

This church was organized in 1887, one mile south and one-half mile west of Eaton. The charter members were: Aaron Heft, Rebecca Heft, Henry Witamyre, Nancy Witamyre, Henry Isgrigg, Barbara Isgrigg, William Schweitzer, Mary Schweitzer, Henry Younce, Margareth Younce. The oldest members now are: Mr. and Mrs. Henry Witamyre, Mrs. Aaron Heft, Mr. and Mrs. Frank Wood, Mr. and Mrs. Ross Thompson, Mr. and Mrs. A. W. Evans, Mr. and Mrs. T. M. McKinley, Mr. and Mrs. Richard Frazee, Mr. and Mrs. Mathias Collins, Mr. and Mrs. William Bowman, Mr. and Mrs. Curtis Cruea, Mr. and Mrs. B. F. Lewis, Mary Eller, Mr. and Mrs. Henry Hoover, Mr. and Mrs. William Miller, Mr. and Mrs. O. V. Cruea, Mr. and Mrs. Henry Hoover, Mr. and Mrs. James Sholtz, Mr. and Mrs. Everett McMahan.

The list of pastors: Rev. W. W. Summers, Rev. L. W. Ditch, Rev. . S. White, Rev. E. D. Burnworth, and present pastor, Rev. C. C. Grisso. A. W. Evans, Secretary.

THE EVANGELICAL.

First Evangelical Lutheran Church, Muncie.

The preliminary meeting for organization of this society was held at the home of B. C. Bowman, February 27, 1889, at which time a constitution was adopted, and the following 15th of March a constitution was adopted and a council elected. The charter members were: B. C. Bowman, Joseph Prutzman, Isaac W. Sayler, Francis W. Koch, Joseph C. McAlister, Virtie McAlister, James . Schaeffer, Jerusha Kirke, Allie Keller, John Cassell, C. E. H. Bowman, Amanda Prutzman, Emma Sayler, Amelia C. Koch, Mary J. McAlister, James . Schaeffer, Matthias Neff, E. A. Bowman, Mary Cassell. Of these all were living at the date of this information except Joseph Prutzman, Jerusha Kirke, Francis W. Koch, John Cassell. At the corner of Howard and Liberty streets a church building was erected and completed in June, 1890, costing about $4,000. The pastors who have served the congregation have been: Charles F. Steck, B. F. Crous, C. U. Larrick, C. R. Dunlap, G. B. Schmitt.

German Evangelical Church, Muncie.

This society was organized October 10, 1894, the first members being: Henry Miller, Louis Edelmann, Charley Fickert, Philip A. Deterling, Martin Klopfer, George Bundel, R. Hartmann, Charles Gass, John Roger, John Langenbeck, Minnie Vogt, Mrs. Harbold, Conrad Davis. The church erected by this congregation cost $3,000, and the parsonage $1,000. The following pastors: Revs. Chumstone, Webber, Hohman, Katterjahn, Gabel.

Cross Roads Evangelical Lutheran Church.

In 1843 Rev. Irvine organized a joint Lutheran and Presbyterian congregation; a church was built on the line between Henry and Delaware counties; the Lutherans predominated and in 1848 Rev. S. Sayford organized the "Richwoods Evangelical Lutheran Church." In course of time a Sunday school was organized in the schoolhouse at Cross Roads and the congregations here were larger than in the old church, so in 1866 Rev. P. G. Bell organized a Lutheran church at Cross Roads; the old organization gave way to the new and in 1868 a new brick church was built at Cross Roads called 'Richwoods Evangelical Lutheran Church," costing $2,900. The names of charter members: Jacob Bowers and wife, Andrew Bowers and wife, George Bowers and wife, Adam Wean and wife, Peter Sheetz and wife, Henry Sheetz and wife, Christian Sourwine and wife, Ephriam

Wurlin and wife, Barnet Gets and wife, David Bowers and wife, David Warner and wife, Mrs. Polly Strickler, Mrs. Mary Sayford, Christian Swigart and wife, Mrs. Dr. Boor, Mrs. Elizabeth Clevenger, Daniel Fultz and wife. The oldest members living are: Mr. John Moreland and wife, Mrs. Mary Cromer, Mrs. Harriet Blazer, Mr. Rush Cromer and wife, Mr. Luther Mowrey, Mr. Cyrus Van Matre. The pastors have been: Samuel Sayford, Peter G. Bell. J. H. Link, J. C. Myers. P. G. Bell, Adam Height, G. W. Enders, A. E. Wagner, W. H. Keller, J. B. Baltzley, E. W. Simon, C. F. Steck, G. G. Clark, J. M. Bramcamp, M. R. Mohler, E. G. Howard, E. C. Harris, H. C. Stuckenberg, Colver, William S. Tomlinson, present pastor.

Miscellaneous.

Society of Spiritualists, Muncie.

The Spiritualists were organized in Muncie in January, 1888. William Lynn was chosen president and Ed. Crossfield secretary of the society, and Hummell Hall was designated as the place of meeting. This notice of an early organization is obtained from a newspaper of that date, but the present society give the time of their organization as 1891, with the following as the first members: J. H. Mendenhall, A. J. Wilson, Mrs. Sarah J. Mong, J. W. Wittemyre, Augustus Baker, A. R. Mock, T. J. Lockwood, J. M. Best, L. H. Harper, Wallace Hibbits, J. J. Shields. The society have held their meetings in halls, and according to custom have had no regular ministers.

Society of Christian Scientists, Muncie.

The Christian Scientists society at Muncie was organized November 2, 1899, with the following charter members: Mr. John D. Wood, Mr. Samuel Cecil, Mrs. Amelia Cecil, Mrs. Laura Dunn, Mrs. Alice Minnick, Mrs. Jean Davis, Mr. Thomas McShea, Mrs. Rowena McShea, Mr. Fred Ritter, Mrs. Elizabeth Ritter, Mr. William Pixley, Mr. Andrew Todd, Mrs. Ella Todd, Mr. Olen Todd, Miss Omole Todd, Mr. A. F. Scott, Mrs. A. F. Scott, Mrs. Anna Collis, Mr. Andrew Fulton, Mrs. Adda Fulton, Mrs. Augusta Anderson, Mr. Henry Cecil. The readers for the society have been: Mrs. Rowena McShea, Mr. J. D. Wood, Mrs. Jean Davis, Mr. Fred Ritter, Mrs. Elizabeth Ritter, Mr. Andrew Todd, Mrs. Rachel Conkling.

Gideonites.

A tabernacle of the Gideon band was established in Muncie at the corner of Ohio avenue and Blaine street and first opened for services August 20, 1906. C. H. Stratton is the leader of the movement in Muncie.

Star of Hope Mission.

This mission on South Walnut street, Muncie, was opened October 7, 1906, with the professed purpose of giving "the Gospel to the poor, lift up the fallen, bring back the erring ones and point sinners to Christ." It is a non-sectarian and chiefly voluntary organization.

Salvation Army of Muncie.

In the chronological record will be found some notice of the early meetings of this organization. It was once in disfavor in Muncie, as in fact in most places, until its objects and the great charity accomplished by the Army became better understood. Of course the Army has no definite organization and regular membership like the other churches, and no history can be given. Some of those who have longest been identified with the work in Muncie are Mr. and Mrs. High, Mr. and Mrs. Keys, and Mr. and Mrs. Smith.

CHAPTER XXVI.

THE SPREAD OF CULTURE THROUGH ORGANIZATION.

WOMAN'S CLUBS—ART, LITERATURE AND MUSIC.

"Culture's hand
Has scattered verdure o'er the land,
And smiles and fragrance rule serene
Where barren wilds usurped the scene."
—BOWRING.

Besides the schools and churches, various other organizations exist whose purpose is linked with these great institutions in effecting mental and moral culture. Usually the activities of a club or literary association are so varied that they cannot properly be considered under the same head with education or religion, and yet are none the less efficient factors in advancing the same cause for which the schools and churches stand. It is proposed in this chapter to consider the principal movements and institutions whose vital purpose is the advancement of esthetic culture, among which belong the woman's clubs (whose activities, however, have a very broad scope), the associations for music and art, and the library.

Woman's Club of Muncie.

In point of time and importance as well, the Muncie Woman's Club is the first to merit attention. When one considers the almost countless number of clubs and fraternal organizations, covering nearly every matter of human interest, that are now active, it seems truly remarkable that this feature of our modern life is less than half a century old. The Masons and a few other orders go back many years, but the host of societies and associations of all kinds that are now catalogued have a history little more than a generation old.

Indiana now advances a claim to having the first woman's club organized in this country, that being the Minerva Club at New Harmony in 1859. The founder, Mrs. Runcie, organized a second club at Madison in 1867, both of which antedate the founding of similar clubs in New York or Boston.

The Muncie Club, which was organized January 29, 1876, at the home of Mrs. Emma Mont. McRae (corner of Adams and Plum streets), is therefore among the pioneer woman's clubs of the state and country. The first membership of the club included the following:

Mrs. Clara Shipley, Mrs. Samantha Bacon, Mrs. Emma Mont. McRae, Mrs. Carrie J. McCulloch, Miss Nellie Smith, Miss Lizzie E. Willard, Mrs. J. A. Husted, Mrs. Marc. Smith, Mrs. Juliette Riley, Mrs. Millie Ethell, Mrs. Susan Kilgore (Templer), Mrs. A. C. Mellette, Mrs. Ella Mellette, Mrs. Hattie L. Patterson, Miss Minnie Young, Mrs. Ellen Smith, Miss Jennie Neely, Mrs. Mary G. Sample, Mrs. Florence C. Brown, Mrs. Mary Marsh, Mrs. Henrietta Hodge, Mrs. Ida A. Harper, Miss Lillie Brotherton, Mrs. A. Winans, Mrs. Mary McC. Smith, Mrs. M. Louise Cassady, Mrs. Mary Little, Miss Mary Little.

The first officers of the club were: Miss Nellie Smith, president; Miss Jennie Neely, vice president; Miss Minnie Young, secretary; Mrs. Carrie J. McCulloch, treasurer; Mrs. Emma Mont. McRae, Mrs. Millie Ethell and Miss Lizzie E. Willard, standing committee.

Originally the club was planned as a reading club with social advantages. It is interesting to note the difference between the object of the club as stated in the constitution twenty-five years ago and that expressed in the present revised form. "The object of this association," asserts the former, 'shall be to present practical methods for improving the mental, moral and physical condition of society, and to secure, as far as possible, united effort toward the higher civilization of humanity." This was a laudable purpose, but too world-wide and general in its intention to be considered practical as a basis for efficient work. Notice the increased definiteness and specification in the revised form—"The object of this club shall be the social and intellectual advancement of women and united effort to further improvement in the community in which we live."

The early meetings were entertaining and popular and the list of members grew rapidly. In the second year, at the suggestion of Mrs. McRae, "History" was made a subject for study and active membership carried with it higher aim and responsibility. A profitable as well as pleasant feature of early meetings was general response to roll call either from assignment or choice of subject.

The anniversaries of the Woman's Club have been events of popular interest and enjoyment—distinguished by the originality and attractive character of the exercises, and entertainment of the guests. Here the club flower, the carnation, bedecks the banquet tables and the club colors, blue and white, are displayed in badge or decoration. These celebrations reached a climax in 1901, when three brilliant social events were given in honor of the Silver Anniversary.

In 1896 the homes of the members could no longer accommodate the increasing membership; a club room was opened with a pleasant session in the Building and Loan block on High street, and the club motto, "Progress," was more in evidence than ever as the work of the club grew into departments, and study classes were organized and conducted in the new room. The club moved the next year to the Streeter block, and here an active interest was taken in school decoration and visiting. In 1900 a re_ vision of the constitution resulted in an old custom, of which the club has been proud, being changed; that of holding meetings once a fortnight, the whole year round. From this time a vacation has been taken through July and August. The work of the Woman's Club has never ceased to benefit and inspire, and its influence has constantly been given to the side of "Prog. ress." At the present time new members are received at almost every busi_ ness meeting and there are now enrolled, active members 56, associates 24.

1906-07.

Besides this year's study of German history and literature, the Woman's Club has taken substantial interest in the Free Kindergartens and aided in establishing the first cooking classes in two of the school buildings. The work of the club is directed through three departments—Literature and Art, History and Current Events, and Sociology and Civics.

The presidents of the club since its organization, including two vice presidents who have presided over the club, have been:

Miss Nellie Smith, Miss M. Jennie Neely (vice president), Mrs. Emma Mont. McRae, Mrs. Carrie J. McCulloch, Mrs. A. Winans, Mrs. Louise Cassady, Mrs. Rose Budd Stewart, Mrs. Mary McCulloch Smith, Mrs. Nellie M. Stouder, Mrs. M. Kuëchmann, Mrs. Martha Carter, Miss Florence Walling (vice president), Mrs. Grace E. Poland, Miss Emma Belle Goodin, Miss Emma Cammack, Mrs. Charles B. Galliher.

The officers of the club, 1906-07, are: President Emeritus, Mrs. Ara- bella Winans; President, Mary B. Galliher; vice president, Mrs. J. V. H. Koons; recording secretary, Mrs. Nellie Warner; corresponding secretary, Mrs. Charlie Jackson; treasurer, Mrs. Donna McCaughn; literary commit- tee, Mrs. Martha Carter chairman, Miss Emma Cammack, Miss Helen Servoss, Miss Julia Fowler, Miss Malita Hutzel; Mrs. Arthur Smith, cus- todian of properties.

The Woman's Club has enrolled many talented and beloved members, but perhaps more than any other has delighted to honor one whose untiring devotion to its interests were given for nearly thirty years. Mrs. Carrie J. McCulloch was identified with the club movement from its earliest days in Indiana. A charter member of the Woman's Club of Muncie in 1876, she continued a regular attendance when in health and in the city until she was present for the last time at the February meeting, 1904, when she took part in the program and was happy at the cordial greetings received from the members present. Mrs. McCulloch served the club as president for thirteen years and was then honored with the title "Emeritus." Her home was a

508

HISTORY OF DELAWARE COUNTY

home for the club many times; her literary efforts were frequent—in essay, address or conversation she willingly gave what she thought would lend in. spiration and helpfulness to her club. Many tender memorials were written and read by her as her kindness of heart made every member her friend and when one was missed she felt the loss a personal one. The Woman's Club shared her honor when Mrs. Carrie J. McCulloch was elected the first president of the City Federation.

A most impressive memorial meeting was held at the Club's first session after her life on earth ended May 14, 1904. One among many loving tributes was written by Mrs. J. V. H. Koons as follows:

IN MEMORIAM.

Earth holds her grand reception, night and day;
Guests come, remain awhile, then go away;
Each has his chosen friends for whom he keeps
An altar fire that never wanes nor sleeps;
But now and then a rare soul comes and fills
The world around with joy, and thrills
The hearts of all with love; such was our friend,
Whose priceless worth her charming presence penned
Indelibly on Memory's sacred page.
We thank thee, God, for such an heritage.

Martha Washington Club.

This club was organized at Muncie, January, 1903, and became a member of the federation in June, 1905. The membership is limited to twenty, who are banded together for literary and social objects. Among the charter members were Mrs. Margaret M. Baily, who was the club's first president, Mrs. John W. Dragoo, Mrs. H. E. Manring, Mrs. C. W. Smeltzer, Mrs. A. B. Wetherill.

Conversation Club.

The Conversation Club of Muncie, which was organized July 27, 1894, at the home of Mrs. Julius A. Heinsohn (Kirby House), originated in a purpose to revive the "lost art of conversation" by the study of literary subjects and the free discussion of them without written notes. The club's endeavors, during the thirteen years of its existence, have been inspired and directed by this purpose, with results that have been very satisfactory and prove the wisdom of the undertaking. The club membership is fixed at twenty, and the harmony and unity with which they have worked are not least of the fruits of the club's efforts. This was the first club to prohibit written papers in its work, and it was the first to give private theatricals. The annual banquet, usually accompanied by a play, has always been an elaborate feature of the club's work.

The charter members of the club were: Mrs. Marie Louise Cowan, Miss Anna Goddard, Mrs. Elizabeth K. Heinsohn, Miss Sarah A. Heinsohn,

Mrs. Mamie S. Heinsohn, Mrs. Louise Haffner, Mrs. Harriet W. Kitts, Mrs. Clara B. Kendall, Mrs. Julia T. Richey, Mrs. Margaret D. Rose, Miss Belle Thomas, Mrs. Sarah P. Wildman. Much of the success of the organization has been attributed to the impetus given by its first president, Mrs. Harriet Kitts, a graduate of Vassar College, and now at the head of the Latin department of the schools of Schenectady, N. Y. Two of its later presidents are Vassar graduates. Two members are finished musicians, two have been successful business women, and one has done original work in educational lines. Nine members have removed from the city, and death has taken away two who were active members.

The officers in 1906-07 are: Miss Julia T. Richey, president; Mrs. Harriet M. Johnston, vice president; Miss Artena Chapin, secretary; Mrs. Mary P. Whitely, treasurer.

Tourist Club.

The Tourist Club of Muncie, which was organized at the home of Mrs. Rose Budd Stewart, November 23, 1899, and was received into the county federation December 1, 1899, and into the Indiana state federation May 2, 1900, was formed by some young ladies for the purpose of studying the life, history and literature of peoples in other lands by means of an imaginary tour around the world. These fictitious journeys to foreign lands have produced many interesting programs. "Although only flights of fancy," writes one of the club members, "our letters describing the various scenes and incidents of travel in almost every country on the globe have been very helpful and delightful. In all, something like 425 letters were written during our years of travel. Each week we met to hear, read and approve the letters written—very few letters were sent home behind time." Occasionally the programs were varied by the presence of real world travelers, who talked informally of foreign scenes. The present year (1906-07), the club took up the study of Shakespeare.

The original members of the club were: Rose Budd Stewart, Ethel Brady Morrison, Alma Budd, Rosa Burmaster, Ola Courtney, Helen Hurd, Blanche Smith, Maude Smith, Etta G. Warner. The officers for 1906-07 were: President, Rosa Burmaster; secretary, Kathryn Postma; treasurer, Louise Lyman; chaperon, Mrs. Rose Budd Stewart; program committee, Rosa Burmaster, Ola Courtney, Etta Warner.

McRae Club.

The McRae Club of Muncie, whose objects are general literary and social, and which has given much attention to elevating the artistic standards in the public schools and has aided in maintaining the manual training departments, was organized at the home of Mrs. John Bloor, March 2, 1894.

Among those first identified with the organization were: Mrs. Ella Cropper, Mrs. Dora Hoover, Mrs. Sadie Baldwin, Mrs. Martha Glass, Mrs. Margaret Hilling, Mrs. Ella Lewellen, Mrs. Evelyn Meeker, Mrs. Carrie Miller, Mrs. Ida Watson, Mrs. Luella Westlake, Mrs. Carrie Guthrie, Mrs. Ida C. Greeley.

The officers for 1906-07 are: Mrs. Carrie Miller, president; Mrs. Irene Kitselman, vice president; Mrs. Etta Griffith, recording secretary; Mrs. Ida Watson, corresponding secretary; Mrs. Ella Cropper, treasurer.

Athenaeum Club.

The Athenaeum Club, which was organized at Muncie February 28, 1894, for "the social and intellectual advancement" of its members, has, while accomplishing this purpose, directed its labors to other worthy objects and has more than once made its influence felt in civic improvement. Each of the twenty-five members resolved to beautify her own home and maintain the best possible sanitary conditions, this being worth while not only for the individual benefit derived but as an example to others. This club also tried to secure enforcement of the anti-spitting ordinance, and among other things has contributed pictures for schoolroom decoration and money to the manual training fund and the free kindergarten.

The members longest connected with the club are:

Mrs. Ida Watson, Mrs. Bertha McElfresh, Mrs. Minnie P. Bennett, Mrs. Harriett Maggs, Mrs. Nellie Hayler, Mrs. Elizabeth Hickson, Mrs. Katherine Jones, Mrs. Lora Witz. The officers for 1906-07 are: President, Mrs. Lora Witz; vice president, Mrs. Leota Botkin; recording secretary, Mrs. Cora Norris; corresponding secretary, Mrs. Katherine Jones; teasurer, Mrs. Blanche Cox.

Culture Club.

The Culture Club of Muncie was organized at the home of Mrs. Tina K. Mann, November 11, 1902, and joined the county federation in 1904 and the state federation in 1905. "We band ourselves together for the sake of intellectual and social improvement," is the purpose expressed in the constitution. The original members of the club include Mrs. Belle Crandall, Mrs. Mary Gorton, Mrs. Kate O. Gleason, Mrs. Lucy S. Hoppes, Mrs. Tina K. Mann, Mrs. Virgie Shaw, Mrs. Ada Williams, Mrs. Catherine Crandall. Originating in a visiting club, the mothers bringing their children to the meeting place, the scope and plan of the club were enlarged until it is now a purely literary club, with a special course of study for the year's work. Once each year the husbands and children are entertained. A fee of ten cents semi-monthly is assessed, the amount being used to purchase books.

The officers of the club for the club year just passed are:

President, Mrs. Lucy S. Hoppes; vice president, Mrs. Ada Williams; recording secretary, Mrs. Fay Sproatt Murray; corresponding secretary, Mrs. Arena Kirkpatrick; treasurer, Mrs. Harriet Maggs; librarian, Mrs. Florence Blease.

Monday Afternoon Club.

A reading circle, that met for the first time February 8, 1892, at the home of Mrs. N. B. Hine, was later changed to the Monday Afternoon Club, which for a number of years has been one of the progressive woman's organizations of Muncie. Besides Mrs. Hine five other ladies were present at the first meeting, thus becoming the charter members; namely, Mrs. Harriet Kemper, Mrs. Elizabeth Long, Mrs. Catharine Johnson, Mrs. Mary E. Maring and Mrs. Susan Moore. These six first organized for the purpose of reading United States history. September 19, 1892, they decided to increase the membership to 12, and the following November 18 limited it to 15. The circle had fifteen members at the time it became a club, and eight of the fifteen are still on the roll book. The club has not yet lost a member by death. Besides its regular program work, the club has been interested in civic improvement and education. The manual training fund has received five dollars each year during the last five from this club, and a picture in the Lincoln schoolhouse was also donated by this club.

Mrs. Harriet Kemper was the first president, elected September 19, 1892, and Mrs. Susan Moore secretary. These served three months until the constitution was adopted. The following have been members since 1893: Mrs. Harriett Kemper, Mrs. Elizabeth Long, Mrs. Mary E. Maring, Mrs. Sue H. Moore, Mrs. Arabella Winans, Mrs. Lucretia Roads, Mrs. Laura Heath, Mrs. Zula M. Valentine. These names were on the first program printed and they are members of the club, at this writing. The present officers are: President, Mrs. Zula M. Valentine; vice president, Laura Shirk; secretary-treasurer, Katharine Kessler; corresponding secretary, Mrs. Martha Long; literary committee, Mrs. Alice Meeks, Mrs. Mary Moore Youse, Mrs. Olive Roberts.

Magazine Club.

The Magazine Club, though now a member of the federation and a regularly organized woman's club, originated in a society whose object, in keeping with the name, was to subscribe for and circulate among the members as many magazines as there were members and to hold social meetings fortnightly. The second year, the subscriptions of the magazines were discontinued and the club became a regularly organized literary society with its object the "social and intellectual advancement of women." Soon afterward it joined the "Federated Club of Clubs of Muncie and Eighth District" and helps in carrying on the work planned by that organization. One of the interesting events of the club activity is the social evening once a month in which the husbands of the members are included.

The Magazine Club was organized October 24, 1893, at the home of Mrs. C. C. Brown, 405 East Adams street. The charter members were: Mrs. Walter H. Ellis, Mrs. C. E. Crandall, Mrs. W. F. Maggs, Mrs. C. C. Brown, Mrs. Lee Coffeen, Mrs. Cary Reid, Mrs. Emmet Smith, Mrs. E. R. Peebles; and among the very early members were Mrs. C. H. Church, Mrs. I. D. Stinson, Mrs. E. F. Tyler, Mrs. A. F. Hickman, Mrs. A. L. Harnott, Mrs. F. L. Dresser, Mrs. M. D. Miller, Miss Kittie Leach, Miss W. H. Sumption, Mrs. Charles F. Koontz, Miss Emma Lowman, and Mrs. J. R. Wick. The present officers are: Mrs. W. L. Holmes, president; Mrs. E. J. Macomber, vice president; Mrs. F. U. Fudge, secretary-treasurer.

Round Table Club.

The Round Table was organized at the home of Mrs. James E. Durham in Muncie, February 22, 1894. Mrs. D. A. McLain, Mrs. C. L. Medsker, Mrs. E. Vatet, Mrs. S. M. Keiser, Miss Emma Wilcoxon are among those longest identified with the club's work. The officers for the current year are: Mrs. F. D. Haimbaugh, president; Mrs. A. W. Long, vice president; Miss Nettie Wood, secretary; Mrs. E. J. Macomber, treasurer.

Yorktown Woman's Club.

This progressive club, of twenty-four active members, meets semi-monthly in the respective homes of members for the study and discussion of programs prepared in the year book. For a number of years the club has been a positive influence in the town life of Yorktown, and the scope of its work has never been limited by strictly literary and social ends. Social and intellectual advancement of the women and homes of the town and community is the stated purpose of the club, the work to be chiefly of an historical, literary and educational nature. In their efforts the members have recognized the necessity for their work to be guided by the higher spirit that does not come from intellect alone. It has been the ambition of this club to leave some marks of improvement in a practical form on the town. Some of these can be seen in the gift of a beautiful window of the M. E. Church; also carefully selected pictures which adorn the walls of each room of the Union school, while the unconsummated plans of a public park are not the least of the club's outlook for future work. It has been the pleasure of the club members to entertain their families at the anniversary in February, each year, also at "Halloween," a summer picnic, and at "Gentleman's Night" in April. In compliment of the latter on May 5, 1903, the gentlemen entertained at a "Ladies' Night" in the I. O. O. F. Hall, giving the most elaborate social function in the town's history.

The club was organized February 11, 1892, and was federated in 1899.

The first meeting was held at the home of Mrs. Martha Flowers, where plans were made and the following persons (representing the charter members) elected officers: Mrs. Cynthia Paulin, Mrs. Elizabeth Matthe, Mrs. Minta Greer, Mrs. Emma Overmire, Mrs. Virena Colvin, Mrs. Mayme Warfel and Miss Melissa Helvie. Mrs. Paulin was elected president. The present officers are: Mrs. Lizzie Downing, president; Mrs. Ella Shirey, vice president; Mrs. Rose Fowler, recording secretary; Mrs. Mary Williamson, corresponding secretary; Mrs. Helen Hensley, treasurer; the literary committee being Mrs. Mayme Warfel, Mrs. Effie Skillen and Mrs. Hester Warfel.

The Mary Martha Club of Delaware County.

The Mary Martha Club of Delaware County is composed almost entirely of the wives and daughters of farmers, the wives of the family physicians and a few women living in the rural village of Selma. There is an article in the constitution prohibiting membership from an incorporate city. The club was organized in 1891 through the efforts of Mrs. Frank Claypool, Mrs. William Truitt, and Mrs. Helen Young. There were seven charter members. The organization was effected one rainy, disagreeable March day at "Ole Homestead," the home of Mrs. Truitt, with three women present: Mrs. Claypool, Mrs. Truitt and Mrs. Helen Young. The second meeting was with Mrs. William Ribble and Mrs. Young at the "Pines." The daughters of the members of the M. M. Club are associate members until they attain the age of eighteen years. They then have the privilege of coming if they so desire into the club as working members.

The name, Mary Martha, was suggested, together with several others, and was taken from the Bible, Luke Chap. 10-41, "And Jesus answered and said unto her, Martha, Martha, thou art careful and troubled about many things. But one thing is needful: And Mary hath chosen that good part, which shall not be taken away from her."

The first program was "Eminent Women of America." The second meeting considered "Eminent Men of America." The club then took up the geography of the United States. The programs are always miscellaneous as the Mary Martha belongs to both the Indiana Union of Literary Clubs, and the State Federation. Keeping in touch with this work, therefore. the next year book will devote one meeting to home economics and one to manual training.

The Mary Martha is also a member of the county federation, and keeps in touch with the county clubs through the club notes that are published in the Muncie *Star*.

The club is popular as a social factor and it has been considered proper to limit it to thirty members when there was a membership of thirty-eight.

With some the query might arise—Where do you get books? The
Muncie Library is open to many of the members because they are city tax
payers, and the club also has access to the traveling library. Magazines are
pooled, so that the Mary Martha is a Magazine Club. The club motto is
the "Actual and the Ideal." The object of this association was the "desire
to obtain a higher degree of literary culture, a greater fund of knowledge,
and a better appreciation of the dignity of womanhood."

The first president of the Mary Martha was Mrs. Emily L. Truitt.
The second was Mrs. Sophia Gilbert Jump. The present officers are:
President, Miss Luick; vice president, Mrs. Cecil; secretary and treasurer,
Mrs. Fay Jump.

Woman's Club of Selma.

The Woman's Club of Selma was organized for literary and social
purposes November 5, 1894, and during the subsequent thirteen years the
club has become an active factor in town life. Among those who have been
identified from the beginning or from early years of the club's existence may
be mentioned Mrs. Hattie M. Black, Mrs. M. J. Orr, Mrs. Ella M. Clark,
Mrs. Louisa M. Skiff, Mrs. Abbie M. Hollopeter, Mrs. May O. Sparks,
Mrs. Kate A. Orr, Mrs. Saidie P. Good, Mrs. Margaret Kline, Mrs. Miriam
P. Hervet, Mrs. Nelia Hill, Mrs. Naomi Dyer, Mrs. Anne E. Hoover, Mrs.
Lizzie Felton, Mrs. Joanne Williams, Miss Mary Graham, Mrs. Jennie
Sherwood, Mrs. Ozora Sherwood. The present officers are: President,
Mrs. Bertha Pittenger; vice president, Mrs. Luella Shroyer; secretary and
treasurer, Mrs. Anna Cunningham; assistant secretary, Miss Della Neel.

Twentieth Century Club of Albany.

Organized at the home of Mrs. N. R. Baker, November 26, 1900, the
Twentieth Century Club has carried out yearly programs of social and
literary interest, and has always stood ready to help in any good undertaking
that concerned the welfare of the town. The oldest members of the club
are: Mrs. Ida Buffington, Mrs. Christine Bosman, Mrs. Maud Hill, Mrs.
Clara Long, Mrs. Maud Murphey, Mrs. Lena Marks, Mrs. Clara Huffman,
Mrs. Aletha Poland, Mrs. Emma Robertson, Mrs. Candace Read, Mrs.
Grace Wingate, Mrs. Orpha Wilson.

The present officers are: President, Mrs. Anna Stright Bouslog; vice
president, Mrs. Orpha Davis Wilson; recording secretary, Mrs. Candace
Jones Read; corresponding secretary, Emma Moffett Barrett; treasurer,
Mrs. Aletha Poland; critic, Mrs. Florence Frushour.

Federate Club of Clubs.

While the individual woman's clubs have been promoting certain objects within the scope of a single club's work, their efforts during the past
ten years have been directed under federate organization to the accomplish-

ment of some very broad ideals. In 1896 was organized the Federate Club of Clubs of Muncie and Delaware, embracing in this the woman's clubs of the county. At the annual meeting of June, 1902, in response to the wishes of several outside clubs, the constitution was changed so as to admit any club within the eighth congressional district, the name being changed to the Federate Club of Clubs of Muncie and the Eighth District.

During its history the Federation has interested itself in many movements that are concerned with the general welfare. Perhaps the general objects to which the efforts of the Federation are directed may be called local improvement in civic affairs and better school advantages. In line with these purposes the Federation has interested itself in the preservation of shade trees, in the promotion of civic art, and in acting as the mouthpiece of public sentiment in claiming such advances in education as the introduction of physical culture in the schools. Almost its first practical work was school-room decoration, each club purchasing a picture or piece of statuary for some school.

The Federation claims the honor of having introduced manual training into the public schools. April 19, 1902, a special meeting for the discussion of this subject was held in the Muncie Baptist church, under the auspices of the Federation. Prof. A. J. Bean, who was an instructor in manual training in the Indianapolis schools, Prof. W. R. Snyder, of the Muncie city schools, T. F. Rose, president of the city school board, and Amos Butler, secretary of the state board of charities, spoke in advocacy of manual training. Lack of funds prevented the immediate realization of any practical plans, though the matter was kept before the public in newspaper discussion. The Federation took the first effective step toward establishing manual training when, in June, 1902, it voted fifty dollars as a special fund to be set apart for this work. This amount was increased to one hundred dollars by individual gifts from Mrs. Emma C. Ball, Mrs. Martha Flowers and Mrs. Kate Patterson and the Art League. Mrs. Ida Watson as custodian of this fund was ordered to pay it to the first school in Delaware county that would use the money in maintaining a course of instruction in the manual arts. By gifts from three of the woman's clubs and from Mrs. Mary W. Spilker, the fund was increased to $135. The Congerville school was the first school to take advantage of the Federation's offer, and a class in wood-working under C. E. Brandon was begun in January, 1906, and a class in sewing by Miss Belle Thomas. The Lincoln and Garfield city schools later introduced the work, and manual training and domestic science are now popular features of the public school work. The Federation makes an annual contribution for this work, and also for the Free Kindergarten.

The officers of the Federation for 1907 are: Mrs. Ida Watson, president; Mrs. Zula N. Valentine, recording secretary and club editor; Mrs. Bessie Blease Ross, financial secretary; Miss Ruby Perkins, treasurer; Mrs. Luella Westlake, custodian of special fund.

Honorary Presidents—
Mrs. Caroline J. McCulloch,
Mrs. Lillian Holmes,
Miss Nannie C. Love,
Mrs. Rose Budd Stewart,
Mrs. Kate Young Kessler,
Mrs. M. Louise Cassady,
Mrs. Martha Flowers,
Miss Emma B. Goodin.

Honorary Secretaries—
Miss Edith Love Drake,
Mrs. Harriet W. Kitts.
Mrs. Harriet Johnston,
Mrs. Rose Budd Stewart,
Miss Jeannette C. Love,
Mrs. Rose S. Caldwell,
Miss Ida Ludlow,
Mrs. Emma Wood Ball,
Miss Maud Smith,
Miss Belle Thomas.

Paul Revere Chapter No. 317, Daughters of American Revolution.

This chapter of the D. A. R. was organized at the Kirby House, January 19, 1897, the first set of officers being: Regent, Mrs. Elizabeth Kirby Heinsohn; vice regent, Mrs. Nannie Hemingray; secretary, Mrs. Ella Edwards Durham; treasurer, Mrs. Harriet Huston Neely; registrar, Miss Nannie C. Love. The principal objects of this national society may be stated as these:

To perpetuate the memory of the spirit of the men and women who achieved American Independence by protecting and acquiring historical spots and erecting monuments, encouraging historical research, and publishing its results, preserving documents and relics. To foster true patriotism and love of country. Any woman may be eligible for membership who is descended from a man or woman who rendered material aid to the cause of American Independence; as a recognized patriot, a soldier, or sailor or civil officer.

The members of the chapter are as follows, each name being followed by the name of the Revolutionary patriot from whom the member traces descent and on whose record her eligibility rests:

Mrs Martha Wysor Marsh, Henry Wysor, Sergeant.
Mrs. Elizabeth Kirby Heinsohn, John Gibson.
Mrs. Arabella Winans, George Wall, Jr., Captain.
Mrs. Mary Winans Spilker, George Wall, Jr., Captain.
Mrs. Carrie Clark Meeks, John Bryant.
Mrs. Sarah Kemper Walterhouse, John Bryant.
Mrs. Judith Kemper Gillam, John Bryant.
Mrs. Zerelda Walterhouse Stewart, John Bryant.

Mrs. Sarah Pierce Wildman, Peter Miller, Lieutenant and Captain.
Mrs. Harriet Huston Neely, John Huston.
Mrs. Ella Edwards Durham, Ebenezer Edwards, Captain.
Mrs. Emma Wells Guffigan, John Grant, Soldier Boston Tea Party.
Mrs. Agnes Howe Jones, Selah Howe.
Miss Emily Howe, Selah Howe.
Mrs. Emma Wood Ball, Ephraim Farrar, Ensign.
Mrs. Virginia Legett Ice, Ignatius Taylor, Captain; Henry Field, Lieutenant.

Miss Ida Ludlow, Cornelius Ludlow, Lieutenant Colonel.

Miss Emma Belle Goodin, William Connett.

Mrs. Cora Webb Morgan, Joshua Webb, Patriot.

Mrs. Anna Martin Fudge, Adam Martin, Captain.

Mrs. Mary Kneedler Munshower, George Shive.

Miss Ola Grace Davis, St. Leger Cowley, Adjutant.

Mrs. Jeunie Townsend Gray, John Townsend.

Mrs. Emeline Bradley Morgan, Timothy Bradley, Jr., Laban Morrell, Lieutenant.

Mrs. Mabel Kennar Haymond, Thomas Curry.

Mrs. Josephine Campbell Kitselman, James Campbell.

Mrs. Ella Wintrode Griffith, Daniel Gray.

Mrs. Eva Hageman Little, Benjamin Dennis.

Mrs. Harriet Hogarty Wilson, Lieutenant Samuel Granger, Captain Joseph King and Joseph Moss.

Mrs. Elizabeth Haymond Andrews, Major William Haymond.

Mrs. Edith Hill Mock, Lieutenant Timothy Church.

Mrs. Rose Budd Stewart, Samuel Sands.

Mrs. Carrie Tennell Miller, George Tennell, Sergeant.

Mrs. Nellie A. W. Dill, John Roach, Zachariah and Peter Norton, Daniel Brown.

Miss Pearle May Boord, James Tappan.

Mrs. Eva Fargo Sharpe, Jeremiah and Simon Mason.

Mrs. Josephine Jones Van Nuys, Major David Page.

Mrs. Mary Tracy Mix, Roger Sherman, Patriot.

Miss Lillian Jackson, Abner Hixon.

Mrs. Edith Jackson Fisher, Abner Hixon.

Mrs. Laura Jackson Mullenix, Abner Hixon.

Mrs. Katherine Young Kessler, Robert Layne.

Mrs. Martha Ellis Ivins, Robert Layne, Eleazer Ellis.

Miss Nellie Jewett, John O'Neile.

Mrs. Electa Chase Murphy, Captain Phineas Castle.

Miss Lola Jackson, Andrew Ice.

Mrs. Ruby Harvey Riddle, Andrew Ice.

Mrs. Maude Dragstrom Crow, Samuel Lovejoy, William Moss.

This chapter gave several hundred dollars to the fund for hospital supplies for the Spanish-American war, being third among the chapter contributors. About three hundred dollars has been given to the memorial Continental Hall at Washington. This year special efforts have been made to locate the graves of Revolutionary soldiers. Those located in this country are Andrew Ice, Mt. Summit, William Whickcar, Strong Cemetery, Albany. The first military funeral in Muncie was in the court house and was that of the Revolutionary soldier, Suel Gilbert, buried in Beech Grove Cemetery. William Blount, Revolutionary soldier and founder of Blountsville, was buried in Muncie on private ground, but his grave has been destroyed. It is remembered by old settlers. Two "Real Daughters" have this year honored our chapter by becoming members of it, Mrs. Nancy Haver Reynolds and Mrs. Sarah Barkley, daughters of John Dennis, Revolutionary soldier.

ART, LITERATURE AND MUSIC.

In June, 1891, some one who evidently had made some close and discriminating observations in Muncie, contributed an article to the Chicago Herald, in which, after referring to the city's previous struggle for wealth and the material boom consequent on the discovery of gas, the writer continues with the statement that Muncie has brought its less material improvements into line with its other achievements.

"So that," to quote the substance of the article, "one coming for the first time to Muncie seems to find a New England town—very busy and very wealthy on one side of its life; very pleasant and very graceful on the other. For instance, there is the Apollo Club, made up of forty men, whose musical entertainments are notable events in the town. Three times a year they give an entertainment, all the numbers being rendered by club members, and twice a year they give a "special," when they call to their assistance the best musical talent obtainable. They have in the past been favored by Mme. Josephine Chatterton, of Chicago, the harpist, and by Charles Abercrombie and Master Glenn Hall. The programs of the past have contained selections from Gounod, Werner, Abt, Handel, Haydn, etc.

"One of the results of this attention to music is the orchestra. Three years ago Muncie had no orchestra, and had to send abroad for all assistance of this kind.

"And the women have been in no wise idle. There is a "Ladies' Matinee Musicale," an association of workers who have devoted themselves so carefully to study that one of their concerts is a surprise—and a pleasant one. It is in this club of women that the ante-gas instruction is seen. Many of the members of the musicale were pupils in the public schools a few years ago, and learned there to tread the easy steps which have led up to excellence. In this work Miss Nannie Love has made Muncie her debtor, an obligation most cheerfully acknowledged on every hand. She is chairman of the executive committee of the State Music Teachers' Association and has succeeded in bringing to this city a three days' session of that body, the meeting to be held in June.

"There is also an 'Ethical Society' where feasts of reason are said to rule; associations of medical men, and a perfect bevy of secret societies.

"But what pleased me most was the 'Woman's Club.' It was formed years ago under the leadership of Mrs. McRae, now occupying the chair of English literature at the Purdue University. It was started with the modest intention of 'learning something,' and that purpose has certainly been accomplished. When Mrs. McRae departed for other fields Mrs. Carrie McCulloch was made president, an office she has since most faithfully filled."

It was about ten years ago, in 1898, that a writer for the Indianapolis News gave a similar resume of the organized movements for culture in the city. This correspondent, after mentioning the sudden growth of Muncie from town to city after 1886, speaks of Mrs. Edmunds, the first born in the town, who was still alive at that time, in proof of the fact that Muncie was still so young that its growth could be measured by a single lifetime. Though social life had been greatly extended, this writer notes the presence among the social leaders of the "old families," who had been here before the gas boom, calling such names as Neely, Patterson, Anthony, Winans,

Little, Wachtell, Willard, McCulloch, Dragoo, Wysor, etc. The women's clubs and Federated Club of Clubs were commended for their interest in city government and their activity in instituting and aiding reforms and promoting education and morals. This writer showed particular appreciation of the Art League and Matinee Musicale, which had taken special fields of work, the former founded by students of J. O. Adams and William Forsyth, and the latter by Miss Nannie Love; also of the Players' Club, which had recently been organized for the promotion of dramatic art; and the free kindergarten association.

Some of the organizations above mentioned are now out of existence or temporarily inactive. The Apollo Club, which deserves great credit for its substantial efforts in creating correct musical taste and in giving creditable performances of classic music, gave its first festival in June, 1889. The club was organized with forty members in February, 1889, nine music-lovers of the city having been foremost in the organization. L. M. Neely was the first president; W. P. Stevens, vice-president; John F. Meredith, secretary; Willis Koontz, treasurer; J. W. Nutt, director. For several years programs of merit were given and then, despite various efforts to revive its activity, the club became inactive. Within the past five years its work has again become a feature of Muncie's music, mention of its concerts being made in the chronological records.

Ladies' Matinee Musicale.

Of organized efforts in promoting the musical interests of Muncie, none has contributed so much of vitalizing and permanent benefit, it is safe to say, as the Ladies' Matinee Musicale. No other musical society has had such a long and continuous career, and from its work has resulted in large part the elevation of musical taste and standard which can justly be said to characterize the better performance of music in the city. The Musicale has succeeded in its primary object, "to advance the interests and promote the culture of musical art in the city of Muncie; also for the mutual improvement of its members."

The Ladies' Matinee Musicale was organized in September, 1889, at the home of Miss Nannie C. Love. In addition to Miss Love, some of those who were identified with this movement from its inception are: Mrs. Mary E. Phinney, Mrs. George F. McCulloch, Mrs. J. M. Maring, Mrs. Eugene Kelley, Mrs. M. Keuchman, Mrs. Laura Keiser, Miss Jeanette C. Love, Mrs. Frank C. Ball, Miss Zula Wilcoxon, Mrs. Loan Franklin, Mrs. M. Louise Cassidy.

The officers for the current year are: Miss Nannie C. Love, President; Miss Helen M. Smith, Secretary; Mrs. Lillian Franklin, Treasurer; Miss Eleanor Smith, Vice-President; Executive Committee, Mrs. Charles Bender,

Mrs. Hal C. Kimbrough, Mrs. Frank C. Ball, Mrs. Lloyd Kimbrough, Miss Mamie Johnson.

Art Associations.

In May, 1907, the Muncie Art Association held its second annual exhibition in the rooms of the Commercial Club. During the twelve days while the exhibit was open to the public, the rooms were visited by several thousand persons, who represented not only those who take special interest in art, but also, and in greater numbers, those who found and expressed a genuine delight in simply "looking at pictures." The attendance at the exhibit and the interest manifested were in themselves the best measure of the value of such an exhibit, but the Art Association merits particular praise because through its agency a considerable proportion of the people of a large community are being familiarized with creditable productions and at the same time being trained to a correct estimation of art.

One must go back at least twenty years to find the beginning of the influences which may be considered to culminate in the work now being done by the Art Association as described above. Nearly coincident with the discovery of natural gas, an art class was begun in Muncie with J. Ottis Adams as its instructor. Mr. Adams, who now resides in Indianapolis, was born in Johnson county, Indiana, and before coming to Muncie had studied seven years in the Royal Academy at Munich. In June, 1888, he held an art reception in the Willard block to view the work of his first class of pupils in Muncie, and this was repeated in the following year, when two or three hundred pictures, some from Fort Wayne and elsewhere, were on exhibition in the Anthony building. Mr. Adams' pupils exhibited more than common enthusiasm in the work, and some of them have been heart and soul of the subsequent movements undertaken for the advancement of art in Muncie.

The first practical organization was the Muncie Art Students' League. Mrs. Arthur Brady and Mrs. William Oves gave the invitation to those interested in art which resulted in a meeting in the kindergarten room of the high school building and the formation of the League in June, 1892. The charter members, most of whom are still members, were: Mrs. J. R. Marsh, Miss Jennie Neely, Mrs. Lon Neely, Mrs. T. F. Rose, Mrs. E. W. Bishop, Mrs. A. J. Williams, Mrs. Harriet Johnston, Mrs. Martha Marsh, Miss Edna Streeter, Mrs. H. M. Winans, Mrs. William Oves, Mrs. George Bard, Mrs. Harry Wysor, Mrs. J. I. Williams, Mrs. Frank Thrall, Mrs. Charles Bennett, Mrs. Thad. Neely, Mrs. Loan Franklin, Mrs. Madison Maring, Miss Florence Walling, Mrs. E. B. Tyler, Mrs. Arthur Brady, Miss Ida Ludlow, Mrs. William Stewart, Mrs. I. N. Trent, Mrs. Thomas Morgan.

The study of the various branches of art, the bringing together of the various art interests of the community in order to promote a spirit of art interest and appreciation, are the professed objects of the League. For some time in the first years a studio was kept open under the supervision of Mr. Adams, and an evening sketch class was maintained. Lecturers are employed to deliver addresses on the history of art, and the picture exhibits have been annual features practically since the first one above mentioned. In 1906 the League, realizing that the annual exhibition had reached proportions where it could not be successfully managed by their organization, directed their efforts toward and became largely responsible for the formation of the Muncie Art Association. The League contributed one hundred dollars toward the purchase of the pictures secured by the Association at the conclusion of the first exhibit. The League has given pictures to the public schools, and through its committee on civic improvement has done much to beautify the city.

The officers of the Art Students' League for 1907 are: President, Mrs. Cora S. Trent, Vice-president, Miss Ida Ludlow; Recording Secretary, Mrs. Grace Spencer; Corresponding Secretary, Mrs. Ella W. Griffith; Treasurer, Mrs. Grace J. Davis; Program Committee, Mrs. Elizabeth Ball, Mrs. Harriet Case, Mrs. Mary Spilker.

Those most prominently identified with the work of the Art Association, as represented by the personnel of the officers and heads of committees during the second annual exhibition, are the following:

George F. McCulloch, president; Mrs. Harriet M. Johnston, first vice-president; Mrs. George A. Ball, second vice-president; Miss Belle Thomas, secretary; Mrs. John P. Kessler, treasurer.

Chairmen of Regular Committees: George L. Roberts, membership; Mrs. F. C. Ball, exhibition; Edmund B. Ball, permanent art museum; George A. Ball, finance; Dr. G. W. H. Kemper, civic art; Ernest P. Wiles, art education.

Directors: George F. McCulloch, George A. Ball, Harriet M. Johnston, George L. Roberts, F. C. Ball, Belle Thomas, Ernest P. Wiles, Sarah Kessler, Susan R. Marsh.

Early Dramatics.

Interest in dramatics and private theatricals has long been a feature of Muncie's culture. Only a few will recall the first organized effort of a dramatic nature. This was the Muncie Dramatic Club, organized during the '60s, the first home talent entertainment having been given in the basement of the Universalist church in 1863. Some of those who took part in the work of that club were A. L. Wright, M. D. Helm, L. M. Neely, W. H. Stewart, J. H. Case, Miss Julia Andrews, Miss May Shipley.

The dramatic club that was active during the nineties has been referred to, and the work of the Conversation Club along that line is mentioned in the sketch of that club. Muncie has contributed several members to the theatrical profession. Walker Whiteside, who for some years has headed a company engaged in creditable productions, and who is popular with theater-goers in most of the cities of America, lived in Muncie for several years, and it is said that his father was born in a house on the site now occupied by Wysor's Grand. Charles Murray, of the Murray & Mack company, one of the superior road companies in comedy and musical plays, is also claimed as a product of Muncie.

Among literary contributors, there are several in Muncie and Delaware county whose names deserve mention. R. I. Patterson and John S. Ellis, both so well known in the official life of the county, have written many verses with reference to passing events or local themes. W. E. Sutton, formerly editor of the Times and later with the Press, is a writer of verse that has been published by the high-class periodicals of the country. With the productions of Mrs. E. S. L. Thompson the people of Muncie and vicin-ity have been familiar for a number of years. Some of her poetry has been issued in book form, and her articles have often appeared in the daily press. Mrs. George H. Koons and Mrs. Minnie Thomas Boyce also occupy a place among Delaware county authors. Mrs. Boyce's "Punkin Holler" sketches first appeared in the Chicago Inter Ocean, and she has also pub-lished short stories of merit and interest. Mrs. Koons has written verses since she was a girl, and has a long list of poems, sketches and stories to her credit.

Delaware County Agricultural and Mechanical Society.

In August, 1907, was held the fifty-fifth annual county fair, which in point of attendance, variety of attractions, and general interest shown was considered the most successful of these annual events, and the directors have succeeded in making good their claim that the Delaware county fair is one of the best held in the state, attracting exhibits not only from Indiana but from many other parts of the Union. Though, in keeping with the tendency shown at all recent fairs and expositions, the number of light amusement concessionaires seem to be increasing, there can be no question that these annual fairs, viewed in the broadest light, fulfill the general purposes of the organization; namely, "to promote the live stock, agricultural and mechanical interests of Delaware and adjoining counties."

The officers and stockholders of the fifty-fifth fair were: Charles H. Anthony, president; H. C. Ziegler, vice president; Benjamin C. Bowman, treasurer; Fred A. Swain, secretary; Frank J. Claypool, Thomas Minton, A. E. Lyman, H. J. McClellan, May Barnet, W. E. Floyd, Ed M. Klein, Marc S. Claypool and H. M. Winans. During the past twenty years the

office of president of the society has been held by two men—William H.
Wood and Charles H. Anthony—while M. S. Claypool has been secretary
and Frank J. Claypool general superintendent.

The memory of a few men still living goes back to the first county fairs.
The first fair was held in the summer or fall of 1852, and the first "agricultural society" for the promotion of such exhibits was formed March 4,
1852. The names of the first officers of the society lend the greater dignity
to this time-honored institution of the county. They were: Martin Galliher, president; Thomas J. Sample, vice president; Daniel Jarrett, secretary; Thomas J. Matthews, treasurer. During those and subsequent years,
others who were prominent in the affairs of the society were Marc Smith,
Judge Joseph Buckles, James Maddy, William M. Petty, Major J. F. Wildman, John M. Graham, Captain Frank Ellis, Samuel Drumm, Samuel
Parkinson, John Fudge, Thomas Tuttle, Joseph Hinton.

It is said that one or two of the first fairs were held on the court house
square. This fact is very suggestive of the extent of the fair of half a
century ago, as compared with the one last witnessed. "Premiums were
offered," so a report of the second fair reads, "on horses, cattle, sheep, swine,
wheat, corn, potatoes, grass seed, butter, cheese, domestic manufactures,
farm implements and various articles displaying mechanical skill, poultry,
fruit and flowers." We can understand how a few tents or wooden shelters
on the square or the halls of the court house itself were used for the display
of these exhibits. Then the other chief attraction was the speaking when
some prominent citizen from home or abroad delivered an address on agricultural and kindred topics. The fair of that time was evidently little more
varied than the average farmers' institute at present, and their objects were
more nearly identical. Evidently racing was not a feature of the earliest
fairs. The fairs were then, much more so than now, a great social com-
mingling of the people from all parts of the county. With only one railroad
through the county, and before the days of pike roads, it was no small
undertaking to journey to the county seat from the outer townships. And
because people came together less frequently than now, they celebrated such
an occasion with the greater heartiness.

By 1854 five acres of ground had been leased and made suitable for
the holding of a fair, and on this land the fairs were held annually until the
termination of the affairs of the first society. A new organization was
effected in January, 1868, of which Judge Buckles was president and J. A.
Wachtell secretary. This association attempted to purchase forty-one acres
north of town, on the site that has ever since been known as the fair
grounds. The association being unable to pay for the land, the county commissioners assumed the debt and the title to the land became vested in the
county.

In 1874, while the grange movement was at its height, another reorganization of the society occurred, under the "Delaware County Agricultural, Horticultural and Mechanical Society." In 1880 another reorganization took place, at which time John M. Graham became president, Thomas Tuttle vice president, William H. Wood superintendent, George Kirby treasurer, Frank Ellis secretary.

Delaware County Children's Home Association.

This philanthropic body was organized and incorporated at Muncie, in January, 1893, the object of its existence, as stated in the constitution, being to maintain a home and asylum for the children of this county whose necessities secure to them the benefactions of this association under the provisions of its articles of association and constitution; to provide for their physical comfort and moral elevation and improvement; and to secure their early and permanent location in families by adoption or indenture.

In line with its purposes, the association has received and placed in permanent homes an average of about sixty dependent children each year during its existence.

The earlier members of the association were: Rev. Frank H. Hays, Dr. Hugh A. Cowing, Hardin Roads, R. A. Andes, Dr. W. E. Driscoll, Mrs. Margaret March, Mrs. Mary A. Goddard, Mrs. Mary Smith, Mrs. Martha James, Mrs. Julia Richey, Mrs. Nellie M. Stouder, Mrs. S. V. Jump.

The present officers are: President, Dr. Hugh A. Cowing; vice president, John W. Dragos; secretary, Mrs. Nellie M. Stouder; treasurer, Hardin Roads.

CHAPTER XXVII.

FRATERNAL AND SOCIAL ORGANIZATIONS.

MASONRY.

Delaware Lodge No. 46, A. F. & A. M.

Delaware Lodge No. 46, the oldest Masonic body in the county, originated in a dispensation dated October 7, 1842, appointing Samuel P. Anthony master, Patrick Justice senior warden and John Brownlee junior warden of the new lodge. The lodge was instituted in the house of Dr. Anthony, March 20, 1843. The present Masonic Temple is located not far from the site of that residence, which was a 2-story frame structure and stood on the east side of High street on the south side of the alley between Main and Jackson. Besides those named, those present at this first meeting were James Hogan, John M. Thomas, John Hupp, Jesse Sythan, James O. Leas, B. Sayre, G. E. Cook. None of these are now living.

May 23, 1843, the lodge was chartered as Delaware Lodge No. 46. A short time later the grand jury room in the court house was obtained as lodge room. From the court house the place of meeting was moved, in 1846, to the house of George B. Norris, northwest corner of Main and Jefferson; thence to a room on the south side of Main street, just east of High. The upper story of the court house was next procured and remodeled for lodge uses. In 1853 a room in the Globe block became the lodge home.

In the spring of 1863 the "Charley Cooper lot," at the southwest corner of the public square, was bought for $1,252, and plans for a Masonic hall laid. The corner stone was laid June 24, 1863, and a three-story brick building erected which served for a lodge home and the purposes of trade and offices until the splendid new temple was built.

The new Masonic temple in Muncie, the corner stone of which was laid November 9, 1905, is one of the most ornate structures dedicated to Masonry, and is a distinct addition to the architectural possessions of the city. Unlike the building it supplanted, which was not to be distinguished in appearance from the business buildings that stood near it, the new home of Masonry has the classic lines of the ancient temple, the symmetry and elegance that consist with art rather than practical business.

The oldest members of the lodge at this writing are: D. H. H. Shewmaker, G. W. H. Kemper, R. S. Gregory, J. B. Ludlow, Cyrus J. Seldomridge, George H. Cannaday, Alonzo Atherton, David Haney, John A. Wachtell, Fred Klopfer, James R. Turner, George Louthian, James Boyce, Samuel O. Budd, John S. Ellis, N. Fuller Ethell, Charles Gass, John N. Kirby, John H. Smith, George Zuber.

The present officers: Emory J. Niday, W. M.; Charles H. Ellis, S. W.; Edward B. Wilson, J. W.; Ralph H. Clark, treasurer; Adam O. Hoppes, secretary; William H. Thompson, S. D.; Charles B. Atherton, J. D.; Ben P. Sargent and Elsworth D. Bishop, stewards; E. W. Swain, tyler.

Relief committee: E. W. Bishop, R. H. Clark, A. T. Eastes.

Finance committee: W. W. Mann, J. N. Retherford, W. F. Stewart.

Trustees: D. H. H. Shewmaker, B. C. Bowman, Joseph E. Davis.

Muncie Lodge No. 433, A. F. & A. M.

November 10, 1870, dispensation was granted a new body of Masons in Muncie, and May 23, 1870, the lodge was organized. The first officers were Asa H. Hodson, W. M.; Isaac Branson, S. W.; H. Clay Hodge, J. W.; Hugh Hughes, treasurer; William L. Little, secretary; W. S. Richey, S. D.; George W. Van Matre, J. D.; J. W. Heath, tyler. This lodge in April, 1879, purchased the old Odd Fellows hall on East Main street, and moved their quarters to that place. About ten years ago the lodge moved to elegant quarters on the fifth floor of the Johnson block, where the meetings are still held.

Of the charter members there are but five living who retain their membership with this lodge, namely: Joseph Hummel, Thomas H. Kirby, Frank Ellis, Nathan H. Long, Webster S. Richey. Joseph Hummel was elected treasurer of the lodge at the annual election in December, 1876, and has been re-elected annually ever since. J. Wallace Perkins was elected secretary of the lodge at the annual election in December, 1879, and has served almost continuously since. The lodge had a membership, January 1, 1907, of 317.

The present officers are: George W. Burt, worshipful master; William D. Whitney, senior warden; J. Lloyd Kimbrough, junior warden; Joseph Hummel, treasurer; J. Wallace Perkins, secretary; Marion A. Norris, senior deacon; E. Stanton Janney, junior deacon; Beecher W. Bennett, tyler; J. Walter Kirkpatrick and Wilbur Ryman, deacons; Charles H. Kimbrough, William H. Wood and Walter S. Parkhurst, trustees.

Muncie Chapter No. 30, R. A. M.

A branch of Royal Arch Masonry has been located in Muncie since 1855. Dispensation to work a Royal Arch Chapter to Anthony Chapter, U. D., and the following appointed officers: S. P. Anthony, H. P.; Thomas Whitney, K.; Joseph A. Hill, S. Under the charter, which bore date May

22, 1856, the name was changed to Muncie Chapter No. 30. Complete organization of the Chapter was not effected until January 22, 1858. By May, 1861, the membership had increased to forty-one, and in 1880 the membership was about 130.

Muncie Commandery No. 18, K. T.

November 9, 1868, fourteen years after the organization of the grand encampment of the State of Indiana, a convention of Knights Templar met at Muncie, and a commandery was instituted under dispensation. The dispensation named the following petitioning Knights: Joseph A. Hill, John Marsh, William Craig, Andrew J. Riley, John Oakerson, John W. Burson, George H. Baxter, George Riley, Jesse K. Jameson, John A. Young. Others who had the degree of knighthood conferred upon them at the first meeting were: Erville B. Bishop, Henry C. Marsh, Thomas S. Walterhouse, Frederick E. Putnam, John M. Kirby, Frank Ellis, George W. Fay, Cyrus G. Neely, Joseph M. Davis, Stephen H. Ladd, S. Ambrose Wilson, Philip F. Davis, James N. Templer, Henry C. Klein, Carlton E. Shipley. The charter, subsequently issued, bears date April 7, 1869. On Jan. 1, 1907, the commandery had 195 members.

The past eminent commanders, in their order of service, have been: William Craig,* Thomas Duncan,* J. Wallace Perkins, Julius C. Wood, J. Edward Haffner, William H. Wood, Eugene W. Kelley,* David H. H. Shewmaker, Carey Franklin, Lee Shaw, George H. Keelor, Theodore F. Rose, Beecher W. Bennett, Frank G. Jackson, Charles B. Fudge, Edward W. Bishop, William C. Ball, Charles E. Miller.

Present officers: Oliver W. Storer, E. C.; James M. Motsenbocker, G.; George W. Wagner, C. G.; Eugene Vatet, S. W.; Walter Shumaker, J. W.; Charles A. Wood, prelate; Charles H. Church, treasurer; Marion A. Morris, recorder; R. Milt Retherford, St. B.; Robert M. Ball, Sw. B.; Walter S. Parkhurst. warden; Samuel U. Huffer, sentinel.

Muncie Council No. 16, R. & S. M.

Cryptic craft Masonry was instituted in Muncie under a dispensation granted December 15, 1863. A charter was granted May 15, 1864, and by the end of the year the Council had a membership of thirty-eight, which had increased in 1880 to about eighty-five. The original petitioners to form the Council were William Roach, John Marsh, Peter H. D. Bandy, George Riley, Peter H. Lemon. G. C. Beeks, James Montgomery, Moses Woolf, George F. Myers. The grand puissant appointed Peter H. D. Bandy, thrice illustrious grand master; John Marsh, thrice illustrious deputy master;

* Deceased.

James Montgomery, principal conductor of work. The first petitions were received from John W. Burson, A. J. Riley, George H. Baxter, William Craig, George Fay, P. F. Davis, I. C. Polsley and Fred E. Putnam.

Present officers: George W. Wagner, illustrious master; Moses E. Black, right illustrious deputy master; Marion A. Norris, illustrious principal conductor of work; Benjamin C. Bowman, treasurer; Thomas L. Westlake, recorder; Charles B. Atherton, captain of the guard; Clarence G. Rea, conductor of the council; Samuel U. Huffer, steward; William S. Martin, guard; George H. Keelor, B. C. Bowman, James B. Ludlow, trustees.

Anthony Lodge No. 171, F. & A. M., Albany.

The dispensation was issued December 12, 1854, and the charter was issued May 30, 1855. For several years the lodge did not grow in membership very rapidly, and the lodge was burned out several times with a complete loss of all their property and fixtures. The last few years the lodge has grown very rapidly and now has about one hundred members.

The following is a list of the charter members: William Krohn, Elisha Bergdoll, Morgan Wilson, James L. Leigh, Ambrose Dixon, Isaiah Sutton, James H. Powers, William Dixon, William Richardson.

It is not known that any of the charter members are still living. For many years about fifteen members kept the lodge alive. Among them were J. W. Wingate, Elisha Wingate, Moses Clark, Andrew Black and Samuel Shroyer, all deceased, and James E. Stafford and Isaiah Dudelston, who are residents of Albany.

William Krohn was the first worshipful master, Elisha Bergdoll senior warden and Morgan Wilson junior warden.

The following are the past masters now living: Andrew Clark, John E. Hill, Joseph H. Pote, Orion O. Faull, Joshua P. Foster, Ivan A. Justice, James M. Vanderburg, Arthur W. Lockhart, Albert M. Poland.

The present officers are: Walter P. McCormick, W. M.; Charles M. Smith, S. W.; Harry Wallar, J. W.; William E. Hodgson, treasurer; Arthur W. Lockhart, secretary; Walter L. Murphy, S. D.; Calvin L. Skinner, J. D.; Simon P. Clouse, tyler.

Whitney Lodge No. 229, F. & A. M., New Burlington.

Whitney Lodge was organized at New Burlington May 28, 1857. It is a child of old Delaware Lodge, all but one of the charter members having demitted from that body. These charter members and the offices they held after organization were: W. M., Dr. Samuel V. Jump; S. W., Jones Harris (of Hagerstown Lodge No. 49); J. W., Thomas Whitney; treasurer, Benjamin G. Cunningham; secretary, John S. Hutchings; S. D., William Quigley; J. D., Samuel Weidner; tyler, Abel Gibson.

William Ribble, who is now a member of Delaware Lodge, was raised in Whitney Lodge November 26, 1857, and is the oldest living person who was made a Mason in Whitney Lodge. Mr. John B. Jackson, present sec. retary of the lodge, has taken pains to compile a list of the oldest members of the lodge still living, their place of residence and the date of raising, and it deserves publishing. It is as follows:

Thornton C. Robe, Oakville, raised May 17, 1862; John A. Powers, Luray, raised August 19, 1862; Jacob Clevenger, New Burlington, raised December 30, 1863; Samuel J. Dragoo, Muncie Route No. 6, raised March 5, 1864; Jacomiah S. Hutchings, Muncie Route No. 7, raised November 19, 1864; Lemuel Dragoo, Muncie Route No. 6, raised June 24, 1865; John Linville, New Burlington, raised May 2, 1866; William Terrell, living near Windsor, raised January 24, 1867; Canty Benbou, Muncie Route No. 6, raised September 12, 1867; Jacob H. Rees, near New Burlington, raised April 11, 1868; George Chalfant, Selma Route No. 2, raised March 27, 1869; Marion A. Cunningham, Selma, raised March 8, 1879; John W. Patterson, Oakville, raised October 8, 1887; John B. Jackson, Muncie Route No. 6, raised August 11, 1888; Frank H. Linvill, a minister, Bluffton, raised July 11, 1896; Parker Marshall, New Burlington, raised September 5, 1896; William L. Lindsey, near New Burlington, raised June 26, 1897; Dr. J. N. Bell, New Burlington, raised November 20, 1897; William Chalfant, near Smithfield, raised November 20, 1897; Eli Walradth, Muncie Route No. 6, raised November 20, 1897.

The present officers of Whitney Lodge are: W. M., Carl U. Williams; S. W., Luther W. Hutchings; J. W., Parker Marshall; treasurer, Dr. J. N. Bell; secretary, John B. Jackson; S. D., John Linville; J. D., Gola Jackson; tyler, Clinton R. Gates.

Eaton Lodge No. 606, F. & A. M.

In 1895 James A. Motsenbocker, Marcus A. Fisher, Robert M. Morris, James M. Atkinson, William Bost, Charles A. Smith, Walter A. Goodrich, Thomas J. Mitchell, Joseph Cramer and Corwello K. Vanbuskirk made application for a dispensation empowering them to meet and work as a lodge of Free and Accepted Masons. A dispensation was issued by Edward O'Rouke, grand master, dated January 13, 1896. In pursuance of this dispensation Eaton Lodge U. D. was organized with the following officers:

James M. Motsenbocker, W. M.; Marcus A. Fisher, S. W.; Robert M. Morris, J. W.; William Bost, treasurer; Corwello K. Vanbuskirk, secretary; William H. Brandt, S. D.; Thomas J. Mitchell, J. D.; Charles A. Smith, tyler.

A charter was granted under date of May 26, 1896. By instructions of the grand master, Eaton Lodge No. 606, F. & A. M., was instituted on June 26, 1896, by Henry W. Mordhurst, acting deputy grand master. The lodge has about sixty members.

The present officers are: Oliver J. Chapman, worshipful master; Shadrach N. Feltz, senior warden; Moses E. Black, junior warden; William H. Brandt, treasurer; Preston H. Feltz, secretary; David B. Blazer, senior deacon; Robert M. Morris, junior deacon; Marcus A. Fisher, tyler.

Muncie Chapter No. 104, O. E. S.

Muncie Chapter of the Eastern Star was organized December 9, 1890, in the Delaware Lodge room at the corner of Main and High streets. The charter members were: Mary Braun, Nannie Crews, Isaac Crews, Susannah Cooper, George E. Dungan, Ida Dungan, S. B. Garrett, Annie L. Garrett, Helen Hartley, Florence Johnson, A. L. Johnson, Lillie Jackson, Andrew Jackson, Clara Klöpfer, Jennie McLaughlin, G. N. McLaughlin, Donna McCaughan, Charles McCaughan, Fred E. Putnam, Kate Reeves, D. H. H. Shewmaker, Nancy Shewmaker, Della Shewmaker, Ella Westlake, Charles Westlake, J. R. Hummel.

The present officers are: Ivy B. Stetter, worthy matron; Moses E. Black, worthy patron; Linnie Thornburg, associate matron; Mary E. Hurst, secretary; Clara S. Klöpfer, conductress; Nellie A. W. Dill, associate conductress; Anna Segelhorst, Adah; Jessie Stephens, Ruth; Edna McDowell, Esther; Sarah E. Edwards, Martha; Rosa Burmaster, Electa; Nettie Eppards, warder; George A. Carpenter, sentinel; Mary Marsh, chaplain; Mabel M. Lewis, marshal; Mary Herbert, organist.

Albany Chapter, O. E. S.

The Eastern Star chapter was organized at Albany March 22, 1899, the earliest members being: Ivan Justice, Cora Justice, William Blankley, Evaline Blankley, Henry Redelsheimer, Mattie Redelsheimer, A. C. Heck, Jennie Heck, Thomas Bracken, Charity Bracken, Clark Shroyer, Lollo Shroyer, John E. Hill, Maud Hill, Norman Russell, John Middlehurst, Florence Middlehurst, John V. Baird, Mary Baird, Robert Stratton, Laura Powers, Bertha Davis, Elisha Wingate, Joseph H. Pope, Emma Pope, Alice Wood, W. C. Huffman, Amanda Wingate.

The present officers are: Worthy matron, Mrs. Ida Dudelston; worthy patron, Isaiah Dudelston; associate matron. Mrs. Candace Reed; secretary, Mrs. Annie L. Hodgson: treasurer, Mrs. Clara Huffman; conductress, Lola Wingate; associate conductress, Mrs. Orena Thomas; chaplain, Mrs. Lillie Barrett.

INDEPENDENT ORDER OF ODD FELLOWS.

Muncie Lodge No. 74, I. O. O. F.

Oddfellowship was introduced into Delaware county in the organization of Muncie Lodge No. 74, which was instituted November 9, 1849. The first set of officers were: David T. Haines, N. G.; John C. Helm, V. G.; Thomas J. Matthews, secretary; John Brady, treasurer; Eli J. Jamison, warden; Theodore J. Riley, conductor; Martin Galliher, R. S. to N. G.; Edward G. Keasby, R. S. S.; William Walling, L. S. S. The organization of this lodge took place in what was then known as Anthony's building, on the south side of Main street, one door east of the southwest corner of the square. Until May 28, 1852, the lodge met in a room in Galliher's building, on Main street between High and Walnut; then for about a year met in Masonic hall. A third floor was built on the Brady building, on the north side of Main, between Walnut and Mulberry, expressly for the use of the Odd Fellows, and the lodge moved to these quarters in May, 1853.

In 1871 the sum of four thousand dollars was paid for a forty-foot lot on the northeast corner of Jackson and Walnut streets, and the taking of a stock subscription for the building of a hall was begun. June 8, 1872, the corner stone was laid, and the new hall was dedicated October 28, 1875. January 1, 1907, the membership of the lodge was 480. The present officers are: W. Claud Hirons, N. G.; Frank V. Langezaal, V. G.; Will S. Stewart, secretary; George W. Brooks, treasurer; John C. Eiler, Will H. F. Young, Frank H. Greely, trustees.

The oldest living members of this lodge are: Nelson Leonard, James Charman, Joseph Hummel, Sr., George W. Blodgett, Joshua C. Bacon, Frank Ellis, Henry P. Roush, Stephen B. Streeter, George Cochren, John C. Eiler, George W. Paxson, Hiram S. Trullender, Elijah J. Reeves, Daniel S. Huffer, Elias P. Smith, Wilson R. Smith, David A. Porterfield, William M. Knapp, Thomas Paxson, Charles Gass, Samuel Q. Brady, William Dunlap, Benjamin F. Bratton, Zachary T. Long, Joseph D. Hoyt, Elias E. Matthews, Anderson Moore, George W. Brooks, James L. Simmon, Will A. Meeks. James W. Meeks, Fred Klöpfer.

Energy Lodge No. 652, I. O. O. F., Muncie.

Energy Lodge was organized October 3, 1889, with the following charter members: William J. Bowen, Samuel Yockey, Thomas Winsor, Mathias H. Shaner, Charles H. Bowers, Isaac N. Trent, John A. Hamilton, John C. Ross, L. M. Tyler, B. K. Rockaway, Andrew Jackson, Harvey A. Richards, Charles F. Gibbs and James M. Gaumer.

Those now filling the lodge offices are: J. R. Rathburn, C. E. Douglass, William Jilbert, J. T. Robinson, Chris. Smith, J. W. Gibson and S. A. Schlechty.

Muncie Encampment No. 30, I. O. O. F.

Muncie Encampment No. 30 was organized January 20, 1852, and on March 24, 1852, was instituted under a charter from the grand encampment. The first officers elected were John C. Helm, C. P.; Jacob Colclazer, H. P.; John H. Jamison, S. W.; Eli J. Jamison, J. W.; William G. Ethell, S.; Edward G. Keasby, treasurer. The formal title of the Encampment was adopted at the second stated meeting.

The oldest members now living, with the date of their initiation, are: Joseph Hummel, February 15, 1864; R. Berger, February 5, 1866; F. Ellis, February 5, 1866; J. C. Bacon, February 19, 1866; H. P. Roush, May 21, 1866; Hiram Trullender, March 15, 1869; Henry Overmire, April 5, 1869; W. R. Smith, February 7, 1870; E. P. Smith, May 16, 1870; Charles Gass, January 11, 1871; James Charman, November 20, 1871; J. C. Eiler, September 2, 1872.

Present officers are: A. C. Case, scribe; Lon Dungan, treasurer; J. F. Mana, George Davis and George Brooks, trustees; B. L. Hollister, chief patriarch; James A. Mason, high priest; James W. Adams, senior warden; W. A. Wagoner, junior warden; R. J. McClellan, inside guard; J. F. Ryan, outside guard; R. J. McClellan, D. D., grand patriarch of Delaware county.

Canton Muncie No. 4, P. M. (I. O. O. F.)

Canton Muncie was organized December 31, 1885, in the lodge rooms of Muncie Lodge No. 74, I. O. O. F. The charter members were: S. C. Humes, C. K. Wright, John Clark, John E. Banta, M. S. Smith, J. R. Fineple, J. W. Meeks, J. M. Williamson, W. L. Lacey, J. O. Lambert, W. J. Kurtz, G. J. Ivens, J. R. Hummel, C. A. Budd, W. S. Stewart, C. W. Lynn, J. D. Hoyt, Charles Gass, B. F. Bratton, J. W. Little, J. A. Brown, Frank Ellis, A. J. Kleinfelder, J. F. Wildman, Joe Hierich, T. F. Rose, Webb Gilbert, Charles Bindschidler, Marion Richmond, George W. Brooks, Lee Joseph, William P. Lake, Arthur Shideler, R. J. Patterson, O. L. Meeks, Karl G. Sample, Will Trullender, M. A. Dolman, Richard Berger, Joseph Hummel, Charles Wildermuth, Marcus Topp, Jacob Vogt, William Dragoo, W. H. M. Cooper, William A. Meeks, William Lynn, Albert Hoyt, John Allen, A. M. Klein, Henry P. Roush, John McConnell, William Morris, H. R. Wysor.

The present officers are: Commandant, Michael Hefner; lieutenant, Wilder L. Maitlue; ensign, Captain G. W. Wagner; clerk, James S. Manor; accountant, Frank H. Greely; drill master, Captain G. W. Wagner.

Lodge No. 772, I. O. O. F., Eaton.

This lodge was organized May 23, 1901, with charter members Moses Peterson, L. D. Larrowe, Sherman Lamar, William M. Burdge, Tabor S. Allis, William E. Brown, Joseph Cramer. The present officers of the lodge are: N. G., C. McFadden; V. G., C. S. Freeman; secretary, E. R. Thompson; chaplain, T. S. Allis; P. G., O. Ν. Rearick; treasurer, Ν. E. Black; trustees, S. Lamar, O. Ν. Rearick, Arthur Lewellen.

Yorktown Lodge No. 345, I. O. O. F.

The charter members, at the organization of this lodge on April 2, 1870, were: Conrad Dippel, Henry Overmire, Hezekiah Stout, D. Ν. Yingling, Jacob Erther, J. H. Williamson. Of these Henry Overmire, Hezekiah Stout and J. H. Williamson are still identified with the lodge. The oldest living initiates are: David Campbell, Andrew Yingling, Ishum Humphries, James R. Applegate, R. J. Stout, J. D. Reynolds, P. V. Stewart, E. F. Alldredge.

The present officers: N. G., Albert Sollers; V. G., J. W. Metzcar; secretary, J. Ν. Warfel; treasurer, W. T. Warfel; trustees, Andrew Yingling, Edward S. Hahn, David Luce.

New Corner Lodge No. 425, I. O. O. F., Gaston.

This lodge was organized in August, 1873, but worked under dispensation until it was chartered on November 23, 1873. The charter members were: J. W. Hannan, Ν. V. Rhoads, Jesse Ayers, Adam Moody, Benjamin F. Buvoy, J. T. Broyles, William S. Null, Joseph Burgess, B. H. McKinley, Benjamin Bartlett, Lamb Graves, John McKinley, David Vannatter, Thomas Stubbs, Ezra Woodring, Madison Bryan, J. H. Boyle.

The present officers: Noble grand, J. C. Brown; vice grand, E. F. Hamilton; treasurer, F. B. McIntosh; secretary, Bruce Roach; recording secretary, H. Ν. Long; trustees, J. C. Brown, J. W. Brock and Allen Oxley.

Cowan Lodge No. 561, I. O. O. F.

This lodge was organized and worked under dispensation for some weeks, until it was formally instituted under charter, November 21, 1878. Of the charter members only J. W. Houck is now living, his fellow members having been J. W. Jones, J. W. Abbott, Peter Quirk, Henry Braun, C. Ν. Kiger, J. W. Poland. For the first few years the membership was very small, but it now numbers 53 and is one of the strong lodges of the county. The officers are: J. E. Rinker, N. G.; D. O. Wert, V. G.; I. A. Kern, secretary; D. Ν. Hays, treasurer; D. S. Koons, Charles Kern, O. P. Bowers, trustees.

Bethel Lodge No. 731, I. O. O. F.

This is one of the recent lodges of Oddfellowship in the county. It was instituted at Bethel November 19, 1897, by the grand master and grand secretary. The charter membership comprised: L. A. Johnson, J. W. Dotson, William A. Jackson, A. S. Parker, W. R. Parker, A. J. Estle, Dr. J. H. Hayden.

The present officers are: Lewis King, N. G.; Christian Berg, V. G.; L. H. Mitchell, recording secretary; B. A. Brunton, secretary; William A. Jackson, Ora King, Christian Berg, trustees.

Charity Lodge No. 785, I. O. O. F., Cammack.

The lodge at Cammack was instituted April 23, 1902, with the following charter members: M. L. Snodgrass, R. M. Snodgrass, John E. Modlin, Hezekiah Stout, George Simpson, Elias Hamilton, Lemuel A. Dawson, Calvin P. Mann (dec.), Hiram W. Summers, Frank Darter, Joseph H. Snodgrass (dec.), J. O. Snodgrass, J. C. Derbyshire, O. P. Snodgrass, William H. Jones, P. M. Rudy.

The present officers: George W. Howell, N. G.; George Simpson, V. G.; Frank Darter, P. G.; David E. Brown, chaplain; T. H. Hankins, secretary; R. M. Snodgrass, treasurer.

Heart and Hand Lodge No. 361, I. O. O. F., Albany.

Heart and Hand Lodge was organized at Albany March 30, 1871, with the following charter members: C. J. Stright, H. J. Lockhart, R. A. Maxwell, David Goings, Adam Boots, John McNelly, William McJohnson, H. C. Nichols, M. A. Wilson. The oldest living members of the lodge are D. M. Bell, J. R. Stafford, Manaen Vincent, B. W. Wingate, M. A. Wilson. The present officers of the lodge are: W. S. Bartow, Elmer Ferguson, C. L. Skinner, M. A. Wilson, J. R. Stafford.

Daleville Lodge No. 309, I. O. O. F.

This lodge was organized June 6, 1868, the following being charter members: L. D. Richman, Santford H. Shoemaker, J. H. Tuttle, William H. Miller, Samuel Dusang, P. M. Rudy. In the same year Cary Fenwick and Joe Lonsdale were initiated, and somewhat later: George W. Brandon, S. B. Garrett, Henry Rader, John Bender.

The present officers of the lodge are: Joe Minnick, N. G.; J. H. Swigers, V. G.; E. B. Shoemaker, P. G.; E. F. Good, treasurer; L. H. Fenwick, secretary.

Wheeling Lodge No. 325, I. O. O. F.

There were seven charter members when this lodge was instituted May 26, 1869, namely: R. W. Rigdon, J. P. Williams, William Lewis, David W. Reynolds, J. C. Ginn, Liberty Hamilton. At the present writing the oldest members of the lodge are George Powers, C. C. Crampton, John Clark, B. H. McKinley, W. W. Hoover, Henry Hyer, George Lewis.

The present officers are: E. S. Rigdon, N. G.; James F. Davis, V. G.; William C. Hamilton, secretary; M. L. Hoover, treasurer; trustees, George Powers, B. H. McKinley, Charles Butcher.

Naomi Rebekah Lodge No. 3, Muncie.

One of the first Rebekah lodges in the state, as its number indicates, the Naomi Daughters of Rebekah were organized January 18, 1869, with the following charter members: Joshua C. Bacon, Samantha A. Bacon, Richard Berger, Amelia Berger, John Hamilton, Anna Hamilton, John A. Huff, Frate Huff, W. H. M. Cooper, Sue M. Cooper, Frank Ellis, Joseph Hummel. Of these there still survive, Joshua C. Bacon, Samantha A. Bacon, Amelia Berger, W. H. M. Cooper, Frank Ellis, Joseph Hummel.

The present officers are: Mrs. Etta Wise, N. G.; Della Parker, V. G.; Elinora M. Gattschalk, Rec. Secy; Carabel Paden, Fin. Secy; Della Babb, Treas.

Omega Rebekah Lodge No. 433, Albany.

The Albany lodge of Rebekahs was organized January 9, 1904, with the following as charter members: Mr. J. R. Stafford, Mrs. Sarah Stafford, Mr. N. Barger, (dec.), Mrs. Anna Barger, Mr. Thomas M. Winagte, Mrs. Sarah E. Wingate, Mr. Thomas B. Clouse, Mrs. Rose E. Clouse.

Present officers: Miss Lizzie Spear, N. G.; Miss Amy Walters, V. G.; Mrs. Etta Ferguson, Rec. Sec.; Mrs. Candace Read, Fin. Sec.; Mrs. Mary Monroe, Treas.; Mrs. Samantha Stanton, Ward; Miss Lissie Burnside, Cond.; Miss Minnie Walters, I. G.; Mrs. Anna Lodge, O. G.; Miss Minnie Burnside, R. S. N. G.; Mrs. Ella Hobbs, L. S. N. G.; Mrs. Matilda Mull, R. S. V. G.; Mrs. Carrie Clark, L. S. V. G.; Miss Sadie Marks, Chap.; Mrs. Florence Trushour, P. N. G.

KNIGHTS OF PYTHIAS.

Welcome Lodge No. 37, K. of P., was instituted at the Odd Fellows' hall in Muncie (then on Main street), August 14, 1873. The charter members of the lodge (the charter was dated January 28, 1874) were: D. B. Shideler, W. D. Jones, J. N. Templer, R. S. Gregory, George W. Spilker, M. S. Claypool, W. R. Maddy, L. L. Hodge, J. F. Saunders, A. Rothschilds, S. P. Anthony Jr., Samuel Huffer, George Higman, William Glenn, Richard Berger, Joseph Fox, John Mann, O. H. Swain, Frank Leon, W. Shick, J. C. Bacon, W. C. Langdon. The Odd Fellows hall continued as the place of meeting until 1879, when a room was obtained in Wysor's opera house.

Some of the oldest members now living are as follows: R. S. Gregory, O. F. Jones, Moses Lutz, August Maick, Charles Gass, Charles Redding, Henry Roush, M. G. Mock, John D. Mock, C. E. Werking, L. H. Harper, E. E. Mathews, Albert G. Morris, Ben Rosenbush.

Present officers: Clarence W. Dearth, Master of Work; Charles Neiswanger, Chancellor Commander; Charles Fisher, Vice Chancellor; William

E. McDougal, Prelate; Parker Thornburg, Master at Arms; Arch H. Hobbs, Keeper of Records; Robert E. Gates, Master of Exchequer; Gola Danner, Master of Finance; Birch Jones, Inner Guard; Harry V. Moore, Outer Guard; August M. Maick, Enos Geiger, Frank L. Gass, trustees; Grand Vice Chancellor, Frank L. Gass.

Silver Shield Lodge No. 403, K. of P., Muncie.

When this lodge of Knights of Pythias was instituted at Muncie, June 12, 1894, there were fifty-two charter members. Since the organization of the lodge, the sum of $4,100 has been paid out in benefits.

The past chancellors of Silver Shield Lodge are: O. E. Baldwin, H. F. Bard, W. F. Benbow, E. E. Botkin, Charles Bowden, O. N. Cranor, J. W. Dragoo, J. Ed Ethel, Ed. J. Gainor, A. F. Goetscheus, L. A. Guthrie, F. T. Harris, H. J. Keller, S. F. Kiser, W. W. Mann, W. A. Mecker, J. A. Meeks, D. A. McLain, U. G. Poland, S. M. Ried, J. K. Ritter, O. T. Sharp, J. Stiffler, J. W. Wilson.

The present officers are: V. E. Silverburg, chanc. com.; W. F. Rutt-ledge, vice-chanc.; E. B. DeVault, prelate; W. S. Elliott, M. of A.; W. F. Benbow, M. of F.; J. W. Dragoo, M. of E.; W. W. Mann, K. of R. & S.; Chas. Bowden, M. of W.; R. Clayton, Inner Guard; F. West, Outer Guard; H. J. Keller, L. M. Glass, O. E. Baldwin, trustees; U. G. Poland, Med. Ex.

Valentine Lodge No. 378, K. of P., Albany.

Valentine Lodge was organized February 14, 1893, with the following charter members: A. C. Wilson, Oscar Wilson, D. W. Slonaker, W. G. Simmons, J. P. H. Casterline, Abraham Campbell, O. H. Tyndal, Harry Wallar, Dr. A. P. Murry.

The present officers are: J. L. Tulley, C. C.; Henry Vincent, V. C.; Earl Wroughton, Prel.; S. P. Dowden, M. of W.; C. L. Wood, K. R. & S.; W. G. Simmons, M. F.; Jno. Barrett, M. Ex.; Will Jacobs, W. A.; Jno. Peterson, I. G.; Fred Garland, O. G.; J. W. St. Clair, W. W. Works, S. P. Dowden, trustees.

Daleville Lodge No 452, K. of P.

This lodge was organized at Daleville December 1, 1897. The charter members were: Santford H. Shoemaker, (dec.), G. O. Driscoll, Jerrie M. Rader, S. A. Cornelius, J. V. Fenwick, S. E. Rinker, C. H. Warron, Frank Feely, D. W. Kabrich, C. F. Thomas, J. W. Overman, H. L. Detrich, W. S. Brandon, L. H. Fenwick, C. L. Richman, O. W. Brandon.

Present officers: W. S. Frazee, C. C.; H. M. Kabrich, V. C.; R. F. Lovin, Prel.; D. W. Kabrich, M. W.; E. C. Stewart, M. F.; A. P. Andrew, M. Ex.; L. H. Fenwick, K. of R.; C. H. Warron, R. A. Haugh, L. H. Fenwick, trustees.

Valentine Temple No. 190, Pythian Sisters, Albany.

The Pythian Sisters were organized at Albany in the K. of P. hall, November 30, 1898, with the following charter members: Martha L. Murray, Hanah Dowden, Carrie Ruth, Etta Orr, Orna Thomas, Ella Rickel, Martha Simmons, Nettie Richey, Norah Brandenburgh, Orilla Burden, Nina Marks, Kate Brann, Margaret Williams, Mollie Robinson, Florence Davidson, Julia Atkinson, Mary Chalk, Myrtle Everhart, Norah Wilson, Phoebe Wickersham, Blanche Manning, Leni Marks, Orpha Wilson, Bessie Dowden, Lena Boothe, Mattie Stout, Mary Johnson, Ida Weaver, Sybil Givans, L. W. Tucker, Wm. Chalk.

The present officers are: Rose Sexton, Past Chief; Lizzie Miller, Most Excellent Chief; Laura Bergdoll, Excellent Senior; Maude Marks, Excellent Junior; Julia Barrette, Manager of Temple; Nina A. Marks, Mistress of Records and Correspondence; Mary L. Chalk, Mistress of Finance; Margaret Williams, Protector of Temple; Alice Kelley, Guard of Outer Temple.

Pythian Sisters Temple No. 28, Muncie.

This temple was organized in Patterson hall, February 26, 1890, with the following charter members: Mesdames McLaughlin (dec.), Stiffler, Cates (dec.), Baldwin, Shafer (dec.), Redding, Zook, Retz, Slinger, Maick, Green, Garrard (dec.), Mack, Geiger, Kiser, Ridgely, Moore, Cunington, Ebenhack, Aydelott, McCaughn, Lutz, Barr.

The present officers are: Anna Nation, P. C.; Carrie Gainor, M. E. C.; Lizzie Stivers, M. E. S.; Lydia Jordon, M. E. J.; Beina Morrow, M. of T.; Hattie Waggoner, M. of R. & C.; Cora Green, M. of F.; Emma Hiatt, P. of T.; Margueit Redding, G. of O. T.; Dessie Gates, Hattie Geiger, Lizzie Rhoads, trustees.

IMPROVED ORDER OF RED MEN.

De Ember Tribe No. 30, I. O. R. M.

The first wigwam of this thoroughly American order was instituted June 26, 1873, at the Willard block, Main and Walnut streets. Meetings were held in the Wysor Opera House hall for about six years, and in 1879 quarters were taken up on the east side of Walnut street, just north of Jackson. The charter members of this order in Muncie were: John R. Ervin, John Kirk, Harry E. Gatrell, William Glenn, J. E. Worcester, James N. Templer, Frank Ellis, Dr. Milton James, Dr. E. C. Kennedy, R. S. Gregory, George L. Elliott. The Tribe has paid out, for burial purposes $2,145, and for sick benefits $15,987.

The present set of officers are: J. O. Newcomb, Sachem; M. J. Snider,

Sr. Sag.; Ed Mauer, Jr. Sag.; Mathias Sux, Prophet; E. C. Yockey, K. of W.; D. A. McLain, C. of R.; S. B. Garrett, N. B. Driscoll, F. C. McGrath, trustees.

Munsy Tribe No. 144, I. O. R. M.

This tribe was organized in the Turner block at Muncie, May 19, 1892. About 150 names are recognized in the charter membership, among them being: Gilbert Hughes, Jacob J. Cope, George Koerner, Thos. Troxell, John O. Lewellen, Ollie Baldwin, Geo. N. McLaughlin, Commodore P. Antrim, Geo. W. Summers, Robt. W. Monroe, David A. Lambert, H. C. Harrington, Samuel A. Kelly, Jerre Garrard, Joseph A. Brown (deceased), Jas. H. Summers, who is filling the office of chief of records for the thirteenth year. John Dooley, now deceased, was the organizer of this tribe.

The present set of officers are: Jesse Flatter, Sachem; Ira Benbow, Sr. Sagamore; Fred Bost, Jr. Sagamore; John C. Cline, Prophet; Thos. Troxell, Keeper of Wampum; Jas. H. Summers, Chief of Records; Gilbert Hughes, Jacob J. Cope and M. J. Hastings, trustees.

Twa Twa Tribe No. 145, I. O. R. M., Muncie.

This tribe, which was organized by John Loth, May 26, 1892, contained among its charter members: John Loth, Hon. Geo. W. Cromer, I. H. Gray, Jno. E. Andrews, G. R. Andrews, W. P. Lake, Jno C. Greisheimes, Frank Smith, R. M. Martin, W. N. Swain, Ed Swain, J. Milt Gray, Moses Hene, Moses Cohen, Hon. G. H. Koons, T. Ben Koons, O. F. Kain, Ed. F. Bender, Prof. A. Damm, N. T. Leager, Jas. M. Best, and 125 others.

The present officers are: Isaac H. Gray, Sachem; B. F. Basha, Sen. Sagamore; N. G. Stainbrook, Jr. Sagamore; John Loth, C. of R.; T. Ben Koons, K. of W.; A. J. Scranton, Prophet; John E. Andrews, I. H. Gray, Frank Smith, trustees; Harry Griffin, D. D. G. S.

Tomahawk Tribe No. 333, I. O. R. M.

This tribe was organized by Perry A. Langdon, in the Turner block at Muncie, June 12, 1902. There were 167 charter members.

The past sachems are: P. A. Langdon, Chas. A. Langdon, H. E. Walk, Annis Joris, Arthur T. Earles, James H. Dowley, Charles Minnick, O. W. Parr, Henry Stepleton, Adam Stepleton and E. M. Stanley.

The present officers: Sachem, William L. Eiler; Sr. Sagamore, James M. Ham; Jr. Sagamore, L. W. McClelland; prophet, Adam Stepleton; trustees, Samuel M. McMillian, E. M. Stanley and Dr. Glen A. Glasgow; G. W., E. M. Stanley; G. W., S. M. McMillian; Custodian of Property, John Shellenbarger; Chief of Records, Elmer E. Botkin; Keeper of Wampum, Sheldon Hickman.

Keechewa Tribe No. 275, I. O. R. M.

The tribe was instituted November 9, 1899, in the building known as the Turner block, located on South Walnut street, Muncie. More than two hundred names comprise the charter membership. The present officers are: Charles Holman, Sachem; Edward Drennen, Senior Sagamore; Hayden Hilton, Junior Sagamore; Elmer Jordan, Prophet; Arch H. Hobbs, Chief of Records; Charles Bowden, Keeper of Wampum; A. E. Needham, Harold Hobbs, Harry Smeltzer, trustees; John M. Hosfield, District Deputy Great Sachem.

Ionia Council No. 92, D. of P., Muncie.

Ionia Council was organized by Lafayette Stogdill, and instituted by G. P. Sue Biddlecome, April 26, 1897, in the Patterson building, corner Main and Walnut streets. The charter members were: Lafayette Stogdill, Mattie Stogdill, Martin G. Mock, Martha D. Mock, Perry Langdon, Sadie V. Langdon, Elizabeth Shafer, Lizzie Allen, Effie Root, L. H. Root, Maggie Hale, Mollie Langdon, Anna Elliott, Johnson Elliott, Elizabeth Elliott, Emma Grice, Luther Gilbert, Alice Gilbert, Samuel Swan, Julia Swan, D. L. Wood, Mollie Wood, Samuel A. Kelly, Emma Kelly, S. J. Simmons, M. E. Simmons, Noah Francis, Frances Francis, Theo. Minnick, Alice Minnick.

The present officers are: Sarah E. Larimer, Pocahontas; Ida M. Corkins, Wenonah; John C. Leonard, Powhatan; Margaret Elliott, Prophetess; Mattie Stogdill, Keeper of Records; Emma Crouse, Keeper of Wampum; Elizabeth Henehan, District Deputy; Lafayette Stogdill, Drill Master; Catherine Furr, Effie Root, Lizzie Allen, trustees.

Washatella Council No. 37, D. of P., Muncie.

Washatella Council was organized September 19, 1892, the charter members being: Mrs. Emma Miller, Bertha Patton, Mary Mason, C. D. Helm, W. H. M. Cooper, G. W. McLaughlin, Ellen Banta, Mrs. Millie Palmer, Mrs. J. E. Andrews, Mrs. Almira Burbage, Frank Smith, Mrs. Barbara Wilson, Mrs. Ora Smith, Mrs. Julia Bennett, William Aydalotte, Mrs. William Aydalotte, Martha Bayless, Dollie Dudley, George Phillips, Mrs. W. H. Postal, Mrs. Eva Heath.

The present officers: Minnie Ingersoll, District Deputy; Mrs. Ella Brown, Pocahontas; Mrs. Mary Mason, Wenona; Mr. Henry Stepeleton, Powhatan; Mrs. Emma Moles, Keeper of Records; Mrs. Mary McConnell, Keeper of Wampum; Charles Ingersoll, Nana Tate, Cora Evans, trustees.

Musco Council No. 7, D. of P., Muncie.

This council was organized with the following charter members: J. J. Johnson, J. O. Newcomb, A. H. Snydman and wife, M. G. Mock and wife,

Joshua Abbott and wife, Joseph Bennett, John Dooley and wife, H. C. Floyd and wife, Eli Hoover and wife, D. A. McLain and wife, J. R. Hunnel, Carl Maitlen, Leroy Freeman, J. N. Lamb and wife, Chas. Gass and wife, J. C. Ross and wife. J. O. Newcomb and Mrs. H. C. Floyd are the only charter members now identified with the council.

The present officers: Prophetess, Carrie Hawk; Pocahontas, Enna Aydelotte; Wenona, Myrtle Prutzman; Powhatan, Chas. Hawk; K. of R., Flora Keeley; K. of W., Amanda Shafer.

Seneca Council No. 150, D. of P., Muncie.

Seneca Council was organized Sept. 6, 1901, on the third floor of the Bishop block at Muncie, Ind., by Martha Mack. The work was done by Ionia Council of Muncie. The charter members were: Mrs. Sarah Sutton, Mary Sutton, Sue McKinley, Hannah Black, Mary James, Mary Thomas, Anna Flemming, Hannah Williams, Dianna Jones, Maria Wasson, Lillie Pippin, Lillian Touhey, Martha Jones, Lizzie Howell, Carrie Bales, Anna Murrey, Verda Murrey, Lizzie Briggs, Mary Bault, Celestina Flatter, Josia Amsden, Sarah Shafer, Emma McCauley, Tilda Shipley, Martha Stanley, Rosa Rock, Edith McCune, John Ellis, Chas. O. Howell, Wm. McKinley, John Cossiboone, John R. Bales.

Present officers: Prophetess, Rosa B. Davore; Pocahontas, Viola Kuhner, Wenona, Lizzie Briggs; Powhatan, Sherman Everist; Keeper of Records, Lizzie Howell; Keeper of Wampum, Josie Oaks; trustees, Wm. Ennis, John R. Bales, Anna Murrey.

Kickapoo Tribe, I. O. R. M., Albany.

This tribe was organized December 20, 1883, some of the oldest members being: L. N. Dowell, Noah Bantz, S. Younce, James Spence, James French, Dr. J. A. Dowell, A. Sipe, D. W. Slonaker.

The present officers are: Sachem, W. E. Chalk; Sen. Sag., W. S. Tewerbaugh; Jr. Sg., Ed. Saffers; Proph., Herbit Whitehair; C. of K. and C. of W., C. L. Wood; K. of W., G. M. Ellis; G. of W., A. Sipe; G. of F., Sim Younce.

Iola Council No. 122, D. of P., Albany.

Iola Council was organized November 22, 1899, with the first membership containing the following: James W., Anna E. and Carrie St. Clair, Chas. L. and Eva Jenkins, A. L. and Laura Godlove, Martin and Clara Phillips, J. W. and Martha Harshman, R. F. and Catherine Brammer, Wm. E. and Cora Richey, Noah and Mary Bantz, Henry and Alice Marquewell, Eli and Mary E. Zehner, Charles and Bell Taylor, Samuel and Mary Sites, Elmer and Mary E. Bartlett, Walter and Esther Bryan, James and Sarah Johnson, E. M. and Mary Wells, L. H. and Ida Stoner, Linnie Goodman, Sarah Hines, Verna Slack, A. Bryan, Ella Jones, Bessie Baldwin.

The present officers are: Prophetess, Sarah Hines; Pocahontas, Mattie E. Jones; Wenona, Martha E. Green; Powhatan, Henry Marquewell; K. of R., Mary L. Chalk; K. of W., Linnie Goodman; first scout, Alice Marquewell; second scout, Emma Smith; first warrior, Wm. Jones; second warrior, Geo. Smith; third warrior, Noah Bantz; fourth warrior, Wm. E. Chalk; G. of T., Ida Stoner; G. of F., James Spence.

Ouray Tribe No. 74, I. O. R. M., Eaton.

Ouray Tribe was organized August 13, 1885, with the following charter members: William H. Younts, George W. Carter, William P. Wagoner, Lewis B. Clark, Lee Pancoast, Henry Shannon, Robert L. Brandt, William Bost, Samuel B. Ames, Alexander Clift, Jacob M. Delph, Charles E. Gunekle, Samuel J. Carmichael, Joel W. Long.

The charter members now living and holding membership: Robert L. Brandt, Lee Pancoast, Samuel J. Carmichael and Joel W. Long.

The present officers are: Gabriel M. Hiatt, Prophet; Albert N. Barrett, Sachem; Oliver J. Chapman, Senior Sagamore; John C. Williams, Junior Sagamore; John R. Thomas, Chief of Records; Otis Edgington, Keeper of Wampum.

Sioux Tribe No. 123, I. O. R. M., Gaston.

Sioux Tribe was organized December 6, 1890, the De Ember Tribe of Muncie, with M. G. Mock as instituting chief, doing the work. The following became members at that time: R. Allwood, J. G. Callahan, H. M. Higdon, S. E. McCreery, J. F. McCreery, Thos. McCreery, N. A. McCreery, S. J. McCreery, J. W. McCreery, Dr. J. F. Julian, J. P. Johnson, C. O. Linn, A. G. Linn, J. F. Hyre, John Lambert, Stephen Fouch, James Gruver, J. C. Driscoll, T. W. Petty, Albert Williams, George Deeter, Benj. Bartlett, William Huffman, Sam. Gwimp, Josh. Furguson, James Hannan, All. Oxley, R. W. Page, Wm. Needham, O. A. Stokes, Sam. McInturf, J. W. Kirklin, James Corn, W. D. Farmer, W. A. Jackson, Geo. Nelson, J. E. Hayden, J. S. Rothel, Wm. Burgess, L. H. Laroo.

The present officers: W. A. Jackson, Sachem; Wilston Linn, Senior Sagamore; L. H. Laroo, Junior Sagamore; Creed Broadwater, Prophet; Allen Oxley, K. of W.; J. C. Driscoll, C. of R., who has held the office since the tribe was instituted and has never missed a meeting night. Dr. H. N. Shaw is D. D. G. S. The Tribe owns property in Gaston and is in good shape financially.

Delaware Tribe No. 77, I. O. R. M., Daleville.

Delaware Tribe was organized October 18, 1887, the first members being: Henry Rader, L. F. Nixon, C. F. Diltz, C. W. Fletcher, Samuel Wanner, J. E. Pitser, Marion Richmond, I. M. Heath, Henry Rader, Franklin Hoel, A. L. Heath, Leonard Leathers, L. O. Hupp, P. A. Rudy, S. B. Garrett, John Price, David Getts, W. A. Pitser, Henry Bronenburg.

The present officers are: Sachem, William O'Briant; S. S., Arlie Thornburg; J. S., John R. Scott; Prophet, Geo. Laboyteaux; C. of R., R. A. Reynolds; K. of W., Joseph Minnick.

Pueblo Tribe No. 234, I. O. R. M., Selma.

Pueblo Tribe was organized April 15, 1897, the original membership comprising the following names: J. L. Huchings, W. G. Bortsfield, Eldon Camaday, J. L. Greenwalt, Wm. Kiger, N. E. Black, W. H. Boots, L. G. Soffer, W. H. Hufferd, J. C. Truitt, J. K. Vance, J. E. Davis, O. W. Cecil, H. H. Fielder, D. J. Leeper, J. A. Neal, P. J. Graham, Taylor Graham, L. L. Denny, L. W. Dickover, J. H. Hill, W. R. Bortsfield, J. E. Dynes, W. A. East, Jr., Harry Bell, J. W. Wingett, Wm. Bergdoll.

The present officers are: Sachem, Ed. McCall; Senior Sag., James Barnes; Junior Sag., J. W. Wingett; Prophet, W. Ross; K. of W., Dr. S. G. Jump; C. of W., Harry Bell; C. of R., J. A. Boots; trustees, L. W. Dickover, O. C. White, Jas. Greenwalt.

Pueblo Council No. 96, D. of P., Selma.

Pueblo Council was instituted June 30, 1897, at first with the name Hiawatha Council, which was later changed to the present name. The charter members were: Sarah Hufford, Joanah Williams, Gertrude Leeper, Viola Wright, Ella Williams, Emma Whitney, Hattie Black, Nelia Hill, Minnie Fielder, Maggie Bailey Jr., Myrtle Williams, Francis Neal, Minnie Naylor, Nannie Hutching, Altenia Hutching, Emma Bortsfield, Hattie Bortsfield, Mary Boots, Elnora Cannaday, Mary Soffer, Ozora Sherwood, Lucy Belle, William Hufford, Wm. H. Williams, Sr., N. E. Black, George Williams, S. S. Anthony, J. H. Hill, H. H. Fielder, Wm. R. Bortsfield, M. M. Bailey, James Greenwalt, J. A. Neal, J. C. Naylor, Eva Stiffler, Caroline Conrad, Elizabeth Bortsfield, Margaret Cecil, Ida Dooley, Mell Hervitte, Laura Davis, J. L. Hutching, Wm. A. East, Jr., A. R. Spangler, J. D. Cannon, J. C. Truitt, J. E. Dynes. Martha Hiatt, Charles Hiatt.

The officers are: Pocahontas, Robbie Earley; Wenona, Rhoda Boots; Prophetess, Emma Black; Powhatan, Edward McCall; Keeper of Records, Hattie Jones; Keeper of Wampum, Minnie Naylor; Collector Wampum, Gertrude Leeper.

Moccasin Tribe, I. O. R. M., Oakville.

Moccasin Tribe was organized May 13, 1904, with the following charter members: W. V. Jones, Frank Ball, Clarence Peckinpaugh, John Ball, P. C. Barnard, Charlie Kern, L. J. Peckinpaugh, Newton Woods, Jesse Veach, T. J. Miller, Scott Robes, George Linkhart, Wm. C. McKinley, Walter Nixon, David Jones, John Snow, Levi Johnson, Charlie Veach, R.

W. Williams, Lee Nixon, Albert Ball, Dan Nixon, Clark Shriver, Andy Ross, Harlie Peckinpaugh, Wm. Ellison, C. A. Burcaw (dec.), Elmer Ball.

The present officers are: Andy Ross, Sachem; Jerry Baney, Sen. Sag.; John Patterson, Jr. Sag.; Charlie Kern, Chief of Records; P. C. Barnard, Keeper of Wampum; James Rutherford, Prophet; Lee Nixon, Isaac Livezey, F. B. Shriver, Trustees.

White Feather Tribe No. 78, I. O. R. M., Cammack.

White Feather Tribe was instituted April 28, 1887, with the following charter members: David Cammack, James McKinley, Joseph Cumerford, James W. Reed, John Cossiboon, George B. Snodgrass, Joseph McKinley, B. F. Plummer, J. W. Williams, Jonas F. Shoemaker, Robert M. Snodgrass, James McGriff, Samuel Snodgrass, Belty S. Dragoo, John Stout, Luther Farr, Amos Tom, David Ayers, Manson Hartley, S. H. Dragoo, James Lee, Charles Fuson, Link Fraizer, William Personett, M. L. Snodgrass.

The present officers are: Sachem, J. C. Hensley; Sr. Sagamore, William H. Snodgrass; Jr. Sagamore, M. J. Shannahan; Prophet, Oscar Ratcliff; Chief of Records, T. H. Hankins; Keeper of Wampum, George Simpson.

Nodawa Tribe No. 241, I. O. R. M., Royerton.

Nodawa Tribe was instituted February 4, 1898, with the following membership: E. E. Richardson, J. P. Alexander, T. M. McKinley, A. Dearth, M. H. McBee, Geo. W. Strohm, N. L. Magee; Geo. A. Kennedy, Lewis T. Lake, E. E. Johnsonbaugh, H. K. Johnsonbaugh, John M. Kennedy, Adam Roach, Robe C. Scott, Geo. R. Mansfield, Clifford. Dearth, Albert Bawlin, Samuel Cochran, Isaac J. Helm, Geo. S. Roach, Authur Lovett, Ira Dearth. D. M. Lovett, Robert Walburn, Wm. P. Campbell, Selva Sanders, John S. Pixley, Walter E. Pixley, Wm. H. Glaze, H. E. Kirkwood, T. J. Mansfield, F. M. Pittenger, D. M. Kirkwood. L. O. Johnsonbaugh, Jos. W. Martin, James D. Ogle, Aaron Sloniker, Frank McLain, D. M. Shafer.

The present officers are: George W. Nelson, Prophet; Earl E. Johnson, Sachem; Geo. W. Strohn, Sr. Sag.; Londus Sloniker, Jr. Sag.; E. E. Johnsonbaugh, C. of R.; Geo. A. Kennedy, K. of W.; C. M. Wilcoxon, D. D. G. S.; D. M. Kirkwood, Adam Roach, D. M. Shafer, Trustees.

Koka Tribe, I. O. R. M., Progress.

Koka Tribe was organized April 23, 1900, the charter members being: Leroy Davis, Joseph Mann, James G. Mann, Columbus Stiffler, Merit Heath, A. L. Ross, J. N. Ross, S. H. Stautamoyer, S. K. Sunderland, L. L. Cooper, John E. Driscoll, Geo. C. Davis, James Crawford, Charles Modlin, E. T. Sharp, S. T. Sharp, John Jordan, Jacob Schaffer, F. M. Sharp, A.

Hornbaker, D. Ν. Hays, W. T. Clark, Cash Funkhouser, Joe Heaton, John Ball.

The present officers are: Spence Ayers, Sachem; W. Ν. Sharp, Sen. Sag.; Web Yingling, Jun. Sag.; A. Vanderburg, Prophet; C. L. Pene, C. of R.; E. T. Sharp, K. of W. The present membership is 112.

KNIGHTS OF THE MACCABEES.

Muncie Tent No. 38, K. O. T. M.

Muncie Tent was organized in the Patterson building, October 18, 1890, with 55 charter members, of whom the following held the first offices: Roscoe Griffith, Wm. R. Snyder, O. F. Raymond, Jno. C. Abbott, C. H. Church, L. A. Clevenger, F. L. Wachtell, E. A. Shields, S. P. Brundage, Wm. E. H. Marsh, J. V. Gilbert, E. M. Lewellen, Quince Walling, W. W. Shick, J. N. Cropper, R. Hummel.

The present officers are: Past Commander, John L. Jones; Commander, Chas. T. Morrison; Lt. Commander, C. A. Taughinbaugh; R. K. & F. K., L. L. Case; Chaplain, Wm. Ramey; Physician, Dr. G. H. Searcey; Sergeant, Arch H. Hobbs; Master at Arms, L. Merle McDowell; first M. of G., J. E. H. Pitzer; second M. of G., Miller Pitzer; Sentinel, B. F. Babb; Picket, Robert McDowell; Trustees, W. B. Austin, Jno. E. H. Pitzer, L. L. Case.

Golden Hive No. 60, L. O. T. M., Muncie.

Golden Hive was organized in the Bishop block, October 20, 1896. The charter members were: Nellie Boomer, Martha Bayless, M. U. Beemer, Kate Beemer, Anna Beardsley, Mary E. Case, Alice Carvel, Emma Guffigan, Ida Greely, Edith Greely Scott, Maggie Hale, Ella Jones, Kate Knowlton, Bessie M. Knapp, Addie Manor, Julia McGill, Ella Mohler, Winnie Palmer, Lettie Rapp, Jennie Rapp, Alice Snell, Amy Seary, Lizzie Seitz, Alice Snell Sutton, Josie Thornburg, Anna Truitt, Ada Winterowd, Lora V. Wagner, Louise Winder, Mary Youngman, Lizzie Zook.

The present officers are: Neva B. Adams, Past Commander; Estelle Keelor, Lady Commander; Lillie Huddleston, Lady Lt. Commander; Bessie M. Knapp, Lady Record Keeper; Minnie Storms, Lady Finance Keeper; Effie Dunnington, Lady Chaplain; Nettie Leonard, Lady Mistress at Arms; Ida B. Vanarsdal, Lady Sergeant; Bessie Fenton, Lady Sentinel; Nannie Millerns, Lady Picket.

Muncie Hive No. 71, L. O. T. M.

Muncie Hive was organized in Bishop block, which was then the K. O. T. M. hall, May 15, 1905. The charter members were: Lydia E. Jones, Martha M. Law, Nancy E. Mills, Mary Martin, Katie Gibson, Myrtle

Humphryville, Addah Brotherton, Elizabeth Longfield, Lillie B. Lawrence, May Sipe, Francis J. Handley, Aurie V. McKenzie, Jennie Ullom, Pearl Murdick, Mabel Doyle, Sue McKinley, Alice Burry, Rosa Bryant, Maud E. Mitchell, Addalaide Williamson, Martha E. Langdon, Jennie Finnerty, Mary E. Jones.

The present officers are: Lady Commander, Anna A. Beach; Lieut. Commander, Elnora Miller; Past Commander, Zora Keppler; Rec. Keeper, Jennie Ullom; Finance Keeper, Frances J. Handley; Chaplain, Margaret Studley; Sergeant, Sarah Bradbury; Mistress-at-Arms, Myrtle Coats; Sentinel, Mildred Shockley; Picket, Emma Frymute.

Albany Tent No. 180, K. O. T. M.

This tent was organized at Albany, May 13, 1896, with the following charter members: Robert P. Arrick, Milton B. Stewart, Wm. H. Nosman, Joseph Lefavour, A. L. Godlove, O. J. Marks, Jas. S. McQuinn, Fred C. Jackson, Jas. L. Thurston, Arthur C. Helm, Eli A. Zehner, L. O. Slonaker, T. M. Grigg, Dill E. Shoemaker, Wm. Z. Taylor, Roy F. Morrical, John W. Wilson, George W. Younts, Fred A. Waller, T. B. Clouse, L. H. Clouse, Dr. J. V. Baird, Chas. R. Austin, Wm. J. Burden, Oliver L. Bergdoll, R. F. Brammer.

The present officers are: Past Commander, T. Buffington; Sir Kt. Commander, W. W. Marks; Lt. Commander, E. E. Ballard; Record Keeper, W. E. Chalk; F. K., Chas. R. Austin; Chaplain, J. W. Hobbs; Sergeant, O. E. Bell; M. of A., Lute. Nensteil; First M. of G., W. S. Barlow; Second M. of G., D. C. Johnson; Sentinel, U. G. Simmons; Picket, J. W. Bond.

Eaton Tent, K. O. T. M.

The tent at Eaton was organized March 28, 1896. The charter members were: Wm. P. McCormick, Jas. M. Motsenboecke, A. G. McCormick, Geo. W. Hoover, Sam A. Gunn, J. F. Palmer, C. McFadden, J. M. Atkinson, D. S. Fisher, J. M. Carmichael, J. D. Chipman, C. A. Bowers, O. R. Winget.

The present officers are: S. Kt. P. Com., W. H. Orr; S. Kt. Com., C. R. Pullen; S. Kt. R. K., Geo. S. Mitchell; Sr. Kt. F. K., Geo. S. Mitchell; Sr. Kt. Chap., H. S. Chase; Sr. Kt. S., D. S. Fisher; Sr. Kt. M. A., Jas. M. Carmichael; Sr. Kt. First G., A. D. Driven; Sr. Kt. Second G., J. H. Barrett; Sr. Kt. Sentinel, Ed. Francey; Sr. Kt. Picket, Jas. O. Lunbuner.

BENEVOLENT AND PROTECTIVE ORDER OF ELKS.
Muncie Lodge No. 245, B. P. O. E.

Muncie Lodge of Elks was organized August 25, 1892, in the Heath Iron building. Though the order is among the more recent in Muncie, it has from the first been one of the strongest, and Muncie has become known as one of the strongholds of the order in Indiana. A few years ago one of the gala weeks in the city's history was celebrated under the auspices of the Elks' convention and carnival. In keeping with the objects and the local strength of the order, the Elk club rooms in Muncie are the most elegantly equipped quarters in the city, the work of remodeling and furnishing having been completed in the spring of 1907.

The charter members of Muncie Lodge were: Carl A. Spilker, Vernon Davis, Thos. K. Heinsohn, Geo. P. Davis, C. E. Shipley, A. E. Kelly, Harry R. Wysor, Henry J. Keller, E. D. Bishop, C. A. Winters, W. R. Youse, John E. Banta, J. R. Sprankle, Harold P. Marsh, Bert F. Bradbury, W. F. Maggs, S. P. Baldus, Charles Woodruff, Quince Walling, Will W. Trullender, J. K. Ritter, Charles O. Fox, R. C. Hemingray, H. M. Winans, C. H. Anthony, C. E. Perrys, Rus Smith, Chas. F. W. Neely, J. O. Sawyer, C. T. Bartlett, R. S. Gregory, H. C. Klein, Robt. T. Winters, D. Cammack, Howard Lewis, A. J. Williams, Everret Moffitt, George W. Cromer.

The present officers are: E. J. Whiteley, Exalted Ruler; Charles Emerson, Esteemed Leading Knight; R. H. Cowan, Esteemed Loyal Knight; H. S. Bowles, Esteemed Lecturing Knight; J. C. O'Harra, Secretary; Robert E. Gates, Treasurer; Milton Gray, Esquire; Charles G. Foresman, Inner Guard; H. F. Morrison, Chaplain; Frank H. Kimbrough, Organist; George B. Glass, Tyler; P. P. Busch, E. G. Clarke, Chas. O. Grafton, Trustees.

MUNCIE COUNCIL NO. 500, KNIGHTS OF COLUMBUS.

The Knights of Columbus were organized in Muncie April 28, 1901, in Union Labor Hall, the first members being: W. H. Tobin, P. J. McArdle, E. J. Manok, J. A. Gallivan, F. F. Frusher, Jas. Flaherty, Thos. J. Hanley, Jas. Rooney, Jas. F. Downs, Cornelius Hanley, Rev. Wm. G. Schmidt, John Kennedy (deceased), Jno. M. Hope, M. T. Hanley, Paul W. Goebel, M. J. McGuff, Leo S. Hope, Rev. F. C. Weichman (deceased), J. L. Barrett, M. F. Downs, Jas. Reiley, Thos. H. Cannon, A. A. Arnold, R. E. Grundy, Fred House, S. Luddy, P. F. McIntyre, Wm. Rahe, M. J. Clark, Chas. Morrow, Jno. Rahe, Edw. Scanlon, Jno. Langan.

The present officers are: Michael T. Hanley, Grand Knight; James F. Ryan, Dep. Grand Knight; Adam J. Traub, Fin. Secy; Michael J. Traub, Rec. Secy; Joseph Grundy, Treasurer; M. J. Clark, Chancellor; Jos. O'Day, Advocate; C. A. Hottinger, Inside Guard; James Throckmorton, Outside Guard; John Rahe, Organist; Frank Balfe, Chorister; Edw. Scanlan, Warden; Rev. Wm. G. Schmidt, Chaplain; Jas. McCabe, Lecturer; Chas. Morrow, E. R. Krug, P. W. Goebel, Trustees.

KNIGHTS AND LADIES OF HONOR.

Protection Lodge No. 346, of this order, was instituted July 20, 1880, in Muncie, with the following members: L. H. Harper, Eleanor Harper,

Noses Lutz, Nancy A. Lutz, John H. Miller, Amanda Miller, Theodore N. Palmer, Joseph R. Paxon, Joseph A. Stahle, Anne E. Stahle, Wilber J. Boyden, Thomas Duncan, Maggie Duncan, L. F. Hardesty, Leroy Heath, Eva Heath, S. U. Huffer, Martha N. Huffer, Martin Shafer, Ben Rosenbush, Sarah Rosenbush, Ida Levy, Guy Sutton, Lillian Key, Isaac Cohen, Albert H. Falk, Peter Mackin, Clem Harding. This order provided for an assessment insurance plan.

The present officers are: Guy N. Sutton, Protector; Albert Falk, Vice Protector; Ben Rosenbush, Secretary; L. H. Harper, Treasurer; Mrs. Ida Levy, Deputy.

COUNCIL NO. 475, CATHOLIC BENEVOLENT LEGION.

This council was organized November 18, 1894, in the St. Lawrence school, Muncie, the first membership list comprising the following: John N. Hope, John J. Schanahan, James P. Grundy, Rev. Wm. Schmidt, George Lyndecker, Edw. J. Manok, Mich Scherkey, Cornelius Courtney, John J. Kelley, John Cramer, John Guffigan, John Norton, Mich L. Mahoney, Mert E. Mahoney, Dennis Dennihan, Lew Norton, Adam Traub, Joseph C. Roy, Joseph T. Walters, James J. Keenan, Wm. J. Getz, Thomas P. Dowd, J. Thomas Ging.

The present officers are: Pres., Wm. Getz; Vice Pres., John Cramer; Sec., James P. Grundy; Treas., Michael Scherkey; Trustees, Harry Dawson, Dennis Shea, Frank Deere.

IMPROVED ORDER OF HEPTASOPHS.

The Muncie branch of the Improved Order of Heptasophs was organized June 26, 1894, by David A. Thorp, of Letonia, Pa., who was sent here for that purpose from the general headquarters of the order at Baltimore. Eighty-seven new members have been added since organization, and there have occurred three deaths, the original or charter membership comprising the following: Robert Richards, David D. Perkins, Lon D. Long, George Derrick, Peter Moran, James G. Parker, Joe Wedlake, Thomas E. James, John N. Wolf, Theo. Cooksey, G. Bucklin, Harveg A. Richards, John Perkins, Francis Allen, Harry Woods, Chas. E. Wilkins, Geo. Williams, Wm. E. Yates, Nelson Parker, Geo. Bell, Garret Fagin, Richard Herron, Isaac N. Trent, Will Blamey, James Creed, Pat. Hazzard, Rufus H. Thorp, Lewis B. Field, Thomas Perkins, John S. Murray, Robert Stevenson, James A. Fields.

The present officers are: Joe Wedlake, Archon; John Buettner, Rec. Sec.; John N. Wolf, Fin. Sec.; Lewis Koegler, Treas.

WOODMEN OF THE WORLD, MUNCIE.

The first lodge of the Woodmen of the World in Muncie became inactive, and on March 8, 1899, a reorganization was effected by the following members: T. H. Barton, W. C. Thomas, Ed. M. Klein, Dr. Bacon, J. S.

Williams, Frank West, Dr. H. H. Baker. The present officers are: S. A. Elliott, Con. Com.; Λ. H. Reece, Adv. Lieut.; J. Λ. Quick, Banker; J. S. Williams, Clerk.

ANCIENT ORDER OF HIBERNIANS.

The Λuncie branch of this order was organized Λay 5, 1892, with the following as charter members: Con Courtney (Hartford City), John P. Λaher, Con Hanley, Λ. F. Downs, Thos. Hartford, Wm. T. Hayes, J. B. Brennan, Daniel E. Kelly, Patrick Bilbow, Wm. Ryan, P. McCarthy.

The present officers are John J. Λechan, County President; Laurence Norton, Sr., President; Geo. Phibbs, Vice President; Wm. O'Meara, Treasurer; R. E. Grundy, Financial Secretary; J. P. Λaher, Recording Secretary.

Ladies' Auxiliary Div. No. 1, A. O. H.

The Ladies' auxiliary of the Hibernians was organized in the old Union Labor Hall at Λuncie by Λrs. J. P. Λaher, October 16, 1898, with the following membership: Λesdames. A. A. Arnold, C. Hanley, Jos. Hinkley, Thos. Hartford, Paul Goebel, Jas. Gallon, Λ. F. Downs, Λichal Thornton, P. Prendergast, Thos. O'Neil, P. McFaddin, J. P. Λaher, Jas. Downs; Λisses Sarah E. Duffy, Hancie Enright, Bessie Doherty, Katherine Fitzgerald, Katherine Shea, Λargaret Unison, Vina O'Meara, Dora O'Meara, Margaret O'Meara, Lizzie O'Meara, Katherine Lawler.

The present officers are: Λrs. E. J. Λahoney, President; Λrs. B. Manning, Vice President; Λrs. C. V. Zeller, Recording Secretary; Λiss Sarah E. Duffy, Financial Secretary; Mrs. D. Cummings, Treasurer; Mrs. Margaret Wolf, Λistress at Arms; Λrs. Wm. McIlvain, Sentinel.

DRAMATIC ORDER KNIGHTS OF KHORASSAN.

El Capitan Temple No. 94, Muncie.

El Capitan Temple was organized July 12, 1900, in the Anthony block, with the following as charter members: Art F. Andrews, C. L. Bender, A. S. Botkin, E. E. Botkin, O. E. Baldwin, August Braun, L. W. Cates, Adam Deems, A. T. Eastes, Chas. B. Fudge, Enos Geiger, Chas. Gass, C. Hanika, A. O. Hoppes, Chas. B. Kirk, J. O. Lewellen, Jos. G. Leffler, Aug. Λaick, S. L. McKimmey, C. W. Neiswanger, G. T. Orr, O. I. Reasoner, Jacob Stiffler, Λark Topp, Sel Votaw, G. G. Williamson, I. J. Young, D. V. Zimmerman.

The present officers are: August Λaick, Royal Vizier; J. O. Lewellen, Grand Emir; O. I. Reasoner, Sheik; J. Harve Leffler, Λahedi; A. O. Hoppes, Secy; F. D. Conyers, Treas.; C. T. Redding, Satrap; Arch Hobbs, Sahib; A. T. Eastes, C. Hanika, Wm. Smith, Trustees.

FRATERNAL ORDER OF EAGLES.

The Muncie Lodge of Eagles was organized in Red Men's hall, corner of High and Jackson streets, May 2, 1902. The membership now numbers 475, and their club and lodge rooms are at 214 South Walnut. The charter members were: Chas. Gwinnup, Geo. P. Davis, Jno. J. Mehan, Jno. P. Weisse, Jno. C. Griesheimer, Geo. R. Andrews, Claud E. Berry, Ed. T. Connell, Thos. Carroll, Jerry Crawley, Jno. Duffy, Wm. Dwyer, Chas. Eby, Aug. Ernst, Ray G. Hickok, Geo. M. Ellis, Wm. Elliott, J. L. Flatter, T. F. Grady, C. A. Griesheimer, Chas. Heffner, Jas. E. Osborn, Wm. Osborn, Jno. Kretschner, A. D. Maddux, S. D. Maddux, A. N. Maddux, Alex. Martin, Asa Kloff, W. A. McIlvain, Walt Newman, W. V. Nickerson, W. Newbold, W. A. Petty, W. E. Petty, C. R. Price, L. L. Perdine, Wm. Pash, Jas. Ryan, M. C. Reardon, D. Shanahan, Jno. Shanahan, W. Shanahan, T. F. Soules, Geo. A. Smith, Jno. M. Seitz, Ralph Shaw, Cal Shaw, Jno. Sullivan, Jere Sullivan, E. O. Streeter, I. Martin, J. B. Swearington, Curt Turner, E. Thrams, N. Thrams, C. A. Weise, Jno. Nuckols, M. A. Wright, A. R. Wolff, W. H. Warfel, F. H. Warner.

The present officers are: C. W. Dearth, Worthy Pres.; Jno. Kretschmer, Worthy Vice Pres.; Jno. Mehan, Past Wor. Pres.; F. H. Young, Wor. Chap.; Jac Melton, Wor. Con.; Geo. P. Davis, Sec.; C. Gwinnup, Treas.; P. T. Moore, Geo. Derrick, D. Shanahan, Wor. Trustees.

Ladies of the Golden Eagle, Albany.

The Albany branch of this order was organized May 27, 1899, with charter members as follows: H. J. Wickersham, Phebe Wickersham, James Werst, L. G. Werst, H. J. Swanders, Ellen Swanders, David Kerns, Lasall Phillips, Mrs. Phillips, Lisban Tully, Moeblie Tully, Rena Houk, Bell Kerns, Ninna Marks, Myrtle Coats, Wm. Whitaker, Mary Whitaker, Maggie Williams, Wm. Bruington, Bert Penington, Frank Hastin, Perl Hasten.

The present officers are: Past Templar, Lizza Spear; Noble Templar, Eva Robertson; V. T., Garnett Wickersham; M. of S., Ida Bantz; G. of R., Phebe Wickersham; G. of E., Mattie Payton; G. of F., Martha Green; Prophetess, Maggie Thompson; Priestess, Estella Penington; G. of M., Bula Robertson; G. of Inner Portal, Vera Adams; G. of Outer Portal, Gerta Bassett; Trustees 6 mo., Alli Wingate; 12 mo. Trustee, Francis Ellis; 18 mo. Trustee, Phillip Payton.

MAGIC CITY GUN CLUB.

The Magic City Gun Club was organized Jan. 6, 1899. For the first year the officers were: F. L. Wachtell, Pres.; Thos. McKillip, V. Pres.; J. G. Otstot, Sec., and C. E. Adamson, Treas. The object of the organization is to perfect its members in the art of shooting and to aid the proper authorities in the preservation and propagation of fish and game. Among those yet active in the club who have been identified with it since its infancy may be named, J. L. Simmons, C. L. Bender, F. L. Wachtell, H. A. Shumack, J. J. Dow, J. W. Farrell, A. C. Spencer, G. G. Williamson, Fred Thompson, Claud Stephens and H. H. Highlands. The present officers are: Fred Thompson, Pres.; G. G. Williamson, Vice Pres., and F. L. Watchtell, Sec.-Treas.

The club is equipped with good grounds and club house opposite the West Side Park. During the season from April to October inclusive the club shoots each Thursday afternoon. Each year a number of prizes are offered in a series of these weekly meetings, to stimulate the interest at these gatherings. The members are divided in two classes according to their average proficiency. Each year in May and September the club holds an open shooting tournament when it is host to large gatherings of the most prominent amateur and professional marksmen in America. The annual shoot of the Trap Shooters' League of Indiana was held under the auspices of the Magic City Gun Club in 1902. At that meeting eighty contestants competed in the several events that covered the two days' meeting. Rolla O. Heikes, William R. Crosby, Chas. Young, Henry Vietmeyer, L. H. Ried, Frederick LeNoir, Frank Riehl and L. R. Barkley are among some of the better known professionals who have at different times participated in the local shooting.

Daniel Boone Rifle Club, Muncie.

This club was organized May 31, 1901, its purpose being sport and improvement in rifle shooting. The club has a rifle range, which is now located on Dr. Trent's farm, and has regular meetings. Some of the oldest active members of the organization are: J. S. Williams, J. A. Stephens, Eugene Brotherton, Quince Walling, Dr. I. N. Trent, Dr. Spickermon, Ed. Harman, Frank Boomer, Frank Mock.

The present officers are: Pres., Quince Walling; Capt., J. A. Stephens; Sec. and Treas., J. S. Williams.

CHAPTER XXVIII.

POLITICS AND CIVIL RECORDS OF COUNTY, TOWNSHIP AND TOWN.

When Delaware county became an independent political division there were two national parties in the field—the Democrats and the Whigs. To follow the lines of party sentiment as it was manifested in the selection of county officials would be an impossible task. Considerations of fitness for office and personal popularity have always broken partisan lines. Notwithstanding that party feeling was shown with more passion and more uncompromisingly fifty and seventy years ago than now, population was less and people knew their neighbors perhaps better than they do now. So that while the party banner counted for more then than now, this fact was neutralized in local politics by personal considerations.

Before proceeding with the details of county politics it is proper to state the remarkable difference in spirit between political contests of this day and those of fifty years ago. In recent elections, especially since the exciting campaign of 1896, there has been a notable absence of excitement or tension among the people, local business goes on as usual, and if the surface of political sentiment is disturbed at all it is due to personal or practical reasons rather than to partisanship. Old-time rallies and political mass meetings have little vogue nowadays, and political speakers must be men of national importance to catch general attention. Half a century ago, and even twenty-five years back, a political campaign was attended with very different features. Partisan discussion, especially in presidential elections, often became virulent, and passionate invective was as frequent as calm debate. There was less discrimination between local and national politics, and the candidate for local office had to bear all the denunciation that was heaped upon his party in general. Processions, bonfires, crowded meetings rapt to enthusiasm by fiery oratory, tense excitement for several weeks before election, characterized a campaign of that period and made it one of the most notable features of American life.

The newspaper and the quicker diffusion of knowledge have undoubtedly had most to do with changing politics from an absorbing excitement to a quietness that often seems apathy. The newspaper reporter with his "interviews" and summaries of speeches, and the editor with his logic, reach more people and appeal more convincingly than the campaign orator, so that now the average citizen sits at home and quietly forms his opinion with the aid of newspapers. Rural free delivery, carrying the daily news into the country districts, renders it unnecessary for the farmer to resort to political speakings to inform himself of the issues. As a result flamboyant oratory is going out, and solid facts are now demanded by the voters as a basis for judgment of men and measures. Furthermore, the words "Democrat" and "Republican" are no longer fetiches. Party name is ceasing to be the shibboleth of political campaigns. Popular conception of political and economic affairs is becoming broader and more analytical, and the party label is no longer a guarantee of the contents. Those engaged in politics find that they must appeal to practical reason less than to sentiment and party ardor, and they attract voters in proportion as they represent practical principles of statecraft.

A brief study may be made of politics according to party divisions in this county before giving the list of county and other officials who have served from time to time in positions of trust. Figures are not at hand to show the political complexion of the county during the earliest years. David Kilgore, who was a Whig, was elected to the legislature in 1832, and in 1836 Andrew Kennedy, who was equally prominent as a Democrat, was elected to the state senate. For some years the two parties were about balanced in the county. In 1842 the Whigs had gained the ascendancy. The seat in the senate that year was contested by James Hodge, Whig, and Judge Buckles, Democrat. The vote by townships for these candidates follows:

Town.	Hodge.	Buckles
Center	240	250
Salem	44	33
Mt. Pleasant	32	42
Harrison	17	17
Union	54	0
Delaware	40	36
Liberty	84	57
Perry	31	46
Monroe	5	16
Niles	96	37
Hamilton	7	6
Washington	25	47
Totals	655	587

In 1844, at the August election, the county was Whig by about 200 majority, and at the presidential elections in November Polk received 732 votes, Henry Clay, the Whig, 940, while Birney, the Free-soiler, got only three votes.

In 1848 Indiana gave the Democratic nominee for president (Gen. Cass) a plurality, but in this county the result of the ballot was 822 votes for General Taylor, the successful Whig, while Cass received 694 and Van Buren (Free Soil) 58.

In 1860, when the crisis of the nation had arrived and the Republican party first became dominant, Delaware county returned a large majority for Lincoln, the vote for the respective presidential candidates of that year being as follows: Lincoln, 1933; Douglas, 1029; Bell, 10; Breckenridge, 98.

In 1872, notwithstanding a decided change in political lines in other parts of the state, Delaware county supported Brown, the Republican nominee for governor, with 2743 votes, against 1557 for Hendricks, the Democratic candidate. In 1880 Porter, Republican, received 3614 votes in this county for the office of governor, against 1843 for Landers and 45 for Gregg. The Democrats were successful in the national campaign of 1884, but in this county the votes resulted as follows: Blaine, Republican, 3540; Cleveland, Democrat, 2016; Butler, Greenback, 88; St. John, Prohibitionist, 30.

In 1888, when the county gave a majority to Benjamin Harrison, it was found that the county contained more than a hundred veteran Whig-Republicans who either in 1836 or 1840 had voted for William Henry Harrison.

In 1890 the Republicans were easily victorious in the county, but it was noticeable that their losses in the off year were greater than those of the Democrats, taking the election 1888 as a basis. In 1891 the Democrats elected the majority of the city officers in Muncie, but with that exception they have had no important victory in city or county during all the remaining years, not even in the Democratic landslide in 1892. Republican majorities have prevailed at all the presidential elections, and it is unnecessary to give the figures in detail.

OFFICIAL LISTS.

Note:—With a few exceptions the official lists for the years up to and including 1880 have been compiled from the old history of the country. Dates before each name generally indicate year in which term of service began, not year of election necessarily.

State Senators.

1828- —Amaziah Morgan.	1845-1849—Richard Winchell.
1829-1831—Daniel Worth.	1849-1853—Joseph S. Buckles.
1832-1835—Samuel Hannah.	1853-1857—Isaac Vandeventer.
1835- —Michael Aker.	1857-1865—Walter March.
1836-1840—Andrew Kennedy.	1865-1869—William A. Bonham.
1840- —Michael Aker.	1869-1871—Milton S. Robinson.
1841- —John Foster.	1871- —John W. Burson*.
1842-1845—James Hodge.	1871-1875—James Orr.

*Burson's seat was contested by Wm. B. Kline and the Senate declared it vacant. James Orr was elected to fill the vacancy.

1875-1877—R. H. Cree.
1877-1879—Charles Doxey.
1879-1881—M. C. Smith.
1881-　　—E. H. Bundy.

1893-1896—Ozro N. Cranon.
1897-1904—Walter L. Ball.
1905-　　—C. M. Kimbrough.

Representatives.

1827-1828—Daniel Worth.
1829-　　—Lemuel G. Jackson.
1830-　　—David Seamans.
1831-　　—Elias Murray.
1832-　　—David Ribble.
1833-1836—David Kilgore.
1836-　　—William Van Matre.
1837-　　—John Richey.
1838-　　—David Kilgore.
1839-　　—Abraham Buckles.
1840-　　—Eleazer Coffeen.
1841-1844—Goldsmith C. Gilbert.
1844-1846—John Tomlinson.
1846-　　—John Trimble.
1847-1850—Samuel Orr.
1850-1853—Michael Thompson.
1853-1855—James Orr.
1855-1857—David Kilgore.
1857-1859—Marcus C. Smith.
1859-1861—Wm. Brotherton.
1861-1863—James Orr.
1863-1867—Alfred Kilgore.
1867-1869—John B. Ervin.
1869-1871—S. V. Jump.

1871-1873—James P. Snodgrass.
1873-1875—Arthur C. Mellette.
1875-1877—William Ribble.
1875-1877—M. A. Smith.
1877-1879—Horatio J. Lockhart.
1877-1879—J. Harvey Koontz.
1879-1881—Walter March.
1879-1881—J. P. C. Shanks.
1881-1882—John W. Ryan.
1883-1884—J. E. Mellette.
1885-1886—J. Linville.
1887-1888—
1889-1890—O. N. Cranor.
1891-1894—Thomas S. Guthrie.
1895-1899—William W. Ross.
1899-1900—William W. Ross.
　　　　　　A. L. Kerwood.
1901-1902—Oliver Carmichael.
　　　　　　Henry L. Hopping.
1903-1904—J. U. Baird.
　　　　　　Oliver Carmichael.
1905-1906—Oliver Carmichael.
　　　　　　Charles A. McGonagle.

Circuit Judges.

1827-1829—Miles C. Eggleston.
1830-1835—Charles H. Test.
1836-1838—Samuel Bigger.
1839-1845—David Kilgore.
1846-1852—Jeremiah Smith.
1853-1858—Joseph Anthony.
1859-1869—Joseph S. Buckles.
1870-1872—Joshua H. Mellett.

1873-　　—John J. Cheney.
　　　　　　Silas Colgrove.
1874-1878—Silas Colgrove.
1879-1885—L. J. Monks.
1885-1892—O. J. Lotz*.
1893-1898—George H. Koons.
1899-　　—Joseph G. Leffler.

Prosecuting Attorneys.

1827-1828—Cyrus Finch.
1829-　　—Martin M. Ray.
1830-1831—James Perry.
1832-1836—Wm. J. Brown.

1837-1838—Samuel W. Parker.
1839-　　—Jehu T. Elliott.
　　　　　　John Brownlee.
1840-1841—Jeremiah Smith.

*The 46th Judicial Circuit consisting of Delaware County was formed by the legislature early in 1885. O. J. Lotz, the defeated candidate the previous fall for Judge of the 25th Circuit, was appointed Judge of the 46th Circuit by the governor.

1842-1843—John N. Wallace.
1844-1845—John Davis.
1846-1847—Joseph S. Buckles.
1848-1849—James H. Swaar.
1850-1852—William Garver.
1853-1854—Silas Colgrove.
1855-   —Andrew J. Neff.
1856-1857—Wm. Brotherton.
1858-1859—David Nation.
1860-1861—David Noss.
1862-1865—John H. Harrison.
1866-1867—L. W. Gooding.
1868-1872—D. W. Chambers.

1873-1874—John W..Ryan.
1875-1876—Alexander Gullett.
1877-1878—Albert O. Marsh.
1879-1882—Josiah E. Mellett.
1883-1884—T. A. Spence.
1885-1886—C. L. Nedsker.
1887-1888—
1889-1890—George W. Cromer.
1891-1894—Joseph G. Lefiler.
1895-1898—Henry L. Hopping.
1899-1900—Edward M. White.
1901-1904—C. W. Dearth.
1905-   —Albert E. Needham.

*County Commissioners.**

1827—Enoch Nation, Valentine Gibson, Aaron Stout.
1828—   .
1829—
1830—
1831—   , ———, Matthew Conner.
1832—   , Isaiah E. Beck, ———
1833—
1834—   , ———, John Richey.
1835—
1836—
1837—John Collins, Stephen Long, Samuel Hutchings.
1838—
1839—
1840—   , William Harvey, John Rees.
1841—Michael Thompson, William Harvey, John Rees.
1842—Michael Thompson, Thomas S. Neely, Eli Boots.
1843—Michael Thompson. Thomas S. Neely, Thomas Hughes.
1844—Michael Thompson. Thomas S. Neely, James Orr.
1847—David Shoemaker, Thomas S. Neely, James Orr.
1848—David Shoemaker, Charles Mansfield, James Orr.

1849—David Shoemaker, Charles Mansfield, Joseph Thomas.
1852—David Shoemaker, Charles Mansfield, Henry Hill.
1853—Abraham Shank, Charles Mansfield, Henry Hill.
1854—Abraham Shank, John B. Babb, Henry Hill.
1855—Abraham Shank, Geo. A. Helvie†, Henry Hill.
1856—Abraham Shank, Volney Willson, Henry Hill.
1857—Abraham Shank, Geo. A. Helvie, Jos. Orr.
1858—Abraham Shank, Geo. A. Helvie, Samuel Weidner.
1859—William Miller, Geo. A. Helvie, Samuel Weidner.
1860—William Miller, Jesse Nixon, Samuel Weidner.
1861—William Miller, Jesse Nixon, John Truitt.
1862—Samuel S. White, Jesse Nixon, John Truitt.
1863—Samuel S. White, Miles Harrold, John Truitt.
1865—John Parker, Miles Harrold, John Truitt.
1866—John Parker, T. J. Matthews, John Truitt.

*On account of defects and loss of records, the exact dates when the Commissioners entered upon their terms of office, after 1827 and prior to 1847, can not be ascertained.

†Geo. A. Helvie served as County Commissioner from Sept. 14, 1855, to Nov. 10, 1855, when he was succeeded by Volney Willson.

1867—John Parker, T. J. Matthews, Benj. F. Smith.
1870—John Parker, Liberty Ginn, William Miller.
1871—Alexander Darter, Liberty Ginn, William Miller.
1873—Alexander Darter, Liberty Ginn, Eli Smith.
1874—James Stewart†, Liberty Ginn, Eli Smith.
1875—W. A. Shoemaker, Liberty Ginn, Eli Smith.
1876—Samuel Davis, Wm. F. Watson, Benj. F. Smith.
1883—C. E. Jones, W. F. Watson, Jas. Barrett.
1885—R. N. Snodgrass, W. F. Watson, — Marshall.
1887—
1889—Thomas Sharp, Matthew McCormick, L. S. Sparks.

1891—Thompson Sharp, Matthew McCormick, N. A. Cunningham.
1893—Thompson Sharp, Matthew McCormick, N. A. Cunningham.
1895—H. C. Schlegel, Matthew McCormick, N. A. Cunningham.
1897—H. C. Schlegel, Lewis G. Cowing, Nathan J. Shroyer.
1899—H. C. Schlegel, Lewis G. Cowing, Nathan J. Shroyer.
1901—John Huffer, Lewis G. Cowing, Nathan J. Shroyer.
1903—John Huffer, J. S. Ellis, Peter Helm.
1905—John Huffer, J. S. Ellis, Peter Helm.

Sheriffs.

1827-1831—Peter Nolin.
1832-1833—Wm. S. Thornburg.
1834-1838—William Gilbert.
1839-   —Joseph Thomas.
            James Howell.
1840-1842—James Howell.
1843-1846—Joseph N. Davis.
1847-1850—H. E. Bowen.
1851-1854—Clark McColly.
1855-1858—William Walling.
1859-1862—John W. Dugan.
1863-1866—D. D. Daugherty.
1867-1868—Wilson R. Smith.

1869-1872—Orlando H. Swain.
1873-1874—C. H. Maitlen.
1875-1876—Andrew J. Slinger.
1877-1880—John W. Dungan.
1881-1884—J. R. McKimmey.
1885-1888—C. H. Maitlen.
. . . .
1889-1892—O. H. Swain.
1893-1896—William P. Sherry.
1897-1900—Thomas Starr.
1901-1904—William N. Swain.
1905-   —Stafford Perdieu.

Recorders.

1827-1833—Wm. Van Matre.
1834-1837—Samuel R. Collier.
1838-   —John Marshall.
            Patrick Justice.
1839-1844—Patrick Justice.
1845-1855—James A. Maddy.
1856-   —George B. Norris*.
1857-1864—T. E. Burt.

1865-1869—W. H. N. Cooper.
1870-1877—Samuel Gayman.
1878-1886—James L. Streeter.
1887-1890—O. N. Wilson.
1891-1894—Thomas E. Harrington.
1895-1898—Reuben Thompson.
1899-1906—George E. Dungan.

†James Stewart resigned as County Commissioner Dec. 5, 1875, and was succeeded by Wm. A. Shoemaker.
*Died in office.

County Treasurers.*

1841-1844—Stephen Long.
1845-1852—Volney Willson.
1853-1856—Fred E. Putnam.
1857-1860—John C. Mathews.
1861-1864—Samuel F. Brady.
1865-1868—Frank Ellis.
1869-1872—Amos L. Wilson.
1873-1876—John Holbert.
1877-1880—Samuel Gibson.

1881-1882—Amos L. Wilson.
1883-1886—J. W. Taylor†.
1887-1888— ....
1889-1890—George Kirby.
1891-1894—Mark Powers.
1895-1898—David A. Lambert.
1899-1902—Charles F. Koontz.
1903-   —James M. Motsenbocker.

County Auditors.

1827-1833—Wm. Van Matre.
1834-1847—Samuel W. Harlan.
1848-1851—Joseph Anthony.
1852-1855—Samuel W. Harlan.
1857-1864—George W. Seitz.
1865-1869—J. S. McClintock.
1870-1873—A. J. Buckles.
1874-1877—William Dragoo.

1878-1882—Wm. H. Murray.
1883-1886—Wm. Dragoo.
1887-1890—Jacob Stiffler.
1891-1894—W. S. Richey.
1895-1898—Robert W. Monroe.
1899-1902—Robert W. Monroe.
1903-   —J. E. Davis.

County Clerks.

1827-1833—Wm. Van Matre.
1834-1847—Samuel W. Harlan.
1848-1858—Thos. J. Mathews.
1859-1866—George W. Spilker.
1867-1874—George W. Greene.
1875-1882—A. L. Kerwood.

1883-1890—G. F. McCulloch.**
1891-1894—C. M. Kimbrough.
1895-1898—John E. Reed.
1899-1902—George R. Mansfield.
1903-   —Robert I. Patterson.

County Surveyors.

1827-1837—John Tomlinson.
1838-1841—Samuel R. Collier.
1842-1845—Stephen C. Collins.
1846-1851—David B. Dowden.
1852-1856—James S. Slack.
1857-1861—Joshua Truitt.
1862-1865—William G. Ethel††.
1866-1871—William Truitt.

1872-1874—Stanton J. Hussey.
        Stanton J. Hussey*.
1875-   —William Truitt.
1876-1882—William Truitt.
1883-1886—E. H. Stradling.
1887-1888—
1889-1894—J. D. Fenwick.
1895-1898—O. W. Storer.
1899-   —Charles Gough.

Coroners.

1827-1833—William Gilbert.
1834-1836—Charles Redpath.
1837-1840—Geo. Cummerford.
1841-1842—Martin Galliher.
1843-1848—James Nottingham.

1849-1858—Charles Rickart.
1859-1866—James Mason.
1867-1869—Milton James.
1870-1874—G. W. H. Kemper††.
1875-1879—W. J. Boyden.

*Prior to 1841, the duties of Treasurer were discharged by Collector and Treasurer jointly, the two offices being first merged into that of Treasurer in 1841.
†Took office August, 1883.
**Took office Aug. 23, 1883.
††Resigned.

1880-1884—D. V. Buchanan.
1885-1886—Chas. W. Smith.
1887-1888—
1889-1892—W. E. Driscoll.

1893-1898—Joseph F. Bowers.
1899-1904—U. G. Poland.
1905-   —A. A. Cecil.

Probate Judges.

1830-   —John Rees.
        Lewis Rees.
1831-1833—S. McCulloch.
        John Tomlinson.

1834-1843—John Tomlinson.
1844-1851—Enoch Nation.
1852—Samuel W. Harlan.

Common Plea Judges.

1852-1855—Walter March.
1856-1859—Henry S. Kelly.

1860-1871—Jacob N. Haynes.
1872-   —John J. Cheney.

Associate Judges.

1827-1830—John Rees, Lewis Rees.
1831-1834—Samuel McCulloch, John
        Tomlinson.
1835-1836—Wm. Van Matre, Wm.
        McCormick.
1837-1838—Eleazer Coffeen, Wm.
        McCormick.

1839-1840—John Richey, Wm. Mc-
        Cormick.
1841-1848—John Richey, John
        Brady.
1849-1852—John A. Gilbert, John
        Brady.

District Attorneys.

1852-1853—Wm. Brotherton.
1854-1855—Henry S. Kelly.
1856-1857—R. T. St. John.
1858-1859—J. D. Chipman.
1860-1861—Thos. J. Hosford.

1862-1863—Enos L. Watson.
1864-1865—John J. Hawkins.
1866-1867—Arthur C. Mellett.
1868-1871—P. A. B. Kennedy.
1872-   —W. H. Lewis.

Township Trustees.
Salem.

John L. McClintock, 1864-65; Jonas Shoemaker, 1866-68; Samuel C. Moffett, 1869; James W. Heath, 1870-73; Peter Suman, 1874-75; W. W. Cornelius, 1876-79; Augustus Mingle, 1880-84; Henry Schlegel, 1885-88; Daniel A. Funkhouser, 1889-1895; Christopher Hollinger, 1896-1899; John M. Hancock, 1899-1904; William Sunderland, 1905-to present.

Liberty.

William J. Moore, 1864-65; John Holbert, 1866-71; William H. Murray, 1872-73; Jacob H. Weirman, 1874-75; Adoniram J. Wells, 1876-77; John F. Dynes, 1878-79; John H. Guthrie, 1880-81; John Current, 1882-85; N. J. Shroyer, 1886-90; W. H. Williams, 1891-95; Joseph E. Davis, 1896-1900; W. H. Williams, 1901-04; Sherman Shroyer, 1905.

Niles.

Calvin Crooks, 1864-65; Amos Wilson, 1866-68; John Barley, 1869-71; Samuel McDonald, 1872-73; Daniel N. Peterson, 1874-79; Samuel McDonald, 1880-83; William Bartlett, 1884-85; D. N. Peterson, 1886-90; George W. Younts, 1891-95; Isaiah Dudelston, 1896-1900; Manacan Vincent, 1901-04; William A. Wilson, 1904.

Delaware.

Archibald Bergdoll, 1864; Eli Smith, 1865-67; John N. Wingate, 1868; Eli Smith, 1869; William M. Smith, 1870-73; George W. Jones; 1874-75; Adam Boots, 1876-77; Benjamin Lockhart, 1878-79; George W. Jones, 1880-81; Lewis G. Sparks, 1882-83; E. Pace, 1884-85; J. R. Stafford, 1886-90; Samuel J. Shroyer, 1891-95; R. F. Brammer, 1896-1900; S. J. Shroyer, 1901; R. F. Brammer, 1902-04; W. E. Pixley, 1905-to present.

Monroe.

Patrick Carmichael, 1864-65; William F. Watson, 1866-73; George W. Himes, 1874-77; Andrew J. Fleming, 1878-81; James Watson, 1882-83; James Oard, 1884-85; V. G. Carmichael, 1886-87; W. W. Ross, 1888-95; W. E. Driscoll, 1896-1900; J. F. Clevenger, 1901-04; E. M. Crandall, 1905; D. S. Koons, 1906.

Washington.

Thomas Dunn. 1864; James G. Williams, 1865-66; George W. Thomas, 1867-68; William Lewis, 1869-71; Thompson Sharp, 1872-73; John Frey, 1874-75; Mark Powers, 1876-79; Thompson Sharp, 1880-83; Mark Powers, 1884-85; Michael Cory, 1886-87; Mark Powers, 1888-90; Henry Hyer, 1891-95; L. F. Miller, 1896-98; Ozora T. Sharp, 1899-1900; William B. Carmin, 1901-04; J. Fletcher Hyer, 1905.

Harrison.

Samuel E. Mitchell, 1864-67; Alexander Darter, 1868-69; Joseph A. Quick, 1870-73; Enoch Drumm, 1874-77; James Rector, 1878-82; Enoch Drumm, 1883-85; Joseph A. Quick, 1886-90; George W. Boxell, 1891-95; Jonas F. Shoemaker, 1896-1900; L. A. Johnson, 1901-04; William Richie, 1905.

Mount Pleasant.

William S. Brundage, 1864-68; Jacob H. Koontz, 1869-73; Daniel T. Reynolds, 1874-77; John Horne, 1878-80; Jacob H. Koontz (appointed October, 1880, vice Horne, deceased), 1881; W. J. Painter, 1882-83. D. M. Yingling, 1884-85; J. W. Crawford, 1886; George B. Snodgrass, 1888-90; Isham Humphries, 1891-95; John S. Huffer, 1896-1900; Isham Humphries, 1901-04; Frank Downing, 1905.

Perry.

George W. Rees, 1864-65; John Linville, 1866-68; Morrison H. Keesling, 1869-73; Albert L. Gates, 1874-79; Albro G. Gates (appointed to succeed Albert L. Gates), 1880; Peter A. Helm. 1881-82: Joseph Mills, 1883-84; M. A. Cunningham, 1885-87; J. B. Cecil, 1888-90; John B. Jackson. 1891-95; Geo. H. Thornburg, 1896-1900; Colwell R. Howell, 1901-04; Geroge H. Thornburg, 1905.

Union.

Jesse Lewis, 1864; Alfred Miller. 1865-66; Martin Brandt. 1867-68; Jonathan L. Martin, 1869; James W. Carter, 1870-71; Jonathan L. Martin, 1872-75; David Gump, 1876-77; Eli Younce, 1878; Joseph S. Kirkwood, 1879-83; Henry Smith, 1884-85; John D. Morris, 1886-90; William Freeman, 1891-92; E. H. Stradling, 1893-1900; Taylor G. Gibson, 1901-04; Mark T. Fisher, 1905.

Hamilton.

Andrew J. Green, 1864; George Johnsonbaugh, 1865-69; Jasper North, 1870-73; Sylvester Stafford, 1874; Philip Cochran (appointed Dec., 1874), 1875; Jasper North, 1876-79; Duncan Williams, 1880-84; Lewis Moore, 1883-85; Anderson Cates, 1886-87; William Campbell, 1888-90; Robert A. Johnson, 1891-95; William Campbell, 1896-1900; John M. Bloss, 1901-04; Harvey West, 1905.

Center.

Warren Stewart, 1864-67; Joseph A. Walling, 1868 (James A. Maddy appointed his successor April, 1877); James A. Maddy, 1877; John Brady, 1878-79; John R. Mason, 1880-83; G. W. Fay, 1884-85; Eph Smell, 1886-88. George N. McLaughlin, 1889-95; Arthur C. Pershing, 1896-1900; J. W. Dragoo, 1901-04; C. E. Lambert, 1905.

CITY OF MUNCIE.

Mayor.	Clerk.	Treasurer.
1865-66—John Brady.	J. F. Duckwall.	William H. Stewart.
1867- —Job Swain.	Ed. W. Gilbert.	Wallace Hibbits.
1868- —Job Swain.	Eugene W. Shipley.	Wallace Hibbits.
1869- —Marcus C. Smith.	E. W. Shipley.	Wallace Hibbits.
1870- —Marcus C. Smith.	S. F. Brady*.	Wallace Hibbits.
	William L. Little.	
1871-72—Marcus C. Smith.	William L. Little.	Wallace Hibbits.
1873- —Marcus C. Smith.	William L. Little.	T. B. Earickson.
1874-76—Marcus C. Smith.	Calvin S. Wachtell.	T. B. Earickson.
1877-78—Wm. F. Jones	C. S. Wachtell.	T. B. Earickson.
1879-80—Chas. W. Kilgore.	C. S. Wachtell.	T. B. Earickson.
1880- —Chas. W. Kilgore.	C. S. Wachtell.	T. B. Earickson.
1881- —Wm. F. Jones.	C. S. Wachtell.	T. B. Earickson.
1882- —Wm. F. Jones.	C. S. Wachtell.	T. B. Earickson.
1883- —Frank Ellis.	C. S. Wachtell.	T. B. Earickson.
1884- —Frank Ellis.	C. S. Wachtell.	T. B. Earickson,†
1885- —Frank Ellis.	C. S. Wachtell.	John E. Banta.
1886- —Frank Ellis.	J. A. Brown.	John E. Banta.
1887- —Frank Ellis.	J. A. Brown.	A. L. Wright.
1888- —Frank Ellis.	J. A. Brown.	A. L. Wright.
1889- —Frank Ellis.	J. A. Brown.	A. L. Wright.
1890- —Frank Ellis.	A. L. Shideler.	A. L. Wright.
1891- —Arthur W. Brady.	A. L. Shideler.	James Williams.
1892-93—Arthur W. Brady.	Frank A. Elrod.	James Williams.
1894-98—Geo. W. Cromer.	Frank A. Elrod.	Thomas H. Barton.
1898- —Edward Tuhey.	Frank W. Clevenger.	Thomas H. Barton.
1902- —C. W. Sherritt.	R. G. Hickok.	Robt. M. Martin.
1904- —C. W. Sherritt.	R. G. Hickok.	Robt. M. Martin.
‡1905- —L. A. Guthrie.	John A. Jackson.	

*Clerk March 16-May 9, 1870.
†Died Dec. 11, 1884, having been treasurer twelve years; Tyler chosen by council for vacancy.
‡‡First city election under new law.

MUNCIE CITY COUNCIL.

*1865—1st, M. Walling, James Truitt and A. M. Klein; 2d, Wm. B. Kline,
    David T. Haines, Franklin Shafer; 3d, John L. Little; Isaac
    Meeks; 4th. Wm. Brotherton, Lewis S. Smith.
1866—1st, M. Walling, A. M. Klein; 2d, David T. Haines, W. B. Kline;
    3d, C. E. Shipley, Isaac Meeks; 4th, Wm. Brotherton, James Dean.
1867—1st, James Truitt,† Alex. Wilson; 2d, D. T. Haines, John W. Little;
    3d, C. E. Shipley, Isaac Meeks; 4th, Wm. Brotherton, Asa H.
    Hodson.
1868—1st, H. A. Stephens, Chas. B. Kline; 2d, D. T. Haines, M. C. Smith;
    3d, C. E. Shipley, Isaac Meeks; 4th, Wm. Brotherton, Asa H.
    Hodson.
1869—1st, A. Kilgore (resgnd), G. L. Elliott, C. B. Kline; 2d, Geo. W.
    Seitz, James Charman; 3d, C. E. Shipley, Isaac Meeks; 4th, Wm.
    Brotherton, Asa H. Hodson.
1870—1st, Geo. L. Elliott, John Parry; 2d, Geo. W. Seitz, Robert Winton;
    3d, C. E. Shipley, C. H. Maitlen; 4th, Wm. Brotherton, A. H.
    Hodson.
1871—1st, Geo. L. Elliott, John Parry; 2d, James Charman, John Brady;
    3d, C. E. Shipley, C. H. Maitlen; 4th, Robt. H. Long, A. H.
    Hodson.
1872—1st, James N. Templer, John Parry; 2d, Philip F. Davis, John
    Brady; 3d, C. E. Shipley, W. F. Jones; 4th, R. H. Long, James
    Boyce.
1873—1st, G. L. Elliott, John Parry; 2d, P. F. Davis, Wallace Hibbits; 3d,
    Benj. F. Gift, W. F. Jones; 4th, A. H. Hodson, James Boyce.
1874—1st, Milton James, O. M. Todd; 2d, Franklin Shafer, Wallace Hib-
    bits: 3d, B. F. Gift, Isaac Meeks; 4th, A. H. Hodson, Elias P.
    Smith.
1875—1st, O. H. Swain, O. M. Todd; 2d, Franklin Shafer, P. F. Davis;
    3d, Wm. Shick, Isaac Meeks: 4th, Richard Berger, E. P. Smith;
    5th, P. H. D. Bandy, T. J. Matthews.
1876—1st, O. H. Swain, Ephraim Smell; 2d, Erville B. Bishop, P. F. Davis;
    3d, Wm. Shick, Isaac Meeks; 4th, R. Berger, James Boyce; 5th,
    Frank Staker (resgnd). P. H. D. Bandy. T. J. Matthews.
1877—1st, B. R. Adamson. Ephraim Emell; 2d, E. B. Bishop, Benj. F. Brat-
    ton; 3d, Wm. Shick. Isaac Meeks; 4th, John S. Reid. James Boyce;
    5th, P. H. D. Bandy, E. E. Matthews.
1878—1st, B. R. Adamson. Ephraim Smell; 2d. Joseph Hummel, B. F.
    Bratton; 3d, Wm. Shick, Joseph A. Hill; 4th, J. S. Reid, G. H.
    Andrews; 5th. Frank M. Horner, John B. Heath.
1879—1st, B. R. Adamson. Ephraim Smell, Wallace
    Hibbits; 3d, Wm. Shick. J. A. Hill; 4th, L. L. Weller, G. H. An-
    drews; 5th, Frank M. Horner, John B. Heath.
1880—1st, B. R. Adamson. Frank Ellis; 2d, Chas. A. Willard, Wallace
    Hibbits (resgnd), F. E. Putnam; 3d, Wm. Shick, J. A. Hill; 4th,
    L. L. Weller, Geo. E. Dungan; 5th, John Fay, John B. Heath.

*Two city elections were held in 1865.
†James Truitt, deceased; H. A. Stephens, appointed to vacancy.

1881—1st, B. R. Adamson, Frank Ellis; 2d, C. A. Willard, F. E. Putnam;
3d, J. A. Hill, T. H. Kirby; 4th, John H. Miller, A. E. Lemmon;
5th, John Fay, Pete Daugherty (dec'd; J: A. Stahle el. to vacancy).
1882—1st (B. R. Adamson, resgnd), John Parry, Frank Ellis; 2d, F. E.
Putnam, G. W. H. Kemper; 3d, T. H. Kirby, W. A. Hoyt; 4th
John H. Miller, Wm. Willard; 5th, J. A. Stable, F. Staker.
    [Note—Numerous changes occurred in the council about this
    time; T. H. Kirby and W. A. Hoyt, resigned March, 1883,
    were succeeded by C. M. Kimbrough and A. E. Lyman].
1883—1st, John Parry, C. W. Kilgore; 2d, G. W. H. Kemper, B. F. Bratton; 3d, C. M. Kimbrough, A. E. Lyman; 4th, Wm. Willard, S. U.
Huffer; 5th, F. Staker, J. A. Stahle.
1884—1st, John Parry, C. W. Kilgore; 2d, B. F. Bratton, G. W. H. Kemper; 3d, A. E. Lyman, Miles Smith; 4th, S. U. Huffer, Wm. Willard; 5th, Frank Staker, J. A. Stahle.
1885—1st, C. W. Kilgore, Henry Hohe; 2d, G. W. H. Kemper, Harry R.
Wysor; 3d, Miles Smith, George Dungan; 4th, Wm. Willard,
John W. Little; 5th, Frank Staker, J. A. Stahle.
1886—
1887—1st, C. W. Kilgore; 2d, H. R. Wysor; 3d, J. D. Hoyt; 4th, E. P.
Smith; 5th, John Galbraith.
1888—1st, C. W. Kilgore, Wm. E. Yost; 2d, H. R. Wysor, J. R. Mason; 3d,
J. D. Hoyt, D. H. H. Shewmaker; 4th, E. P. Smith, James Carpenter: 5th, John Galbraith, Thomas L. Zook.
1889—1st, Wm. E. Yost, C. W. Kilgore; 2d, J. R. Mason, Geo. L. Lenon;
3d, D. H. H. Shewmaker, John C. Johnson; 4th, James Carpenter,
John A. Keener; 5th, Thomas L. Zook, W. Bent Meeker.
1890—1st, C. W. Kilgore, J. C. Eiler; 2d, Geo. L. Lenon, J. L. Streeter;
3d, J. C. Johnson, D. H. H. Shewmaker; 4th, J. A. Keener, W. L.
Little; 5th, W. B. Meeker, Jesse Williamson.
    In 1890 the proposition to divide the fifth ward, creating ward 6,
    carried, the boundaries of the 6th being south of the Big Four
    track and east of Madison street. Election was held May 29,
    for one new councilman in each ward, James O'Neil being
    elected from the fifth, and N. B. Powers from the 6th.
1891—1st, John M. Graham, Jacob Dodson; 2d, J. L. Streeter, Homer
Highlands; 3d, J. C. Johnson, John J. Hartley; 4th, Philip W.
Patterson, W. L. Little; 5th, Jesse Williamson, John O'Neil; 6th,
N. B. Powers, W. B. Meeker.
1892—1st, J. M. Graham, O. W. Crabbs; 2d, Homer Highlands, G. L.
Lenon; 3d, J. J. Hartley, W. E. Driscoll; 4th, P. W. Patterson,
A. E. Lyman; 5th, W. H. Moreland, B. F. Day; 6th, W. B. Meeker,
Joseph Porter.
    Beginning with the election of May, 1894, councilmen and all
    city officers were elected for terms of four years, councilmen
    only being chosen in 1896 and each four years thereafter.
1894—1st, Henry C. Haymond; 2d, Milton Gray; 3d, J. C. Johnson. T. H.
Kirby; 4th, James Boyce; 5th, Thos. L. Zook; 6th. J. Q. Mitchell.
1896—1st, H. C. Haymond. O. W. Crabbs; 2d. Milton Gray. C. H. Anthony; 3d, J. C. Johnson, T. H. Kirby; 4th, R. Berger, Will

Meeker; 5th, T. L. Zook, Frank A. Clevenger; 6th, J. Q. Mitchell, C. Allen Budd.

1898—1st, O. W. Crabbs, H. C. Haymond; 2d, C. H. Anthony, W. R. Youse; 3d, T. H. Kirby, J. O. Lewellen; 4th, R. Berger, Milton Gra_v_; 5th, F. A. Clevenger, C. Hanika; 6th, C. A. Budd, Frank O. Gill.

1900—1st, Daniel Topp, H. C. Haymond; 2d, C. H. Anthony, W. R. Youse; 3d, Albert ·Wright, J. O. Lewellen; 4th, Richard Berger, J. M. Gray; 5th, Henry Kehlenbeck, C. Hanika; 6th, Frank Lafferty, F. O. Gill.

1902—1st, Chris. Heckenhaur, T. J. Ault; 2d, E. B. Steck, Frank Reed; 3d, A. L. Wright (T. H. Kirby el. successor June, 1902), Luther W. Cates; 4th, M. J. McGuff, John A. Keener (E. M. White succeeds July, 1903); 5th, C. L. Nihart, C. M. Shanks; 6th, A. C. Budd (W. H. McClung succeeds Dec., 1902), Joseph Porter.

1904—1st, P. P. Busch, D. A. McLain; 2d, W. A. Petty, W. H. White; 3d, L. W. Cates, J. E. Ethel; 4th, M. J. McGuff, E. M. White; 5th, C. L. Nihart, C. M. Shanks; 6th, Joseph Porter, James P. English.

1905—(November election under new law) 1st, D. A. McLain; 2d, W. F. White; 3d, L. W. Cates; 4th, M. J. McGuff; 5th, W. D. Carter; 6th, John O'Day. Councilmen at large—Philip P. Busch, James E. Durham, Peter K. Morrison.

The Muncie city government as constituted in 1907, is as follows: Leonidas A. Guthrie, Mayor; John A. Jackson, City Clerk; H. C. Haymond, Controller; James M. Motsenbocker, City Treasurer; Robe Carl White, City Attorney; John O. Potter, City Engineer; Frank L. Gass, City Judge; Harry McCullough, Electrical Inspector; Van Benbow, Supt. of Police; Oscar W. Crabbs, Supt. of Cemetery; Harry L. Gallivan, Supt. of Fire Department; Albert Stephens, Supt. of Garbage Furnace; Harry Smeltzer, Street Foreman.

Members of Common Council: Councilmen-at-Large, Philip P. Busch, P. K. Morrison, James E. Durham; First Ward, David A. McLain; Second Ward, William F. White; Third Ward, Luther W. Cates; Fourth Ward, Michael J. McGuff; Fifth Ward, William D. Carter; Sixth Ward, Joseph O'Day.

Committees: Cemetery, Busch, McLain, Durham; Education, Carter, Morrison. McGuff; Election, O'Day, Busch, Carter; Fee and Salary, Carter, White, McLain; Finance, White, McGuff, Cates; Fire Department, McLain, O'Day, McGuff; Garbage. O'Day, Morrison, Cates; Hospital, McGuff, Durham. O'Day; Judiciary, Cates, White, Busch; Library, Morrison, Durham, Carter; Market Places and Parks, Busch, Carter, Durham; Ordinances, Cates, White, Morrison: Public Buildings, White, McLain, Busch; Railways, Durham, O'Day, McLain; Sewers, Morrison, Busch, White; Streets and Alleys, McGuff, Carter, McLain; Street Lights, Durham, Carter, White; Waterworks, McLain, Carter, White.

Board of Public Works: Dr. George R. Green, President; Frederick F. McClellan, Francis J. Lafferty; John A. Jackson, Clerk; Milton Thomas, Deputy Clerk.

Board of Health and Charity: Dr. Harry R. Spickermon, Secretary; Dr. Will W. Kemper, Dr. Clarence G. Rea.

The Publishers take this opportunity, in the closing pages of this volume, to speak a few words in appreciation of the enthusiasm and pains-taking interest displayed by the Editor, Dr. Kemper, in all departments of the work by which this History of Delaware county has been perfected. By a long residence in the county Dr. Kemper has become identified not only in a prominent manner with the medical profession, of which he is now the dean of active practitioners, but also with the life and affairs of the county in general, so that he was a natural choice as editor of a work which has endeavored to include all the numerous interests of a city and county with a history extending back more than three-quarters of a century. A brief sketch of the life of the Editor will be of interest.

General William Harrison Kemper, named in honor of the first governor of Indiana, was born in Richland township, Rush county, Indiana, December 16, 1839. In the early pages of this history much was said about the sources from which the first settlers of the county came. It is noteworthy in this connection that Dr. Kemper is a member of an early Indiana family that came to the state from Kentucky, and originally from the state of Virginia, where John Kemper, the progenitor of the Kemper family in America, had settled in 1714, having emigrated to this country from his birthplace at Muesen, Germany.

Dr. Kemper's father was Arthur Smith Kemper, who was born in Garrard county, Kentucky, May 4, 1794, was a farmer, and followed that occupation after coming to Rush county, in 1834, where he died in 1849, when scarcely more than fifty-five years of age. The mother of Dr. Kemper was Patience Bryant, who was born in Garrard county, Kentucky, February 9, 1802, and died at Muncie, October 30, 1881. While her husband was German, she was of English and French Huguenot stock. her grandfather, James Bryant, having come from England in 1700 and settled at Manakinton, Virginia. Her father, John Bryant, was a soldier of the Revolutionary war.

Dr. Kemper was reared on a farm, attending the schools at Clarksburg and Greensburg, and in 1856, when seventeen years old, went west to the comparatively new country of Iowa, where he lived for three years. Two years of this time he worked in a printing office, of the Montezuma *Republican* at Montezuma. Returning to Indiana in the fall of 1859, on the first day of January, 1861, he began the study of medicine under the preceptorship of Dr. J. W. Moodey at Greensburg. But this was a period of national trial and excitement conflicting with all the calm pursuits of men, and only a few days after the breaking out of the Civil war he had enlisted as a private (April 18, 1861) in Company B, Seventh Regiment, Indiana Volunteers, for a term of three months. His first engagement was the battle of Philippi, West Virginia, June 3, 1861, and while a member of the Seventh Regiment he was also engaged at Laurel Hill and Carrick's Ford. On the expiration of his first enlistment, he re-enlisted and served as hospital steward in the Seventeenth Regiment, Indiana Volunteers, from September 25, 1861, to July 27, 1864. His experience in the war is outlined in the battles at which he was present during these three years, namely: Hoover's Gap, Chattanooga, Ringgold, Lett's Tanyard, Chickamauga, Thompson's Cove, Murfreesboro Road, Shelbyville Pike and Farmington, Missionary Ridge, Cleveland, siege of Knoxville, Charleston, Dallas, Big Shanty, Noonday Creek, Kenesaw Mountain, and the battles before Atlanta. Dr. Kemper is a member of Williams Post No. 78, G. A. R., being a past commander of the post, and is also a member of the Military Order of the Loyal Legion, Insignia No. 4648.

Immediately after his return from the field of war, he resumed the study of medicine, attending lectures in the medical department of the University of Michigan during 1864-65, and during the spring of 1865 at the Long Island College Hospital, Brooklyn, N. Y., where he was graduated in June of 1865. Two months later he had entered upon the practice at Muncie which has been continued now for more than forty-two years. No other physician in the county is now in active practice who was here at that time. Success in his work and the high esteem of his colleagues have marked his career here, and the distinctions that have come to him in a professional way are too many to detail in this sketch. In 1886 he took a post-graduate course in the New York Polyclinic, and has always been a close student of his profession. His writings on medical subjects are voluminous, over fifty articles having been read before medical societies or published in medical journals. He has also written for the layman from his professional standpoint, these writings entitling him to consideration among Indiana authors. His little volume, "Uses of Suffering," which appeared in 1896, had been written as a lecture, and contains a proof of the goodness of God exhibited through suffering and disease. "The World's Anatomists" is another attractive brochure bearing the doctor's name. In 1898 the Indiana Commandery of the Loyal Legion published a volume of "War Papers" to which Dr. Kemper contributed the article "The Seventh Regiment." He is a member of the Delaware County Medical Society, the Indiana State Medical Society and the American Medical Association. He was treasurer of the state society from 1879 to 1885 and president in 1886-87. For many years he has been local surgeon for the Big Four and Lake Erie railroads.

In politics Dr. Kemper has in the main supported the men and measures of the Republican party. While he has not sought political honors, he has at several times been identified with local affairs outside of his profession. He served as coroner 1870-75, and during the '80s was a member of the city council. From 1872 to 1893, with the exception of two years, he was United States examining surgeon for pensions, and in 1902 was reappointed to this position, which he still holds. He has been an active member of the High Street Methodist Episcopal church for years, and has a record of twenty-one years' service as superintendent of the Sunday-school, from 1867 to 1888. His fondness for travel has led him to many diverse parts of the world, to continental Europe, the Holy Land and other regions about the Mediterranean, besides extensive travels in his own country. The Kemper collection of historical relics, antiquities and curios is the result of many years of search, and is one of the most varied and extensive private collections to be found anywhere. It will not be improper for the writer to say that such a long life of useful and varied activity has produced, in addition to a well-rounded character, a certain richness of personal charm, a positiveness of judgment, and a readiness and elevation of discourse, that are appreciated by all who have had the privilege of his acquaintance.

Dr. Kemper married, August 15, 1865, Miss Harriet Kemper, of Oskaloosa, Iowa. Mrs. Kemper has for many years been prominent in woman's club work in Muncie. Their three children are Georgette Moodey, wife of John Lawrence Smith; Arthur Thomson and William Winton.

Arthur Thomson Kemper, M. D., who is one of the firm of Drs. Kemper, was born at Muncie, September 7, 1870, and after graduating from the Muncie high school in 1889 and from the Medical College of Indiana in 1897, has practiced his profession in association with his father. In 1906 he took a post-graduate course at the Chicago Polyclinic. He is a member of the Delaware County and the Indiana State Medical Societies, is a Royal Arch Mason, a Knight of Pythias, and is a member of the Methodist Episcopal church; in politics a Republican. He married, in 1897, Miss Effice Bradford, of Dayton, Ohio.

William Winton Kemper, M. D., also a member of the firm, was born at Muncie, June 13, 1877, and like his brother was educated in the city schools and graduated from the Medical College of Indiana in 1904, since which time he has practiced with father and brother. He is a member of the county and state medical societies, and at the present time is a member of the Muncie board of health. He is a Mason, a Republican in politics, and a member of the Methodist Episcopal church. He married, in 1906, Miss Helen, daughter of J. W. Garner, D. D. S., of Muncie.